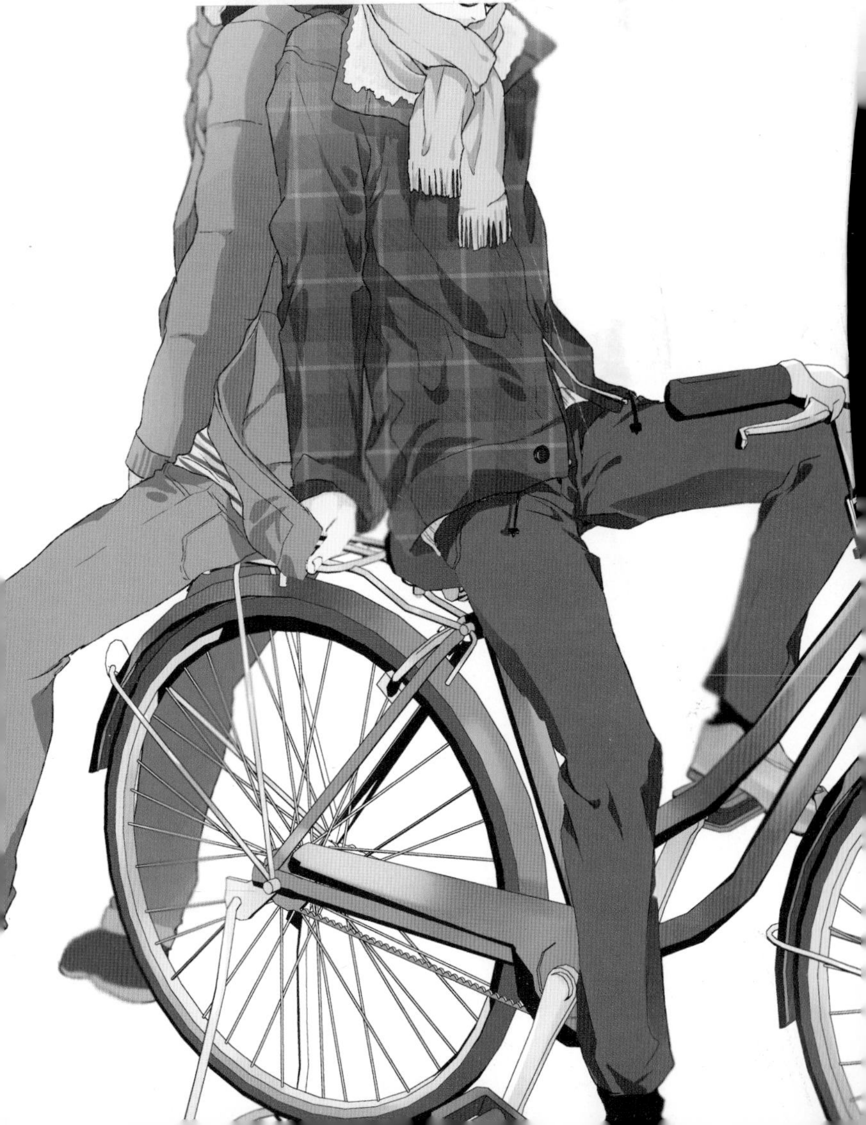

Escape Journey

Story and Art by **Ogeretsu Tanaka** volume **1**

CONTENTS

1st Escape 003

2nd Escape 041

3rd Escape 073

4th Escape 115

5th Escape 151

Last Escape 189

Bonus Story 239

Afterword 257

SUBLIME
SuBLime Manga Edition

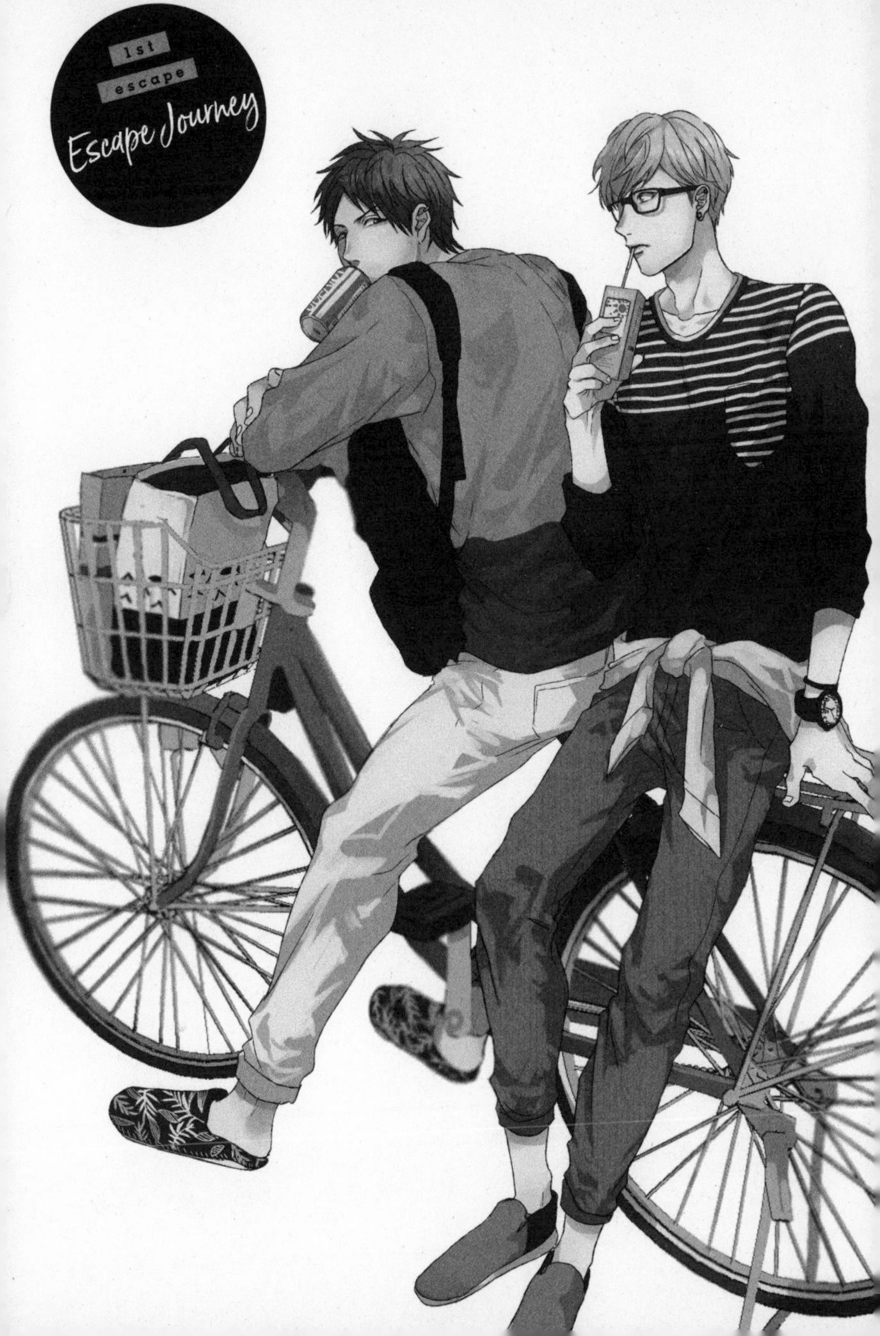
1st
escape
Escape Journey

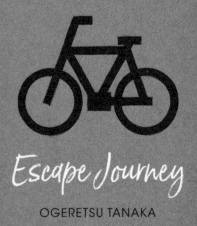

Escape Journey

OGERETSU TANAKA

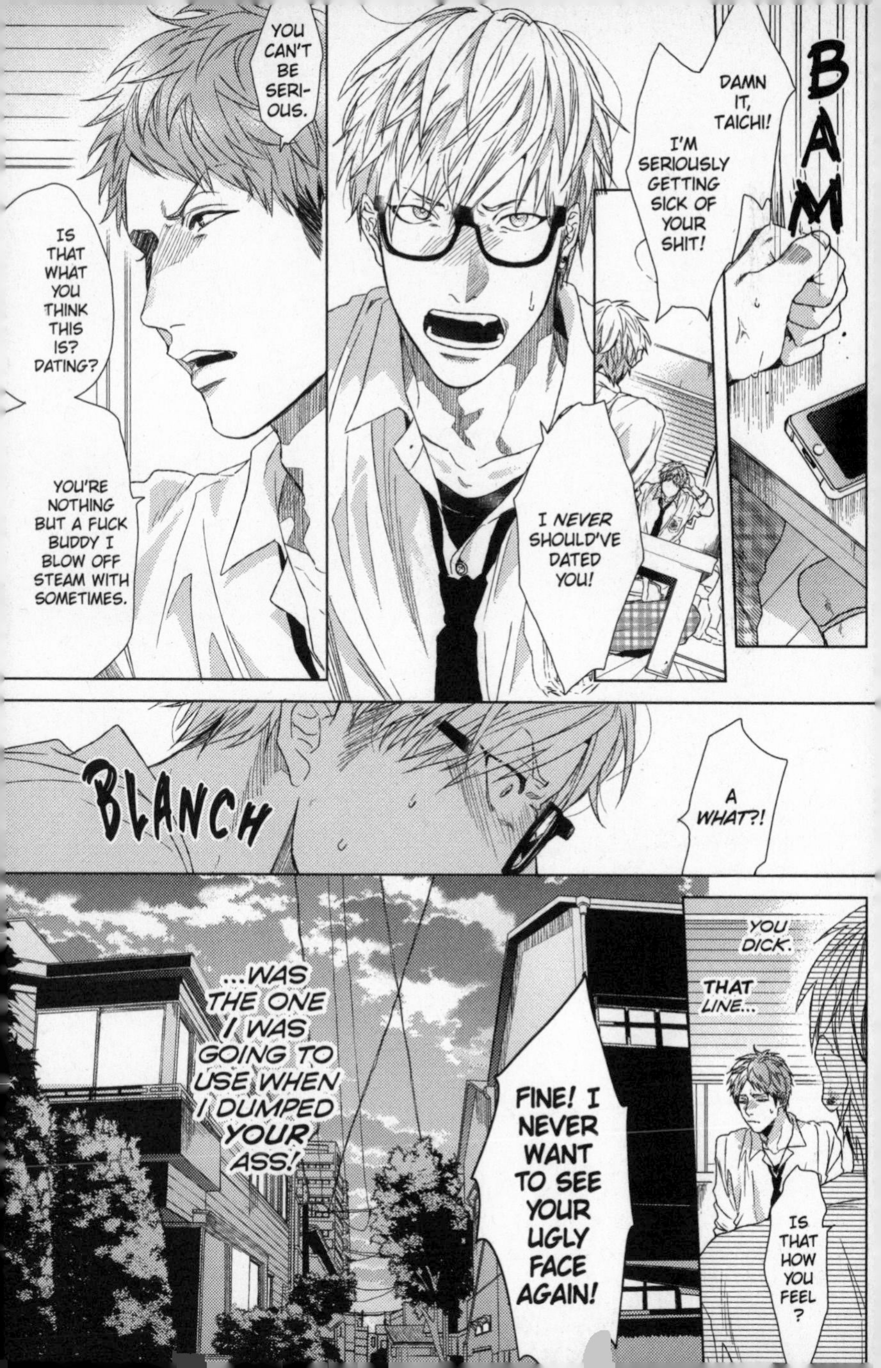
BAM
DAMN IT, TAICHI!
I'M SERIOUSLY GETTING SICK OF YOUR SHIT!
I *NEVER* SHOULD'VE DATED YOU!
YOU CAN'T BE SERI-OUS.
IS THAT WHAT YOU THINK THIS IS? DATING?
YOU'RE NOTHING BUT A FUCK BUDDY I BLOW OFF STEAM WITH SOMETIMES.
A *WHAT*?!
BLANCH
YOU DICK.
THAT LINE...
IS THAT HOW YOU FEEL?
FINE! I NEVER WANT TO SEE YOUR UGLY FACE AGAIN!
...WAS THE ONE I WAS GOING TO USE WHEN I DUMPED YOUR ASS!

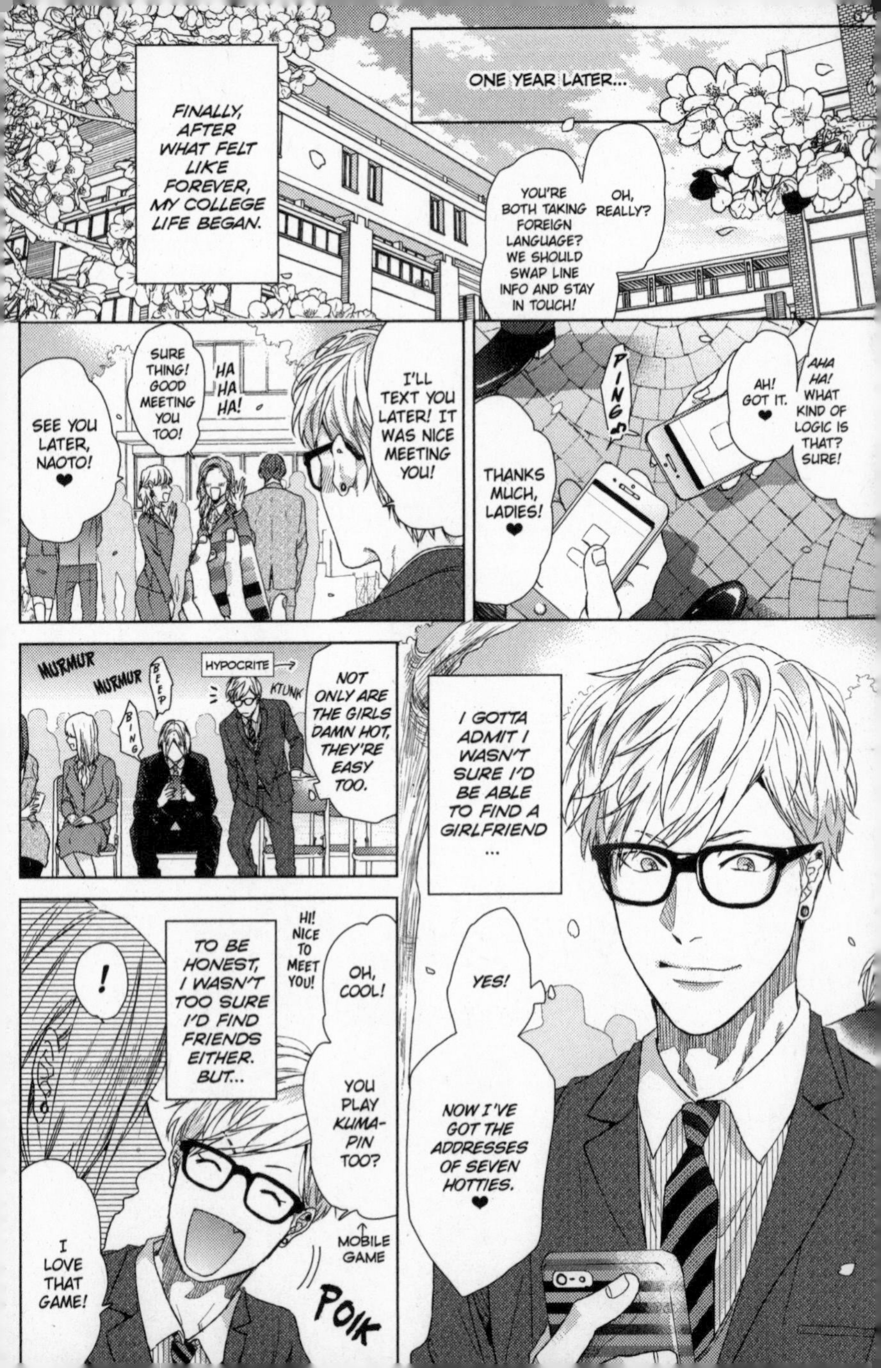
ONE YEAR LATER...
FINALLY, AFTER WHAT FELT LIKE FOREVER, MY COLLEGE LIFE BEGAN.
OH, REALLY?
YOU'RE BOTH TAKING FOREIGN LANGUAGE? WE SHOULD SWAP LINE INFO AND STAY IN TOUCH!
AHA HA! WHAT KIND OF LOGIC IS THAT? SURE!
AH! GOT IT. ♥
PING
THANKS MUCH, LADIES! ♥
I'LL TEXT YOU LATER! IT WAS NICE MEETING YOU!
HA HA HA!
SURE THING! GOOD MEETING YOU TOO!
SEE YOU LATER, NAOTO! ♥
I GOTTA ADMIT I WASN'T SURE I'D BE ABLE TO FIND A GIRLFRIEND...
YES!
NOW I'VE GOT THE ADDRESSES OF SEVEN HOTTIES. ♥
NOT ONLY ARE THE GIRLS DAMN HOT, THEY'RE EASY TOO.
KTUNK
HYPOCRITE →
BEEP
BING
MURMUR
MURMUR
HI! NICE TO MEET YOU!
OH, COOL!
TO BE HONEST, I WASN'T TOO SURE I'D FIND FRIENDS EITHER. BUT...
!
YOU PLAY KUMA-PIN TOO?
MOBILE GAME
I LOVE THAT GAME!
POIK

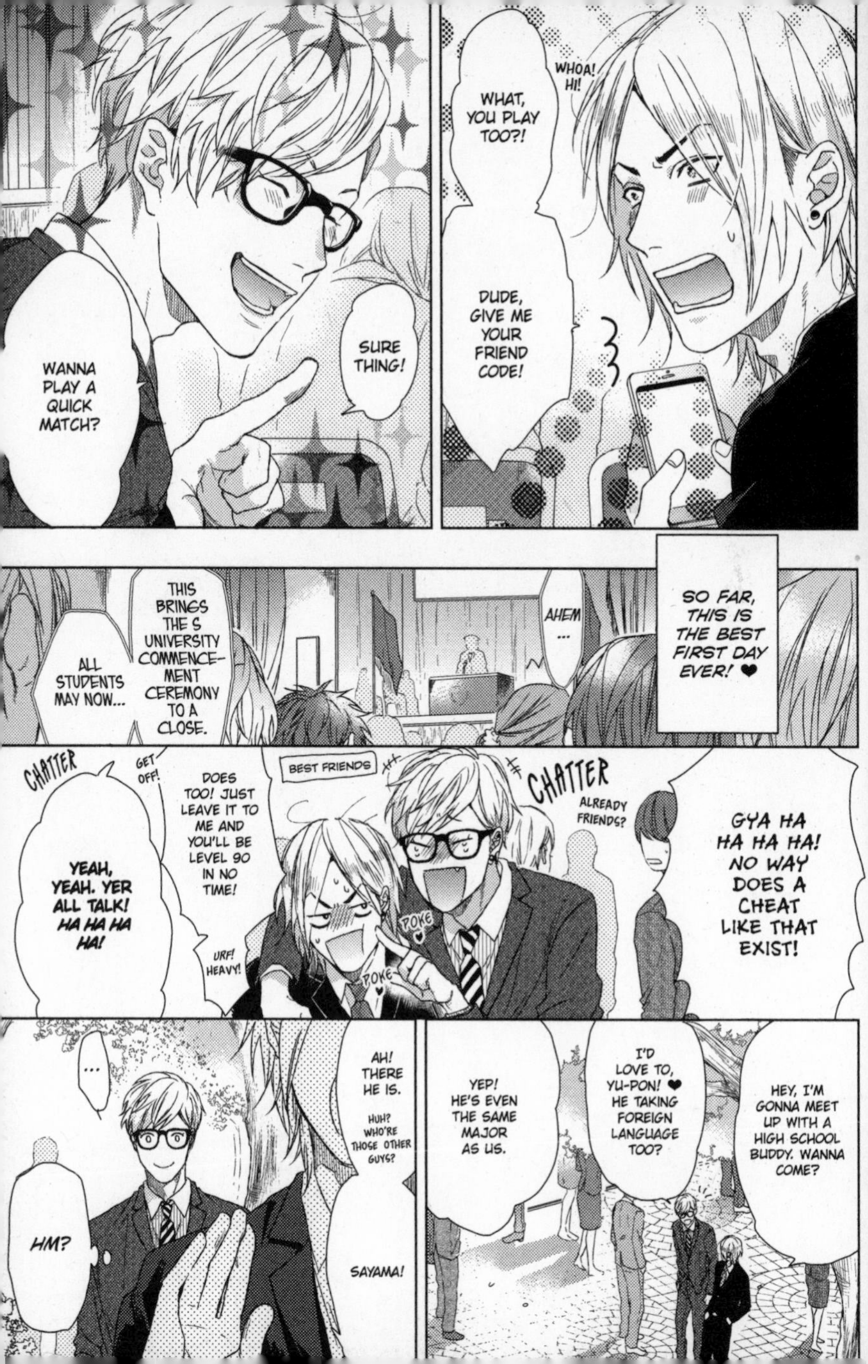
WHOA! HI!
WHAT, YOU PLAY TOO?!
DUDE, GIVE ME YOUR FRIEND CODE!
SURE THING!
WANNA PLAY A QUICK MATCH?
SO FAR, THIS IS THE BEST FIRST DAY EVER! ❤
AHEM ...
THIS BRINGS THE S UNIVERSITY COMMENCE-MENT CEREMONY TO A CLOSE.
ALL STUDENTS MAY NOW...
GYA HA HA HA HA! NO WAY DOES A CHEAT LIKE THAT EXIST!
CHATTER
ALREADY FRIENDS?
BEST FRIENDS
DOES TOO! JUST LEAVE IT TO ME AND YOU'LL BE LEVEL 90 IN NO TIME!
GET OFF!
CHATTER
YEAH, YEAH. YER ALL TALK! HA HA HA HA!
POKE ❤
POKE ❤
URF! HEAVY!
HEY, I'M GONNA MEET UP WITH A HIGH SCHOOL BUDDY. WANNA COME?
I'D LOVE TO, YU-PON! ❤ HE TAKING FOREIGN LANGUAGE TOO?
YEP! HE'S EVEN THE SAME MAJOR AS US.
AH! THERE HE IS.
HUH? WHO'RE THOSE OTHER GUYS?
SAYAMA!
...
HM?

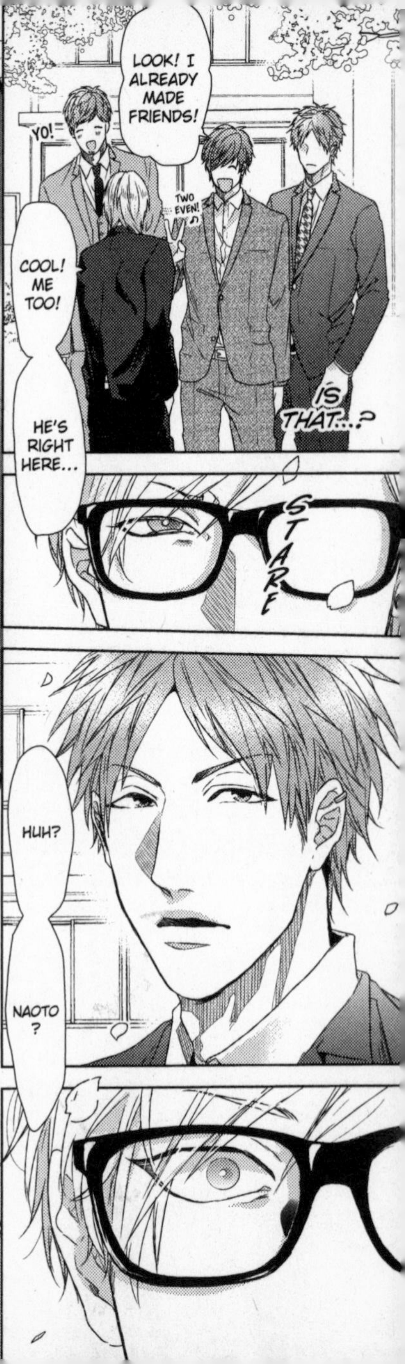
LOOK! I ALREADY MADE FRIENDS!
YO!
TWO EVEN! ♪
COOL! ME TOO!
HE'S RIGHT HERE...
IS THAT...?
STARE
HUH?
NAOTO?
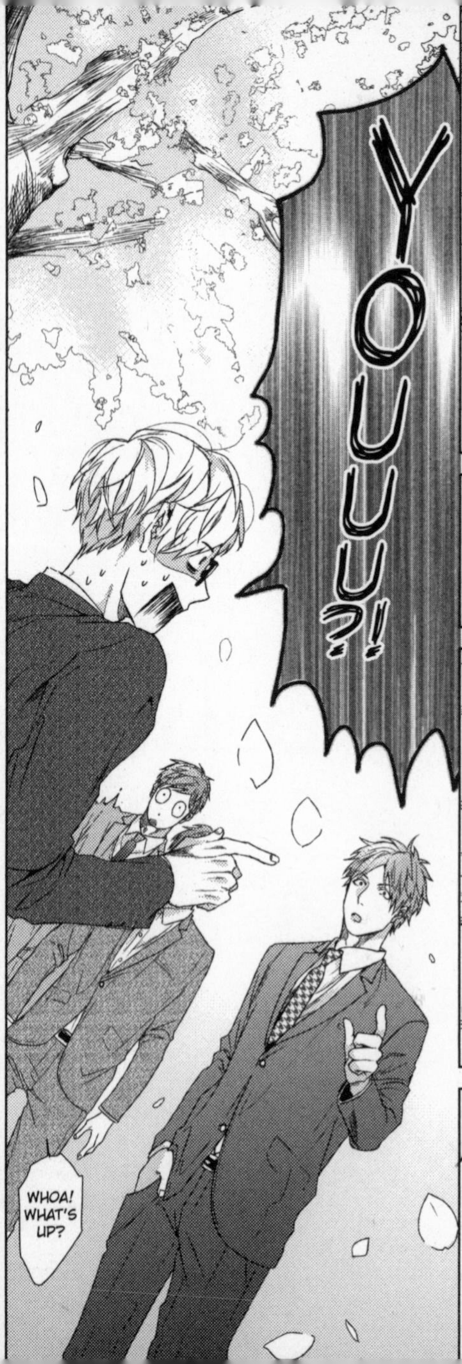
YOUUUU?!
WHOA! WHAT'S UP?

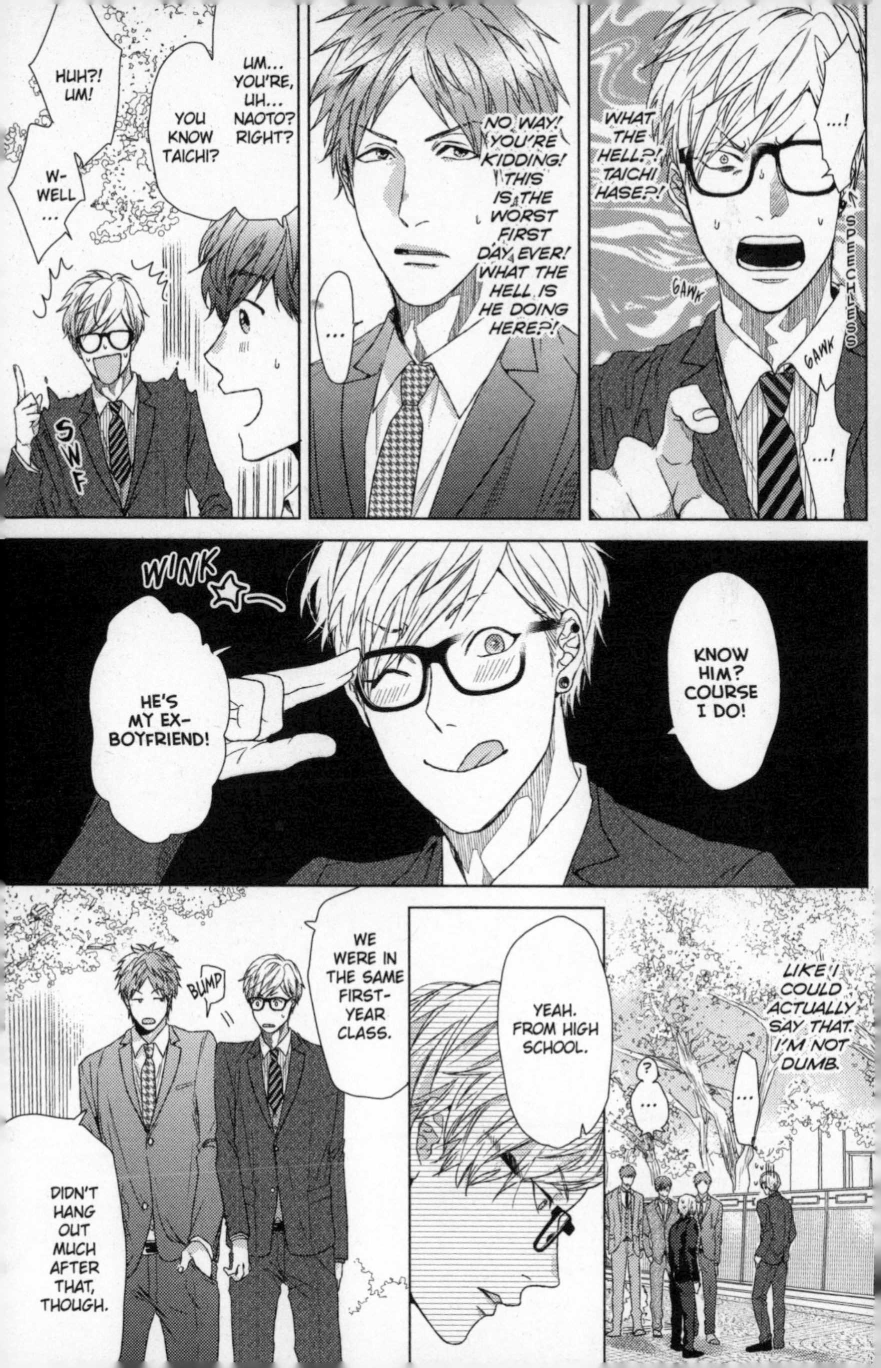

...!
WHAT THE HELL?! TAICHI HASE?!
SPEECHLESS
GAWK
GAWK
...!
NO WAY! YOU'RE KIDDING! THIS IS THE WORST FIRST DAY EVER! WHAT THE HELL IS HE DOING HERE?!
...
UM... YOU'RE, UH... NAOTO? RIGHT?
YOU KNOW TAICHI?
HUH?! UM!
W-WELL ...
SWF
KNOW HIM? COURSE I DO!
WINK
HE'S MY EX-BOYFRIEND!
LIKE I COULD ACTUALLY SAY THAT. I'M NOT DUMB.
...
?
...
YEAH. FROM HIGH SCHOOL.
WE WERE IN THE SAME FIRST-YEAR CLASS.
BUMP
DIDN'T HANG OUT MUCH AFTER THAT, THOUGH.

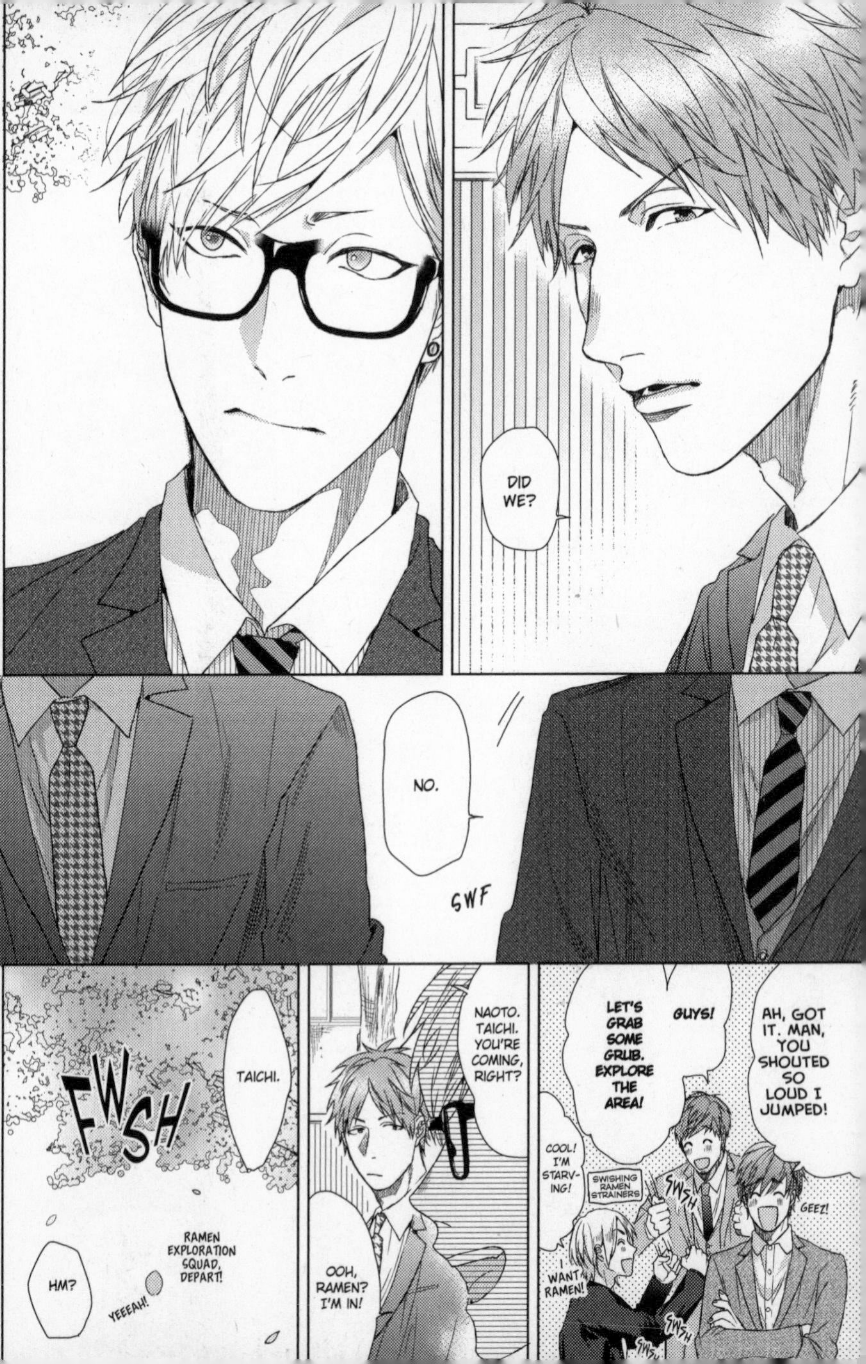
DID WE?
NO.
SWF
AH, GOT IT. MAN, YOU SHOUTED SO LOUD I JUMPED!
GUYS!
LET'S GRAB SOME GRUB. EXPLORE THE AREA!
GEEZ!
COOL! I'M STARV-ING!
SWISHING RAMEN STRAINERS
SWSH
I WANT RAMEN!
SWSH
NAOTO. TAICHI. YOU'RE COMING, RIGHT?
OOH, RAMEN? I'M IN!
TAICHI.
FWSH
RAMEN EXPLORATION SQUAD, DEPART!
HM?
YEEEAH!

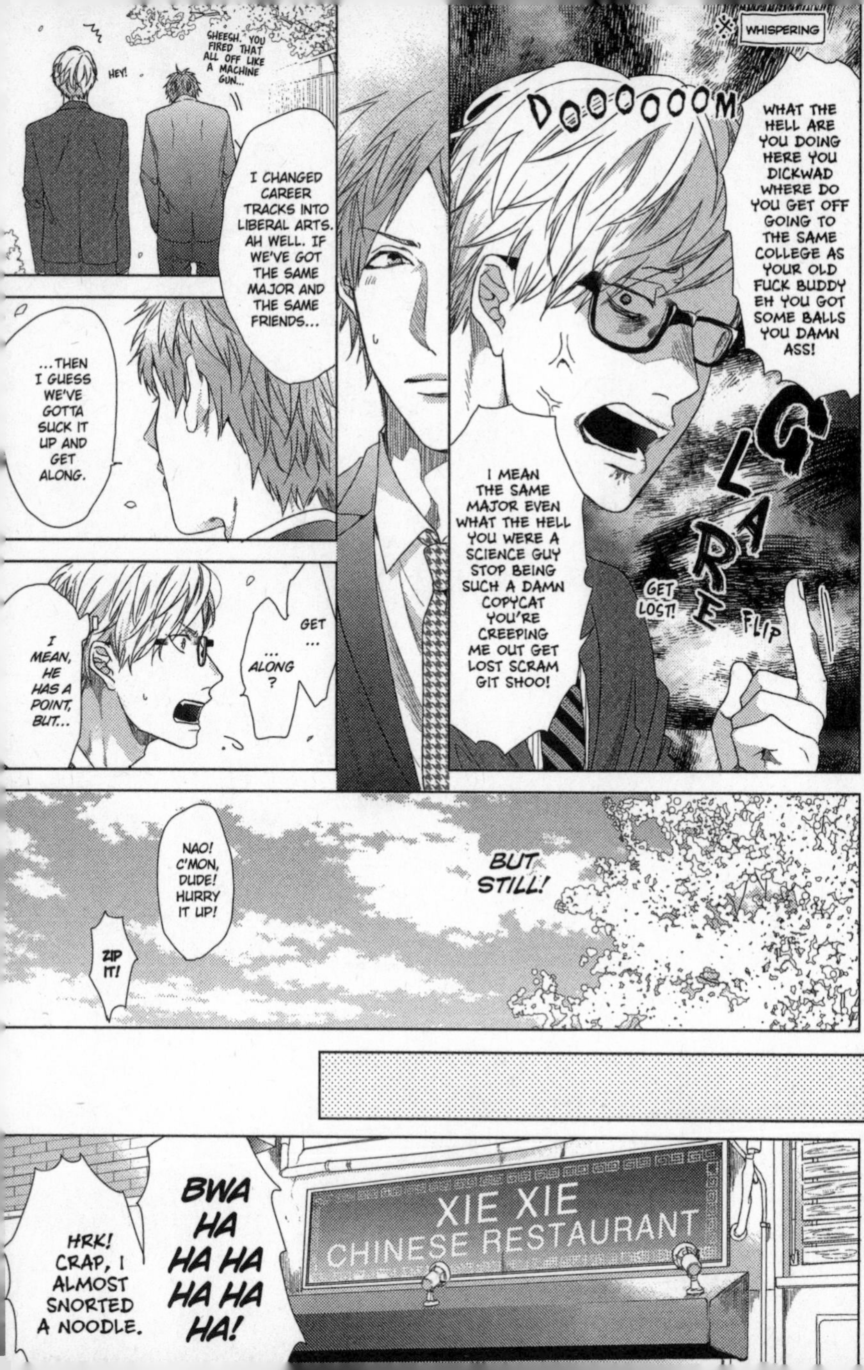
※ WHISPERING
DOOOOOOM
WHAT THE HELL ARE YOU DOING HERE YOU DICKWAD WHERE DO YOU GET OFF GOING TO THE SAME COLLEGE AS YOUR OLD FUCK BUDDY EH YOU GOT SOME BALLS YOU DAMN ASS!
I MEAN THE SAME MAJOR EVEN WHAT THE HELL YOU WERE A SCIENCE GUY STOP BEING SUCH A DAMN COPYCAT YOU'RE CREEPING ME OUT GET LOST SCRAM GIT SHOO!
GLARE
GET LOST!
FLIP
I CHANGED CAREER TRACKS INTO LIBERAL ARTS. AH WELL. IF WE'VE GOT THE SAME MAJOR AND THE SAME FRIENDS...
SHEESH. YOU FIRED THAT ALL OFF LIKE A MACHINE GUN...
HEY!
...THEN I GUESS WE'VE GOTTA SUCK IT UP AND GET ALONG.
GET ... ... ALONG?
I MEAN, HE HAS A POINT, BUT...
BUT STILL!
NAO! C'MON, DUDE! HURRY IT UP!
ZIP IT!
XIE XIE
CHINESE RESTAURANT
BWA HA HA HA HA HA HA!
HRK! CRAP, I ALMOST SNORTED A NOODLE.

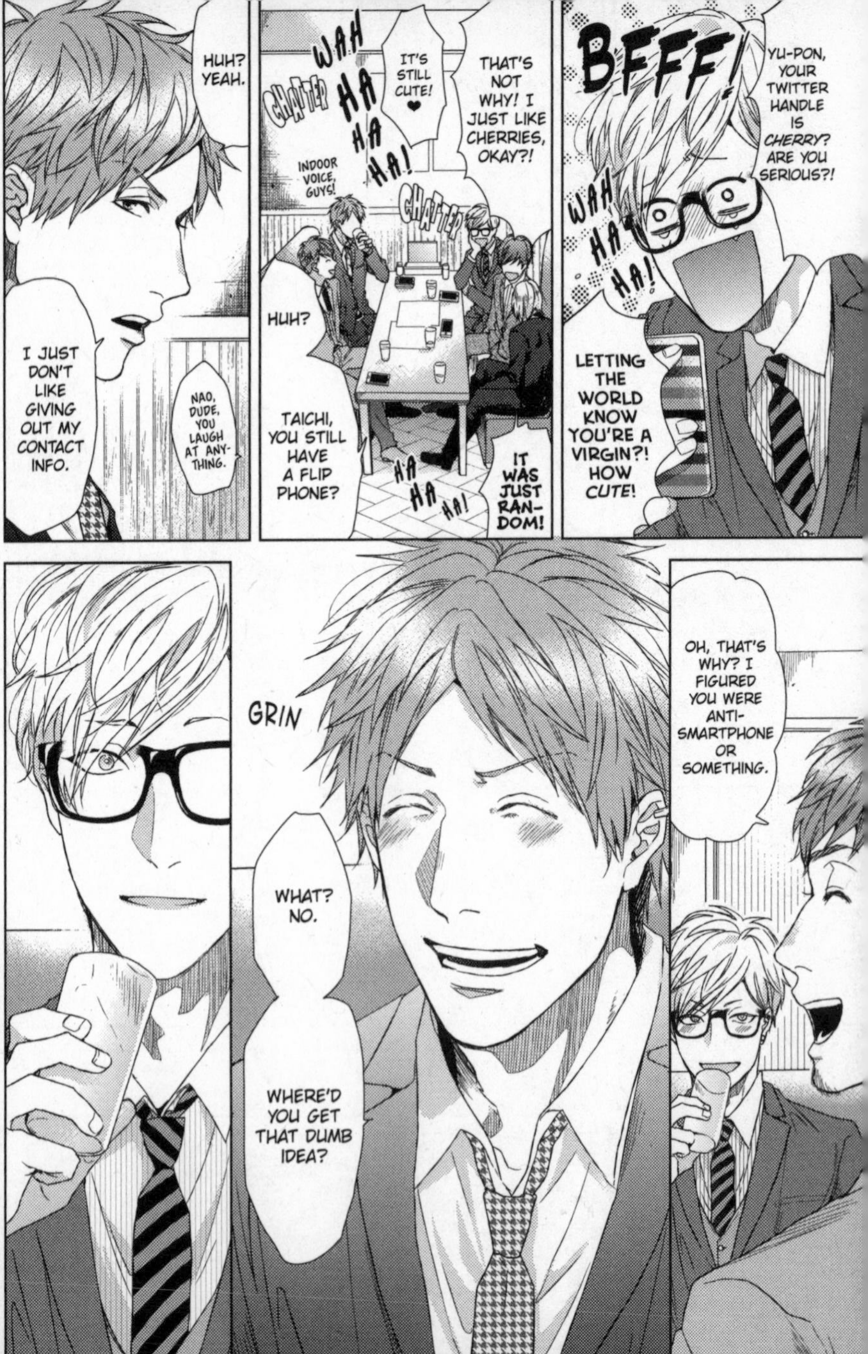
BFFF!
YU-PON, YOUR TWITTER HANDLE IS CHERRY? ARE YOU SERIOUS?!
WAH HA HA!
LETTING THE WORLD KNOW YOU'RE A VIRGIN?! HOW CUTE!
THAT'S NOT WHY! I JUST LIKE CHERRIES, OKAY?!
IT'S STILL CUTE! ♥
WAH HA HA HA!
CHATTER
CHATTER
INDOOR VOICE, GUYS!
IT WAS JUST RAN-DOM!
HA HA HA!
HUH?
TAICHI, YOU STILL HAVE A FLIP PHONE?
HUH? YEAH.
NAO, DUDE, YOU LAUGH AT ANY-THING.
I JUST DON'T LIKE GIVING OUT MY CONTACT INFO.
OH, THAT'S WHY? I FIGURED YOU WERE ANTI-SMARTPHONE OR SOMETHING.
GRIN
WHAT? NO.
WHERE'D YOU GET THAT DUMB IDEA?

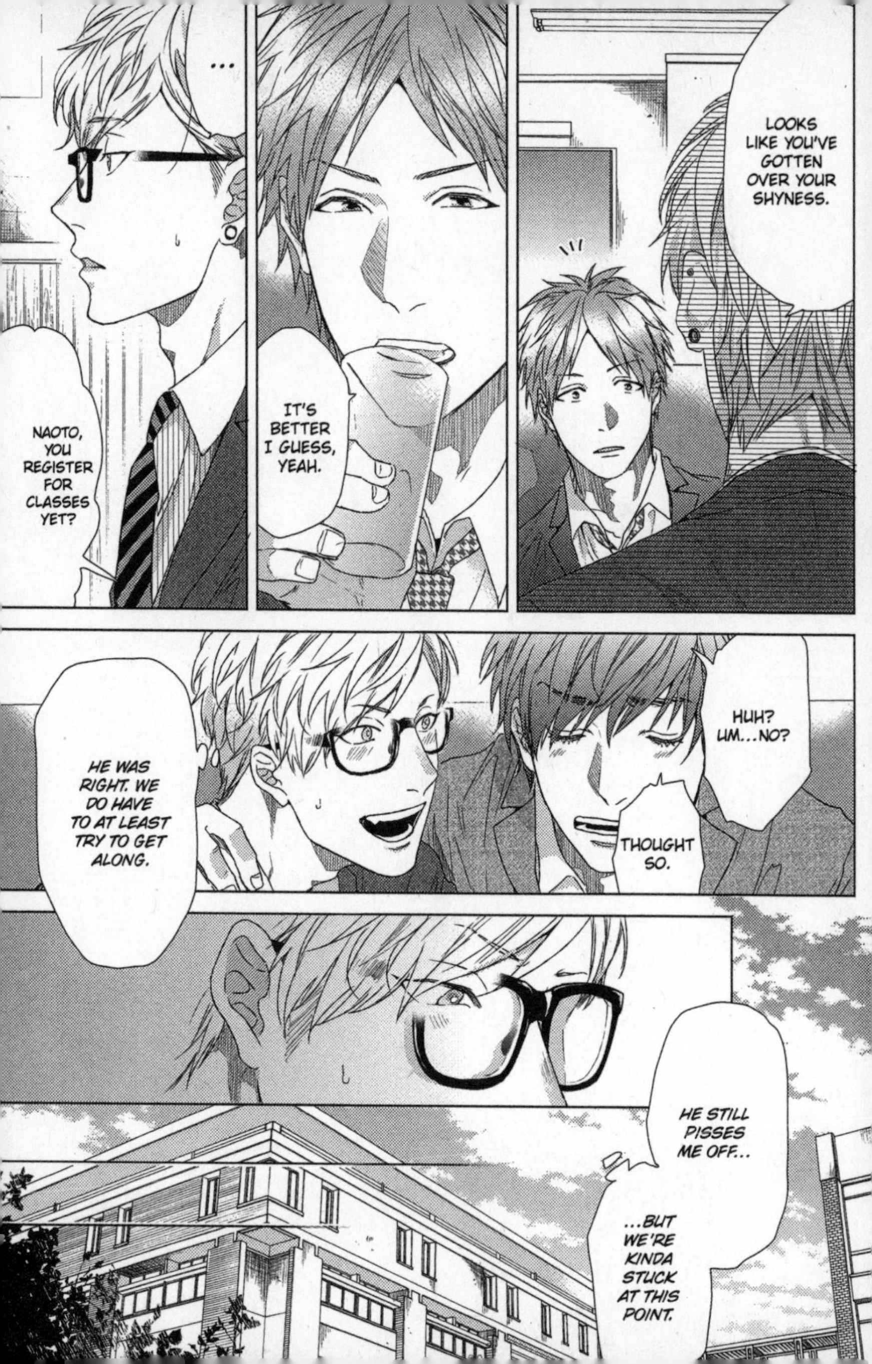
LOOKS LIKE YOU'VE GOTTEN OVER YOUR SHYNESS.
IT'S BETTER I GUESS, YEAH.
...
NAOTO, YOU REGISTER FOR CLASSES YET?
HUH? UM...NO?
THOUGHT SO.
HE WAS RIGHT. WE DO HAVE TO AT LEAST TRY TO GET ALONG.
HE STILL PISSES ME OFF...
...BUT WE'RE KINDA STUCK AT THIS POINT.

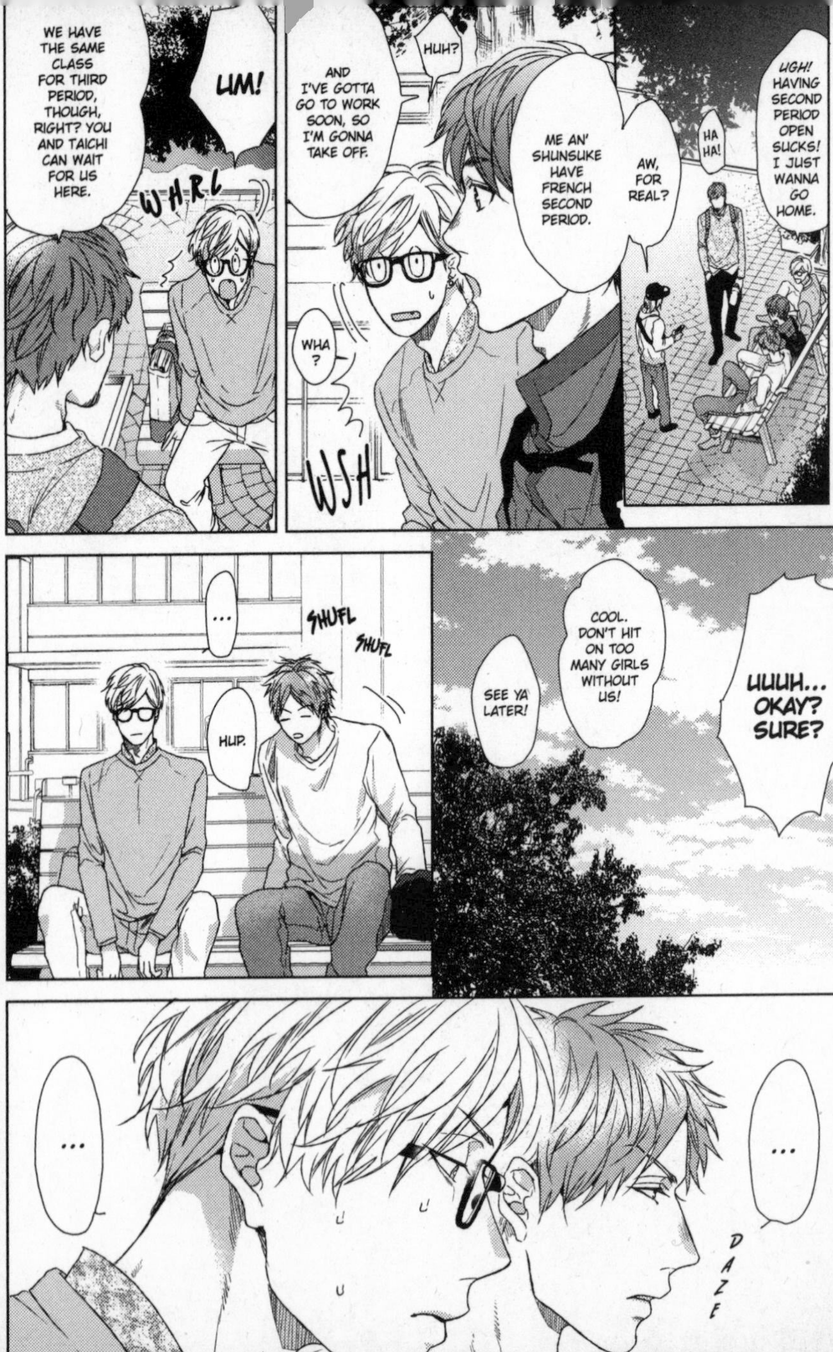
UGH! HAVING SECOND PERIOD OPEN SUCKS! I JUST WANNA GO HOME.
HA HA!
AW, FOR REAL?
ME AN' SHUNSUKE HAVE FRENCH SECOND PERIOD.
HUH?
AND I'VE GOTTA GO TO WORK SOON, SO I'M GONNA TAKE OFF.
WHA?
WSH
UM!
WE HAVE THE SAME CLASS FOR THIRD PERIOD, THOUGH, RIGHT? YOU AND TAICHI CAN WAIT FOR US HERE.
WHRL
UUUH... OKAY? SURE?
COOL. DON'T HIT ON TOO MANY GIRLS WITHOUT US!
SEE YA LATER!
SHUFL
SHUFL
...
HUP.
...
DAZE
...

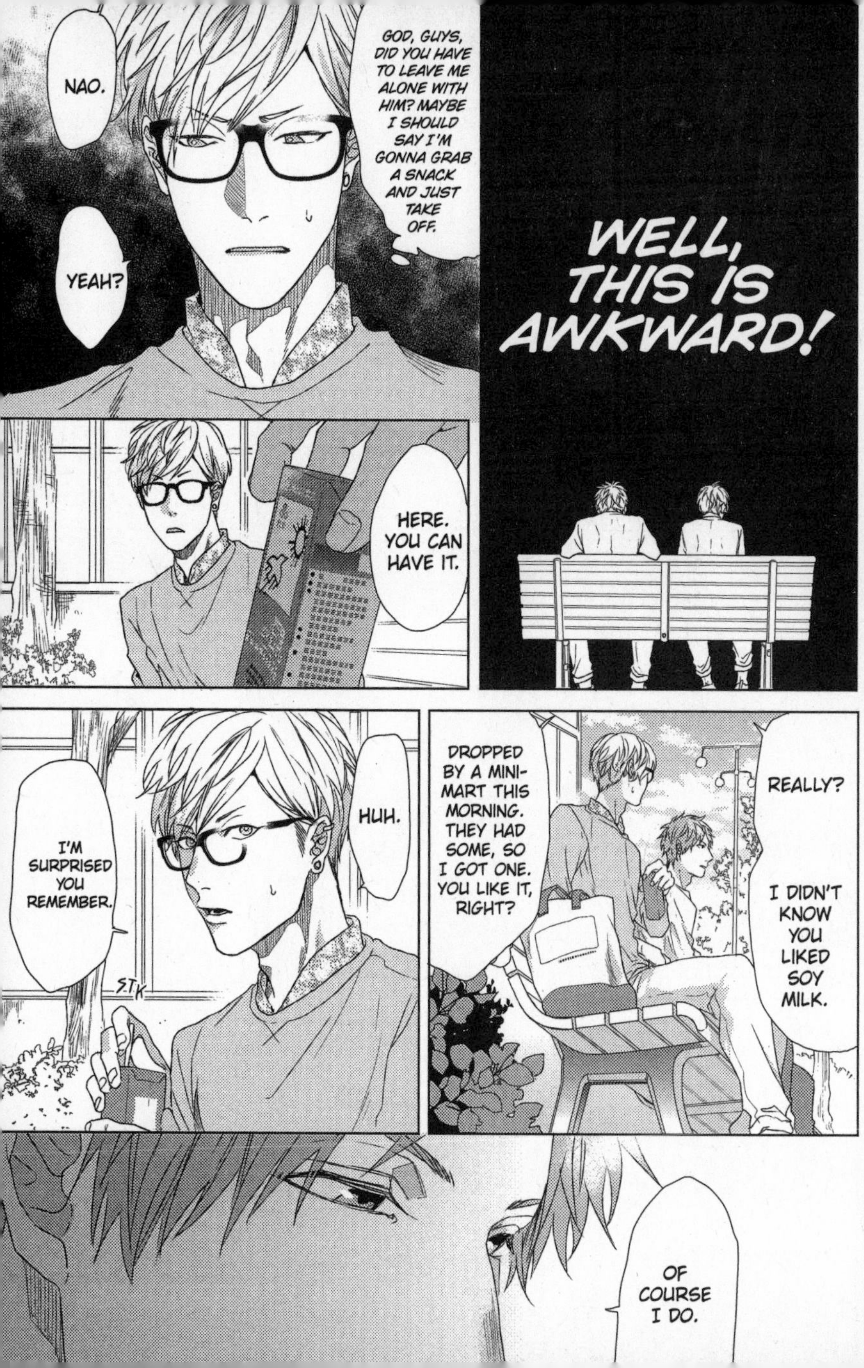
WELL, THIS IS AWKWARD!
GOD, GUYS, DID YOU HAVE TO LEAVE ME ALONE WITH HIM? MAYBE I SHOULD SAY I'M GONNA GRAB A SNACK AND JUST TAKE OFF.
NAO.
YEAH?
HERE. YOU CAN HAVE IT.
REALLY?
I DIDN'T KNOW YOU LIKED SOY MILK.
DROPPED BY A MINI-MART THIS MORNING. THEY HAD SOME, SO I GOT ONE. YOU LIKE IT, RIGHT?
HUH.
I'M SURPRISED YOU REMEMBER.
STK
OF COURSE I DO.

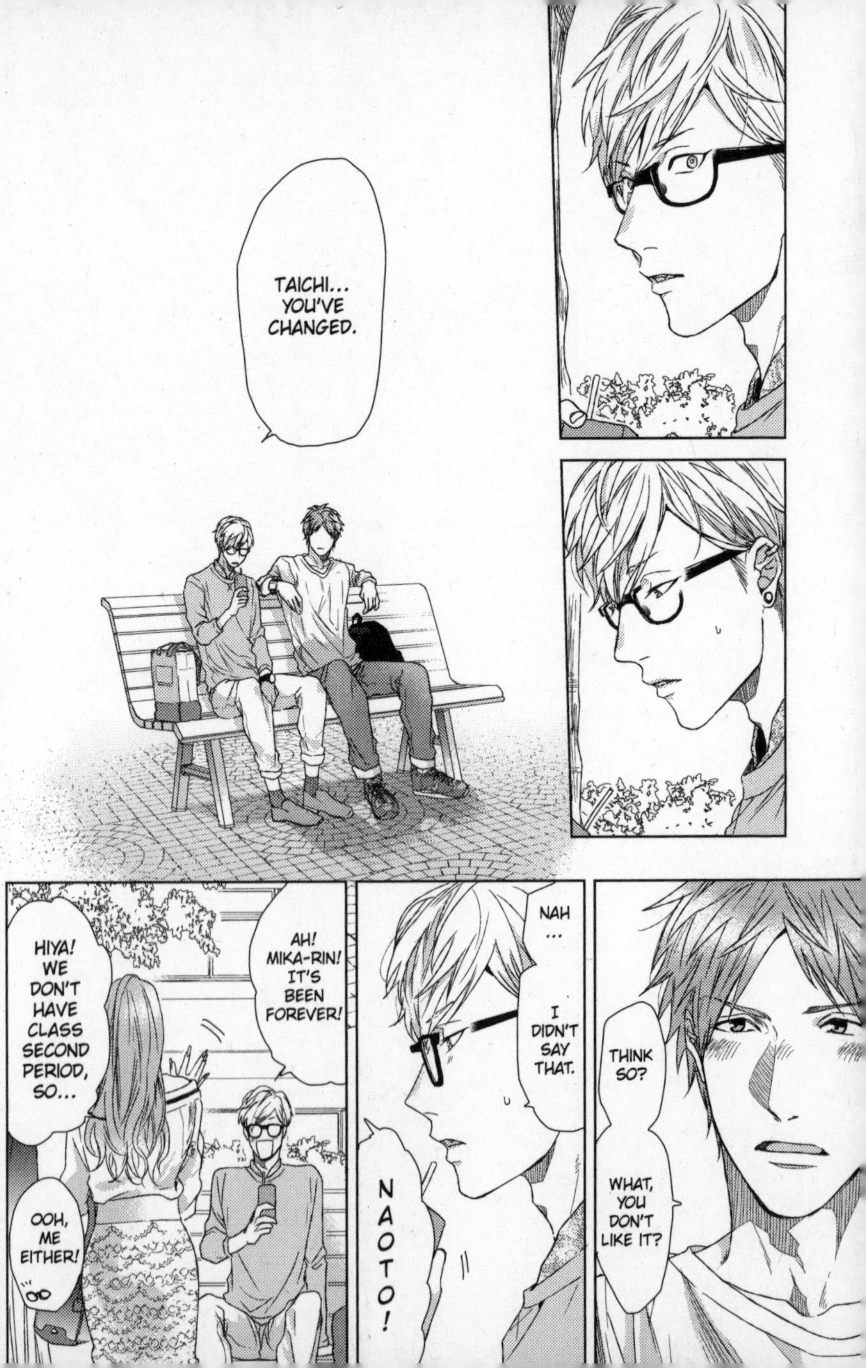
TAICHI... YOU'VE CHANGED.
THINK SO?
WHAT, YOU DON'T LIKE IT?
NAH ... I DIDN'T SAY THAT.
NAOTO!
AH! MIKA-RIN! IT'S BEEN FOREVER!
HIYA! WE DON'T HAVE CLASS SECOND PERIOD, SO...
OOH, ME EITHER!

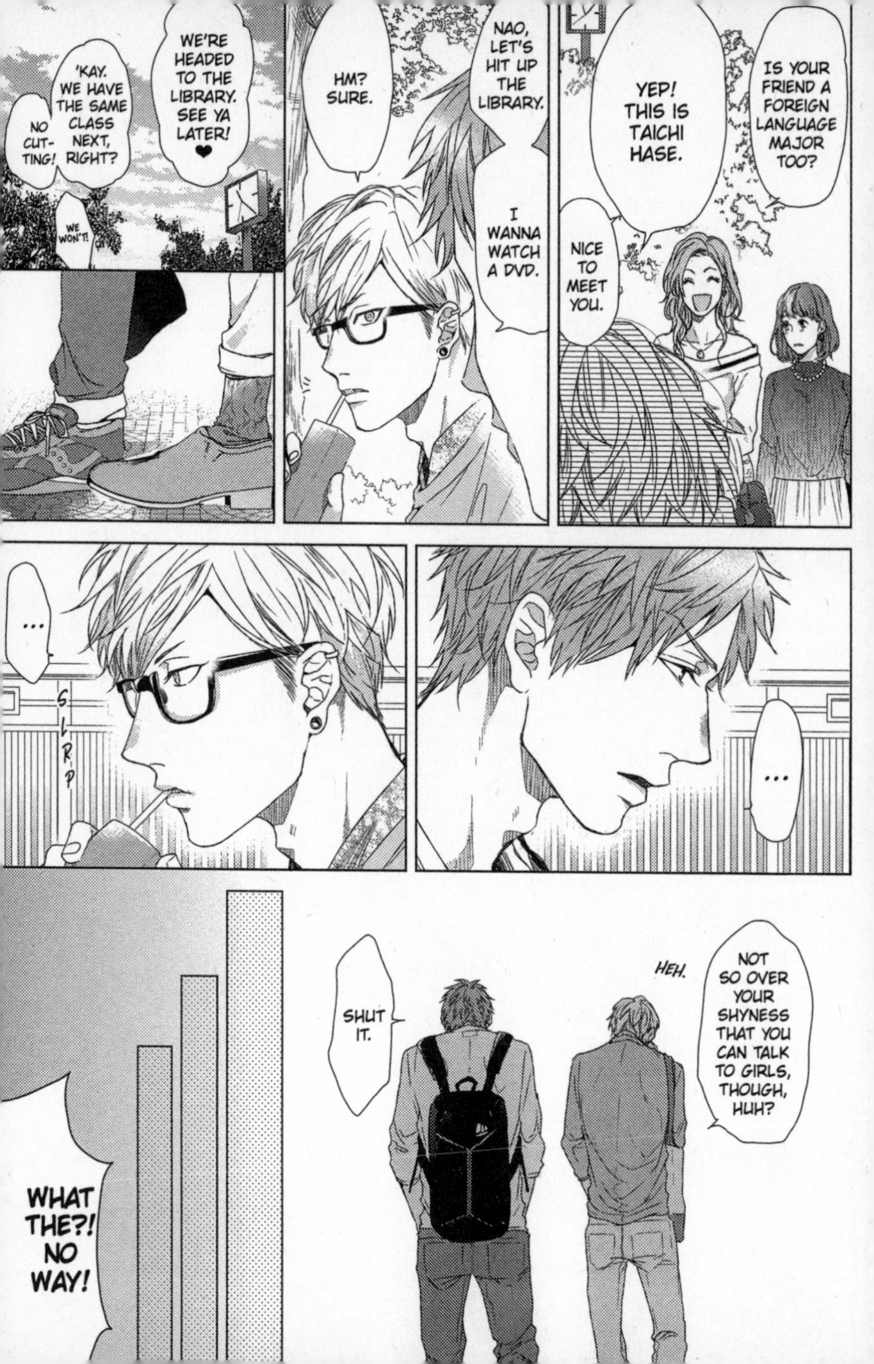
IS YOUR FRIEND A FOREIGN LANGUAGE MAJOR TOO?
YEP! THIS IS TAICHI HASE.
NICE TO MEET YOU.
NAO, LET'S HIT UP THE LIBRARY.
I WANNA WATCH A DVD.
HM? SURE.
WE'RE HEADED TO THE LIBRARY. SEE YA LATER! ❤
'KAY. WE HAVE THE SAME CLASS NEXT, RIGHT?
NO CUT-TING!
WE WON'T!
...
...
SLRP
NOT SO OVER YOUR SHYNESS THAT YOU CAN TALK TO GIRLS, THOUGH, HUH?
HEH.
SHUT IT.
WHAT THE?! NO WAY!

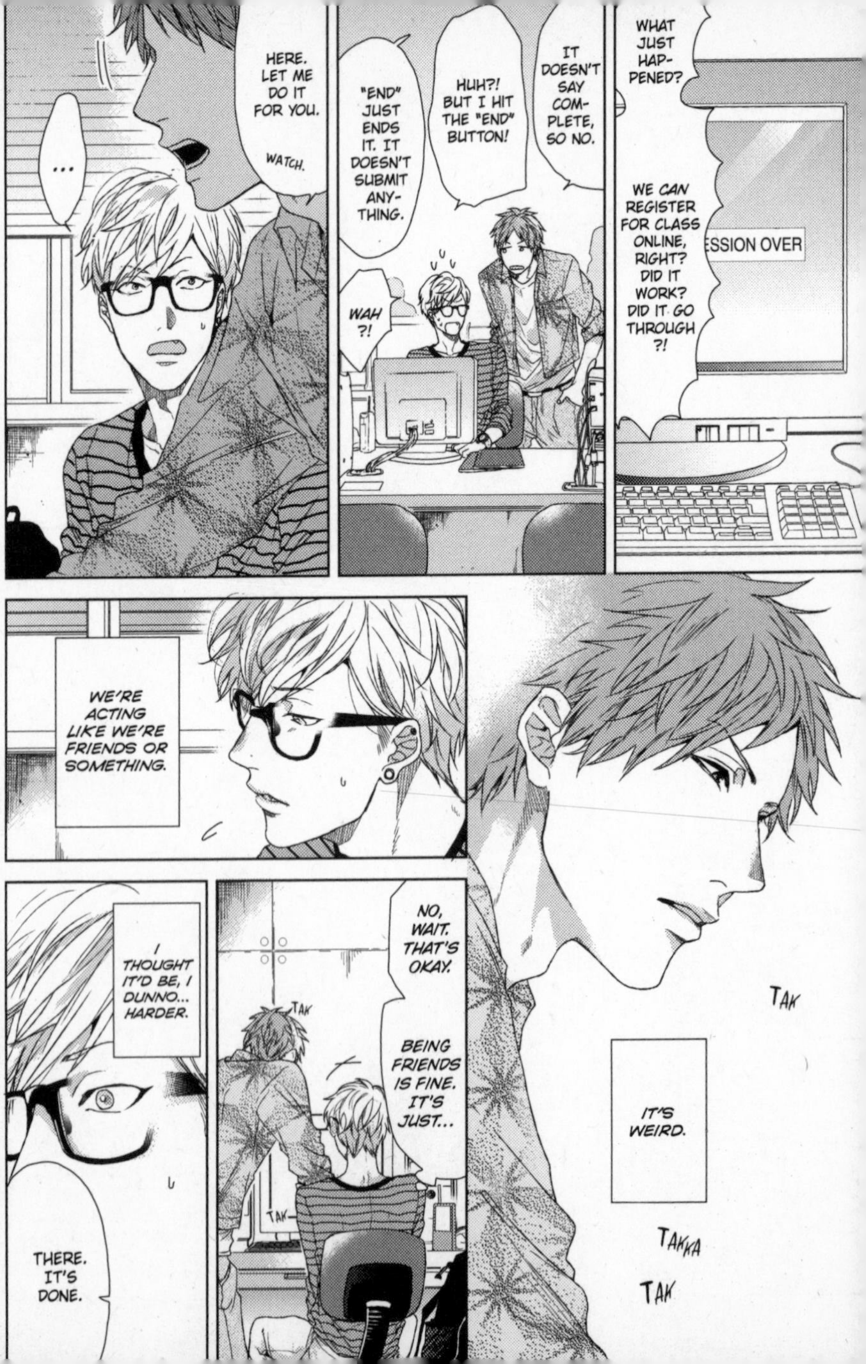
WHAT JUST HAP-PENED?
WE CAN REGISTER FOR CLASS ONLINE, RIGHT? DID IT WORK? DID IT GO THROUGH?!
ESSION OVER
IT DOESN'T SAY COM-PLETE, SO NO.
HUH?! BUT I HIT THE "END" BUTTON!
"END" JUST ENDS IT. IT DOESN'T SUBMIT ANY-THING.
WAH?!
HERE. LET ME DO IT FOR YOU.
WATCH.
...
TAK
IT'S WEIRD.
TAKKA
TAK
WE'RE ACTING LIKE WE'RE FRIENDS OR SOMETHING.
NO, WAIT. THAT'S OKAY.
TAK
BEING FRIENDS IS FINE. IT'S JUST...
TAK
I THOUGHT IT'D BE, I DUNNO... HARDER.
THERE. IT'S DONE.

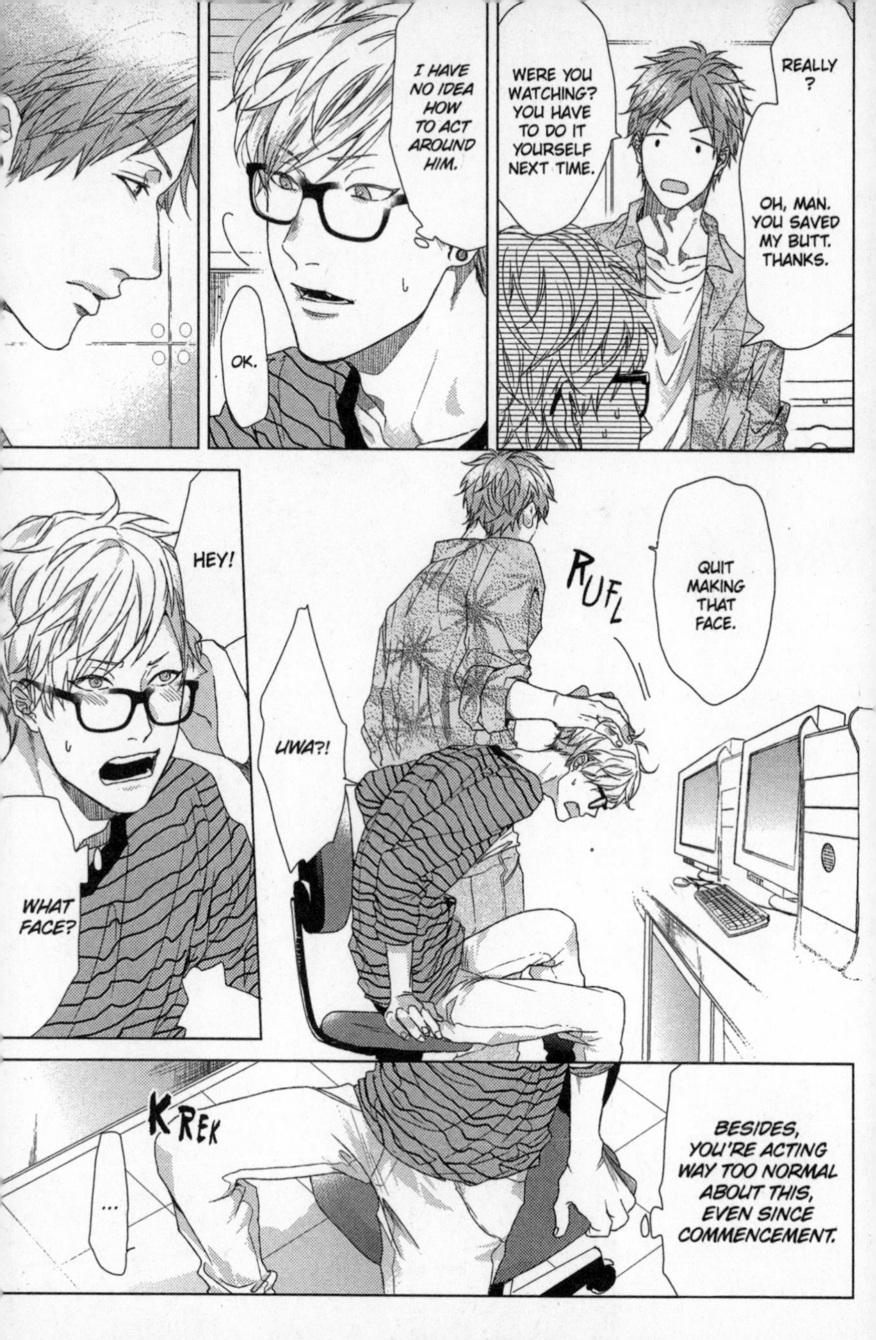
REALLY?
OH, MAN. YOU SAVED MY BUTT. THANKS.
WERE YOU WATCHING? YOU HAVE TO DO IT YOURSELF NEXT TIME.
I HAVE NO IDEA HOW TO ACT AROUND HIM.
OK.
QUIT MAKING THAT FACE.
RUFL
UWA?!
HEY!
WHAT FACE?
BESIDES, YOU'RE ACTING WAY TOO NORMAL ABOUT THIS, EVEN SINCE COMMENCEMENT.
KREK
...

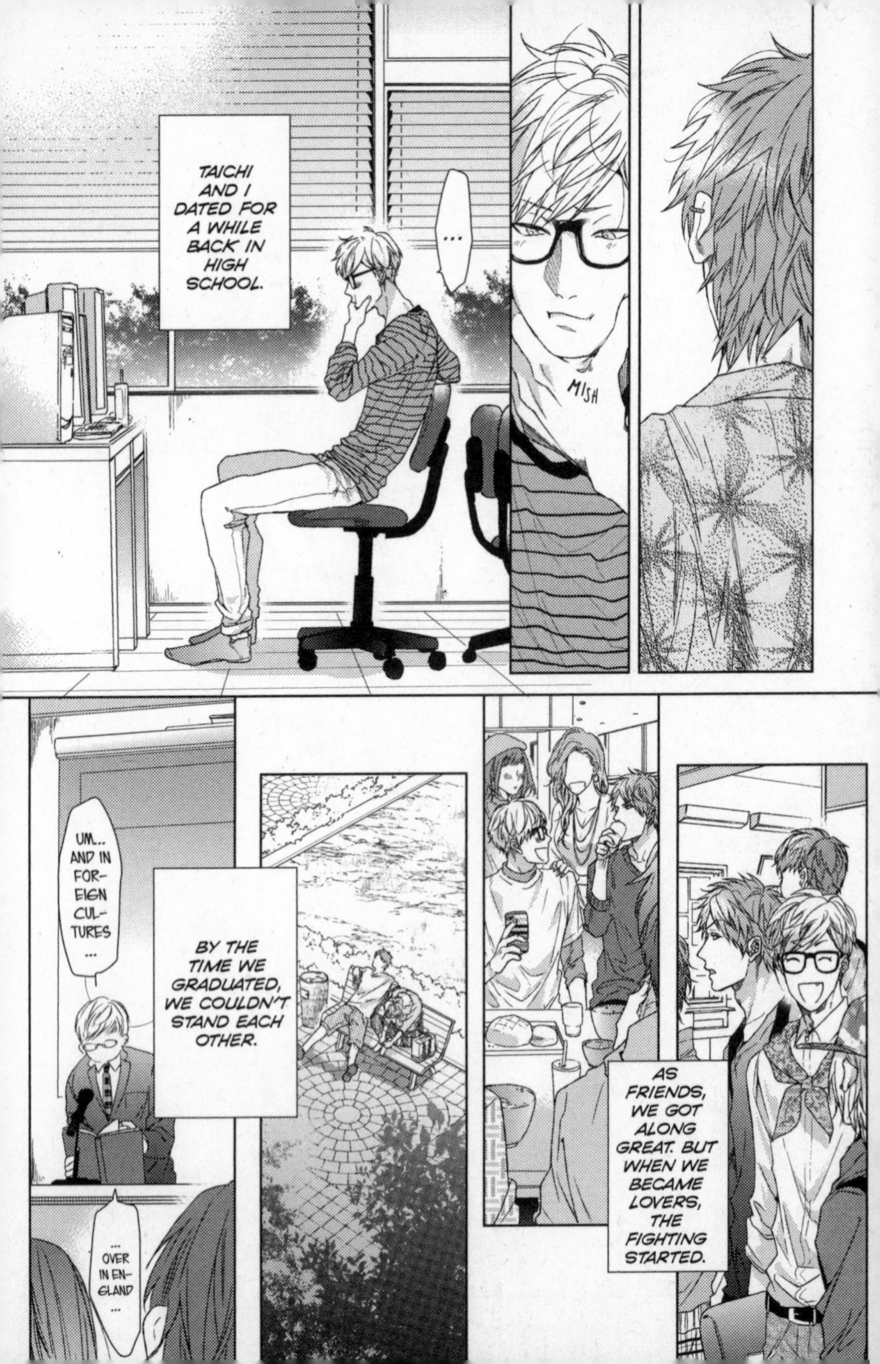
MISH
TAICHI AND I DATED FOR A WHILE BACK IN HIGH SCHOOL.
...
AS FRIENDS, WE GOT ALONG GREAT. BUT WHEN WE BECAME LOVERS, THE FIGHTING STARTED.
BY THE TIME WE GRADUATED, WE COULDN'T STAND EACH OTHER.
UM... AND IN FOR-EIGN CUL-TURES ...
... OVER IN EN-GLAND ...

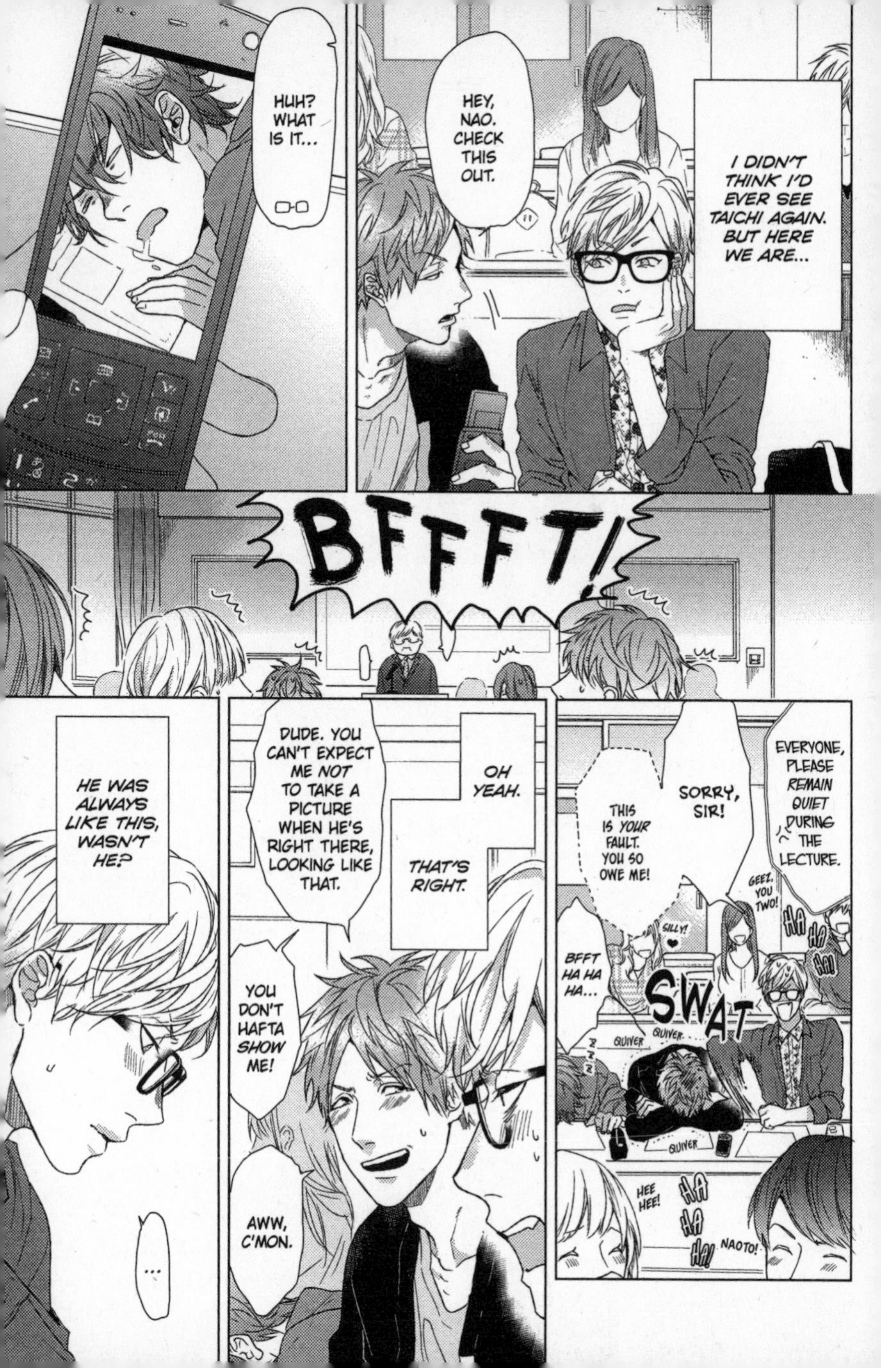
I DIDN'T THINK I'D EVER SEE TAICHI AGAIN. BUT HERE WE ARE...
HEY, NAO. CHECK THIS OUT.
HUH? WHAT IS IT...
BFFFT!
EVERYONE, PLEASE *REMAIN* QUIET DURING THE LECTURE.
SORRY, SIR!
THIS IS *YOUR* FAULT. YOU SO OWE ME!
GEEZ, YOU TWO!
HA HA HA!
SILLY!
BFFT HA HA HA...
SWAT
QUIVER QUIVER
QUIVER
HEE HEE!
HA HA HA!
NAOTO!
OH YEAH.
DUDE. YOU CAN'T EXPECT ME *NOT* TO TAKE A PICTURE WHEN HE'S RIGHT THERE, LOOKING LIKE THAT.
THAT'S RIGHT.
YOU DON'T HAFTA *SHOW* ME!
AWW, C'MON.
HE WAS ALWAYS LIKE THIS, WASN'T HE?
...

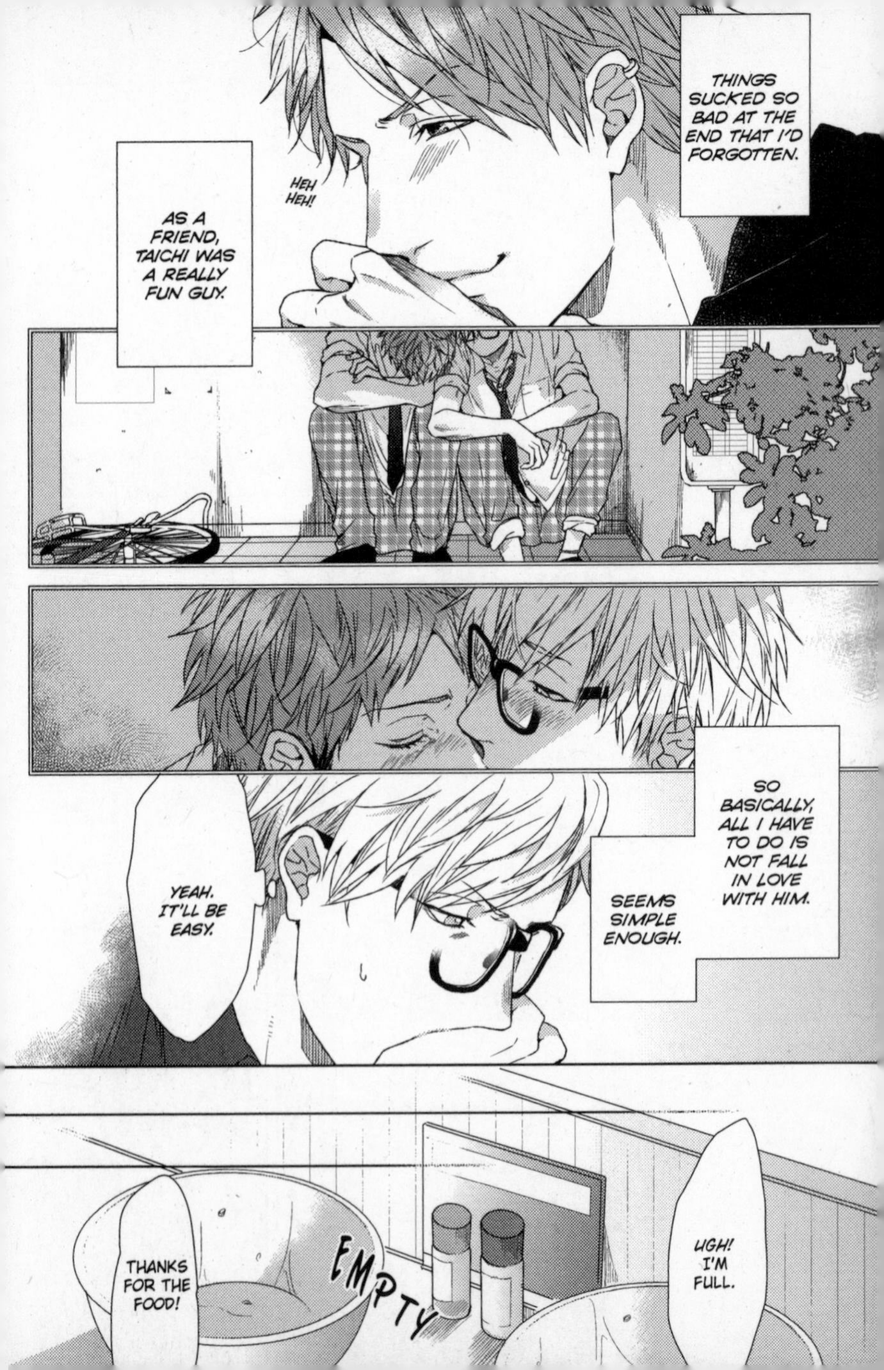
THINGS SUCKED SO BAD AT THE END THAT I'D FORGOTTEN.
HEH HEH!
AS A FRIEND, TAICHI WAS A REALLY FUN GUY.
SO BASICALLY, ALL I HAVE TO DO IS NOT FALL IN LOVE WITH HIM.
SEEMS SIMPLE ENOUGH.
YEAH. IT'LL BE EASY.
UGH! I'M FULL.
EMPTY
THANKS FOR THE FOOD!

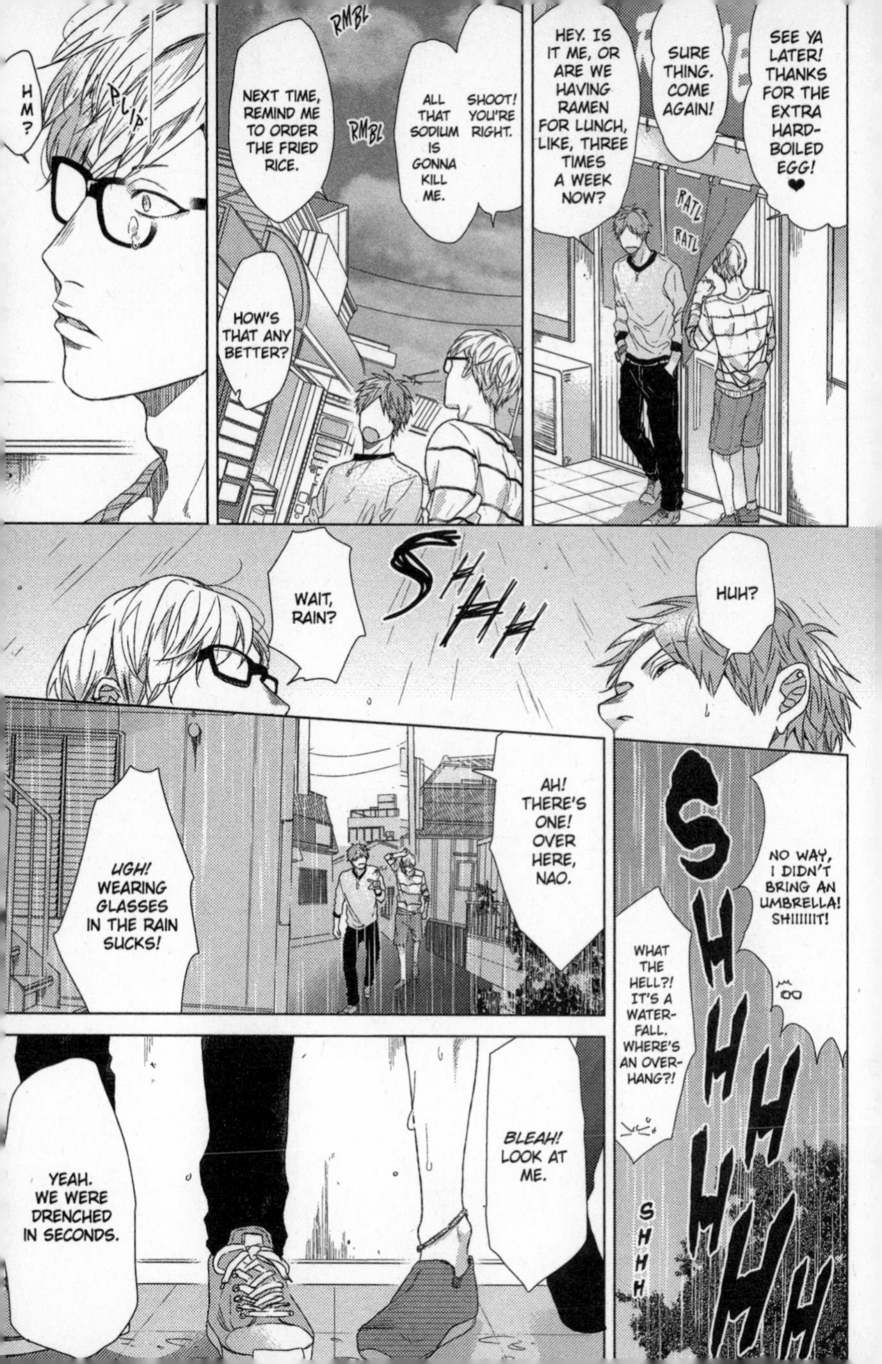
SEE YA LATER! THANKS FOR THE EXTRA HARD-BOILED EGG! ❤
SURE THING. COME AGAIN!
RATL RATL
HEY. IS IT ME, OR ARE WE HAVING RAMEN FOR LUNCH, LIKE, THREE TIMES A WEEK NOW?
RMBL
SHOOT! YOU'RE RIGHT.
ALL THAT SODIUM IS GONNA KILL ME.
RMBL
NEXT TIME, REMIND ME TO ORDER THE FRIED RICE.
HOW'S THAT ANY BETTER?
PLIP
HM?
HUH?
SHHH
WAIT, RAIN?
SHHHHHHH
NO WAY, I DIDN'T BRING AN UMBRELLA! SHIIIIIIT!
WHAT THE HELL?! IT'S A WATER-FALL. WHERE'S AN OVER-HANG?!
SHHH
AH! THERE'S ONE! OVER HERE, NAO.
UGH! WEARING GLASSES IN THE RAIN SUCKS!
BLEAH! LOOK AT ME.
YEAH. WE WERE DRENCHED IN SECONDS.

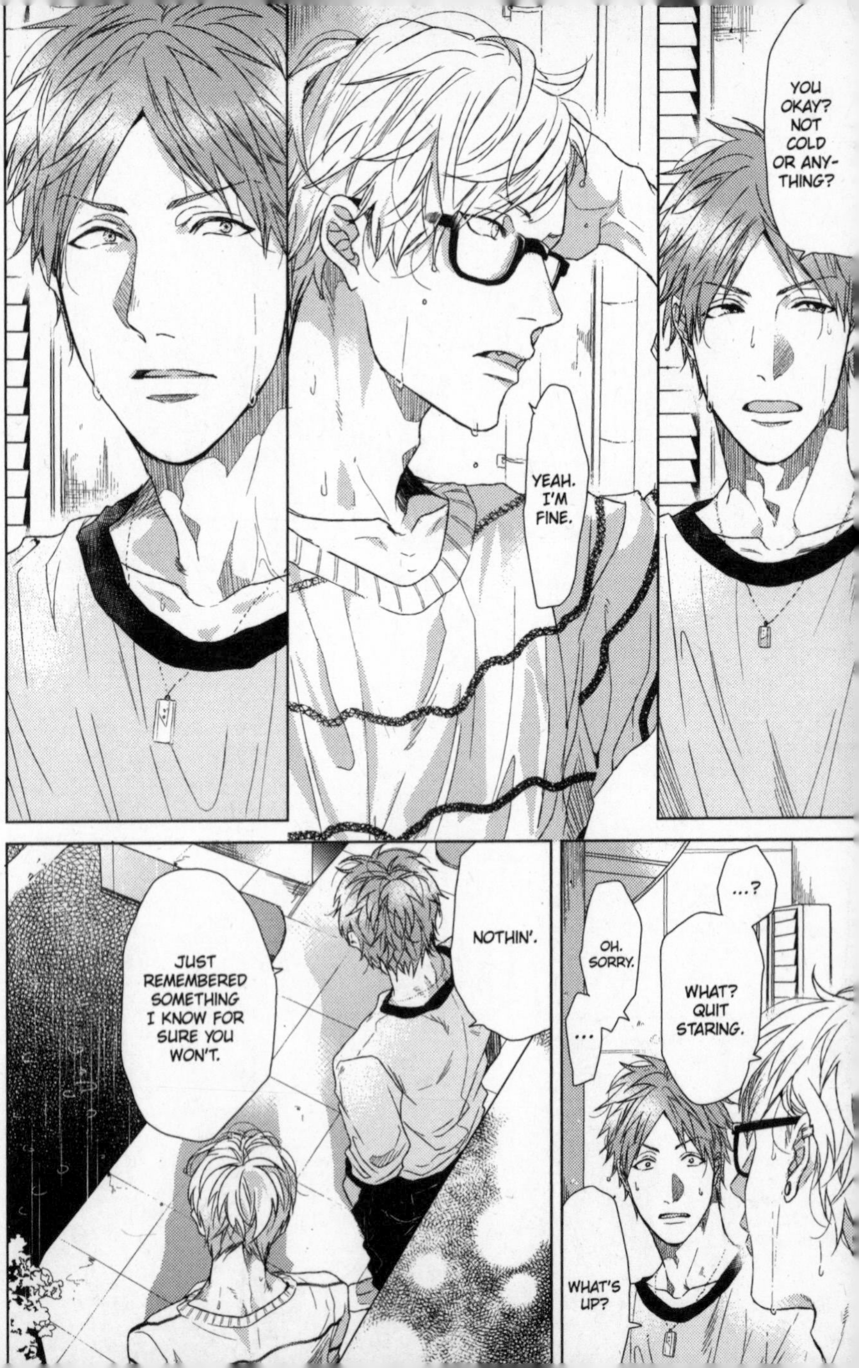
YOU OKAY? NOT COLD OR ANY-THING?
YEAH. I'M FINE.
...?
WHAT? QUIT STARING.
OH. SORRY.
...
WHAT'S UP?
NOTHIN'.
JUST REMEMBERED SOMETHING I KNOW FOR SURE YOU WON'T.

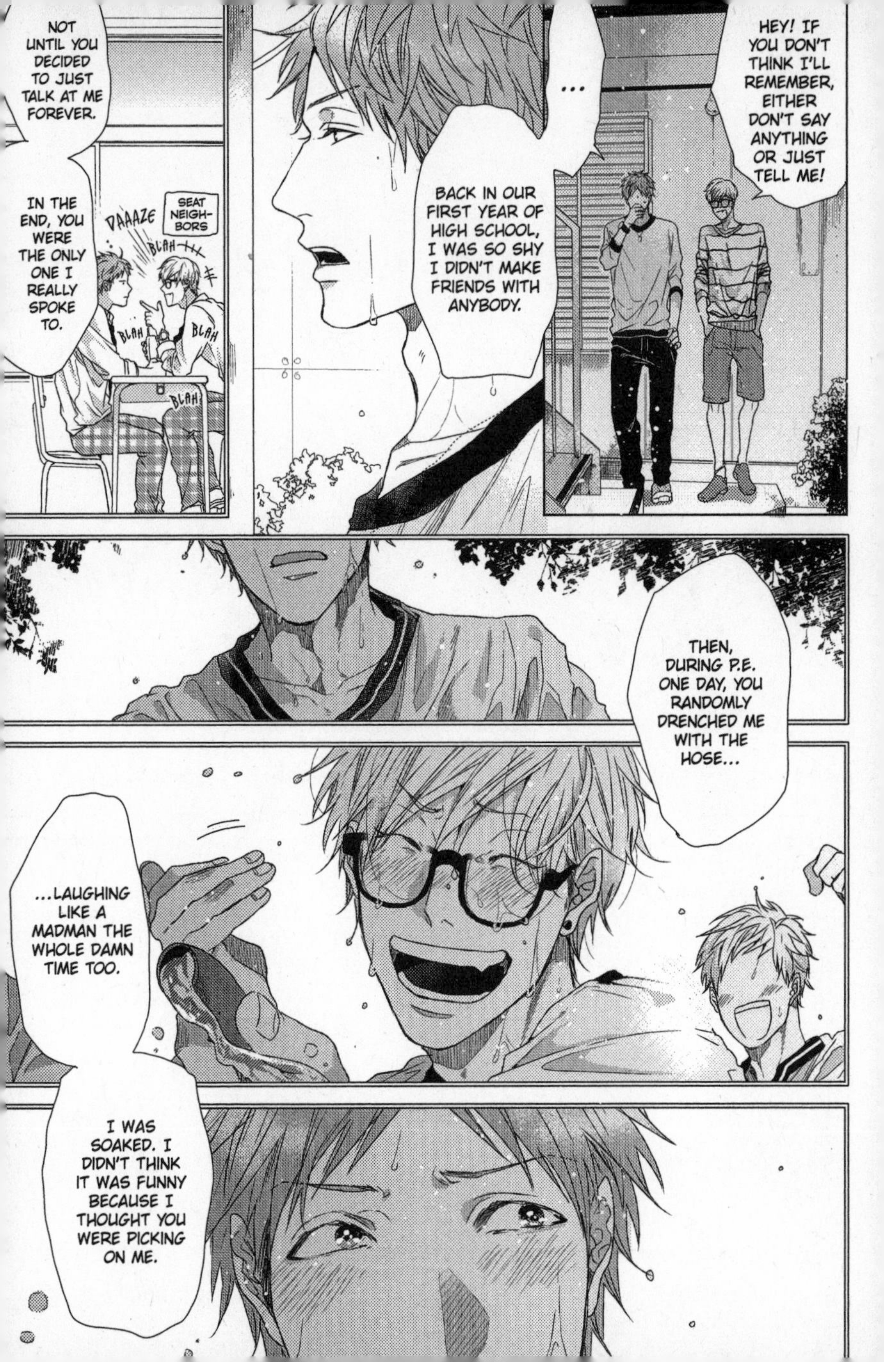
HEY! IF YOU DON'T THINK I'LL REMEMBER, EITHER DON'T SAY ANYTHING OR JUST TELL ME!
...
BACK IN OUR FIRST YEAR OF HIGH SCHOOL, I WAS SO SHY I DIDN'T MAKE FRIENDS WITH ANYBODY.
NOT UNTIL YOU DECIDED TO JUST TALK AT ME FOREVER.
SEAT NEIGHBORS
DAAAZE
BLAH
BLAH
BLAH
BLAH
IN THE END, YOU WERE THE ONLY ONE I REALLY SPOKE TO.
THEN, DURING P.E. ONE DAY, YOU RANDOMLY DRENCHED ME WITH THE HOSE...
...LAUGHING LIKE A MADMAN THE WHOLE DAMN TIME TOO.
I WAS SOAKED. I DIDN'T THINK IT WAS FUNNY BECAUSE I THOUGHT YOU WERE PICKING ON ME.

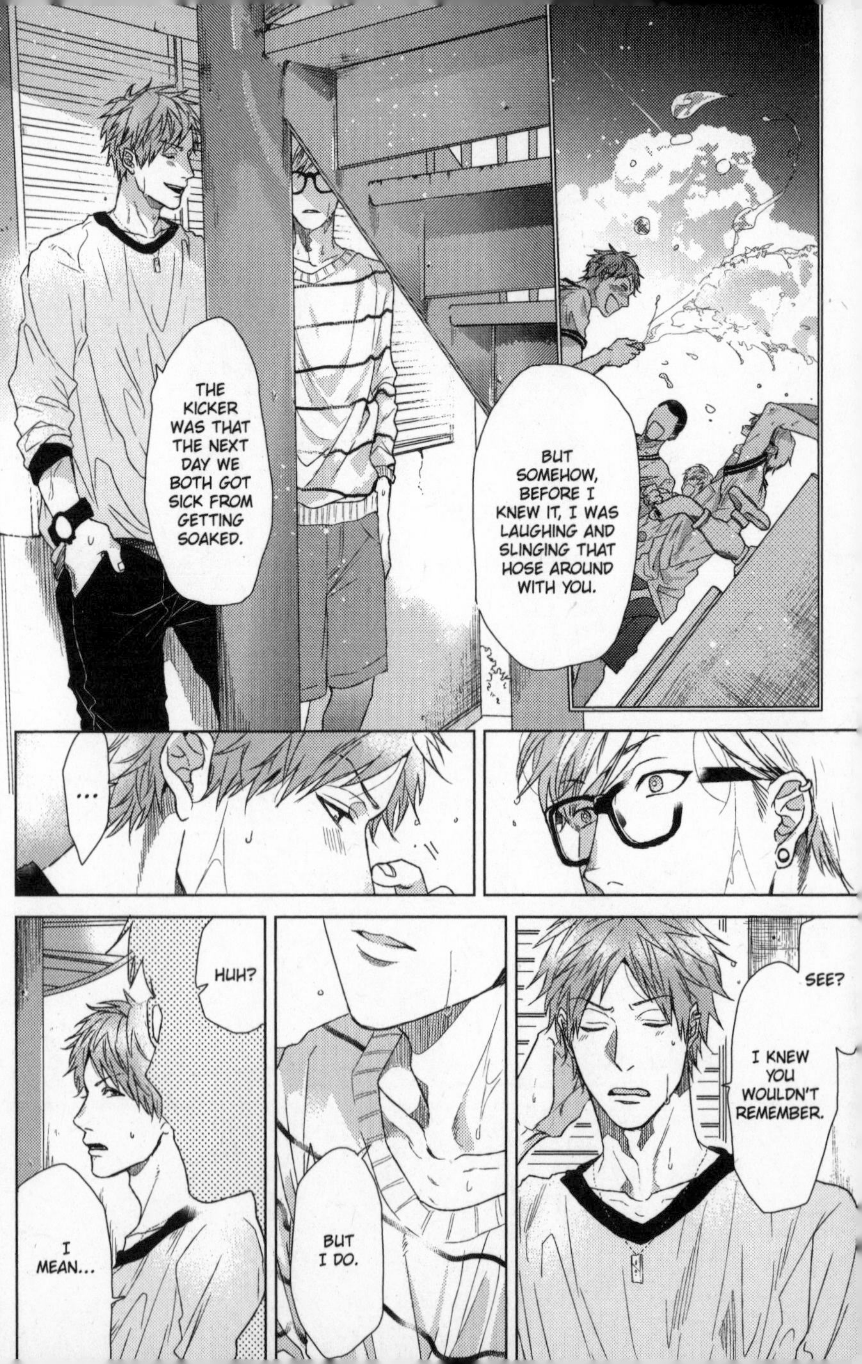
BUT SOMEHOW, BEFORE I KNEW IT, I WAS LAUGHING AND SLINGING THAT HOSE AROUND WITH YOU.
THE KICKER WAS THAT THE NEXT DAY WE BOTH GOT SICK FROM GETTING SOAKED.
...
SEE?
I KNEW YOU WOULDN'T REMEMBER.
BUT I DO.
HUH?
I MEAN...

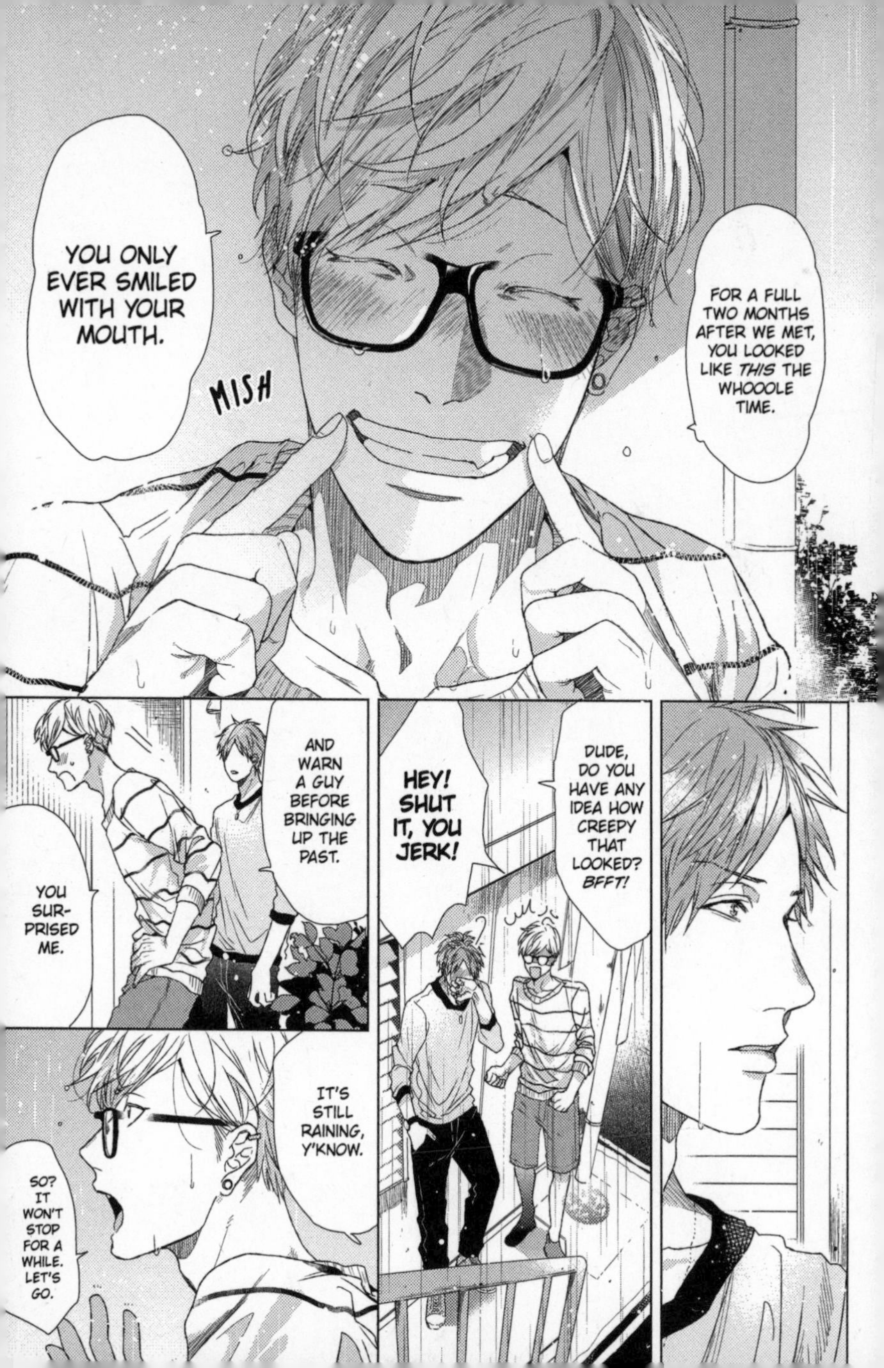
FOR A FULL TWO MONTHS AFTER WE MET, YOU LOOKED LIKE *THIS* THE WHOOOLE TIME.
MISH
YOU ONLY EVER SMILED WITH YOUR MOUTH.
DUDE, DO YOU HAVE ANY IDEA HOW CREEPY THAT LOOKED? *BFFT!*
HEY! SHUT IT, YOU JERK!
AND WARN A GUY BEFORE BRINGING UP THE PAST.
YOU SUR-PRISED ME.
IT'S STILL RAINING, Y'KNOW.
SO? IT WON'T STOP FOR A WHILE. LET'S GO.

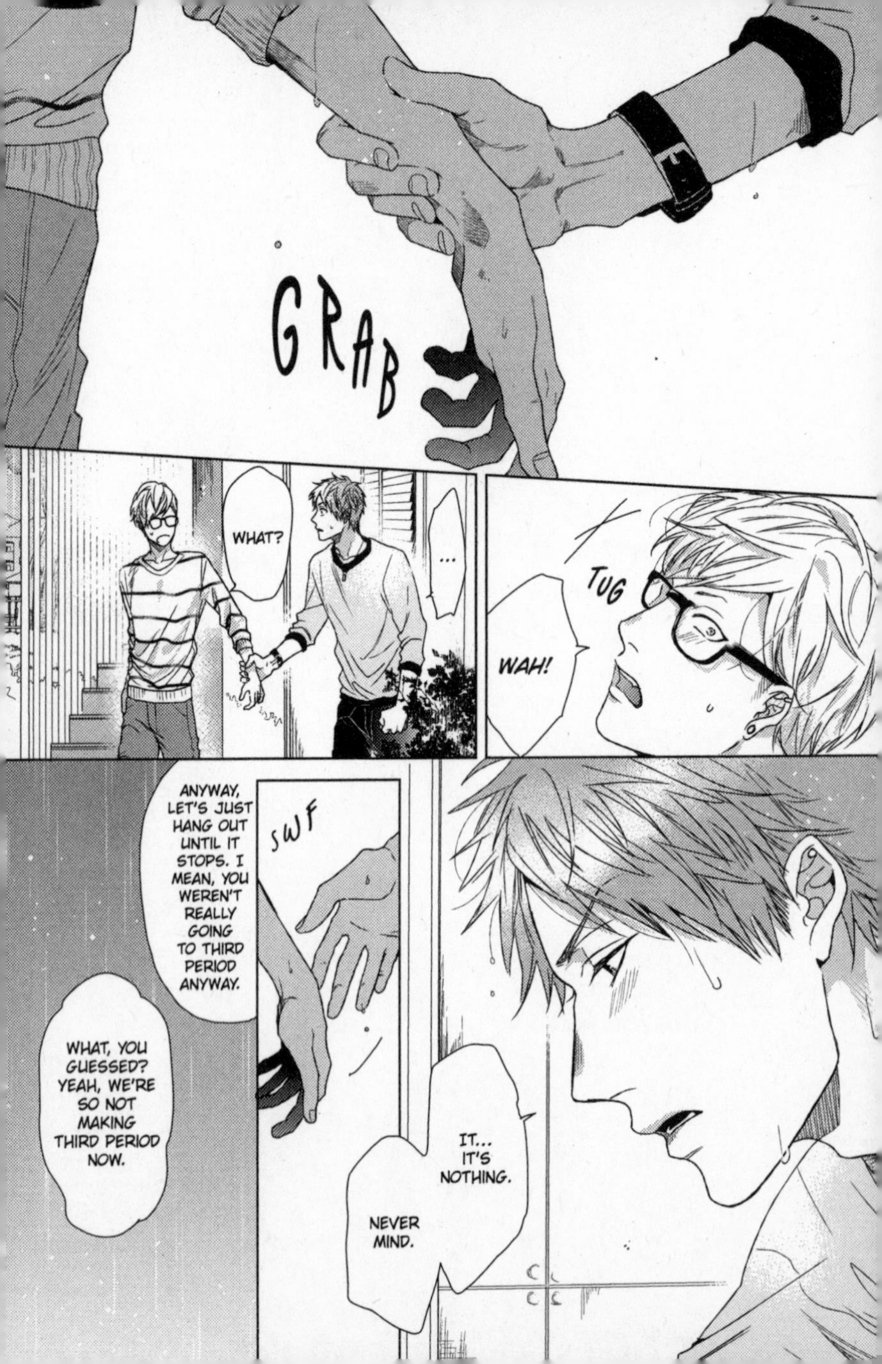
GRAB
WAH!
TUG
...
WHAT?
SWF
IT... IT'S NOTHING.
NEVER MIND.
ANYWAY, LET'S JUST HANG OUT UNTIL IT STOPS. I MEAN, YOU WEREN'T REALLY GOING TO THIRD PERIOD ANYWAY.
WHAT, YOU GUESSED? YEAH, WE'RE SO NOT MAKING THIRD PERIOD NOW.

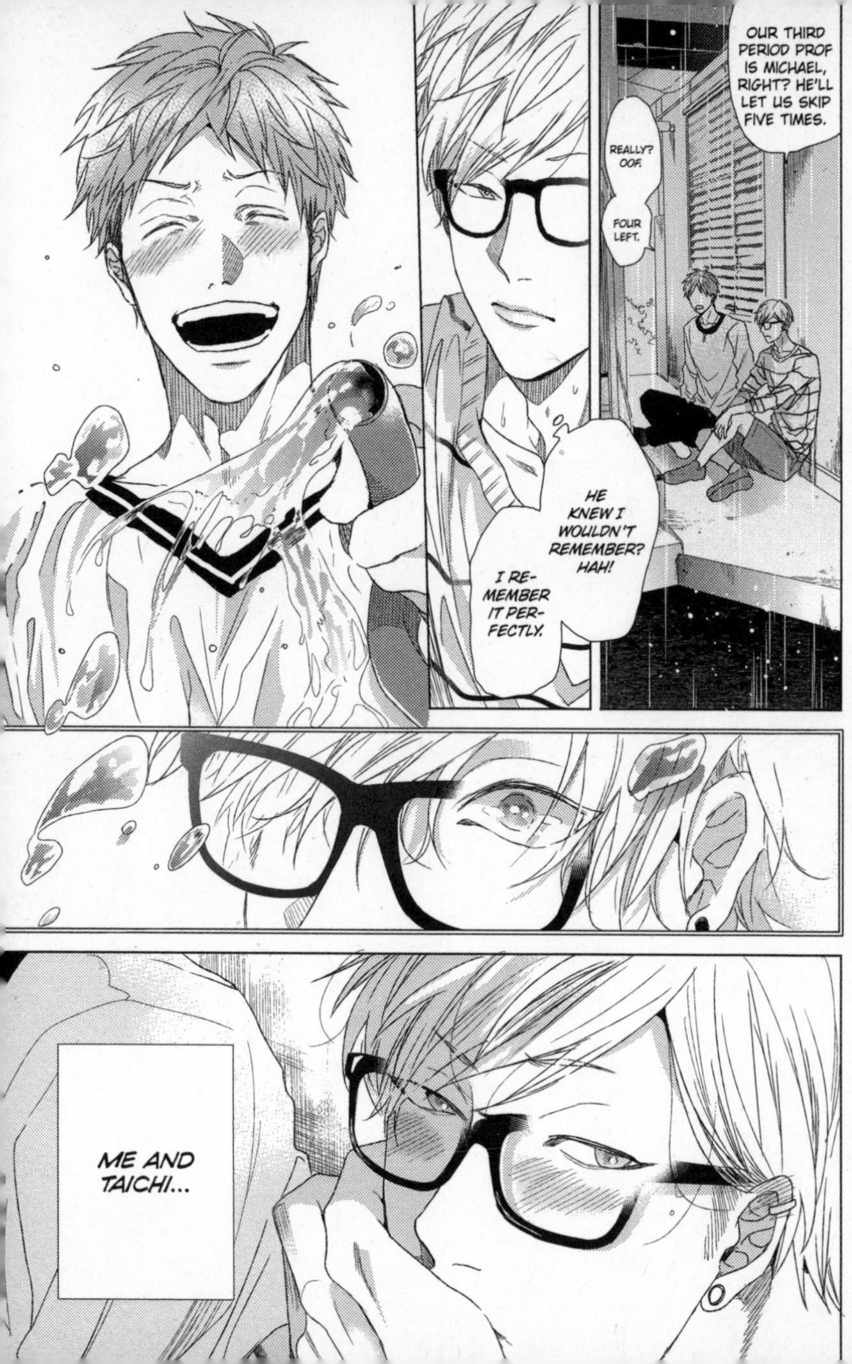
OUR THIRD PERIOD PROF IS MICHAEL, RIGHT? HE'LL LET US SKIP FIVE TIMES.
REALLY? OOF.
FOUR LEFT.
HE KNEW I WOULDN'T REMEMBER? HAH!
I RE-MEMBER IT PER-FECTLY.
ME AND TAICHI...

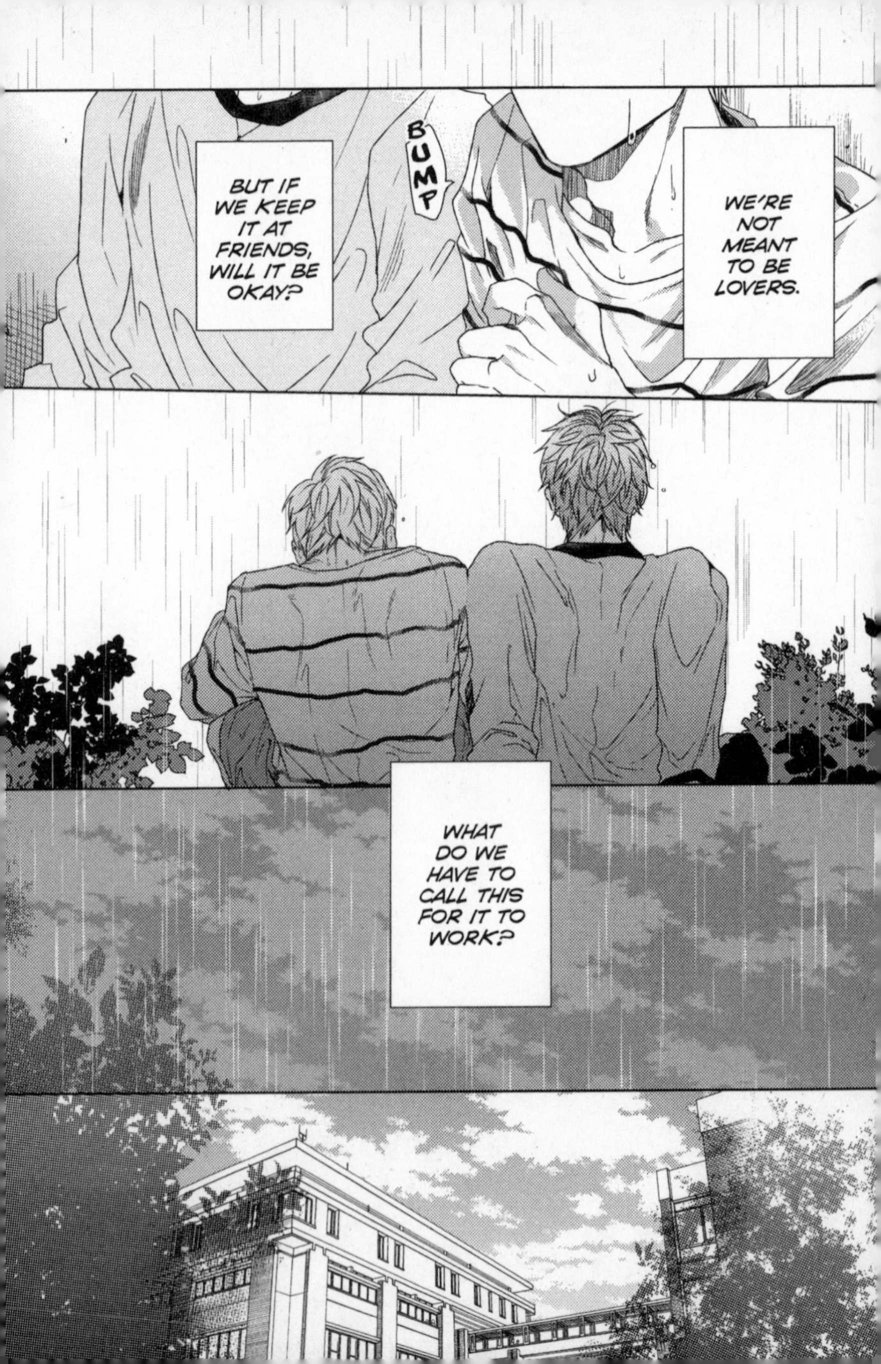
WE'RE NOT MEANT TO BE LOVERS.
BUMP
BUT IF WE KEEP IT AT FRIENDS, WILL IT BE OKAY?
WHAT DO WE HAVE TO CALL THIS FOR IT TO WORK?

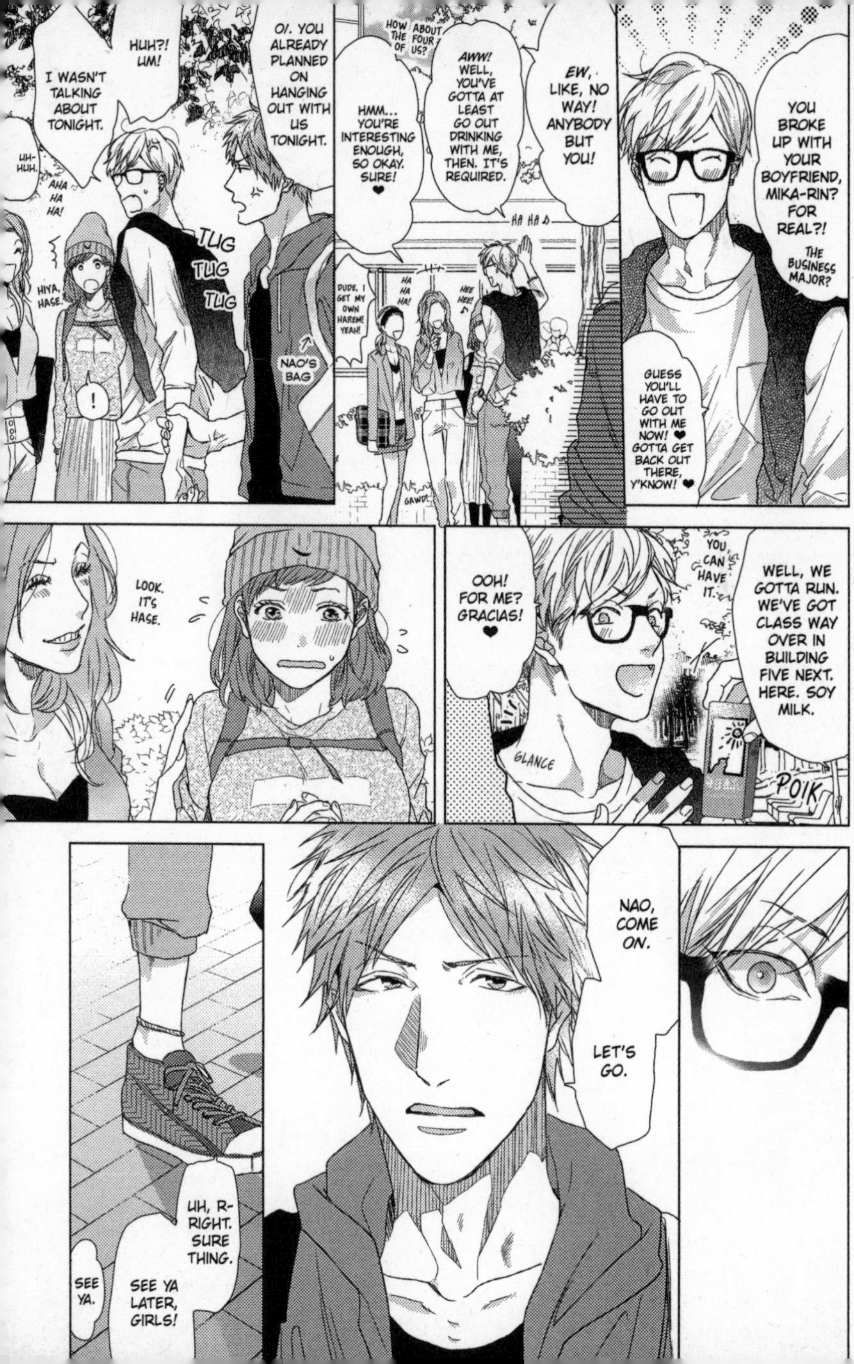
YOU BROKE UP WITH YOUR BOYFRIEND, MIKA-RIN? FOR REAL?!
THE BUSINESS MAJOR?
GUESS YOU'LL HAVE TO GO OUT WITH ME NOW! ❤ GOTTA GET BACK OUT THERE, Y'KNOW! ❤
EW, LIKE, NO WAY! ANYBODY BUT YOU!
AWW! WELL, YOU'VE GOTTA AT LEAST GO OUT DRINKING WITH ME, THEN. IT'S REQUIRED.
HOW ABOUT THE FOUR OF US?
HMM... YOU'RE INTERESTING ENOUGH, SO OKAY. SURE! ❤
HA HA ♪
HEE HEE! ♪
HA HA HA!
DUDE, I GET MY OWN HAREM! YEAH!
GAWD!
OI. YOU ALREADY PLANNED ON HANGING OUT WITH US TONIGHT.
HUH?! UM!
I WASN'T TALKING ABOUT TONIGHT.
UH-HUH.
AHA HA HA!
TUG TUG TUG
HIYA, HASE.
!
NAO'S BAG
WELL, WE GOTTA RUN. WE'VE GOT CLASS WAY OVER IN BUILDING FIVE NEXT. HERE. SOY MILK.
YOU CAN HAVE IT.
POIK
OOH! FOR ME? GRACIAS! ❤
GLANCE
LOOK. IT'S HASE.
NAO, COME ON.
LET'S GO.
UH, R-RIGHT. SURE THING.
SEE YA LATER, GIRLS!
SEE YA.

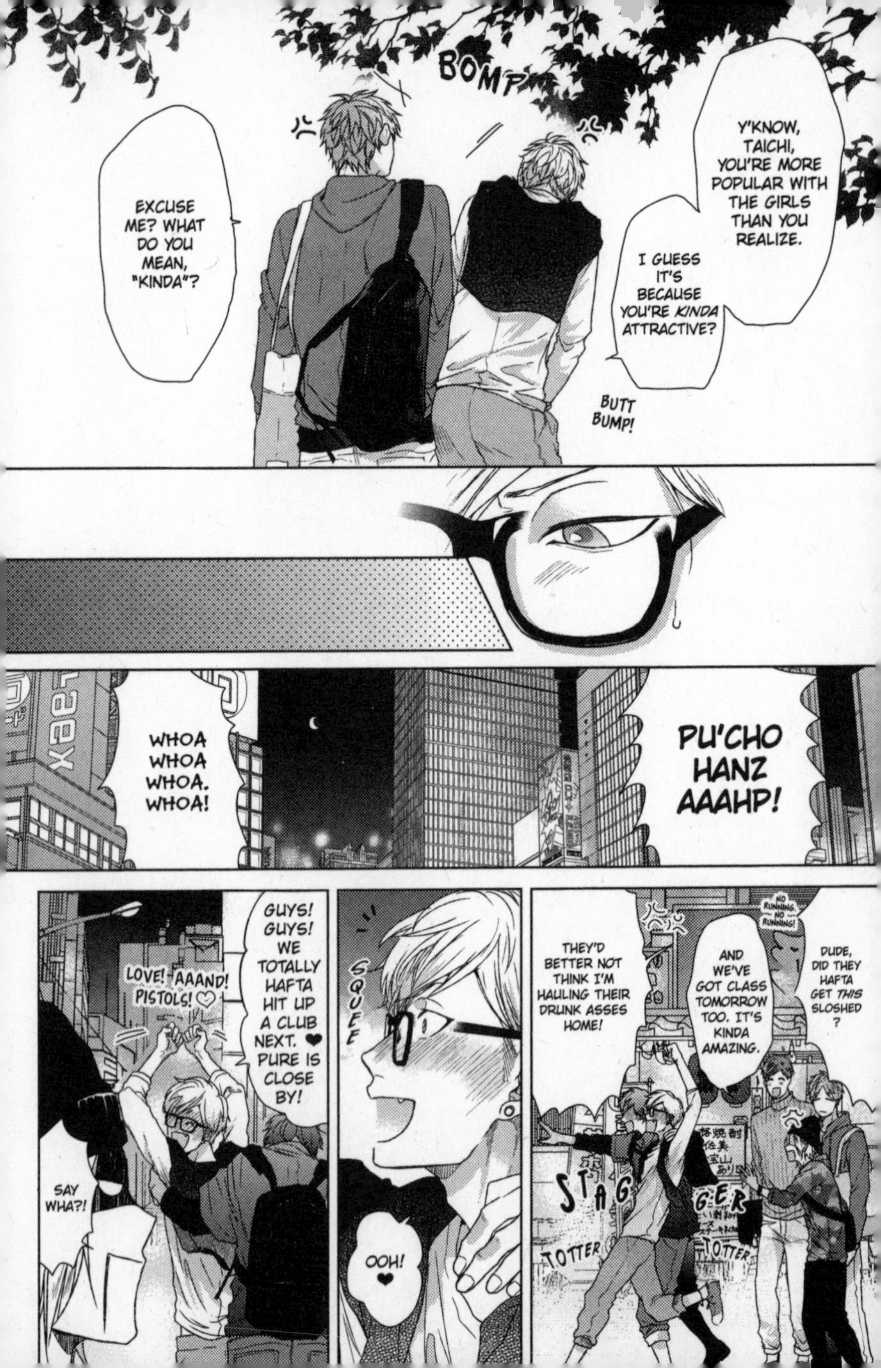
BOMP
Y'KNOW, TAICHI, YOU'RE MORE POPULAR WITH THE GIRLS THAN YOU REALIZE.
I GUESS IT'S BECAUSE YOU'RE *KINDA* ATTRACTIVE?
BUTT BUMP!
EXCUSE ME? WHAT DO YOU MEAN, "KINDA"?
PU'CHO HANZ AAAHP!
WHOA WHOA WHOA. WHOA!
NO RUNNING. NO RUNNING!
DUDE, DID THEY HAFTA GET *THIS* SLOSHED?
AND WE'VE GOT CLASS TOMORROW TOO. IT'S KINDA AMAZING.
THEY'D BETTER NOT THINK I'M HAULING THEIR DRUNK ASSES HOME!
STAGGER
TOTTER
TOTTER
SQUEE
OOH! ♥
GUYS! GUYS! WE TOTALLY HAFTA HIT UP A CLUB NEXT. ♥ PURE IS CLOSE BY!
LOVE! AAAND! PISTOLS! ♡
SAY WHA?!

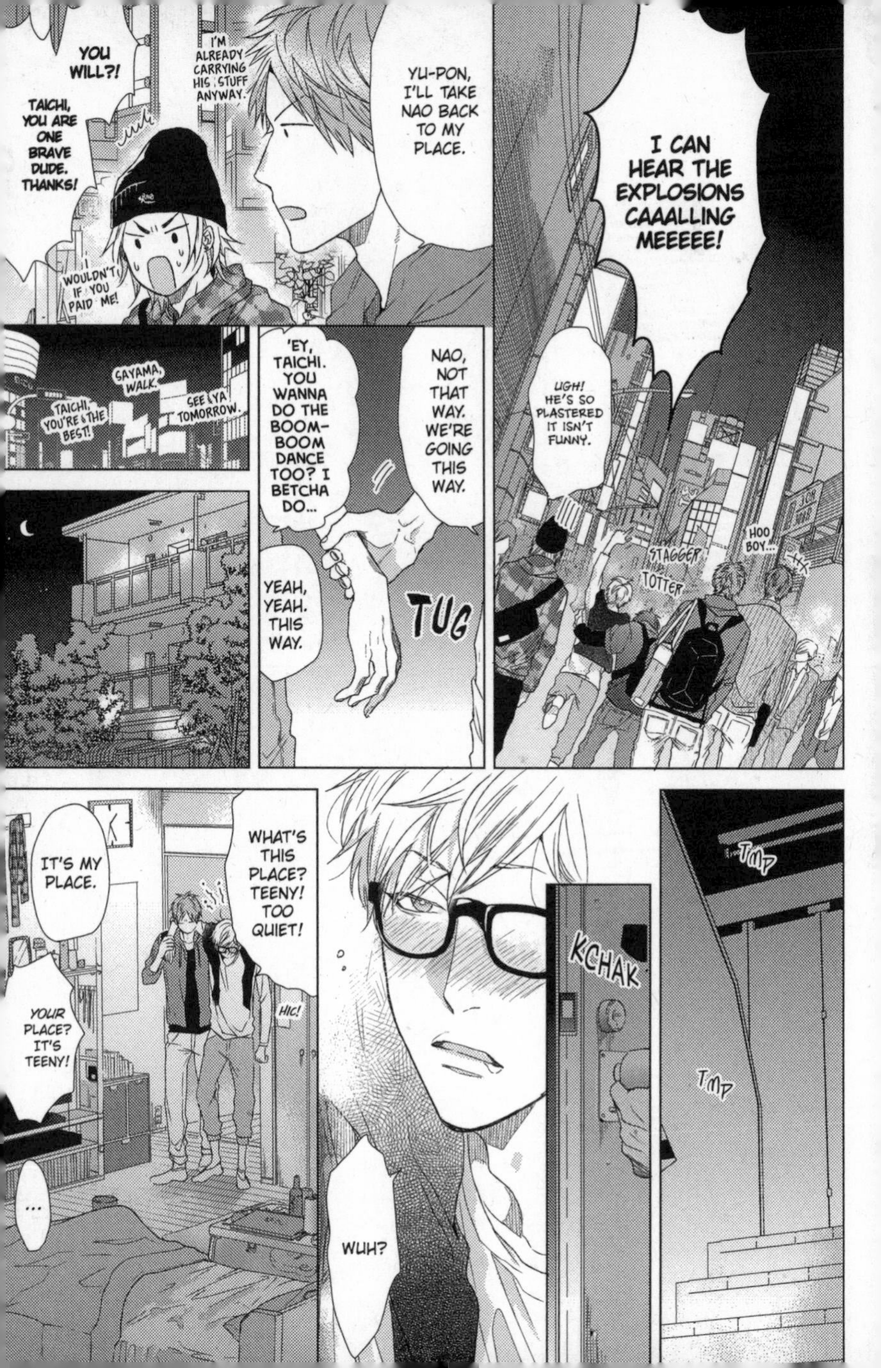

I CAN HEAR THE EXPLOSIONS CAAALLING MEEEEE!
UGH! HE'S SO PLASTERED IT ISN'T FUNNY.
HOO BOY...
STAGGER TOTTER
YU-PON, I'LL TAKE NAO BACK TO MY PLACE.
I'M ALREADY CARRYING HIS STUFF ANYWAY.
YOU WILL?!
TAICHI, YOU ARE ONE BRAVE DUDE. THANKS!
I WOULDN'T IF YOU PAID ME!
NAO, NOT THAT WAY. WE'RE GOING THIS WAY.
'EY, TAICHI. YOU WANNA DO THE BOOM-BOOM DANCE TOO? I BETCHA DO...
YEAH, YEAH. THIS WAY.
TUG
SEE YA TOMORROW.
SAYAMA, WALK.
TAICHI, YOU'RE THE BEST!
TMP
TMP
KCHAK
WUH?
WHAT'S THIS PLACE? TEENY! TOO QUIET!
IT'S MY PLACE.
HIC!
YOUR PLACE? IT'S TEENY!
...

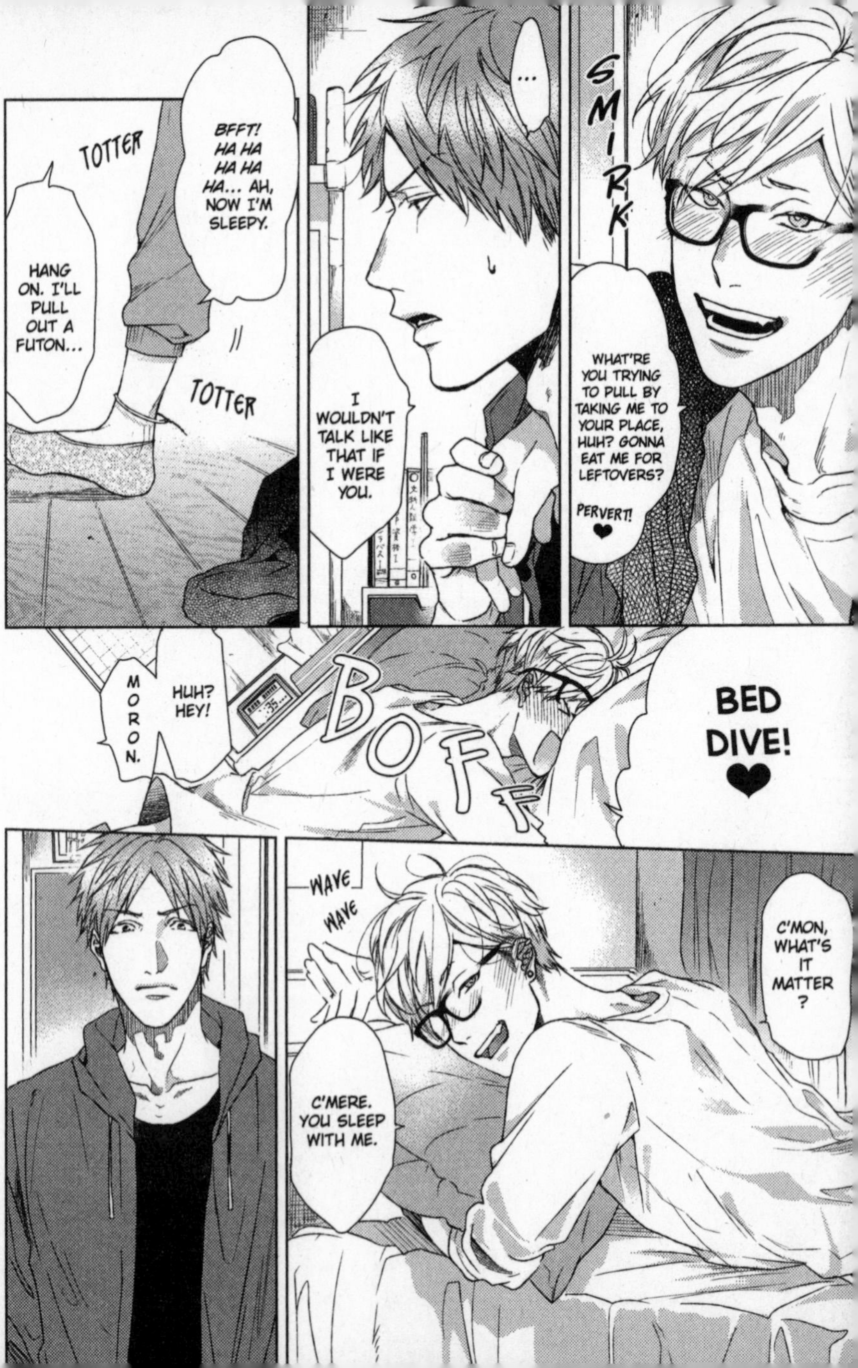
SMIRK
WHAT'RE YOU TRYING TO PULL BY TAKING ME TO YOUR PLACE, HUH? GONNA EAT ME FOR LEFTOVERS?
PERVERT! ❤
...
I WOULDN'T TALK LIKE THAT IF I WERE YOU.
BFFT! HA HA HA HA HA... AH, NOW I'M SLEEPY.
TOTTER
TOTTER
HANG ON. I'LL PULL OUT A FUTON...
BED DIVE! ❤
BOFF
HUH? HEY!
MORON.
C'MON, WHAT'S IT MATTER?
WAVE
WAVE
C'MERE. YOU SLEEP WITH ME.

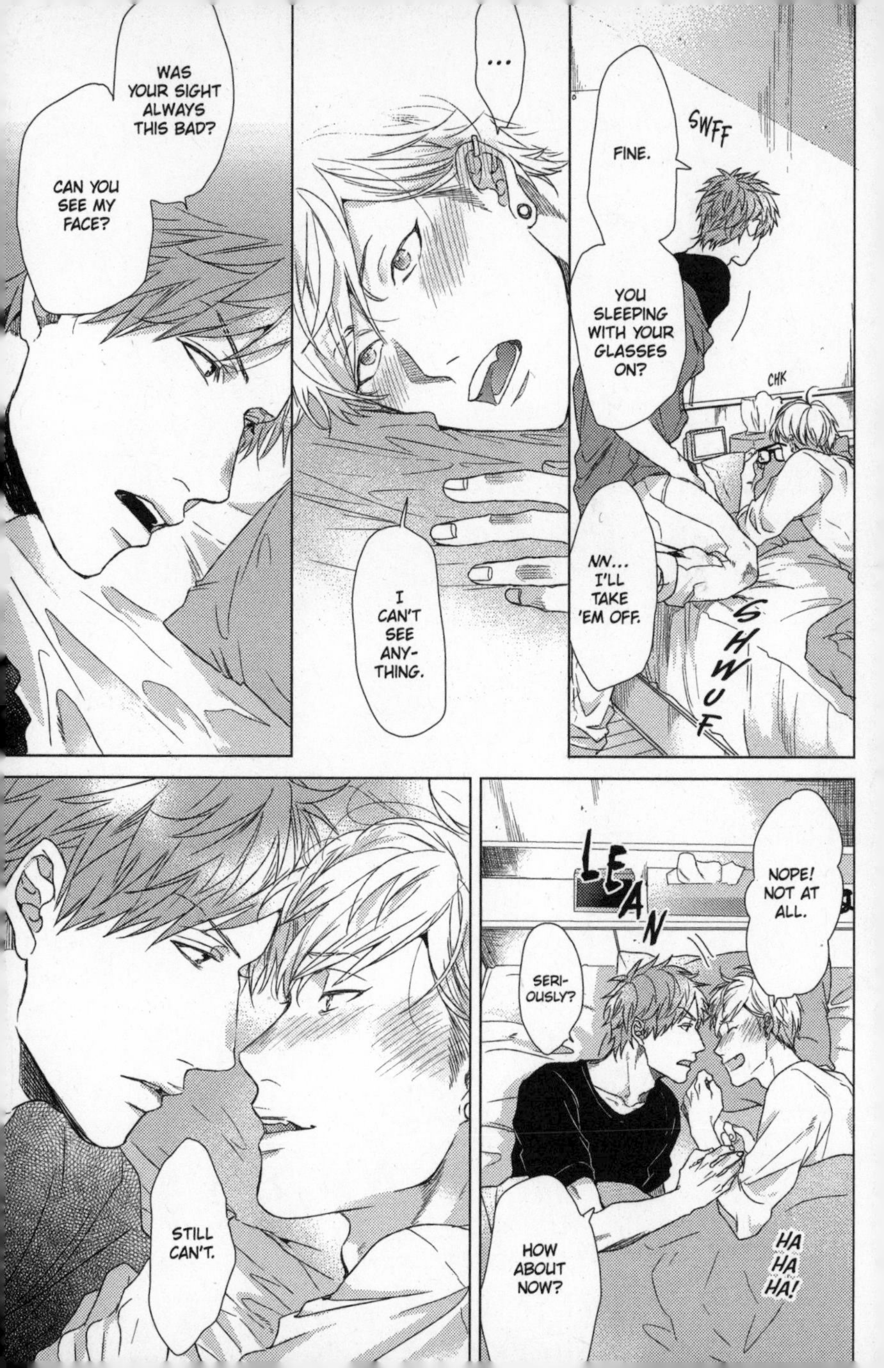
FINE.
SWFF
YOU SLEEPING WITH YOUR GLASSES ON?
CHK
NN... I'LL TAKE 'EM OFF.
SHWUF
...
I CAN'T SEE ANYTHING.
WAS YOUR SIGHT ALWAYS THIS BAD?
CAN YOU SEE MY FACE?
NOPE! NOT AT ALL.
LEAN
SERIOUSLY?
HA HA HA!
HOW ABOUT NOW?
STILL CAN'T.

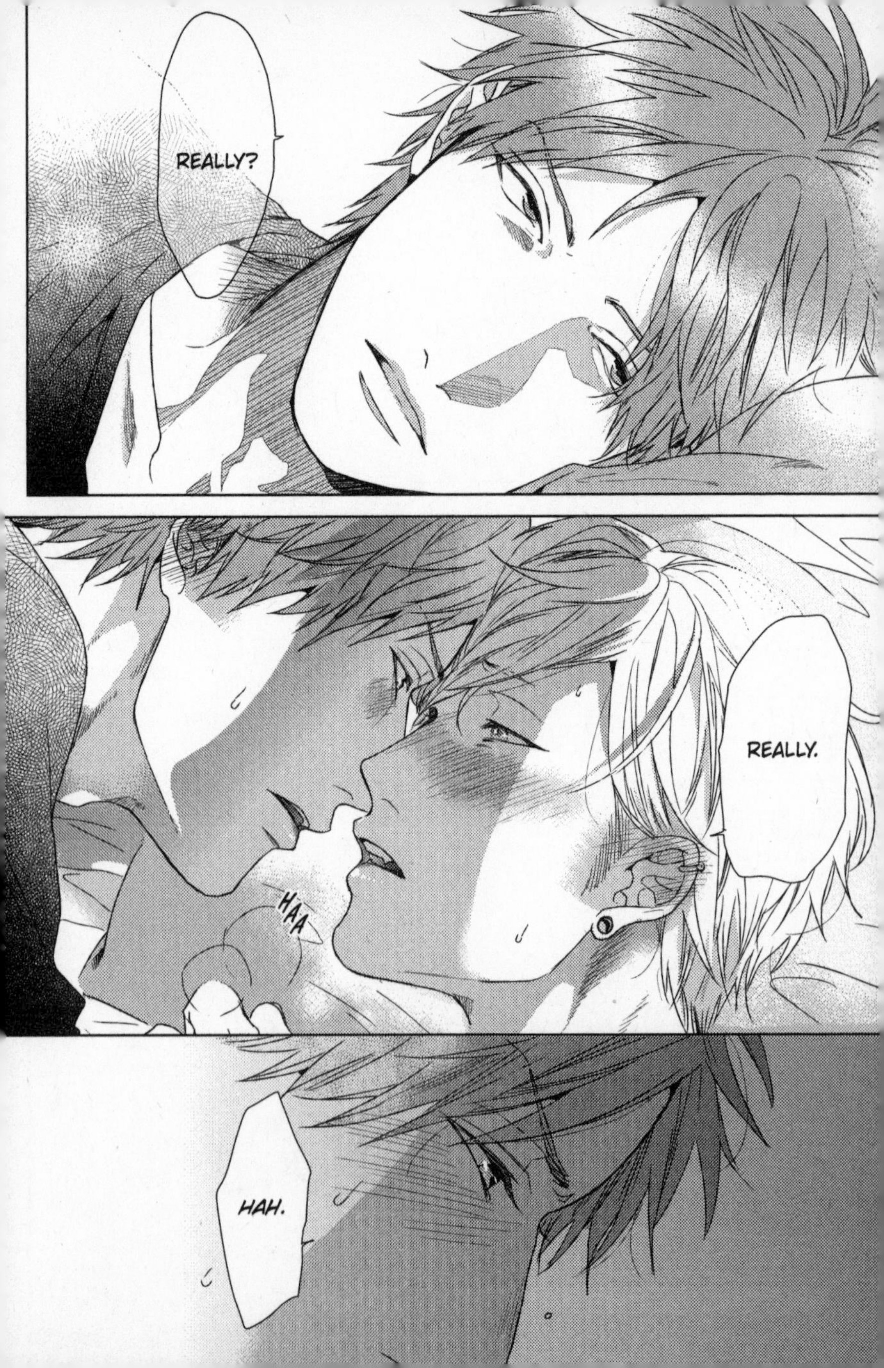
REALLY?
REALLY.
HAA
HAH.

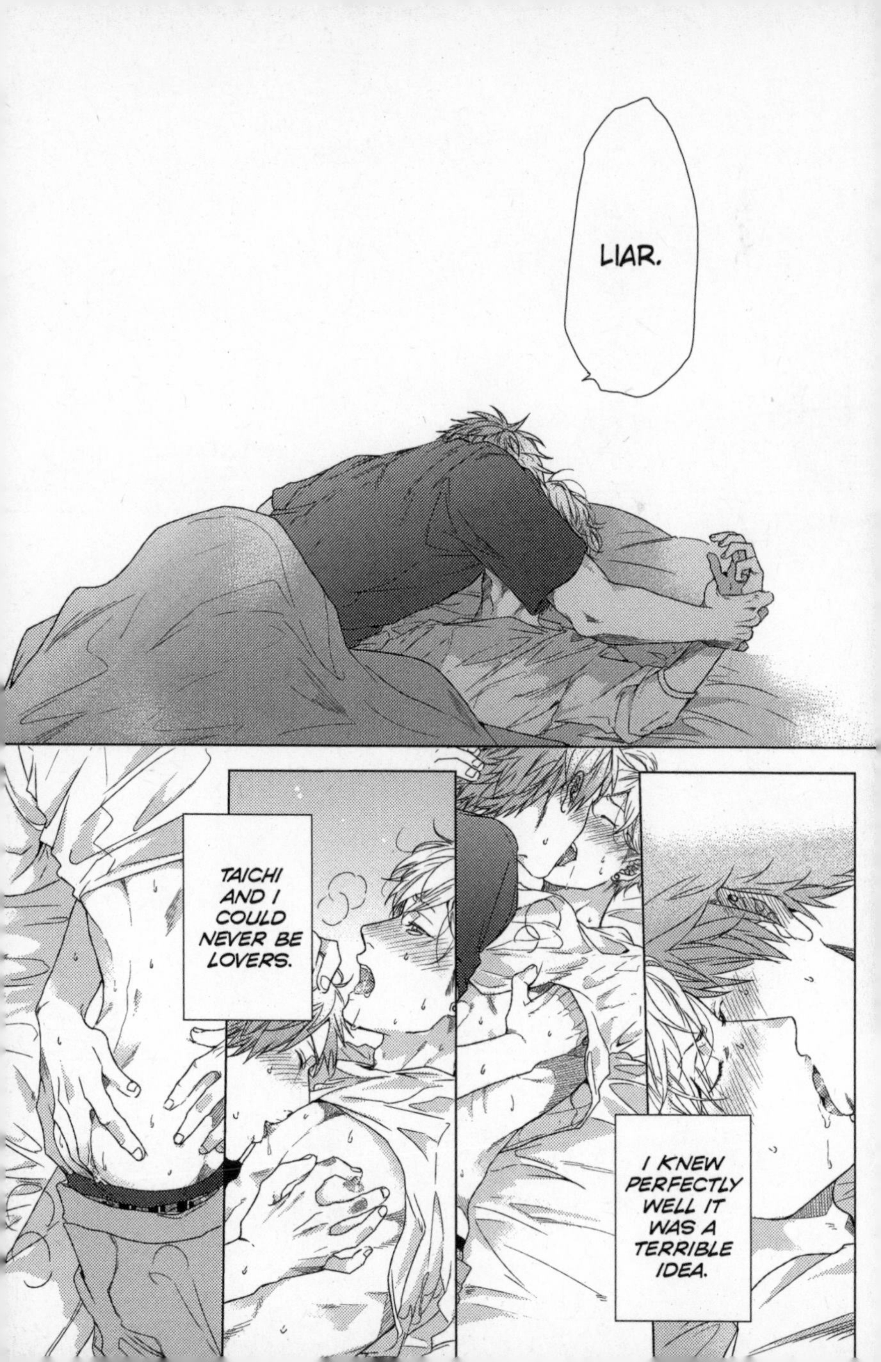
LIAR.
I KNEW PERFECTLY WELL IT WAS A TERRIBLE IDEA.
TAICHI AND I COULD NEVER BE LOVERS.

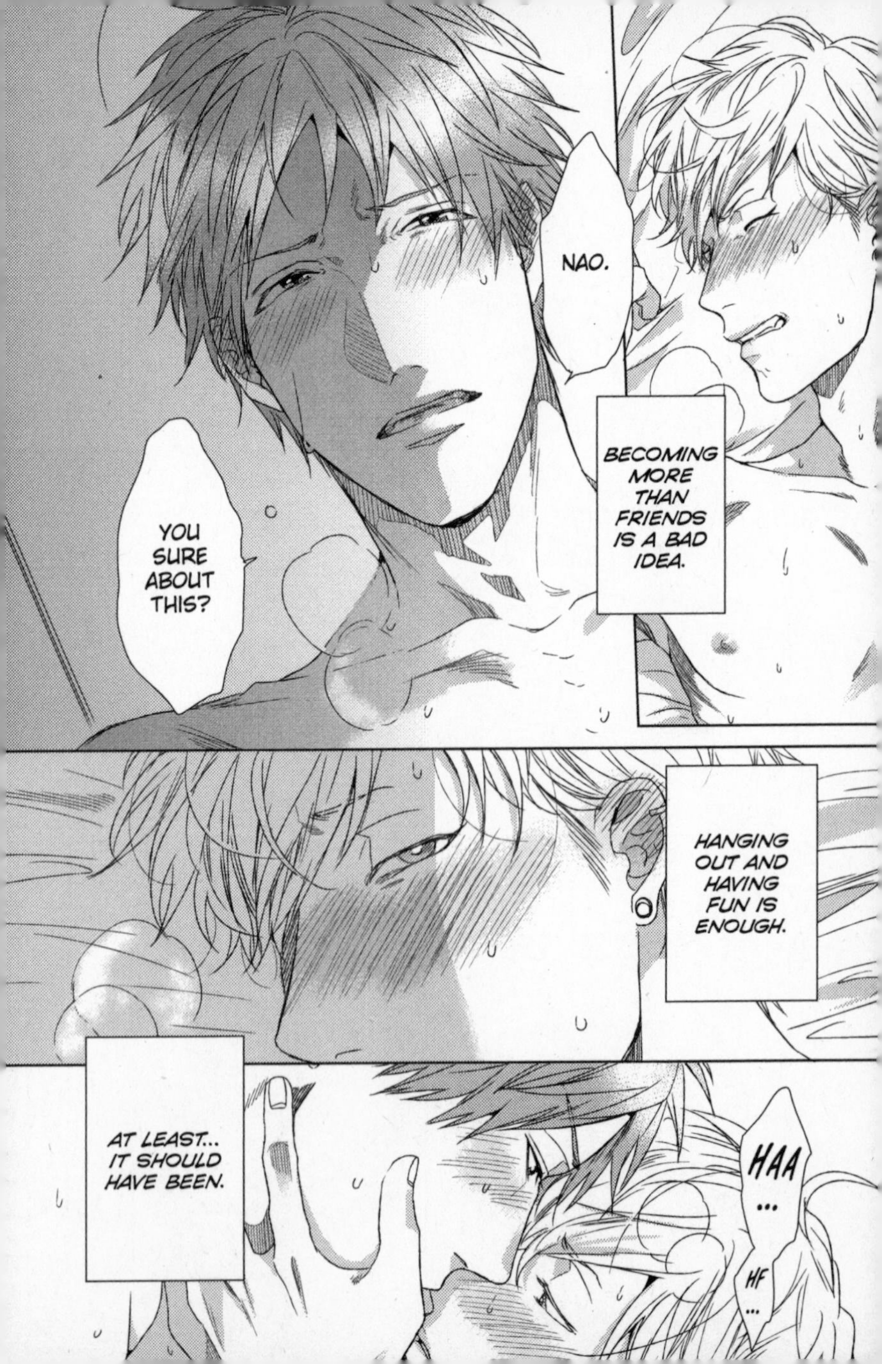
NAO.
BECOMING MORE THAN FRIENDS IS A BAD IDEA.
YOU SURE ABOUT THIS?
HANGING OUT AND HAVING FUN IS ENOUGH.
AT LEAST... IT SHOULD HAVE BEEN.
HAA...
HF...

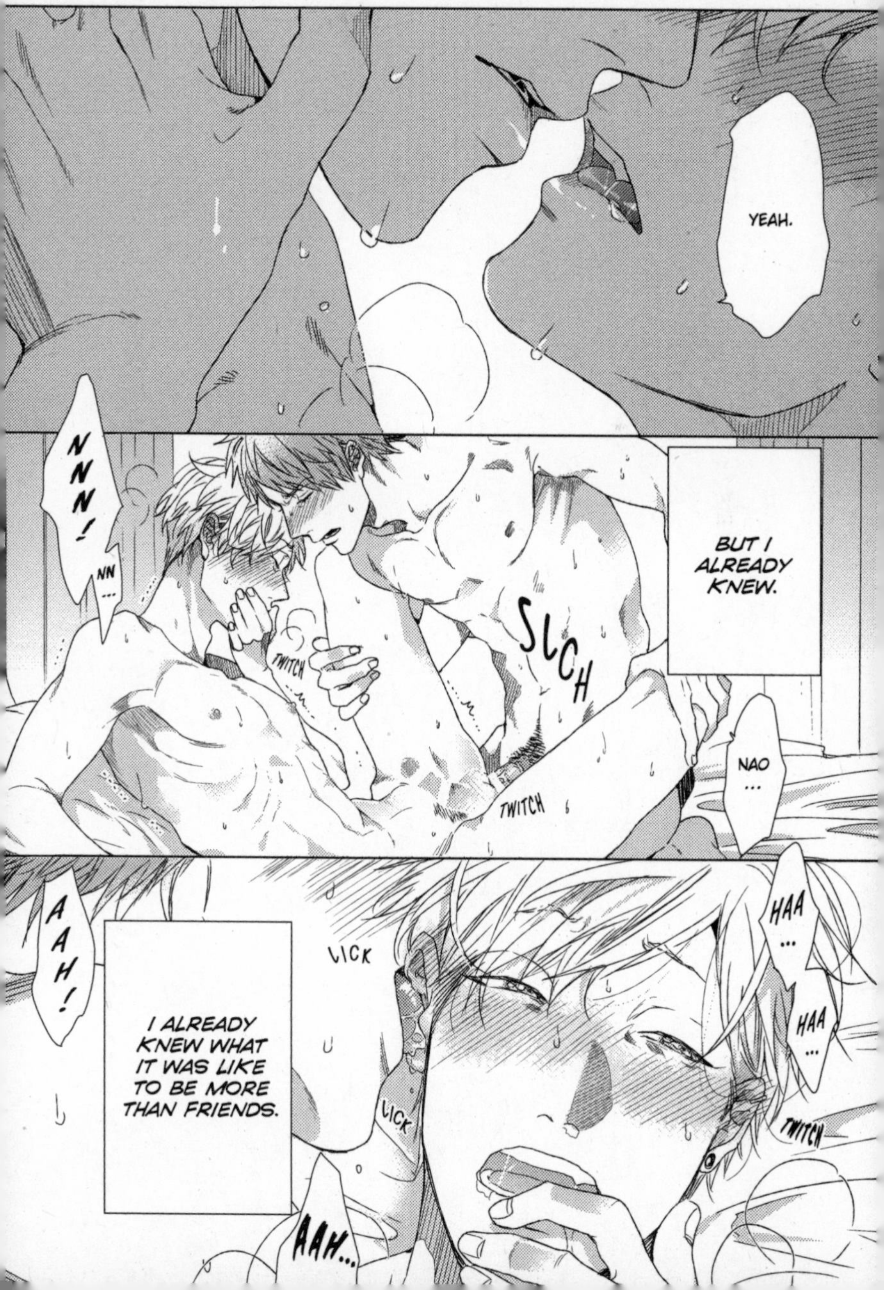
YEAH.
BUT I ALREADY KNEW.
NAO ...
SLCH
TWITCH
NNN!
NN ...
TWITCH
HAA ...
HAA ...
TWITCH
LICK
LICK
I ALREADY KNEW WHAT IT WAS LIKE TO BE MORE THAN FRIENDS.
AAH!
AAH...

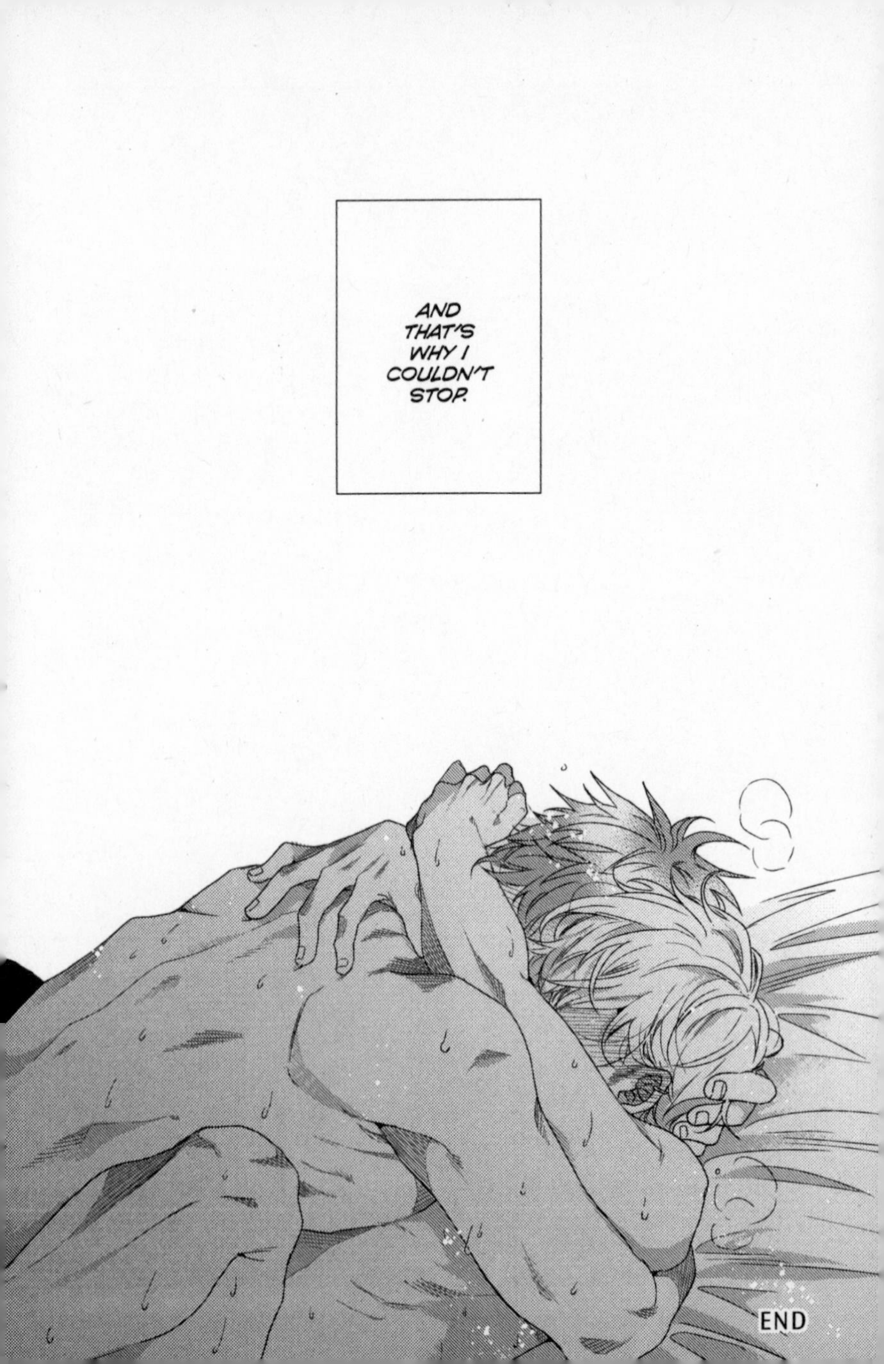
AND THAT'S WHY I COULDN'T STOP.
END

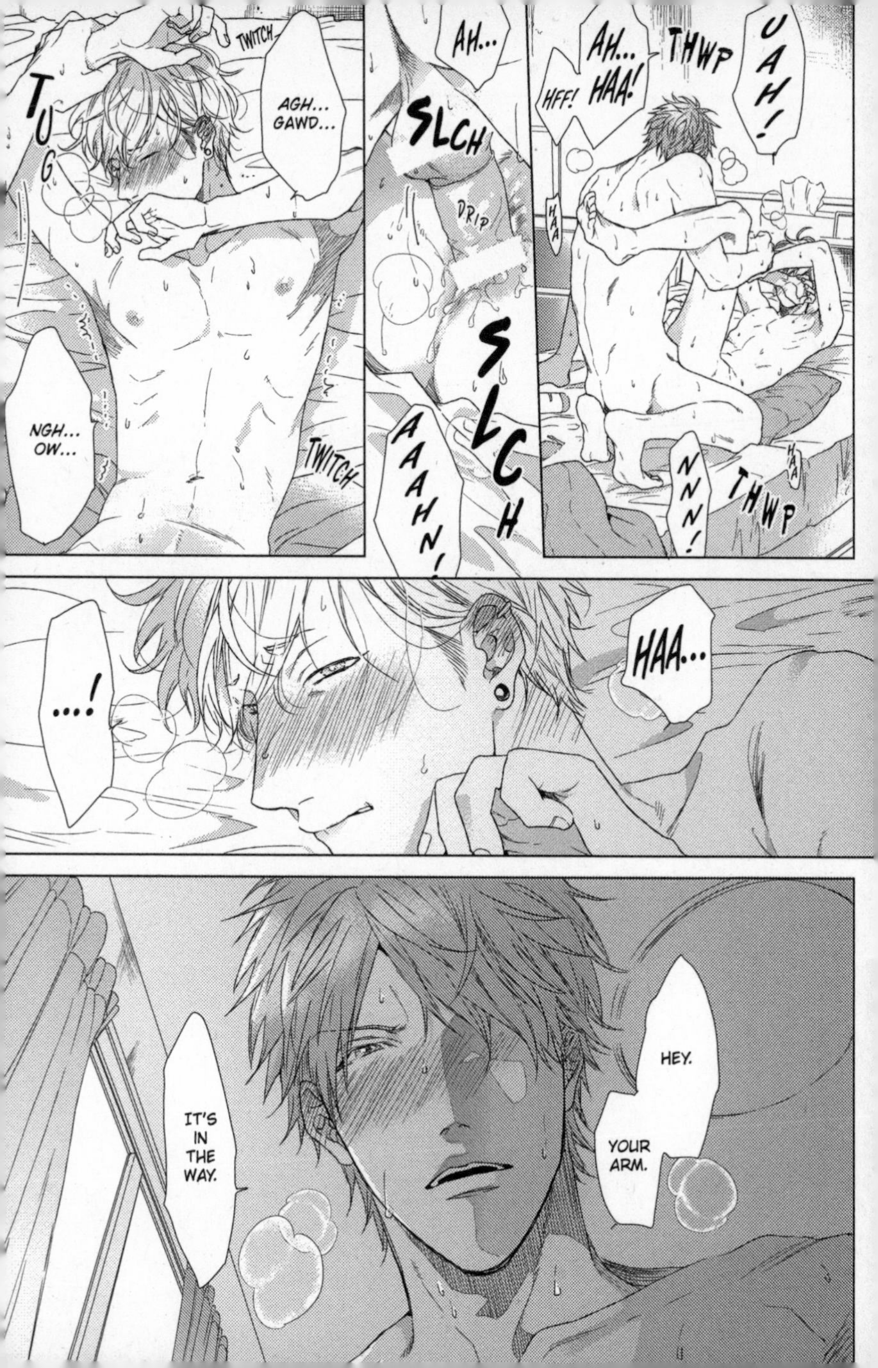
UAH!
THWP
AH... HAA!
HFF!
HAA
HAA
THWP
NNN!
AH...
SLCH
DRIP
SLCH
AAAHN!
TWITCH
AGH... GAWD...
TUG
NGH... OW...
TWITCH
HAA...
...!
HEY.
YOUR ARM.
IT'S IN THE WAY.

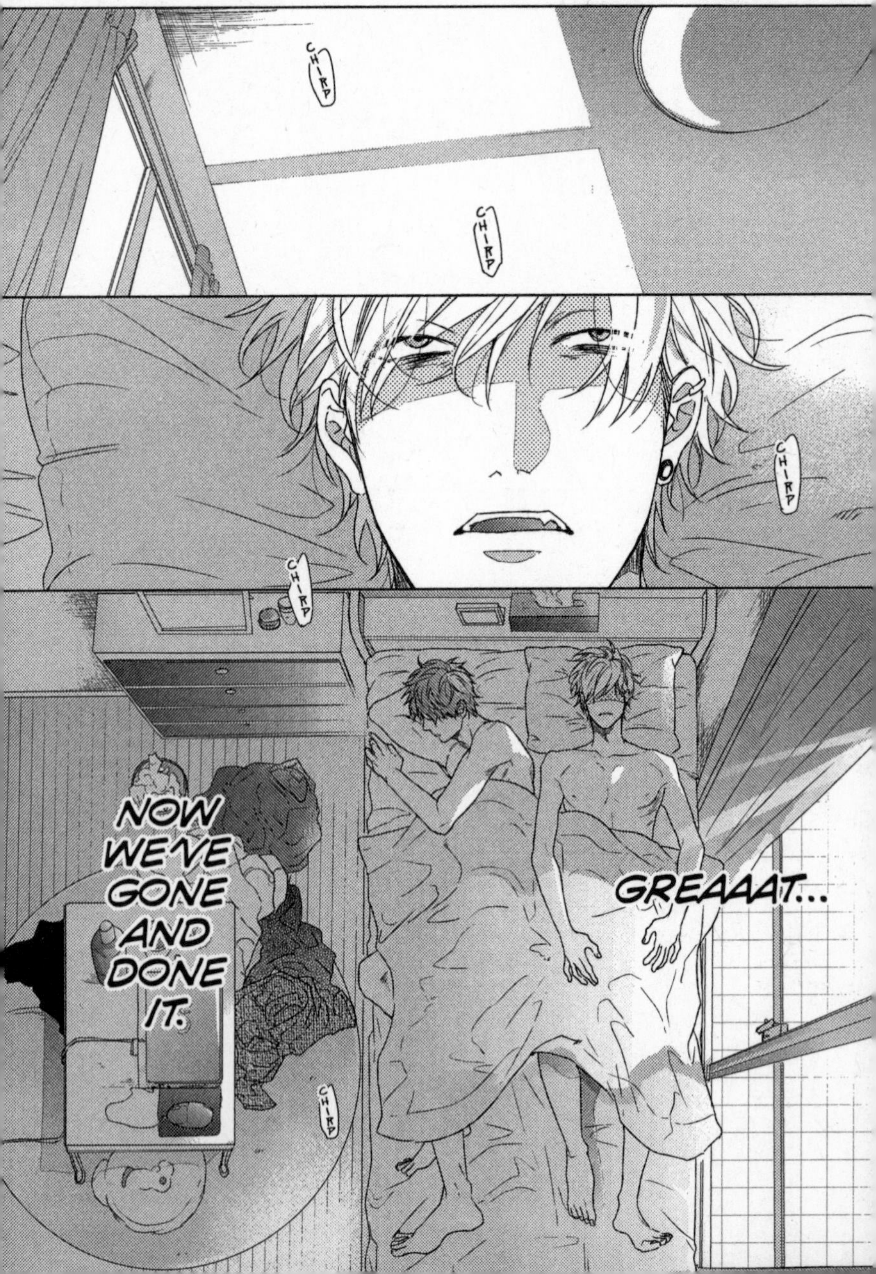
CHIRP
CHIRP
CHIRP
CHIRP
CHIRP
GREAAAT...
NOW WE'VE GONE AND DONE IT.
CHIRP

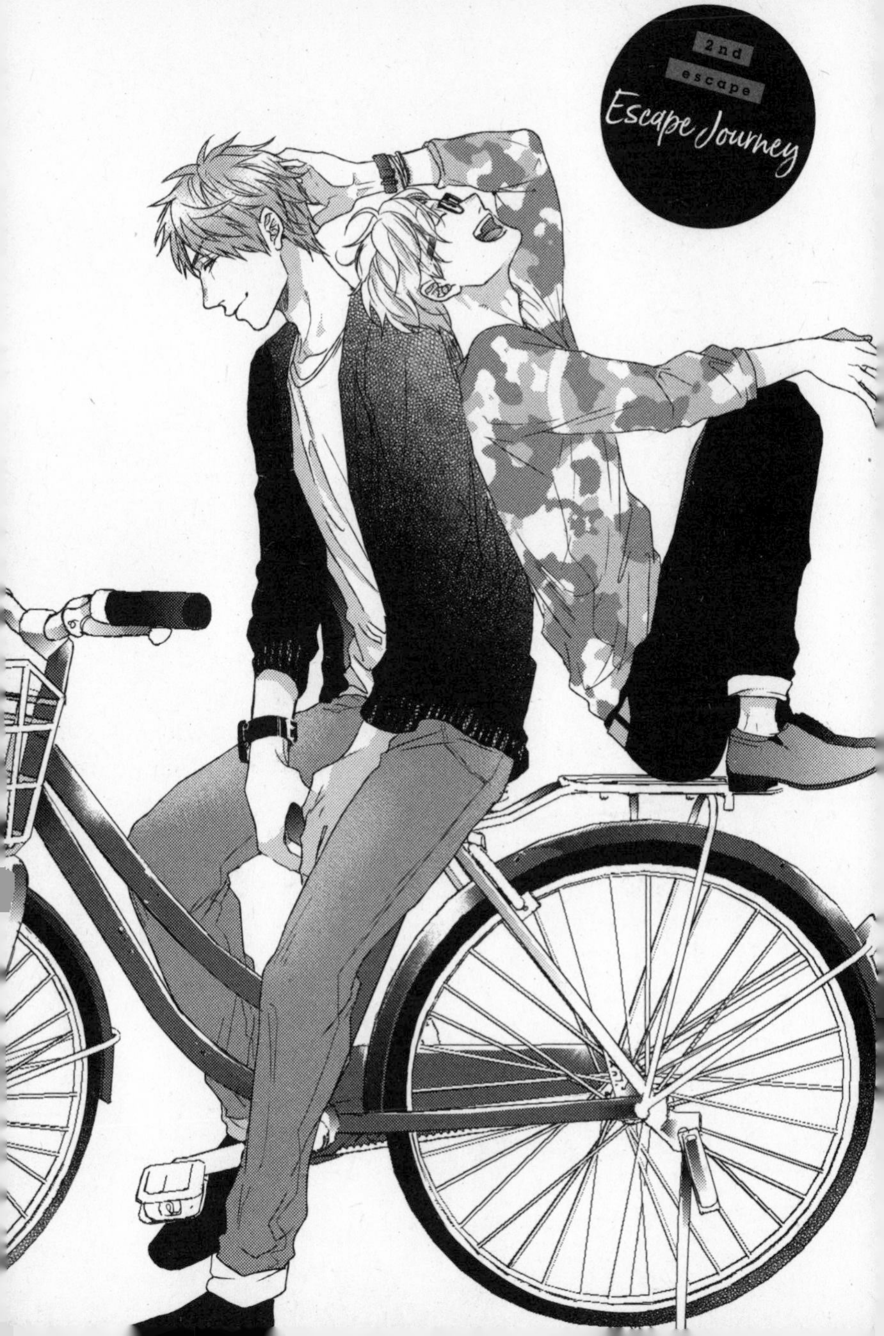
2nd
escape
Escape Journey

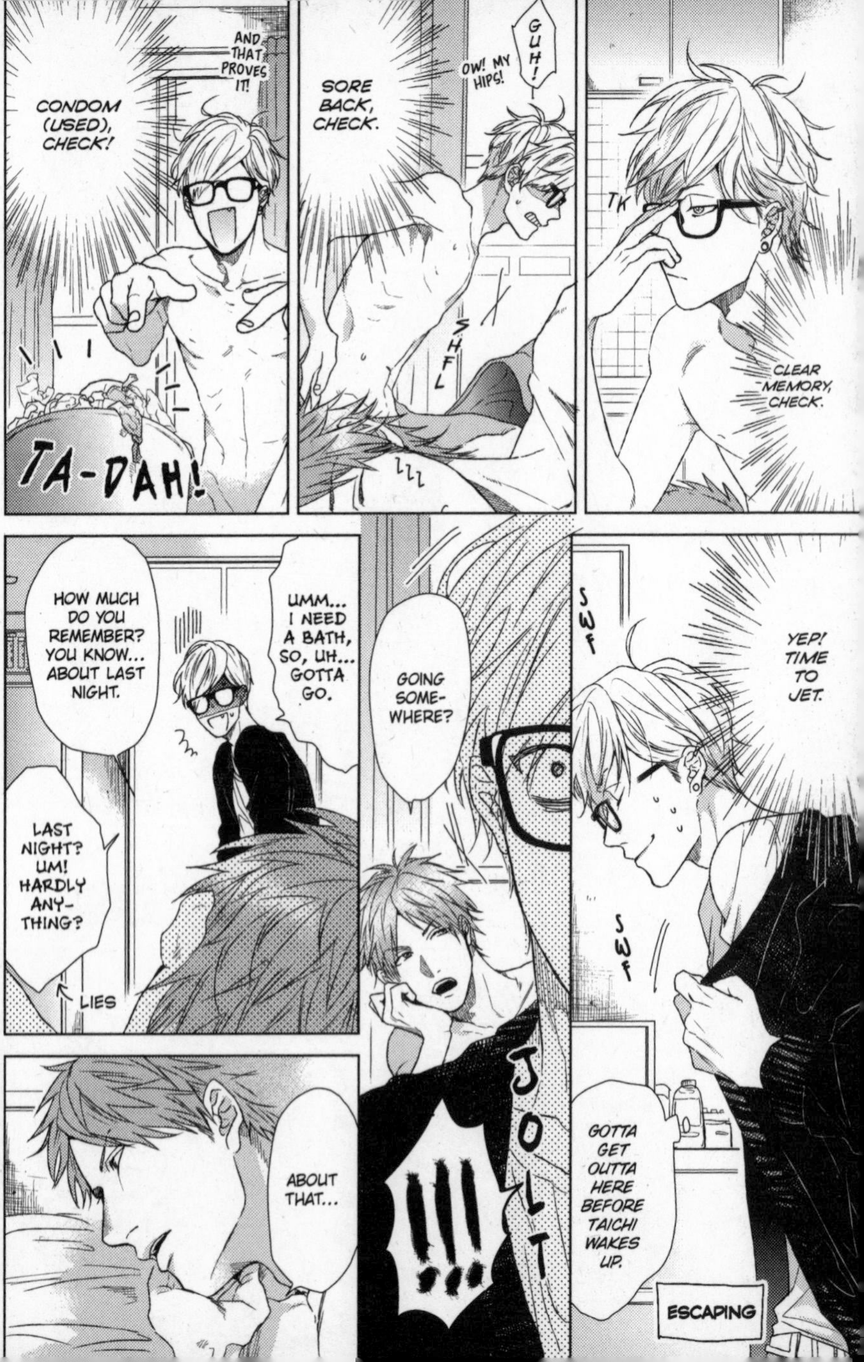
TK
CLEAR MEMORY, CHECK.
GUH!
OW! MY HIPS!
SORE BACK, CHECK.
SHFL
ZZZ
AND THAT PROVES IT!
CONDOM (USED), CHECK!
TA-DAH!
YEP! TIME TO JET.
SWF
SWF
GOTTA GET OUTTA HERE BEFORE TAICHI WAKES UP.
ESCAPING
GOING SOME-WHERE?
JOLT
!!!
UMM... I NEED A BATH, SO, UH... GOTTA GO.
HOW MUCH DO YOU REMEMBER? YOU KNOW... ABOUT LAST NIGHT.
LAST NIGHT? UM! HARDLY ANY-THING?
LIES
ABOUT THAT...

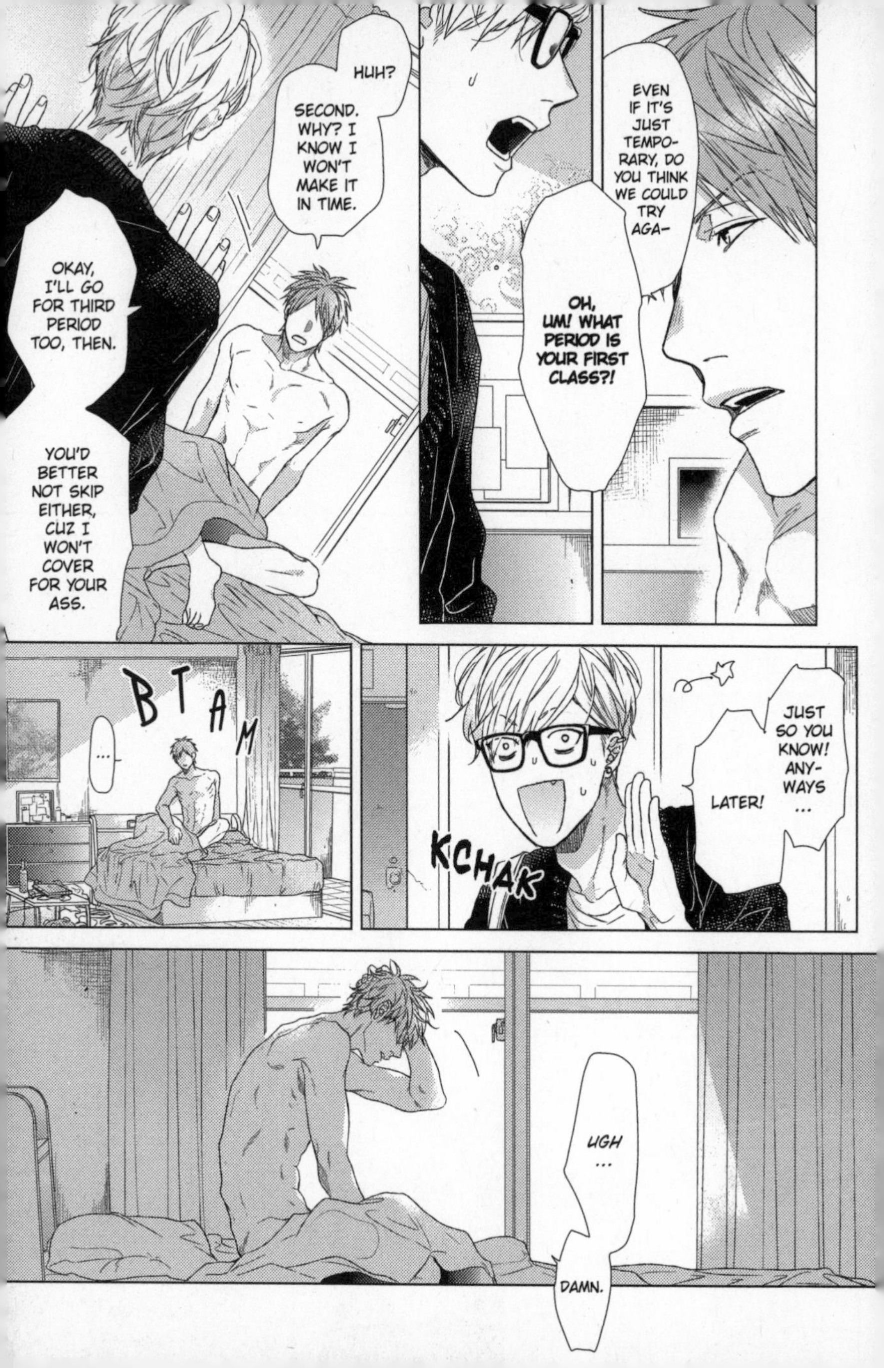
EVEN IF IT'S JUST TEMPO-RARY, DO YOU THINK WE COULD TRY AGA-
OH, UM! WHAT PERIOD IS YOUR FIRST CLASS?!
HUH?
SECOND. WHY? I KNOW I WON'T MAKE IT IN TIME.
OKAY, I'LL GO FOR THIRD PERIOD TOO, THEN.
YOU'D BETTER NOT SKIP EITHER, CUZ I WON'T COVER FOR YOUR ASS.
JUST SO YOU KNOW! ANY-WAYS ...
LATER!
KCHAK
BTAM
...
UGH ...
DAMN.

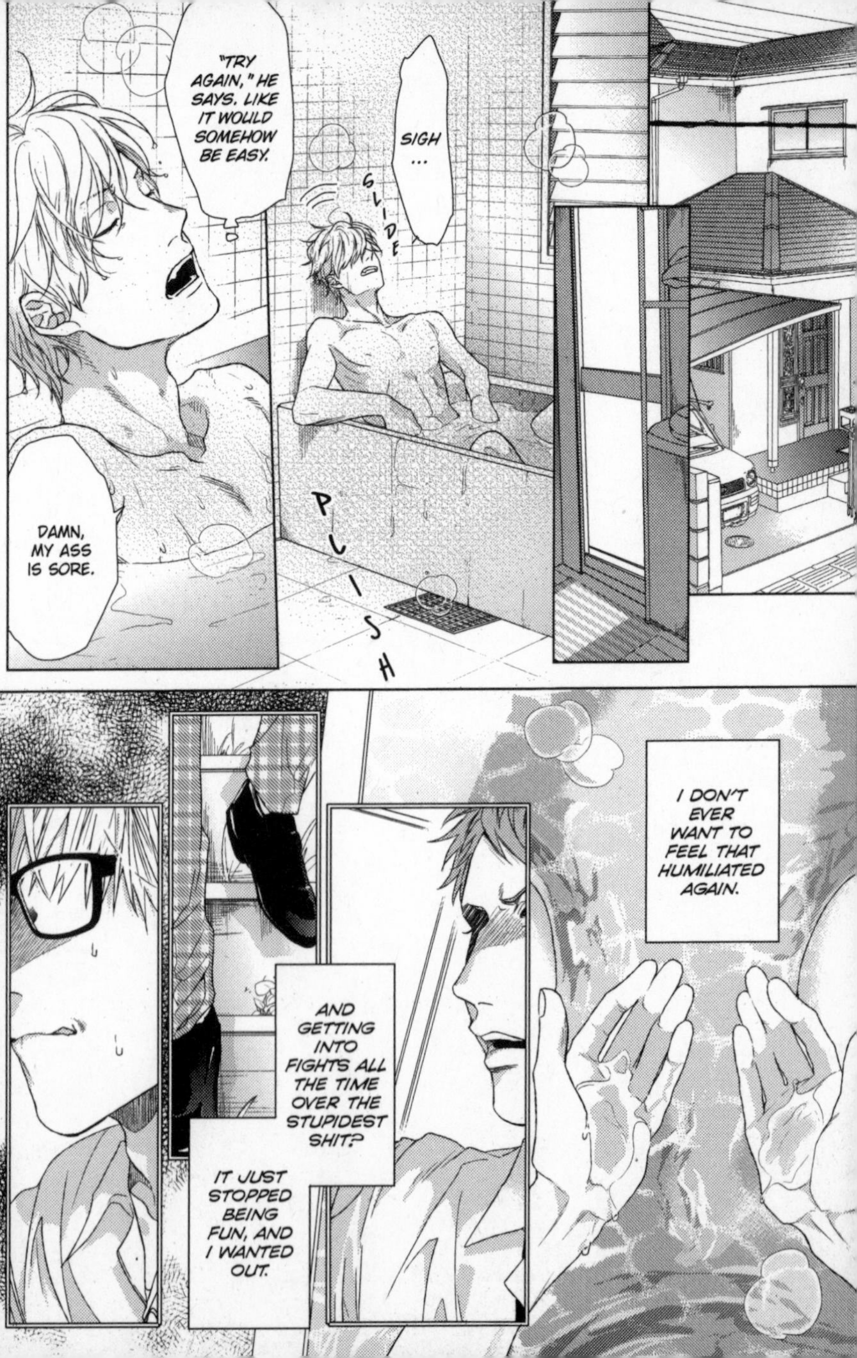
SIGH ...
GLIDE
PUSH
"TRY AGAIN," HE SAYS. LIKE IT WOULD SOMEHOW BE EASY.
DAMN, MY ASS IS SORE.
I DON'T EVER WANT TO FEEL THAT HUMILIATED AGAIN.
AND GETTING INTO FIGHTS ALL THE TIME OVER THE STUPIDEST SHIT?
IT JUST STOPPED BEING FUN, AND I WANTED OUT.

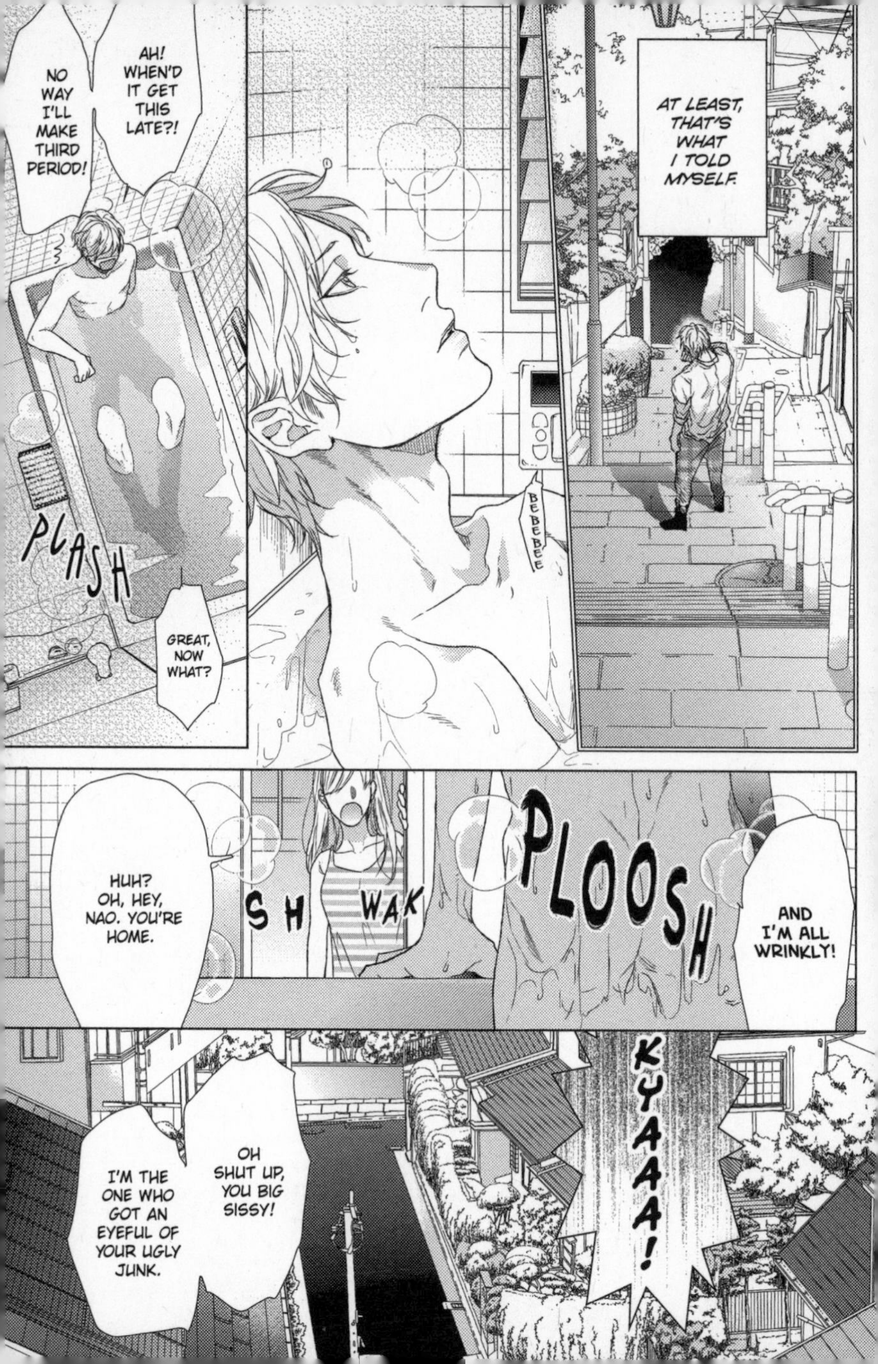
AT LEAST, THAT'S WHAT I TOLD MYSELF.
BEBEBEBEE
AH! WHEN'D IT GET THIS LATE?!
NO WAY I'LL MAKE THIRD PERIOD!
PLASH
GREAT, NOW WHAT?
AND I'M ALL WRINKLY!
PLOOSH
SH WAK
HUH? OH, HEY, NAO. YOU'RE HOME.
KYAAAA!
OH SHUT UP, YOU BIG SISSY!
I'M THE ONE WHO GOT AN EYEFUL OF YOUR UGLY JUNK.

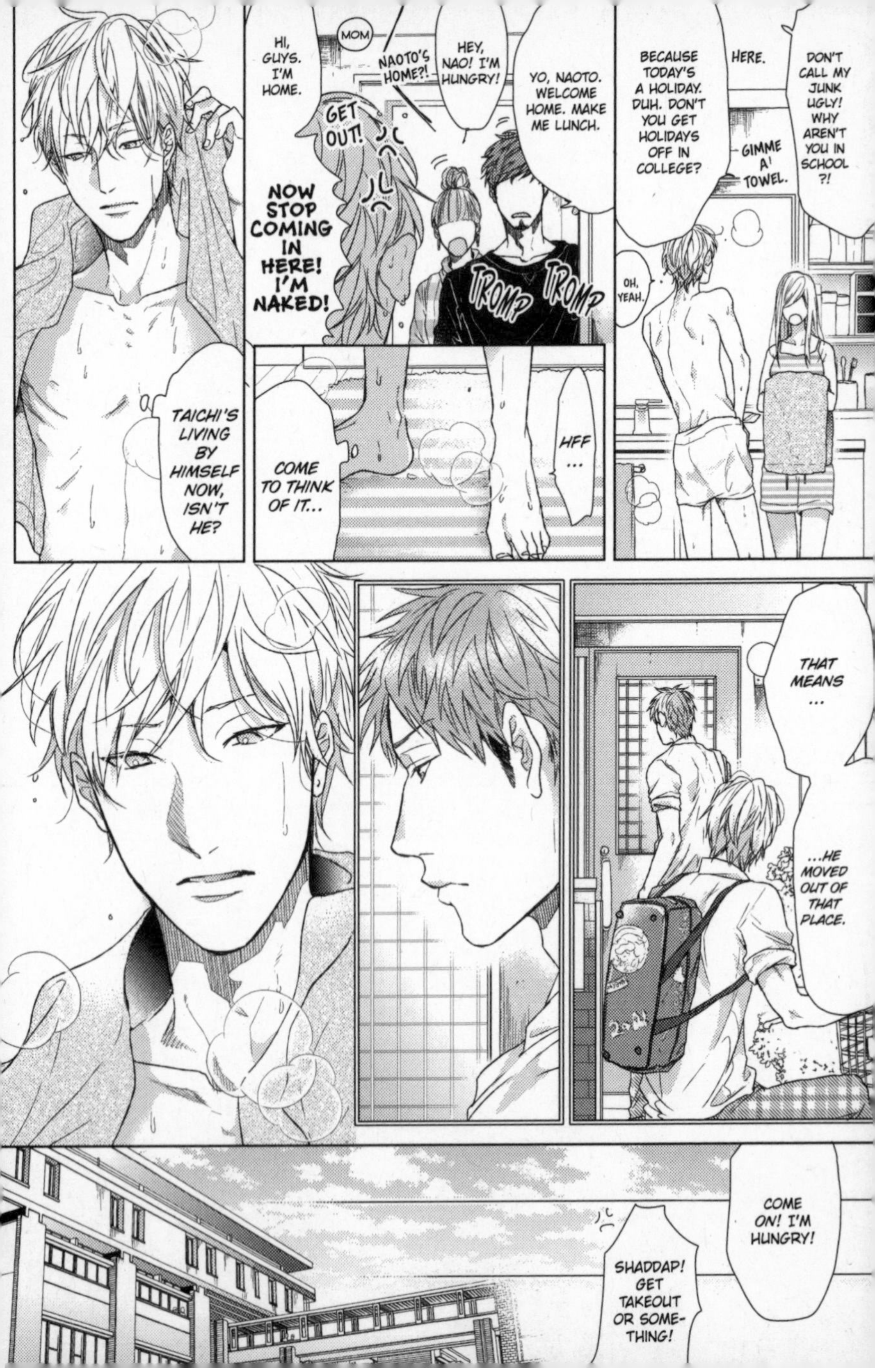
DON'T CALL MY JUNK UGLY! WHY AREN'T YOU IN SCHOOL?!
HERE.
BECAUSE TODAY'S A HOLIDAY. DUH. DON'T YOU GET HOLIDAYS OFF IN COLLEGE?
GIMME A' TOWEL.
OH, YEAH.
YO, NAOTO. WELCOME HOME. MAKE ME LUNCH.
HEY, NAO! I'M HUNGRY!
MOM
NAOTO'S HOME?!
HI, GUYS. I'M HOME.
GET OUT!
TROMP TROMP
NOW STOP COMING IN HERE! I'M NAKED!
HFF ...
COME TO THINK OF IT...
TAICHI'S LIVING BY HIMSELF NOW, ISN'T HE?
THAT MEANS ...
...HE MOVED OUT OF THAT PLACE.
COME ON! I'M HUNGRY!
SHADDAP! GET TAKEOUT OR SOME-THING!

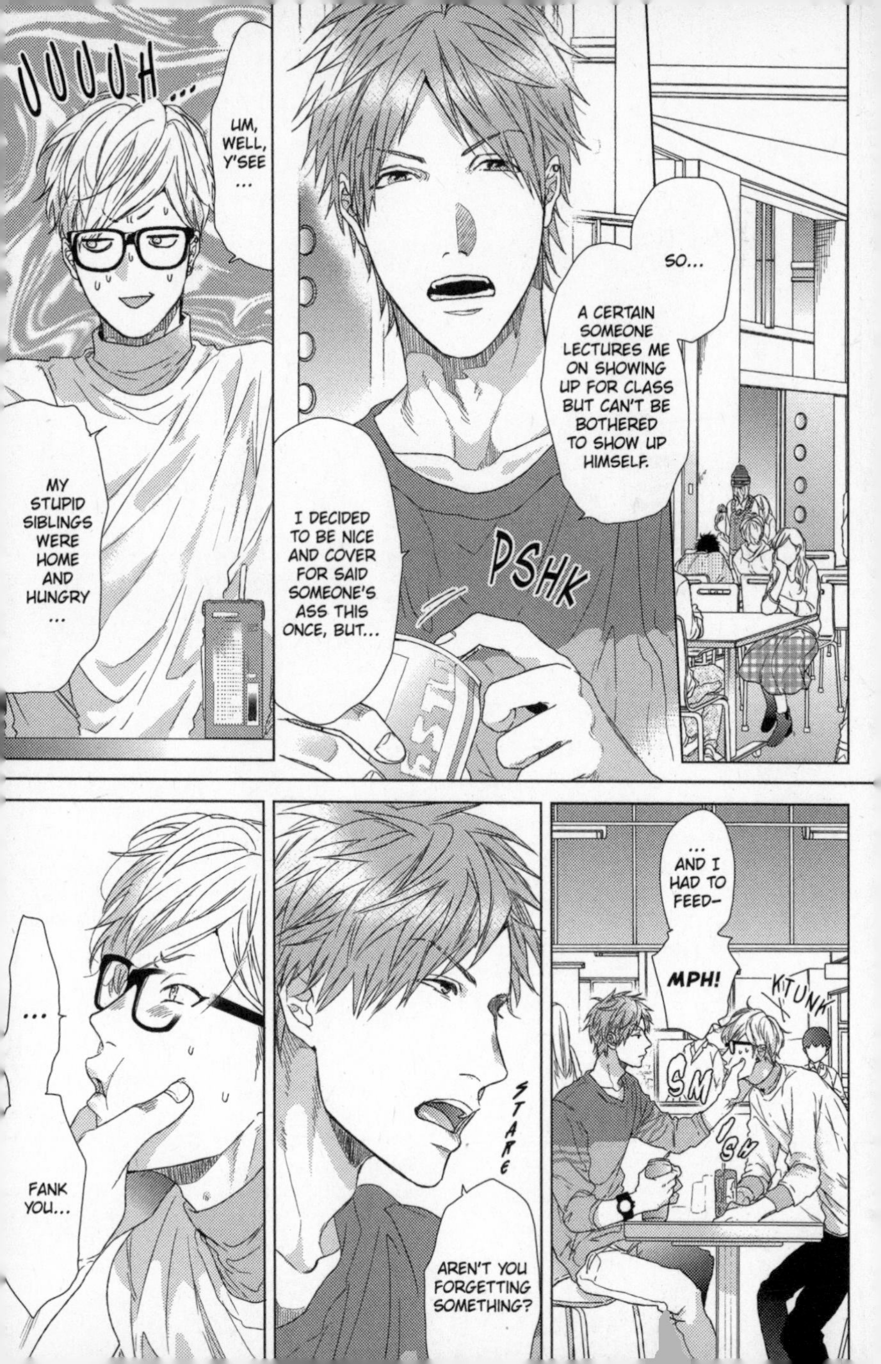
SO...
A CERTAIN SOMEONE LECTURES ME ON SHOWING UP FOR CLASS BUT CAN'T BE BOTHERED TO SHOW UP HIMSELF.
I DECIDED TO BE NICE AND COVER FOR SAID SOMEONE'S ASS THIS ONCE, BUT...
PSHK
UUUUH...
UM, WELL, Y'SEE ...
MY STUPID SIBLINGS WERE HOME AND HUNGRY ...
... AND I HAD TO FEED-
MPH!
KTUNK
SMISH
STARE
AREN'T YOU FORGETTING SOMETHING?
...
FANK YOU...

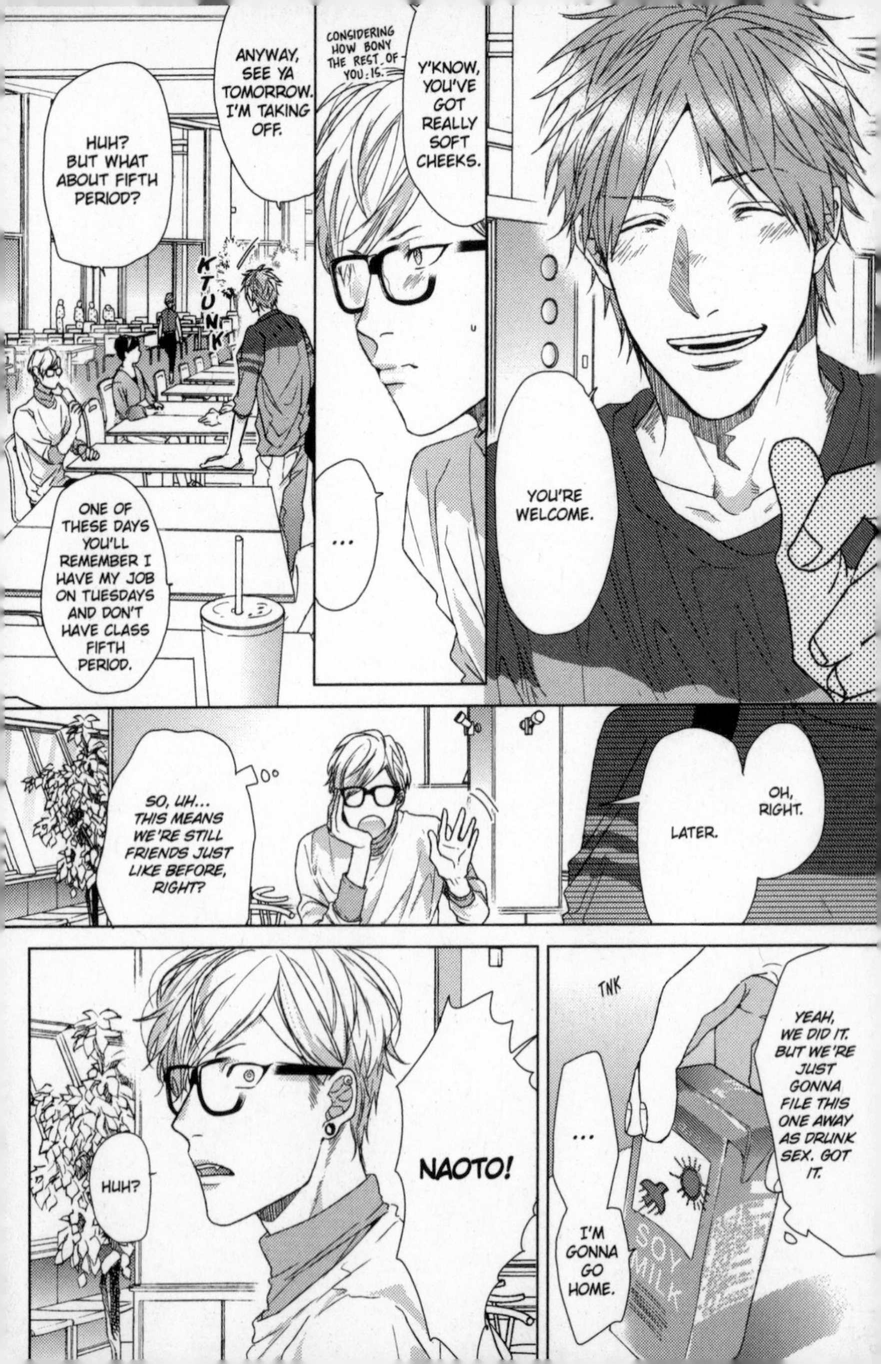
YOU'RE WELCOME.
Y'KNOW, YOU'VE GOT REALLY SOFT CHEEKS.
CONSIDERING HOW BONY THE REST OF YOU IS.
...
ANYWAY, SEE YA TOMORROW. I'M TAKING OFF.
HUH? BUT WHAT ABOUT FIFTH PERIOD?
KTUNK
ONE OF THESE DAYS YOU'LL REMEMBER I HAVE MY JOB ON TUESDAYS AND DON'T HAVE CLASS FIFTH PERIOD.
OH, RIGHT.
LATER.
SO, UH... THIS MEANS WE'RE STILL FRIENDS JUST LIKE BEFORE, RIGHT?
TNK
YEAH, WE DID IT. BUT WE'RE JUST GONNA FILE THIS ONE AWAY AS DRUNK SEX. GOT IT.
...
I'M GONNA GO HOME.
SOY MILK
NAOTO!
HUH?

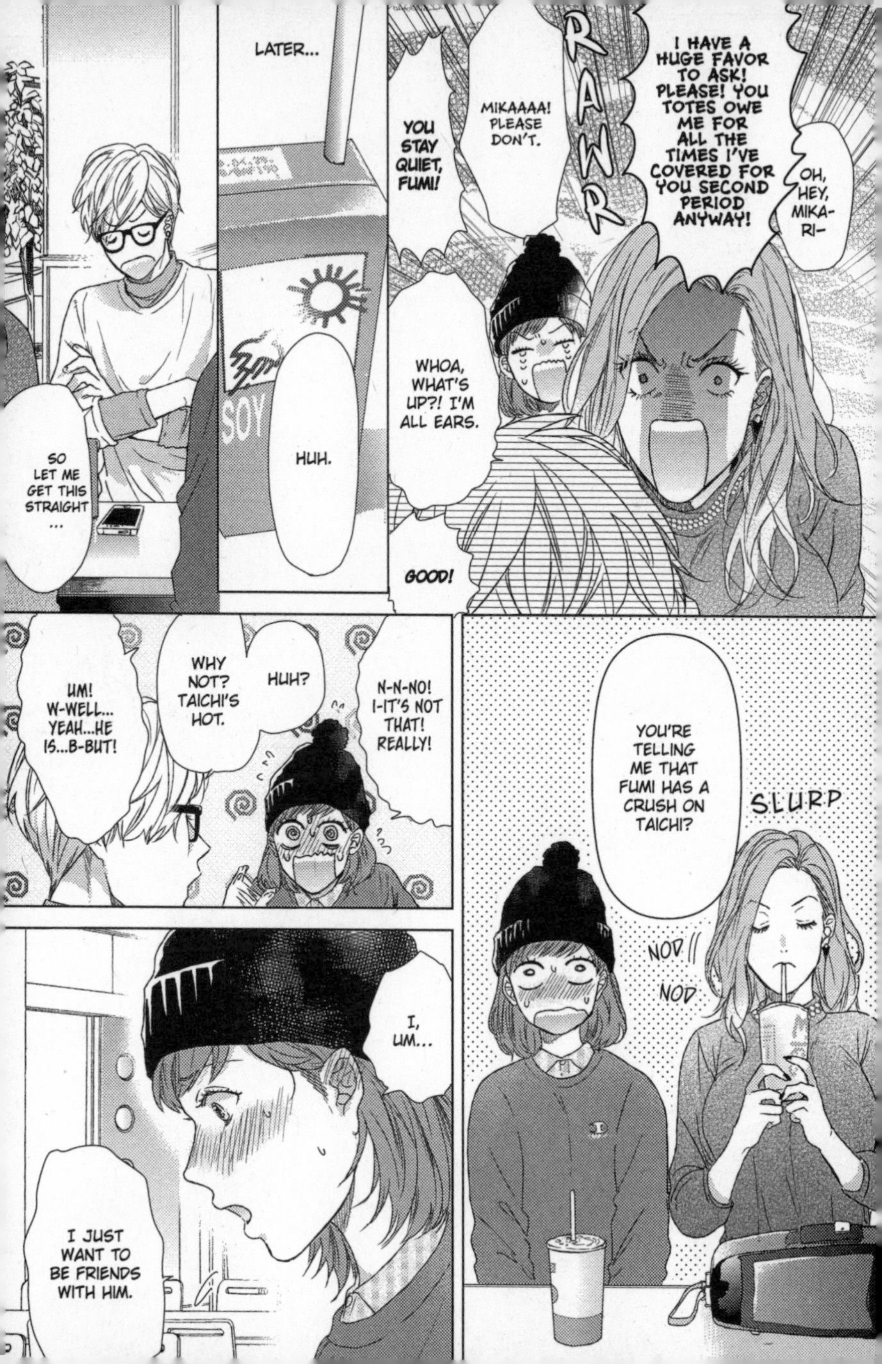
OH, HEY, MIKA-RI-
I HAVE A HUGE FAVOR TO ASK! PLEASE! YOU TOTES OWE ME FOR ALL THE TIMES I'VE COVERED FOR YOU SECOND PERIOD ANYWAY!
RAWR
MIKAAAA! PLEASE DON'T.
YOU STAY QUIET, FUMI!
WHOA, WHAT'S UP?! I'M ALL EARS.
GOOD!
LATER...
HUH.
SO LET ME GET THIS STRAIGHT ...
YOU'RE TELLING ME THAT FUMI HAS A CRUSH ON TAICHI?
SLURP
NOD
NOD
N-N-NO! I-IT'S NOT THAT! REALLY!
HUH?
WHY NOT? TAICHI'S HOT.
UM! W-WELL... YEAH...HE IS...B-BUT!
I, UM...
I JUST WANT TO BE FRIENDS WITH HIM.

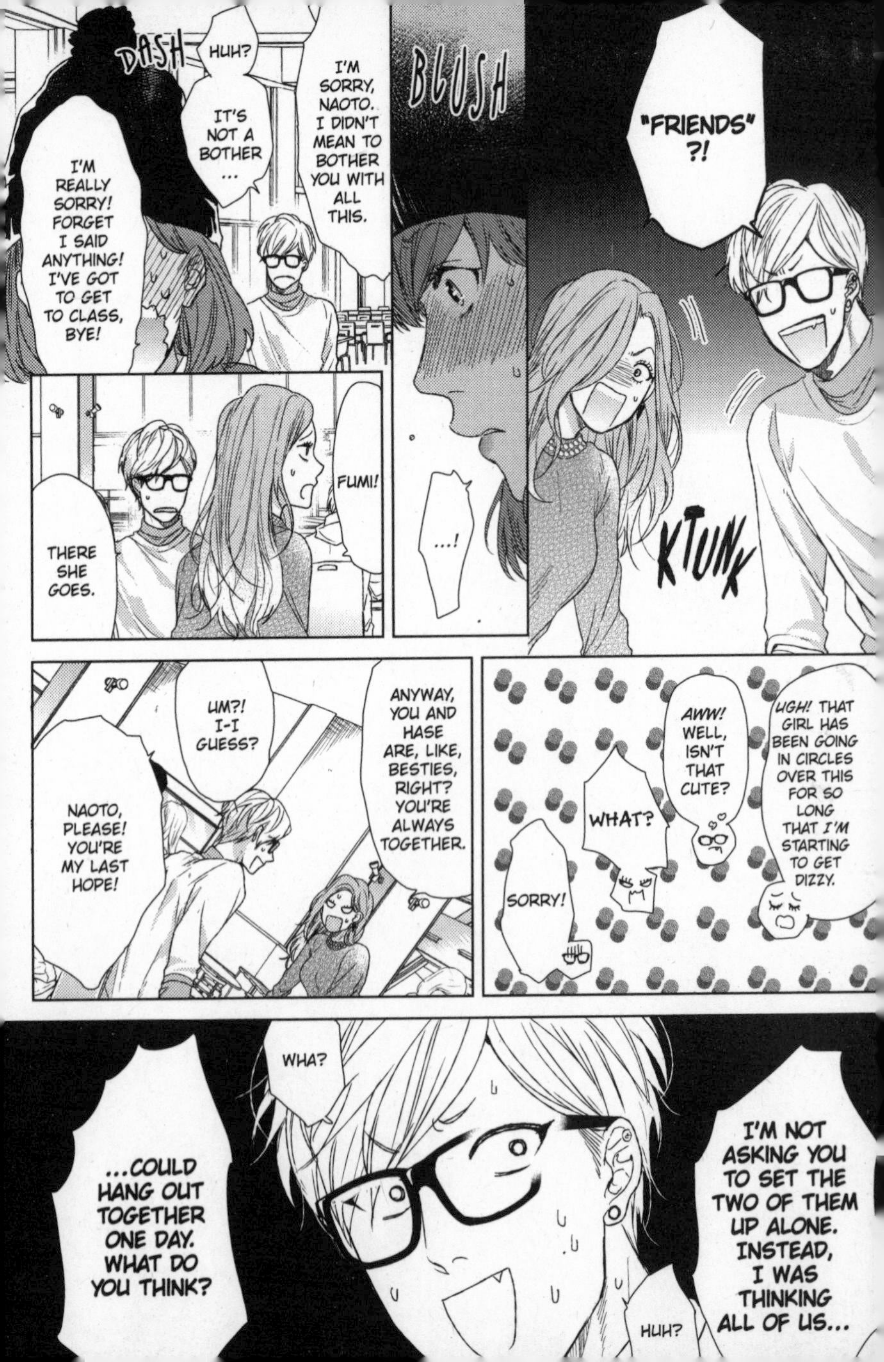
"FRIENDS" ?!
KTUNK
BLUSH
...!
I'M SORRY, NAOTO. I DIDN'T MEAN TO BOTHER YOU WITH ALL THIS.
HUH?
IT'S NOT A BOTHER ...
DASH
I'M REALLY SORRY! FORGET I SAID ANYTHING! I'VE GOT TO GET TO CLASS, BYE!
FUMI!
THERE SHE GOES.
UGH! THAT GIRL HAS BEEN GOING IN CIRCLES OVER THIS FOR SO LONG THAT I'M STARTING TO GET DIZZY.
AWW! WELL, ISN'T THAT CUTE?
WHAT?
SORRY!
ANYWAY, YOU AND HASE ARE, LIKE, BESTIES, RIGHT? YOU'RE ALWAYS TOGETHER.
UM?! I-I GUESS?
NAOTO, PLEASE! YOU'RE MY LAST HOPE!
WHA?
I'M NOT ASKING YOU TO SET THE TWO OF THEM UP ALONE. INSTEAD, I WAS THINKING ALL OF US...
...COULD HANG OUT TOGETHER ONE DAY. WHAT DO YOU THINK?
HUH?

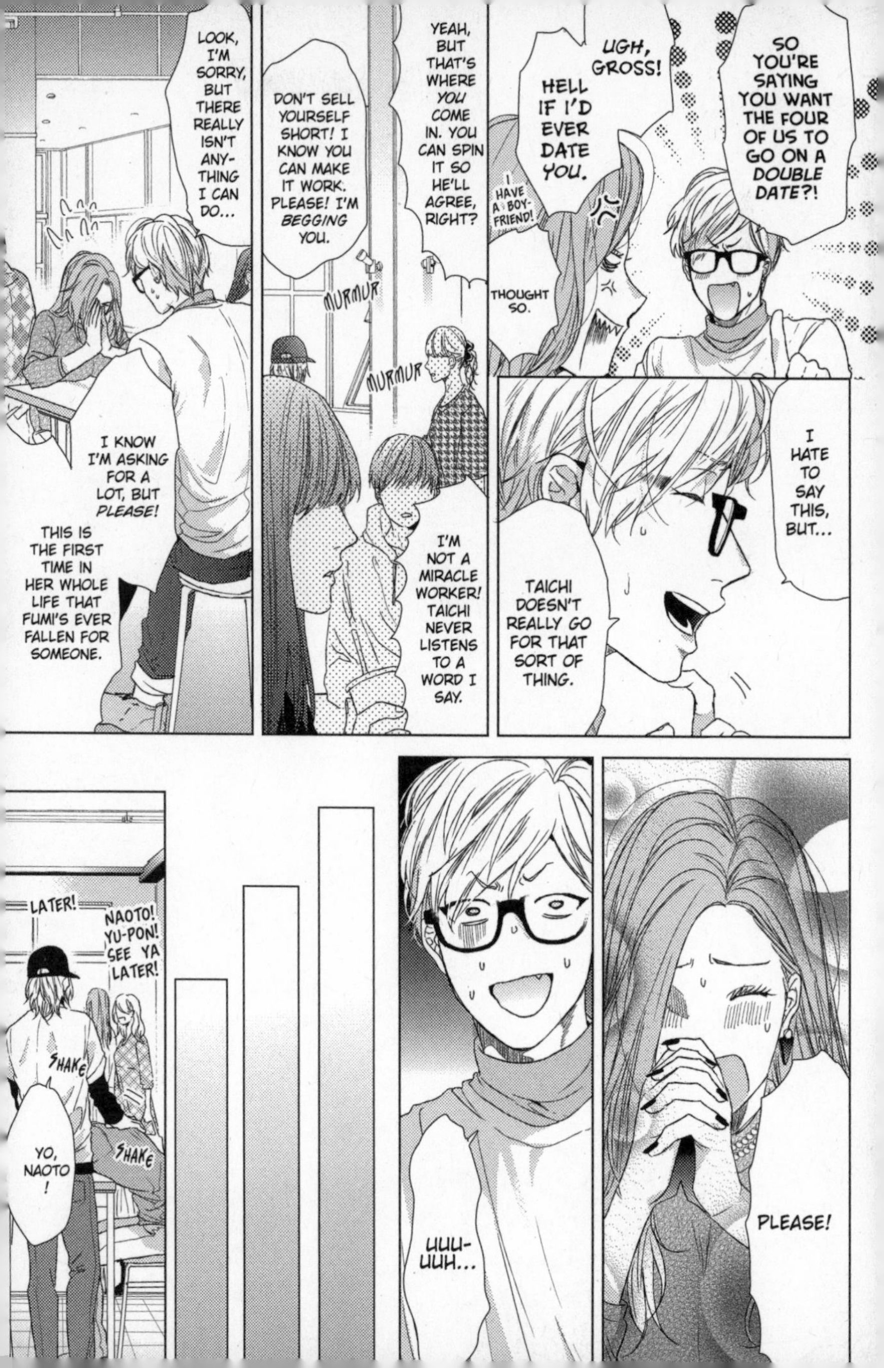

SO YOU'RE SAYING YOU WANT THE FOUR OF US TO GO ON A *DOUBLE DATE?!*
UGH, GROSS!
HELL IF I'D EVER DATE *YOU.*
I HAVE A BOY-FRIEND!
THOUGHT SO.
I HATE TO SAY THIS, BUT...
TAICHI DOESN'T REALLY GO FOR THAT SORT OF THING.
YEAH, BUT THAT'S WHERE *YOU* COME IN. YOU CAN SPIN IT SO HE'LL AGREE, RIGHT?
DON'T SELL YOURSELF SHORT! I KNOW YOU CAN MAKE IT WORK. PLEASE! I'M *BEGGING* YOU.
MURMUR
MURMUR
I'M NOT A MIRACLE WORKER! TAICHI NEVER LISTENS TO A WORD I SAY.
LOOK, I'M SORRY, BUT THERE REALLY ISN'T ANY-THING I CAN DO...
I KNOW I'M ASKING FOR A LOT, BUT *PLEASE!*
THIS IS THE FIRST TIME IN HER WHOLE LIFE THAT FUMI'S EVER FALLEN FOR SOMEONE.
PLEASE!
UUU-UUH...
NAOTO! YU-PON! SEE YA LATER!
LATER!
SHAKE
SHAKE
YO, NAOTO!

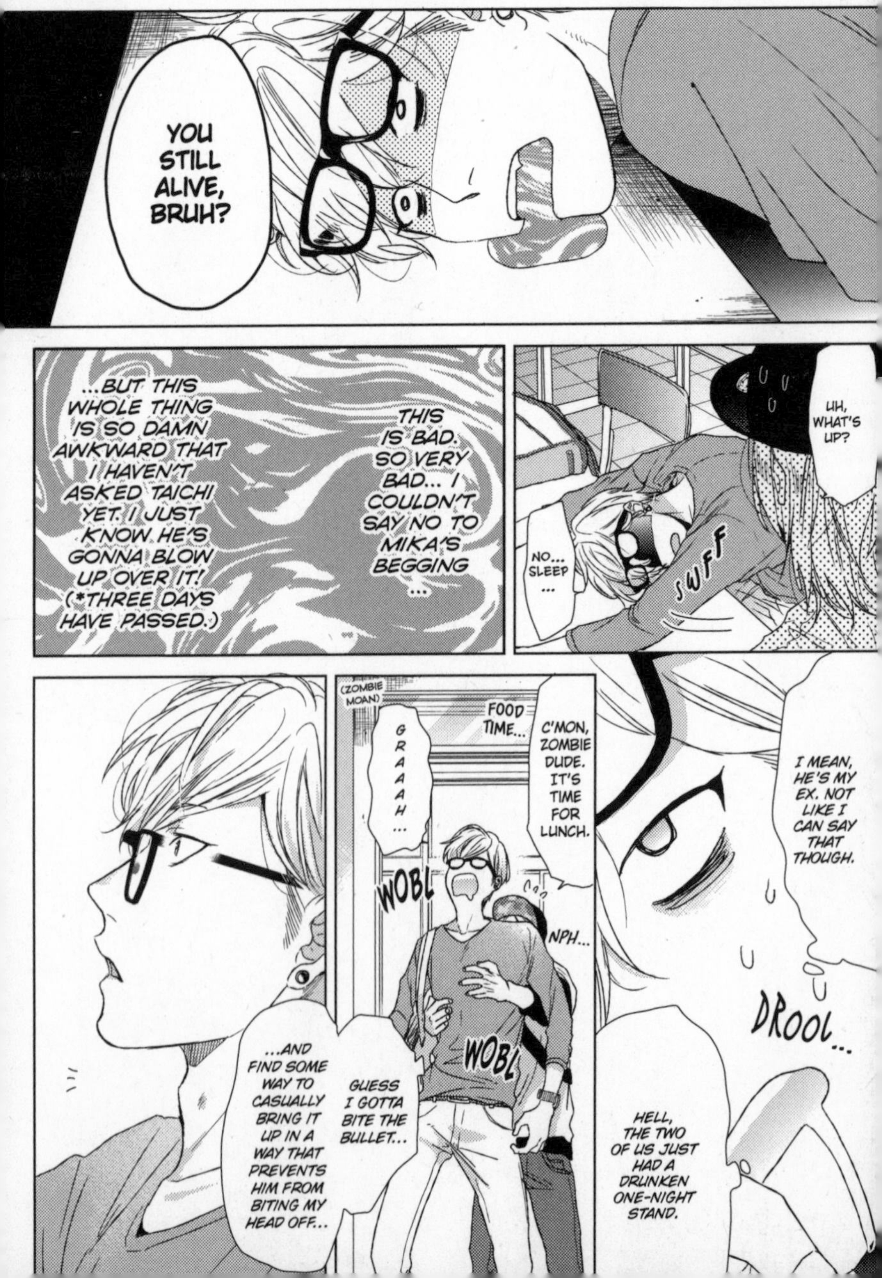
YOU STILL ALIVE, BRUH?
UH, WHAT'S UP?
NO... SLEEP ...
SWFF
THIS IS BAD. SO VERY BAD... I COULDN'T SAY NO TO MIKA'S BEGGING ...
...BUT THIS WHOLE THING IS SO DAMN AWKWARD THAT I HAVEN'T ASKED TAICHI YET. I JUST KNOW HE'S GONNA BLOW UP OVER IT! (*THREE DAYS HAVE PASSED.)
I MEAN, HE'S MY EX. NOT LIKE I CAN SAY THAT THOUGH.
DROOL...
HELL, THE TWO OF US JUST HAD A DRUNKEN ONE-NIGHT STAND.
C'MON, ZOMBIE DUDE. IT'S TIME FOR LUNCH.
FOOD TIME...
(ZOMBIE MOAN)
GRAAAAH...
WOBL
NPH...
WOBL
GUESS I GOTTA BITE THE BULLET...
...AND FIND SOME WAY TO CASUALLY BRING IT UP IN A WAY THAT PREVENTS HIM FROM BITING MY HEAD OFF...

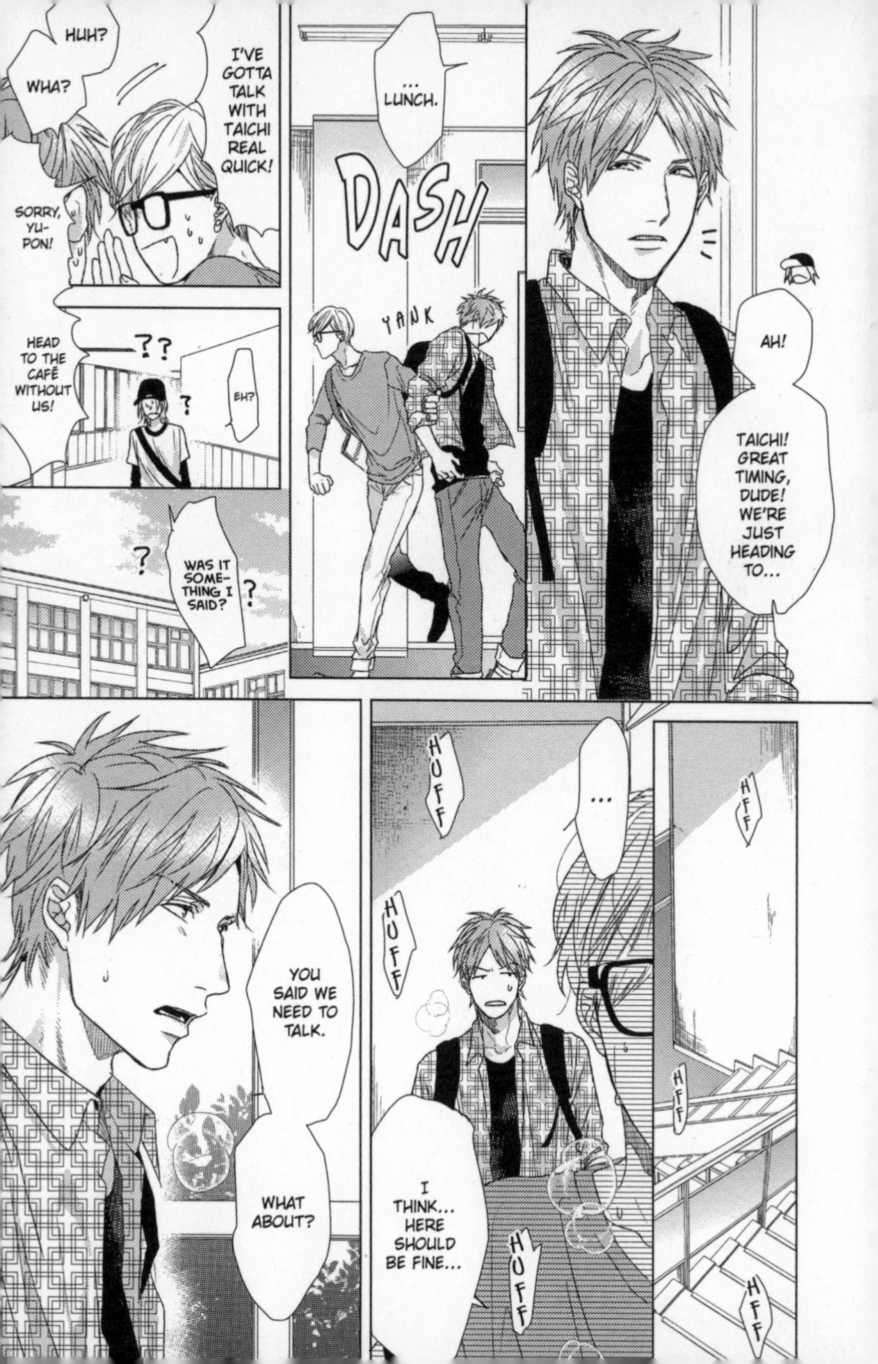
AH!
TAICHI! GREAT TIMING, DUDE! WE'RE JUST HEADING TO...
... LUNCH.
DASH
YANK
I'VE GOTTA TALK WITH TAICHI REAL QUICK!
HUH?
WHA?
SORRY, YU-PON!
HEAD TO THE CAFÉ WITHOUT US!
??
EH?
?
?
WAS IT SOMETHING I SAID?
?
HFF
HFF
HFF
...
HUFF
HUFF
I THINK... HERE SHOULD BE FINE...
HUFF
YOU SAID WE NEED TO TALK.
WHAT ABOUT?

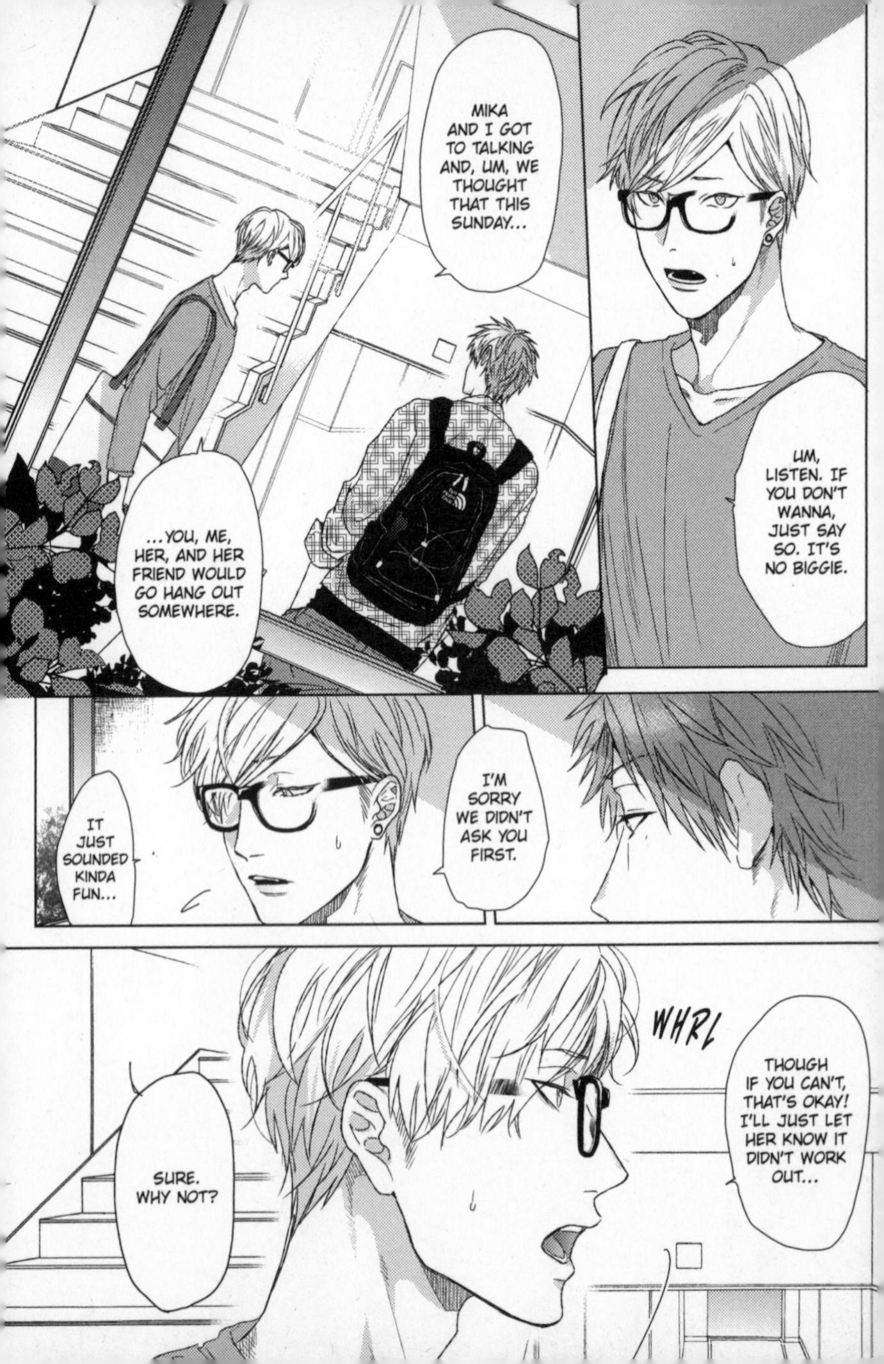
UM, LISTEN. IF YOU DON'T WANNA, JUST SAY SO. IT'S NO BIGGIE.
MIKA AND I GOT TO TALKING AND, UM, WE THOUGHT THAT THIS SUNDAY...
...YOU, ME, HER, AND HER FRIEND WOULD GO HANG OUT SOMEWHERE.
I'M SORRY WE DIDN'T ASK YOU FIRST.
IT JUST SOUNDED KINDA FUN...
WHRL
THOUGH IF YOU CAN'T, THAT'S OKAY! I'LL JUST LET HER KNOW IT DIDN'T WORK OUT...
SURE. WHY NOT?

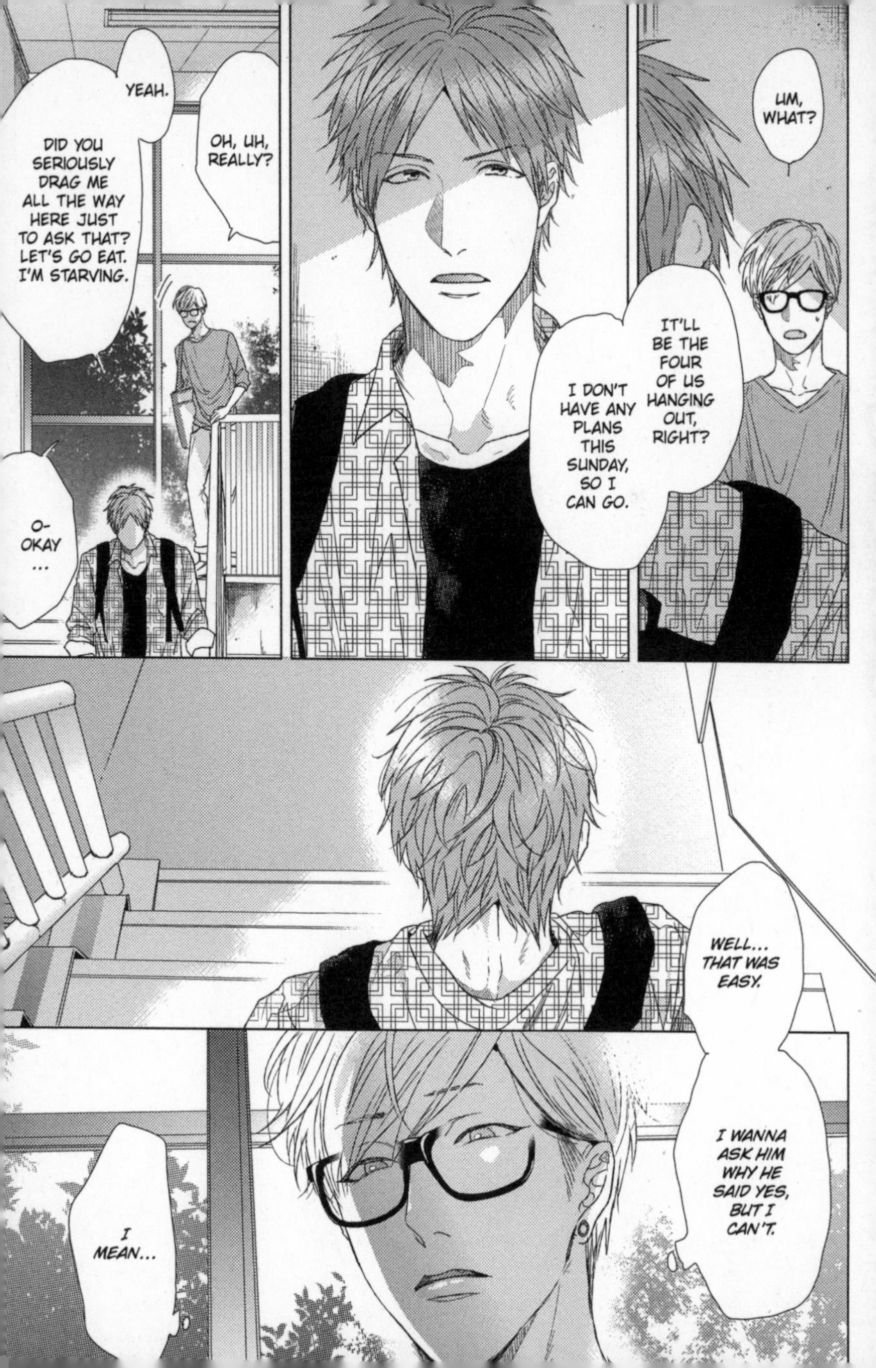
UM, WHAT?
IT'LL BE THE FOUR OF US HANGING OUT, RIGHT?
I DON'T HAVE ANY PLANS THIS SUNDAY, SO I CAN GO.
OH, UH, REALLY?
YEAH.
DID YOU SERIOUSLY DRAG ME ALL THE WAY HERE JUST TO ASK THAT? LET'S GO EAT. I'M STARVING.
O-OKAY...
WELL... THAT WAS EASY.
I WANNA ASK HIM WHY HE SAID YES, BUT I CAN'T.
I MEAN...

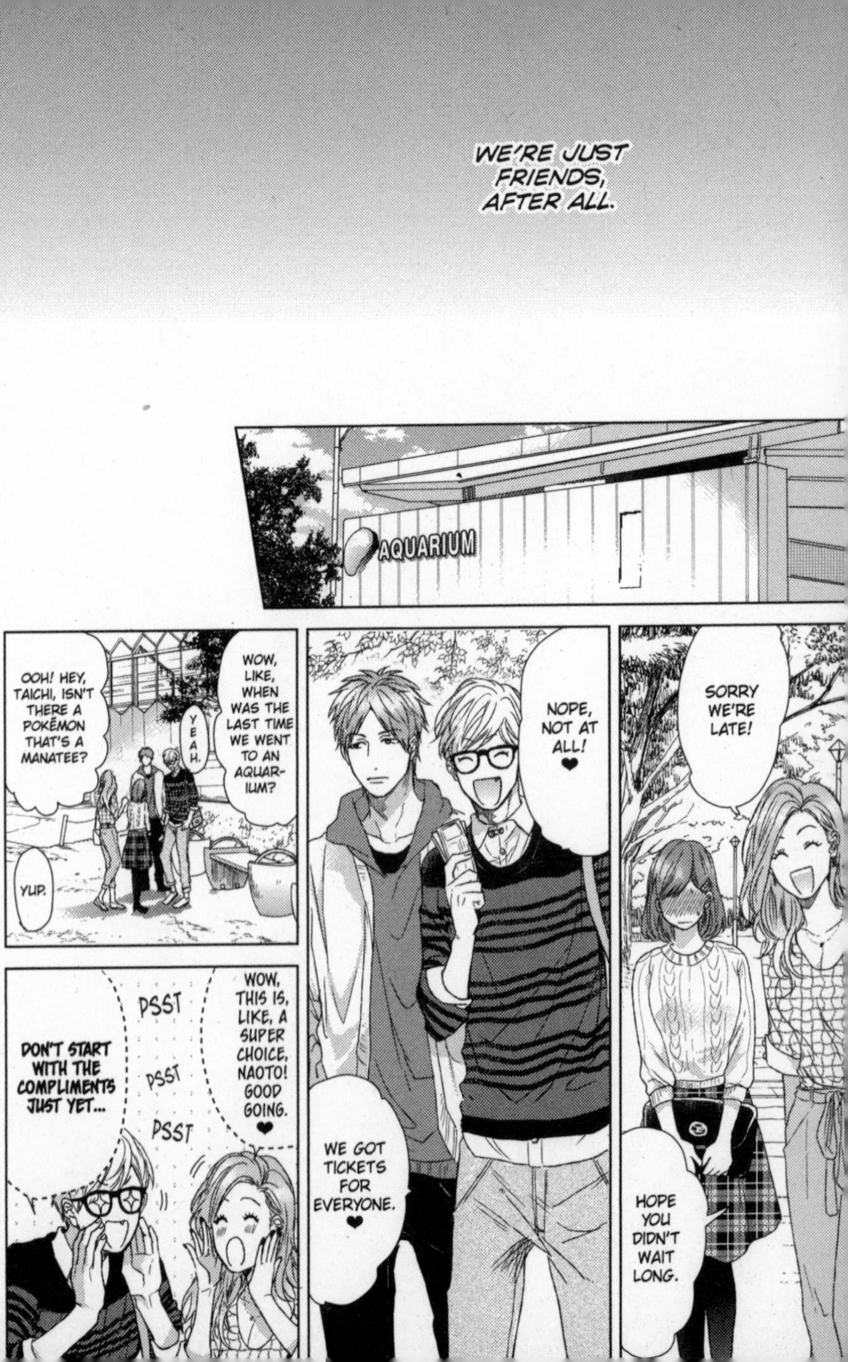
WE'RE JUST FRIENDS, AFTER ALL.
AQUARIUM
SORRY WE'RE LATE!
HOPE YOU DIDN'T WAIT LONG.
NOPE, NOT AT ALL! ❤
WE GOT TICKETS FOR EVERYONE. ❤
WOW, LIKE, WHEN WAS THE LAST TIME WE WENT TO AN AQUARIUM?
YEAH.
OOH! HEY, TAICHI, ISN'T THERE A POKÉMON THAT'S A MANATEE?
YUP.
WOW, THIS IS, LIKE, A SUPER CHOICE, NAOTO! GOOD GOING. ❤
PSST
PSST
PSST
DON'T START WITH THE COMPLIMENTS JUST YET...

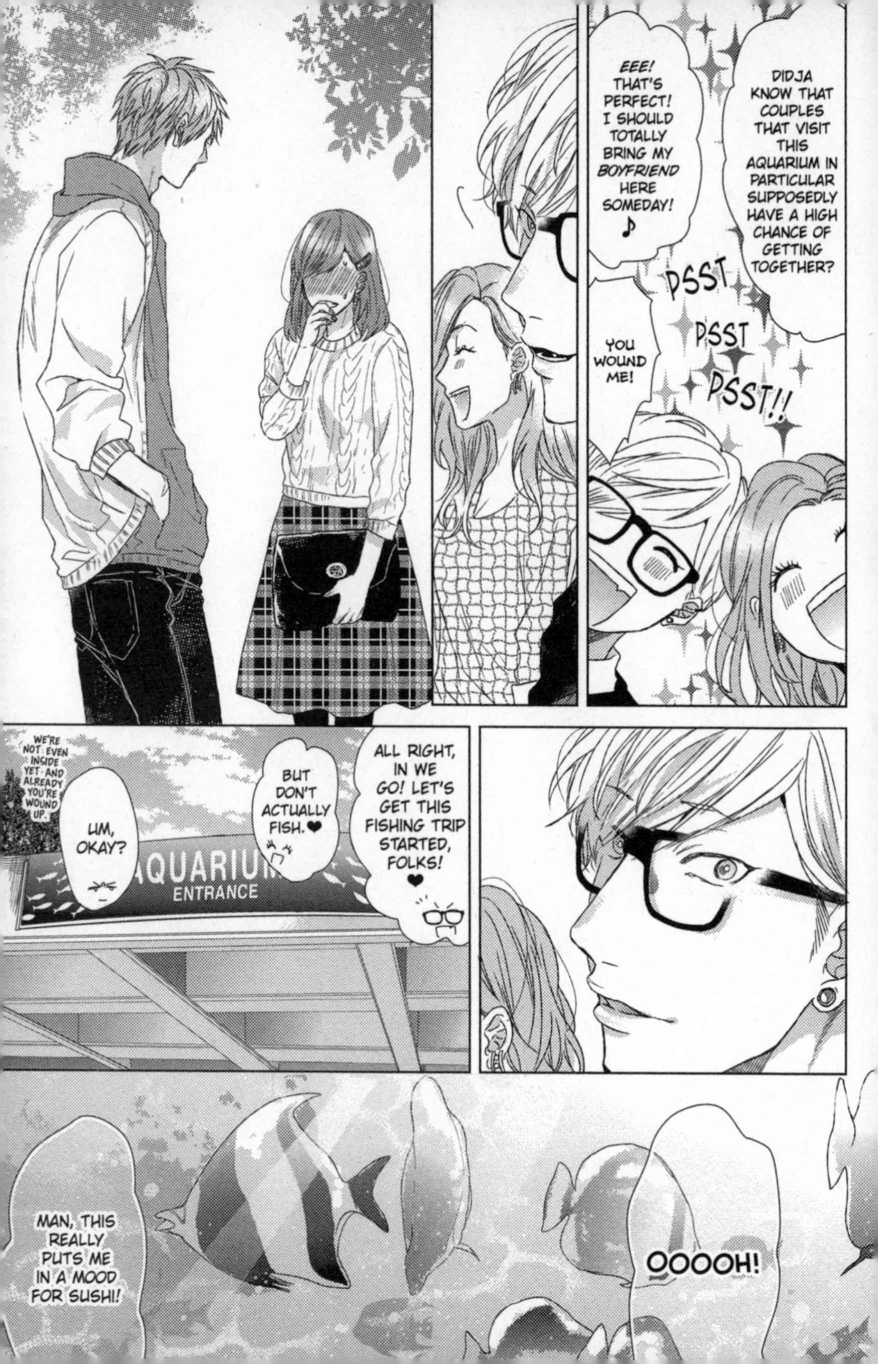
DIDJA KNOW THAT COUPLES THAT VISIT THIS AQUARIUM IN PARTICULAR SUPPOSEDLY HAVE A HIGH CHANCE OF GETTING TOGETHER?
PSST PSST PSST!!
EEE! THAT'S PERFECT! I SHOULD TOTALLY BRING MY BOYFRIEND HERE SOMEDAY! ♪
YOU WOUND ME!
ALL RIGHT, IN WE GO! LET'S GET THIS FISHING TRIP STARTED, FOLKS! ❤
BUT DON'T ACTUALLY FISH. ❤
WE'RE NOT EVEN INSIDE YET AND ALREADY YOU'RE WOUND UP.
UM, OKAY?
ENTRANCE
OOOOH!
MAN, THIS REALLY PUTS ME IN A MOOD FOR SUSHI!

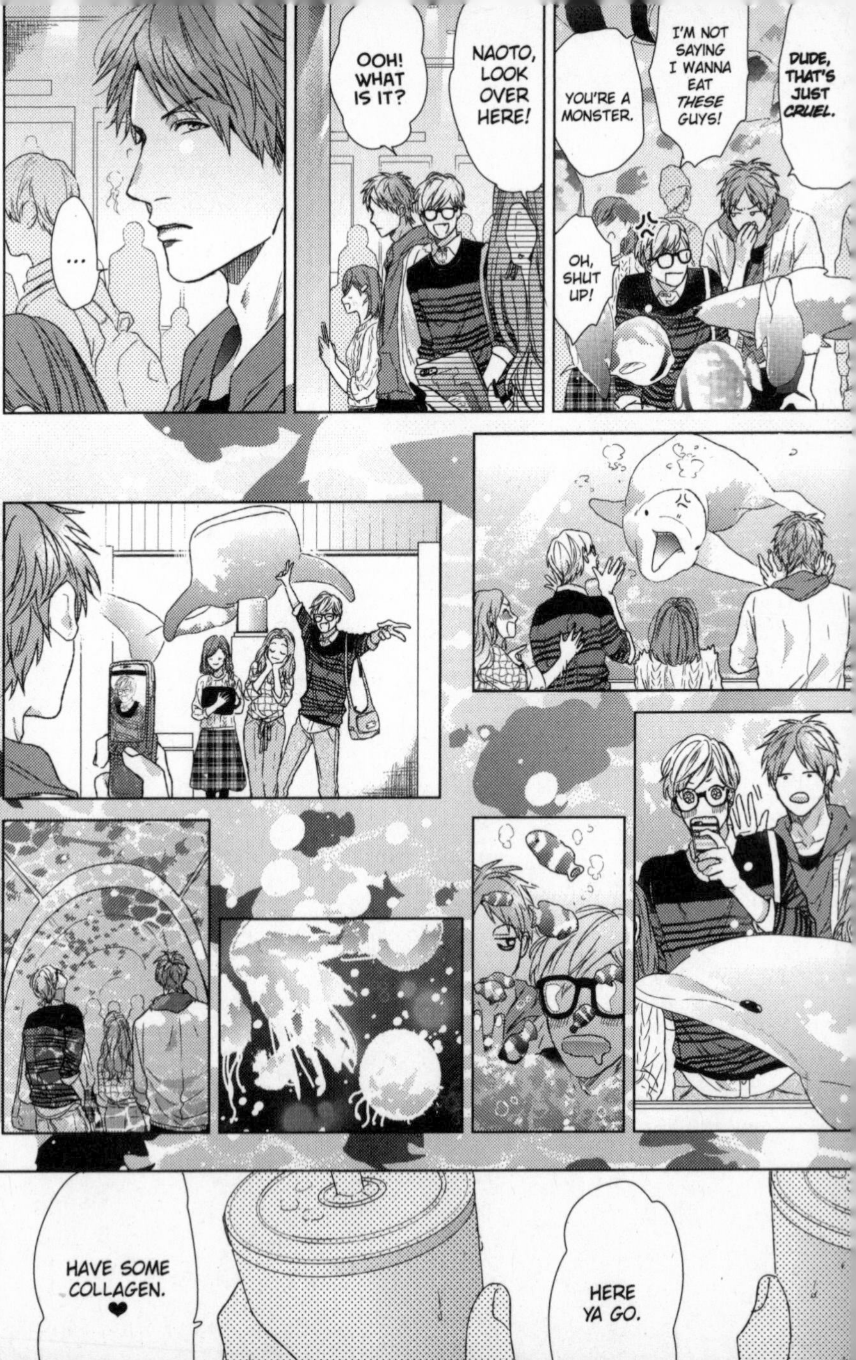
DUDE, THAT'S JUST CRUEL.
I'M NOT SAYING I WANNA EAT THESE GUYS!
YOU'RE A MONSTER.
OH, SHUT UP!
NAOTO, LOOK OVER HERE!
OOH! WHAT IS IT?
...
HERE YA GO.
HAVE SOME COLLAGEN. ❤

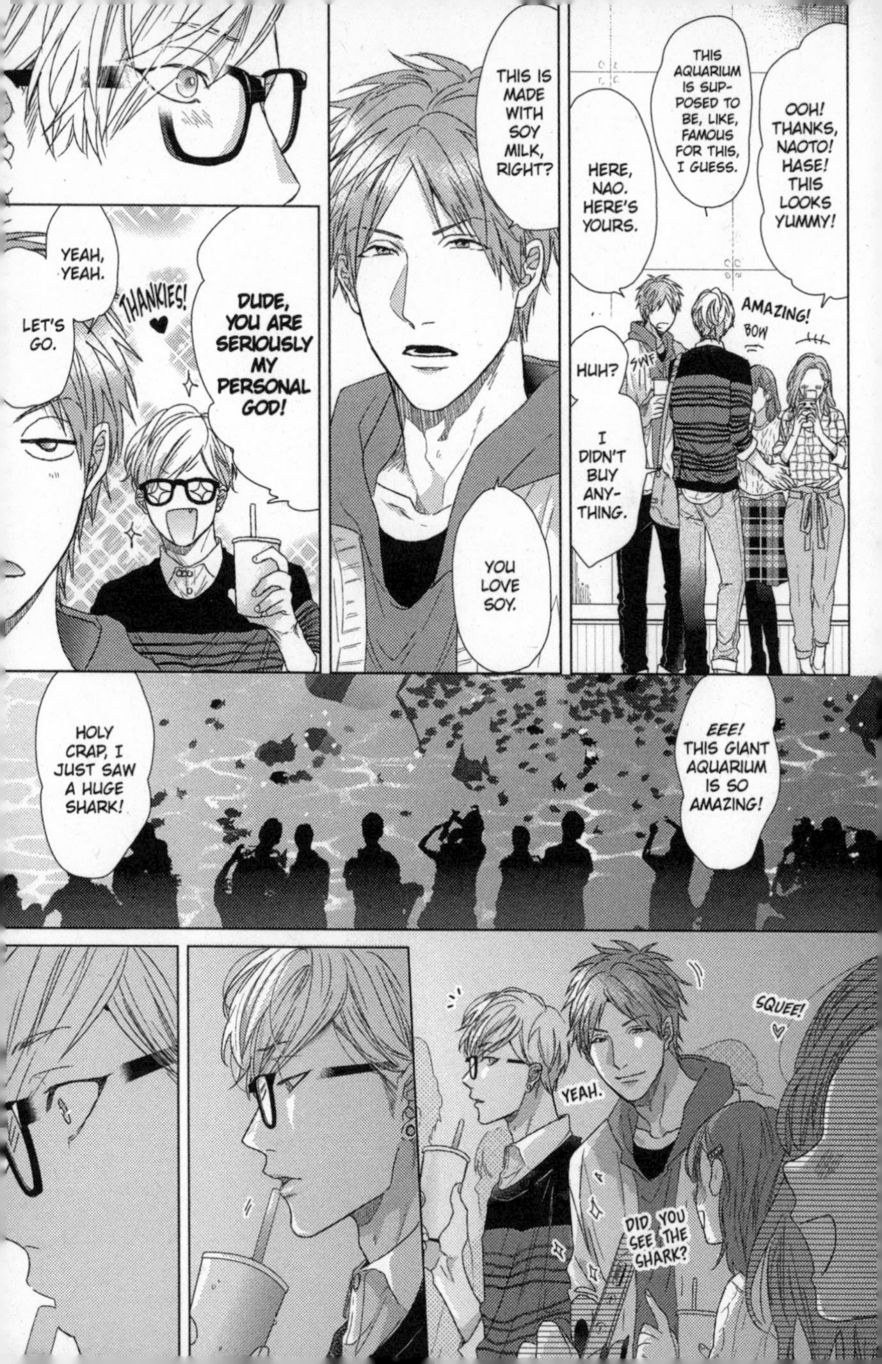
OOH! THANKS, NAOTO! HASE! THIS LOOKS YUMMY!
THIS AQUARIUM IS SUPPOSED TO BE, LIKE, FAMOUS FOR THIS, I GUESS.
HERE, NAO. HERE'S YOURS.
AMAZING!
BOW
HUH?
SWF
I DIDN'T BUY ANYTHING.
THIS IS MADE WITH SOY MILK, RIGHT?
YOU LOVE SOY.
DUDE, YOU ARE SERIOUSLY MY PERSONAL GOD!
THANKIES! ♥
YEAH, YEAH.
LET'S GO.
EEE! THIS GIANT AQUARIUM IS SO AMAZING!
HOLY CRAP, I JUST SAW A HUGE SHARK!
SQUEE! ♥
YEAH.
DID YOU SEE THE SHARK?

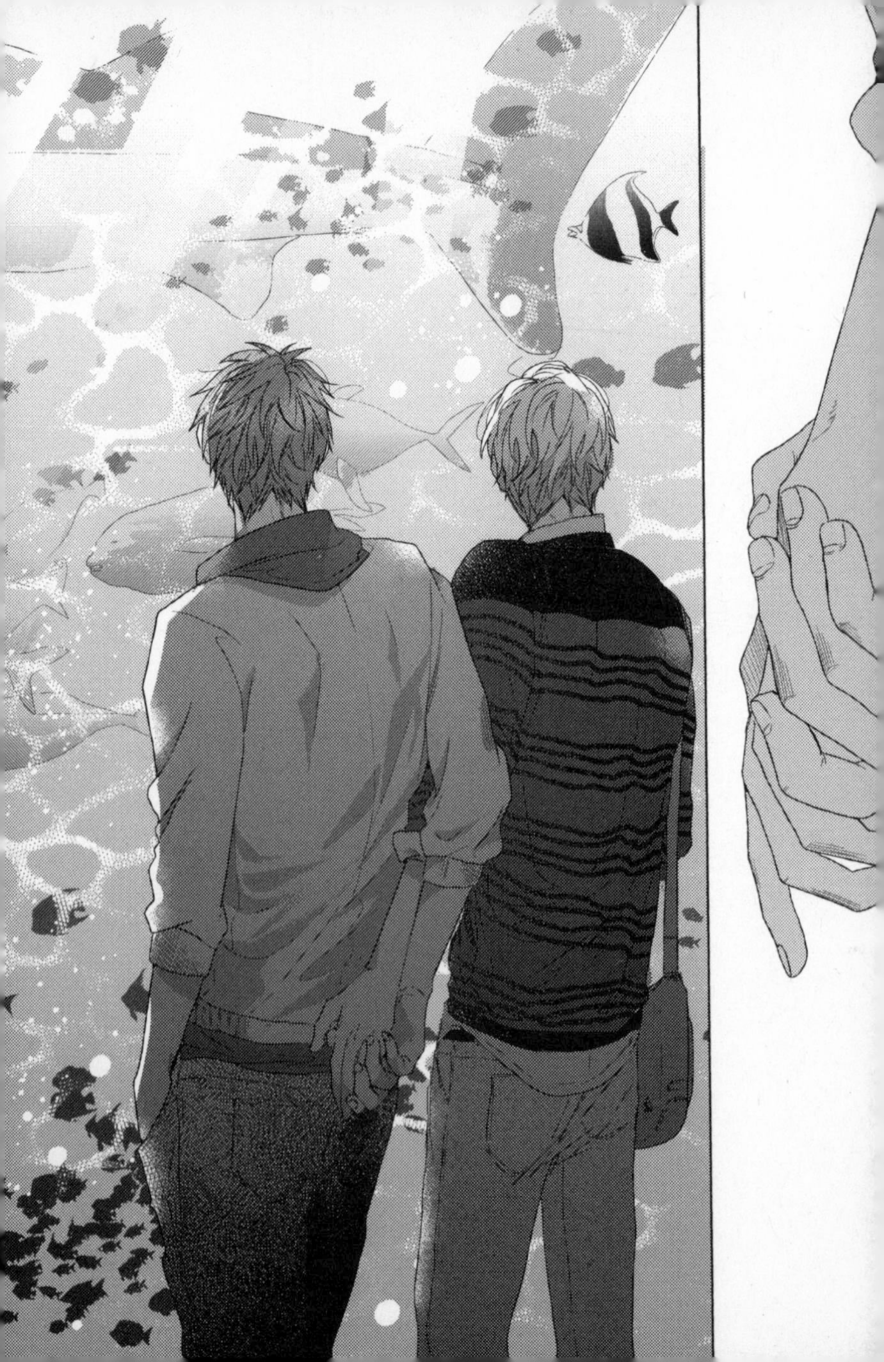

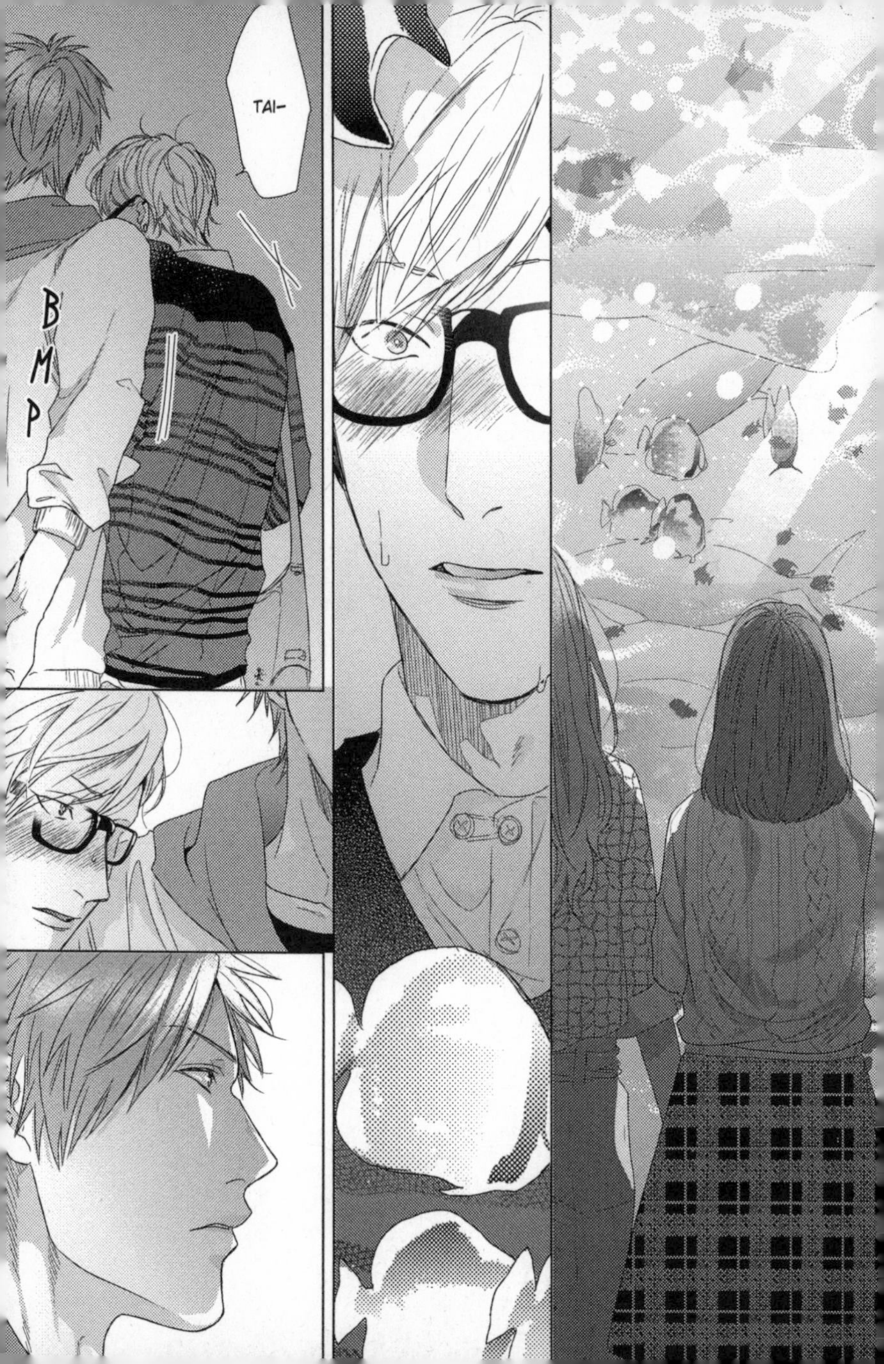
TAI-
BMP

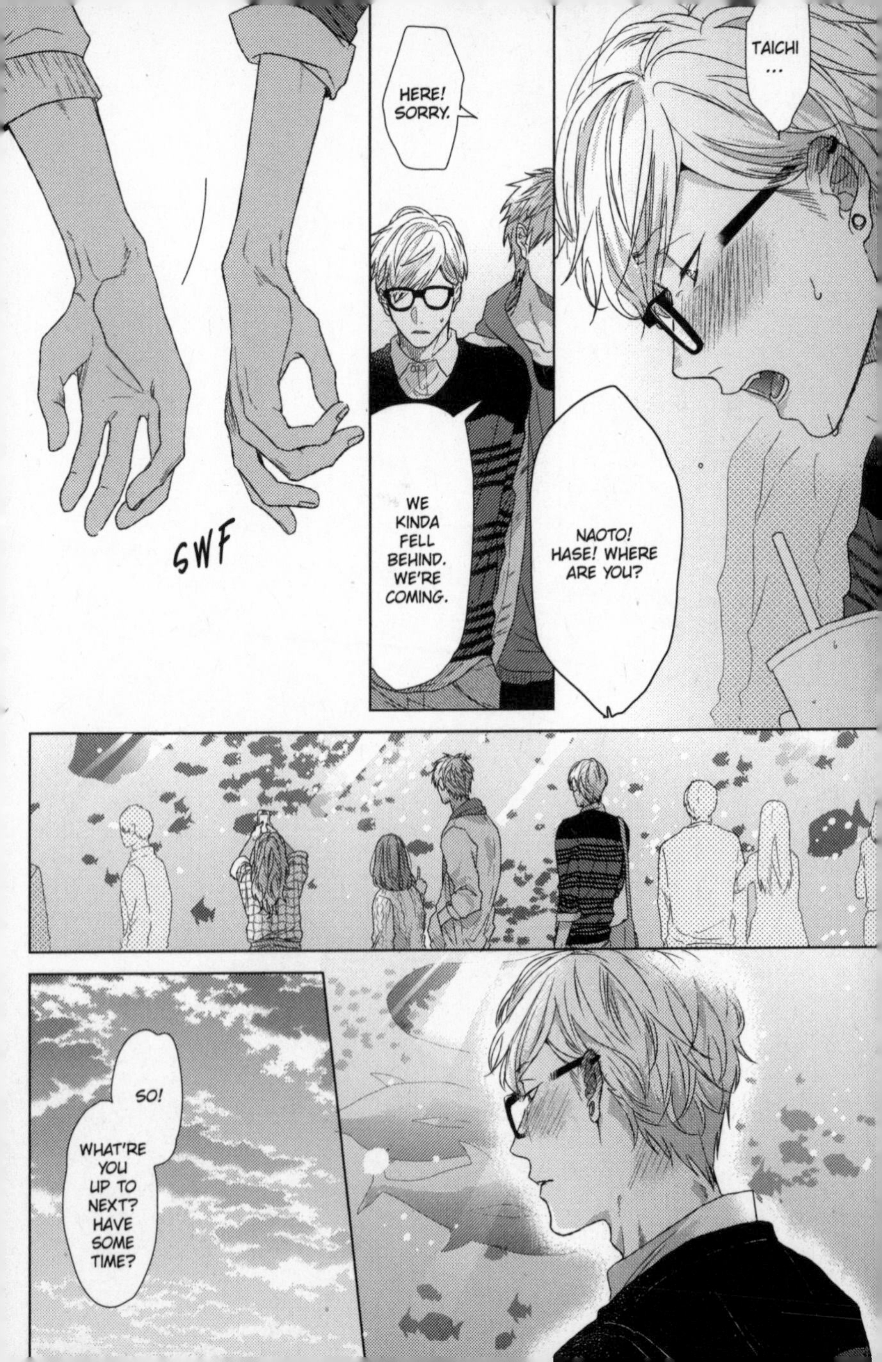
TAICHI ...
NAOTO! HASE! WHERE ARE YOU?
HERE! SORRY.
WE KINDA FELL BEHIND. WE'RE COMING.
SWF
SO!
WHAT'RE YOU UP TO NEXT? HAVE SOME TIME?

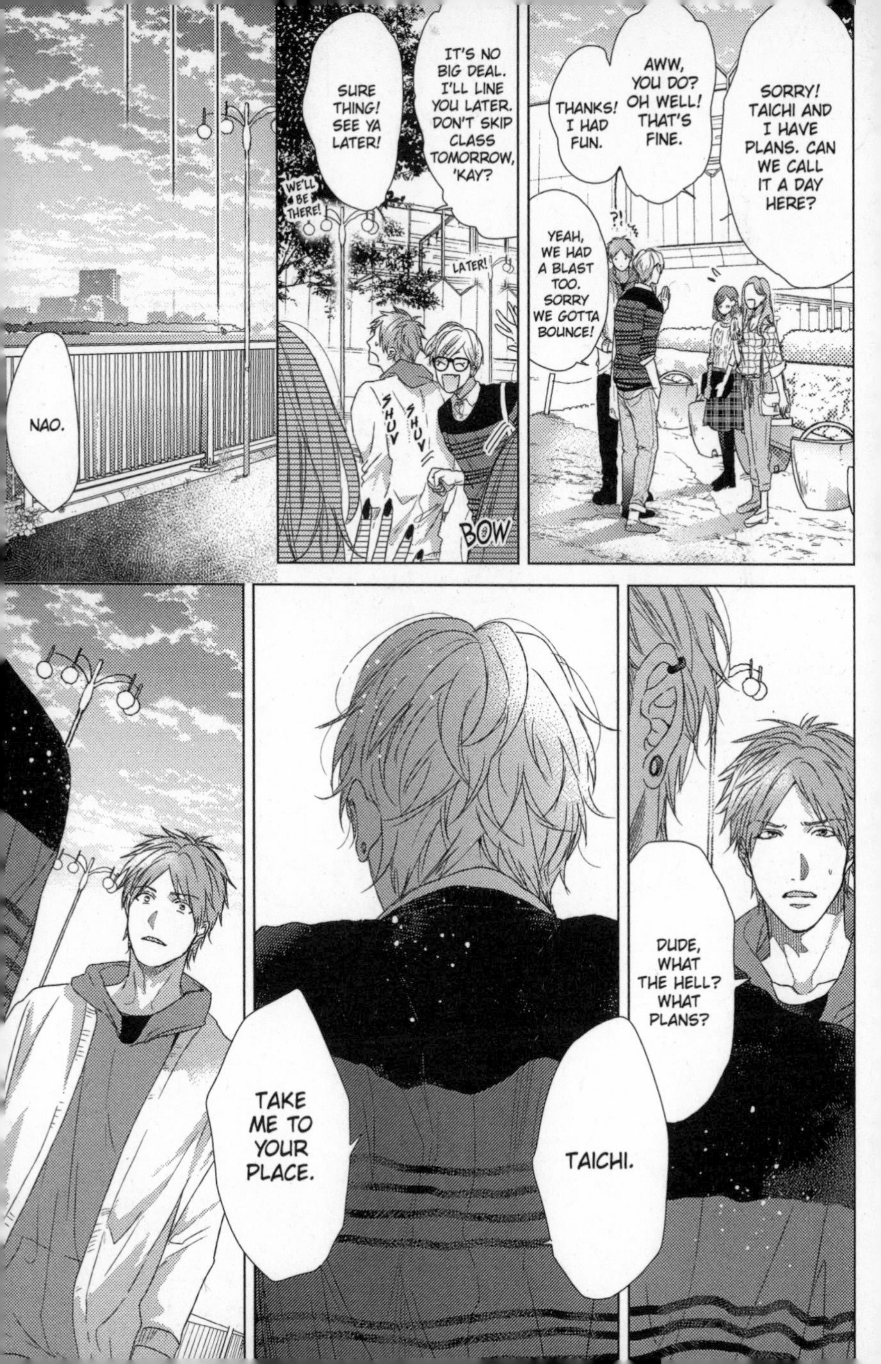
SORRY! TAICHI AND I HAVE PLANS. CAN WE CALL IT A DAY HERE?
AWW, YOU DO? OH WELL! THAT'S FINE.
THANKS! I HAD FUN.
?!
YEAH, WE HAD A BLAST TOO. SORRY WE GOTTA BOUNCE!
IT'S NO BIG DEAL. I'LL LINE YOU LATER. DON'T SKIP CLASS TOMORROW, 'KAY?
SURE THING! SEE YA LATER!
LATER!
WE'LL BE THERE!
SHUV
SHUV
BOW
NAO.
DUDE, WHAT THE HELL? WHAT PLANS?
TAICHI.
TAKE ME TO YOUR PLACE.

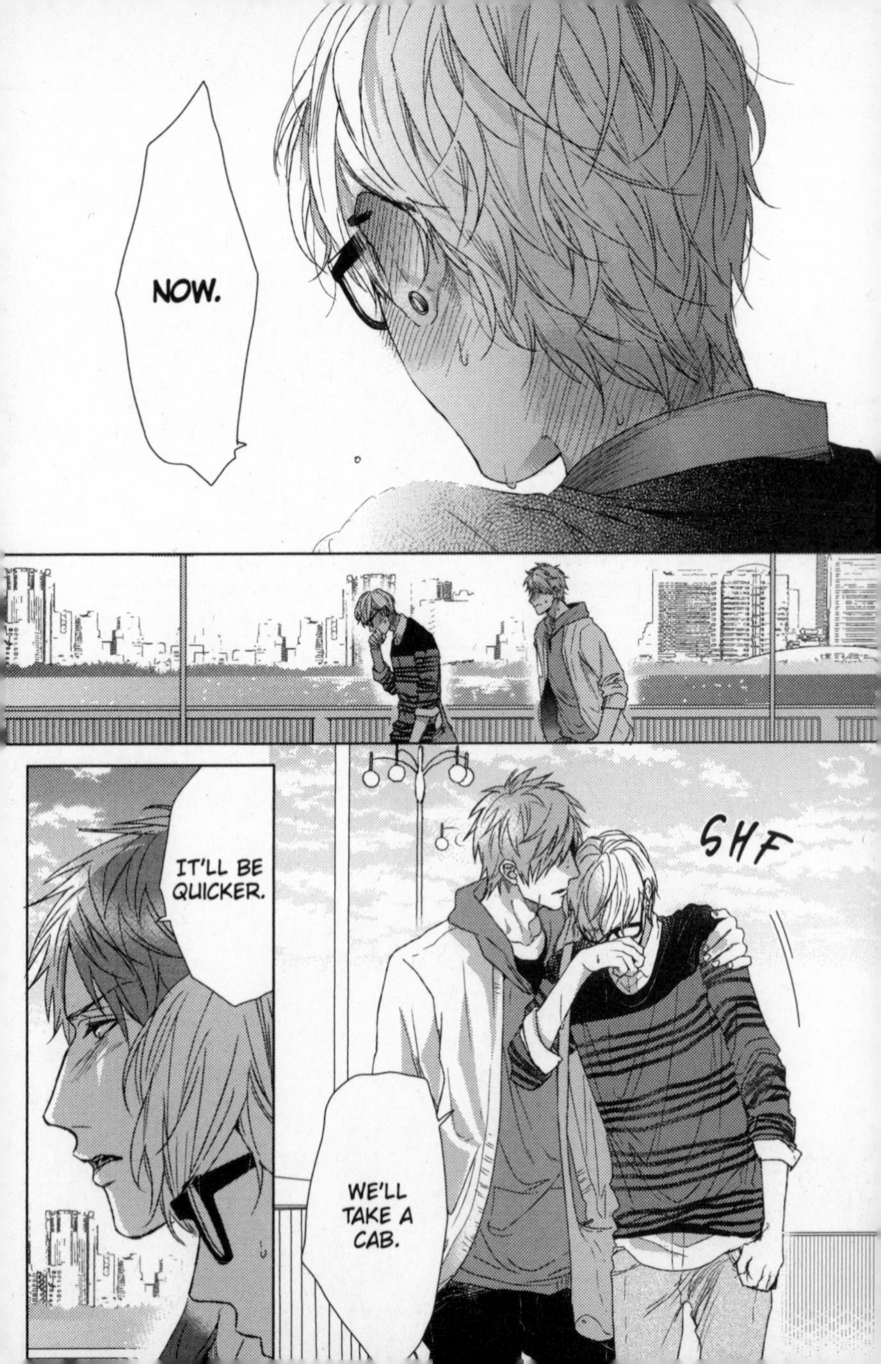
NOW.
SHF
WE'LL TAKE A CAB.
IT'LL BE QUICKER.

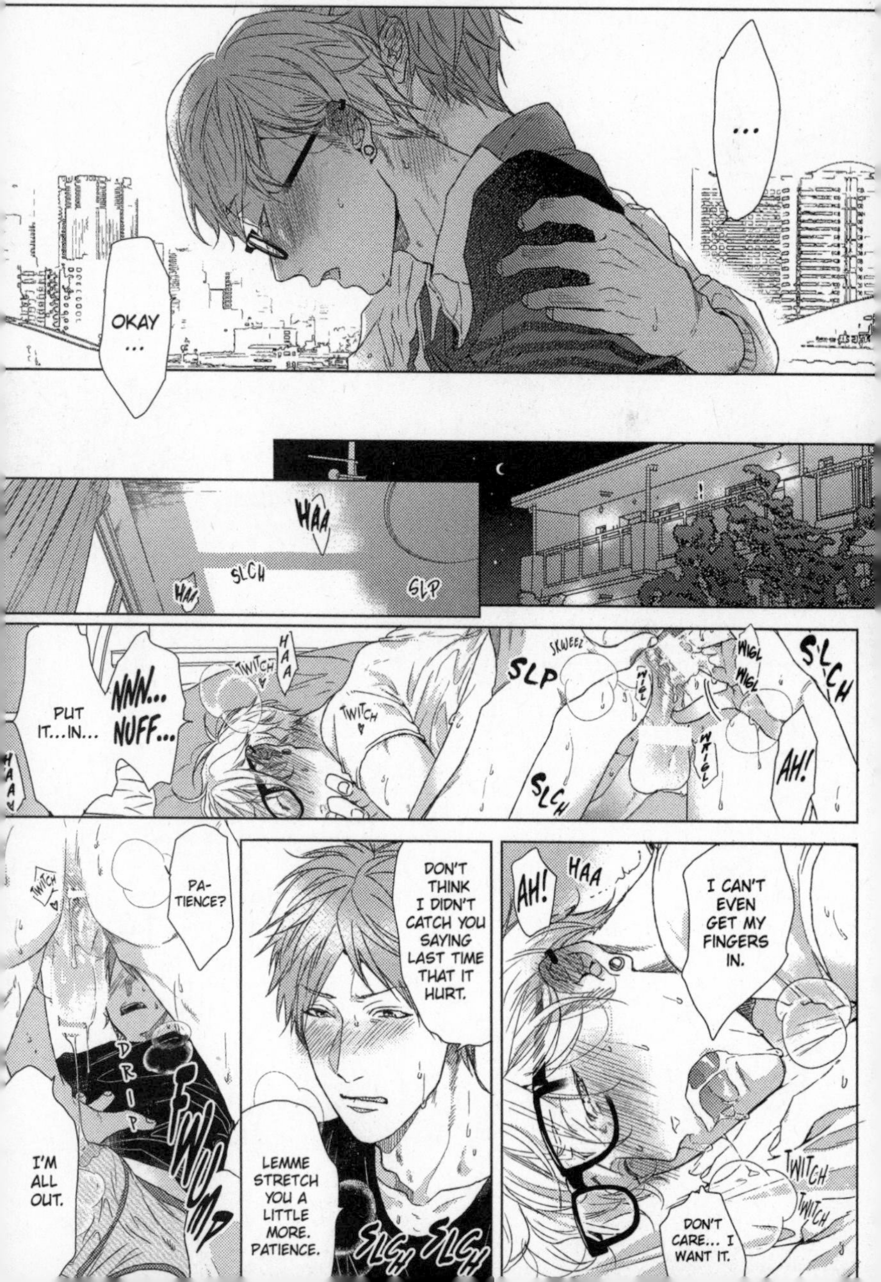
…
OKAY …
HAA
SLCH
SLP
HAA
S'L'CH
WIGL
WIGL
AH!
SKWEEZ
SLP
WIGL
WRIGL
SLCH
TWITCH
HAA
TWITCH
NNN… NUFF…
PUT IT…IN…
HAAA
I CAN'T EVEN GET MY FINGERS IN.
AH!
HAA
TWITCH
TWITCH
DON'T CARE… I WANT IT.
DON'T THINK I DIDN'T CATCH YOU SAYING LAST TIME THAT IT HURT.
LEMME STRETCH YOU A LITTLE MORE. PATIENCE.
SLCH SLCH
PA-TIENCE?
TWITCH
DRIP
FWUMP
I'M ALL OUT.

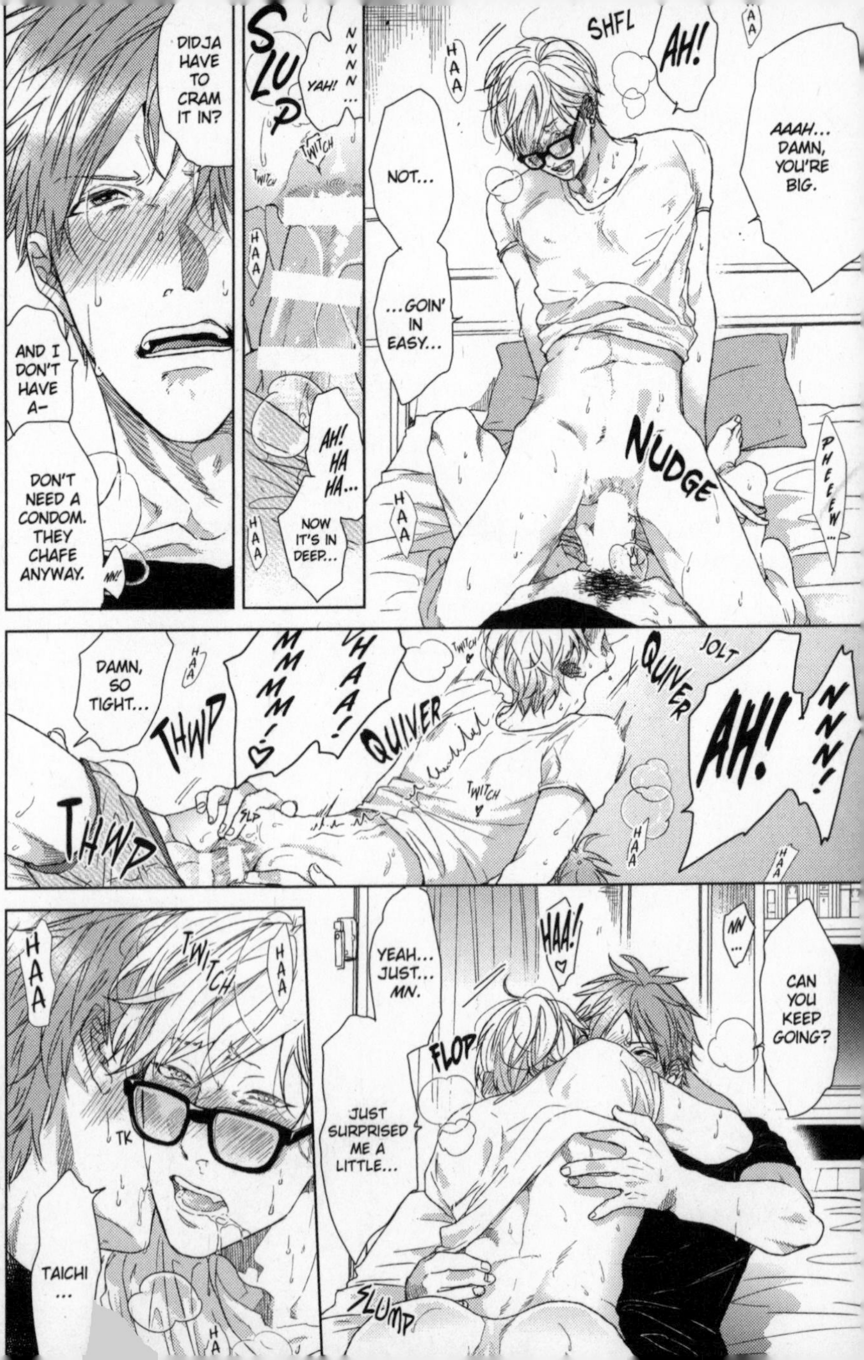
HAA
AH!
SHFL
AAAH... DAMN, YOU'RE BIG.
HAA
NOT...
...GOIN' IN EASY...
PHEEEW...
NUDGE
NNNNN...
YAH!
SLURP
TWITCH
TWITCH
HAA
AH! HA HA...
NOW IT'S IN DEEP...
HAA
HAA
DIDJA HAVE TO CRAM IT IN?
AND I DON'T HAVE A-
DON'T NEED A CONDOM. THEY CHAFE ANYWAY.
MN!
NNNN!
AH!
JOLT
QUIVER
HAA
HAA
TWITCH
HAAA!
MMMM!♡
QUIVER
TWITCH
HAA
DAMN, SO TIGHT...
THWP
SLP
THWP
NN...
CAN YOU KEEP GOING?
HAA!♡
YEAH... JUST... MN.
FLOP
JUST SURPRISED ME A LITTLE...
SLUMP
HAA
TWITCH
HAA
TK
TAICHI...
HA

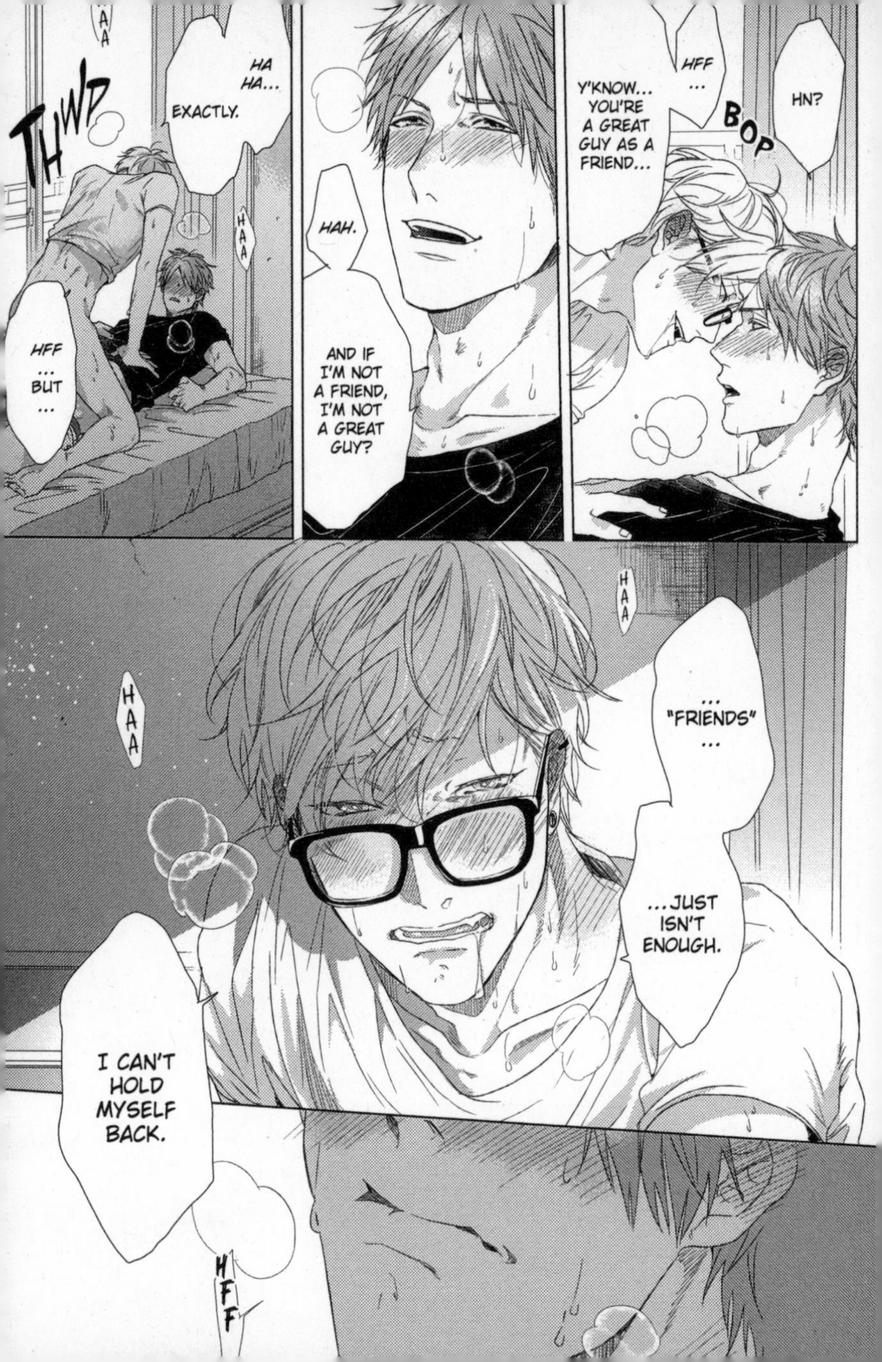
HN?
BOP
HFF ...
Y'KNOW... YOU'RE A GREAT GUY AS A FRIEND...
HAH.
AND IF I'M NOT A FRIEND, I'M NOT A GREAT GUY?
HAA
HA HA... EXACTLY.
THWP
HAA
HFF ... BUT ...
HAA
... "FRIENDS" ...
...JUST ISN'T ENOUGH.
HAA
I CAN'T HOLD MYSELF BACK.
HFF

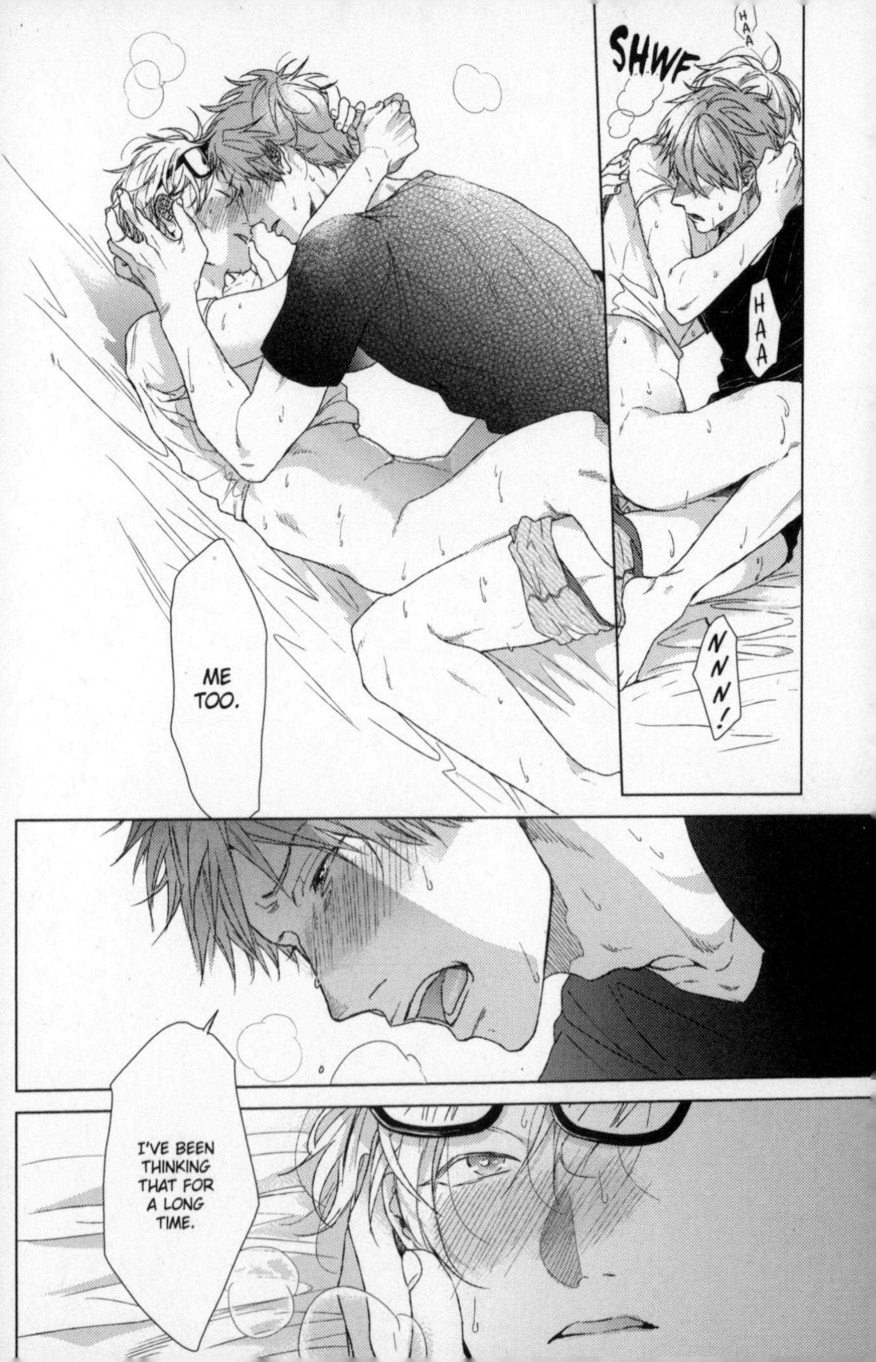
HAA
SHWF
HAA
NNN!
ME TOO.
I'VE BEEN THINKING THAT FOR A LONG TIME.

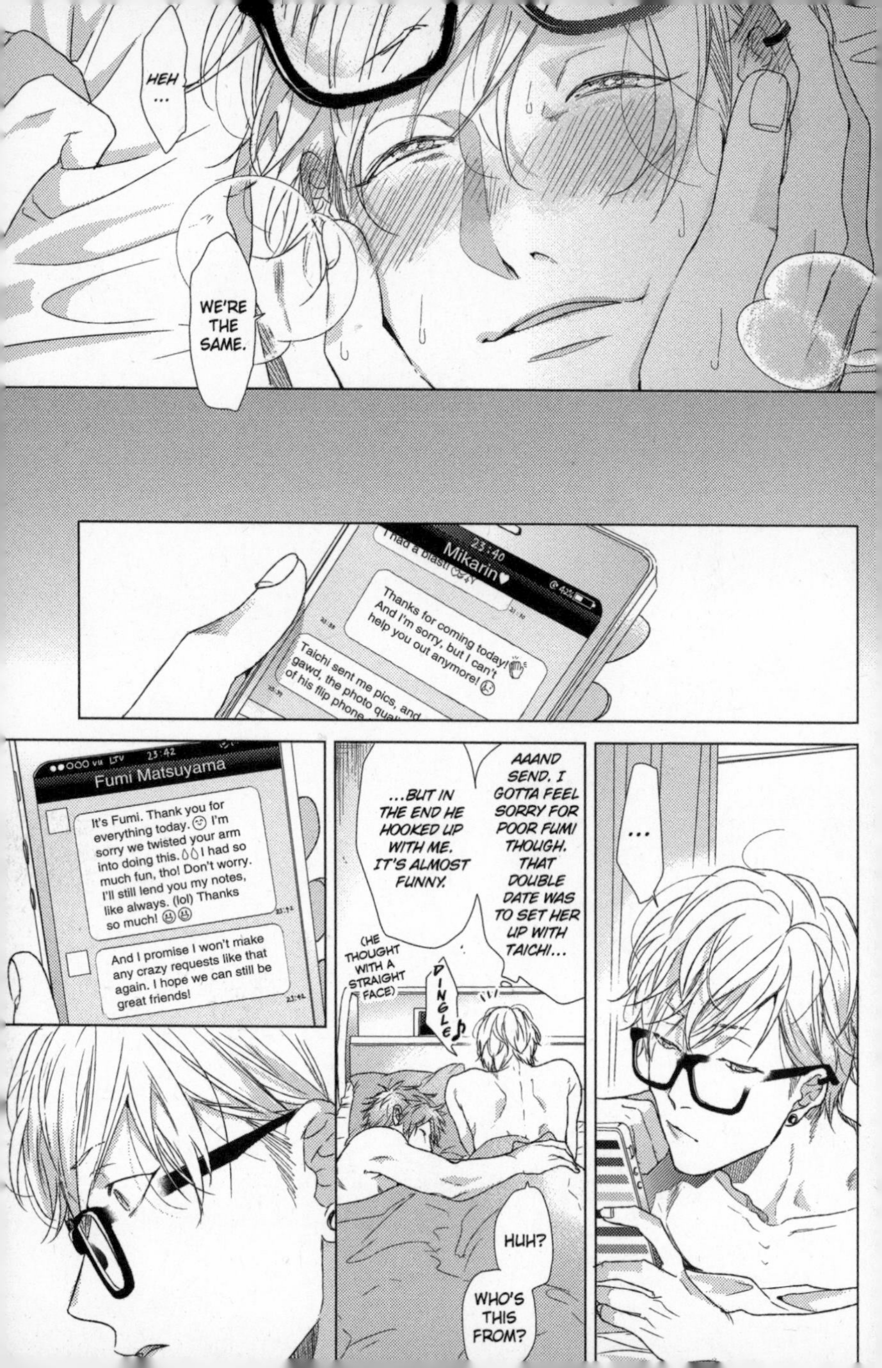
HEH ...
WE'RE THE SAME.
23:40
Mikarin♥
I had a blast!
Thanks for coming today! And I'm sorry, but I can't help you out anymore!
Taichi sent me pics, and gawd, the photo qua of his flip phone
...
AAAND SEND. I GOTTA FEEL SORRY FOR POOR FUMI THOUGH. THAT DOUBLE DATE WAS TO SET HER UP WITH TAICHI...
...BUT IN THE END HE HOOKED UP WITH ME. IT'S ALMOST FUNNY.
(HE THOUGHT WITH A STRAIGHT FACE)
DINGLE
HUH?
WHO'S THIS FROM?
23:42
Fumi Matsuyama
It's Fumi. Thank you for everything today. I'm sorry we twisted your arm into doing this. I had so much fun, tho! Don't worry. I'll still lend you my notes, like always. (lol) Thanks so much!
And I promise I won't make any crazy requests like that again. I hope we can still be great friends!

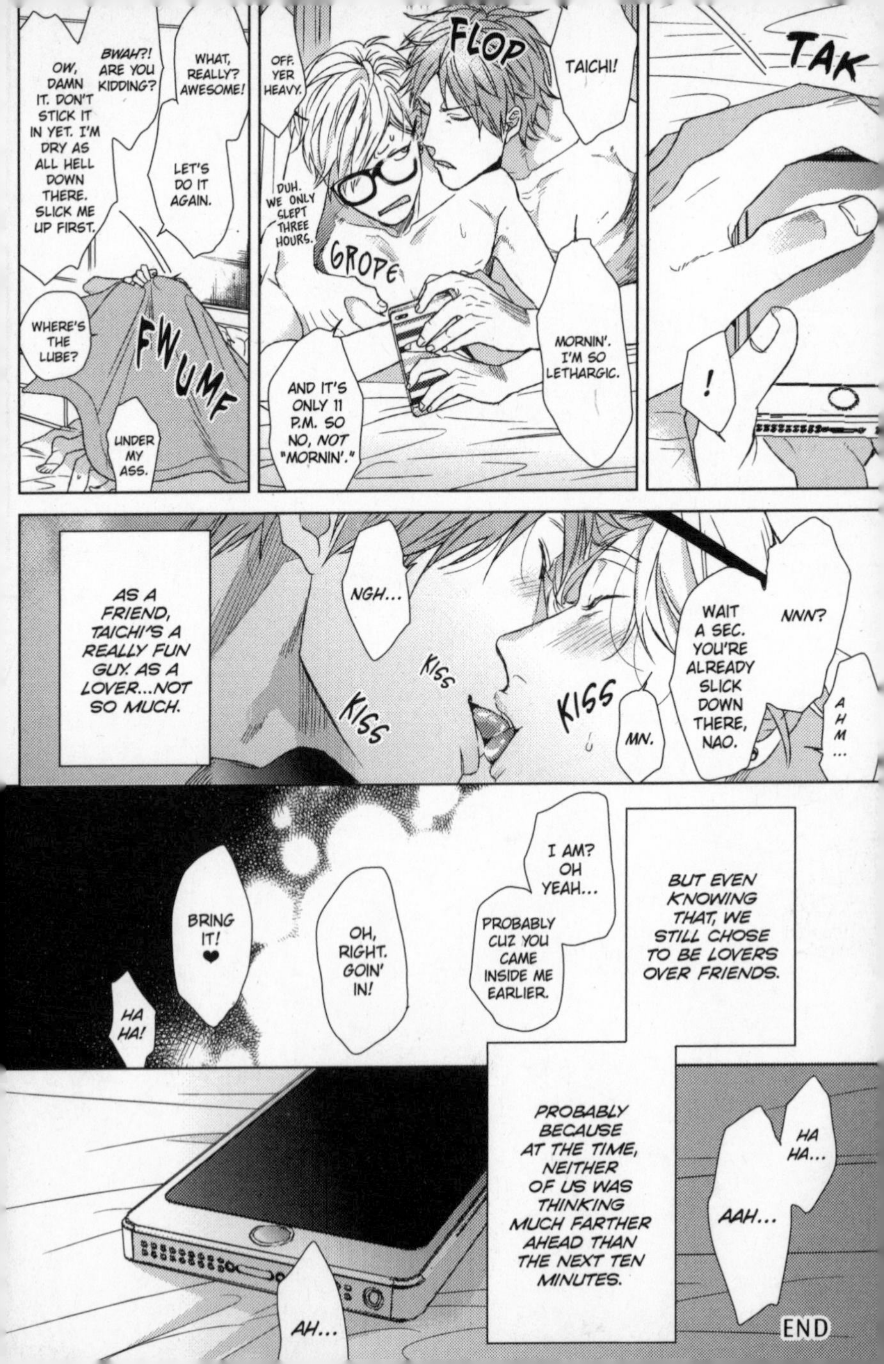
TAK
!
FLOP
TAICHI!
MORNIN'. I'M SO LETHARGIC.
OFF. YER HEAVY.
DUH. WE ONLY SLEPT THREE HOURS.
GROPE
AND IT'S ONLY 11 P.M. SO NO, NOT "MORNIN'."
WHAT, REALLY? AWESOME!
LET'S DO IT AGAIN.
BWAH?! ARE YOU KIDDING?
OW, DAMN IT. DON'T STICK IT IN YET. I'M DRY AS ALL HELL DOWN THERE. SLICK ME UP FIRST.
WHERE'S THE LUBE?
FWUMF
UNDER MY ASS.
AHM...
NNN?
WAIT A SEC. YOU'RE ALREADY SLICK DOWN THERE, NAO.
MN.
KISS
KISS
NGH...
KISS
AS A FRIEND, TAICHI'S A REALLY FUN GUY. AS A LOVER...NOT SO MUCH.
BUT EVEN KNOWING THAT, WE STILL CHOSE TO BE LOVERS OVER FRIENDS.
I AM? OH YEAH...
PROBABLY CUZ YOU CAME INSIDE ME EARLIER.
OH, RIGHT. GOIN' IN!
BRING IT! ❤
HA HA!
HA HA...
AAH...
PROBABLY BECAUSE AT THE TIME, NEITHER OF US WAS THINKING MUCH FARTHER AHEAD THAN THE NEXT TEN MINUTES.
AH...
END

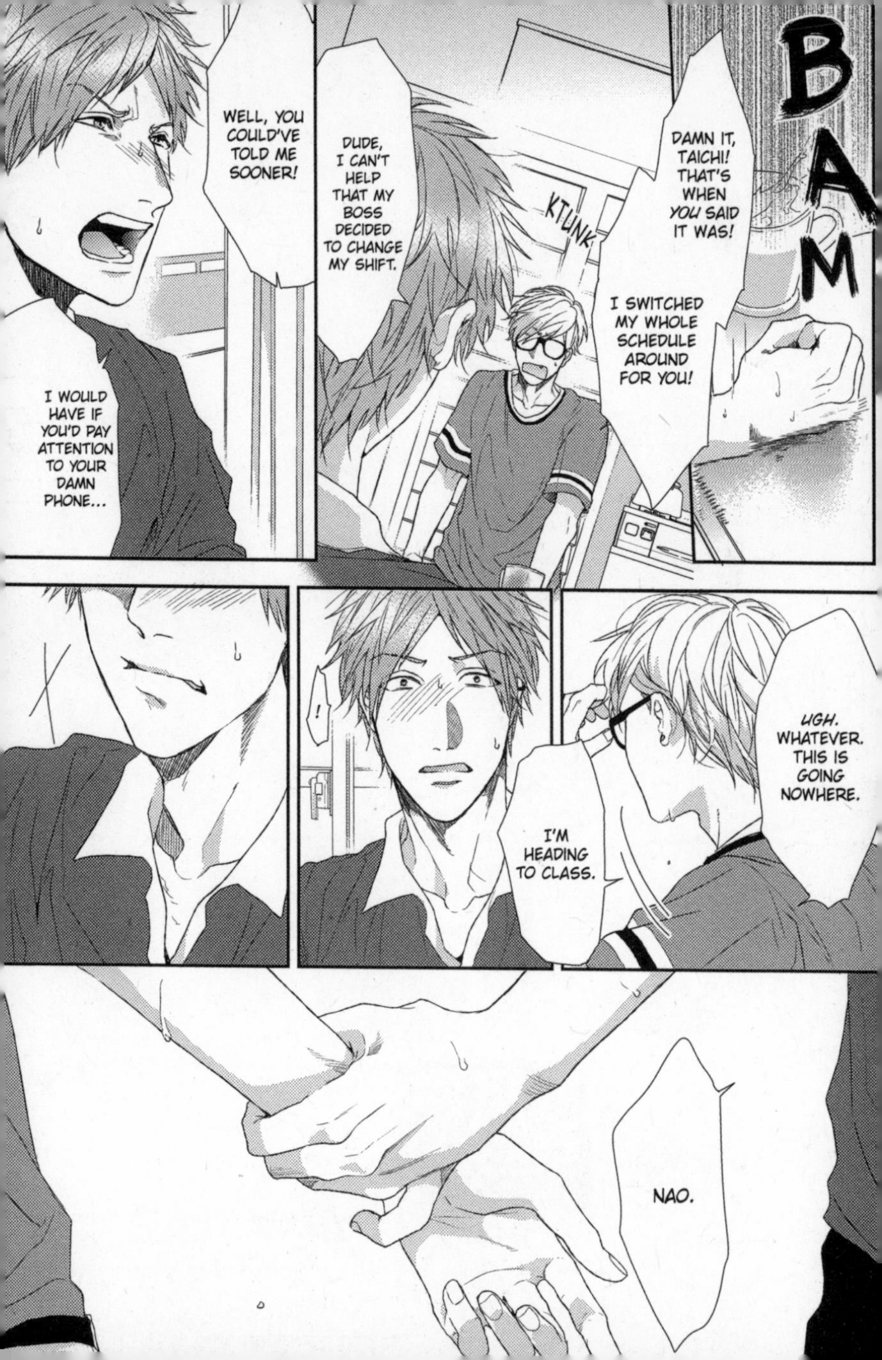
BAM
DAMN IT, TAICHI! THAT'S WHEN *YOU* SAID IT WAS!
I SWITCHED MY WHOLE SCHEDULE AROUND FOR YOU!
KTUNK
DUDE, I CAN'T HELP THAT MY BOSS DECIDED TO CHANGE MY SHIFT.
WELL, YOU COULD'VE TOLD ME SOONER!
I WOULD HAVE IF YOU'D PAY ATTENTION TO YOUR DAMN PHONE...
UGH. WHATEVER. THIS IS GOING NOWHERE.
I'M HEADING TO CLASS.
!
NAO.

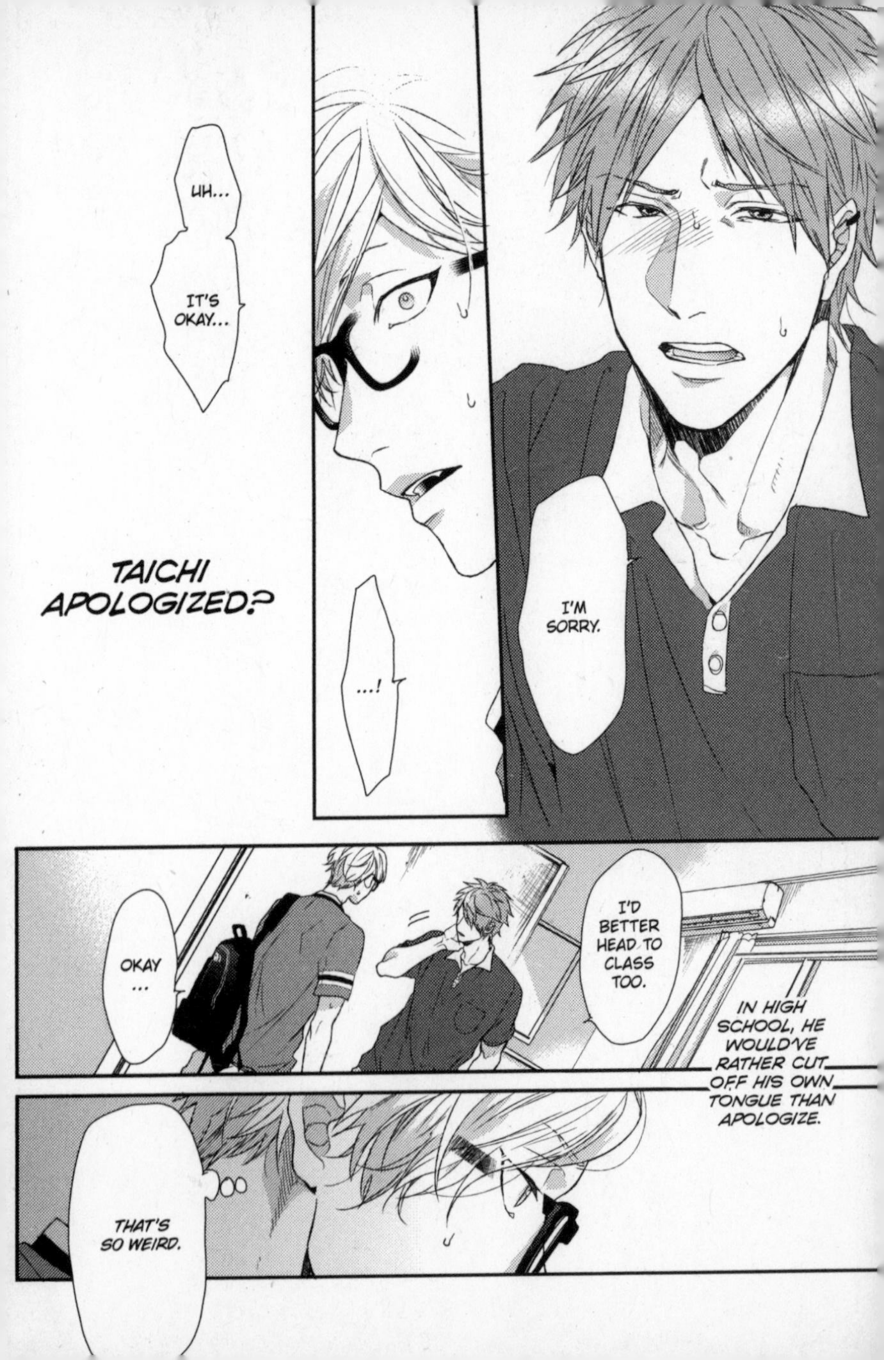
I'M SORRY.
...!
UH...
IT'S OKAY...
TAICHI APOLOGIZED?
I'D BETTER HEAD TO CLASS TOO.
OKAY ...
IN HIGH SCHOOL, HE WOULD'VE RATHER CUT OFF HIS OWN TONGUE THAN APOLOGIZE.
THAT'S SO WEIRD.

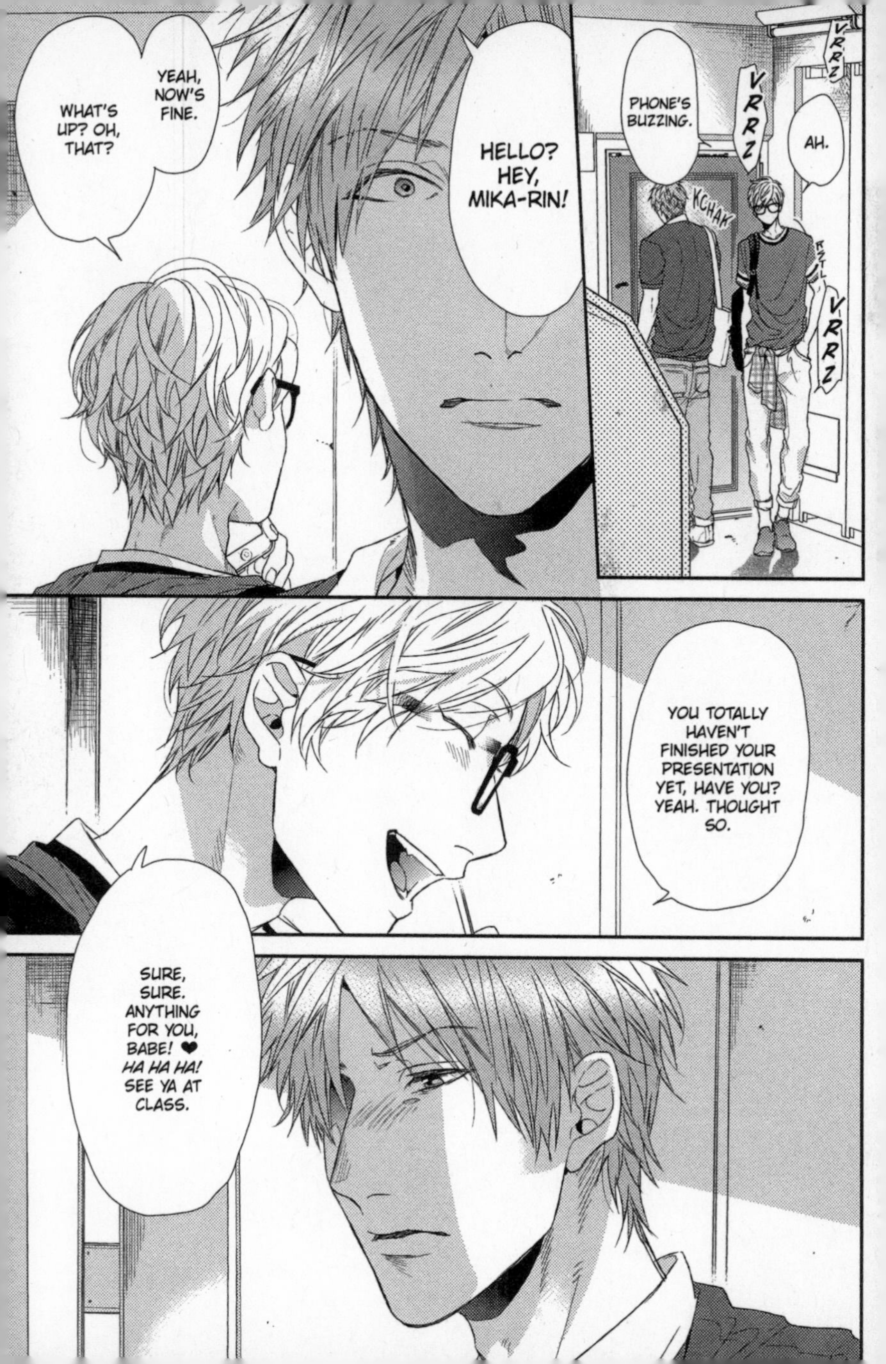
VRRZ
AH.
VRRZ
PHONE'S BUZZING.
KCHAK
RZTL
VRRZ
HELLO? HEY, MIKA-RIN!
YEAH, NOW'S FINE.
WHAT'S UP? OH, THAT?
YOU TOTALLY HAVEN'T FINISHED YOUR PRESENTATION YET, HAVE YOU? YEAH. THOUGHT SO.
SURE, SURE. ANYTHING FOR YOU, BABE! ❤ *HA HA HA!* SEE YA AT CLASS.

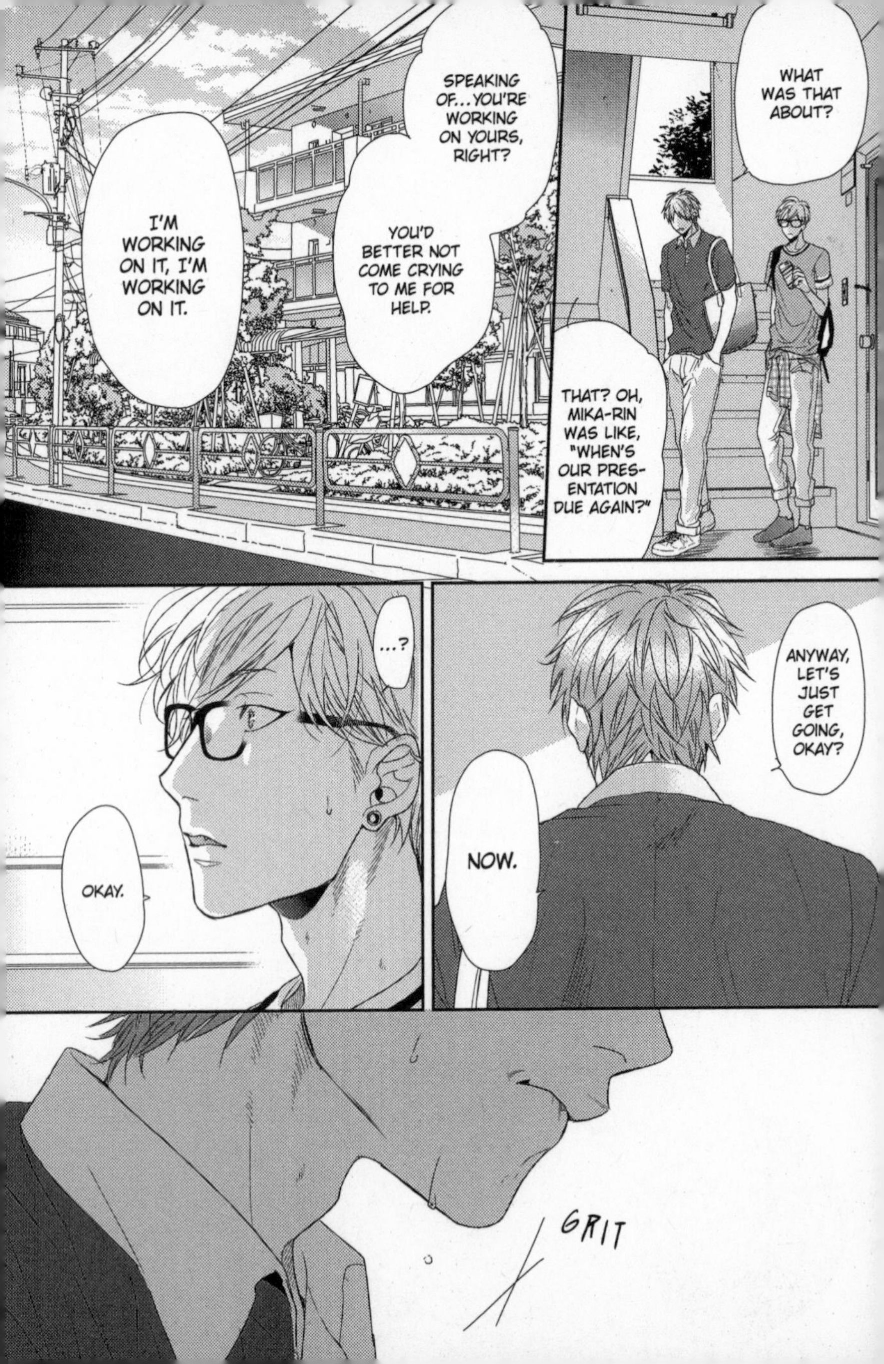
WHAT WAS THAT ABOUT?
THAT? OH, MIKA-RIN WAS LIKE, "WHEN'S OUR PRES-ENTATION DUE AGAIN?"
SPEAKING OF...YOU'RE WORKING ON YOURS, RIGHT?
YOU'D BETTER NOT COME CRYING TO ME FOR HELP.
I'M WORKING ON IT, I'M WORKING ON IT.
ANYWAY, LET'S JUST GET GOING, OKAY?
NOW.
...?
OKAY.
GRIT

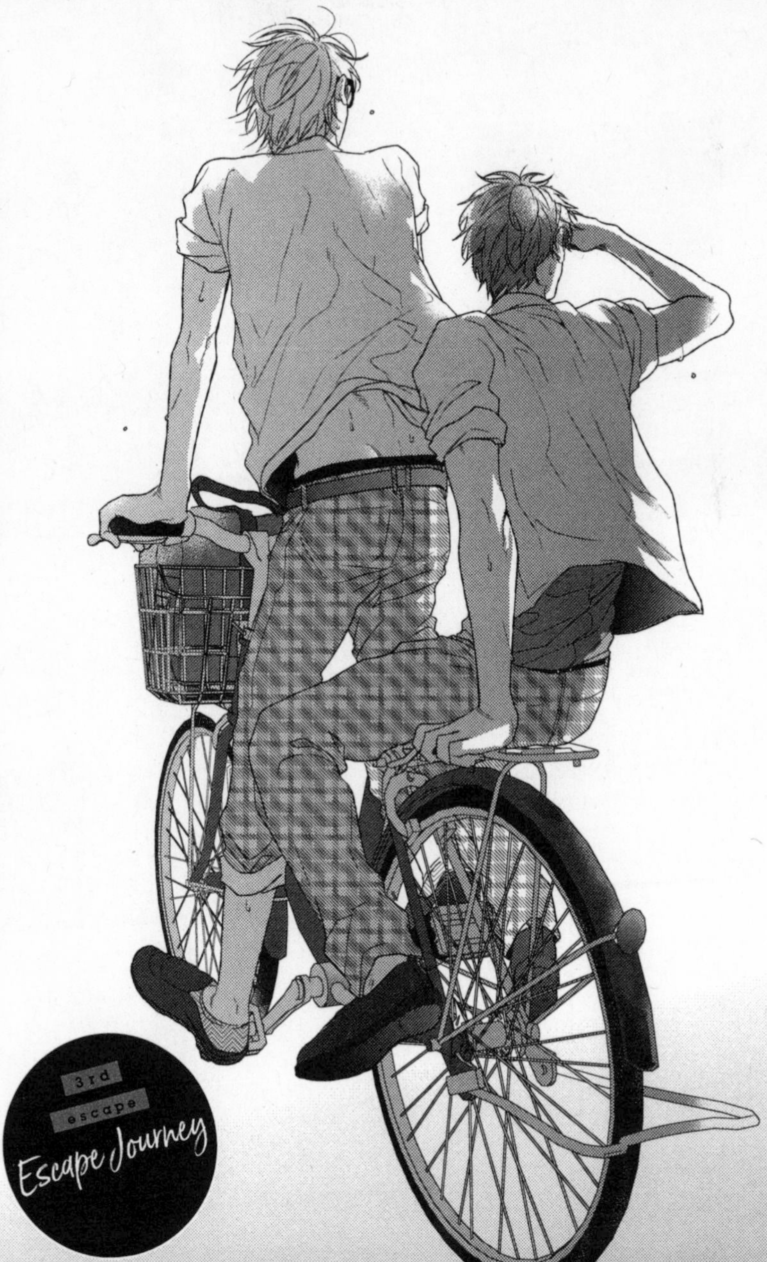
3rd
escape
Escape Journey

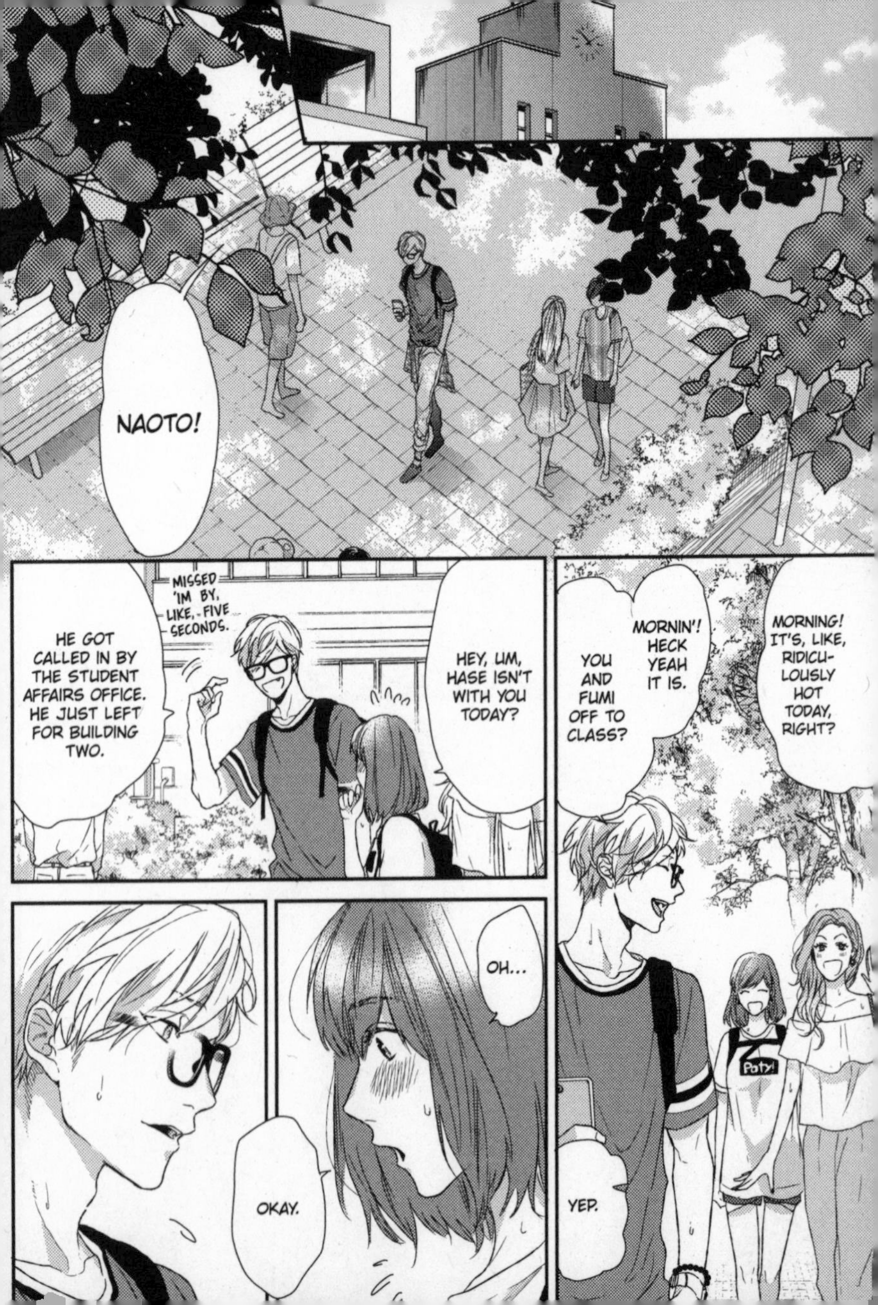
NAOTO!
MORNING! IT'S, LIKE, RIDICU-LOUSLY HOT TODAY, RIGHT?
MORNIN'! HECK YEAH IT IS.
YOU AND FUMI OFF TO CLASS?
YEP.
HEY, UM, HASE ISN'T WITH YOU TODAY?
HE GOT CALLED IN BY THE STUDENT AFFAIRS OFFICE. HE JUST LEFT FOR BUILDING TWO.
MISSED 'IM BY, LIKE, FIVE SECONDS.
OH...
OKAY.

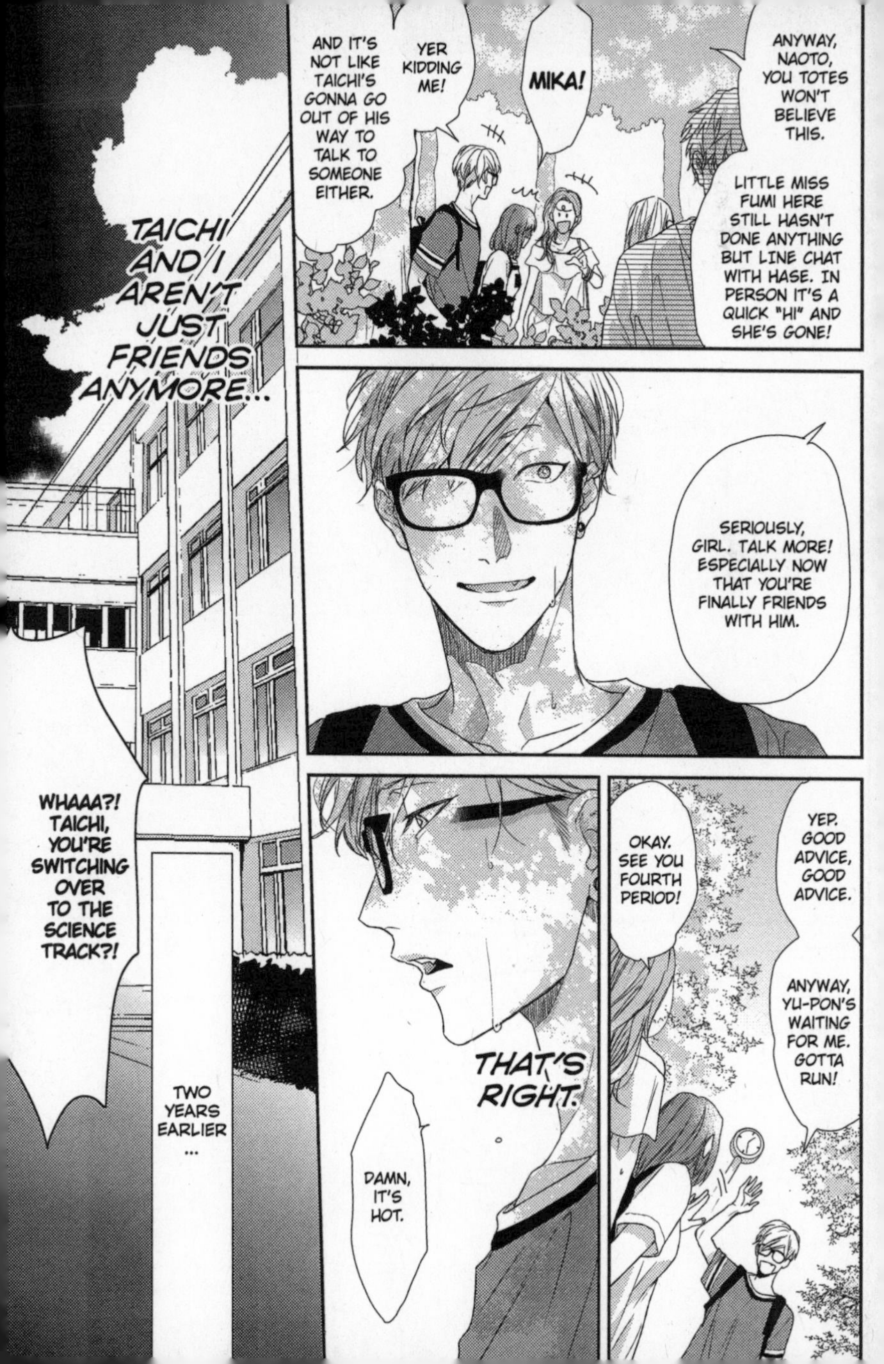
ANYWAY, NAOTO, YOU TOTES WON'T BELIEVE THIS.
LITTLE MISS FUMI HERE STILL HASN'T DONE ANYTHING BUT LINE CHAT WITH HASE. IN PERSON IT'S A QUICK "HI" AND SHE'S GONE!
MIKA!
YER KIDDING ME!
AND IT'S NOT LIKE TAICHI'S GONNA GO OUT OF HIS WAY TO TALK TO SOMEONE EITHER.
SERIOUSLY, GIRL. TALK MORE! ESPECIALLY NOW THAT YOU'RE FINALLY FRIENDS WITH HIM.
YEP. GOOD ADVICE, GOOD ADVICE.
ANYWAY, YU-PON'S WAITING FOR ME. GOTTA RUN!
OKAY. SEE YOU FOURTH PERIOD!
THAT'S RIGHT.
DAMN, IT'S HOT.
TAICHI AND I AREN'T JUST FRIENDS ANYMORE...
WHAAA?! TAICHI, YOU'RE SWITCHING OVER TO THE SCIENCE TRACK?!
TWO YEARS EARLIER...

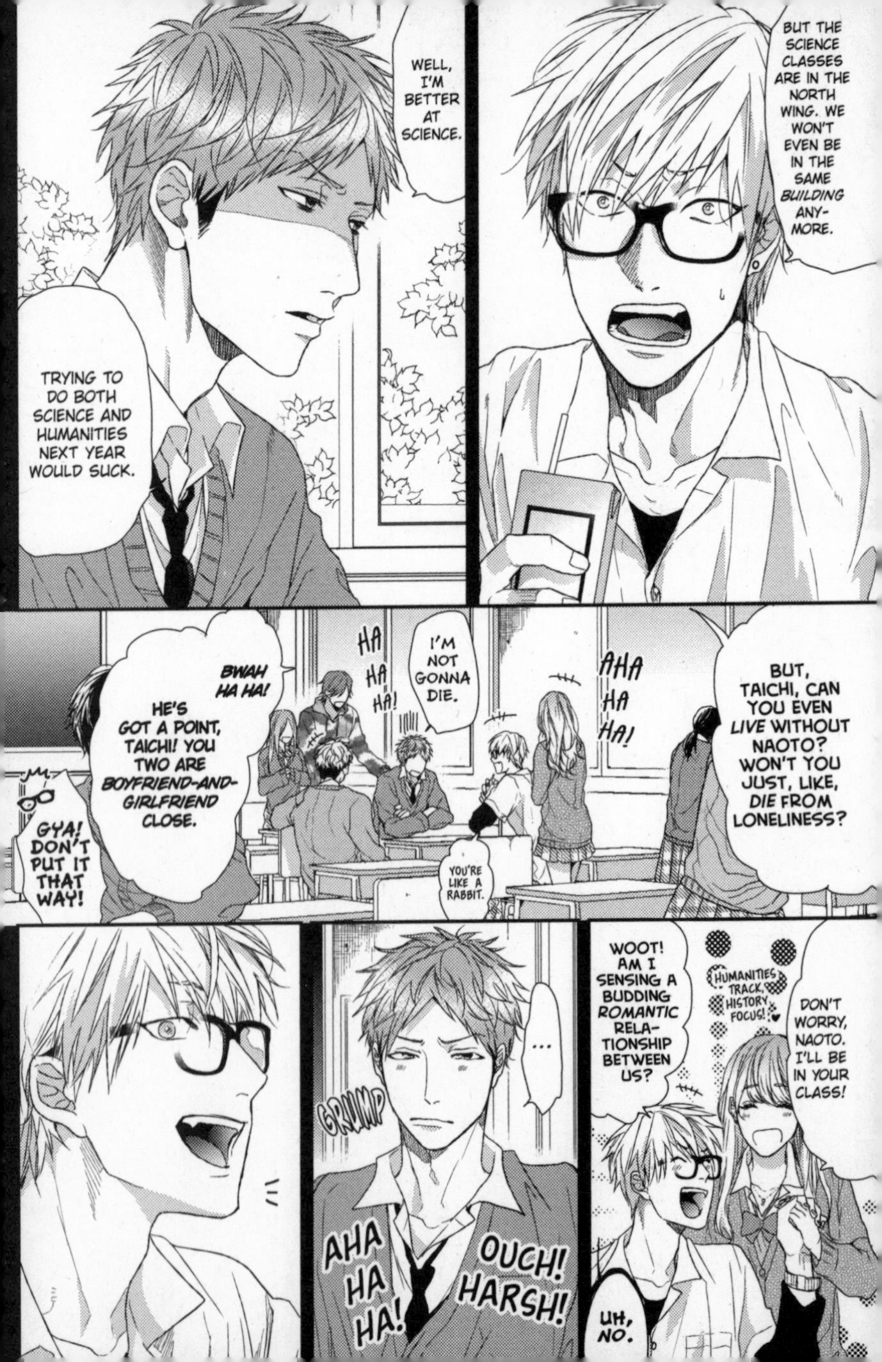
BUT THE SCIENCE CLASSES ARE IN THE NORTH WING. WE WON'T EVEN BE IN THE SAME *BUILDING* ANYMORE.
WELL, I'M BETTER AT SCIENCE.
TRYING TO DO BOTH SCIENCE AND HUMANITIES NEXT YEAR WOULD SUCK.
BUT, TAICHI, CAN YOU EVEN *LIVE* WITHOUT NAOTO? WON'T YOU JUST, LIKE, *DIE* FROM LONELINESS?
AHA HA HA!
I'M NOT GONNA DIE.
HA HA HA!
YOU'RE LIKE A RABBIT.
BWAH HA HA!
HE'S GOT A POINT, TAICHI! YOU TWO ARE *BOYFRIEND-AND-GIRLFRIEND* CLOSE.
GYA! DON'T PUT IT THAT WAY!
DON'T WORRY, NAOTO. I'LL BE IN YOUR CLASS!
HUMANITIES TRACK, HISTORY FOCUS!
WOOT! AM I SENSING A BUDDING *ROMANTIC* RELATIONSHIP BETWEEN US?
UH, NO.
...
GRUMP
OUCH! HARSH!
AHA HA HA!

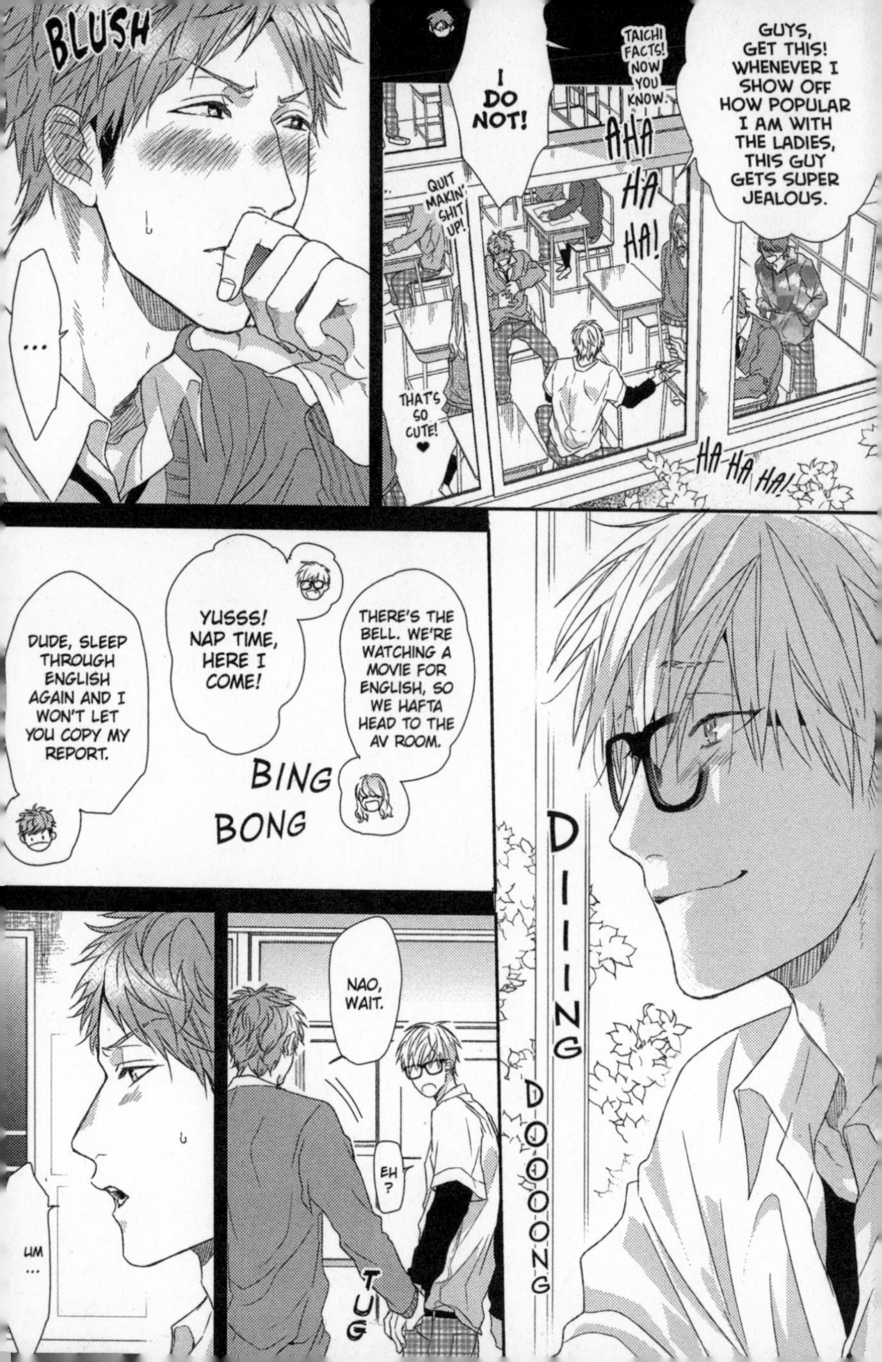
GUYS, GET THIS! WHENEVER I SHOW OFF HOW POPULAR I AM WITH THE LADIES, THIS GUY GETS SUPER JEALOUS.
TAICHI FACTS! NOW YOU KNOW.
I DO NOT!
AHA HA HA!
QUIT MAKIN' SHIT UP!
THAT'S SO CUTE! ♥
HA HA HA!
BLUSH
...
DIIING
DOOOONG
THERE'S THE BELL. WE'RE WATCHING A MOVIE FOR ENGLISH, SO WE HAFTA HEAD TO THE AV ROOM.
YUSSS! NAP TIME, HERE I COME!
DUDE, SLEEP THROUGH ENGLISH AGAIN AND I WON'T LET YOU COPY MY REPORT.
BING BONG
NAO, WAIT.
EH?
TUG
UM ...

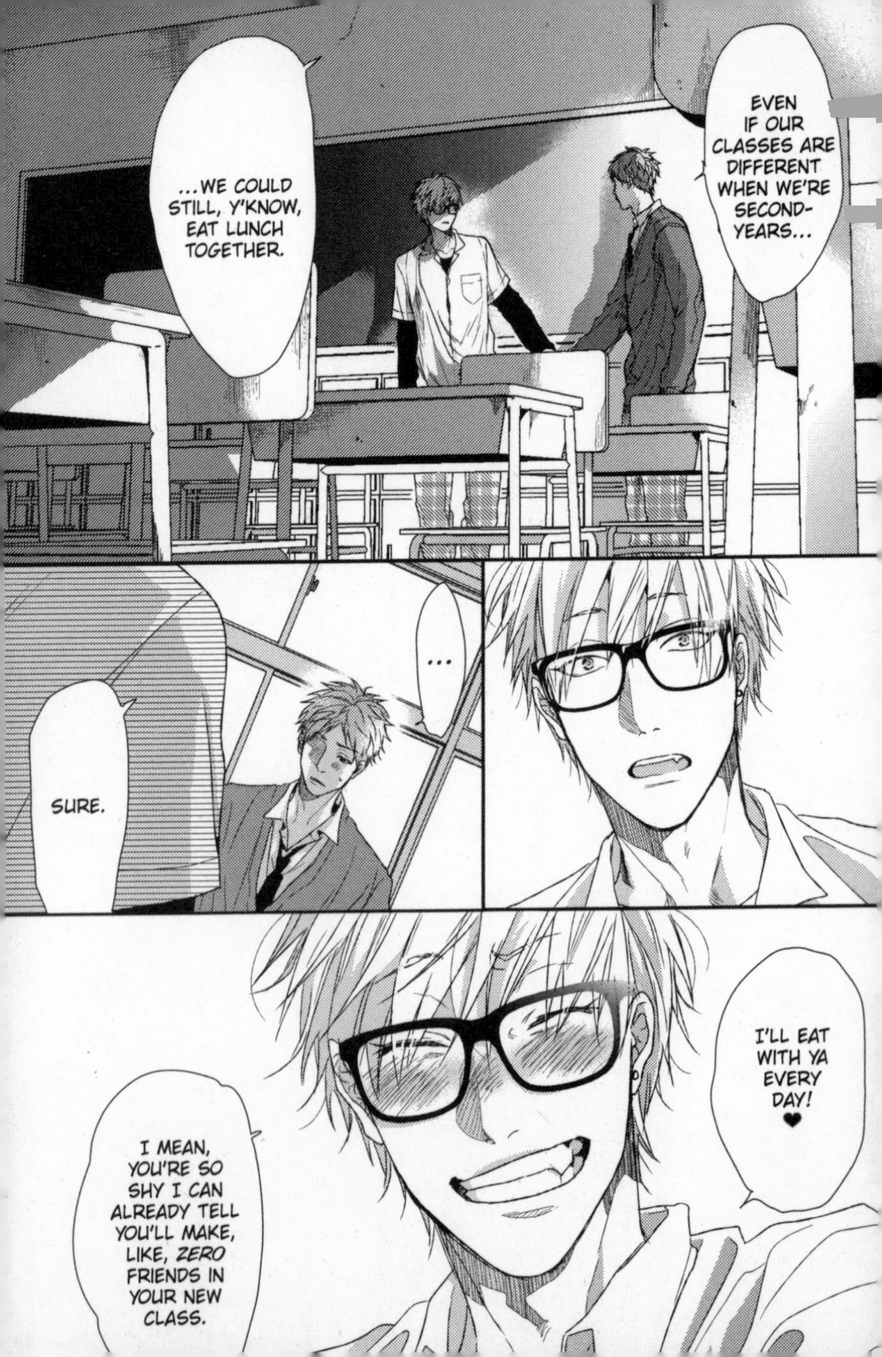
EVEN IF OUR CLASSES ARE DIFFERENT WHEN WE'RE SECOND-YEARS...
...WE COULD STILL, Y'KNOW, EAT LUNCH TOGETHER.
...
SURE.
I'LL EAT WITH YA EVERY DAY! ♥
I MEAN, YOU'RE SO SHY I CAN ALREADY TELL YOU'LL MAKE, LIKE, ZERO FRIENDS IN YOUR NEW CLASS.

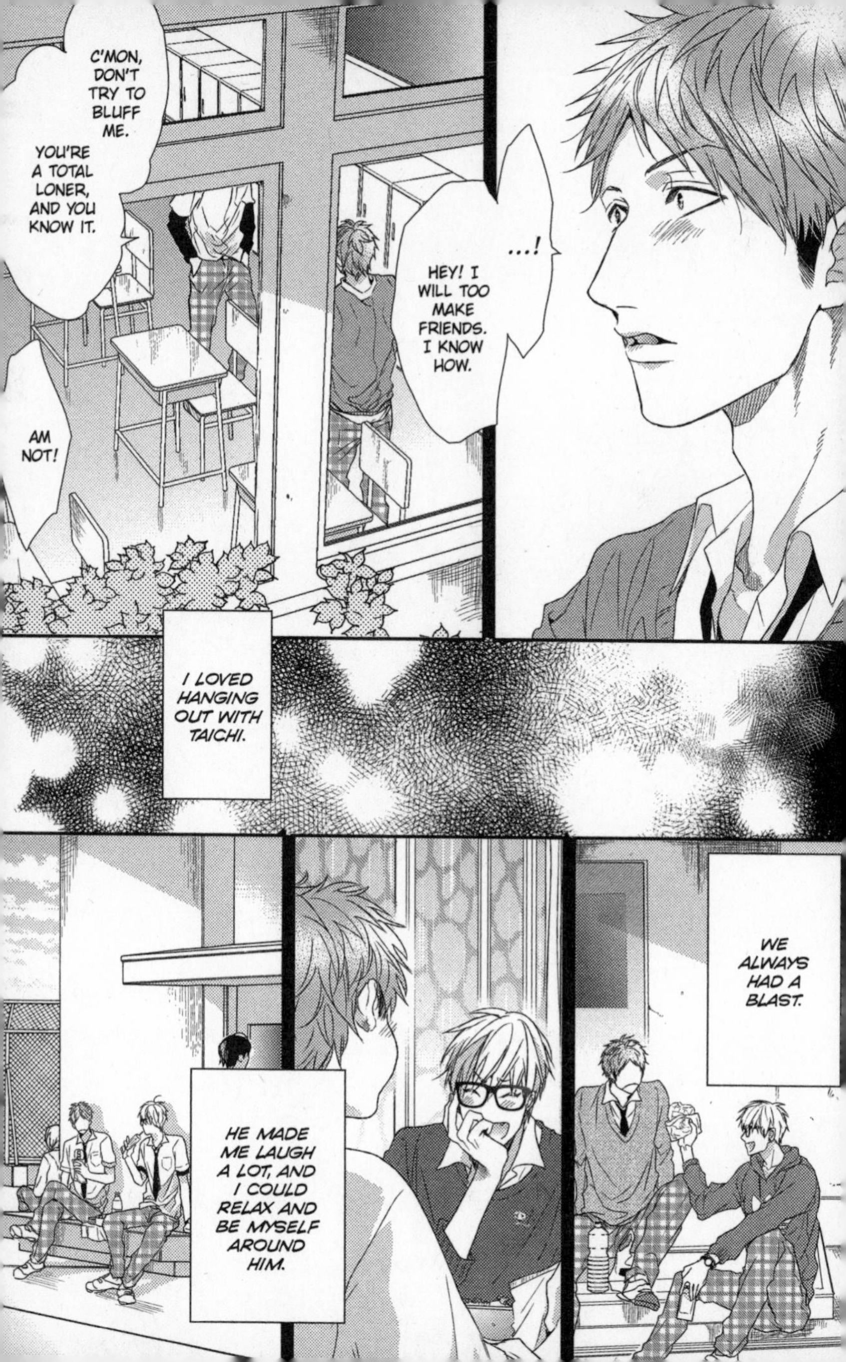
...!
HEY! I WILL TOO MAKE FRIENDS. I KNOW HOW.
C'MON, DON'T TRY TO BLUFF ME.
YOU'RE A TOTAL LONER, AND YOU KNOW IT.
AM NOT!
I LOVED HANGING OUT WITH TAICHI.
WE ALWAYS HAD A BLAST.
HE MADE ME LAUGH A LOT, AND I COULD RELAX AND BE MYSELF AROUND HIM.

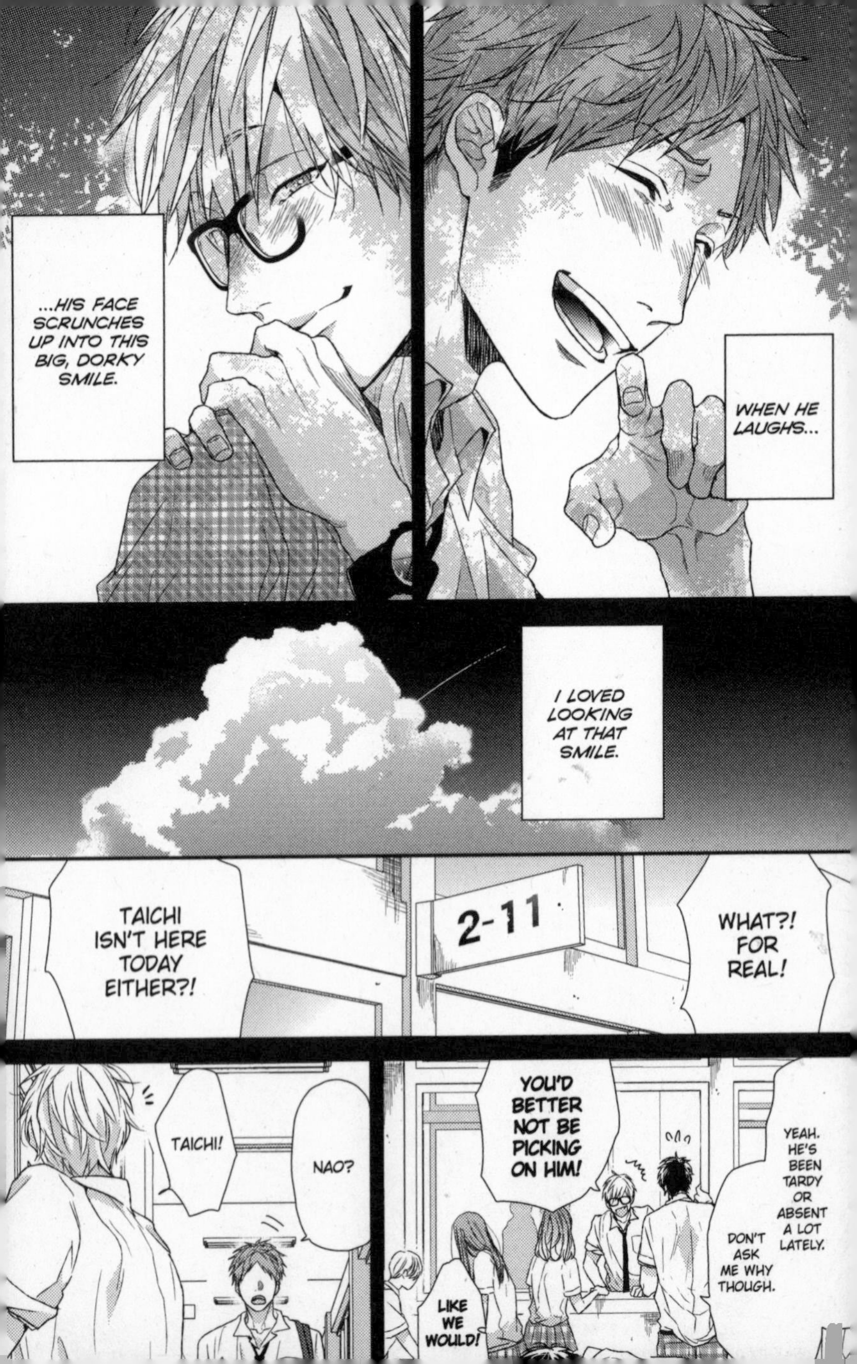
WHEN HE LAUGHS...
...HIS FACE SCRUNCHES UP INTO THIS BIG, DORKY SMILE.
I LOVED LOOKING AT THAT SMILE.
WHAT?! FOR REAL!
2-11
TAICHI ISN'T HERE TODAY EITHER?!
YEAH. HE'S BEEN TARDY OR ABSENT A LOT LATELY.
DON'T ASK ME WHY THOUGH.
YOU'D BETTER NOT BE PICKING ON HIM!
LIKE WE WOULD!
NAO?
TAICHI!

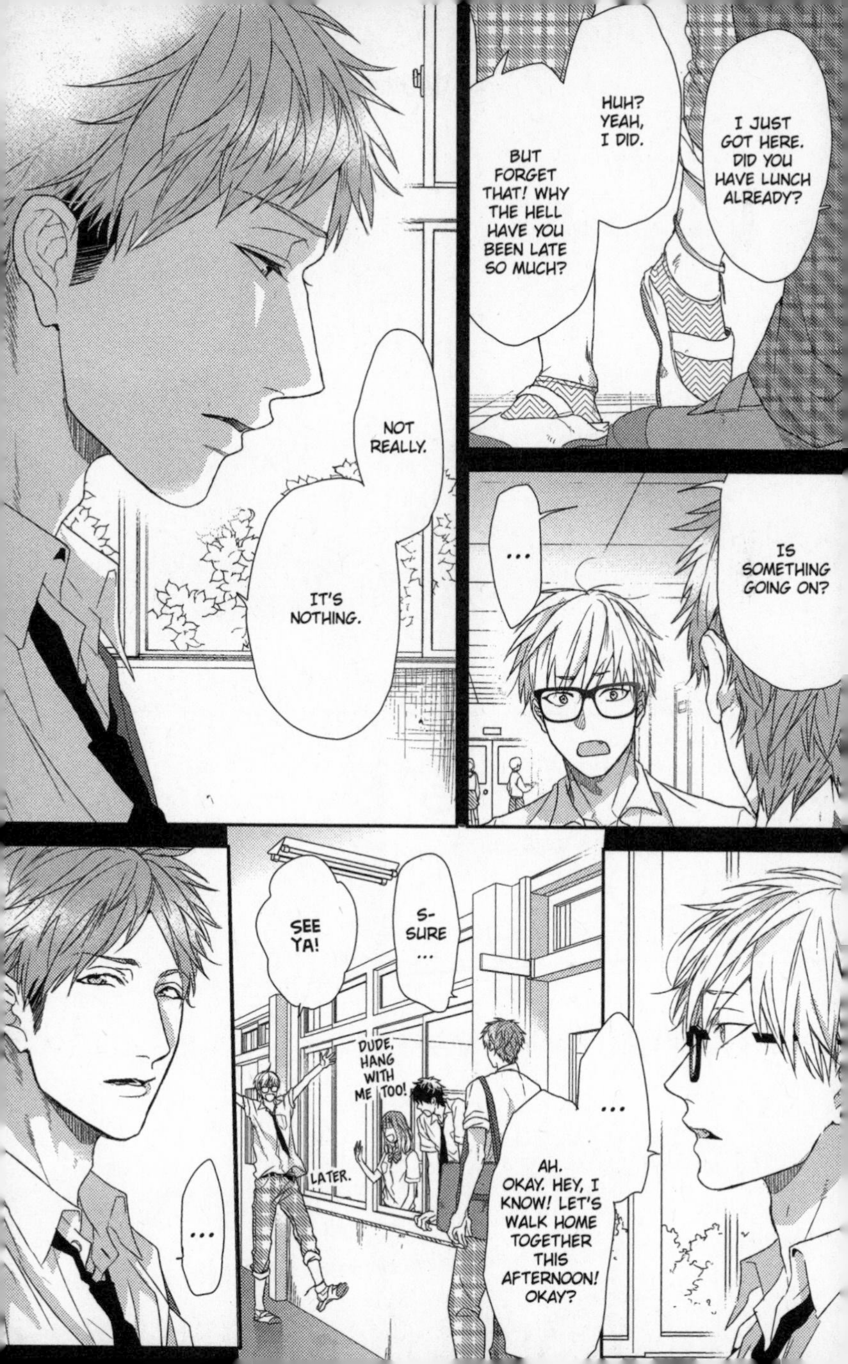
I JUST GOT HERE. DID YOU HAVE LUNCH ALREADY?
HUH? YEAH, I DID.
BUT FORGET THAT! WHY THE HELL HAVE YOU BEEN LATE SO MUCH?
IS SOMETHING GOING ON?
...
NOT REALLY.
IT'S NOTHING.
...
AH. OKAY. HEY, I KNOW! LET'S WALK HOME TOGETHER THIS AFTERNOON! OKAY?
S-SURE...
SEE YA!
DUDE, HANG WITH ME TOO!
LATER.
...

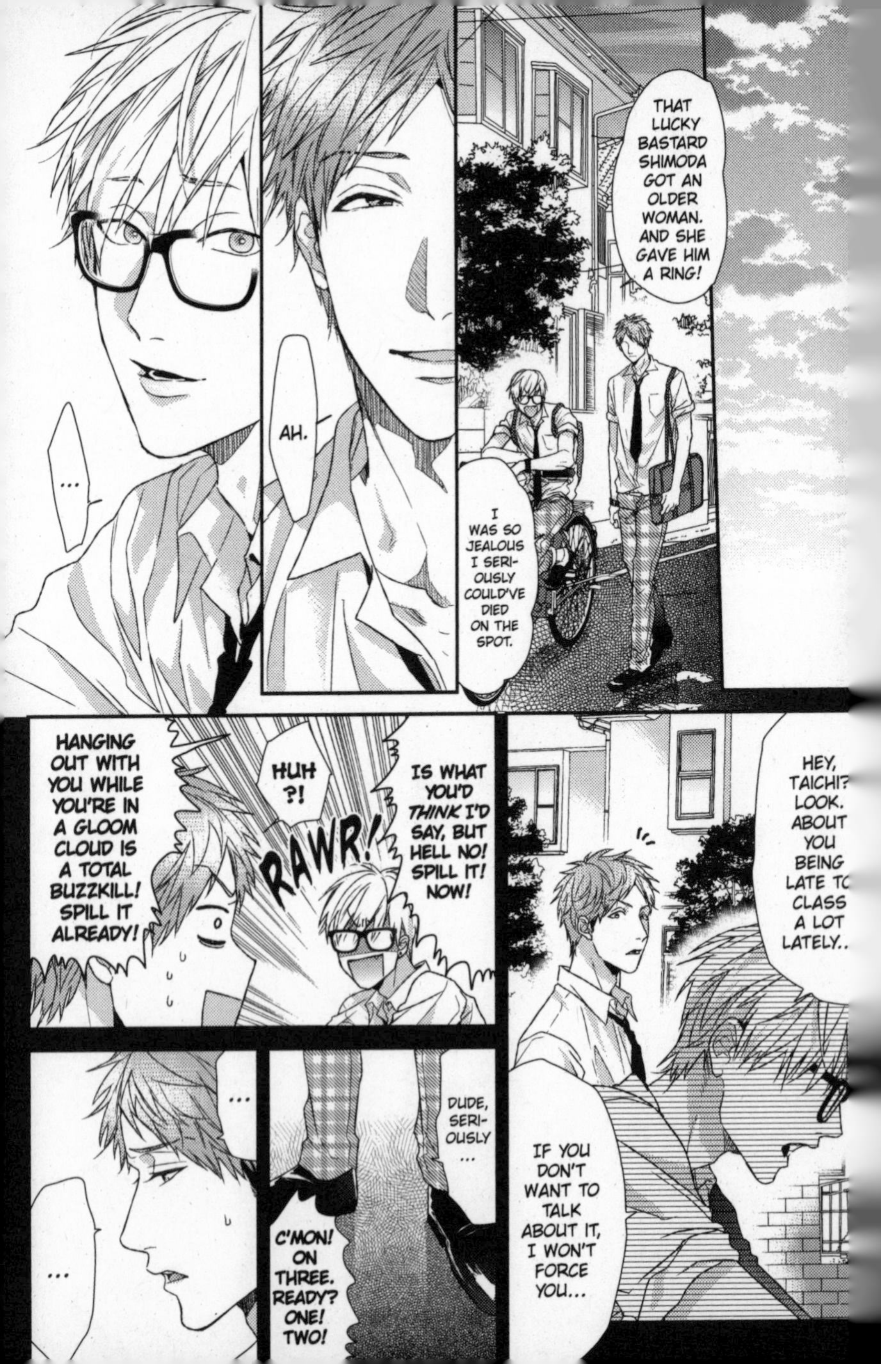
THAT LUCKY BASTARD SHIMODA GOT AN OLDER WOMAN. AND SHE GAVE HIM A RING!
I WAS SO JEALOUS I SERIOUSLY COULD'VE DIED ON THE SPOT.
AH.
...
HEY, TAICHI? LOOK. ABOUT YOU BEING LATE TO CLASS A LOT LATELY..
IF YOU DON'T WANT TO TALK ABOUT IT, I WON'T FORCE YOU...
IS WHAT YOU'D *THINK* I'D SAY, BUT HELL NO! SPILL IT! NOW!
HUH ?!
RAWR!
HANGING OUT WITH YOU WHILE YOU'RE IN A GLOOM CLOUD IS A TOTAL BUZZKILL! SPILL IT ALREADY!
DUDE, SERIOUSLY ...
C'MON! ON THREE. READY? ONE! TWO!
...
...

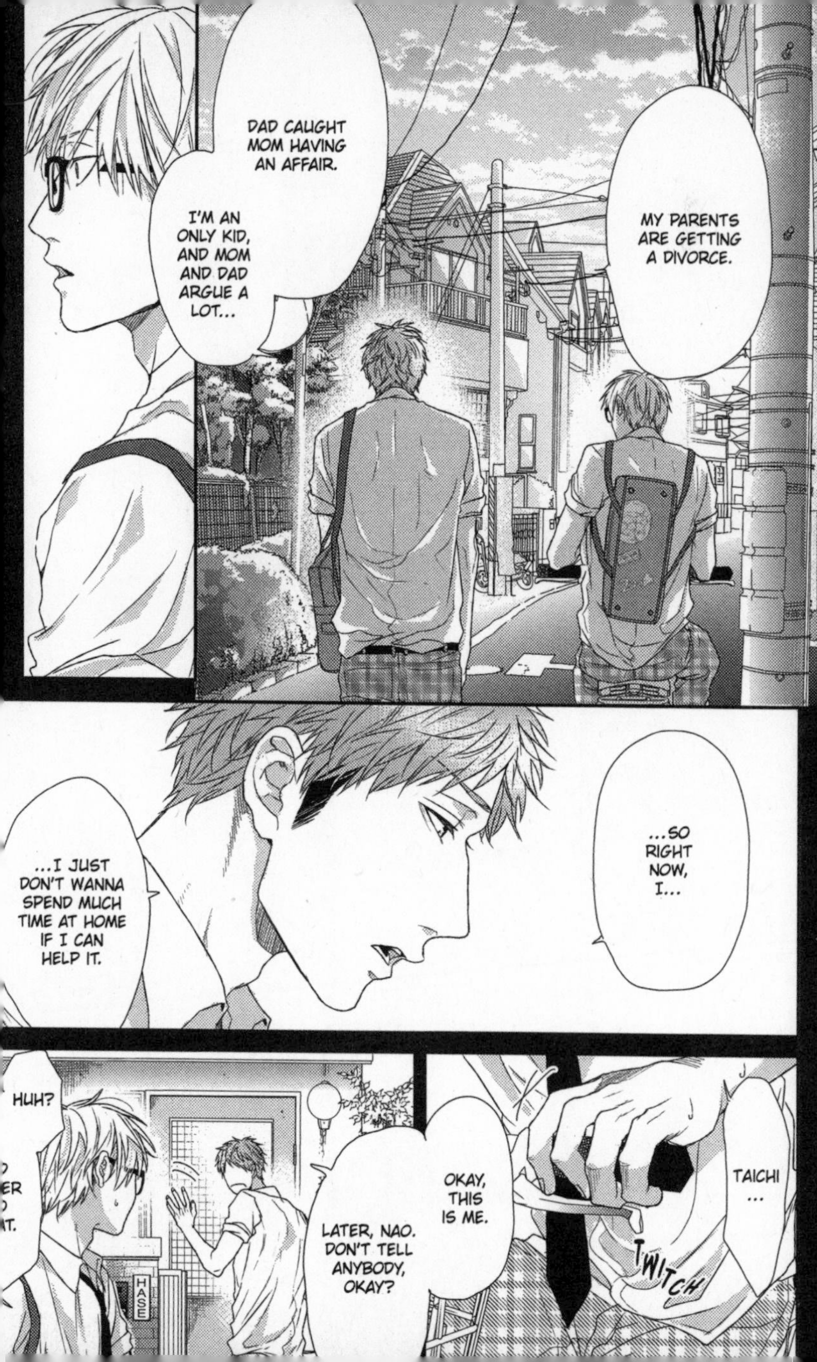
MY PARENTS ARE GETTING A DIVORCE.
DAD CAUGHT MOM HAVING AN AFFAIR.
I'M AN ONLY KID, AND MOM AND DAD ARGUE A LOT...
...SO RIGHT NOW, I...
...I JUST DON'T WANNA SPEND MUCH TIME AT HOME IF I CAN HELP IT.
TAICHI ...
TWITCH
OKAY, THIS IS ME.
LATER, NAO. DON'T TELL ANYBODY, OKAY?
HASE
HUH?

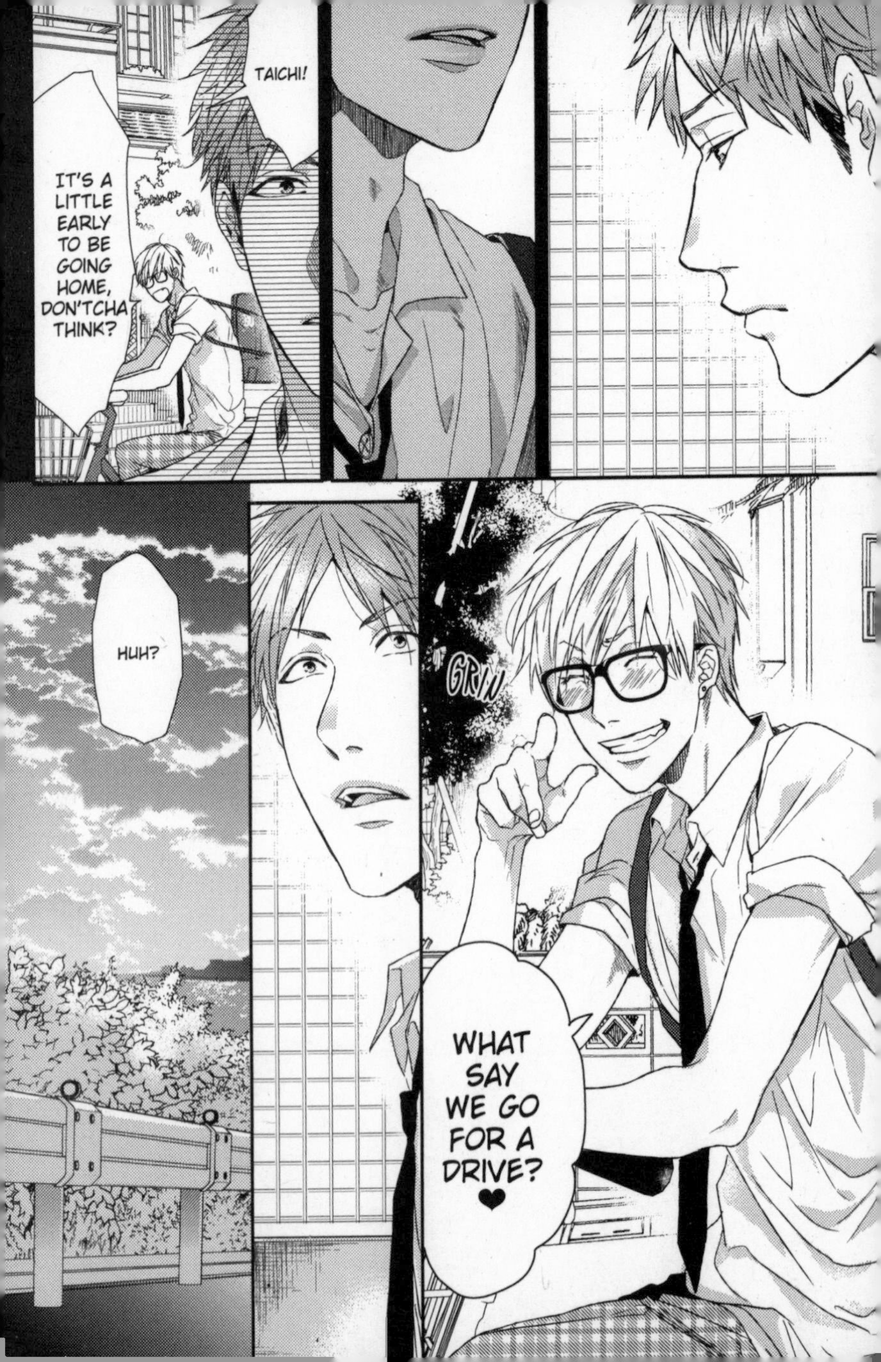
TAICHI!
IT'S A LITTLE EARLY TO BE GOING HOME, DON'TCHA THINK?
GRIN
WHAT SAY WE GO FOR A DRIVE? ♥
HUH?

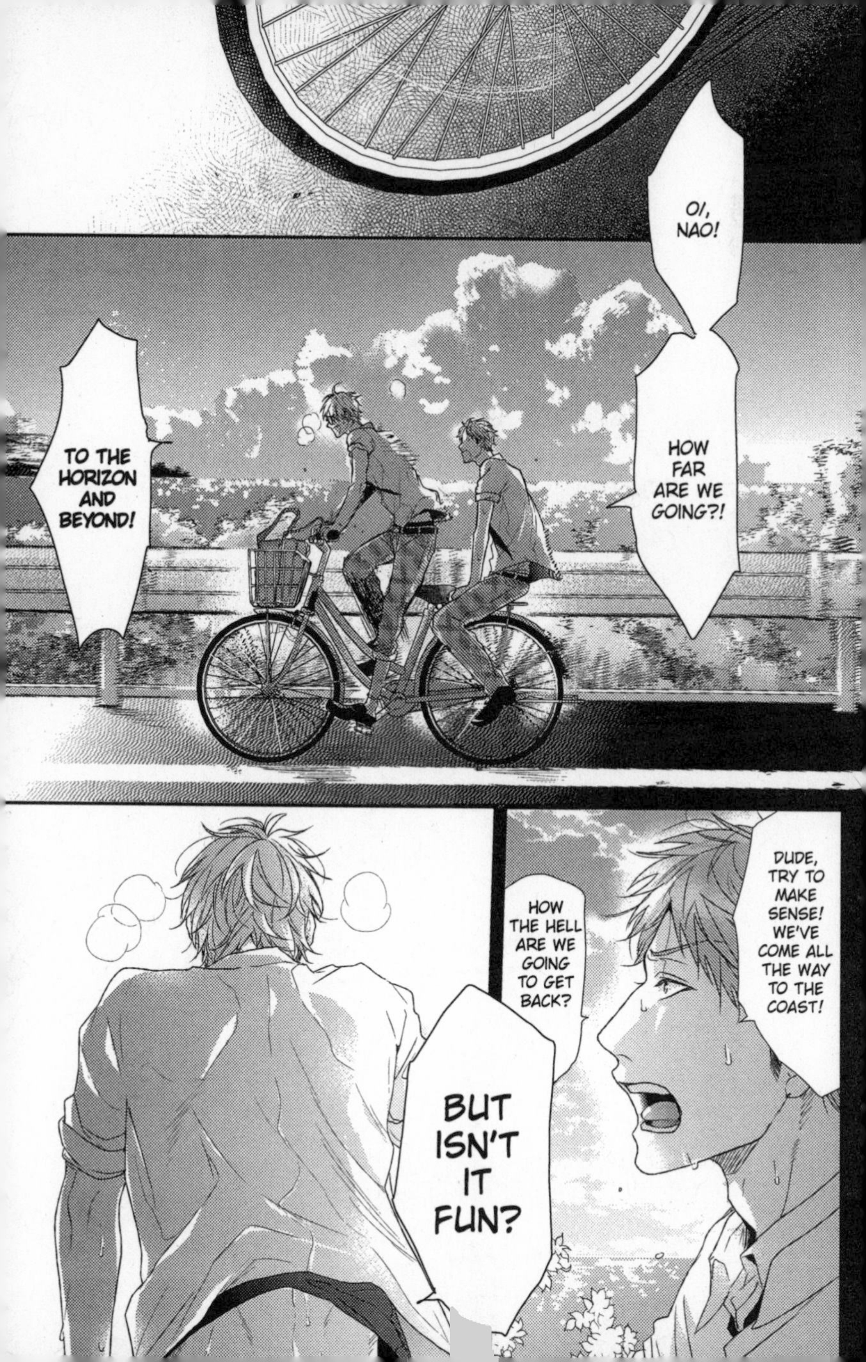
OI, NAO!
HOW FAR ARE WE GOING?!
TO THE HORIZON AND BEYOND!
DUDE, TRY TO MAKE SENSE! WE'VE COME ALL THE WAY TO THE COAST!
HOW THE HELL ARE WE GOING TO GET BACK?
BUT ISN'T IT FUN?

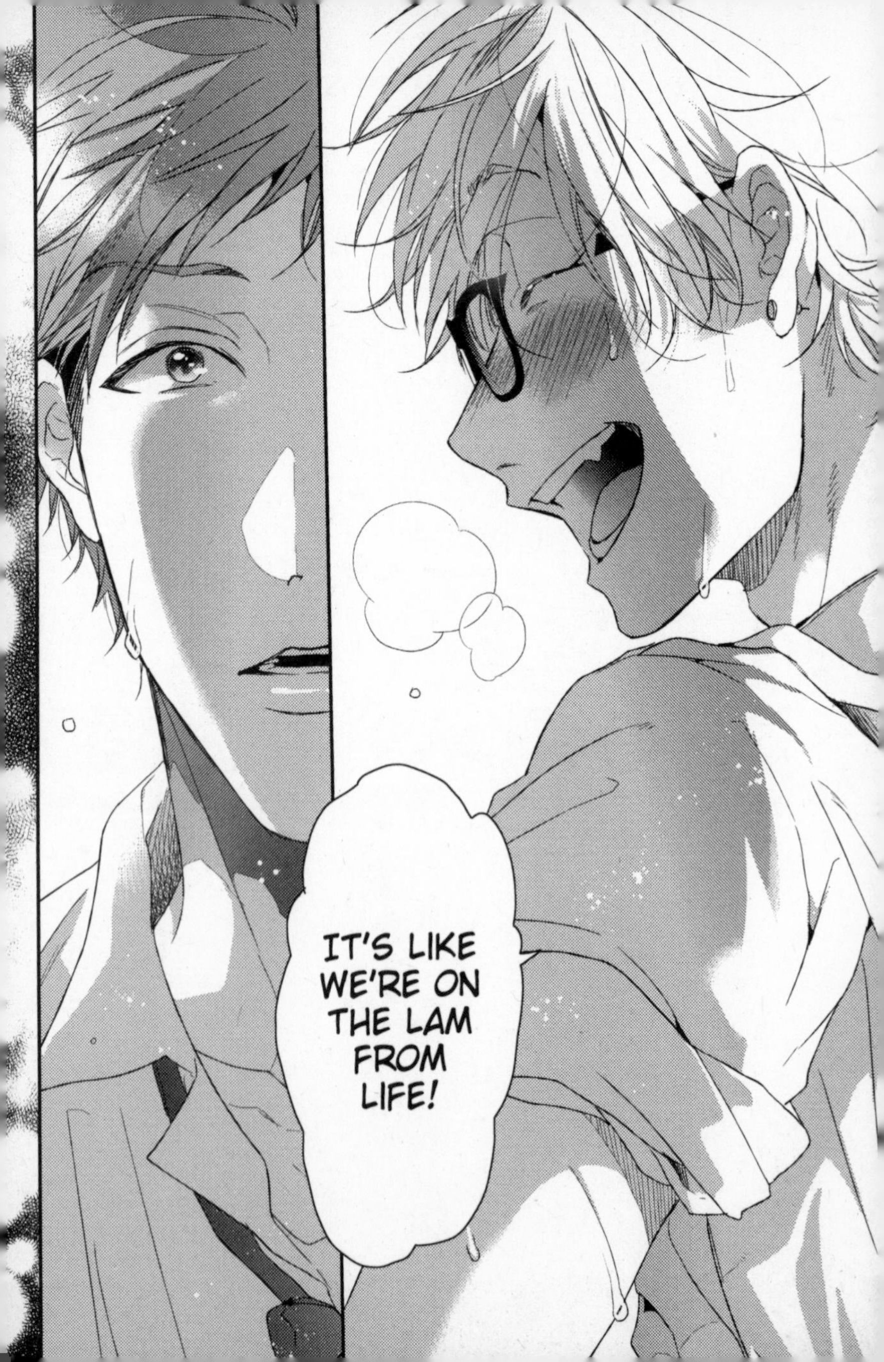
IT'S LIKE WE'RE ON THE LAM FROM LIFE!

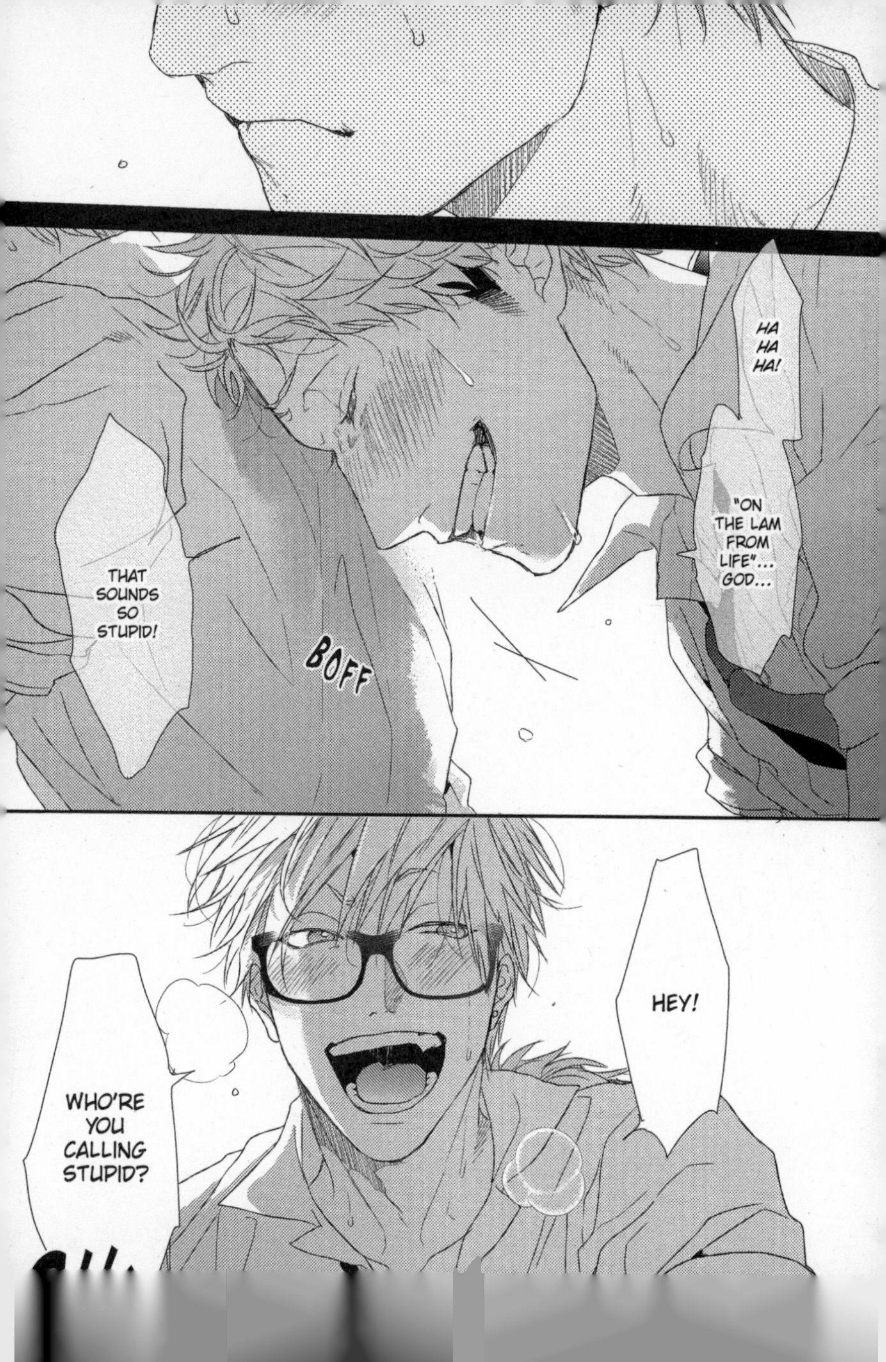
HA HA HA!
"ON THE LAM FROM LIFE"... GOD...
BOFF
THAT SOUNDS SO STUPID!
HEY!
WHO'RE YOU CALLING STUPID?

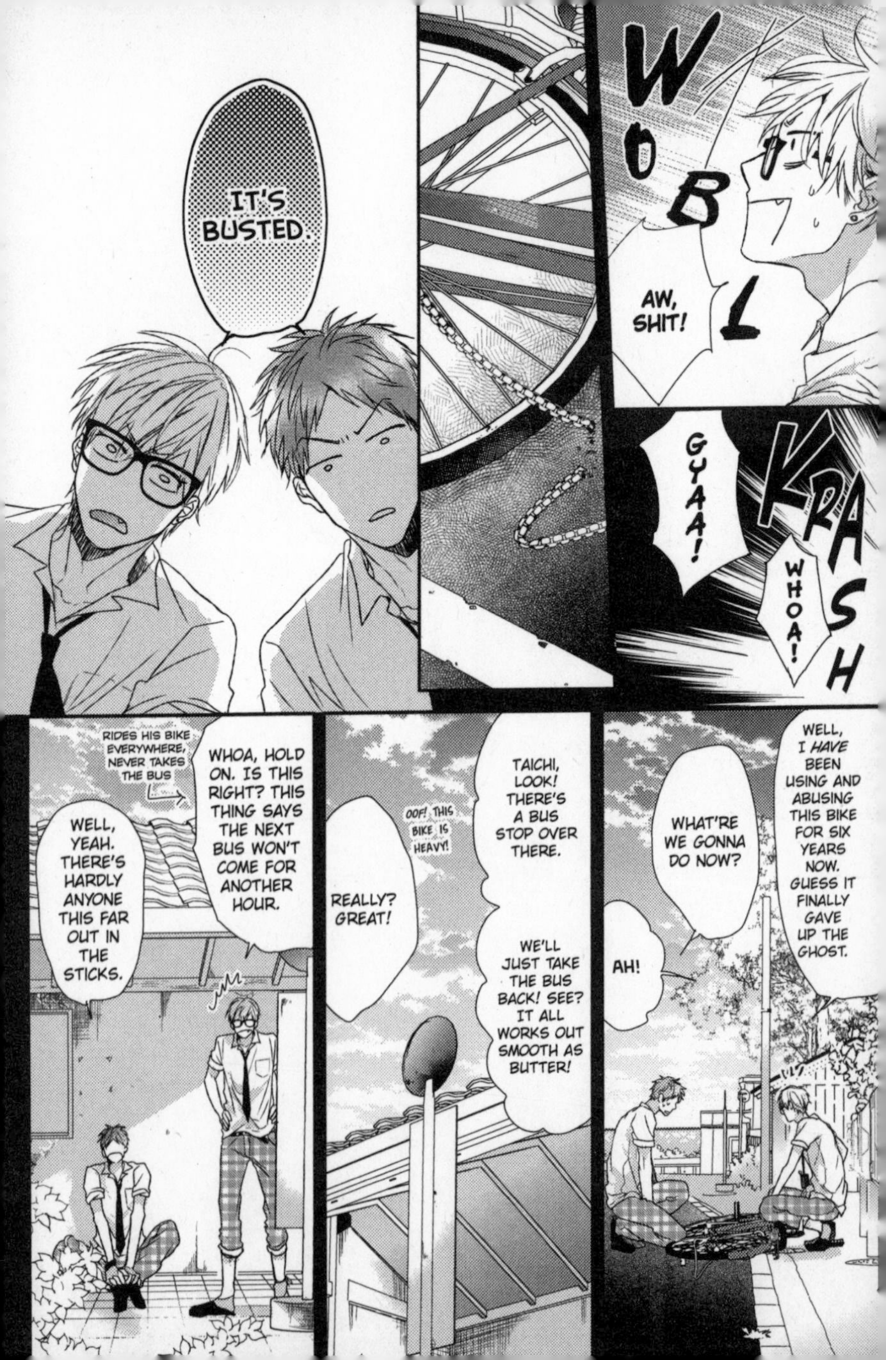
WOBBL
AW, SHIT!
KRASH
GYAA!
WHOA!
IT'S BUSTED.
WELL, I *HAVE* BEEN USING AND ABUSING THIS BIKE FOR SIX YEARS NOW. GUESS IT FINALLY GAVE UP THE GHOST.
WHAT'RE WE GONNA DO NOW?
AH!
TAICHI, LOOK! THERE'S A BUS STOP OVER THERE.
OOF! THIS BIKE IS HEAVY!
REALLY? GREAT!
WE'LL JUST TAKE THE BUS BACK! SEE? IT ALL WORKS OUT SMOOTH AS BUTTER!
RIDES HIS BIKE EVERYWHERE, NEVER TAKES THE BUS
WHOA, HOLD ON. IS THIS RIGHT? THIS THING SAYS THE NEXT BUS WON'T COME FOR ANOTHER HOUR.
WELL, YEAH. THERE'S HARDLY ANYONE THIS FAR OUT IN THE STICKS.

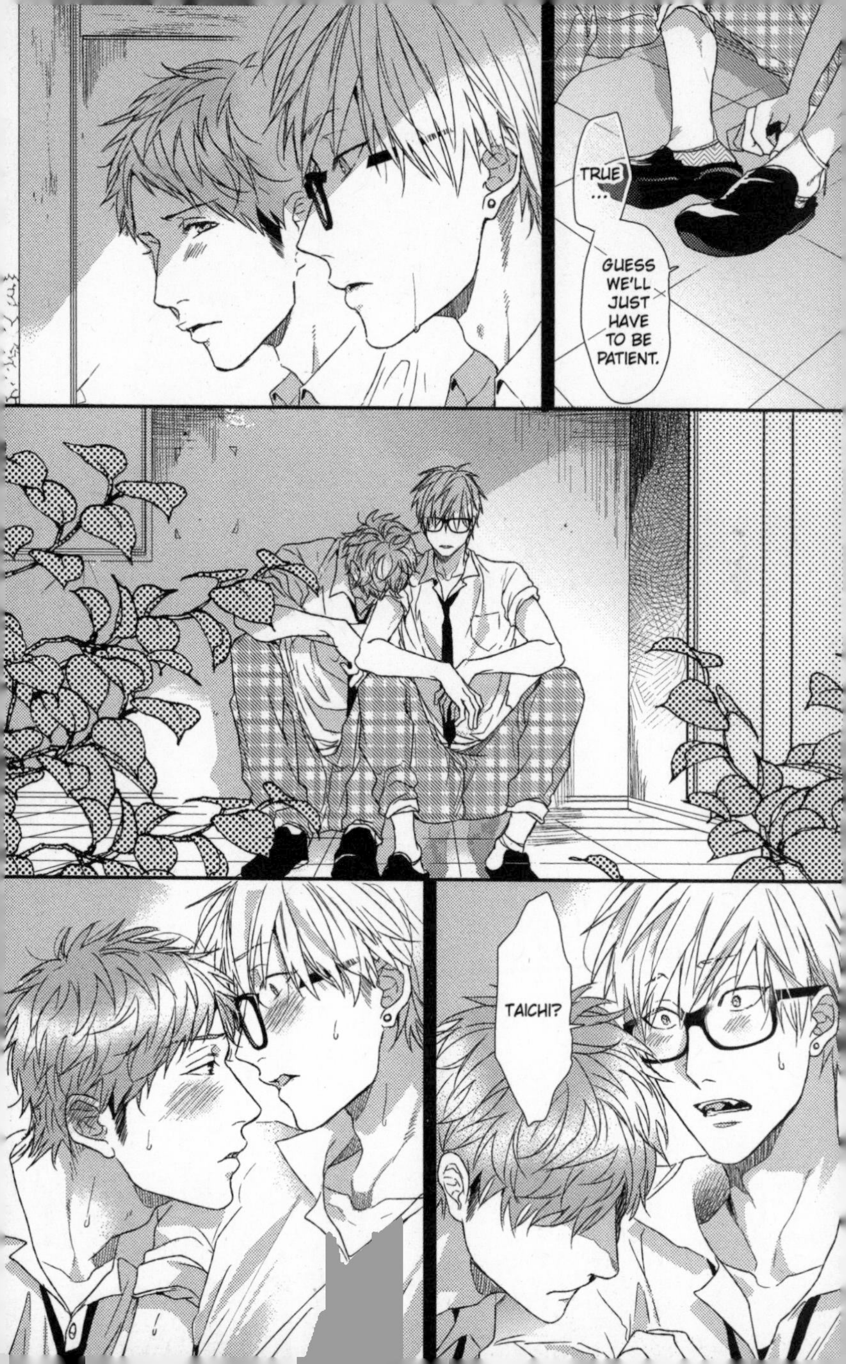
TRUE ...
GUESS WE'LL JUST HAVE TO BE PATIENT.
TAICHI?

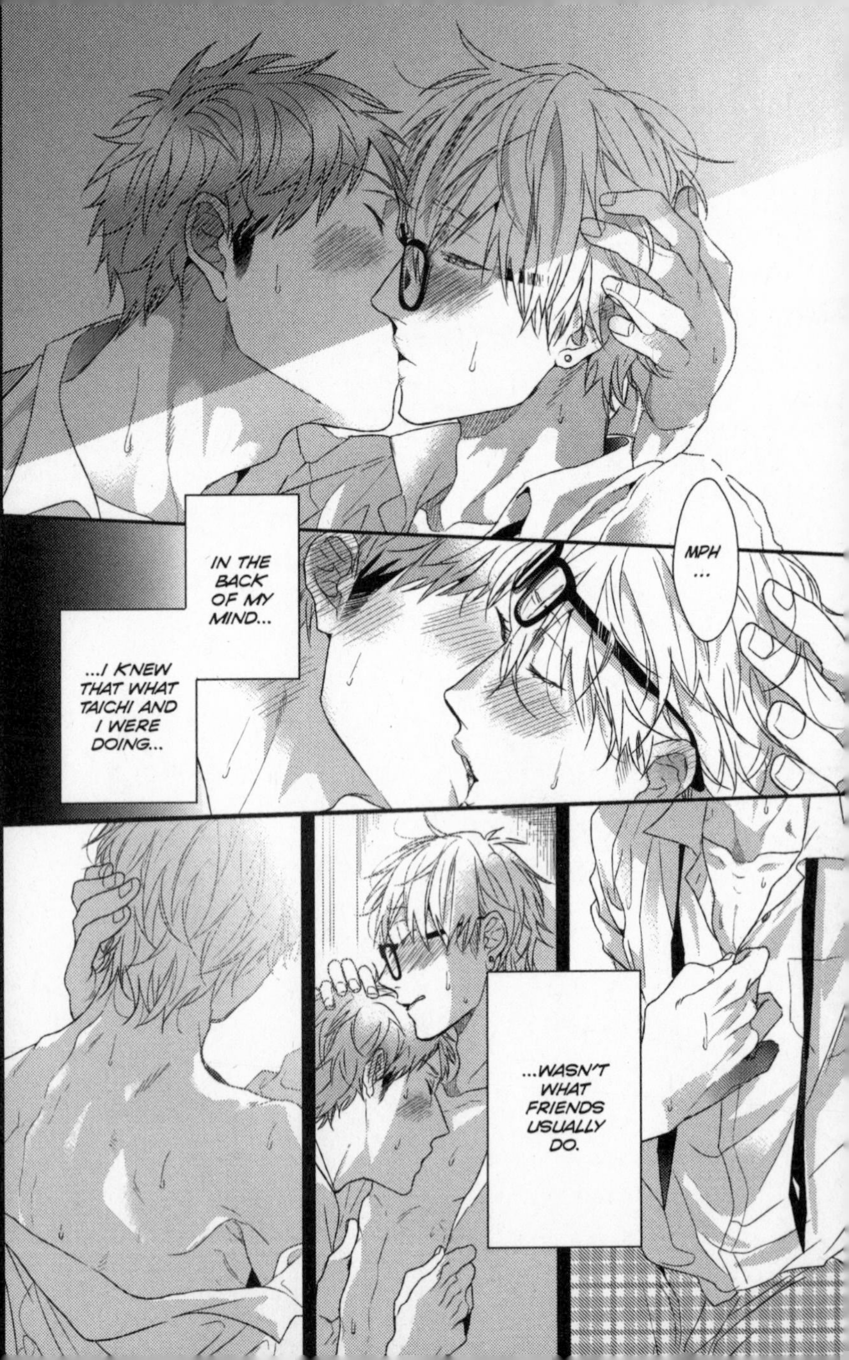
MPH ...
IN THE BACK OF MY MIND...
...I KNEW THAT WHAT TAICHI AND I WERE DOING...
...WASN'T WHAT FRIENDS USUALLY DO.

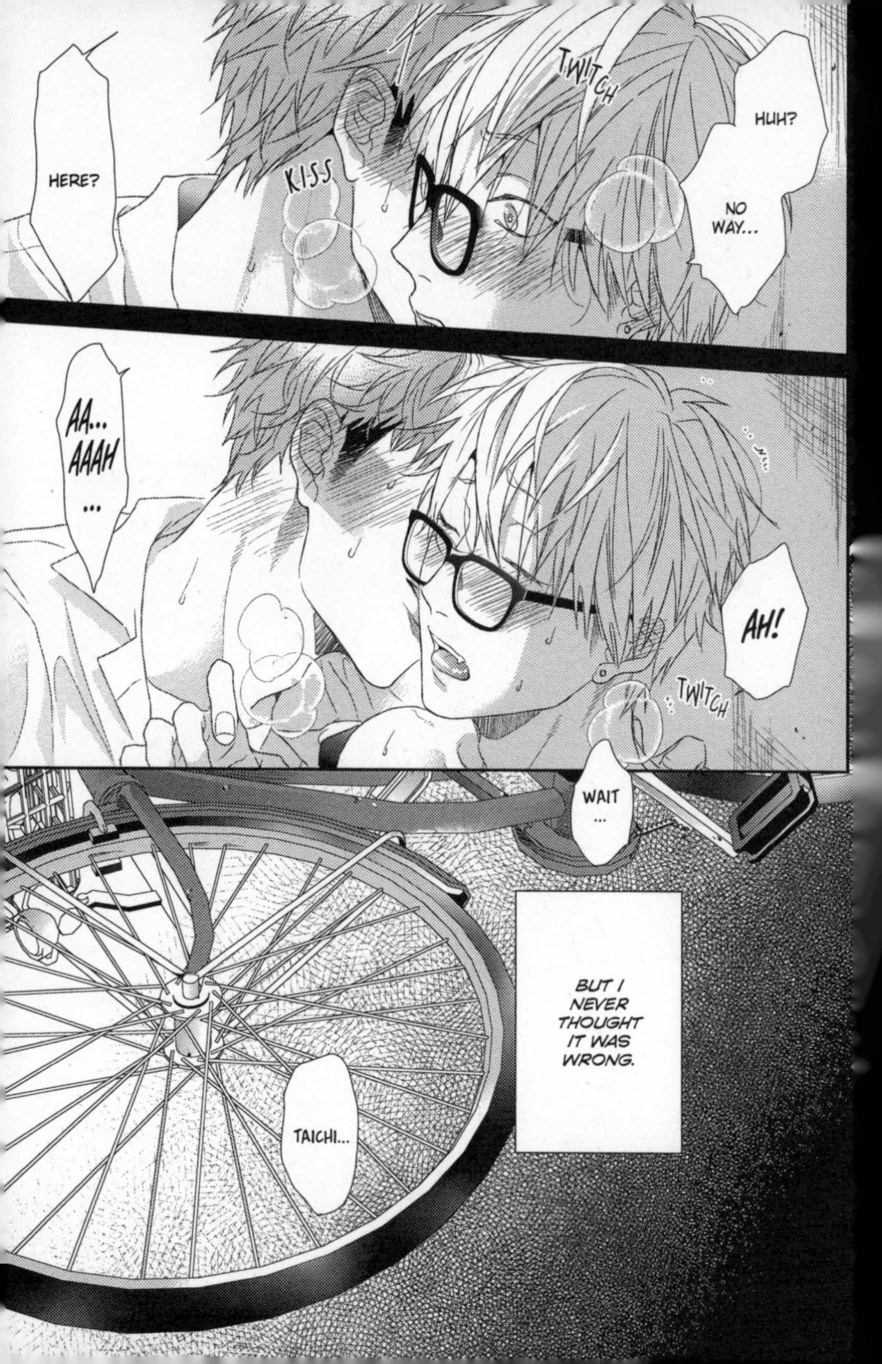
HUH?
NO WAY...
TWITCH
KISS
HERE?
AH!
TWITCH
AA... AAAH ...
WAIT ...
BUT I NEVER THOUGHT IT WAS WRONG.
TAICHI...

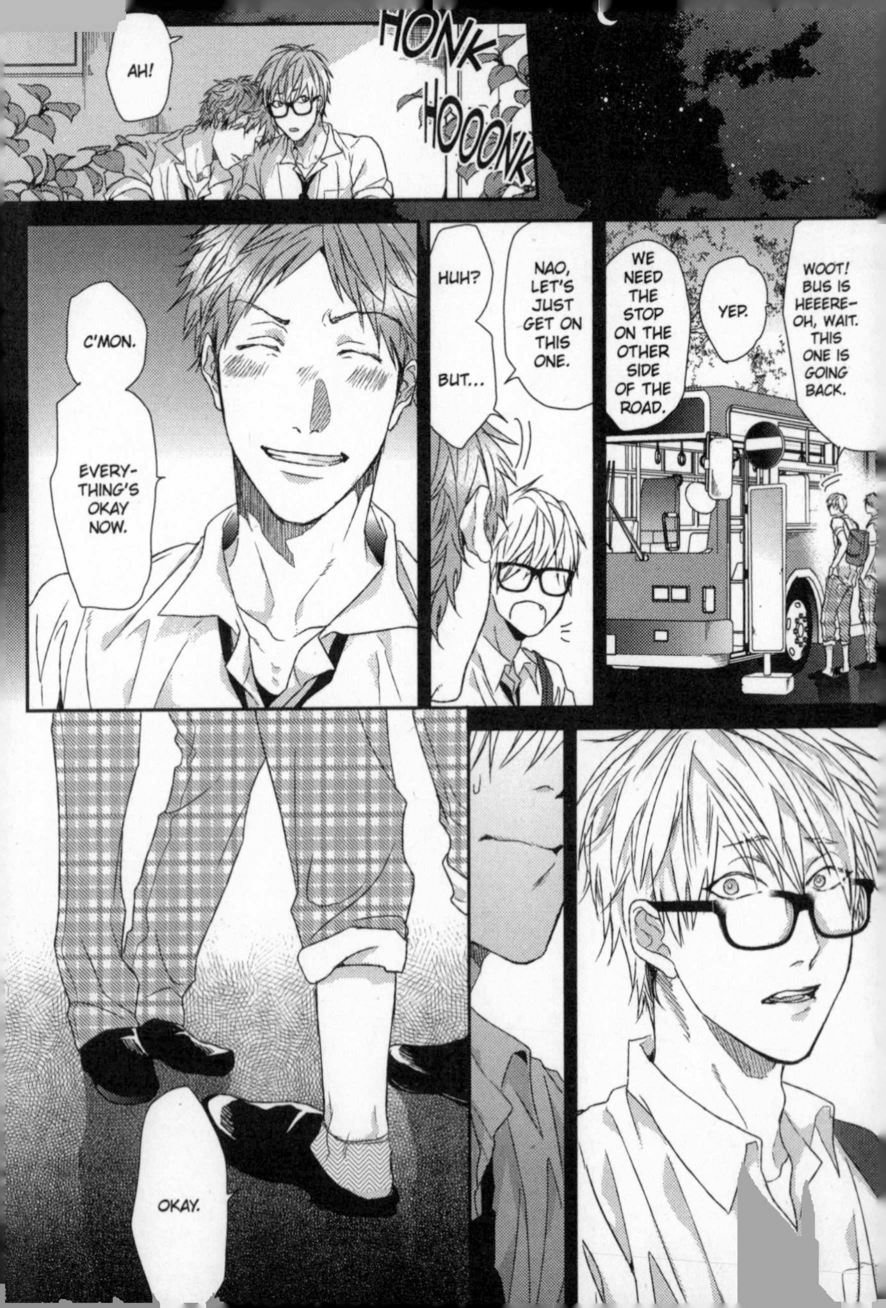
HONK
HOOONK
AH!
WOOT! BUS IS HEEERE—OH, WAIT. THIS ONE IS GOING BACK.
YEP.
WE NEED THE STOP ON THE OTHER SIDE OF THE ROAD.
NAO, LET'S JUST GET ON THIS ONE.
HUH?
BUT...
C'MON.
EVERY-THING'S OKAY NOW.
OKAY.

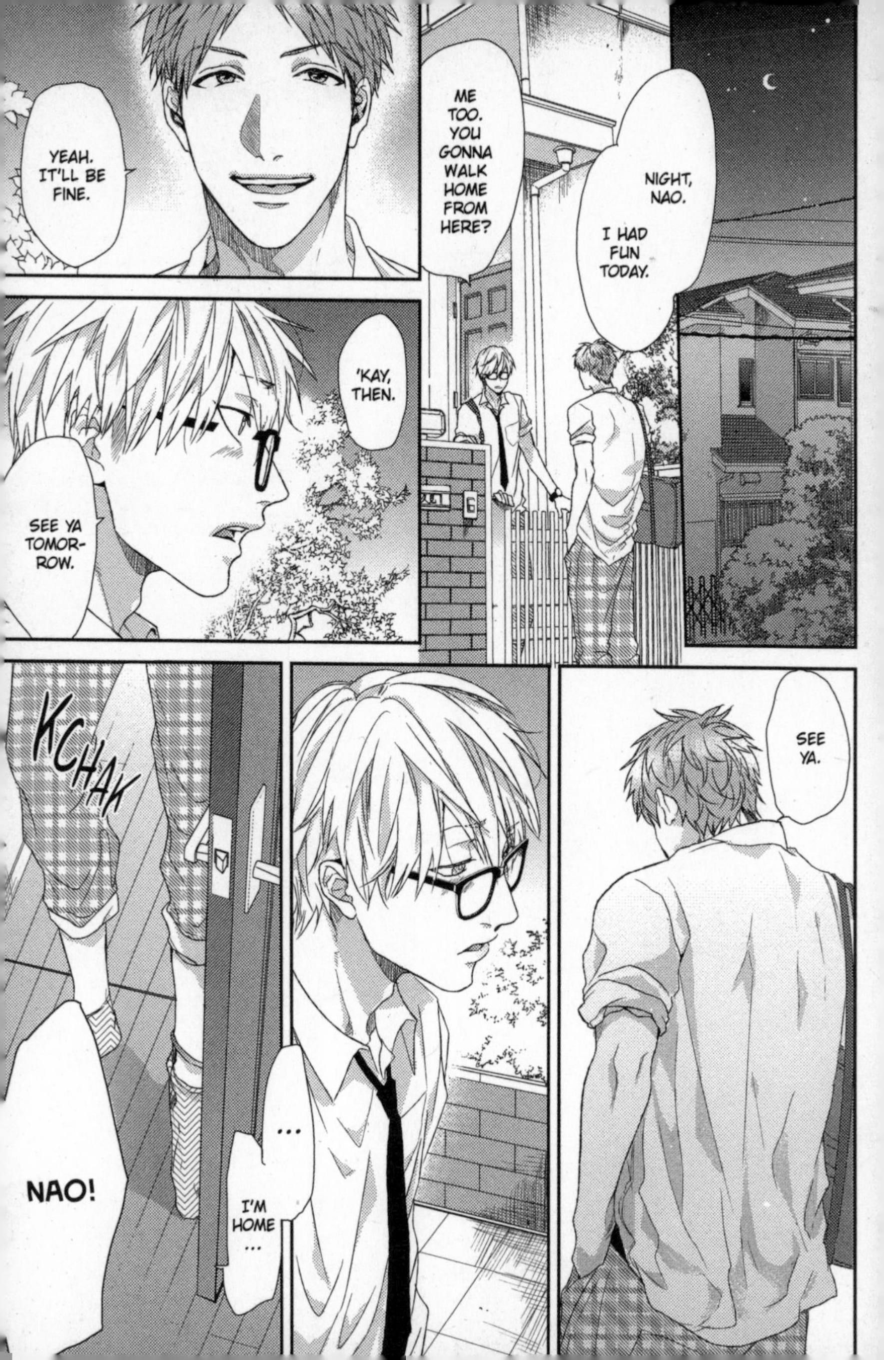
NIGHT, NAO.
I HAD FUN TODAY.
ME TOO. YOU GONNA WALK HOME FROM HERE?
YEAH. IT'LL BE FINE.
'KAY, THEN.
SEE YA TOMORROW.
SEE YA.
...
I'M HOME ...
KCHAK
NAO!

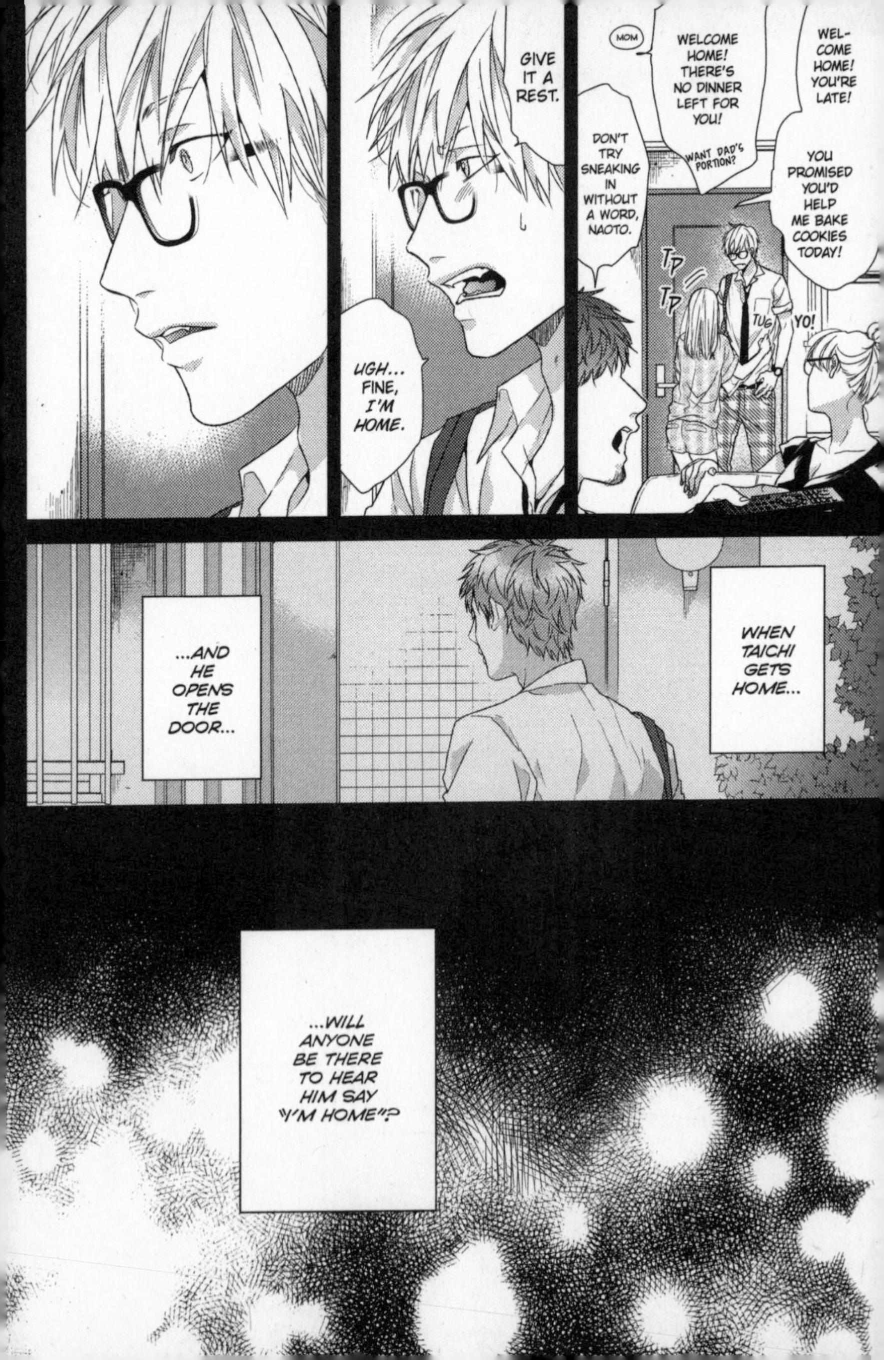
WEL-COME HOME! YOU'RE LATE!
MOM
WELCOME HOME! THERE'S NO DINNER LEFT FOR YOU!
WANT DAD'S PORTION?
YOU PROMISED YOU'D HELP ME BAKE COOKIES TODAY!
DON'T TRY SNEAKING IN WITHOUT A WORD, NAOTO.
TP
TP
YO!
TUG
GIVE IT A REST.
UGH... FINE, I'M HOME.
WHEN TAICHI GETS HOME...
...AND HE OPENS THE DOOR...
...WILL ANYONE BE THERE TO HEAR HIM SAY "I'M HOME"?

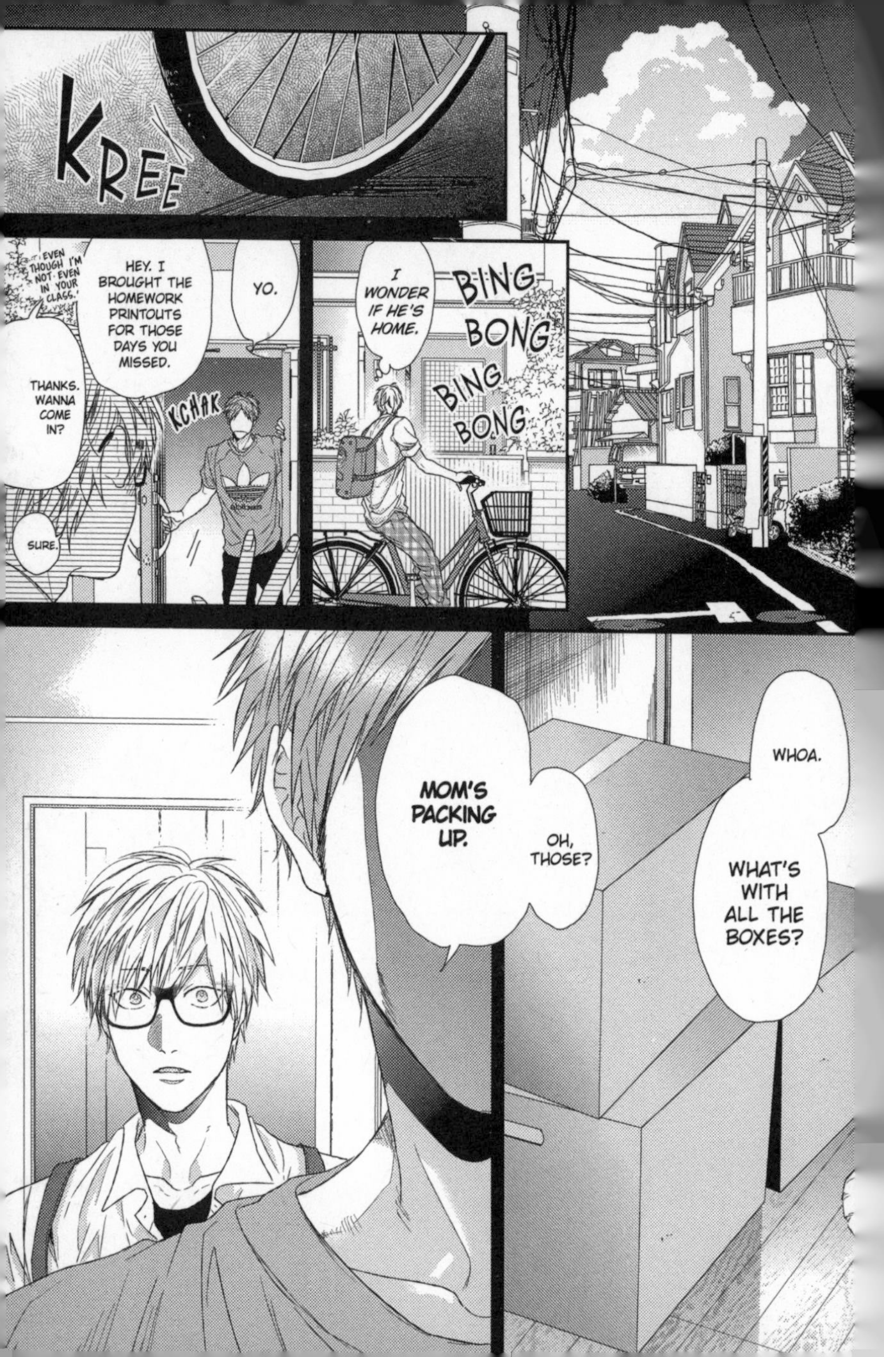
KREE
I WONDER IF HE'S HOME.
BING BONG
BING BONG
YO.
HEY. I BROUGHT THE HOMEWORK PRINTOUTS FOR THOSE DAYS YOU MISSED.
EVEN THOUGH I'M NOT EVEN IN YOUR CLASS.
KCHAK
THANKS. WANNA COME IN?
SURE.
WHOA.
WHAT'S WITH ALL THE BOXES?
OH, THOSE?
MOM'S PACKING UP.

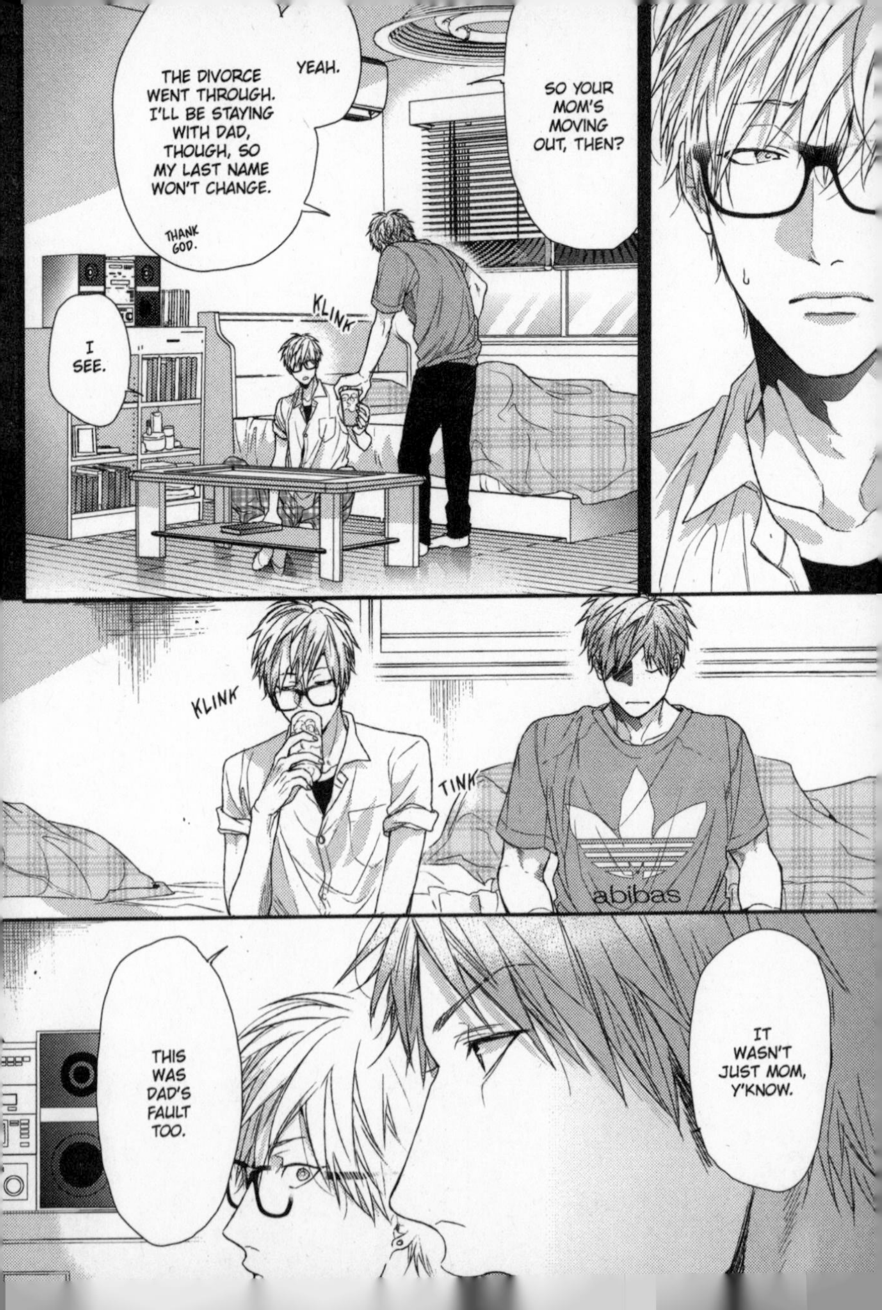
SO YOUR MOM'S MOVING OUT, THEN?
YEAH.
THE DIVORCE WENT THROUGH. I'LL BE STAYING WITH DAD, THOUGH, SO MY LAST NAME WON'T CHANGE.
THANK GOD.
KLINK
I SEE.
TINK
abibas
KLINK
IT WASN'T JUST MOM, Y'KNOW.
THIS WAS DAD'S FAULT TOO.

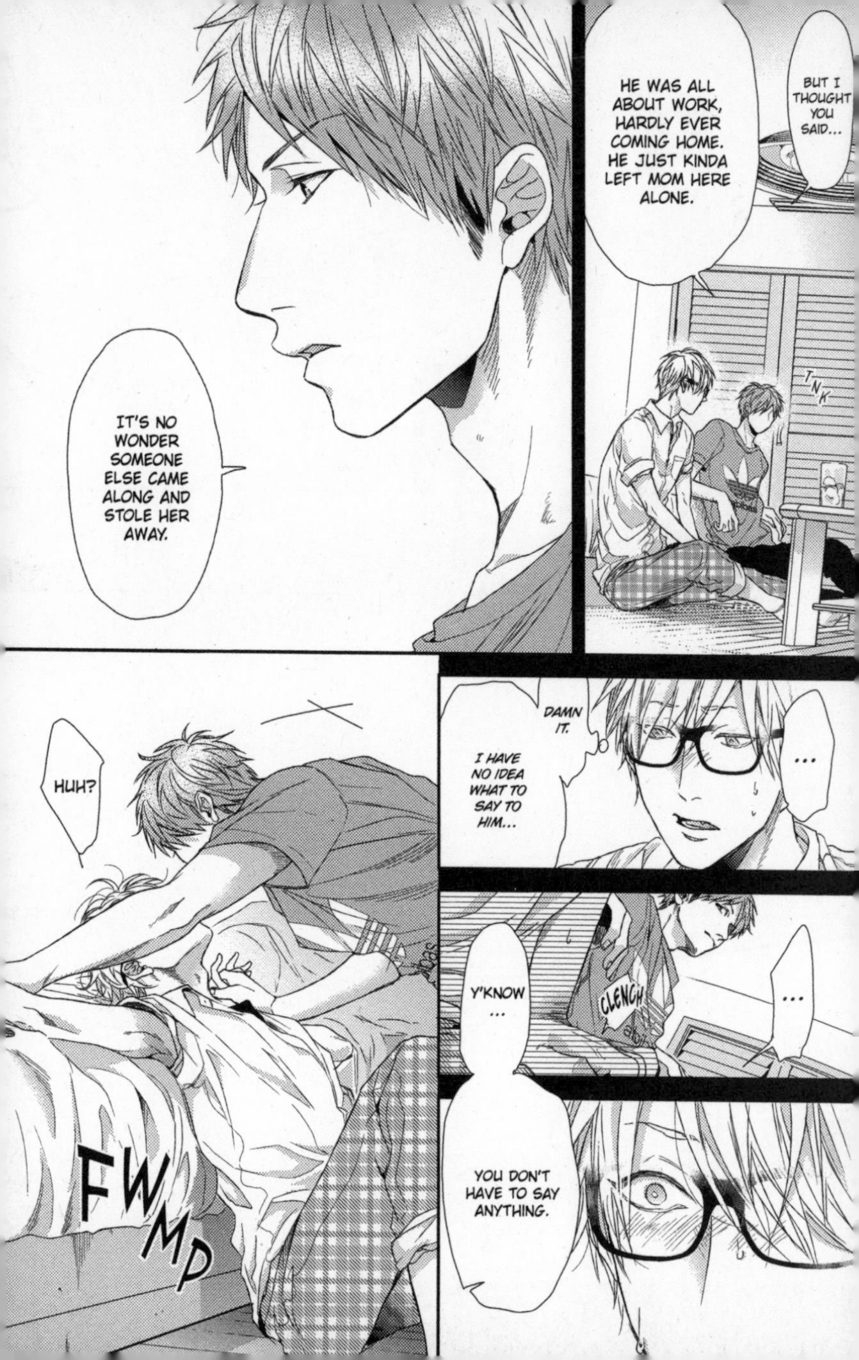
BUT I THOUGHT YOU SAID...
HE WAS ALL ABOUT WORK, HARDLY EVER COMING HOME. HE JUST KINDA LEFT MOM HERE ALONE.
TNK
IT'S NO WONDER SOMEONE ELSE CAME ALONG AND STOLE HER AWAY.
...
DAMN IT.
I HAVE NO IDEA WHAT TO SAY TO HIM...
...
CLENCH
Y'KNOW...
YOU DON'T HAVE TO SAY ANYTHING.
HUH?
FWMP

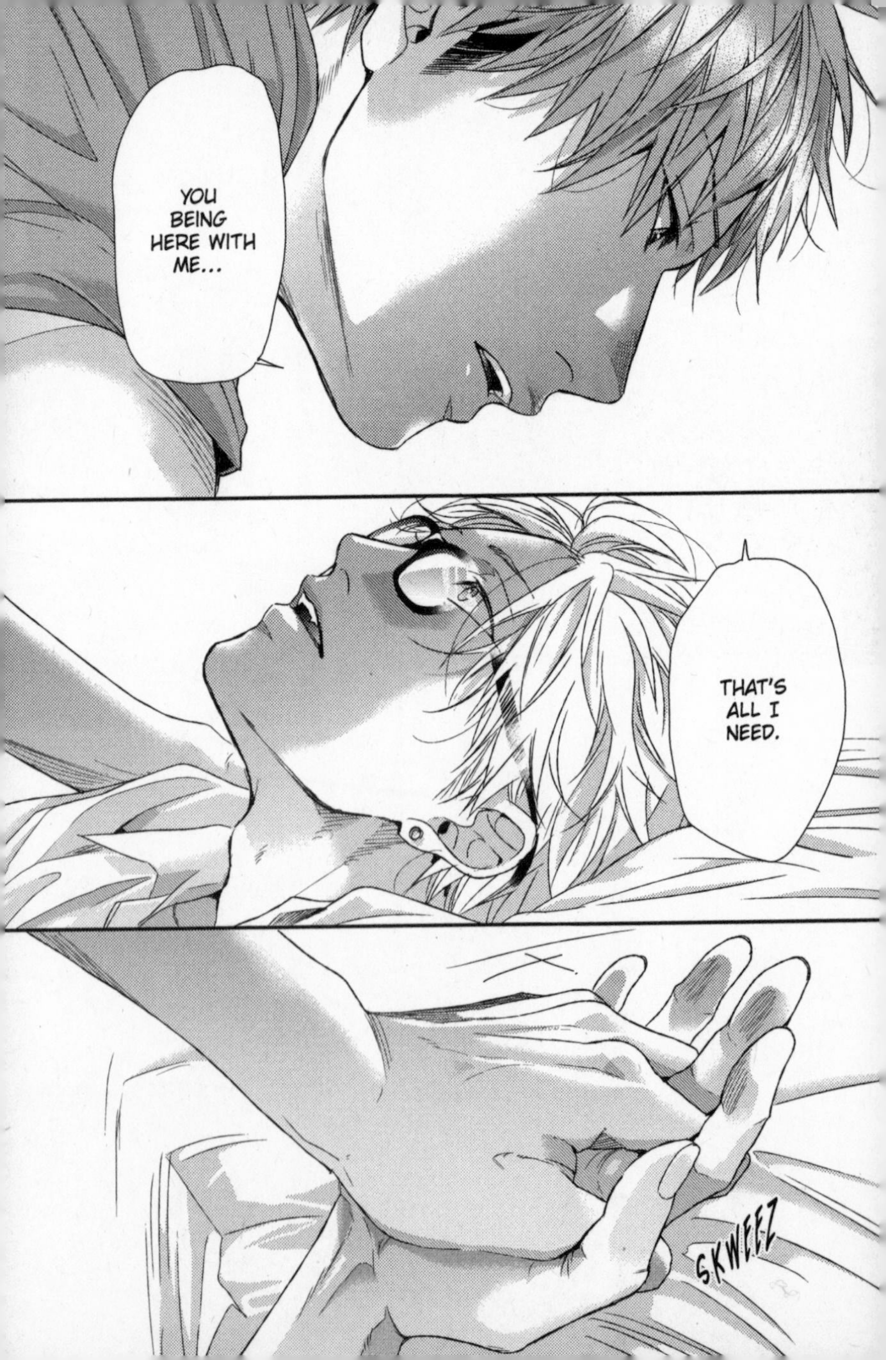
YOU BEING HERE WITH ME...
THAT'S ALL I NEED.
SKWEEZ

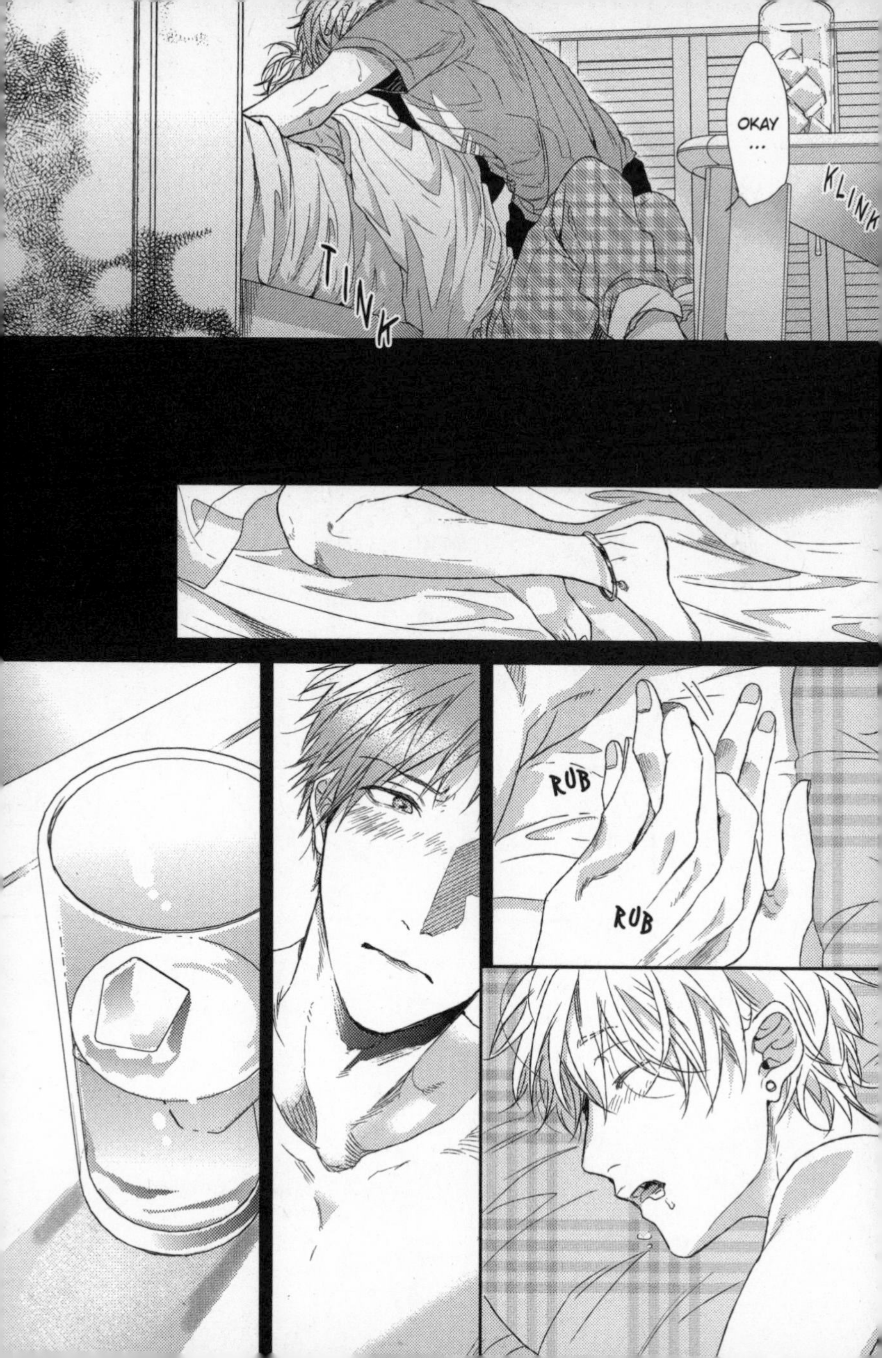
OKAY ...
KLINK
TINK
RUB
RUB

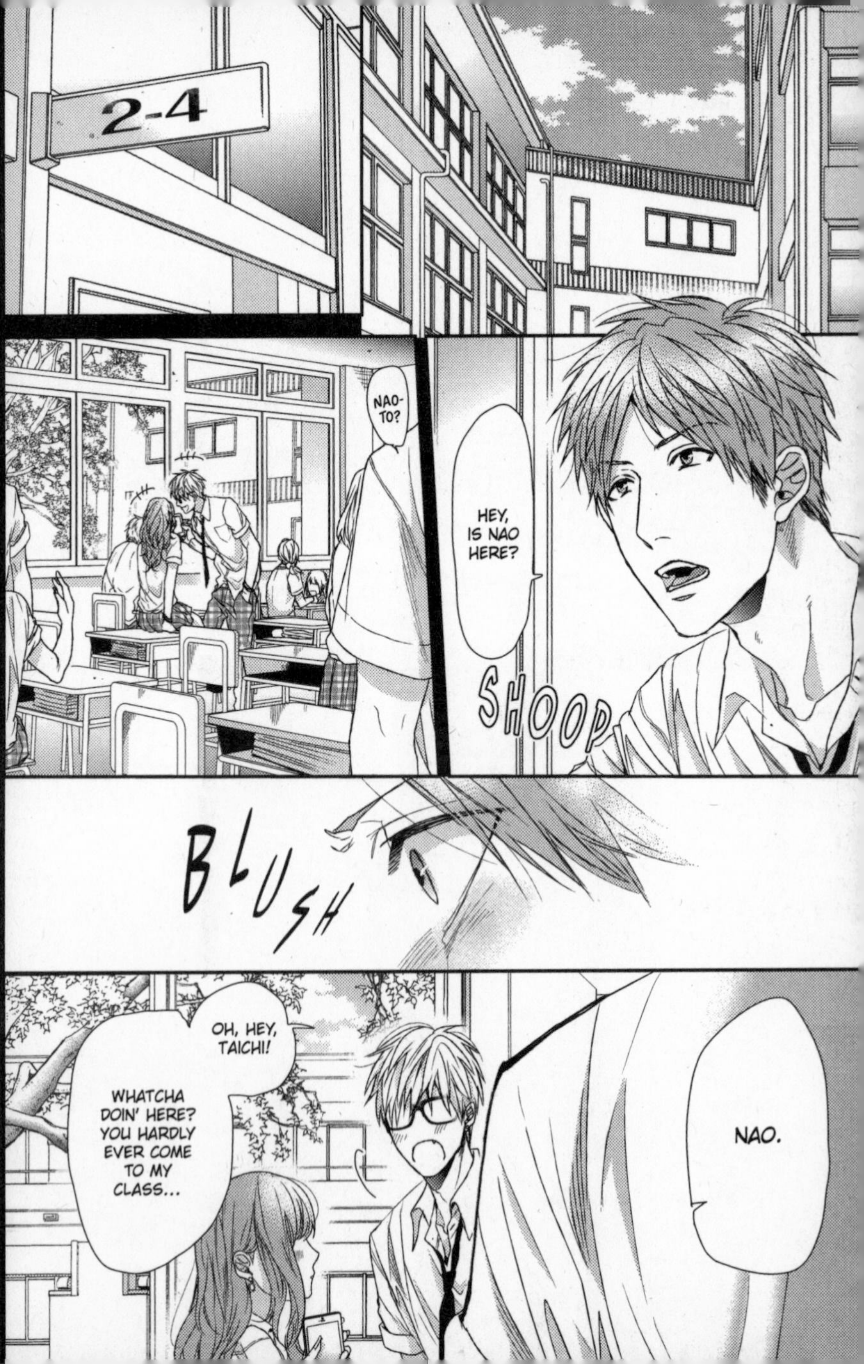
2-4
HEY, IS NAO HERE?
SHOOP
NAO-TO?
BLUSH
NAO.
OH, HEY, TAICHI!
WHATCHA DOIN' HERE? YOU HARDLY EVER COME TO MY CLASS...

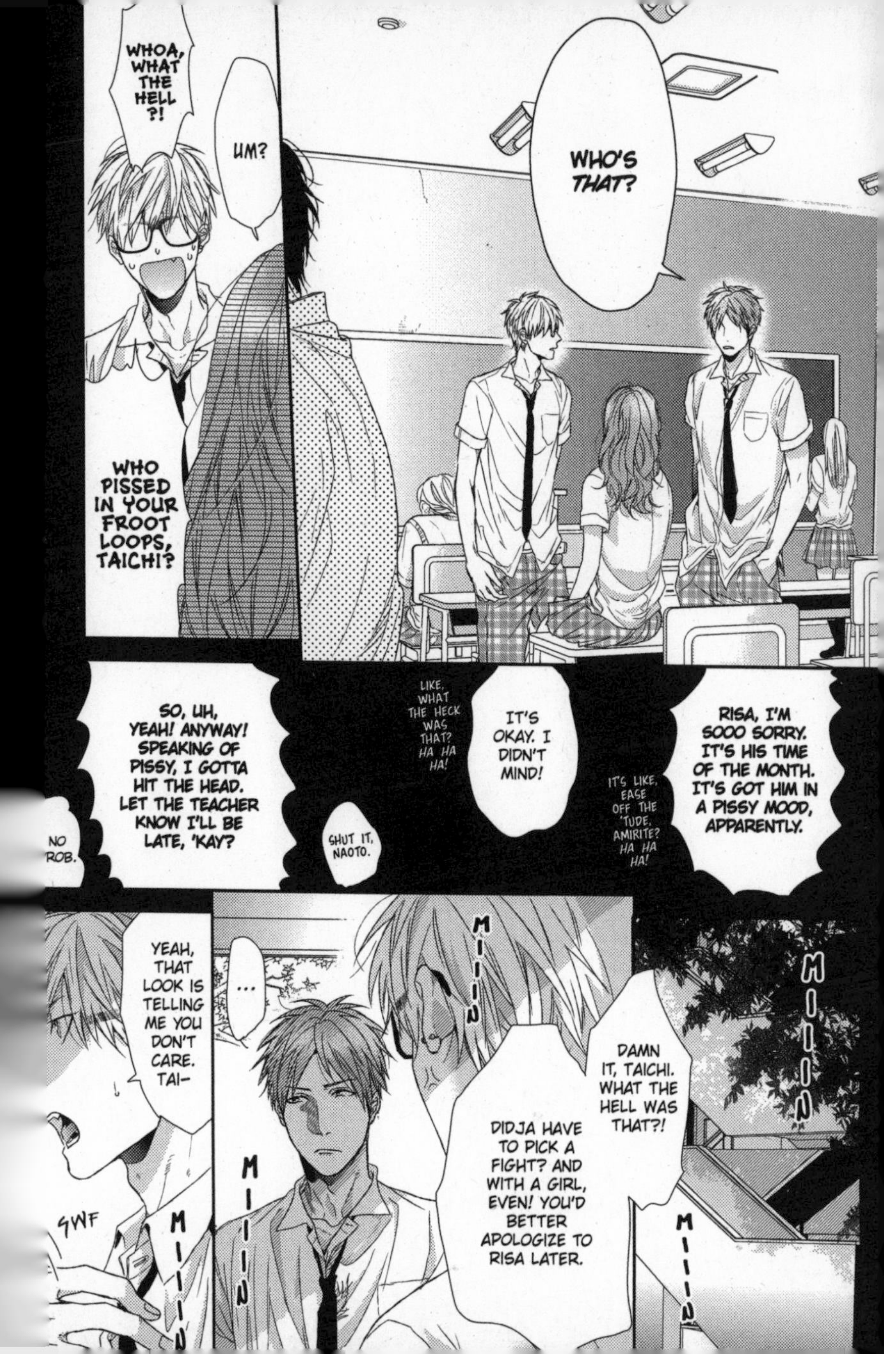
WHO'S *THAT?*
UM?
WHOA, WHAT THE HELL ?!
WHO PISSED IN YOUR FROOT LOOPS, TAICHI?
RISA, I'M SOOO SORRY. IT'S HIS TIME OF THE MONTH. IT'S GOT HIM IN A PISSY MOOD, APPARENTLY.
IT'S LIKE, EASE OFF THE 'TUDE, AMIRITE? HA HA HA!
IT'S OKAY. I DIDN'T MIND!
LIKE, WHAT THE HECK WAS THAT? HA HA HA!
SHUT IT, NAOTO.
SO, UH, YEAH! ANYWAY! SPEAKING OF PISSY, I GOTTA HIT THE HEAD. LET THE TEACHER KNOW I'LL BE LATE, 'KAY?
NO PROB.
MIIIN
DAMN IT, TAICHI. WHAT THE HELL WAS THAT?!
DIDJA HAVE TO PICK A FIGHT? AND WITH A GIRL, EVEN! YOU'D BETTER APOLOGIZE TO RISA LATER.
MIIIN
MIIIN
...
MIIIN
YEAH, THAT LOOK IS TELLING ME YOU DON'T CARE. TAI-
SWF
MIIIN

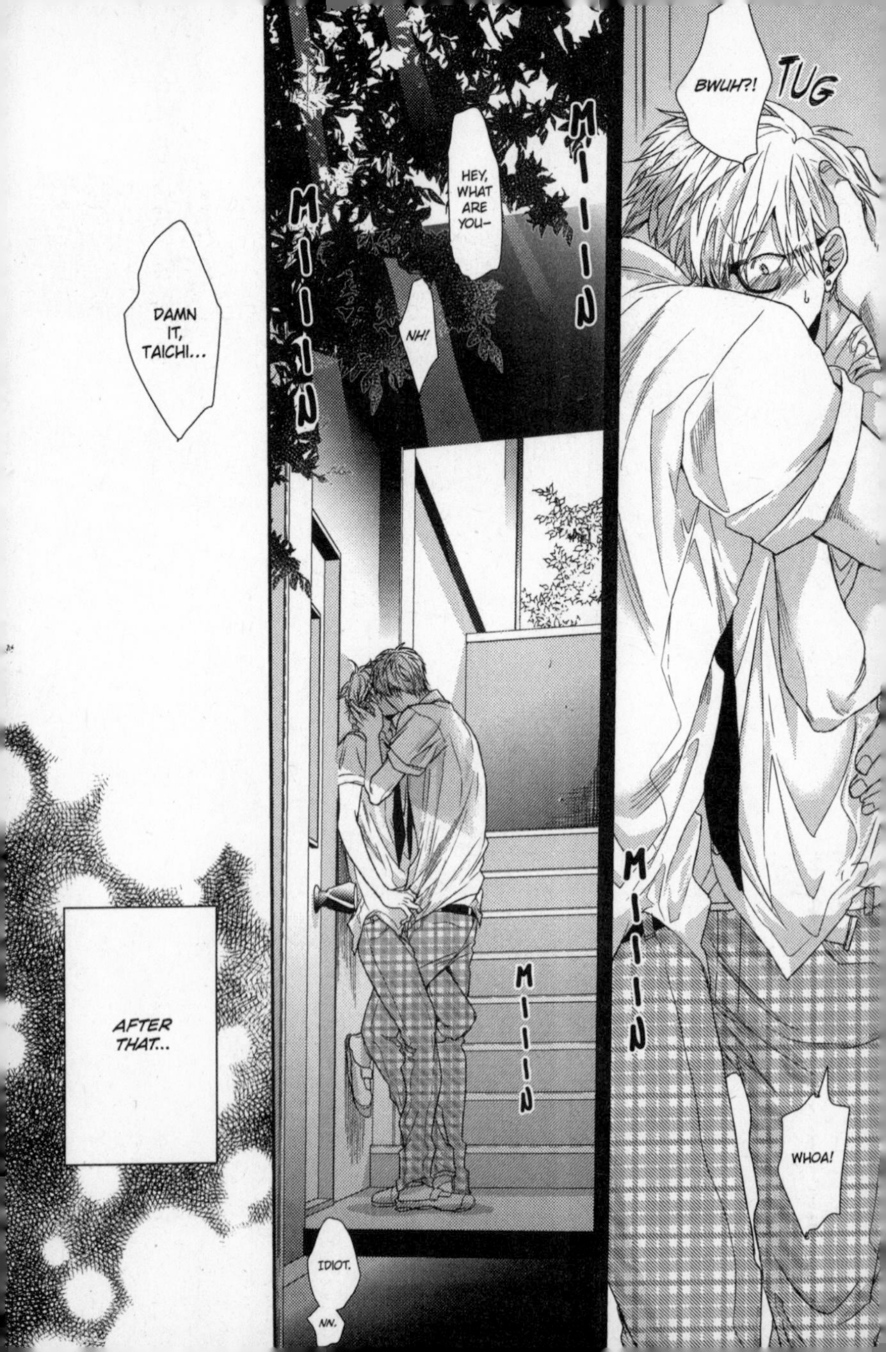
BWUH?!
TUG
MIIIN
WHOA!
HEY, WHAT ARE YOU-
MIIIN
MIIIN
NH!
MIIIN
IDIOT.
NN.
DAMN IT, TAICHI...
AFTER THAT...

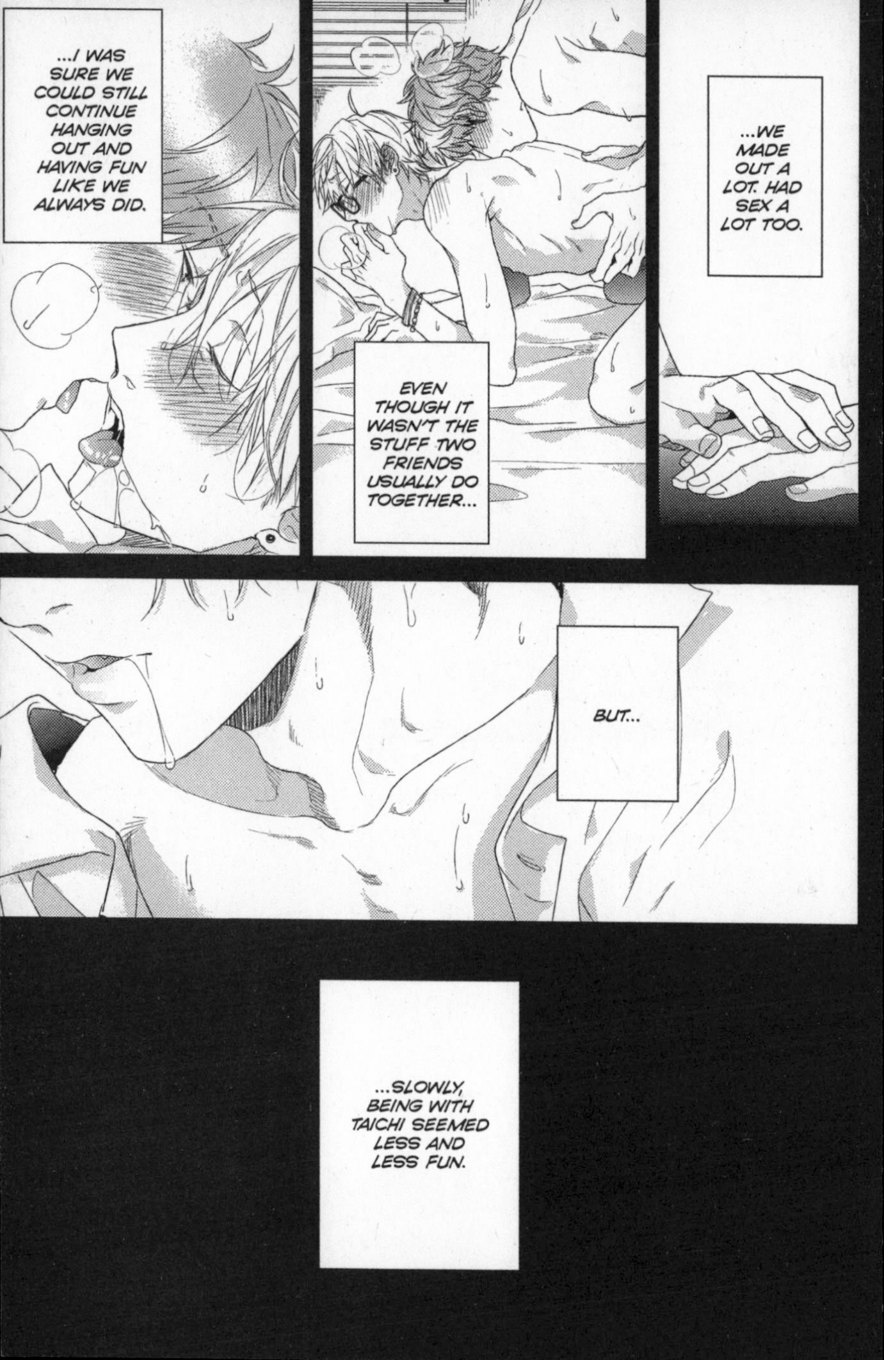
...WE MADE OUT A LOT. HAD SEX A LOT TOO.
EVEN THOUGH IT WASN'T THE STUFF TWO FRIENDS USUALLY DO TOGETHER...
...I WAS SURE WE COULD STILL CONTINUE HANGING OUT AND HAVING FUN LIKE WE ALWAYS DID.
BUT...
...SLOWLY, BEING WITH TAICHI SEEMED LESS AND LESS FUN.

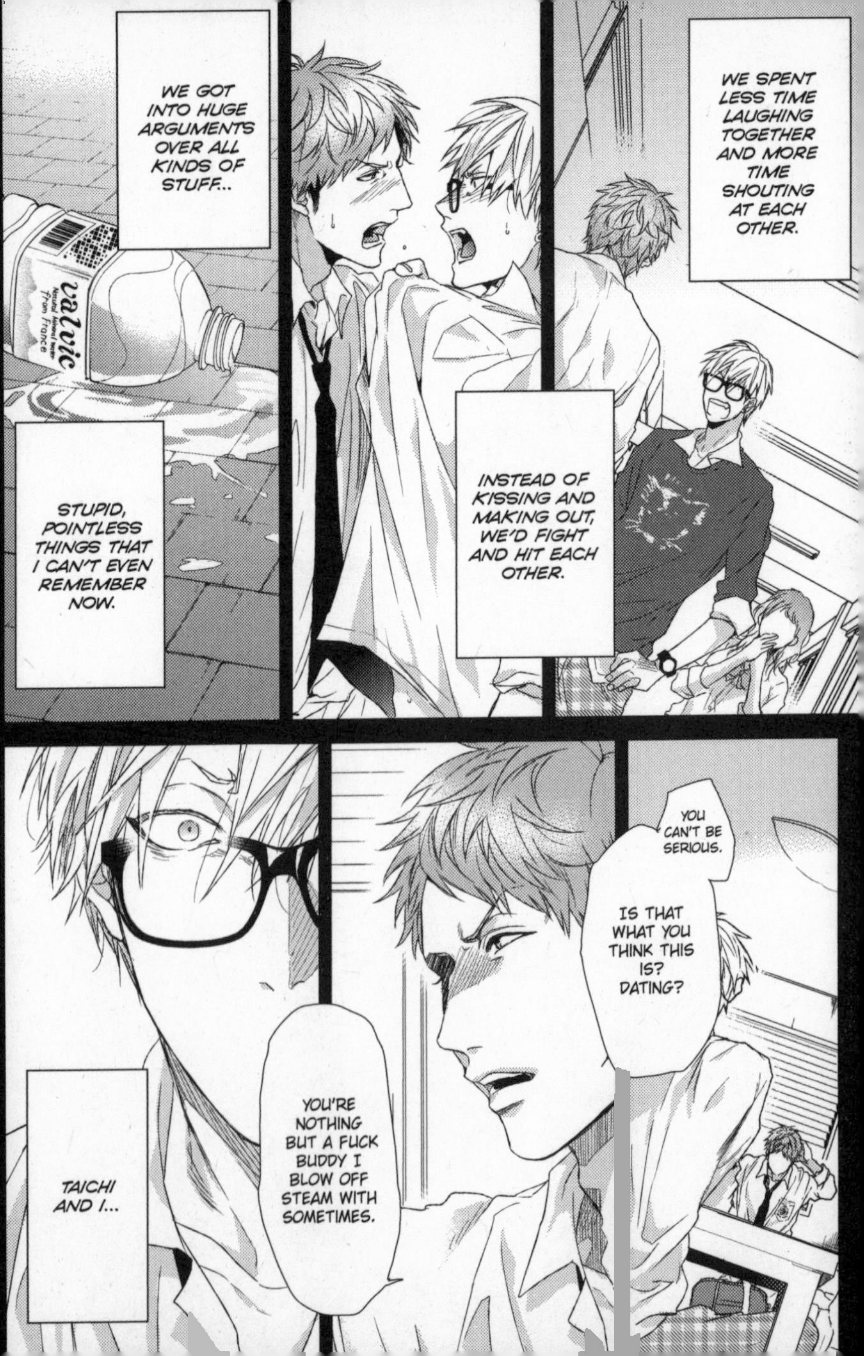
WE SPENT LESS TIME LAUGHING TOGETHER AND MORE TIME SHOUTING AT EACH OTHER.
INSTEAD OF KISSING AND MAKING OUT, WE'D FIGHT AND HIT EACH OTHER.
WE GOT INTO HUGE ARGUMENTS OVER ALL KINDS OF STUFF...
valvic
STUPID, POINTLESS THINGS THAT I CAN'T EVEN REMEMBER NOW.
YOU CAN'T BE SERIOUS.
IS THAT WHAT YOU THINK THIS IS? DATING?
YOU'RE NOTHING BUT A FUCK BUDDY I BLOW OFF STEAM WITH SOMETIMES.
TAICHI AND I...

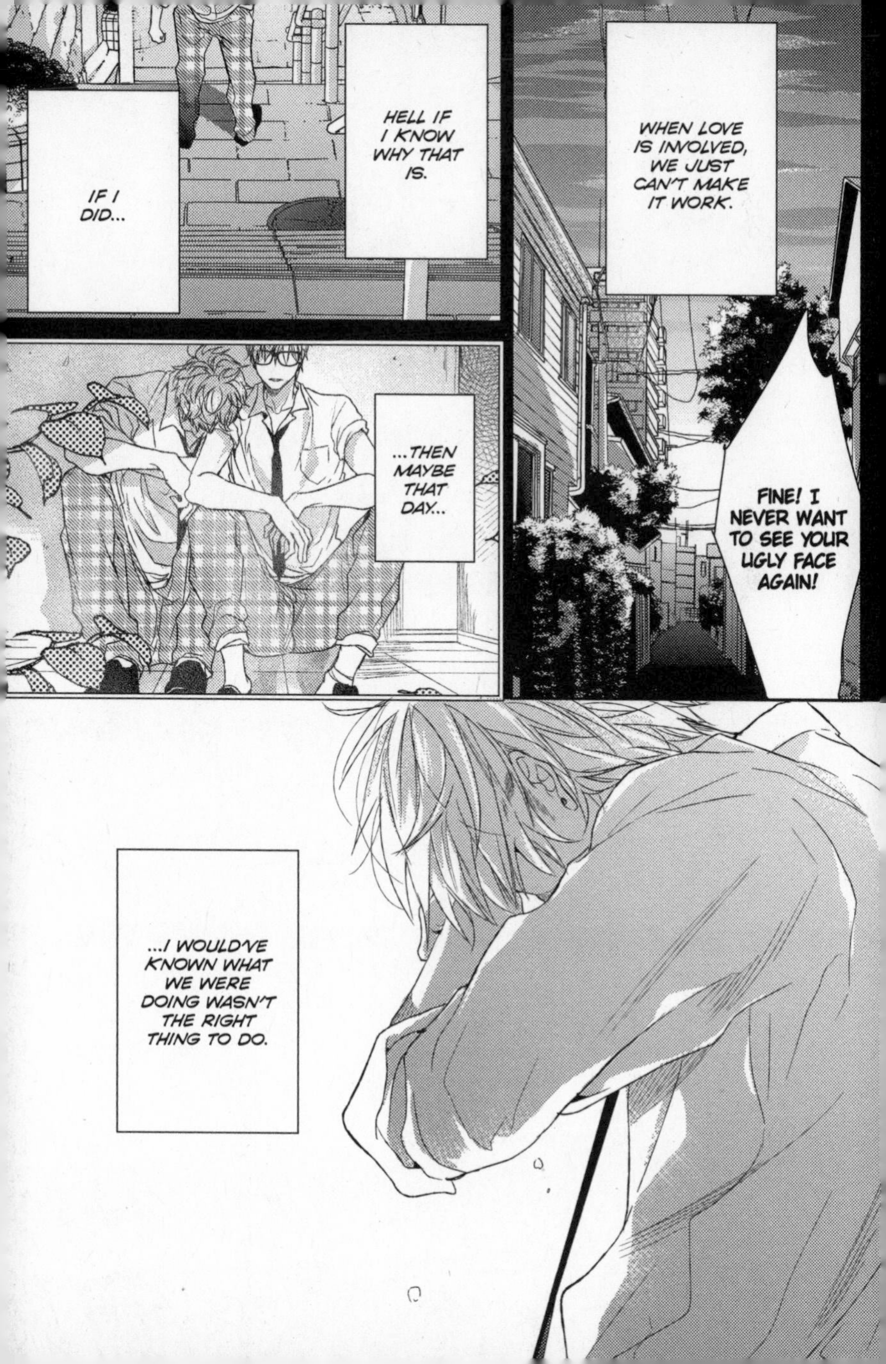
WHEN LOVE IS INVOLVED, WE JUST CAN'T MAKE IT WORK.
FINE! I NEVER WANT TO SEE YOUR UGLY FACE AGAIN!
HELL IF I KNOW WHY THAT IS.
IF I DID...
...THEN MAYBE THAT DAY...
...I WOULD'VE KNOWN WHAT WE WERE DOING WASN'T THE RIGHT THING TO DO.

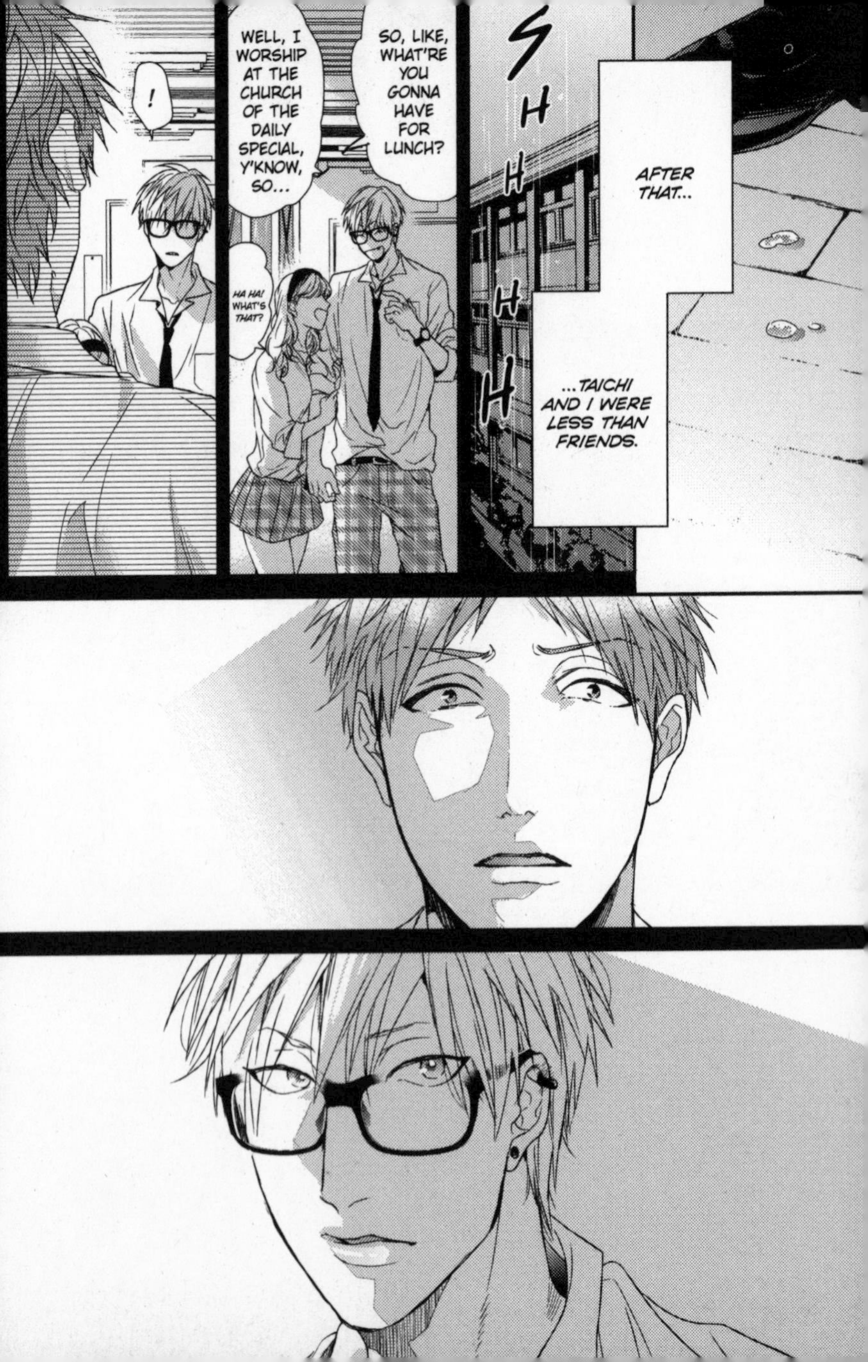
AFTER THAT...
SHHHH
...TAICHI AND I WERE LESS THAN FRIENDS.
SO, LIKE, WHAT'RE YOU GONNA HAVE FOR LUNCH?
WELL, I WORSHIP AT THE CHURCH OF THE DAILY SPECIAL, Y'KNOW, SO...
HA HA! WHAT'S THAT?
!

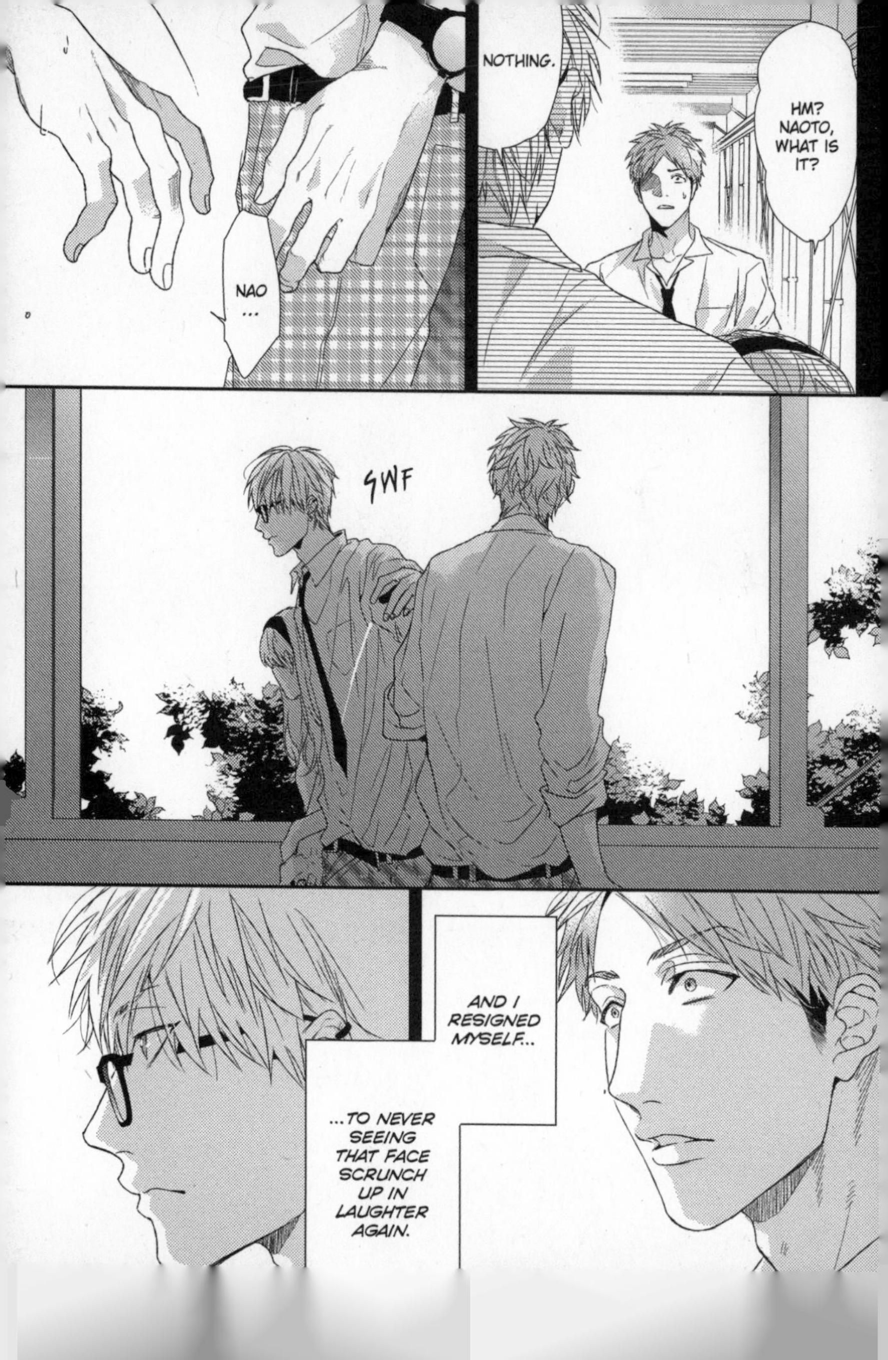
HM? NAOTO, WHAT IS IT?
NOTHING.
NAO...
SWF
AND I RESIGNED MYSELF...
...TO NEVER SEEING THAT FACE SCRUNCH UP IN LAUGHTER AGAIN.

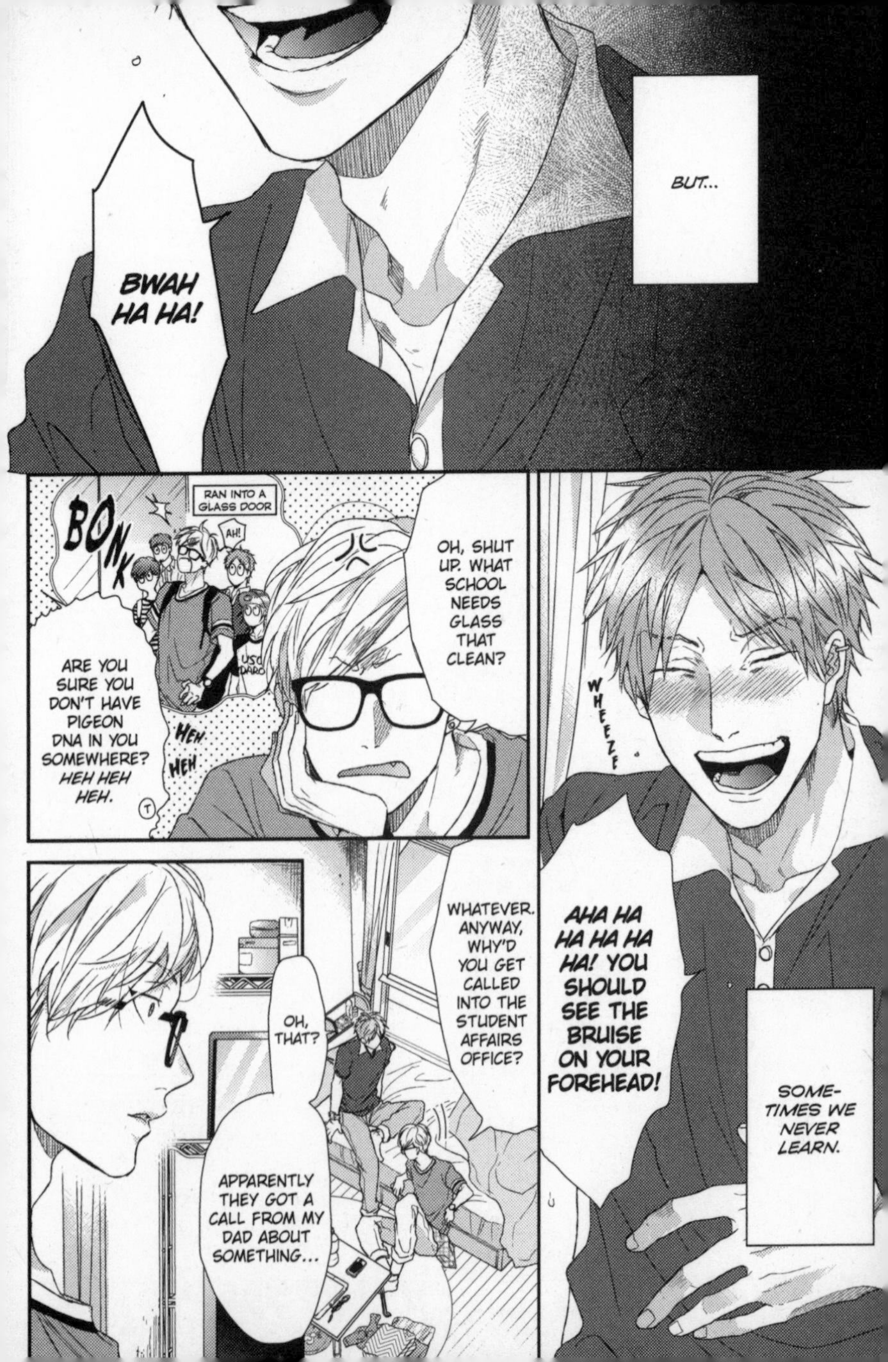
BUT...
BWAH HA HA!
WHEEZE
AHA HA HA HA HA HA! YOU SHOULD SEE THE BRUISE ON YOUR FOREHEAD!
SOMETIMES WE NEVER LEARN.
OH, SHUT UP. WHAT SCHOOL NEEDS GLASS THAT CLEAN?
RAN INTO A GLASS DOOR
BONK
AH!
ARE YOU SURE YOU DON'T HAVE PIGEON DNA IN YOU SOMEWHERE? HEH HEH HEH.
HEH HEH
WHATEVER. ANYWAY, WHY'D YOU GET CALLED INTO THE STUDENT AFFAIRS OFFICE?
OH, THAT?
APPARENTLY THEY GOT A CALL FROM MY DAD ABOUT SOMETHING...

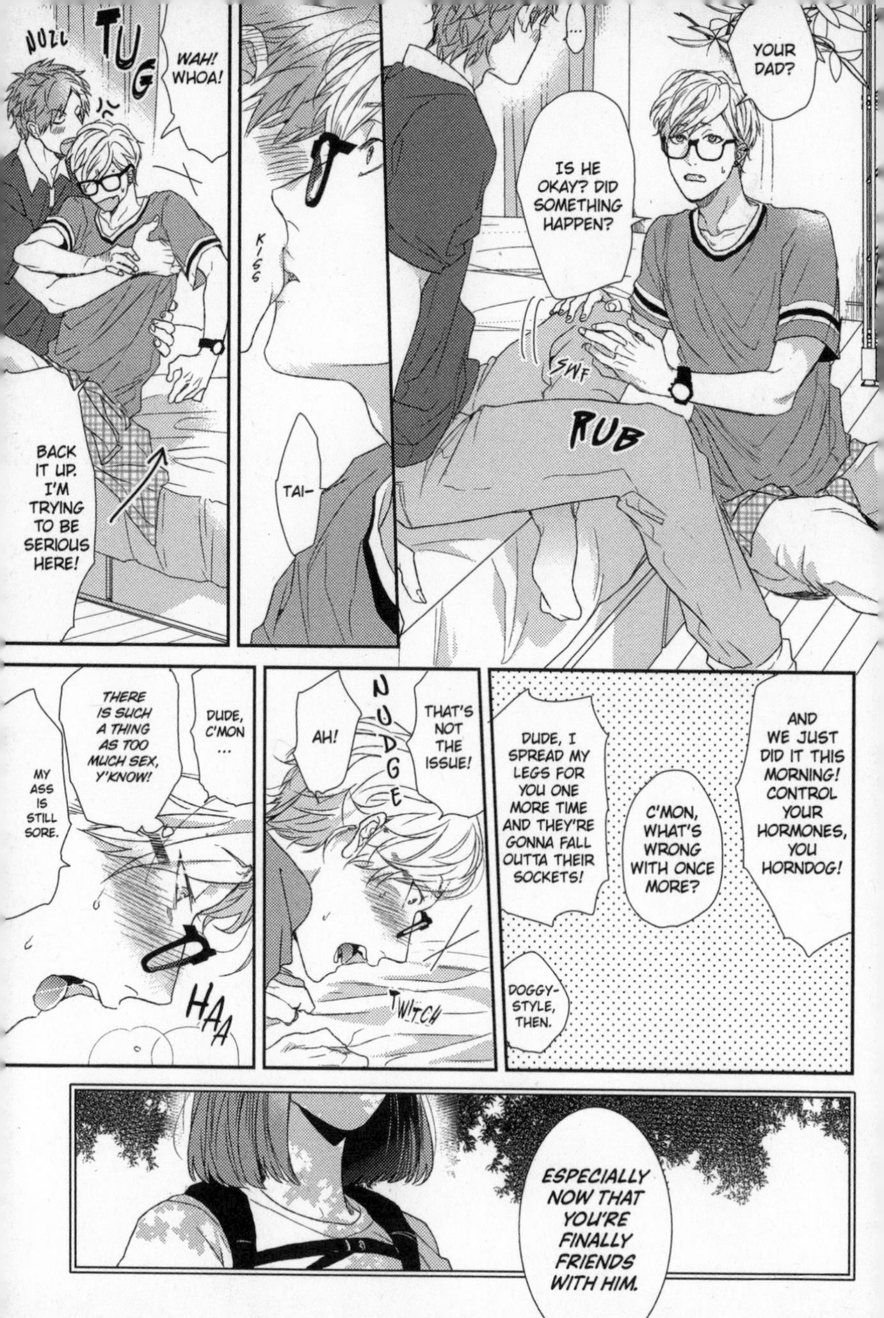
YOUR DAD?
...
IS HE OKAY? DID SOMETHING HAPPEN?
SWF
RUB
KISS
TAI-
WAH! WHOA!
TUG
NUZZ
BACK IT UP. I'M TRYING TO BE SERIOUS HERE!
AND WE JUST DID IT THIS MORNING! CONTROL YOUR HORMONES, YOU HORNDOG!
C'MON, WHAT'S WRONG WITH ONCE MORE?
DUDE, I SPREAD MY LEGS FOR YOU ONE MORE TIME AND THEY'RE GONNA FALL OUTTA THEIR SOCKETS!
DOGGY-STYLE, THEN.
THAT'S NOT THE ISSUE!
NUDGE
AH!
TWITCH
DUDE, C'MON ...
THERE IS SUCH A THING AS TOO MUCH SEX, Y'KNOW!
MY ASS IS STILL SORE.
HAA
ESPECIALLY NOW THAT YOU'RE FINALLY FRIENDS WITH HIM.

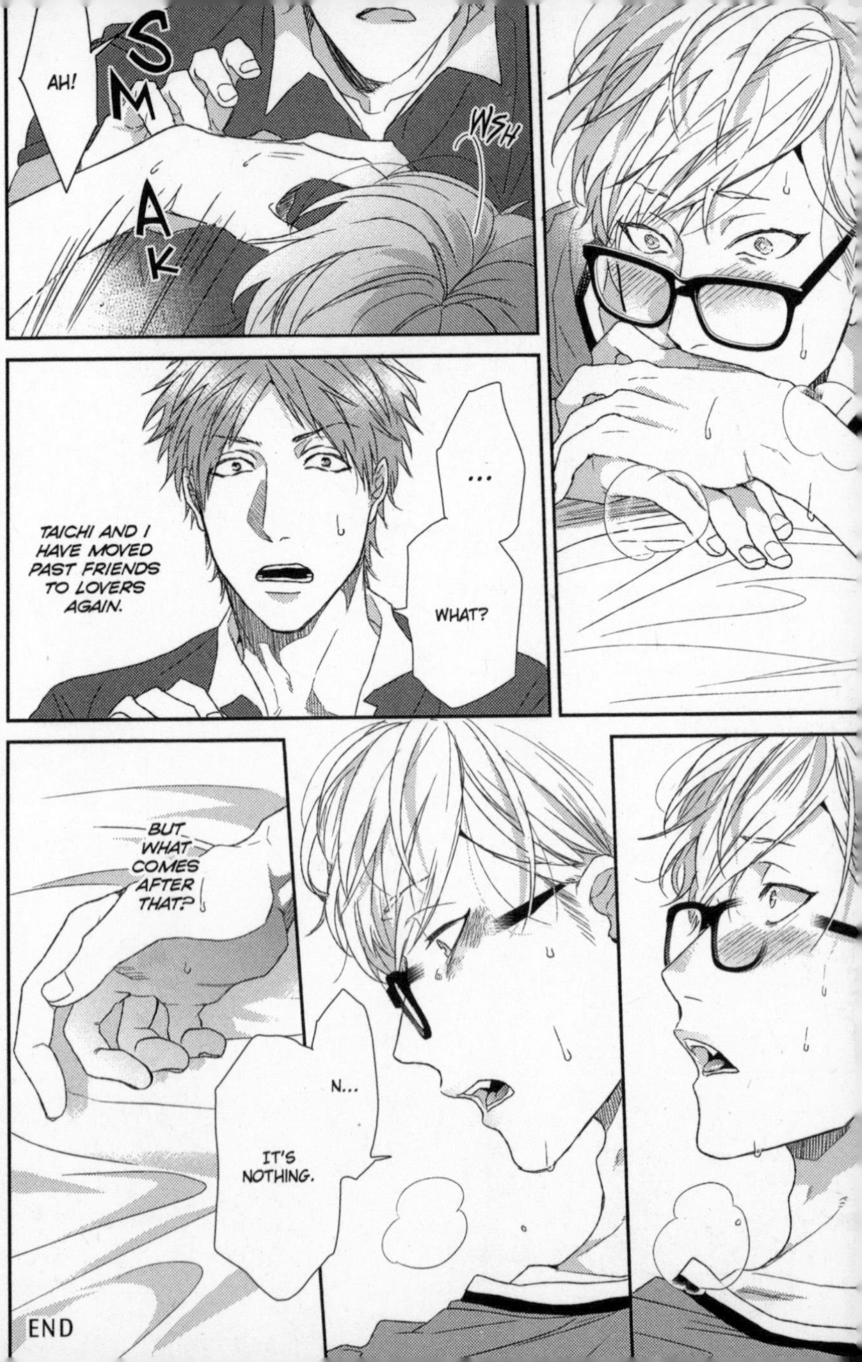
WSH
SMACK
AH!
...
WHAT?
TAICHI AND I HAVE MOVED PAST FRIENDS TO LOVERS AGAIN.
BUT WHAT COMES AFTER THAT?
N...
IT'S NOTHING.
END

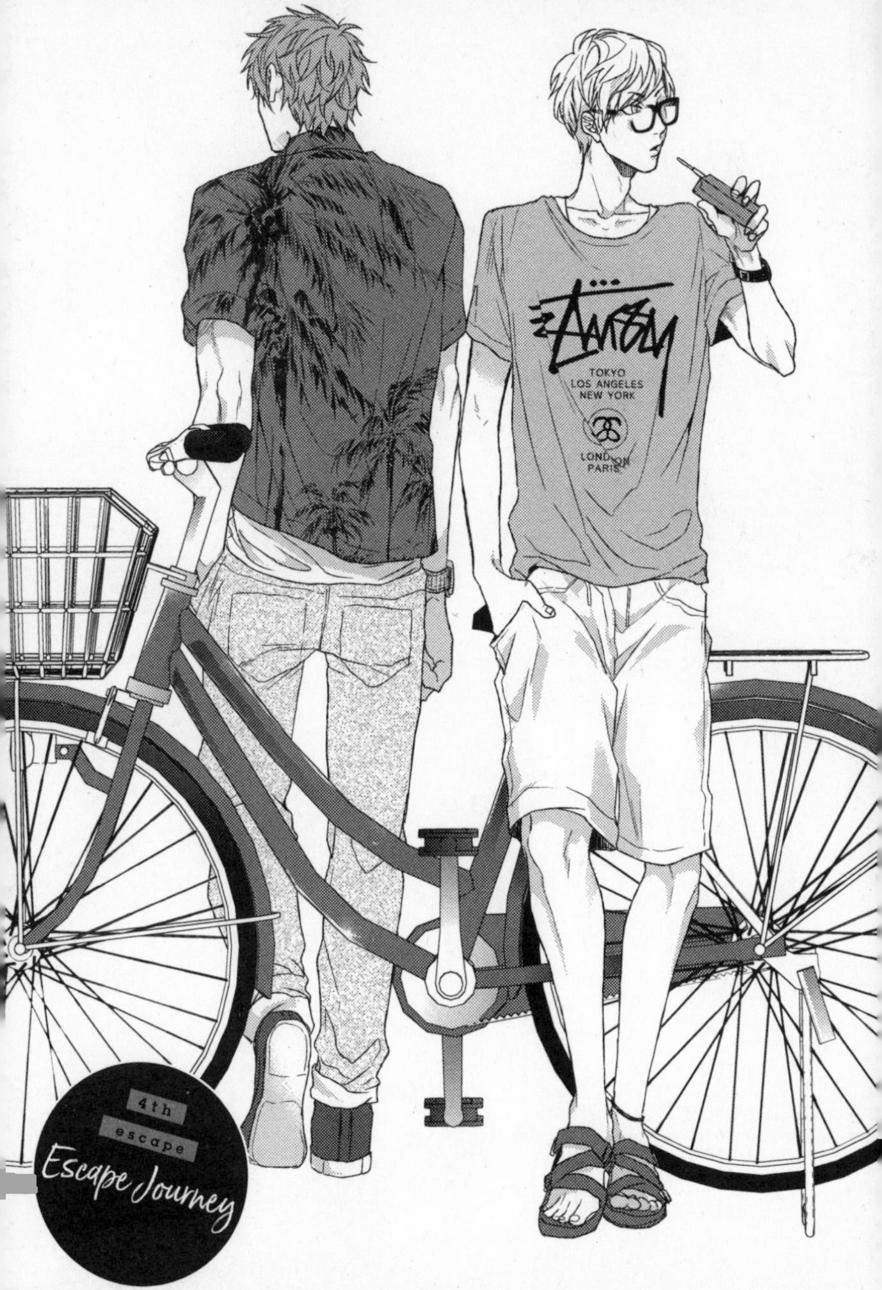
TOKYO
LOS ANGELES
NEW YORK
LONDON
PARIS
4th
escape
Escape Journey

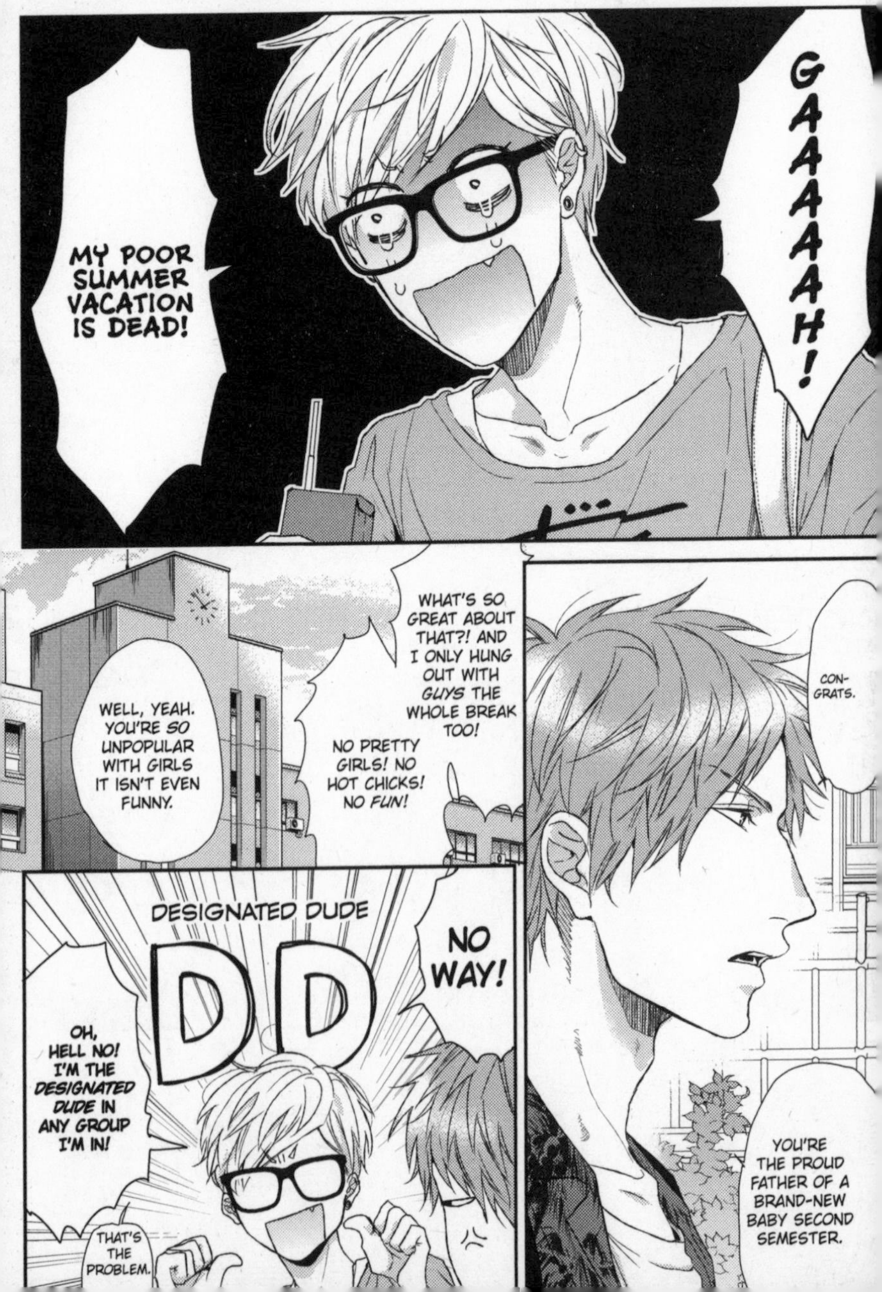
GAAAAAH!
MY POOR SUMMER VACATION IS DEAD!
CON-GRATS.
YOU'RE THE PROUD FATHER OF A BRAND-NEW BABY SECOND SEMESTER.
WHAT'S SO GREAT ABOUT THAT?! AND I ONLY HUNG OUT WITH *GUYS* THE WHOLE BREAK TOO!
NO PRETTY GIRLS! NO HOT CHICKS! NO *FUN*!
WELL, YEAH. YOU'RE *SO* UNPOPULAR WITH GIRLS IT ISN'T EVEN FUNNY.
NO WAY!
DESIGNATED DUDE
DD
OH, HELL NO! I'M THE *DESIGNATED DUDE* IN ANY GROUP I'M IN!
THAT'S THE PROBLEM.

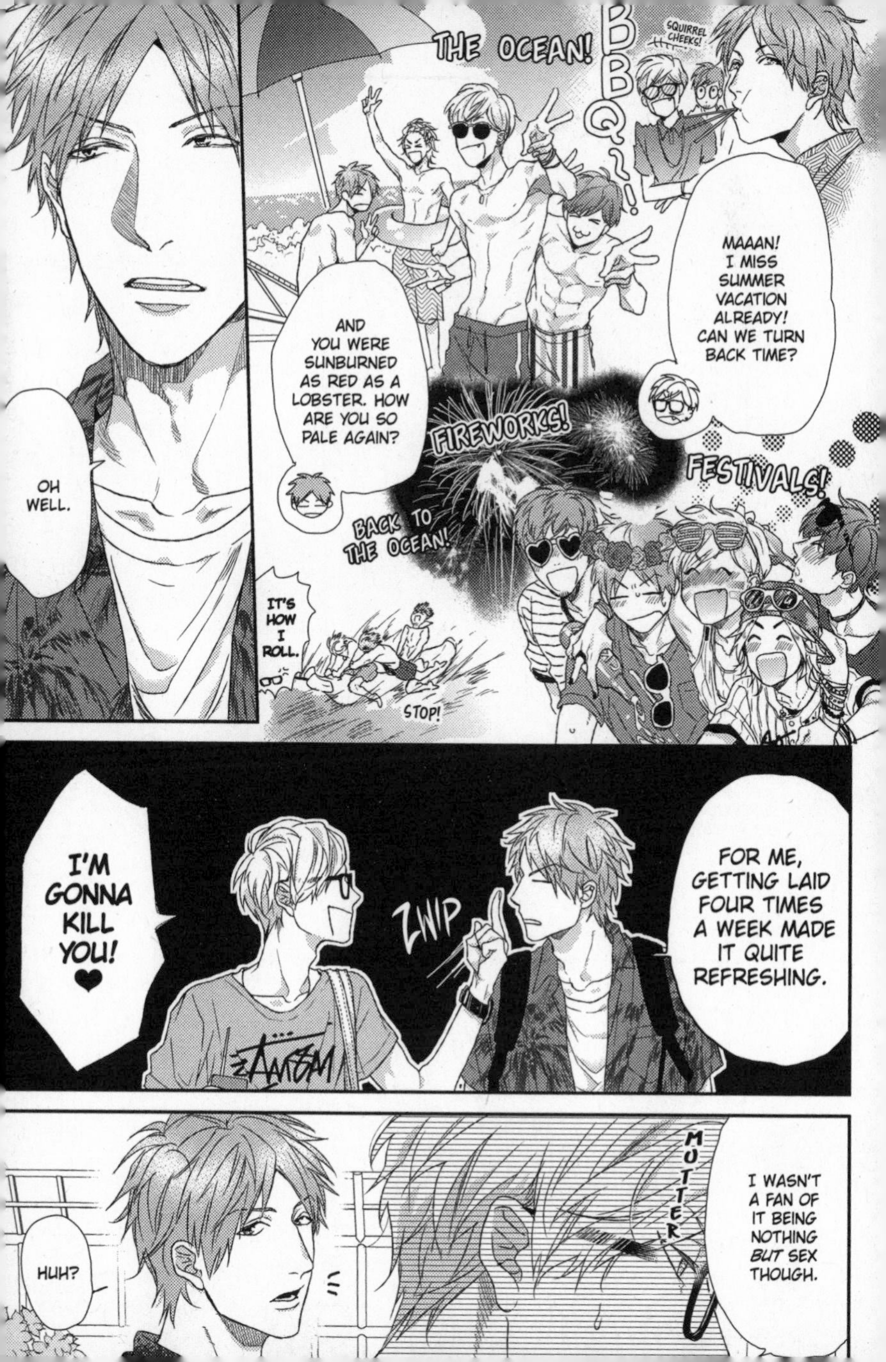
SQUIRREL CHEEKS!
BBQ~!
THE OCEAN!
MAAAN! I MISS SUMMER VACATION ALREADY! CAN WE TURN BACK TIME?
AND YOU WERE SUNBURNED AS RED AS A LOBSTER. HOW ARE YOU SO PALE AGAIN?
FIREWORKS!
FESTIVALS!
BACK TO THE OCEAN!
IT'S HOW I ROLL.
STOP!
OH WELL.
FOR ME, GETTING LAID FOUR TIMES A WEEK MADE IT QUITE REFRESHING.
ZWIP
I'M GONNA KILL YOU! ❤
I WASN'T A FAN OF IT BEING NOTHING *BUT* SEX THOUGH.
MUTTER
HUH?

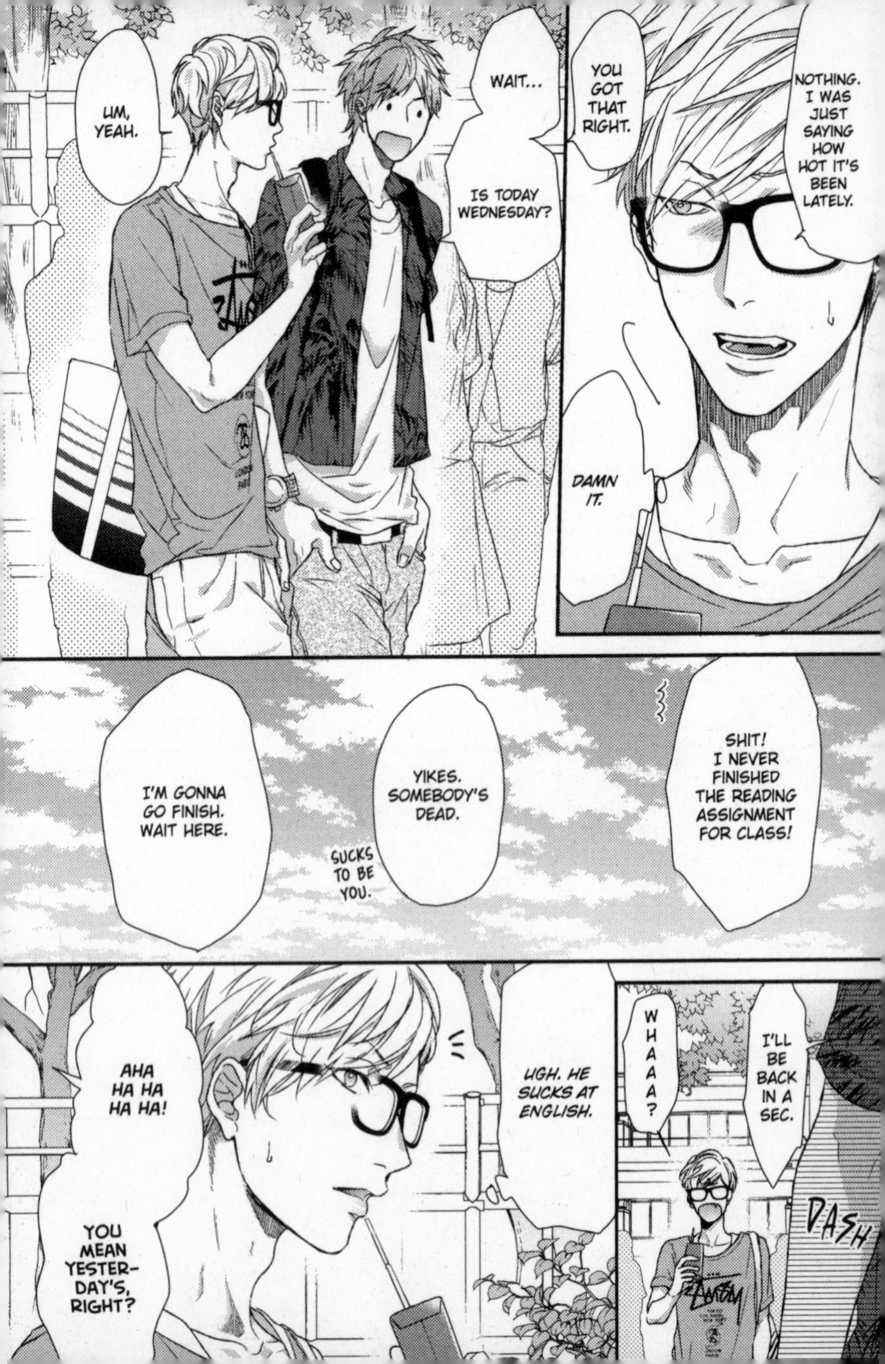
NOTHING. I WAS JUST SAYING HOW HOT IT'S BEEN LATELY.
YOU GOT THAT RIGHT.
DAMN IT.
WAIT...
IS TODAY WEDNESDAY?
UM, YEAH.
SHIT! I NEVER FINISHED THE READING ASSIGNMENT FOR CLASS!
YIKES. SOMEBODY'S DEAD.
SUCKS TO BE YOU.
I'M GONNA GO FINISH. WAIT HERE.
I'LL BE BACK IN A SEC.
WHAAAA?
DASH
UGH. HE SUCKS AT ENGLISH.
AHA HA HA HA HA!
YOU MEAN YESTER-DAY'S, RIGHT?

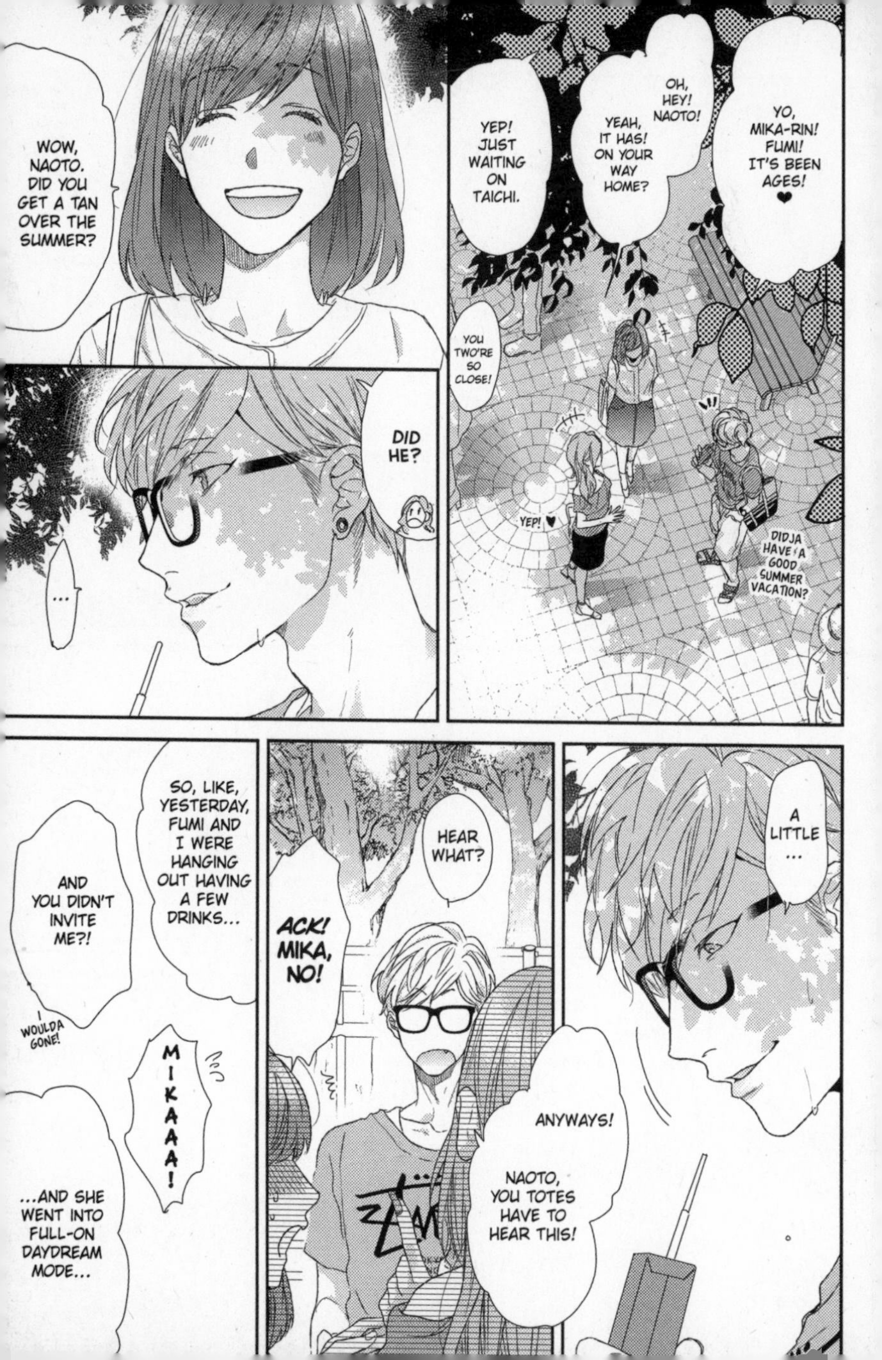
YO, MIKA-RIN! FUMI! IT'S BEEN AGES! ❤
OH, HEY! NAOTO!
YEAH, IT HAS! ON YOUR WAY HOME?
YEP! JUST WAITING ON TAICHI.
YOU TWO'RE SO CLOSE!
YEP! ❤
DIDJA HAVE A GOOD SUMMER VACATION?
WOW, NAOTO. DID YOU GET A TAN OVER THE SUMMER?
DID HE?
...
A LITTLE ...
ANYWAYS!
NAOTO, YOU TOTES HAVE TO HEAR THIS!
HEAR WHAT?
ACK! MIKA, NO!
SO, LIKE, YESTERDAY, FUMI AND I WERE HANGING OUT HAVING A FEW DRINKS...
AND YOU DIDN'T INVITE ME?!
I WOULDA GONE!
MIKAAAA!
...AND SHE WENT INTO FULL-ON DAYDREAM MODE...

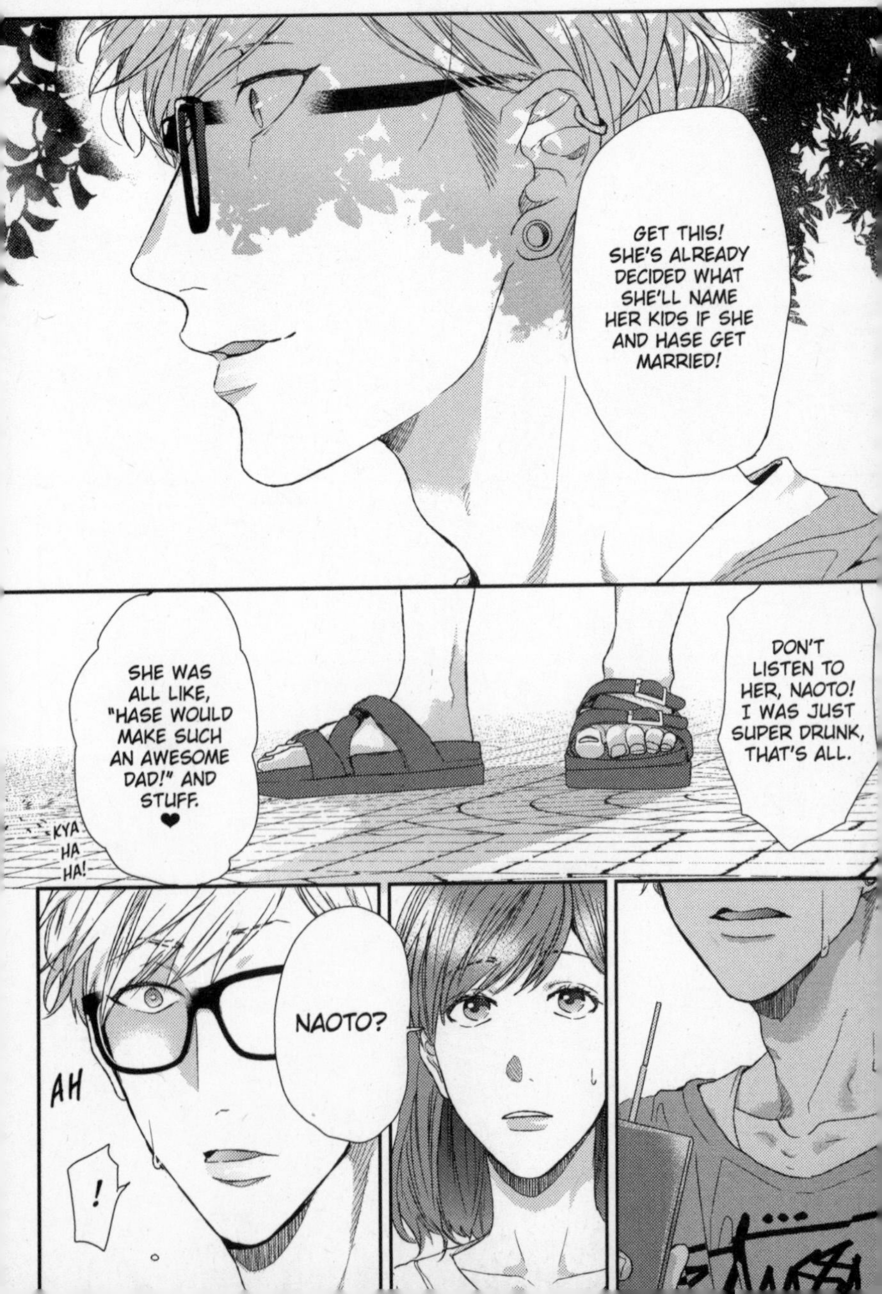
GET THIS! SHE'S ALREADY DECIDED WHAT SHE'LL NAME HER KIDS IF SHE AND HASE GET MARRIED!
DON'T LISTEN TO HER, NAOTO! I WAS JUST SUPER DRUNK, THAT'S ALL.
SHE WAS ALL LIKE, "HASE WOULD MAKE SUCH AN AWESOME DAD!" AND STUFF. ❤
KYA HA HA!
NAOTO?
AH
!

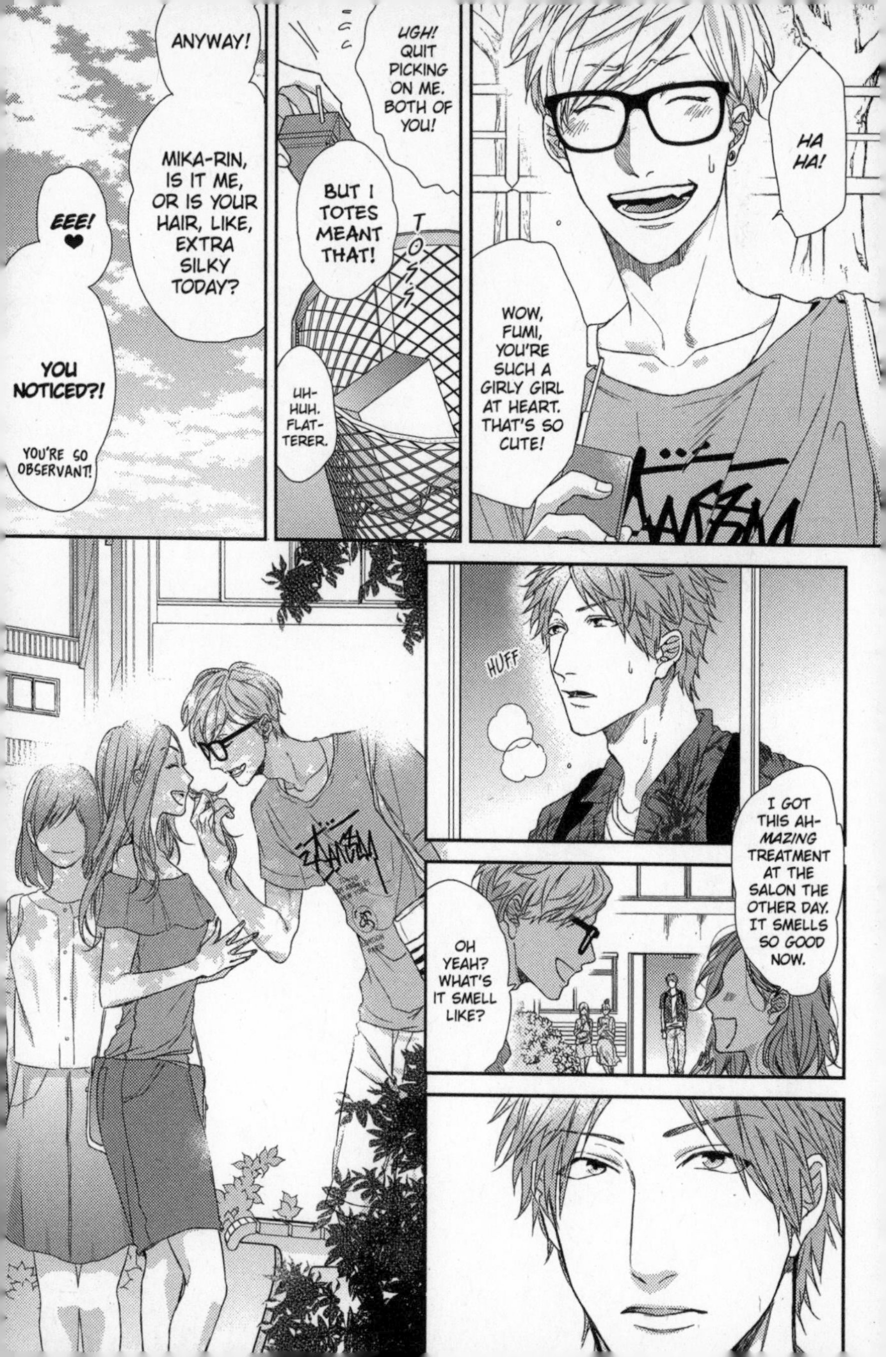
HA HA!
WOW, FUMI, YOU'RE SUCH A GIRLY GIRL AT HEART. THAT'S SO CUTE!
UGH! QUIT PICKING ON ME. BOTH OF YOU!
BUT I TOTES MEANT THAT!
TOSS
UH-HUH. FLATTERER.
ANYWAY!
MIKA-RIN, IS IT ME, OR IS YOUR HAIR, LIKE, EXTRA SILKY TODAY?
EEE! ❤
YOU NOTICED?!
YOU'RE SO OBSERVANT!
HUFF
I GOT THIS AH-*MAZING* TREATMENT AT THE SALON THE OTHER DAY. IT SMELLS SO GOOD NOW.
OH YEAH? WHAT'S IT SMELL LIKE?

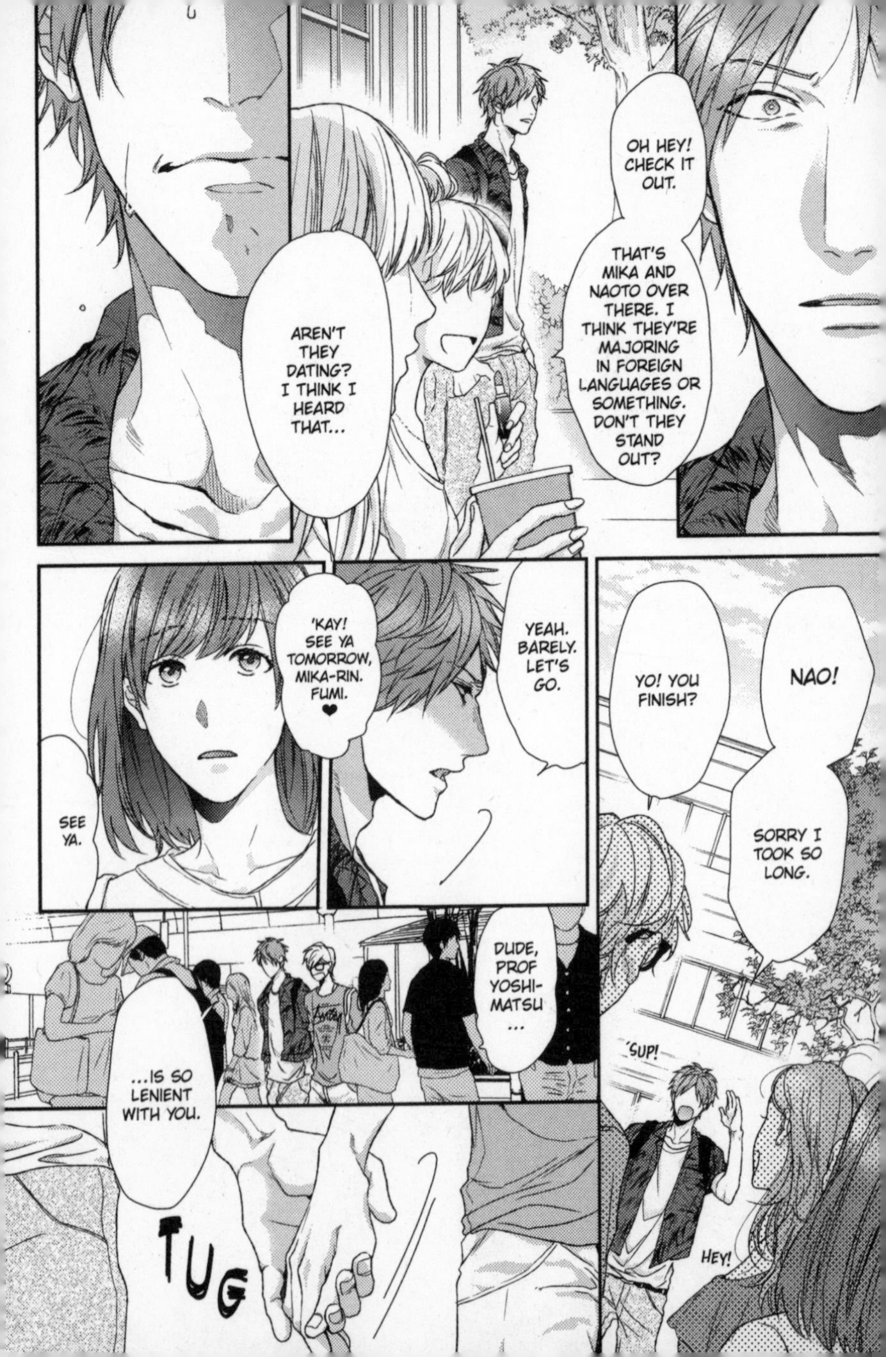
OH HEY! CHECK IT OUT.
THAT'S MIKA AND NAOTO OVER THERE. I THINK THEY'RE MAJORING IN FOREIGN LANGUAGES OR SOMETHING. DON'T THEY STAND OUT?
AREN'T THEY DATING? I THINK I HEARD THAT...
NAO!
YO! YOU FINISH?
SORRY I TOOK SO LONG.
'SUP!
HEY!
YEAH. BARELY. LET'S GO.
'KAY! SEE YA TOMORROW, MIKA-RIN. FUMI. ❤
SEE YA.
DUDE, PROF YOSHI-MATSU ...
...IS SO LENIENT WITH YOU.
TUG

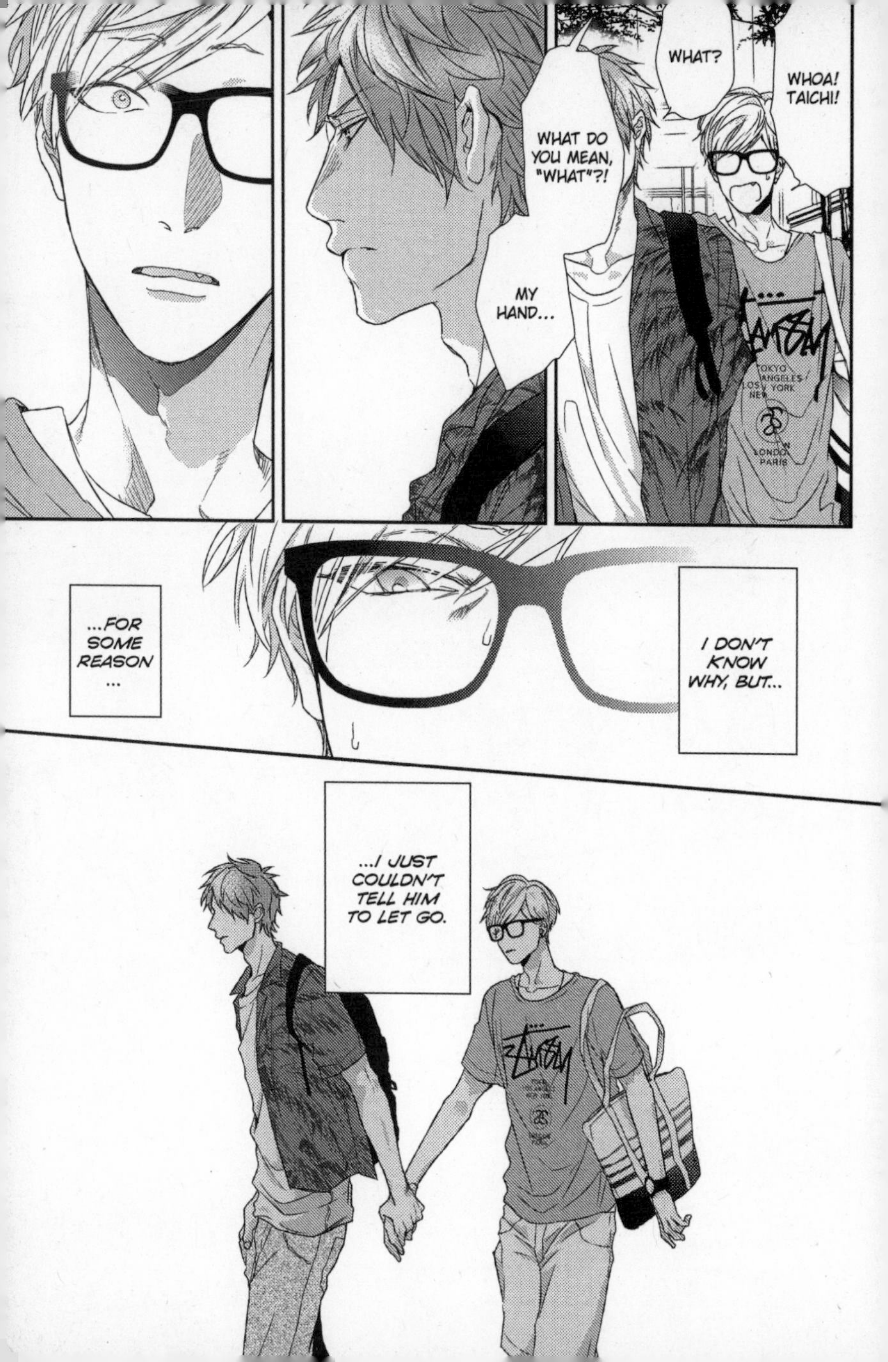
WHOA! TAICHI!
WHAT?
WHAT DO YOU MEAN, "WHAT"?!
MY HAND...
I DON'T KNOW WHY, BUT...
...FOR SOME REASON ...
...I JUST COULDN'T TELL HIM TO LET GO.

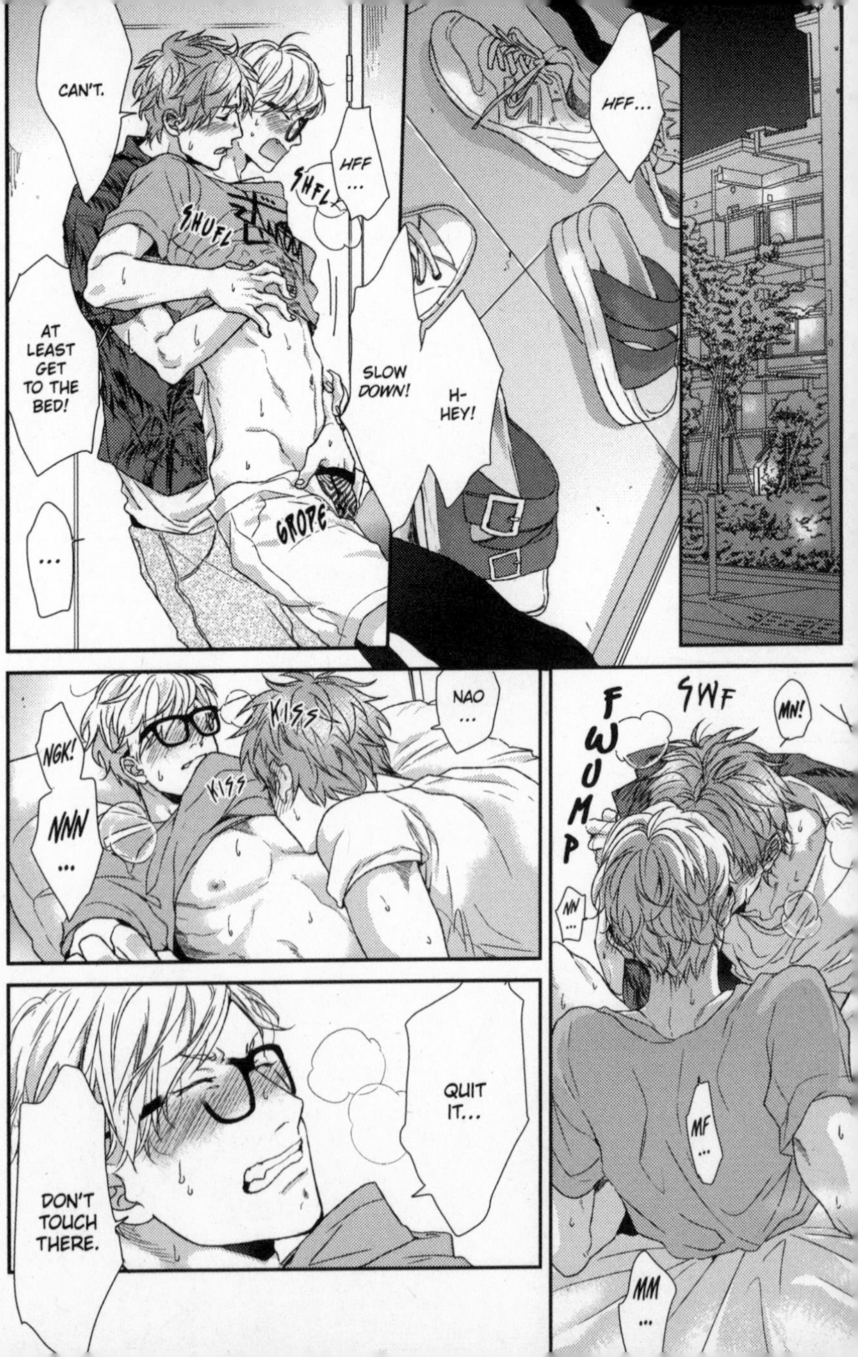
HFF...
H-
HEY!
SLOW DOWN!
HFF ...
SHFL
CAN'T.
SHUFL
AT LEAST GET TO THE BED!
GROPE
...
SWF
MN!
FWUMP
NN ...
MF ...
MM ...
NAO ...
KISS
KISS
NGK!
NNN ...
QUIT IT...
DON'T TOUCH THERE.

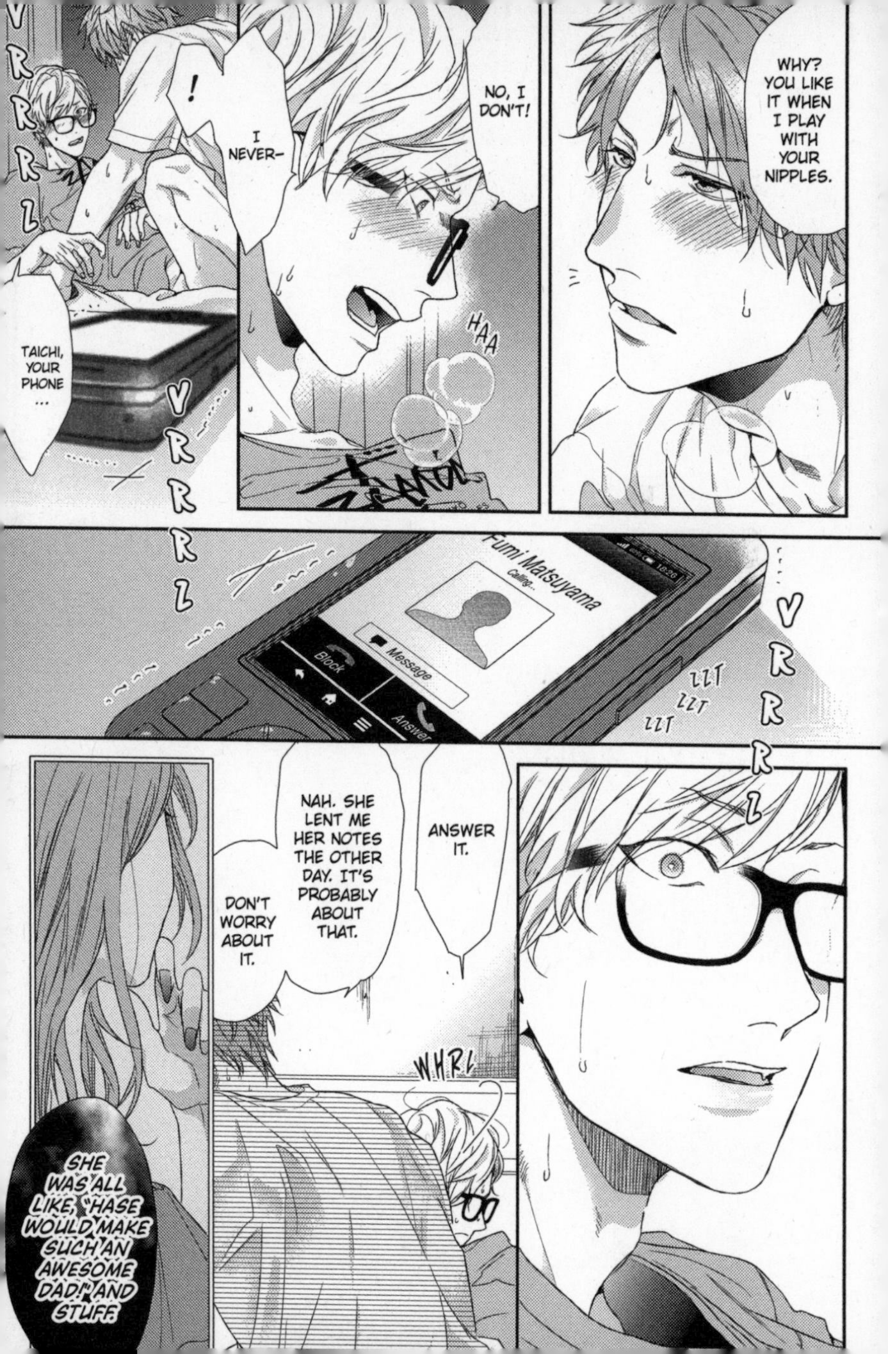
WHY? YOU LIKE IT WHEN I PLAY WITH YOUR NIPPLES.
NO, I DON'T!
I NEVER—
HAA
!
VRRRZ
TAICHI, YOUR PHONE ...
VRRRZ
Fumi Matsuyama
Calling...
Block
Message
Answer
VRRRZ
ZZT
ZZT
ZZT
ANSWER IT.
NAH. SHE LENT ME HER NOTES THE OTHER DAY. IT'S PROBABLY ABOUT THAT.
DON'T WORRY ABOUT IT.
WHRL
SHE WAS ALL LIKE, "HASE WOULD MAKE SUCH AN AWESOME DAD!" AND STUFF.

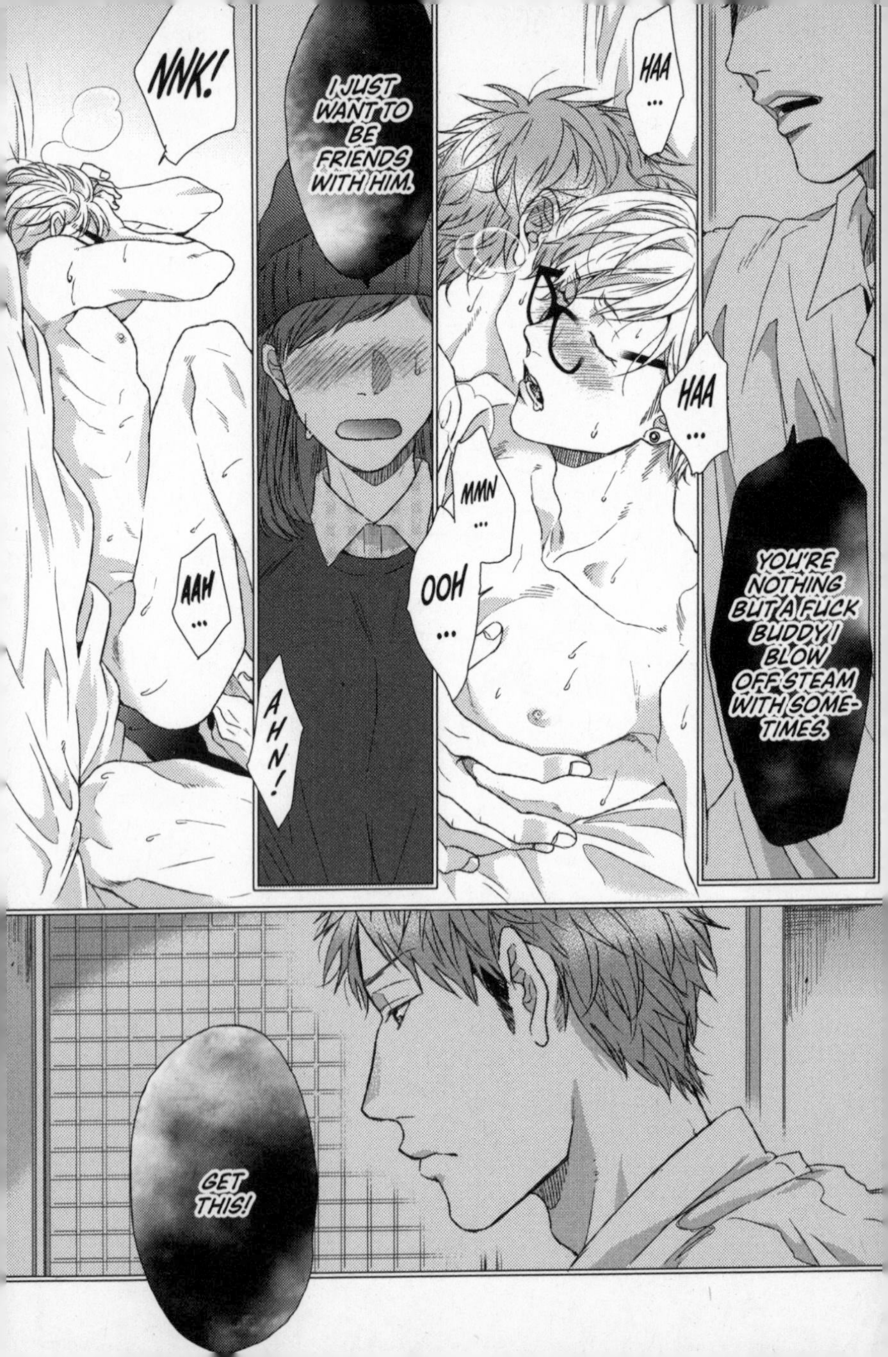
YOU'RE NOTHING BUT A FUCK BUDDY I BLOW OFF STEAM WITH SOME-TIMES.
HAA ...
HAA ...
MMN ...
OOH ...
I JUST WANT TO BE FRIENDS WITH HIM.
AHN!
NNK!
AAH ...
GET THIS!

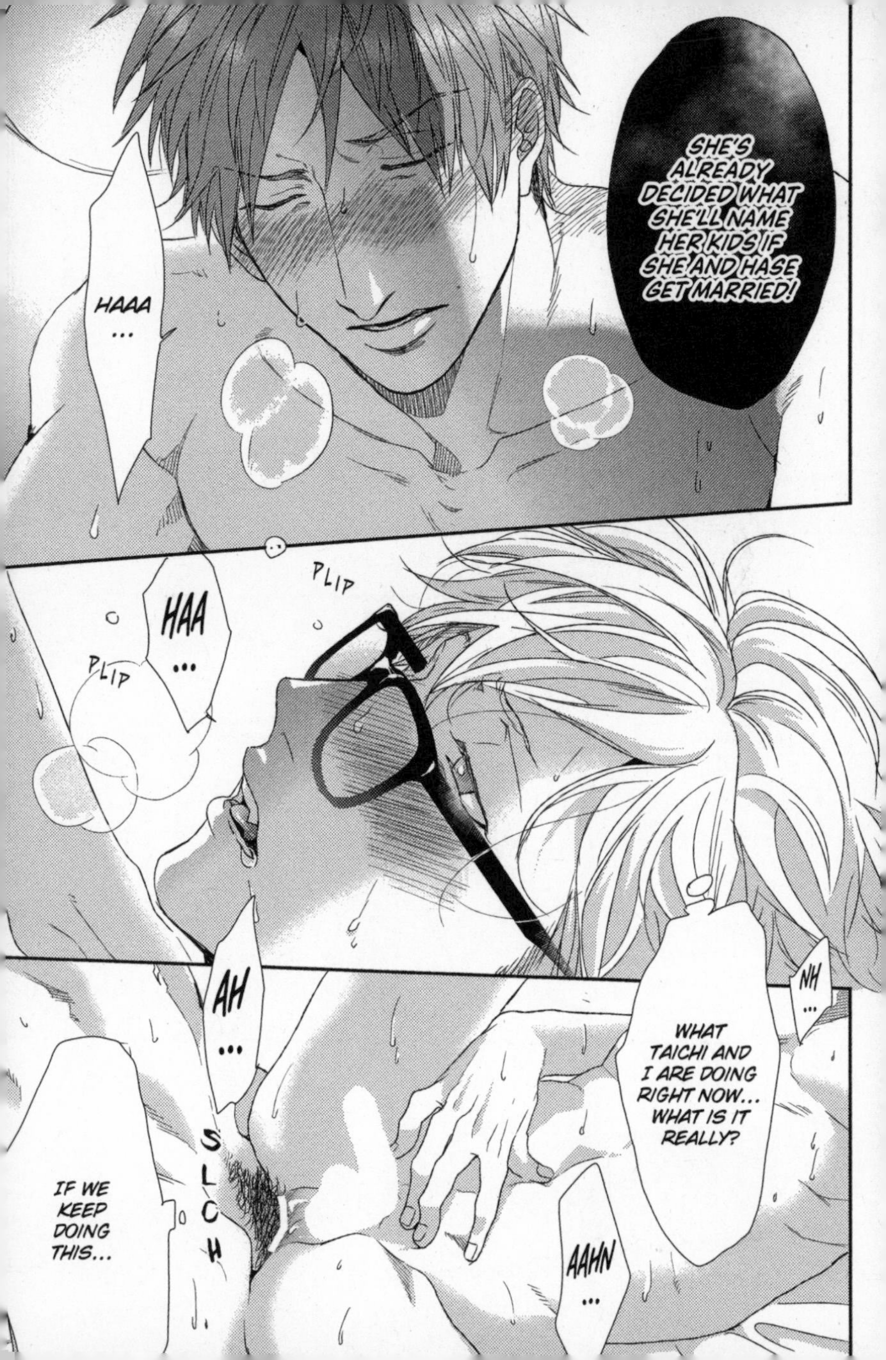
SHE'S ALREADY DECIDED WHAT SHE'LL NAME HER KIDS IF SHE AND HASE GET MARRIED!
HAAA...
PLIP
HAA...
PLIP
NH...
WHAT TAICHI AND I ARE DOING RIGHT NOW... WHAT IS IT REALLY?
AAHN...
AH...
SLCH
IF WE KEEP DOING THIS...

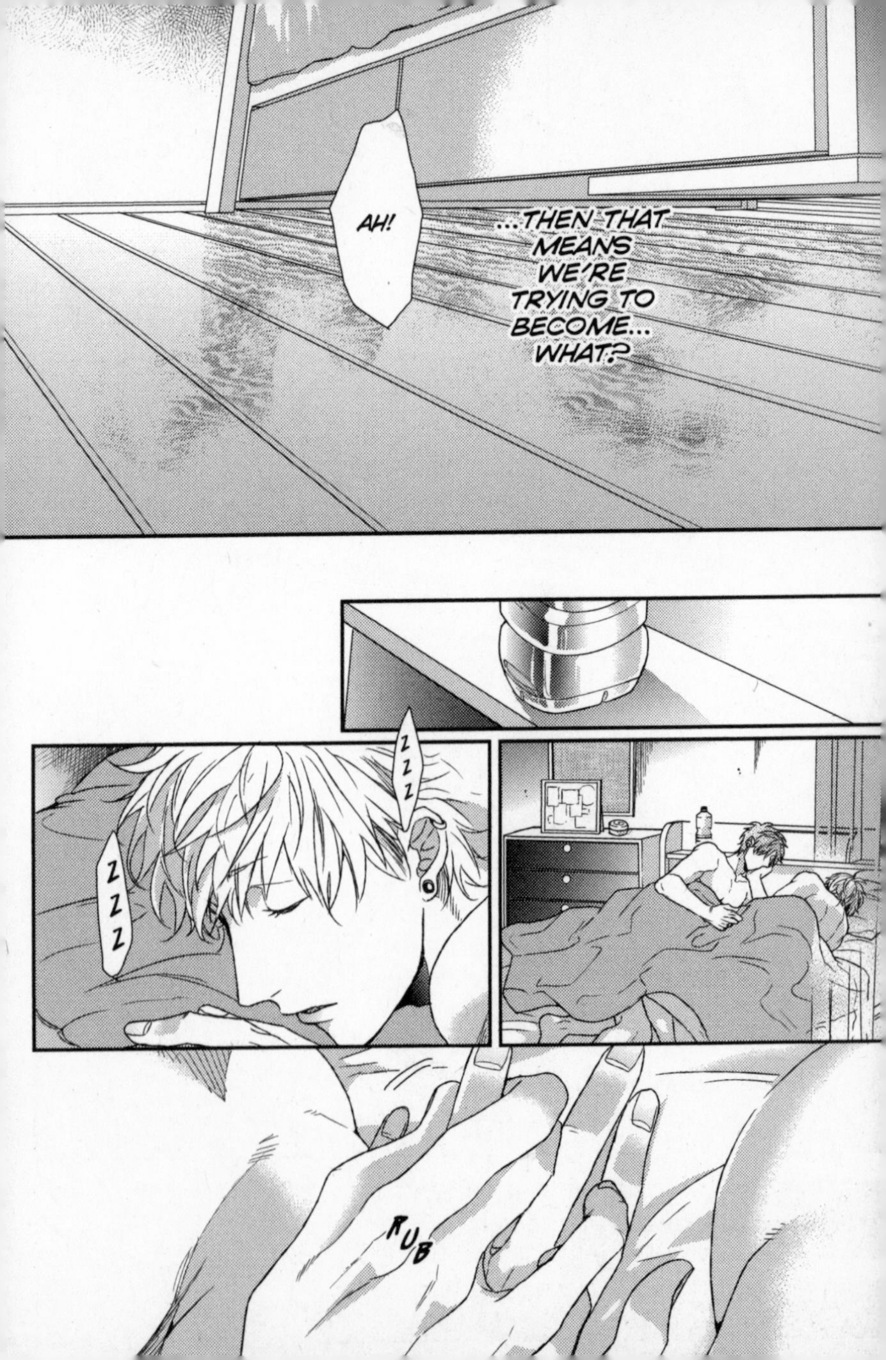
...THEN THAT MEANS WE'RE TRYING TO BECOME... WHAT?
AH!
ZZZ
ZZZ
RUB

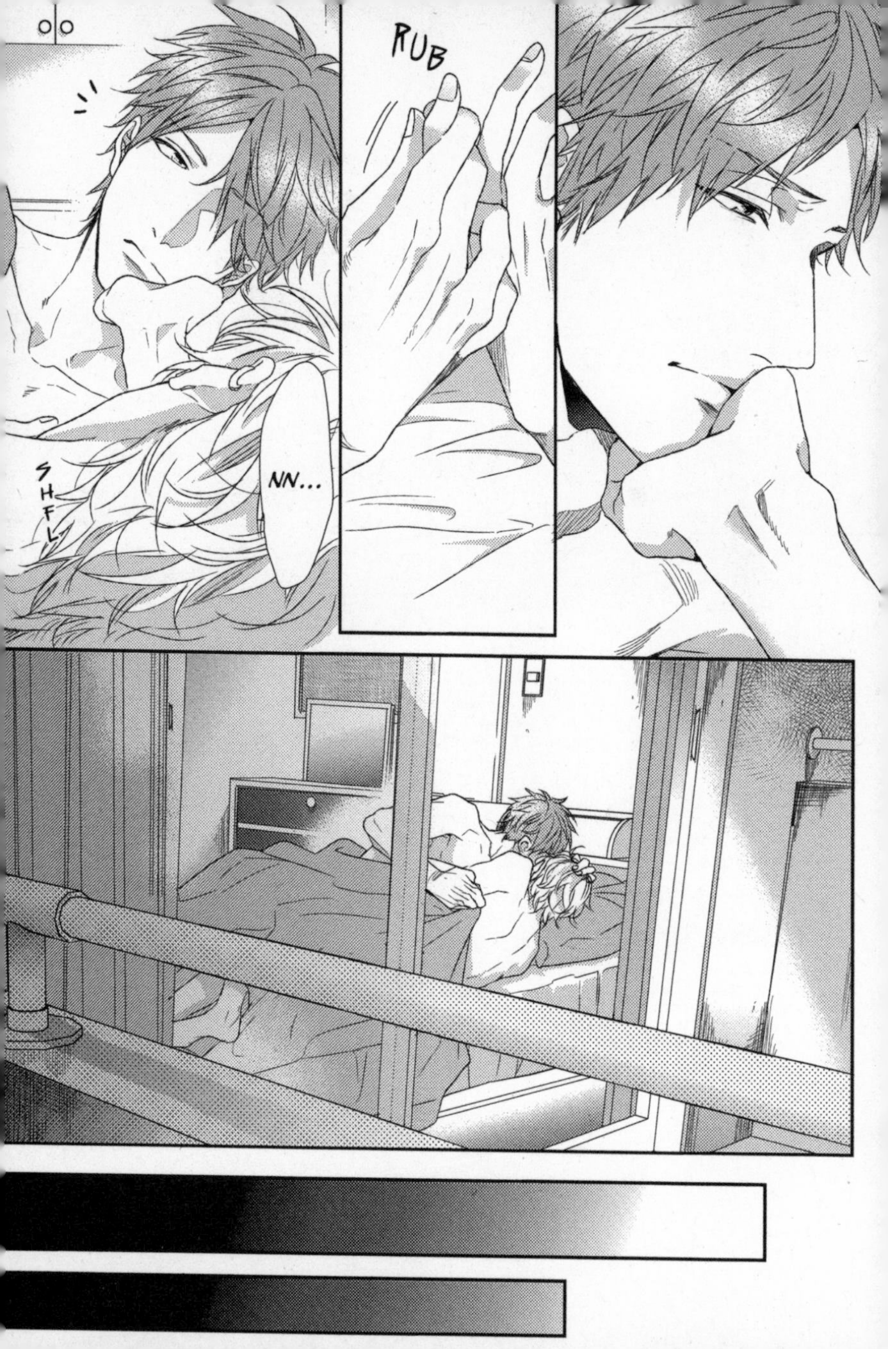
RUB
NN...
SHFL

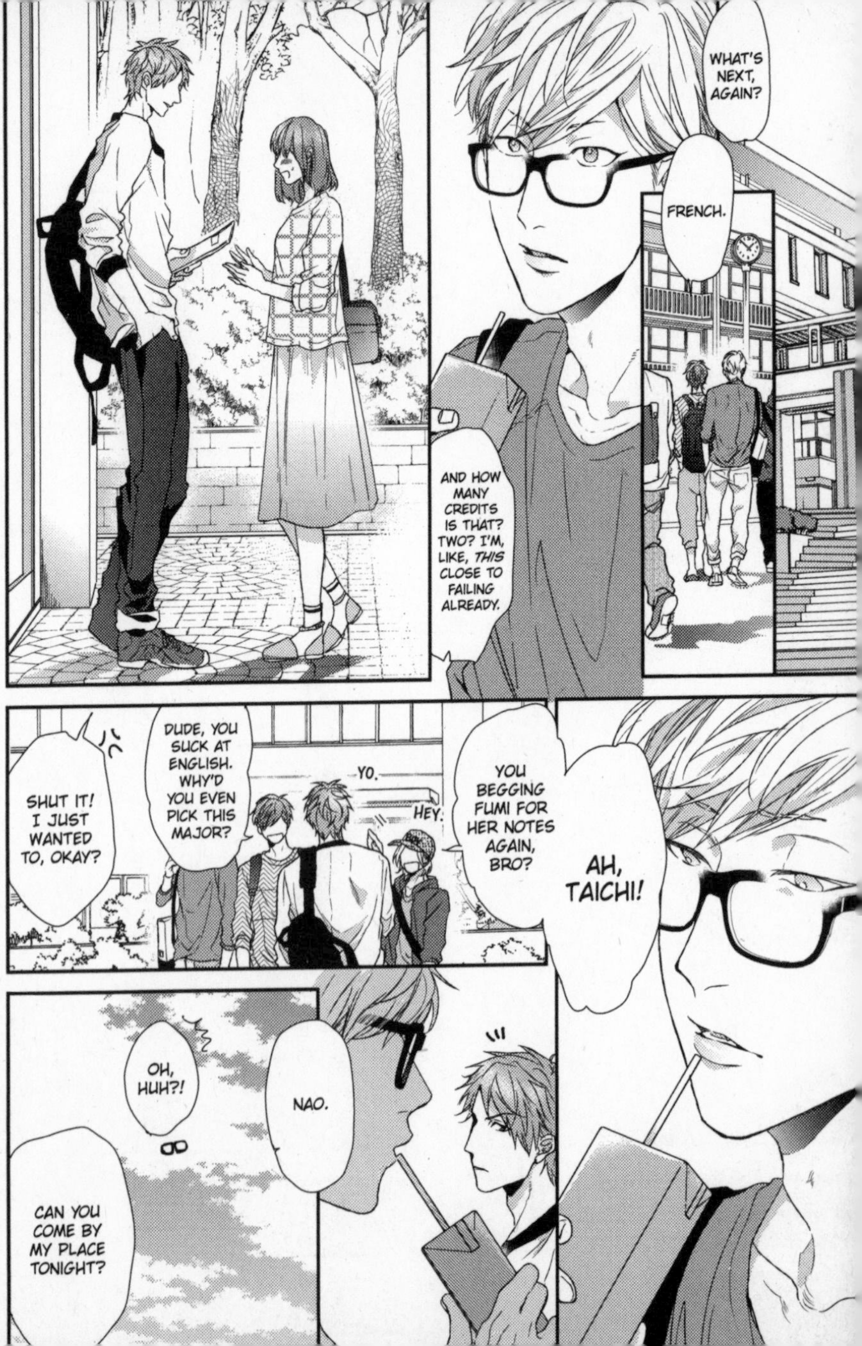
WHAT'S NEXT, AGAIN?
FRENCH.
AND HOW MANY CREDITS IS THAT? TWO? I'M, LIKE, *THIS* CLOSE TO FAILING ALREADY.
AH, TAICHI!
YO.
HEY.
YOU BEGGING FUMI FOR HER NOTES AGAIN, BRO?
DUDE, YOU SUCK AT ENGLISH. WHY'D YOU EVEN PICK THIS MAJOR?
SHUT IT! I JUST WANTED TO, OKAY?
NAO.
OH, HUH?!
CAN YOU COME BY MY PLACE TONIGHT?

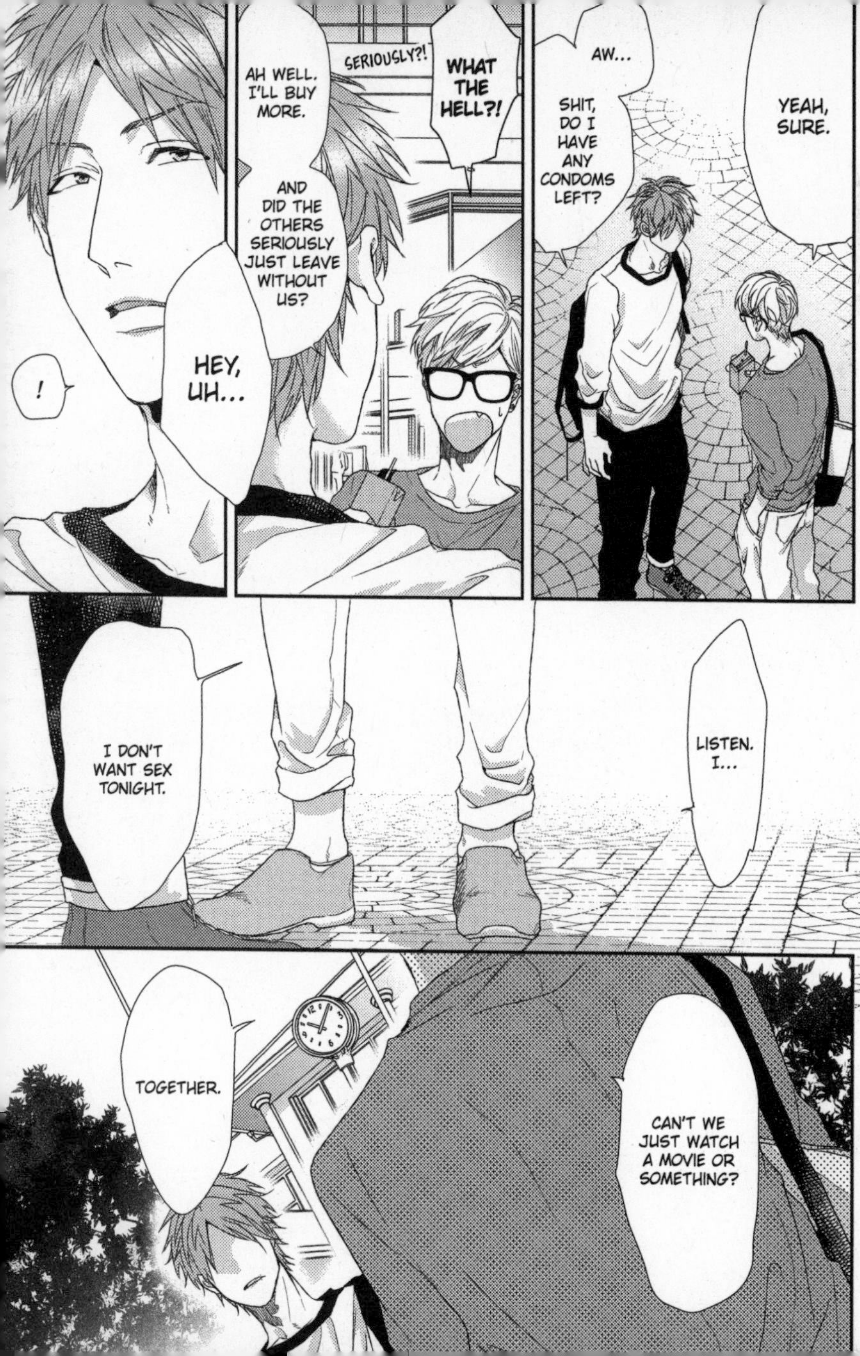
YEAH, SURE.
AW...
SHIT, DO I HAVE ANY CONDOMS LEFT?
WHAT THE HELL?!
SERIOUSLY?!
AH WELL. I'LL BUY MORE.
AND DID THE OTHERS SERIOUSLY JUST LEAVE WITHOUT US?
HEY, UH...
!
LISTEN. I...
I DON'T WANT SEX TONIGHT.
CAN'T WE JUST WATCH A MOVIE OR SOMETHING?
TOGETHER.

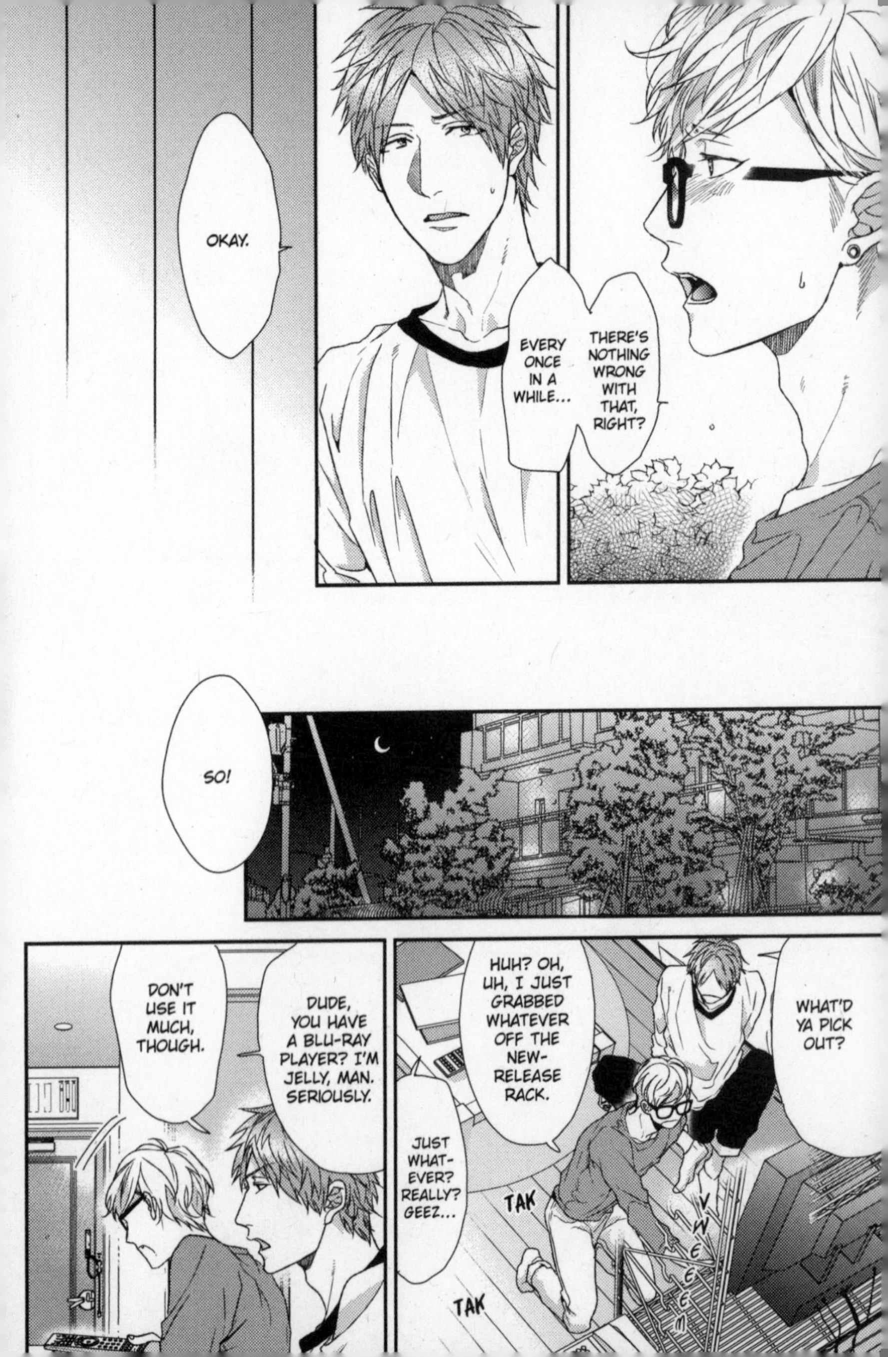
THERE'S NOTHING WRONG WITH THAT, RIGHT?
EVERY ONCE IN A WHILE...
OKAY.
SO!
WHAT'D YA PICK OUT?
HUH? OH, UH, I JUST GRABBED WHATEVER OFF THE NEW-RELEASE RACK.
JUST WHAT-EVER? REALLY? GEEZ...
VWEEEEM
TAK
TAK
DUDE, YOU HAVE A BLU-RAY PLAYER? I'M JELLY, MAN. SERIOUSLY.
DON'T USE IT MUCH, THOUGH.

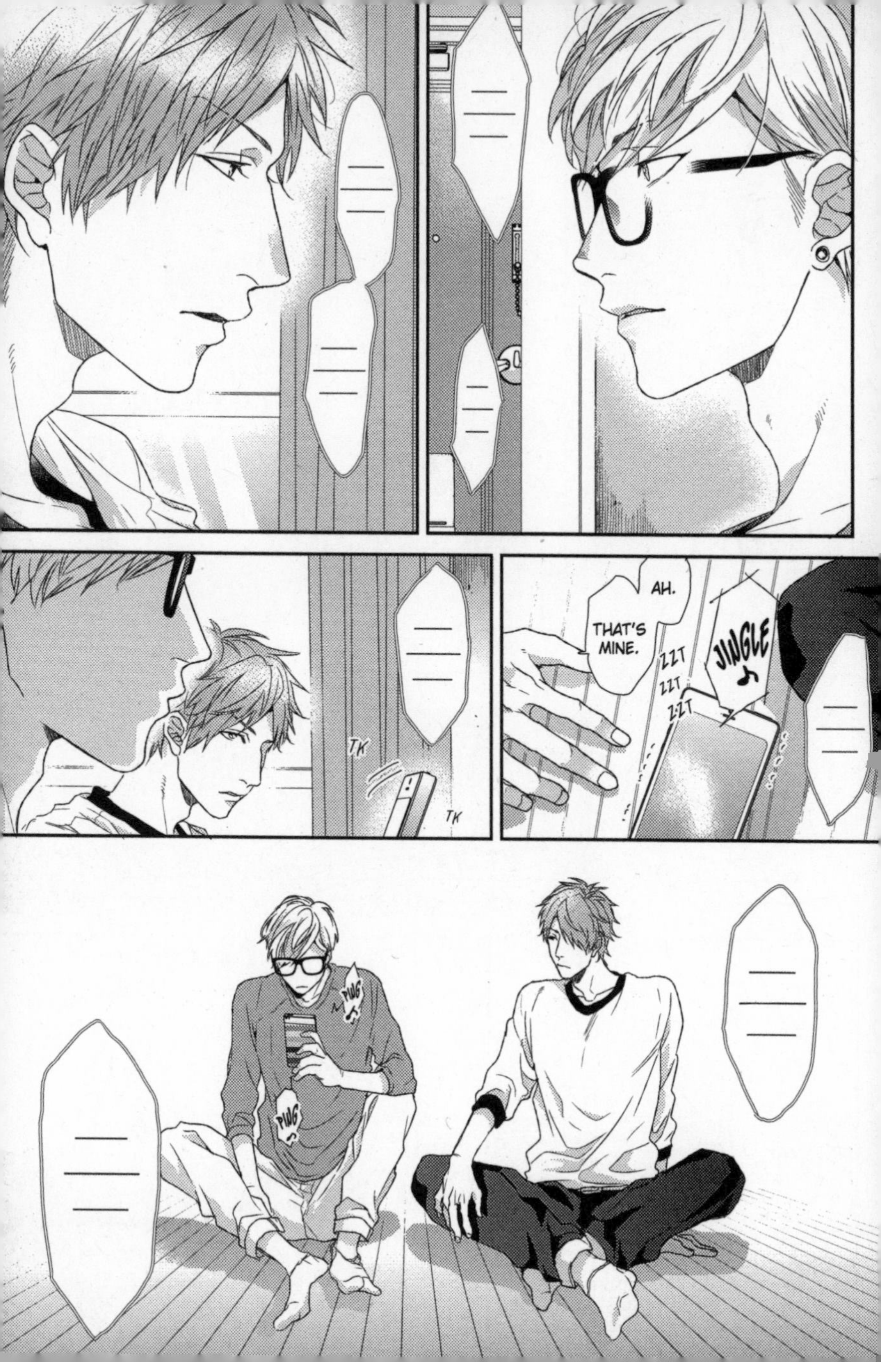
JINGLE ♪
AH.
THAT'S MINE.
ZZT
ZZT
ZZT
TK
TK
PLING
PLING

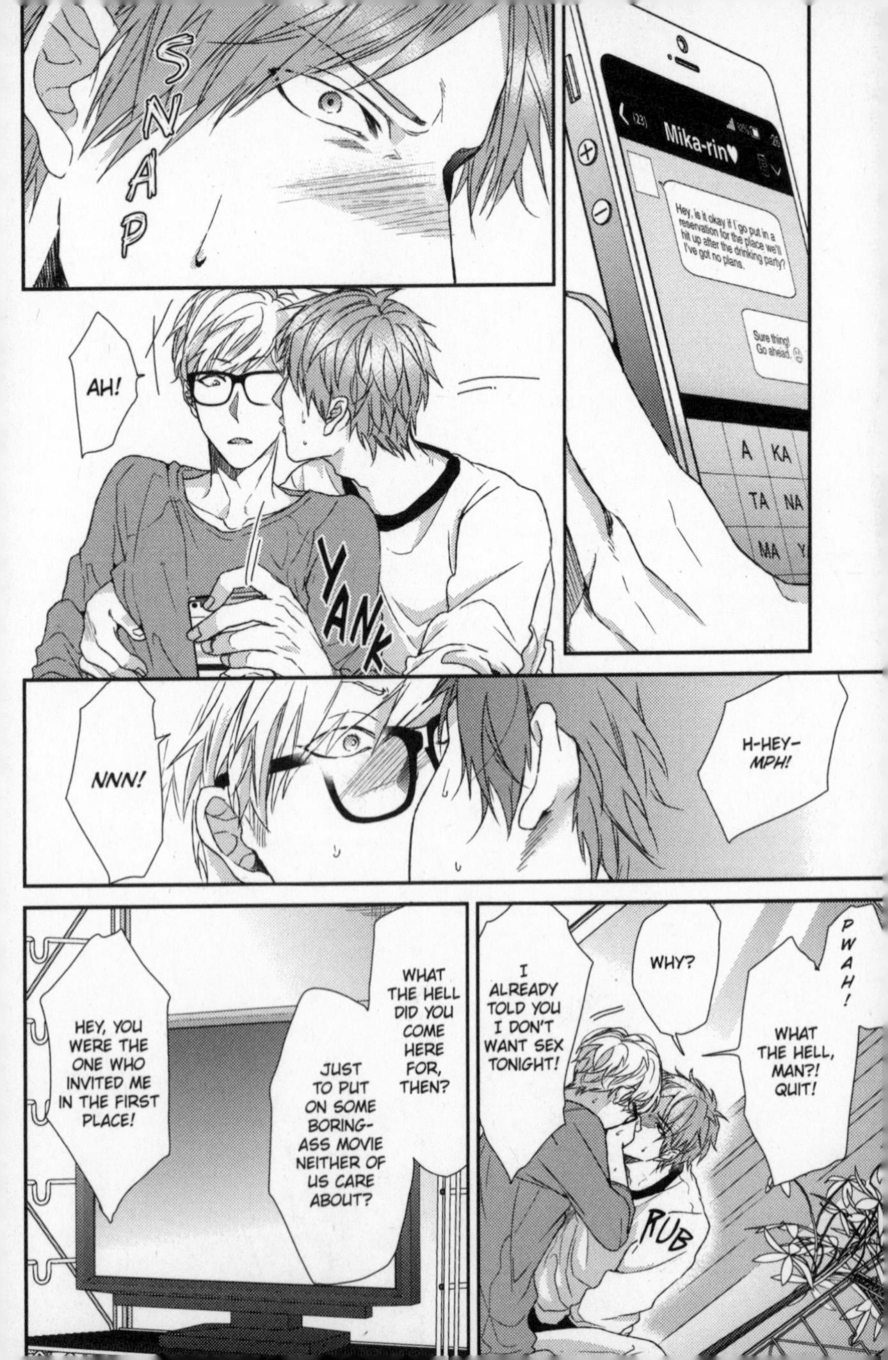

Mika-rin♥
Hey, is it okay if I go put in a reservation for the place we'll hit up after the drinking party? I've got no plans.
Sure thing! Go ahead.
A KA
TA NA
MA
SNAP
AH!
YANK
H-HEY- MPH!
NNN!
PWAH!
WHAT THE HELL, MAN?! QUIT!
WHY?
I ALREADY TOLD YOU I DON'T WANT SEX TONIGHT!
RUB
WHAT THE HELL DID YOU COME HERE FOR, THEN?
JUST TO PUT ON SOME BORING-ASS MOVIE NEITHER OF US CARE ABOUT?
HEY, YOU WERE THE ONE WHO INVITED ME IN THE FIRST PLACE!

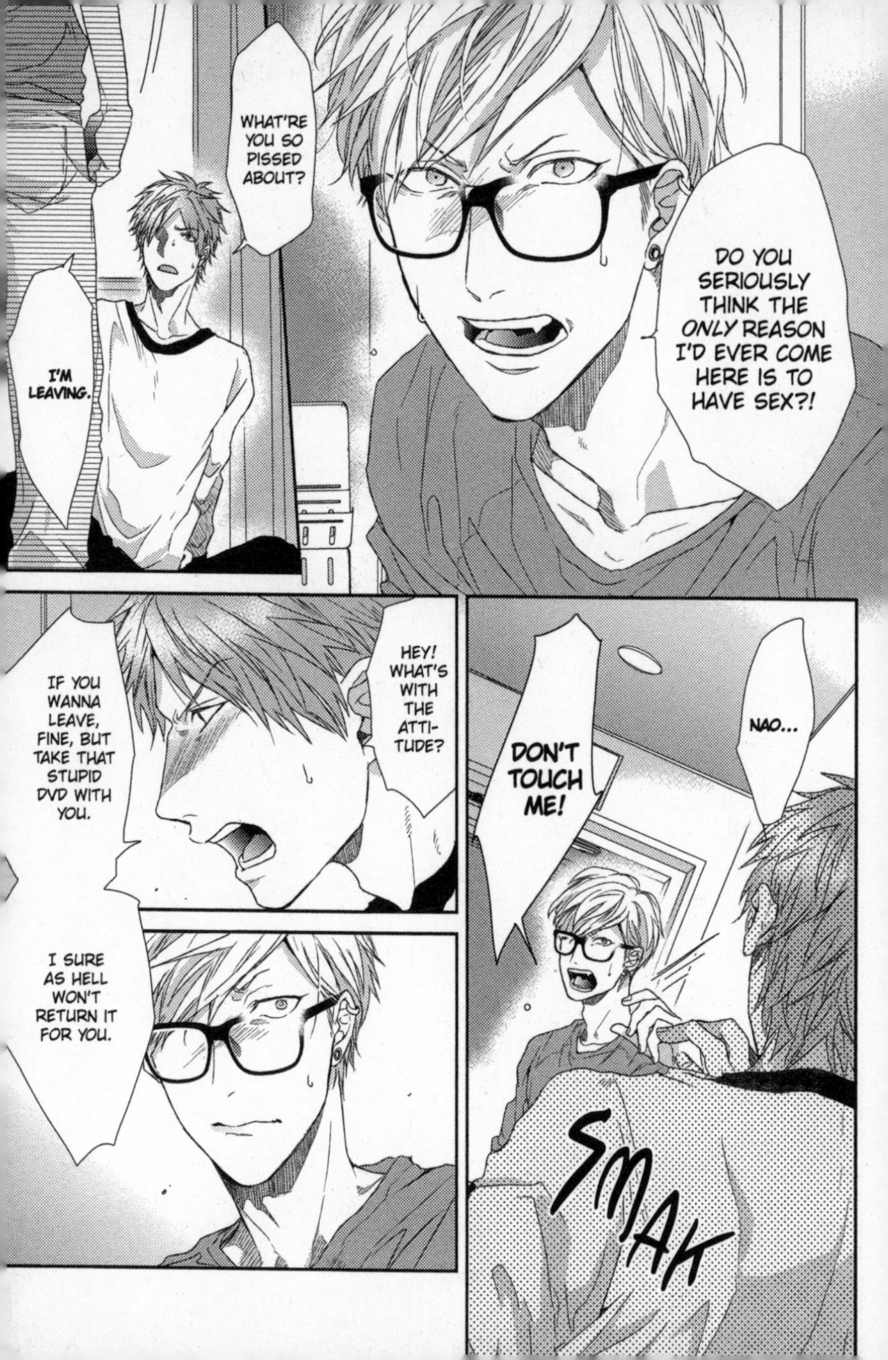
DO YOU SERIOUSLY THINK THE *ONLY* REASON I'D EVER COME HERE IS TO HAVE SEX?!
WHAT'RE YOU SO PISSED ABOUT?
I'M LEAVING.
NAO...
DON'T TOUCH ME!
SMAK
HEY! WHAT'S WITH THE ATTI-TUDE?
IF YOU WANNA LEAVE, FINE, BUT TAKE THAT STUPID DVD WITH YOU.
I SURE AS HELL WON'T RETURN IT FOR YOU.

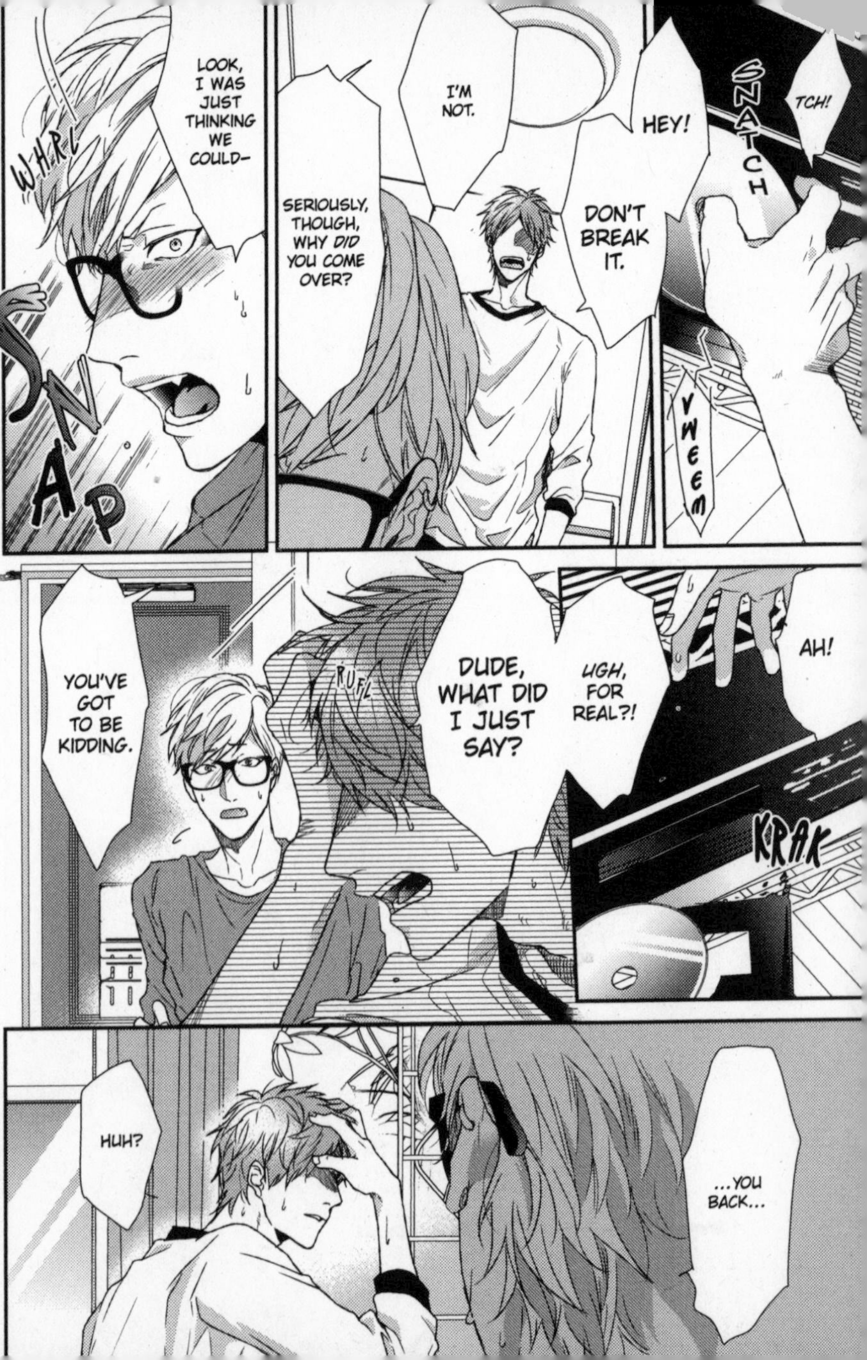
TCH!
SNATCH
HEY!
DON'T BREAK IT.
VWEEM
I'M NOT.
SERIOUSLY, THOUGH, WHY *DID* YOU COME OVER?
LOOK, I WAS JUST THINKING WE COULD–
WHRL
SNAP
AH!
UGH, FOR REAL?!
KRAK
DUDE, WHAT DID I JUST SAY?
RUFL
YOU'VE GOT TO BE KIDDING.
...YOU BACK...
HUH?

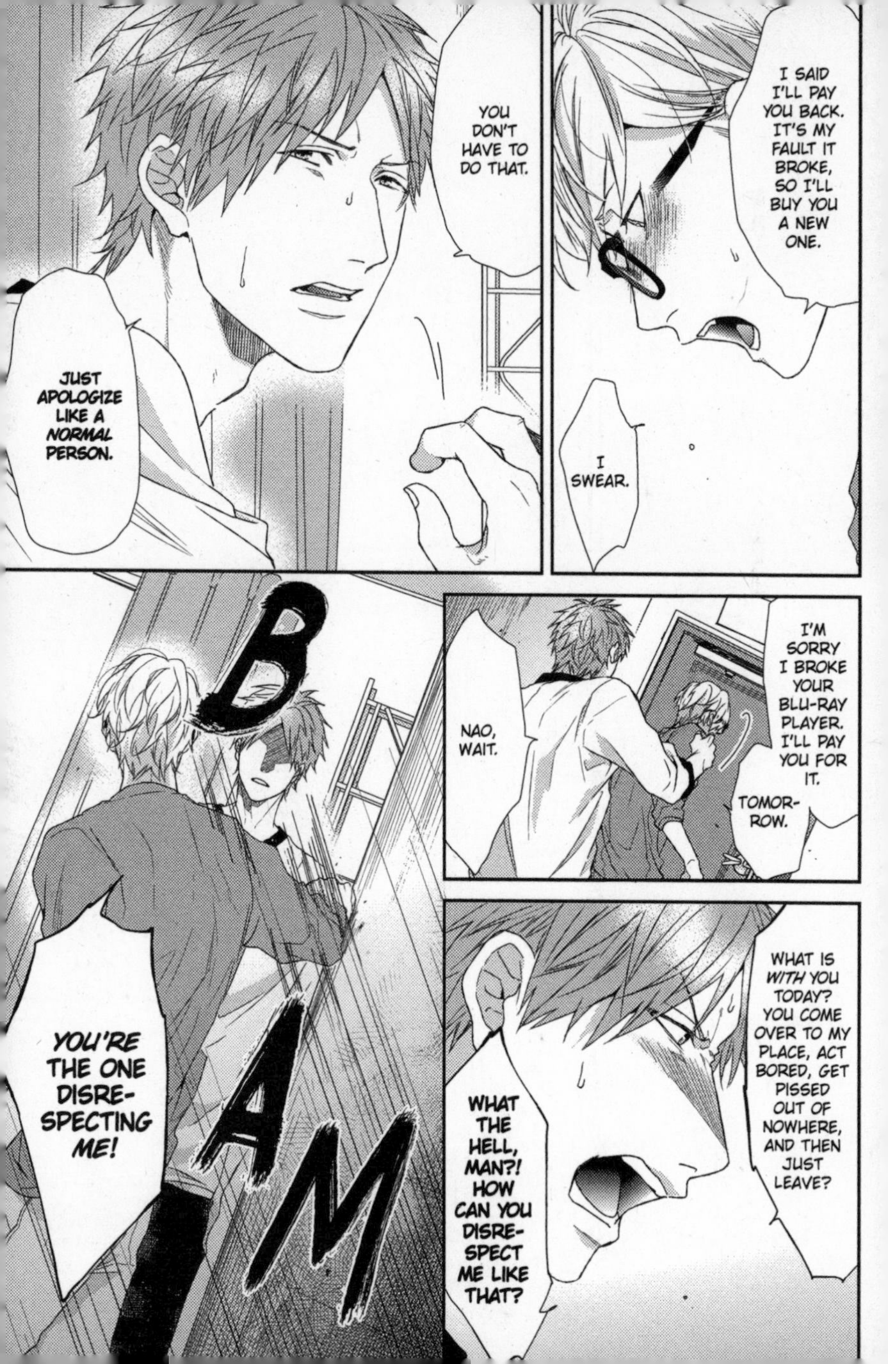
I SAID I'LL PAY YOU BACK. IT'S MY FAULT IT BROKE, SO I'LL BUY YOU A NEW ONE.
I SWEAR.
YOU DON'T HAVE TO DO THAT.
JUST APOLOGIZE LIKE A *NORMAL* PERSON.
I'M SORRY I BROKE YOUR BLU-RAY PLAYER. I'LL PAY YOU FOR IT.
TOMOR-ROW.
NAO, WAIT.
WHAT IS *WITH* YOU TODAY? YOU COME OVER TO MY PLACE, ACT BORED, GET PISSED OUT OF NOWHERE, AND THEN JUST LEAVE?
WHAT THE HELL, MAN?! HOW CAN YOU DISRE-SPECT ME LIKE THAT?
YOU'RE THE ONE DISRE-SPECTING *ME!*
BAM

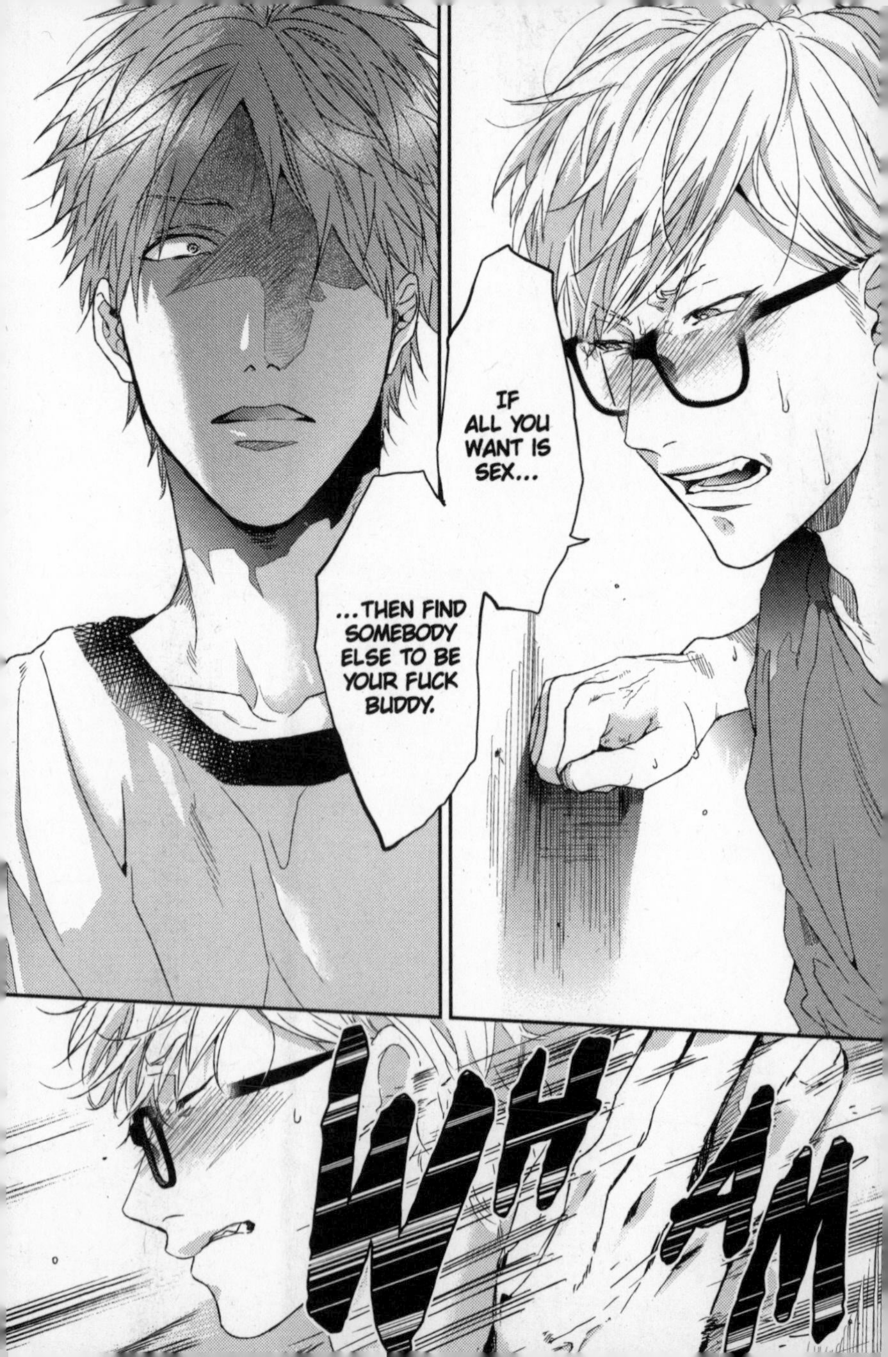
IF ALL YOU WANT IS SEX...
...THEN FIND SOMEBODY ELSE TO BE YOUR FUCK BUDDY.
WHAM

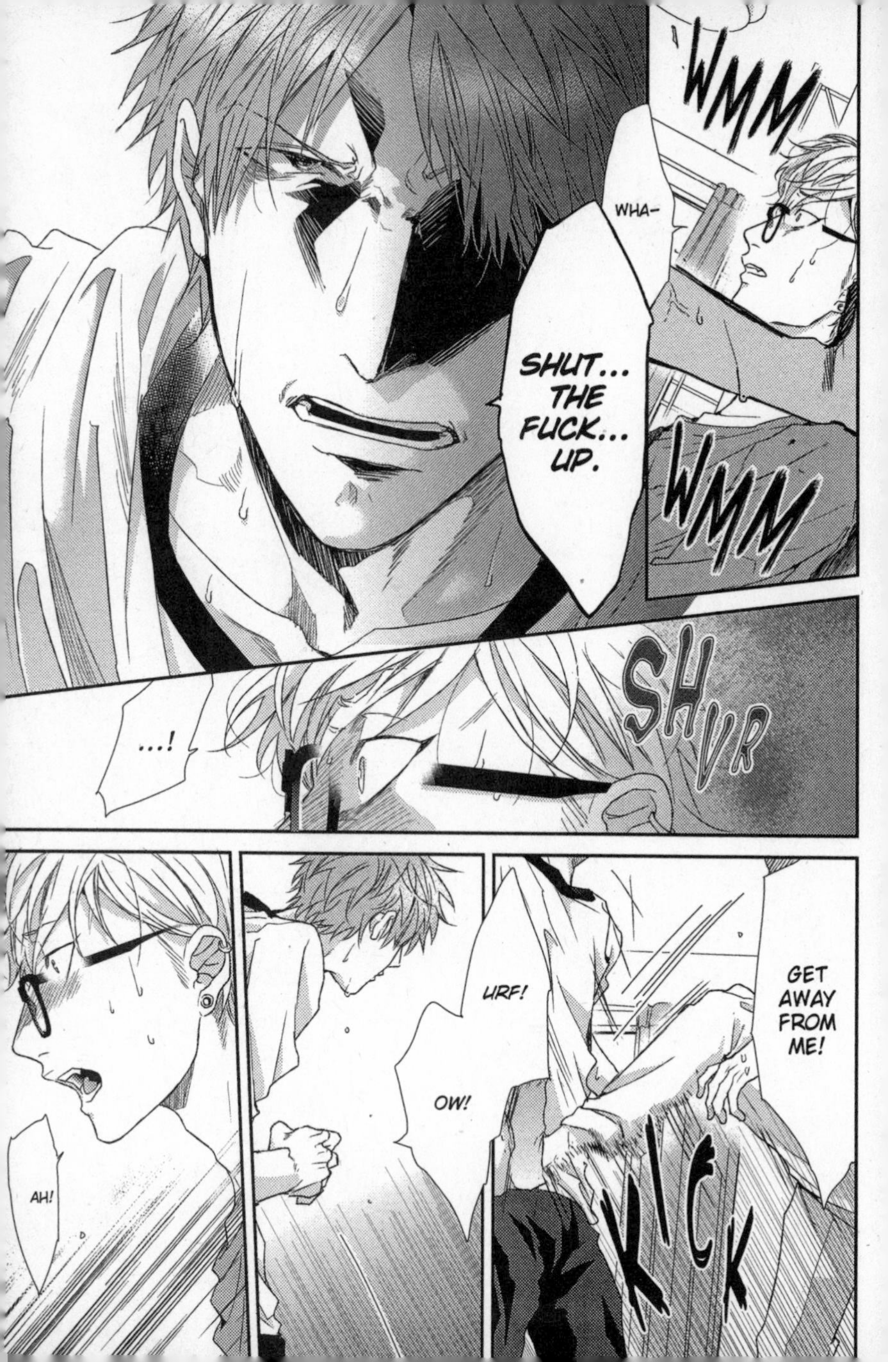
WMM
WHA-
WMM
SHUT... THE FUCK... UP.
SHVR
...!
GET AWAY FROM ME!
KICK
URF!
OW!
AH!

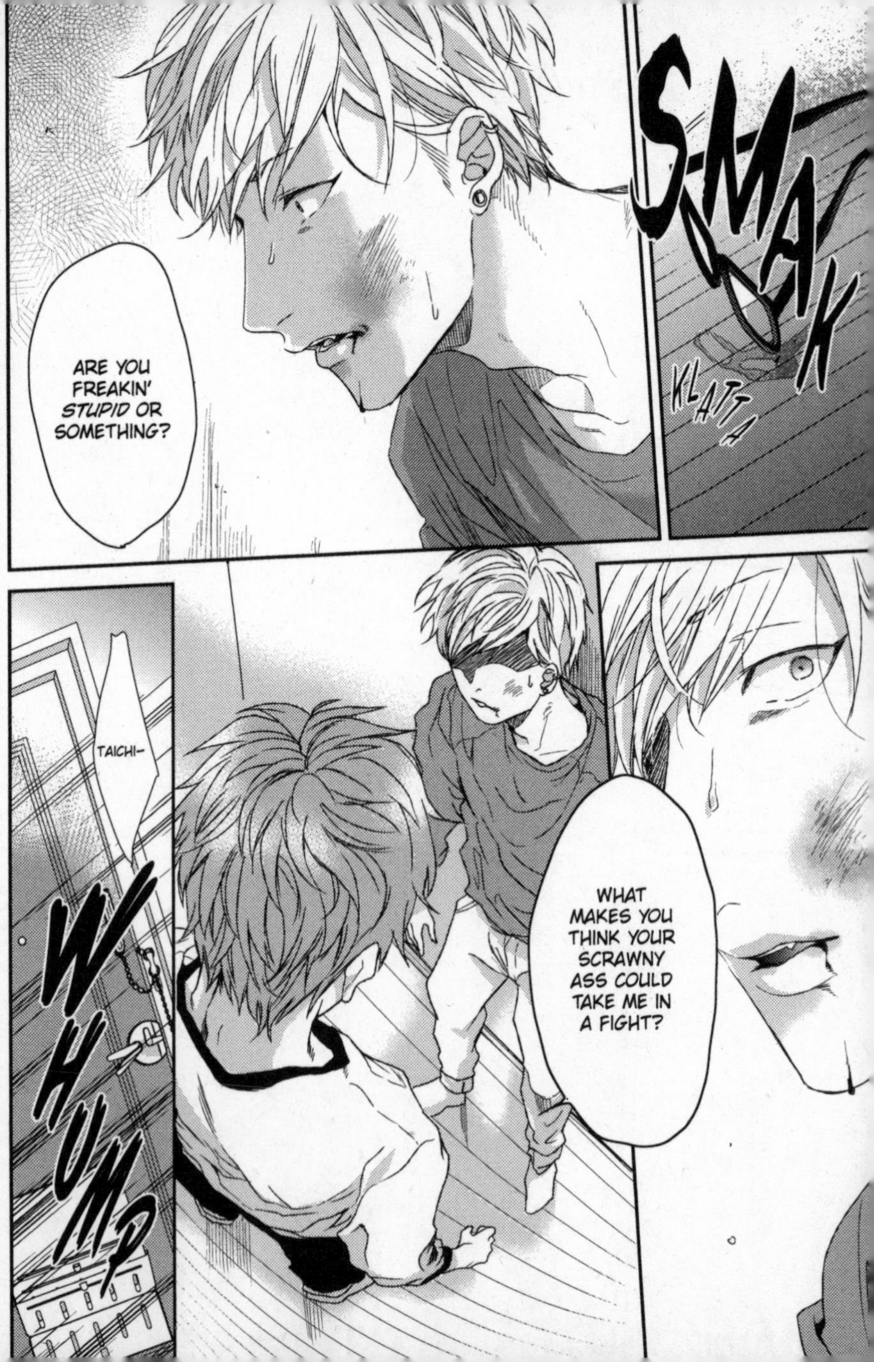
SMAK
KLATTA
ARE YOU FREAKIN' *STUPID* OR SOMETHING?
WHAT MAKES YOU THINK YOUR SCRAWNY ASS COULD TAKE ME IN A FIGHT?
TAICHI-
WHUMP

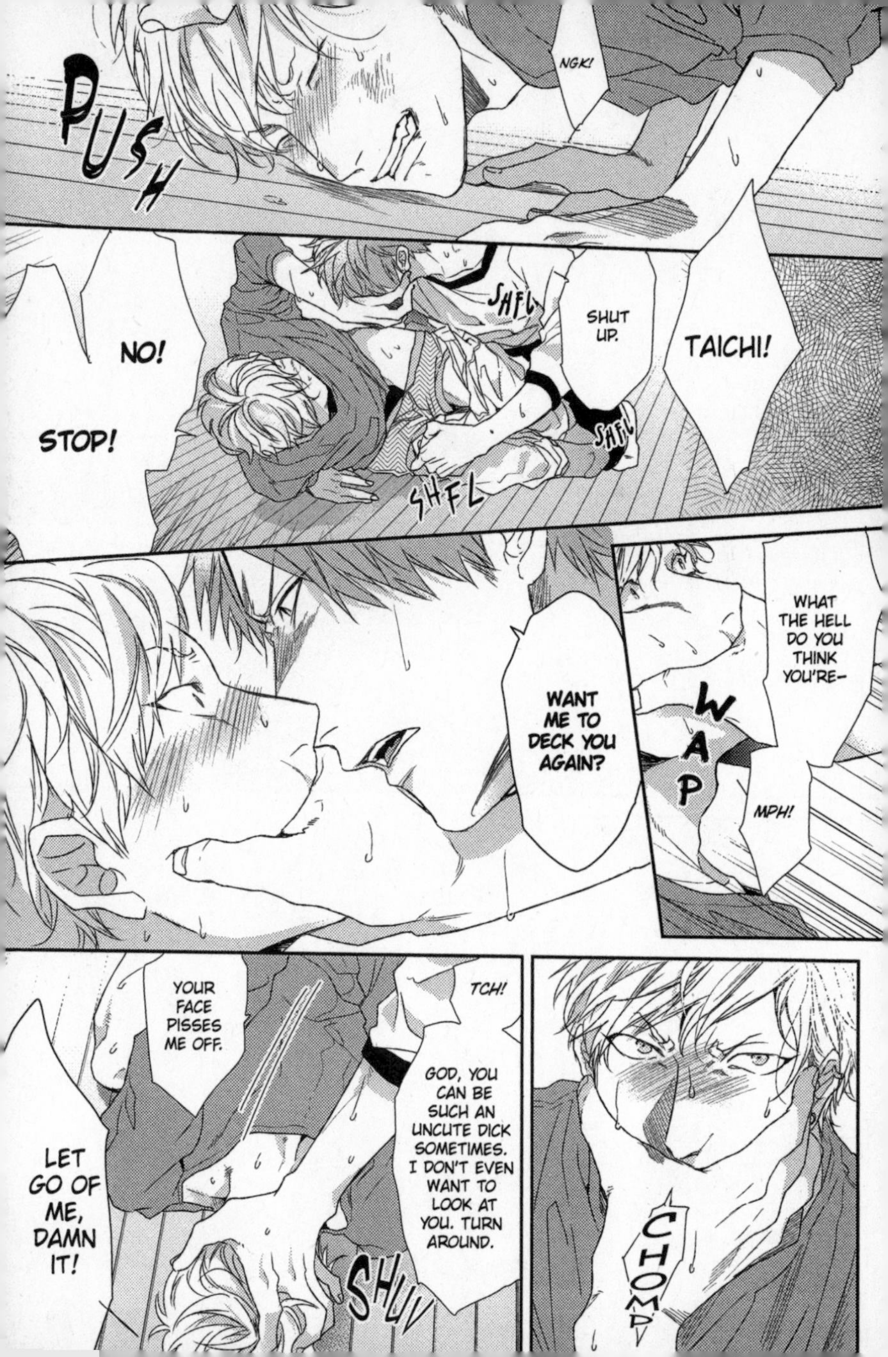
NGK!
PUSH
TAICHI!
SHUT UP.
SHFL
SHFL
SHFL
NO!
STOP!
WHAT THE HELL DO YOU THINK YOU'RE-
WAP
MPH!
WANT ME TO DECK YOU AGAIN?
CHOMP
TCH!
YOUR FACE PISSES ME OFF.
GOD, YOU CAN BE SUCH AN UNCUTE DICK SOMETIMES. I DON'T EVEN WANT TO LOOK AT YOU. TURN AROUND.
LET GO OF ME, DAMN IT!
SHUV

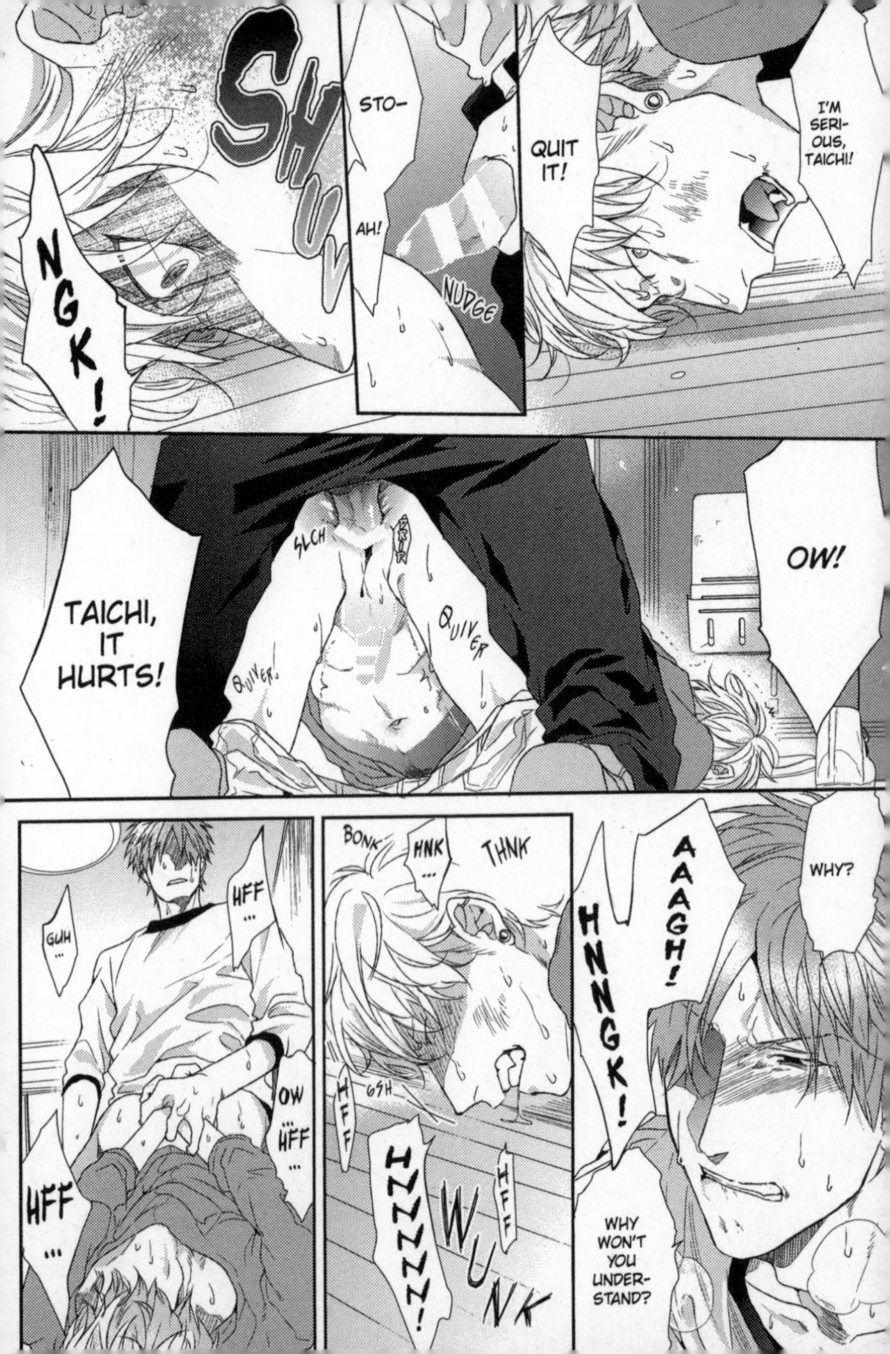

I'M SERI-OUS, TAICHI!
QUIT IT!
STO–
AH!
NUDGE
SHUU
NGK!
OW!
SLCH
DRIP
QUIVER
QUIVER
TAICHI, IT HURTS!
WHY?
AAAGH!
HNNNGK!
WHY WON'T YOU UNDER-STAND?
THNK
HNK...
BONK
HFF
GSH
HNNNNN!
WUNK
HFF
HFF...
GUH...
OW... HFF...
HFF...

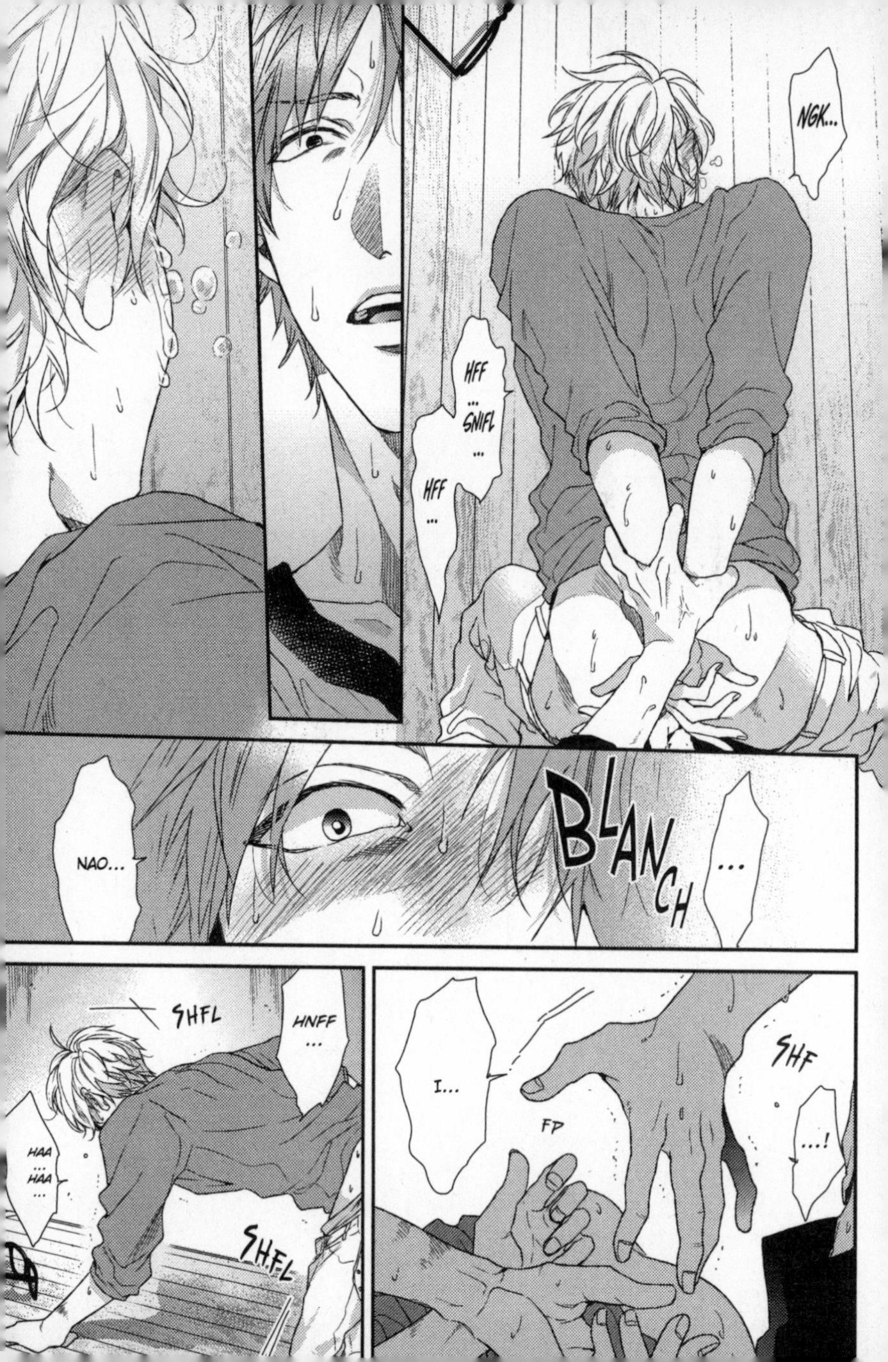
NGK...
HFF ... SNIFL ... HFF ...
...
BLANCH
NAO...
SHF
...!
I...
FP
HNFF ...
SHFL
HAA ... HAA ...
SHFL

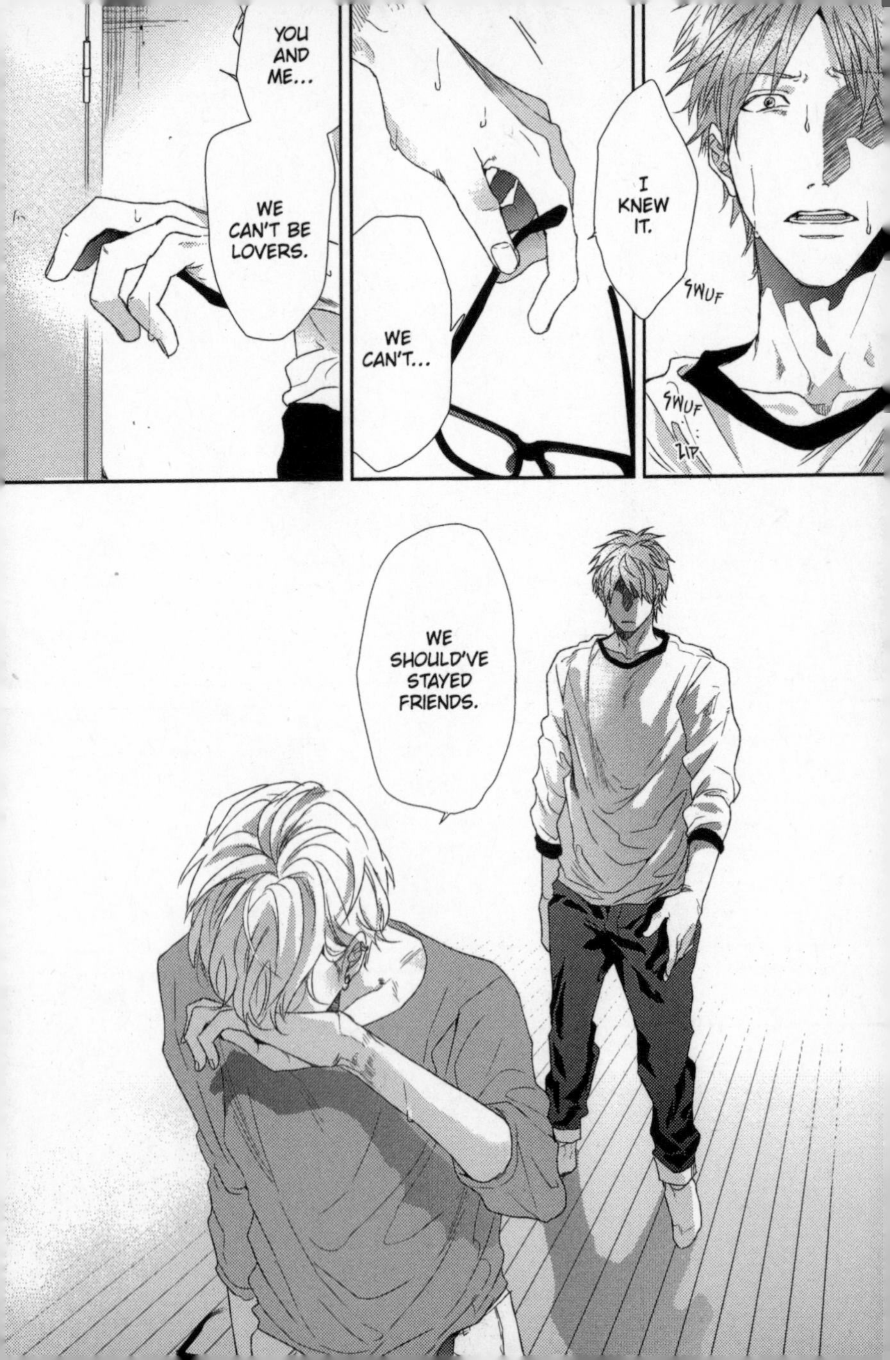

I KNEW IT.
SWUF
SWUF
ZIP
WE CAN'T...
YOU AND ME...
WE CAN'T BE LOVERS.
WE SHOULD'VE STAYED FRIENDS.

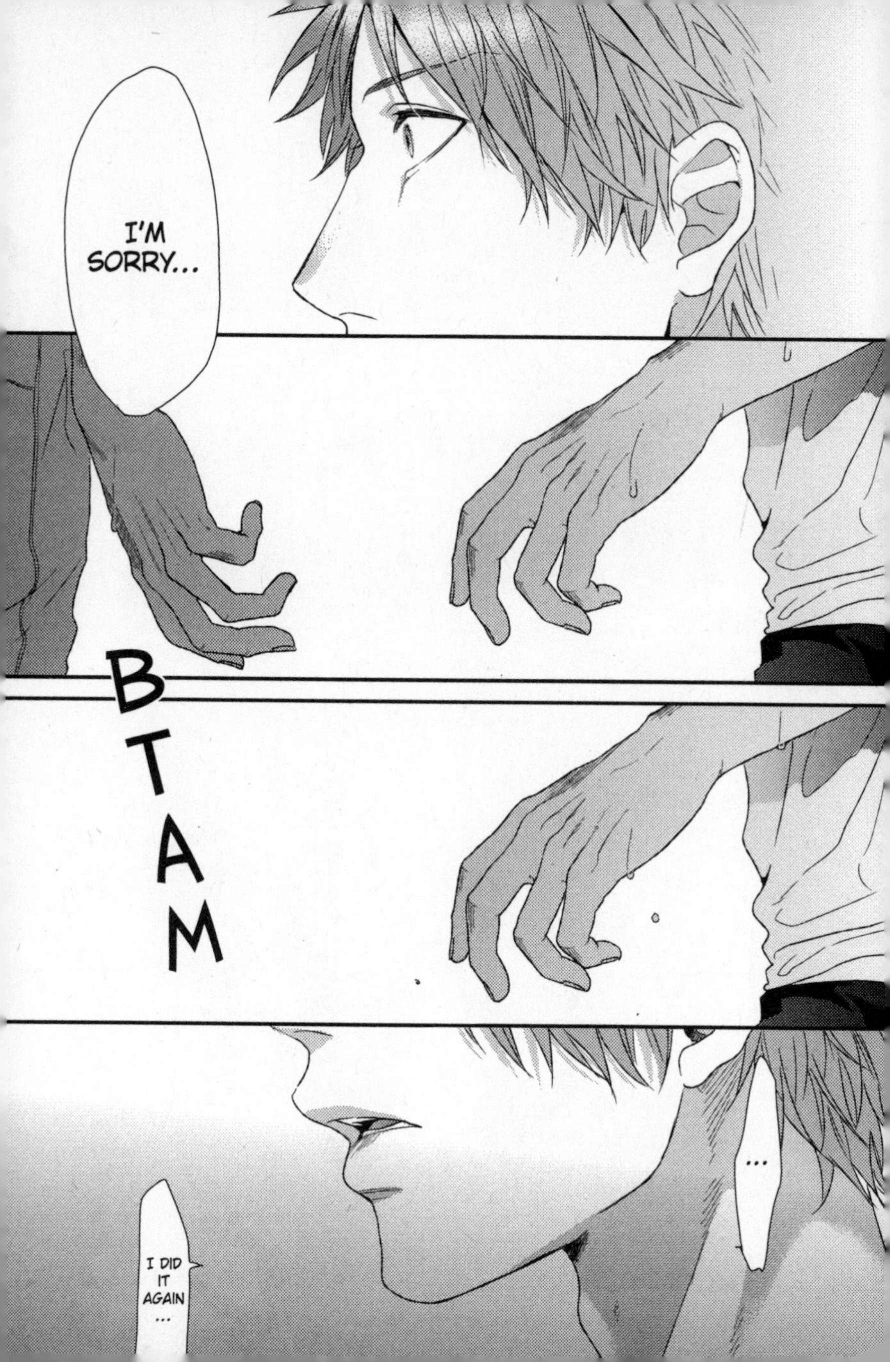
I'M SORRY...
BTAM
...
I DID IT AGAIN ...

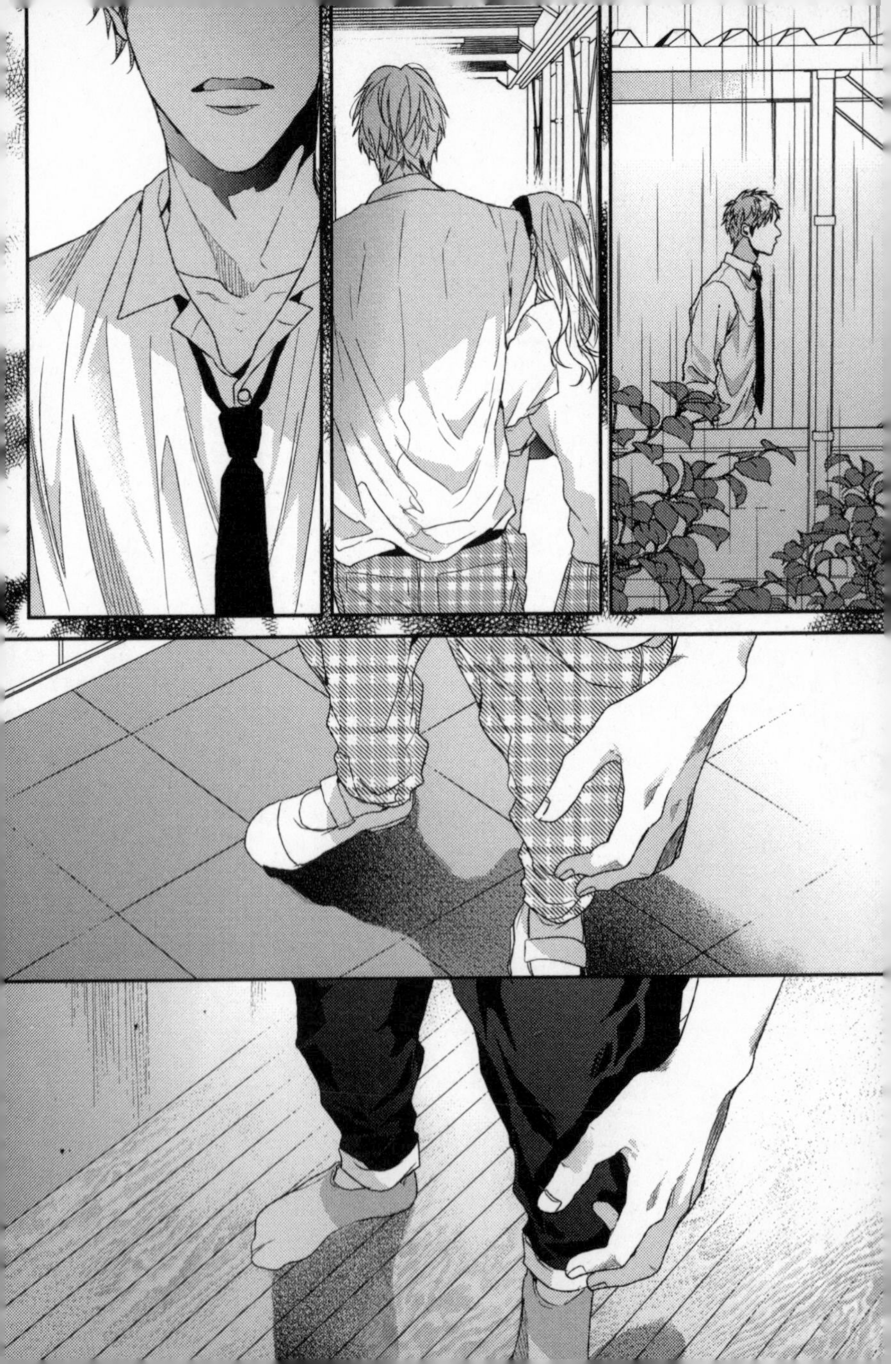

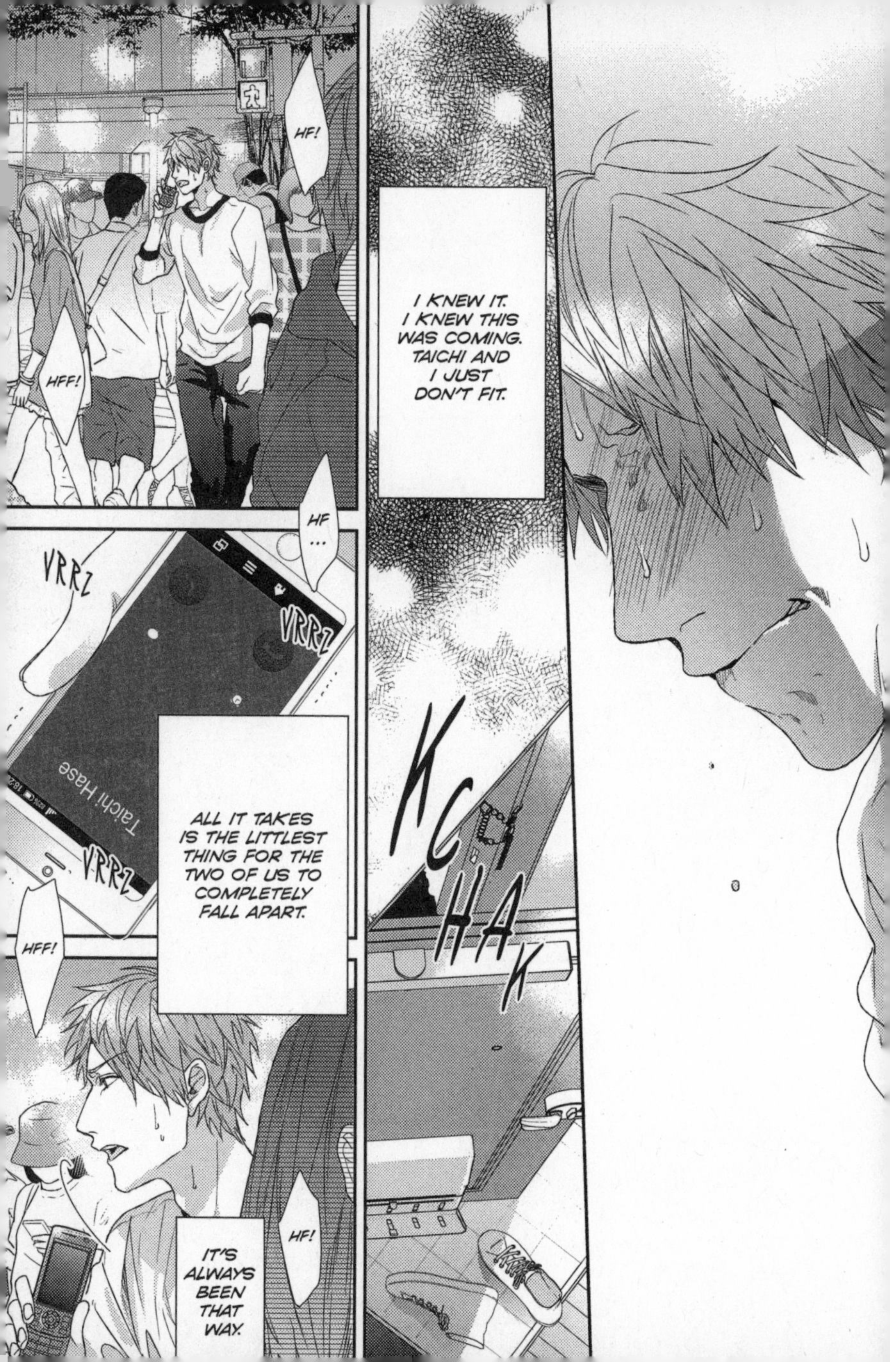
I KNEW IT. I KNEW THIS WAS COMING. TAICHI AND I JUST DON'T FIT.
KCHAK
HF!
HFF!
HF ...
VRRZ
VRRZ
Taichi Hase
VRRZ
ALL IT TAKES IS THE LITTLEST THING FOR THE TWO OF US TO COMPLETELY FALL APART.
HFF!
HF!
IT'S ALWAYS BEEN THAT WAY.

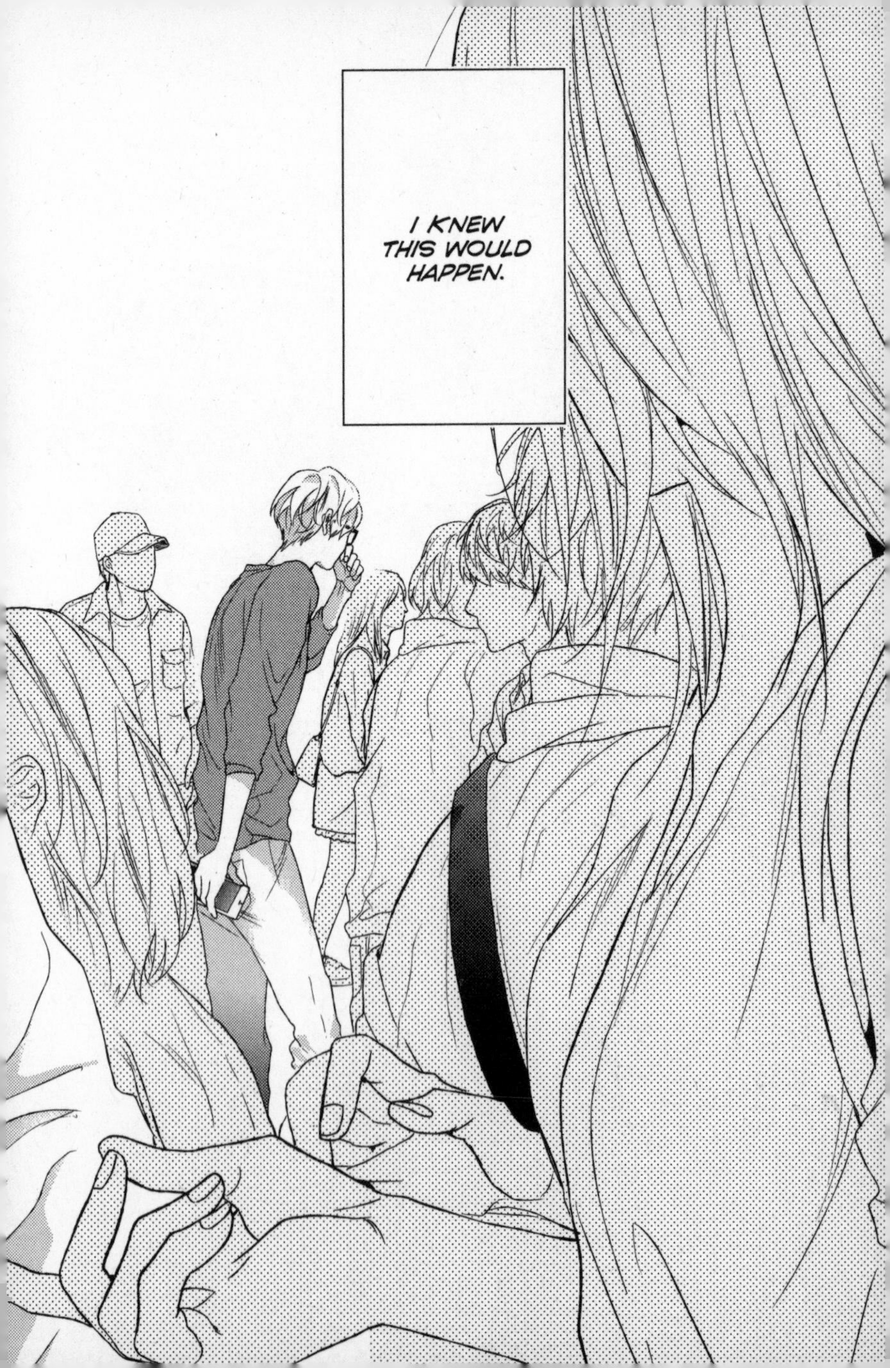
I KNEW THIS WOULD HAPPEN.

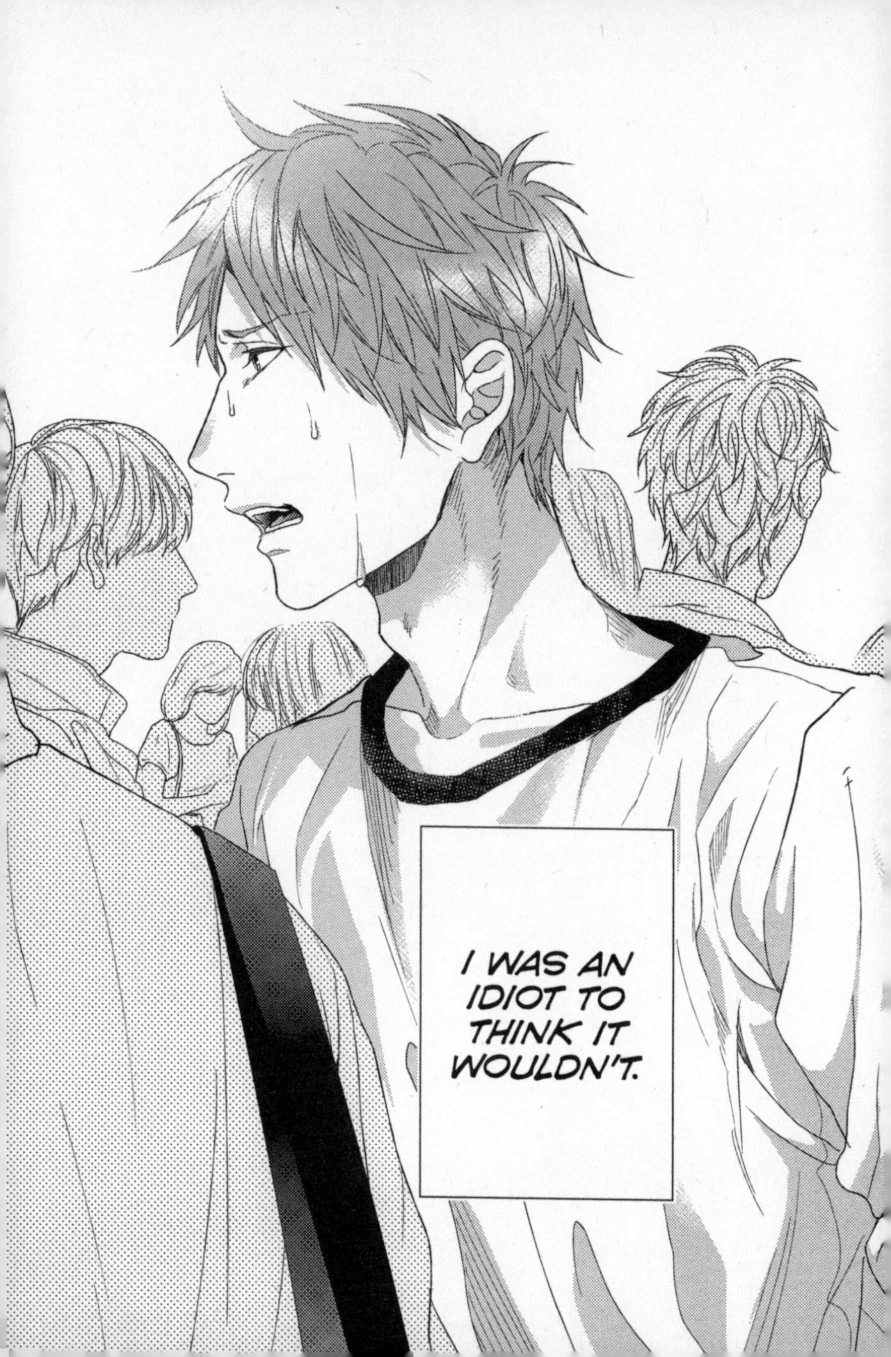
I WAS AN IDIOT TO THINK IT WOULDN'T.

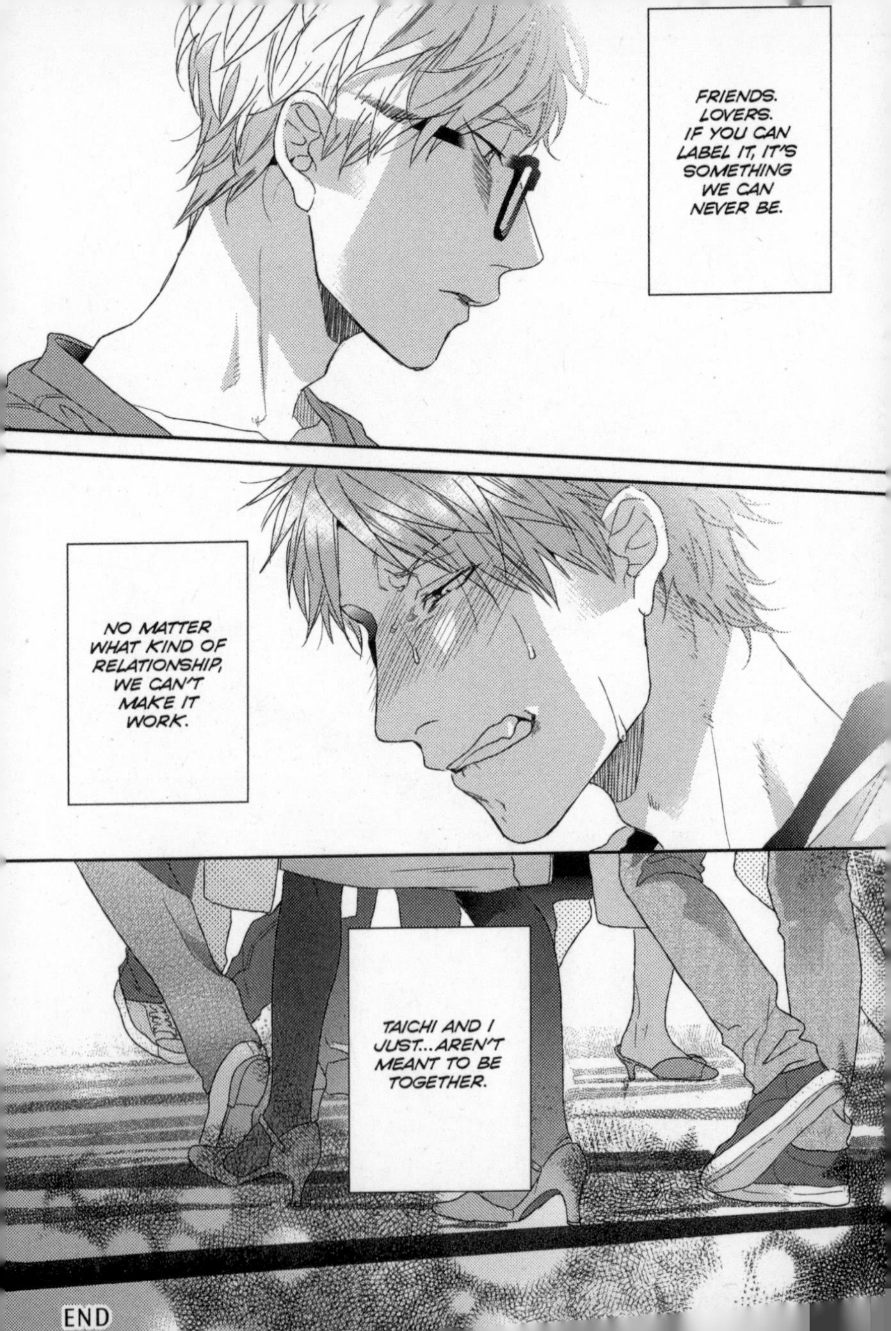

FRIENDS. LOVERS. IF YOU CAN LABEL IT, IT'S SOMETHING WE CAN NEVER BE.
NO MATTER WHAT KIND OF RELATIONSHIP, WE CAN'T MAKE IT WORK.
TAICHI AND I JUST...AREN'T MEANT TO BE TOGETHER.
END

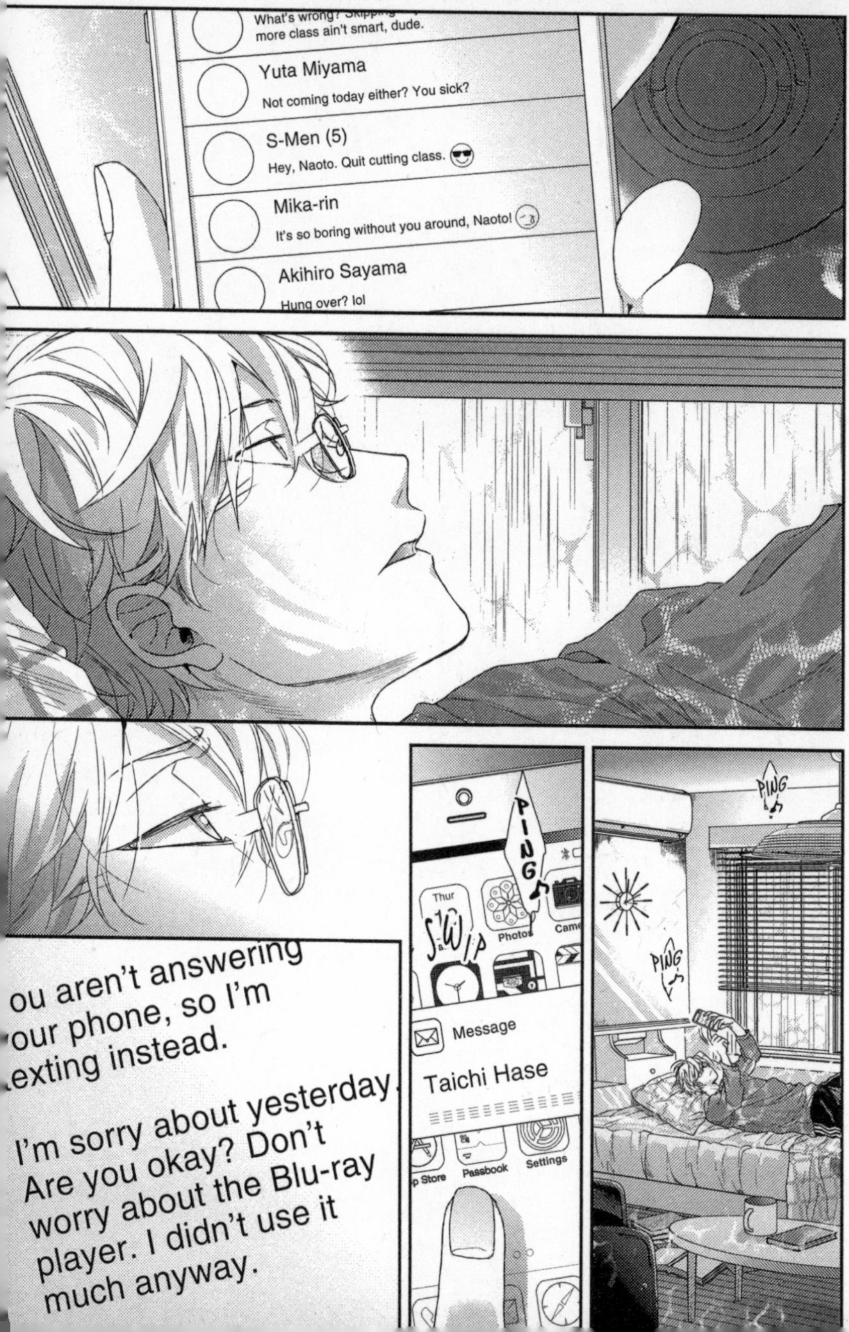
What's wrong? Skipping
more class ain't smart, dude.
Yuta Miyama
Not coming today either? You sick?
S-Men (5)
Hey, Naoto. Quit cutting class.
Mika-rin
It's so boring without you around, Naoto!
Akihiro Sayama
Hung over? lol
PING
PING
PING
SWIP
Thur
Photos
Message
Taichi Hase
Passbook
Settings
ou aren't answering
our phone, so I'm
exting instead.
I'm sorry about yesterday.
Are you okay? Don't
worry about the Blu-ray
player. I didn't use it
much anyway.

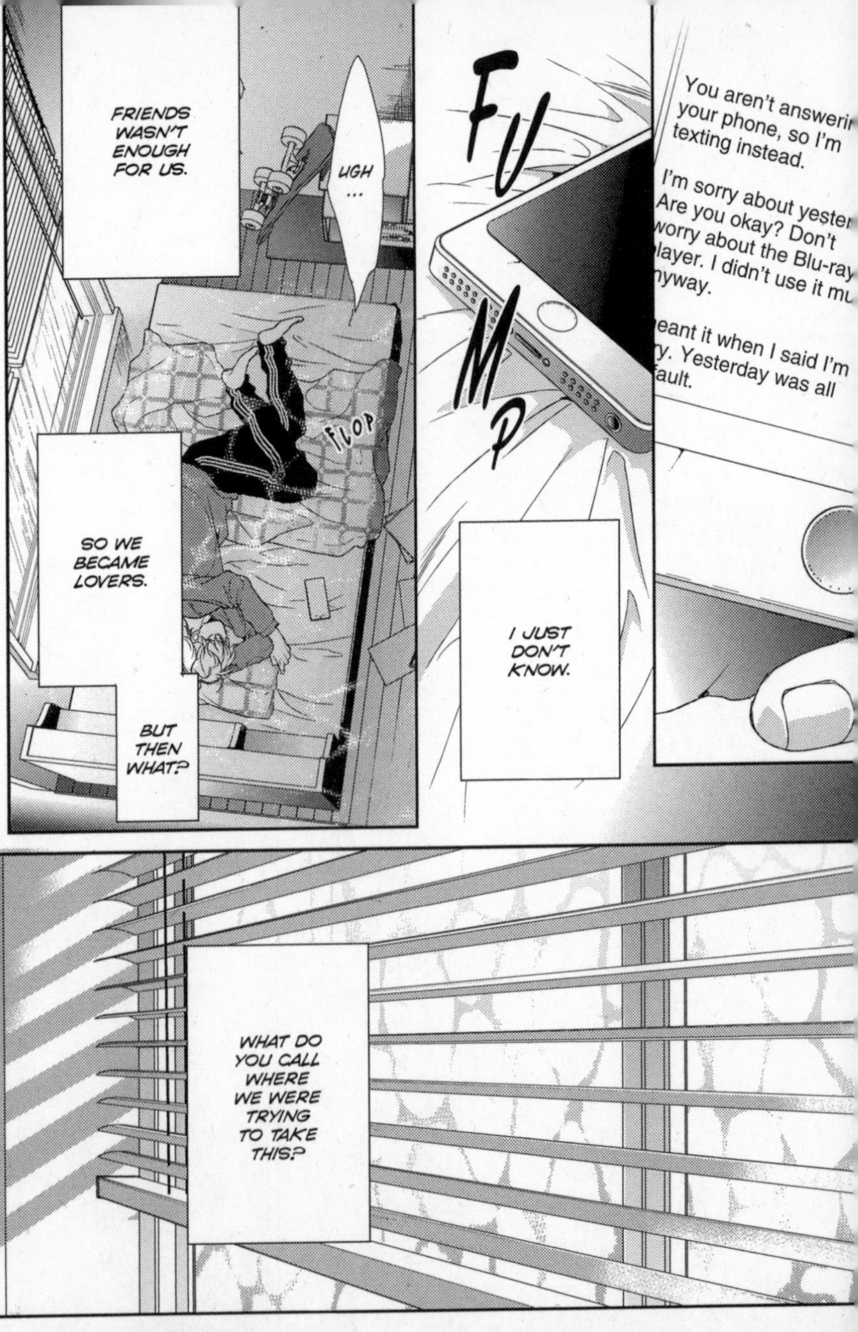
You aren't answeri
your phone, so I'm
texting instead.
I'm sorry about yester
Are you okay? Don't
worry about the Blu-ray
layer. I didn't use it mu
nyway.
eant it when I said I'm
y. Yesterday was all
fault.
FUMP
I JUST DON'T KNOW.
FRIENDS WASN'T ENOUGH FOR US.
UGH ...
FLOP
SO WE BECAME LOVERS.
BUT THEN WHAT?
WHAT DO YOU CALL WHERE WE WERE TRYING TO TAKE THIS?

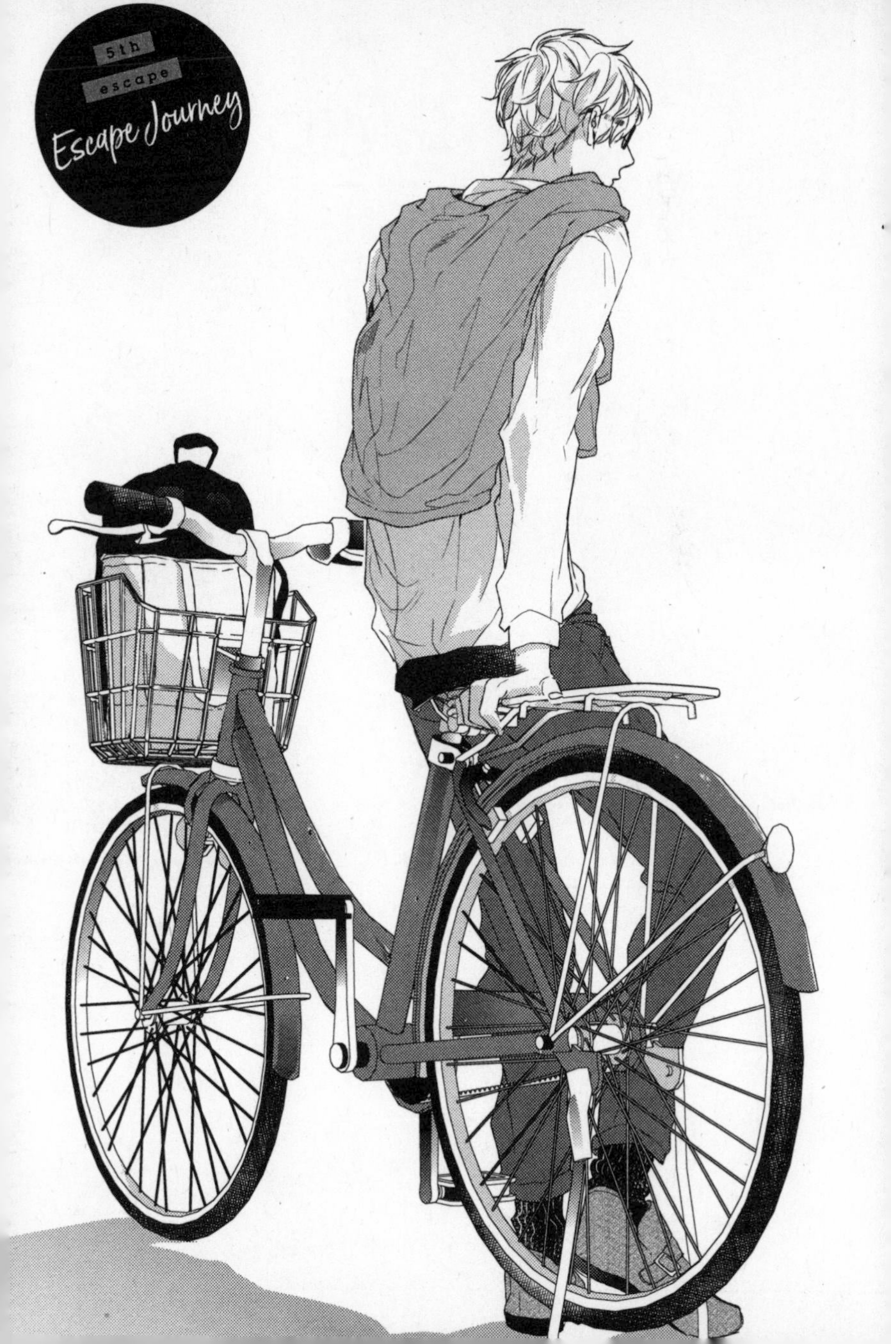
5th
escape
Escape Journey

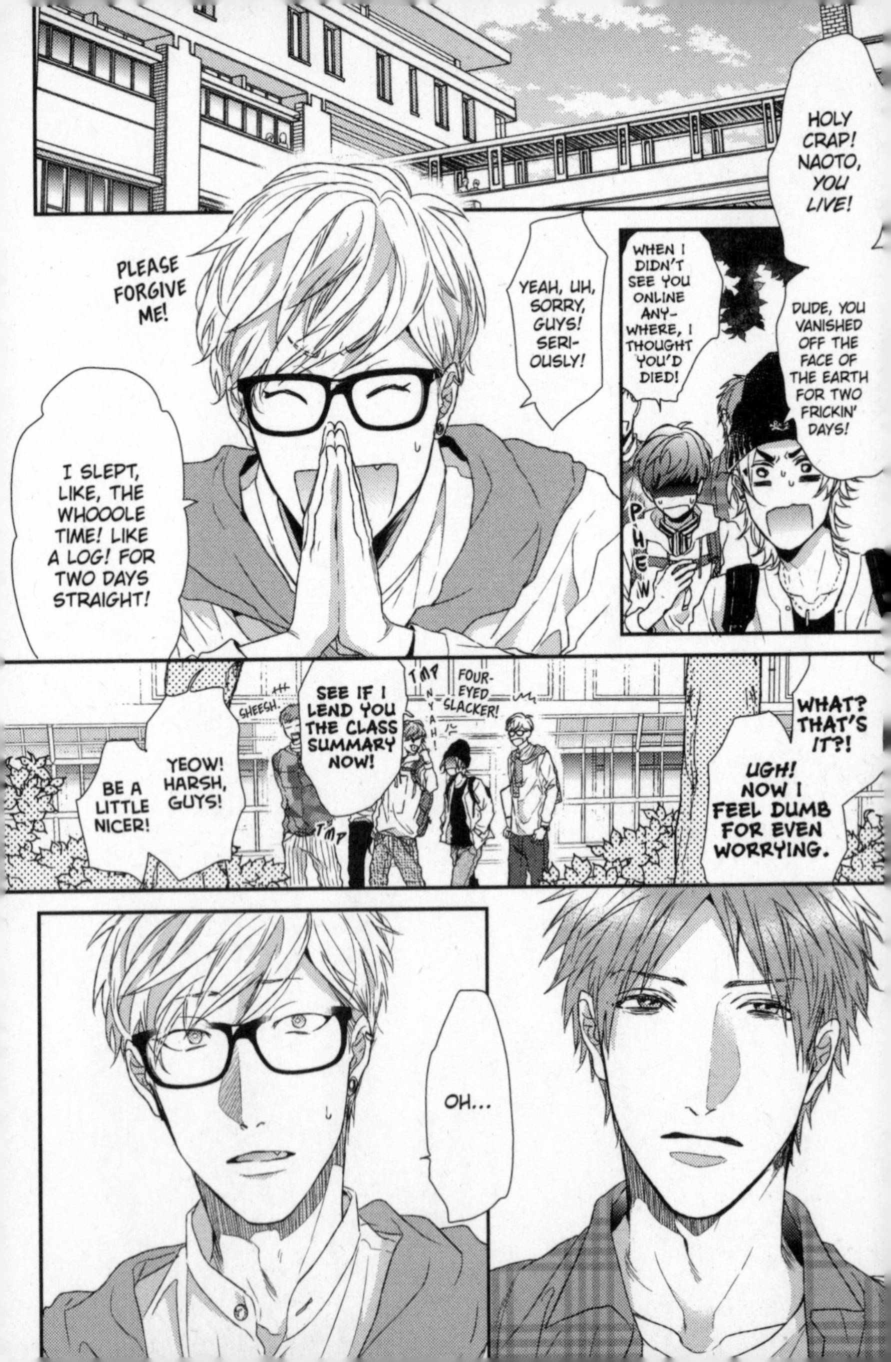
HOLY CRAP! NAOTO, YOU LIVE!
DUDE, YOU VANISHED OFF THE FACE OF THE EARTH FOR TWO FRICKIN' DAYS!
WHEN I DIDN'T SEE YOU ONLINE ANY-WHERE, I THOUGHT YOU'D DIED!
PHEW
YEAH, UH, SORRY, GUYS! SERI-OUSLY!
PLEASE FORGIVE ME!
I SLEPT, LIKE, THE WHOOOLE TIME! LIKE A LOG! FOR TWO DAYS STRAIGHT!
WHAT? THAT'S IT?!
UGH! NOW I FEEL DUMB FOR EVEN WORRYING.
FOUR-EYED SLACKER!
TMP
NYAH!
SEE IF I LEND YOU THE CLASS SUMMARY NOW!
SHEESH.
YEOW! HARSH, GUYS!
BE A LITTLE NICER!
TMP
OH...

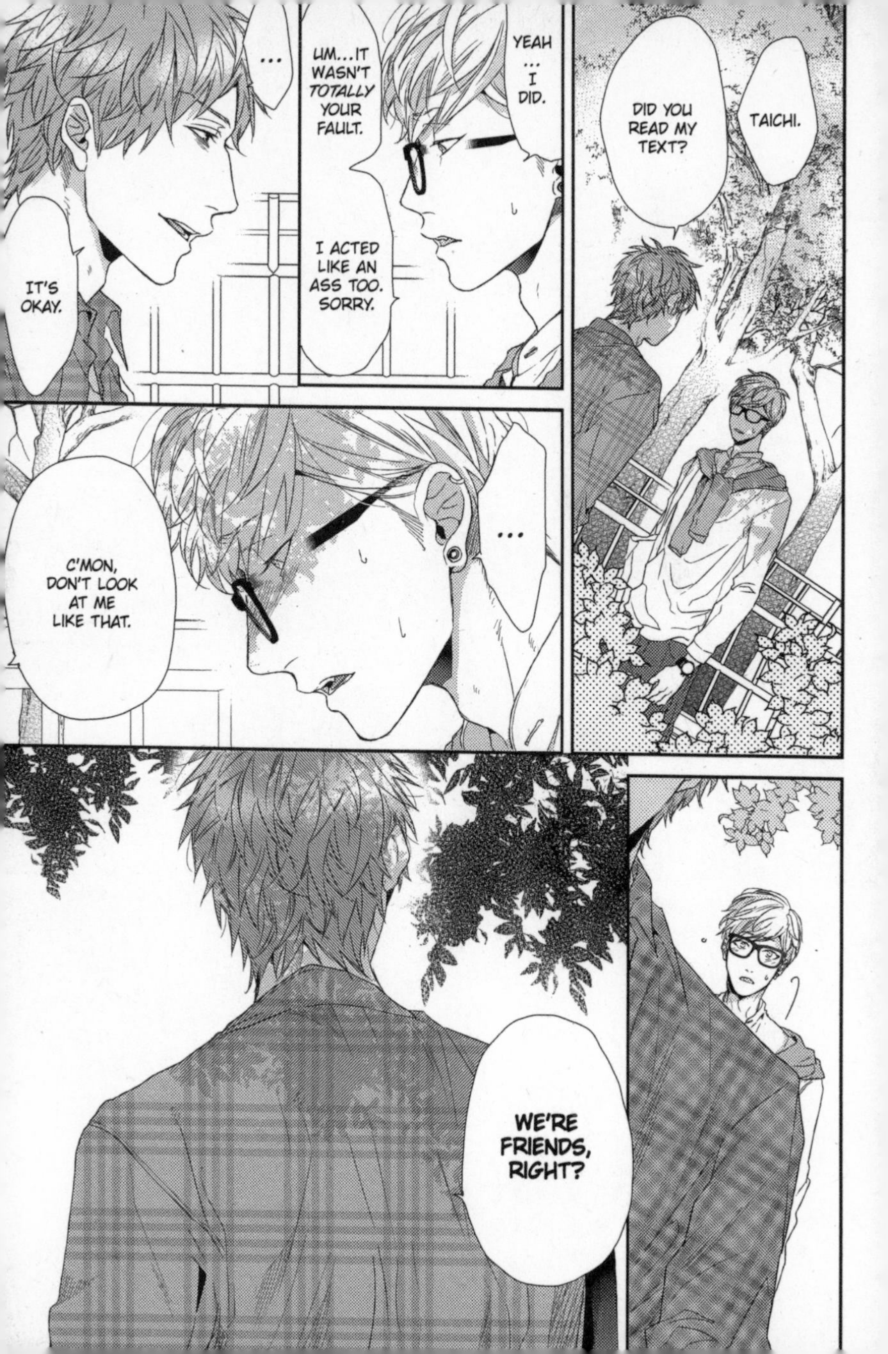
TAICHI.
DID YOU READ MY TEXT?
YEAH ... I DID.
UM...IT WASN'T *TOTALLY* YOUR FAULT.
I ACTED LIKE AN ASS TOO. SORRY.
...
IT'S OKAY.
...
C'MON, DON'T LOOK AT ME LIKE THAT.
WE'RE FRIENDS, RIGHT?

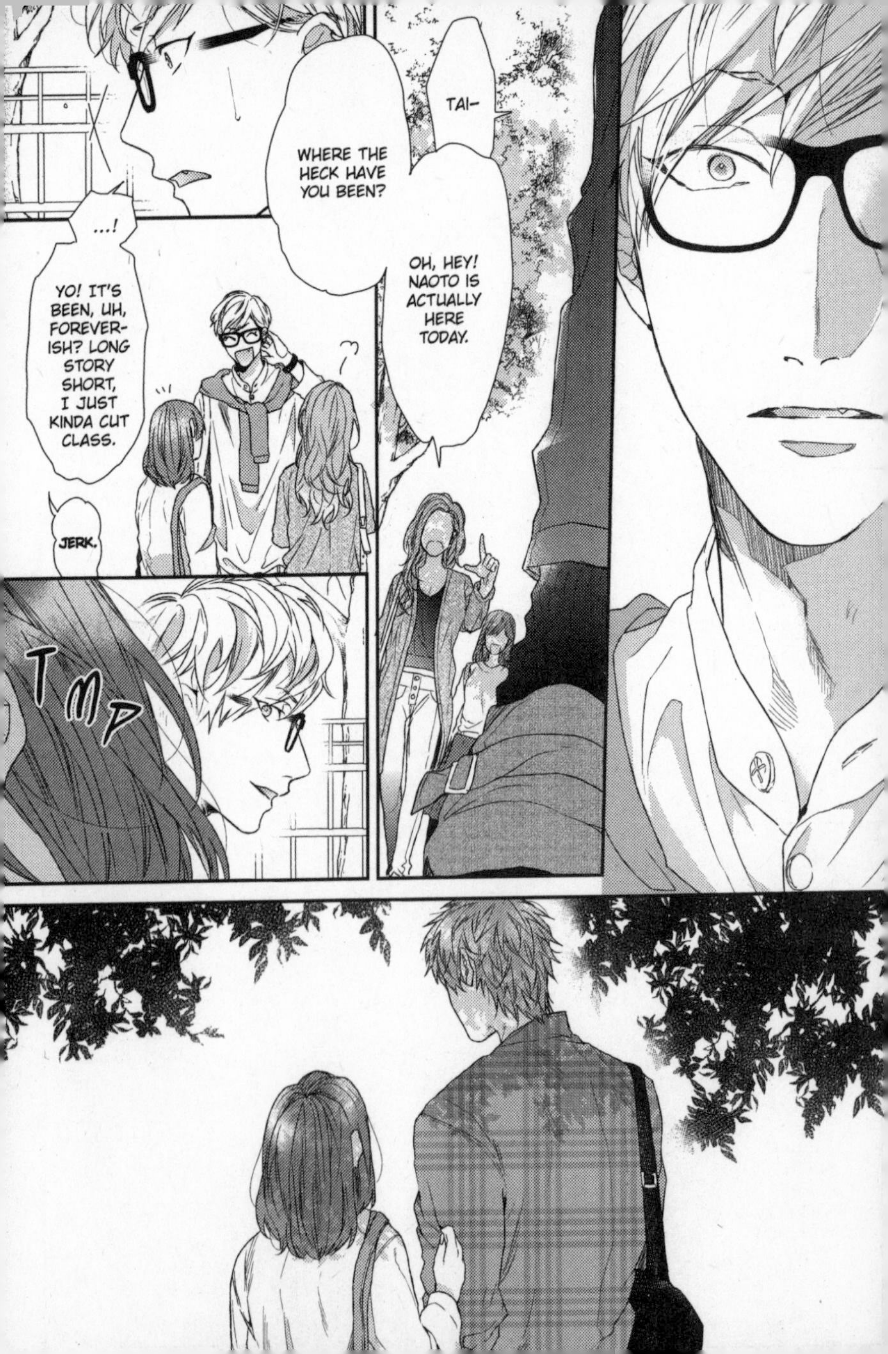
TAI-
WHERE THE HECK HAVE YOU BEEN?
OH, HEY! NAOTO IS ACTUALLY HERE TODAY.
...!
YO! IT'S BEEN, UH, FOREVER-ISH? LONG STORY SHORT, I JUST KINDA CUT CLASS.
JERK.
TMP

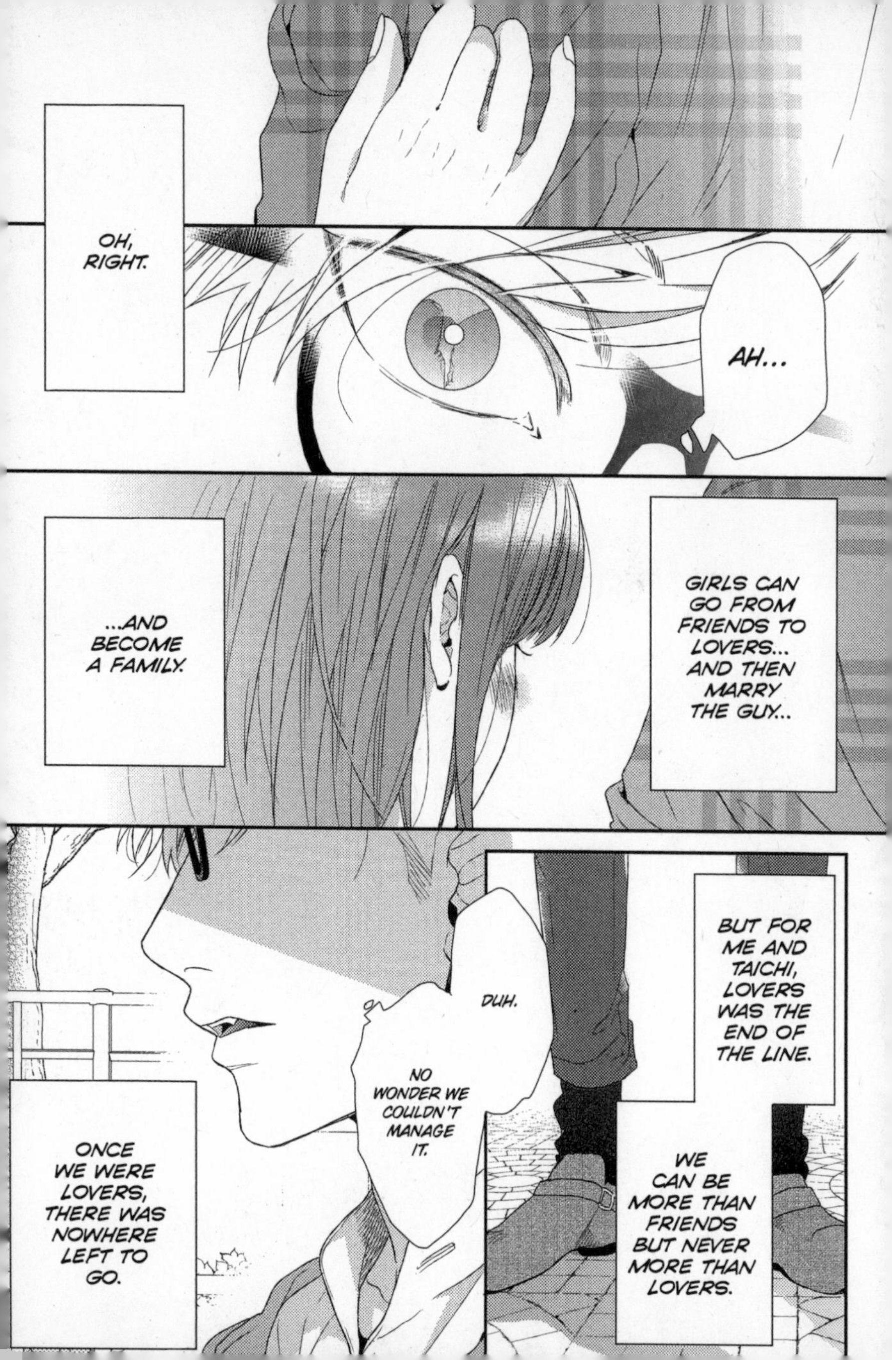
AH...
OH, RIGHT.
GIRLS CAN GO FROM FRIENDS TO LOVERS... AND THEN MARRY THE GUY...
...AND BECOME A FAMILY.
BUT FOR ME AND TAICHI, LOVERS WAS THE END OF THE LINE.
WE CAN BE MORE THAN FRIENDS BUT NEVER MORE THAN LOVERS.
DUH.
NO WONDER WE COULDN'T MANAGE IT.
ONCE WE WERE LOVERS, THERE WAS NOWHERE LEFT TO GO.

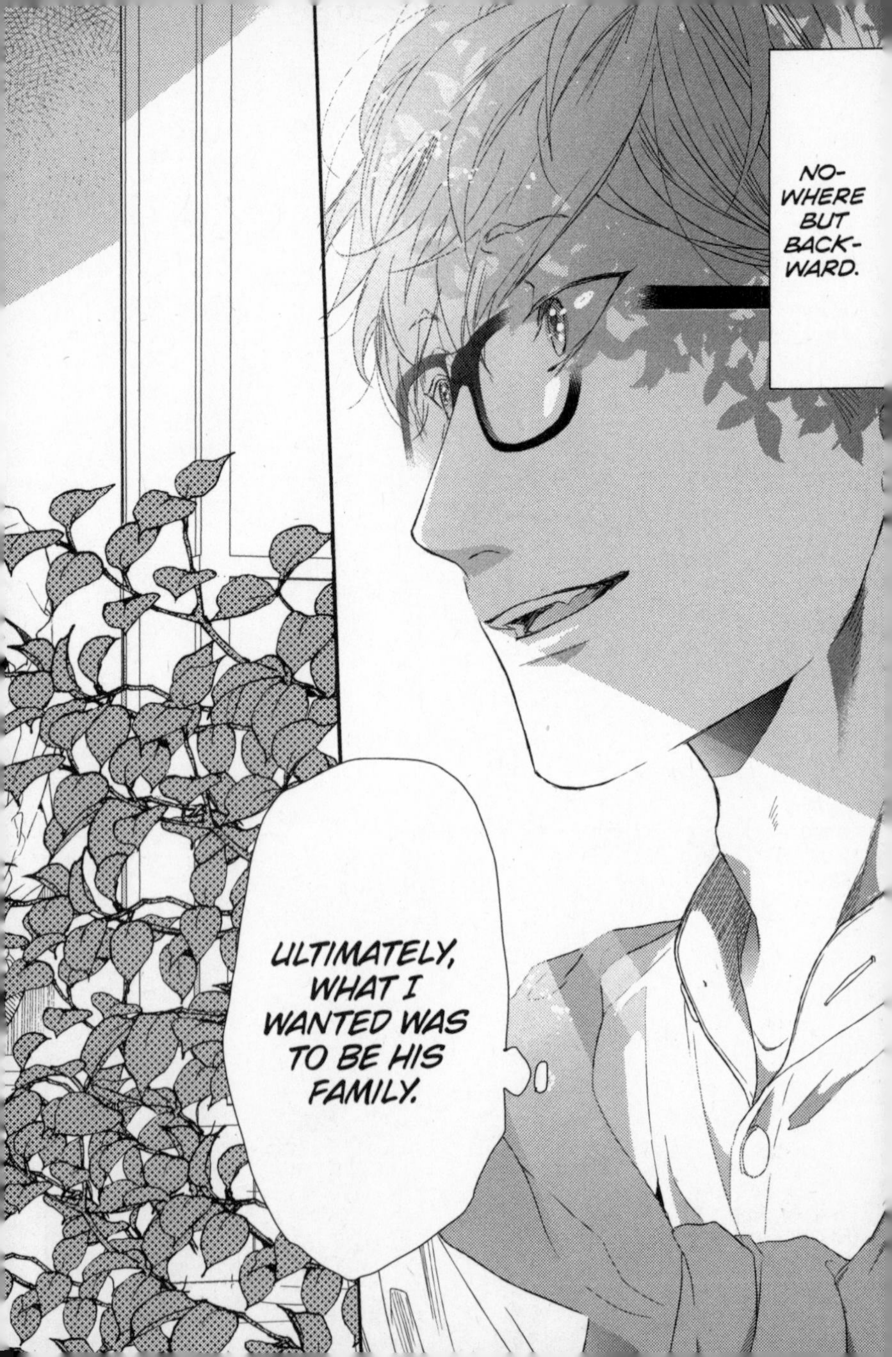
NO-WHERE BUT BACK-WARD.
ULTIMATELY, WHAT I WANTED WAS TO BE HIS FAMILY.

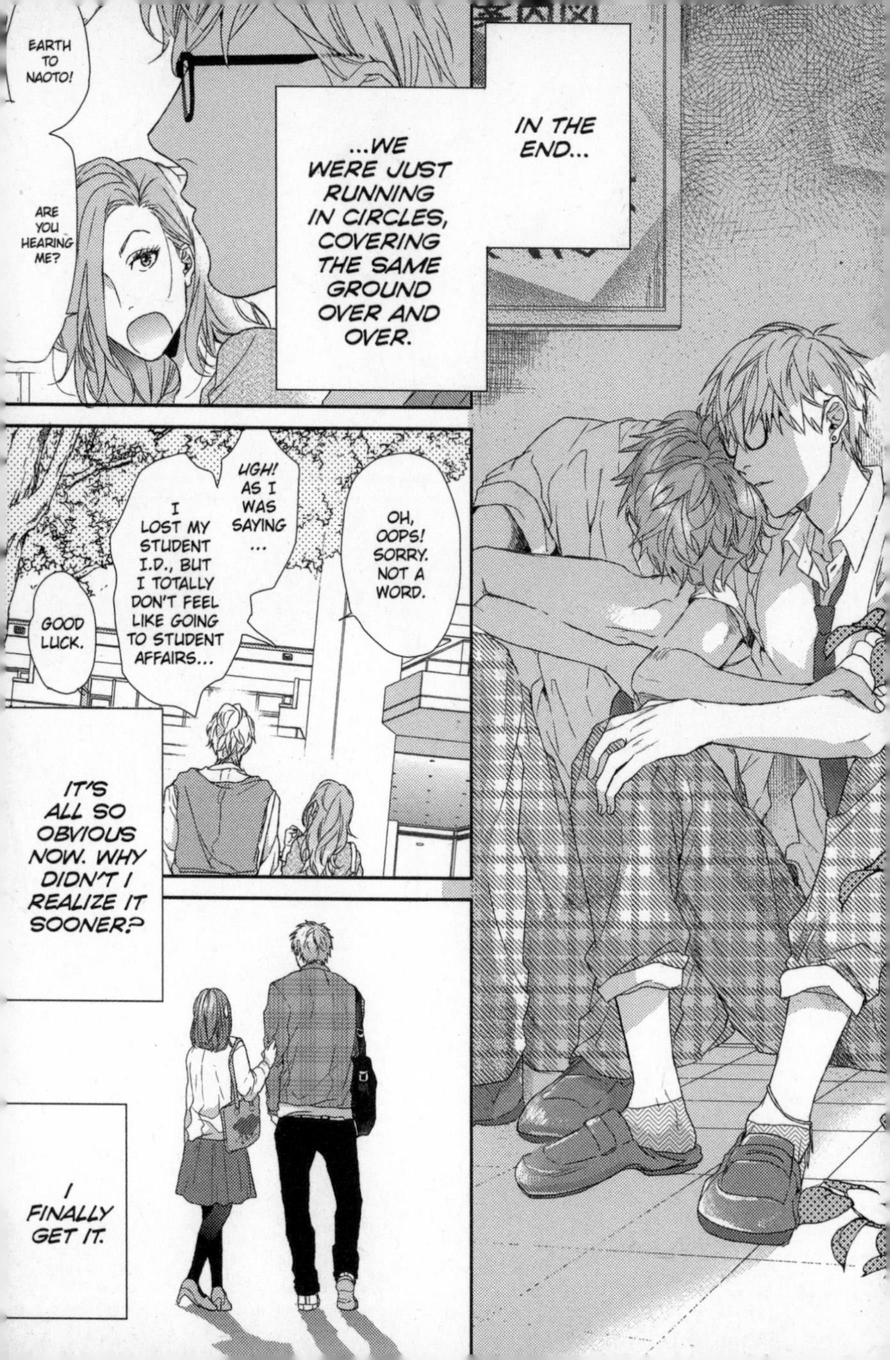
IN THE END...
...WE WERE JUST RUNNING IN CIRCLES, COVERING THE SAME GROUND OVER AND OVER.
EARTH TO NAOTO!
ARE YOU HEARING ME?
OH, OOPS! SORRY. NOT A WORD.
UGH! AS I WAS SAYING...
I LOST MY STUDENT I.D., BUT I TOTALLY DON'T FEEL LIKE GOING TO STUDENT AFFAIRS...
GOOD LUCK.
IT'S ALL SO OBVIOUS NOW. WHY DIDN'T I REALIZE IT SOONER?
I FINALLY GET IT.

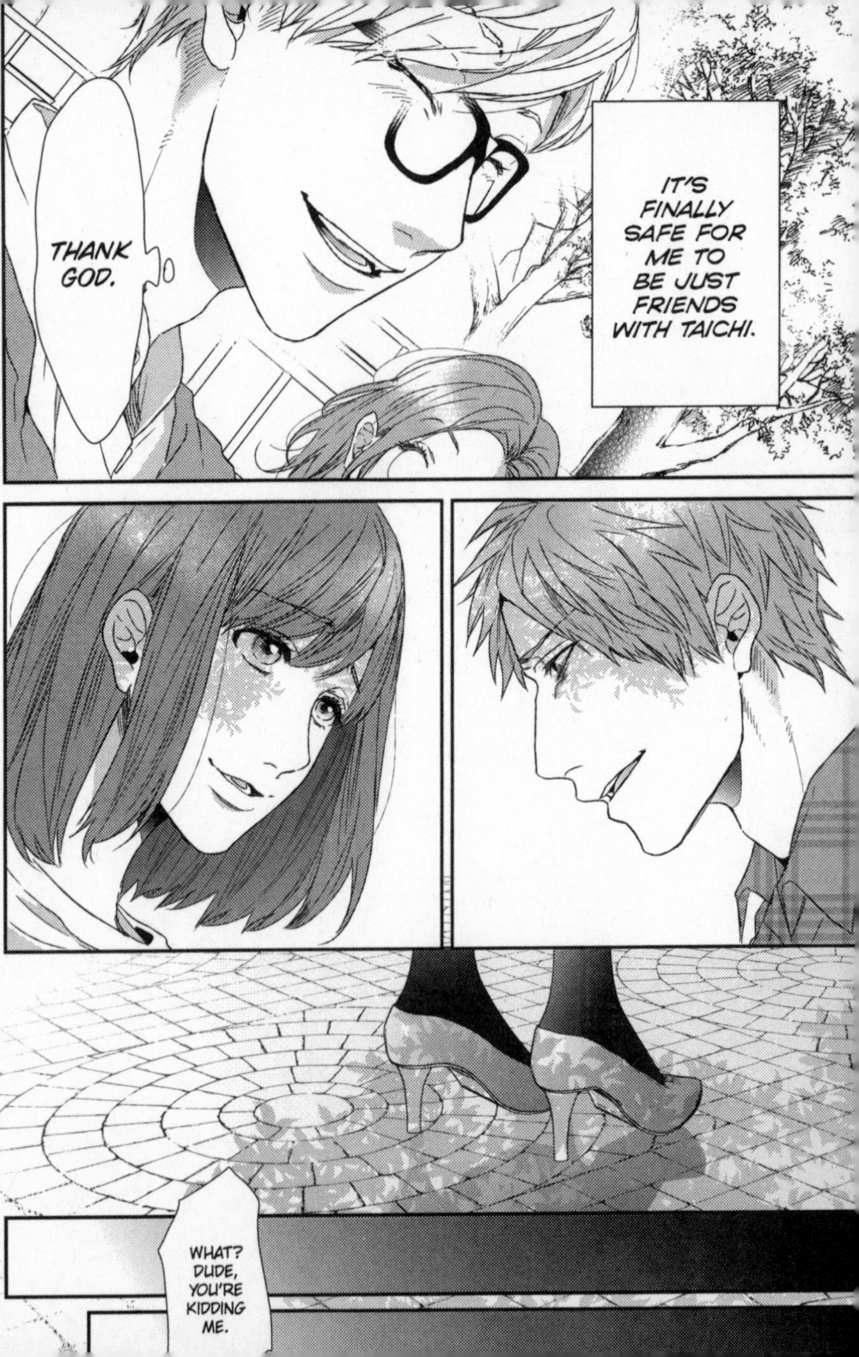
IT'S FINALLY SAFE FOR ME TO BE JUST FRIENDS WITH TAICHI.
THANK GOD.
WHAT? DUDE, YOU'RE KIDDING ME.

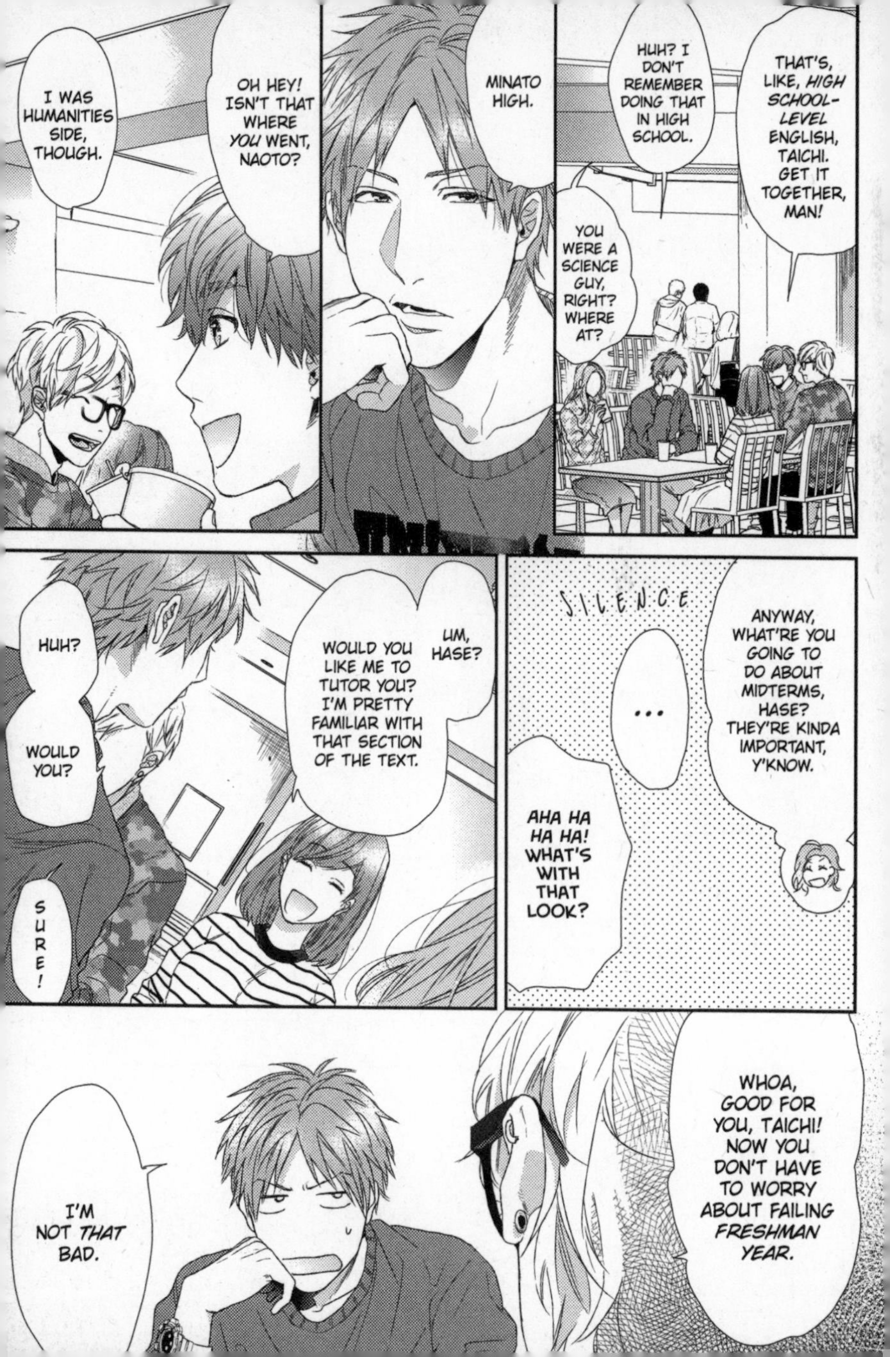
THAT'S, LIKE, *HIGH SCHOOL-LEVEL* ENGLISH, TAICHI. GET IT TOGETHER, MAN!
HUH? I DON'T REMEMBER DOING THAT IN HIGH SCHOOL.
YOU WERE A SCIENCE GUY, RIGHT? WHERE AT?
MINATO HIGH.
OH HEY! ISN'T THAT WHERE *YOU* WENT, NAOTO?
I WAS HUMANITIES SIDE, THOUGH.
SILENCE
ANYWAY, WHAT'RE YOU GOING TO DO ABOUT MIDTERMS, HASE? THEY'RE KINDA IMPORTANT, Y'KNOW.
...
AHA HA HA HA! WHAT'S WITH THAT LOOK?
UM, HASE?
WOULD YOU LIKE ME TO TUTOR YOU? I'M PRETTY FAMILIAR WITH THAT SECTION OF THE TEXT.
HUH?
WOULD YOU?
SURE!
WHOA, GOOD FOR YOU, TAICHI! NOW YOU DON'T HAVE TO WORRY ABOUT FAILING *FRESHMAN YEAR*.
I'M NOT *THAT* BAD.

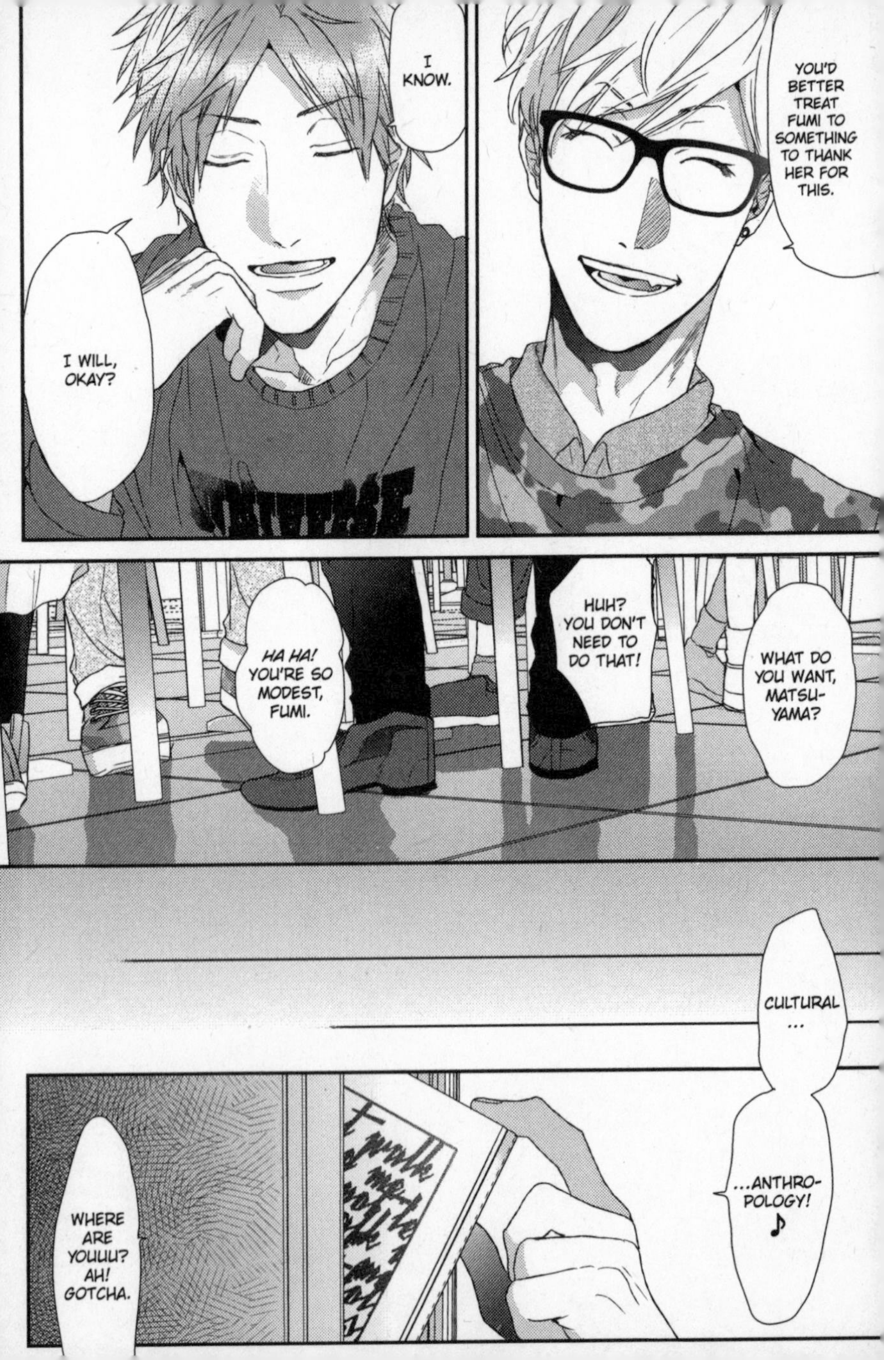
YOU'D BETTER TREAT FUMI TO SOMETHING TO THANK HER FOR THIS.
I KNOW.
I WILL, OKAY?
WHAT DO YOU WANT, MATSU-YAMA?
HUH? YOU DON'T NEED TO DO THAT!
HA HA! YOU'RE SO MODEST, FUMI.
CULTURAL ...
...ANTHRO-POLOGY! ♪
WHERE ARE YOUUU? AH! GOTCHA.

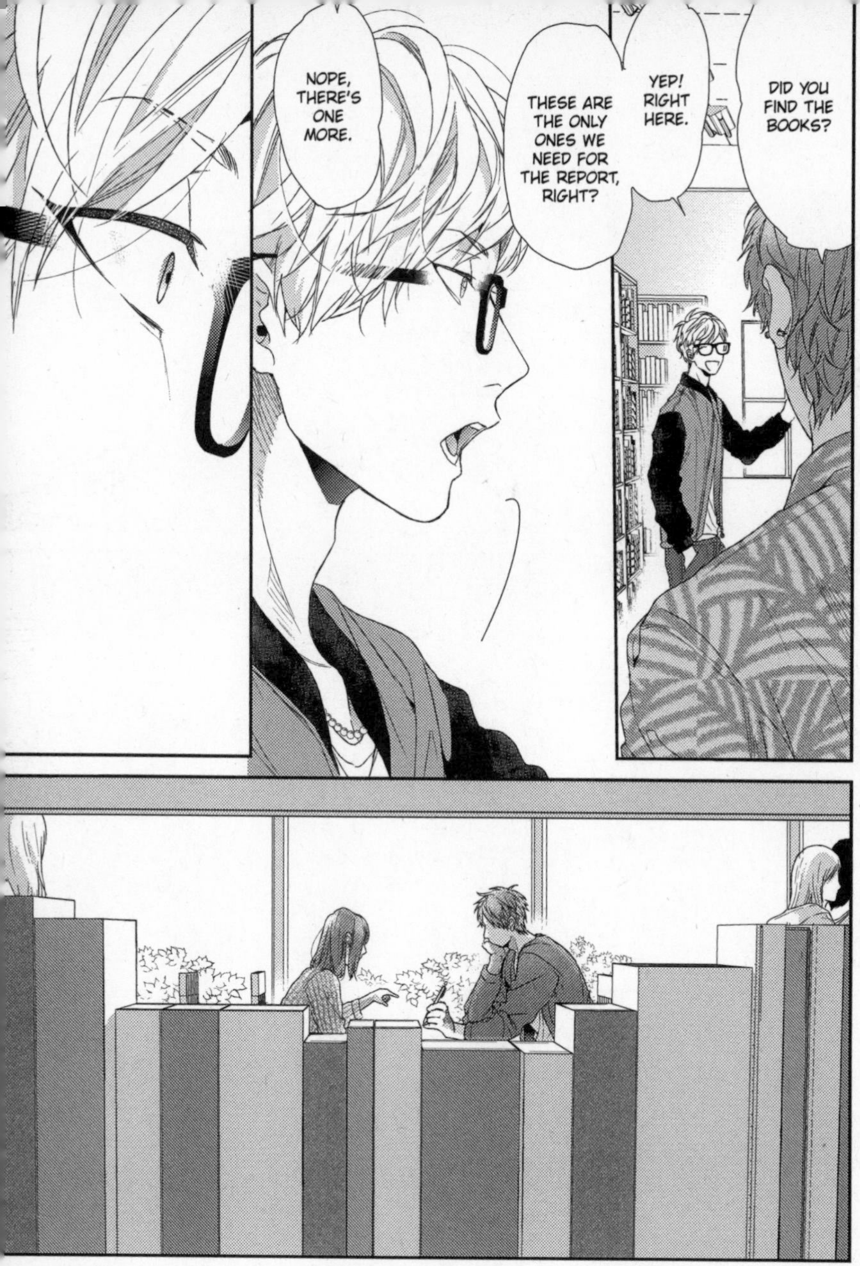
DID YOU FIND THE BOOKS?
YEP! RIGHT HERE.
THESE ARE THE ONLY ONES WE NEED FOR THE REPORT, RIGHT?
NOPE, THERE'S ONE MORE.

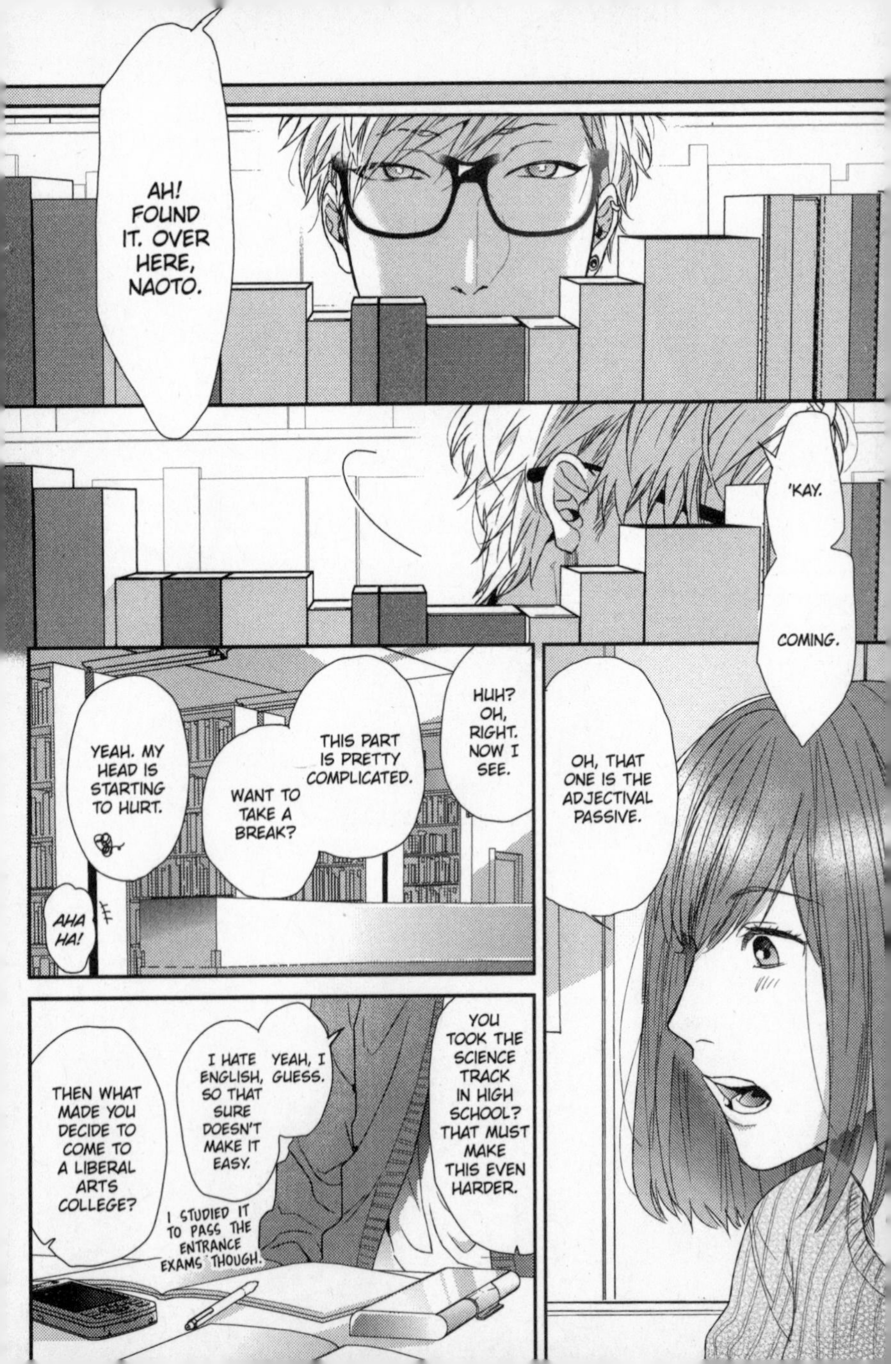
AH! FOUND IT. OVER HERE, NAOTO.
'KAY.
COMING.
OH, THAT ONE IS THE ADJECTIVAL PASSIVE.
HUH? OH, RIGHT. NOW I SEE.
THIS PART IS PRETTY COMPLICATED.
WANT TO TAKE A BREAK?
YEAH. MY HEAD IS STARTING TO HURT.
AHA HA!
YOU TOOK THE SCIENCE TRACK IN HIGH SCHOOL? THAT MUST MAKE THIS EVEN HARDER.
YEAH, I GUESS.
I HATE ENGLISH, SO THAT SURE DOESN'T MAKE IT EASY.
I STUDIED IT TO PASS THE ENTRANCE EXAMS THOUGH.
THEN WHAT MADE YOU DECIDE TO COME TO A LIBERAL ARTS COLLEGE?

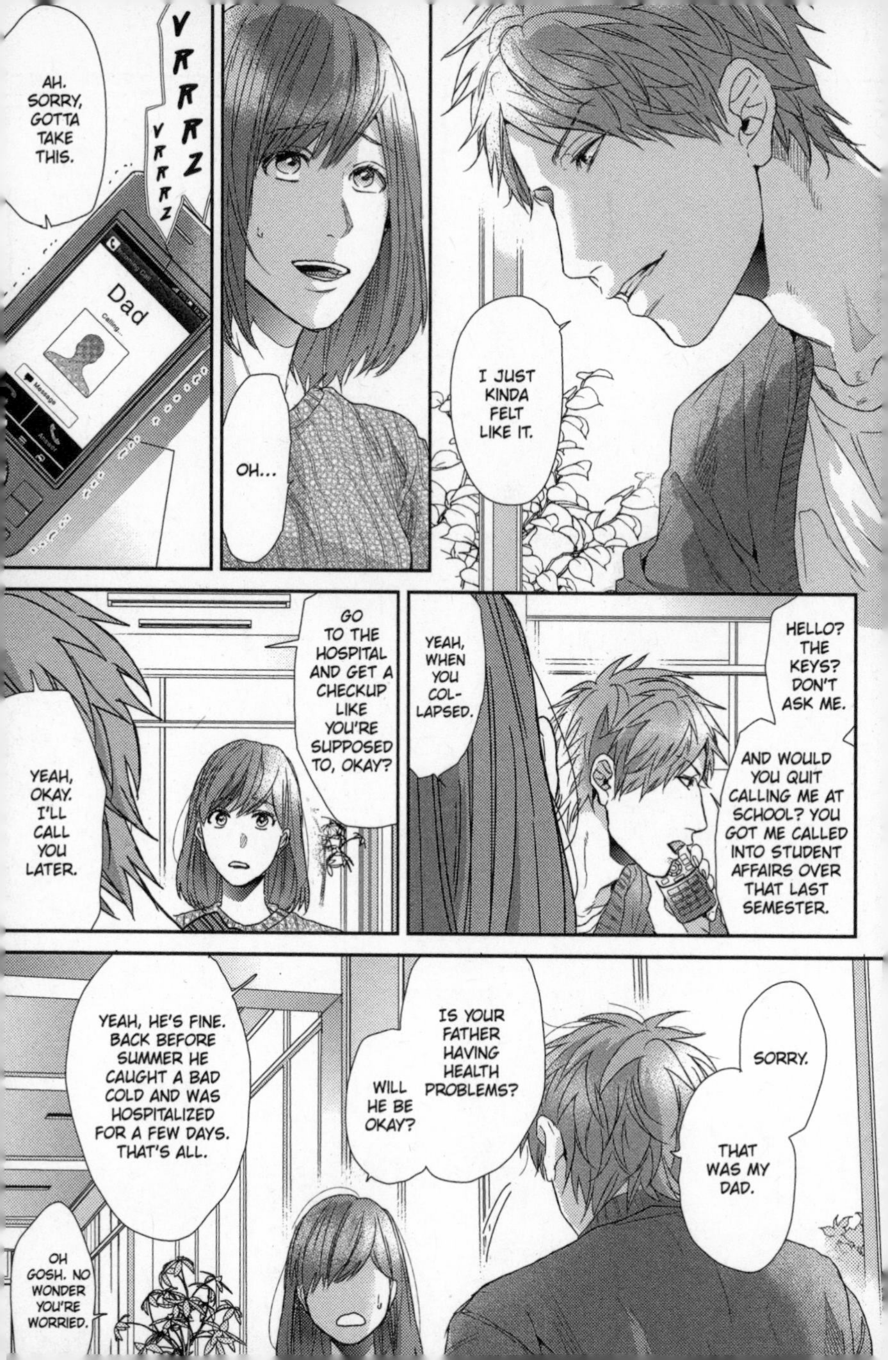
I JUST KINDA FELT LIKE IT.
OH...
VRRRZ
VRRRZ
AH. SORRY, GOTTA TAKE THIS.
Dad
Calling...
Message
Answer
HELLO? THE KEYS? DON'T ASK ME.
AND WOULD YOU QUIT CALLING ME AT SCHOOL? YOU GOT ME CALLED INTO STUDENT AFFAIRS OVER THAT LAST SEMESTER.
YEAH, WHEN YOU COL-LAPSED.
GO TO THE HOSPITAL AND GET A CHECKUP LIKE YOU'RE SUPPOSED TO, OKAY?
YEAH, OKAY. I'LL CALL YOU LATER.
SORRY.
THAT WAS MY DAD.
IS YOUR FATHER HAVING HEALTH PROBLEMS?
WILL HE BE OKAY?
YEAH, HE'S FINE. BACK BEFORE SUMMER HE CAUGHT A BAD COLD AND WAS HOSPITALIZED FOR A FEW DAYS. THAT'S ALL.
OH GOSH. NO WONDER YOU'RE WORRIED.

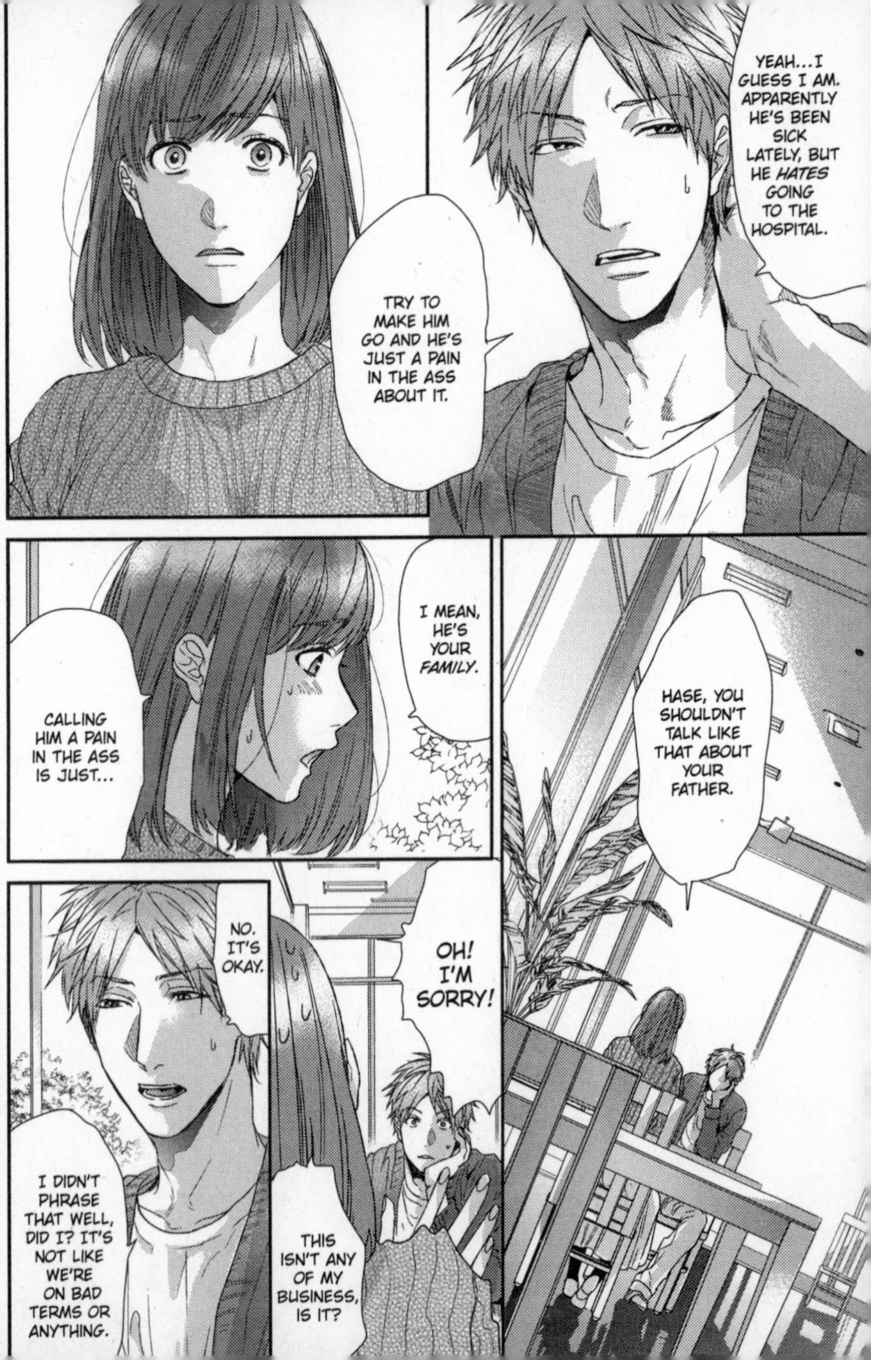
YEAH...I GUESS I AM. APPARENTLY HE'S BEEN SICK LATELY, BUT HE *HATES* GOING TO THE HOSPITAL.
TRY TO MAKE HIM GO AND HE'S JUST A PAIN IN THE ASS ABOUT IT.
HASE, YOU SHOULDN'T TALK LIKE THAT ABOUT YOUR FATHER.
I MEAN, HE'S YOUR *FAMILY*.
CALLING HIM A PAIN IN THE ASS IS JUST...
OH! I'M SORRY!
THIS ISN'T ANY OF MY BUSINESS, IS IT?
NO. IT'S OKAY.
I DIDN'T PHRASE THAT WELL, DID I? IT'S NOT LIKE WE'RE ON BAD TERMS OR ANYTHING.

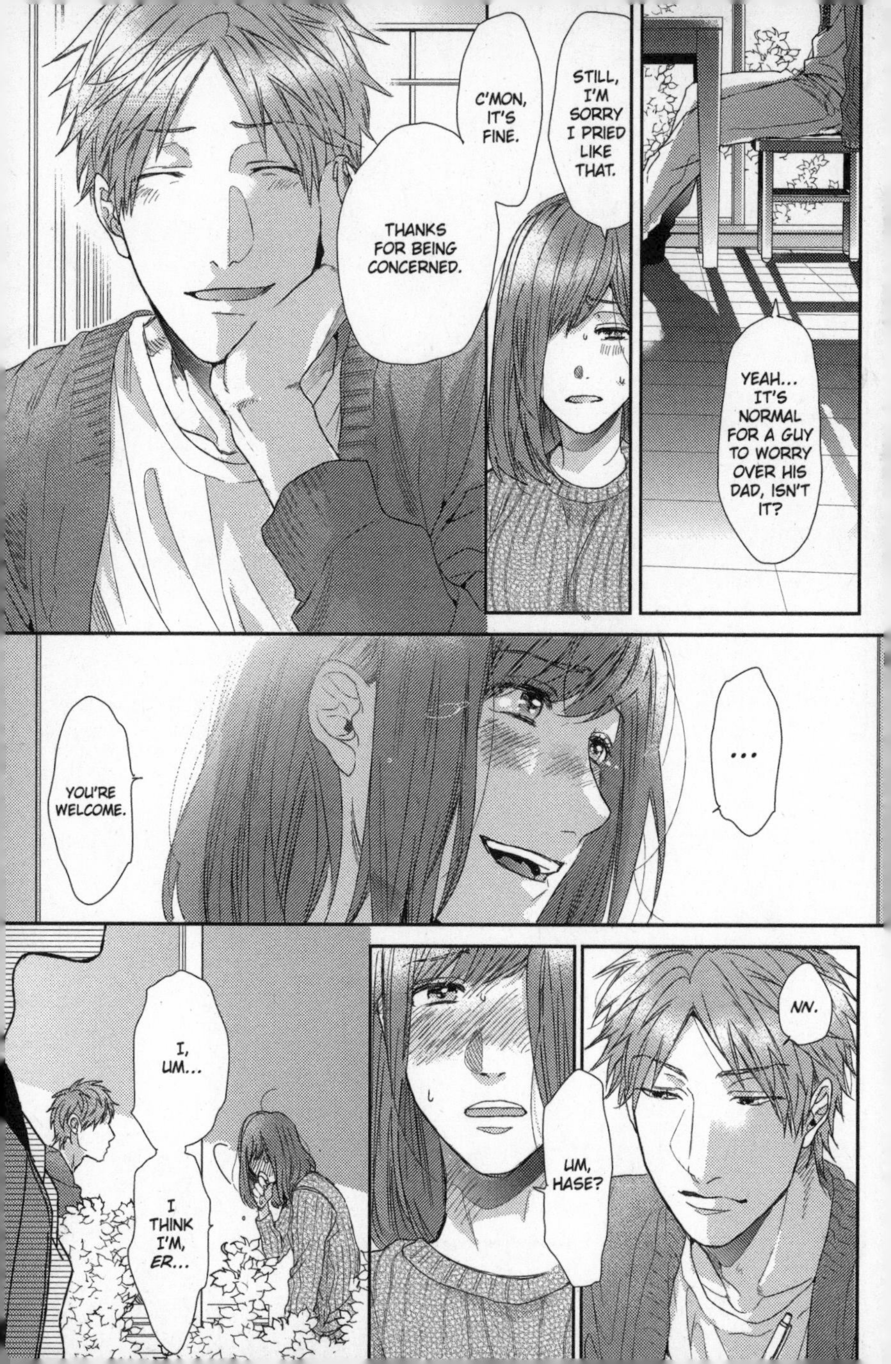
YEAH... IT'S NORMAL FOR A GUY TO WORRY OVER HIS DAD, ISN'T IT?
STILL, I'M SORRY I PRIED LIKE THAT.
C'MON, IT'S FINE.
THANKS FOR BEING CONCERNED.
...
YOU'RE WELCOME.
NN.
UM, HASE?
I, UM...
I THINK I'M, ER...

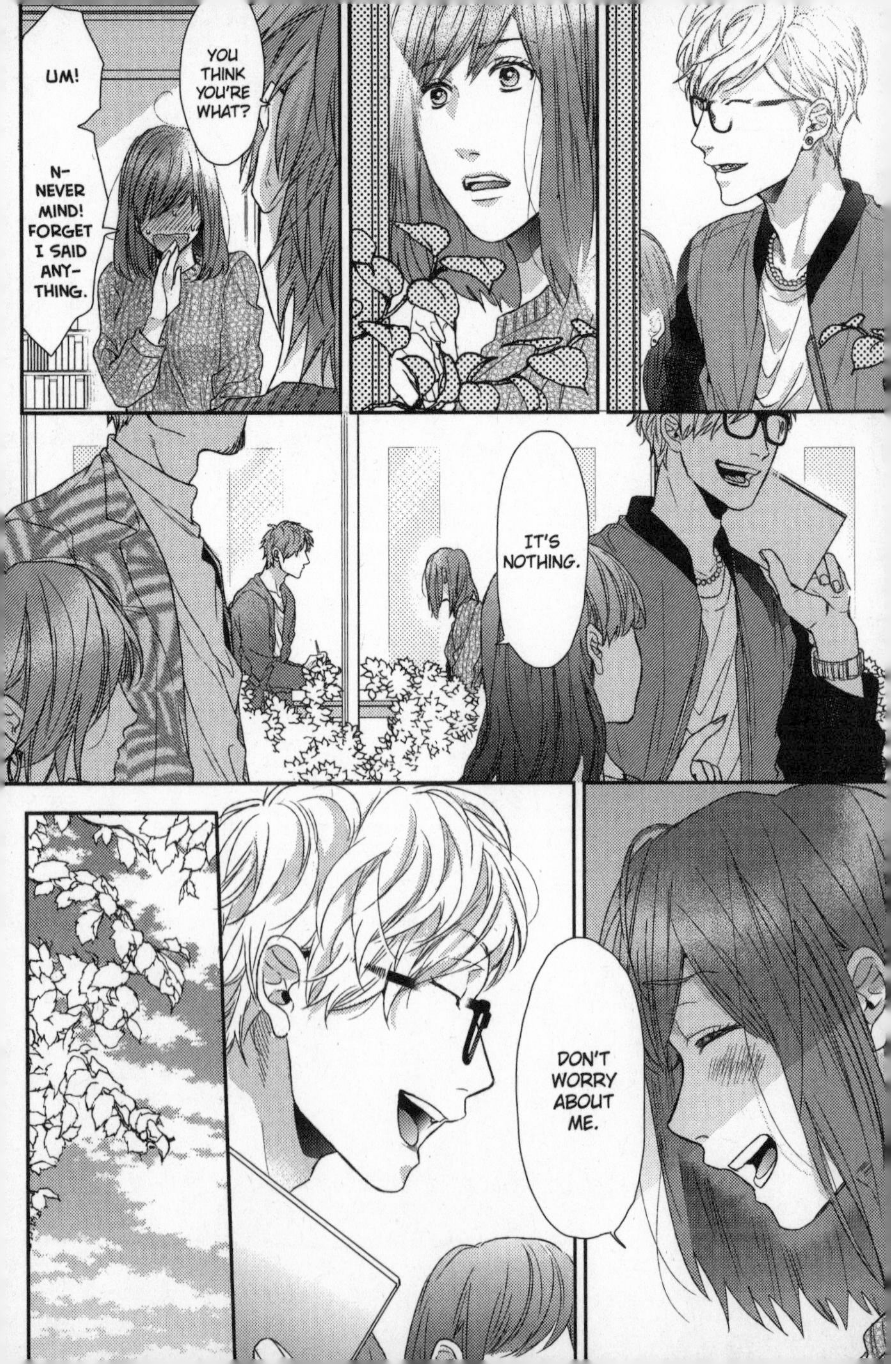
YOU THINK YOU'RE WHAT?
UM!
N-NEVER MIND! FORGET I SAID ANY-THING.
IT'S NOTHING.
DON'T WORRY ABOUT ME.

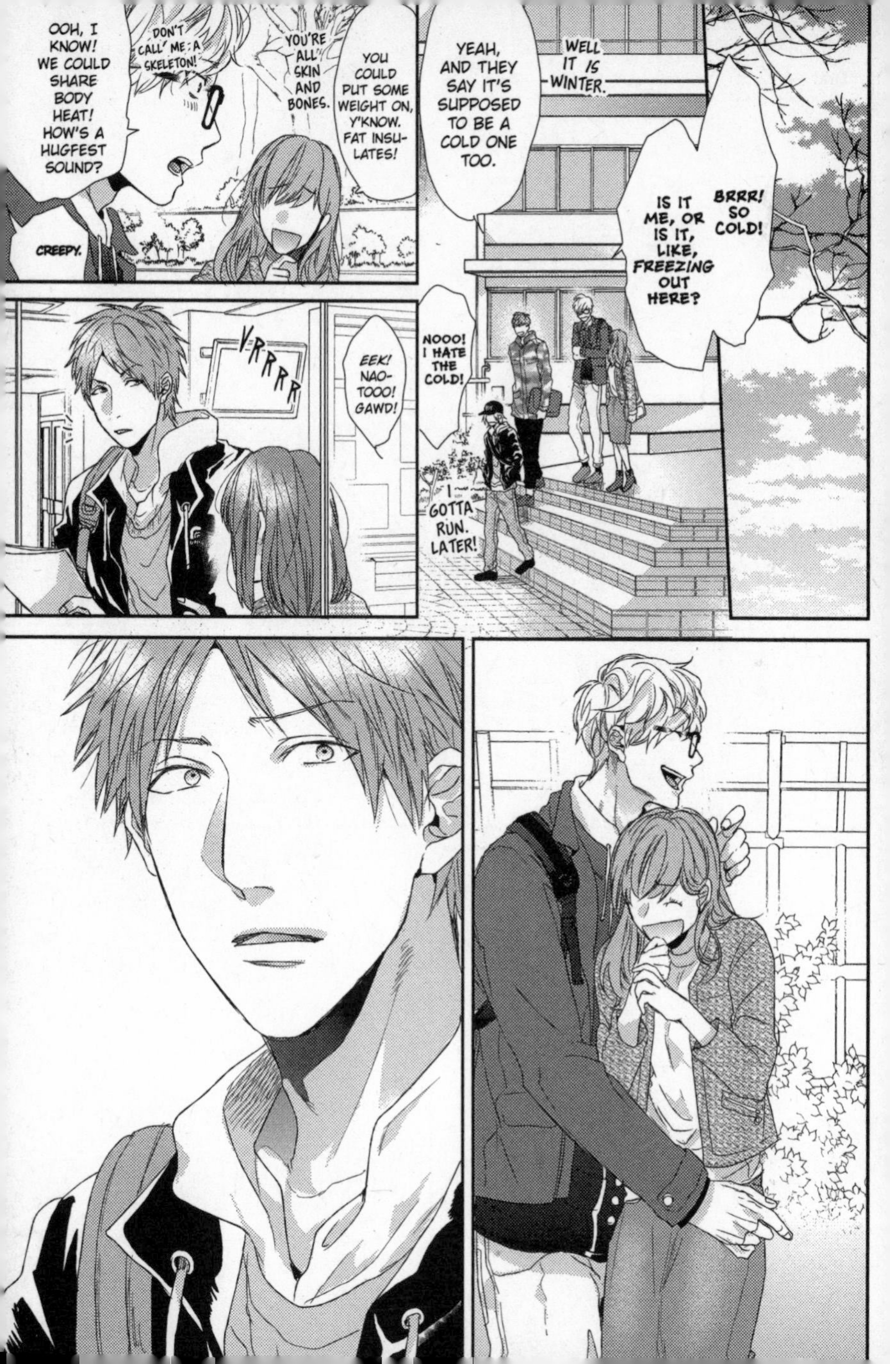
BRRR! SO COLD!
IS IT ME, OR IS IT, LIKE, FREEZING OUT HERE?
WELL IT IS WINTER.
YEAH, AND THEY SAY IT'S SUPPOSED TO BE A COLD ONE TOO.
NOOO! I HATE THE COLD!
I GOTTA RUN. LATER!
YOU COULD PUT SOME WEIGHT ON, Y'KNOW. FAT INSULATES!
YOU'RE ALL SKIN AND BONES.
DON'T CALL ME A SKELETON!
OOH, I KNOW! WE COULD SHARE BODY HEAT! HOW'S A HUGFEST SOUND?
CREEPY.
EEK! NAO-TOOO! GAWD!
VRRRR

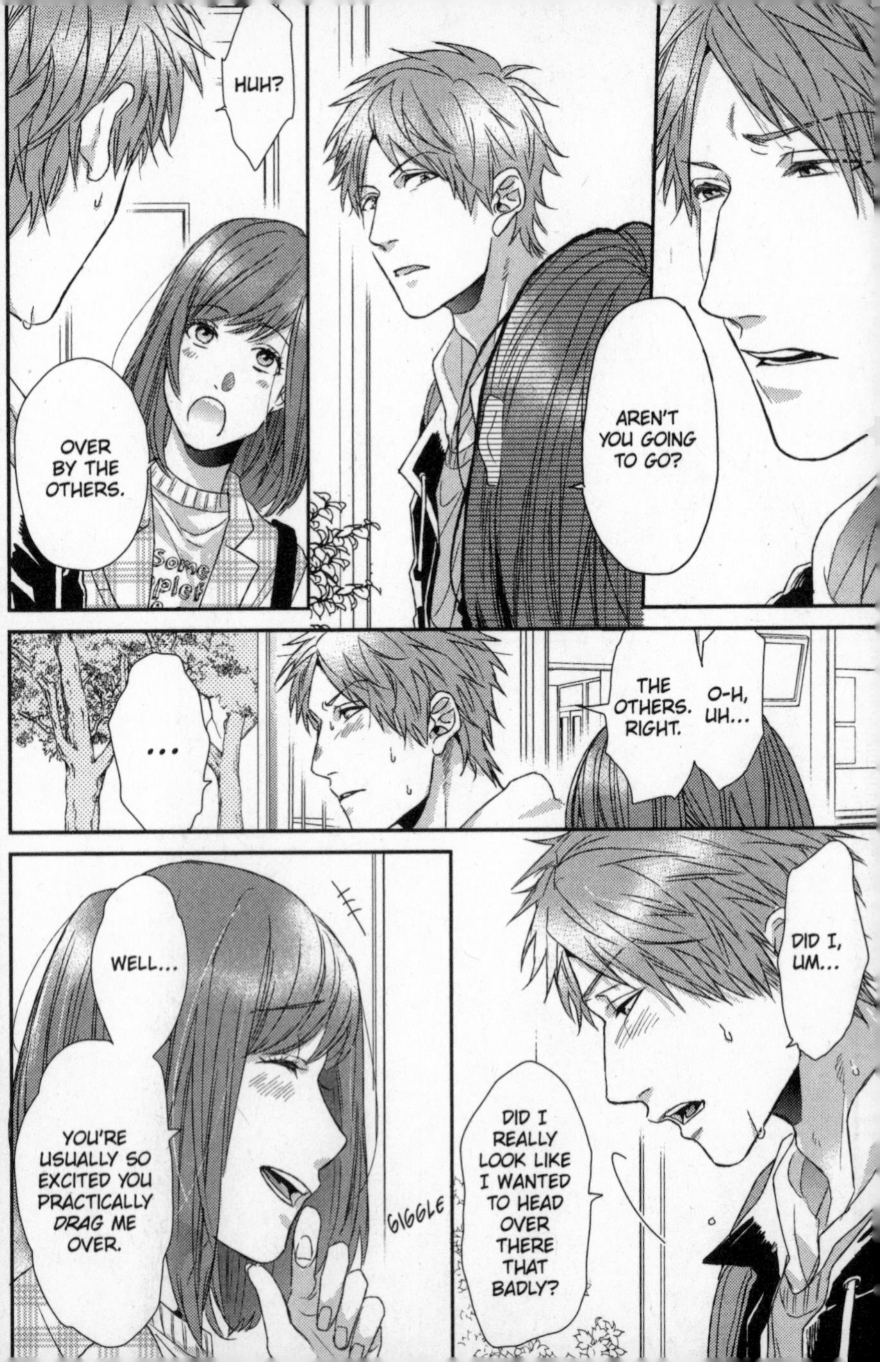
AREN'T YOU GOING TO GO?
HUH?
OVER BY THE OTHERS.
O-H, UH...
THE OTHERS. RIGHT.
...
DID I, UM...
DID I REALLY LOOK LIKE I WANTED TO HEAD OVER THERE THAT BADLY?
WELL...
YOU'RE USUALLY SO EXCITED YOU PRACTICALLY DRAG ME OVER.
GIGGLE

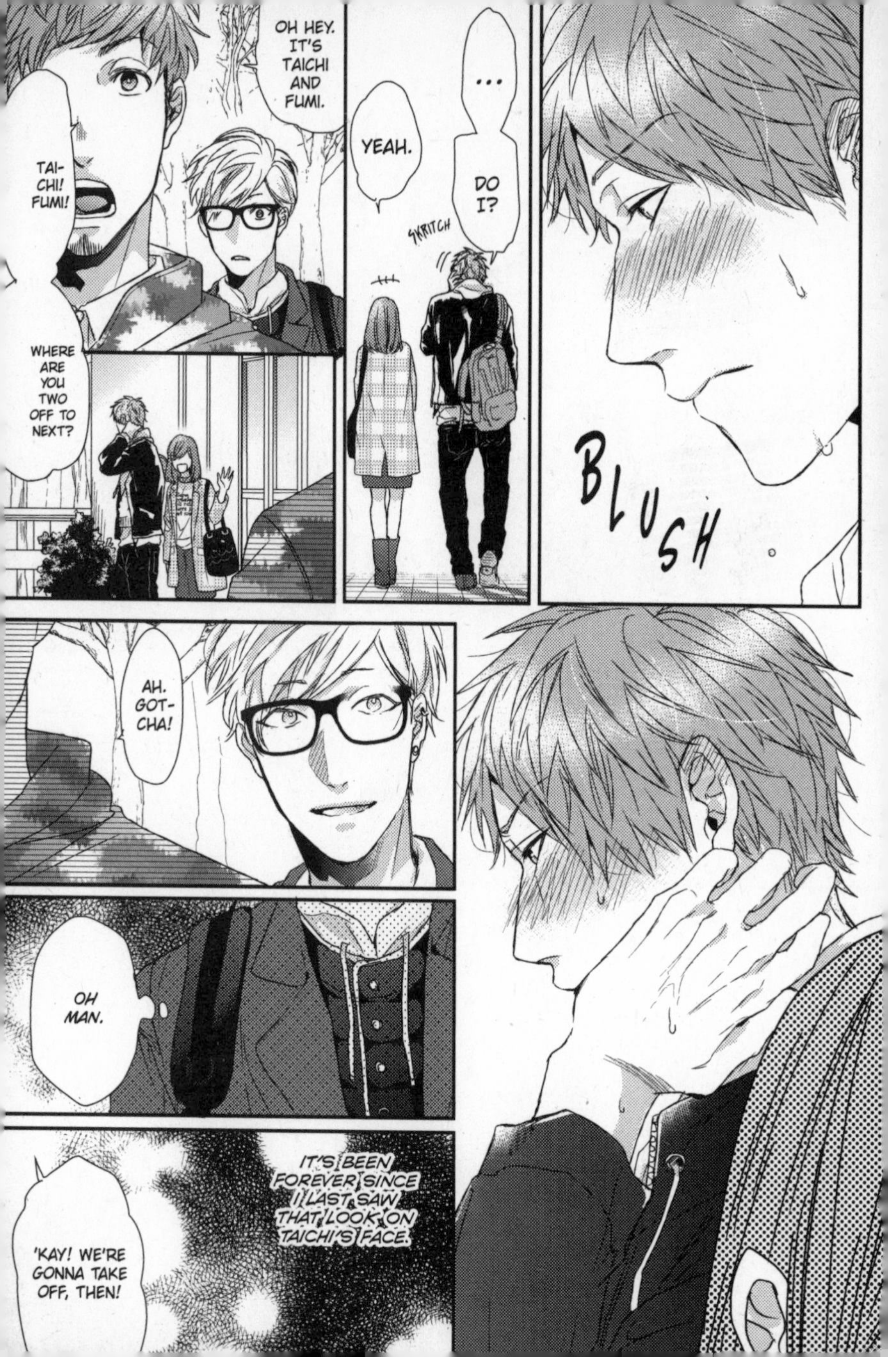
BLUSH
...
DO I?
YEAH.
SKRITCH
OH HEY. IT'S TAICHI AND FUMI.
TAI-CHI! FUMI!
WHERE ARE YOU TWO OFF TO NEXT?
AH. GOT-CHA!
OH MAN.
IT'S BEEN FOREVER SINCE I LAST SAW THAT LOOK ON TAICHI'S FACE.
'KAY! WE'RE GONNA TAKE OFF, THEN!

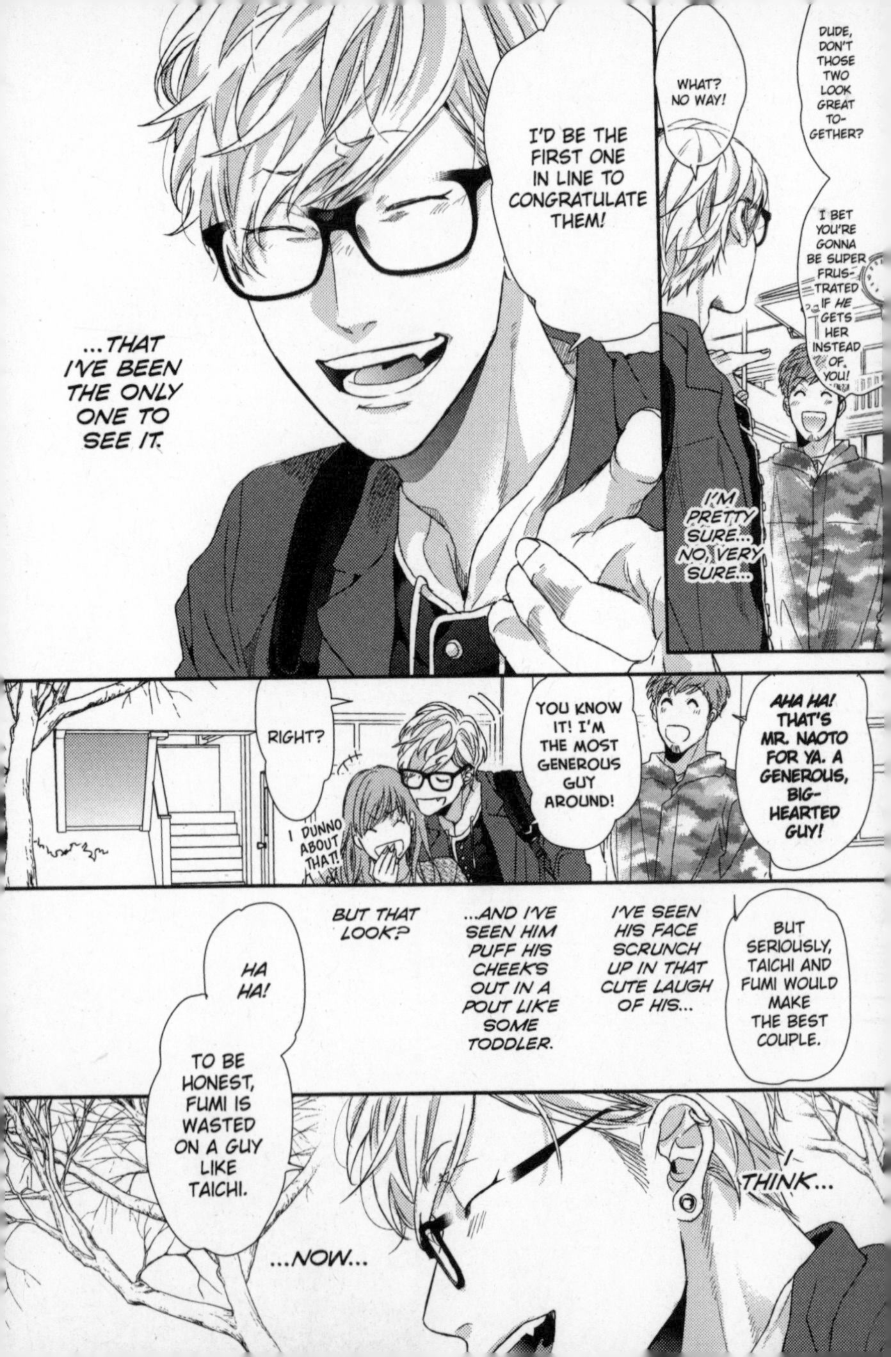
DUDE, DON'T THOSE TWO LOOK GREAT TO-GETHER?
WHAT? NO WAY!
I BET YOU'RE GONNA BE SUPER FRUS-TRATED IF HE GETS HER INSTEAD OF YOU!
I'M PRETTY SURE... NO, VERY SURE...
I'D BE THE FIRST ONE IN LINE TO CONGRATULATE THEM!
...THAT I'VE BEEN THE ONLY ONE TO SEE IT.
AHA HA! THAT'S MR. NAOTO FOR YA. A GENEROUS, BIG-HEARTED GUY!
YOU KNOW IT! I'M THE MOST GENEROUS GUY AROUND!
RIGHT?
I DUNNO ABOUT THAT!
BUT SERIOUSLY, TAICHI AND FUMI WOULD MAKE THE BEST COUPLE.
I'VE SEEN HIS FACE SCRUNCH UP IN THAT CUTE LAUGH OF HIS...
...AND I'VE SEEN HIM PUFF HIS CHEEKS OUT IN A POUT LIKE SOME TODDLER.
BUT THAT LOOK?
HA HA!
TO BE HONEST, FUMI IS WASTED ON A GUY LIKE TAICHI.
I THINK...
...NOW...

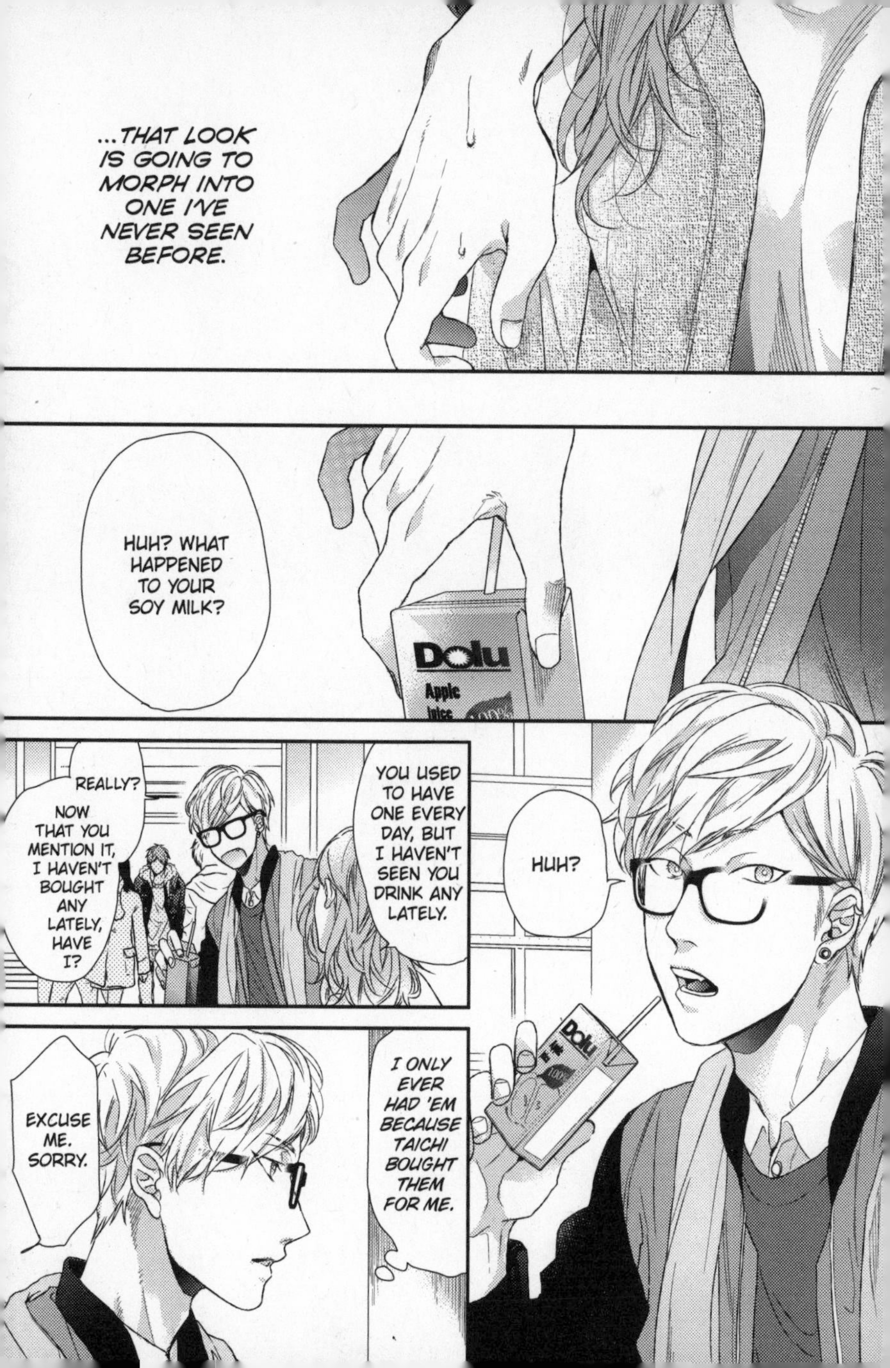
...THAT LOOK IS GOING TO MORPH INTO ONE I'VE NEVER SEEN BEFORE.
HUH? WHAT HAPPENED TO YOUR SOY MILK?
Dolu
Apple
HUH?
Dolu
YOU USED TO HAVE ONE EVERY DAY, BUT I HAVEN'T SEEN YOU DRINK ANY LATELY.
REALLY?
NOW THAT YOU MENTION IT, I HAVEN'T BOUGHT ANY LATELY, HAVE I?
I ONLY EVER HAD 'EM BECAUSE TAICHI BOUGHT THEM FOR ME.
EXCUSE ME. SORRY.

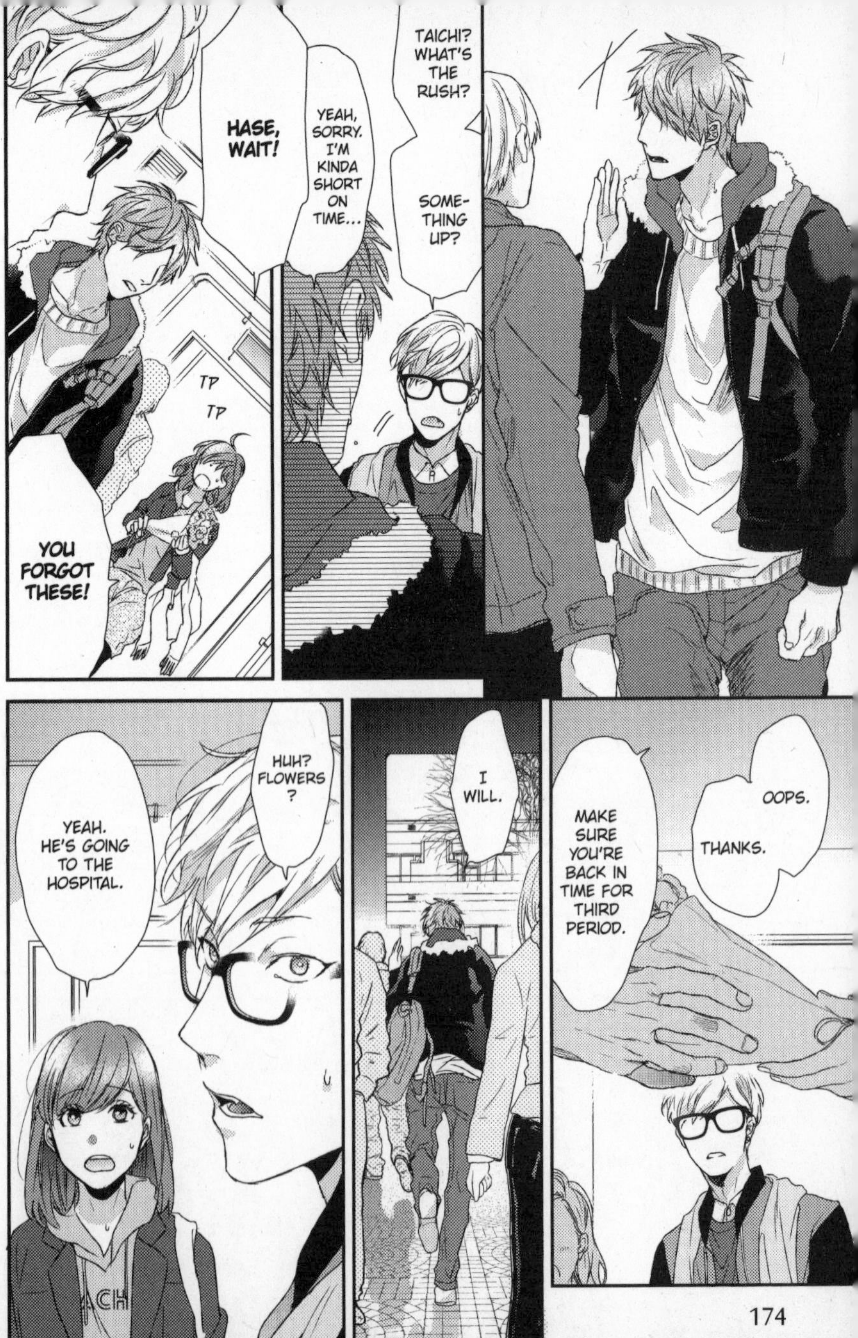
TAICHI? WHAT'S THE RUSH?
YEAH, SORRY. I'M KINDA SHORT ON TIME...
SOME-THING UP?
HASE, WAIT!
TP
TP
YOU FORGOT THESE!
OOPS.
THANKS.
MAKE SURE YOU'RE BACK IN TIME FOR THIRD PERIOD.
I WILL.
HUH? FLOWERS?
YEAH. HE'S GOING TO THE HOSPITAL.

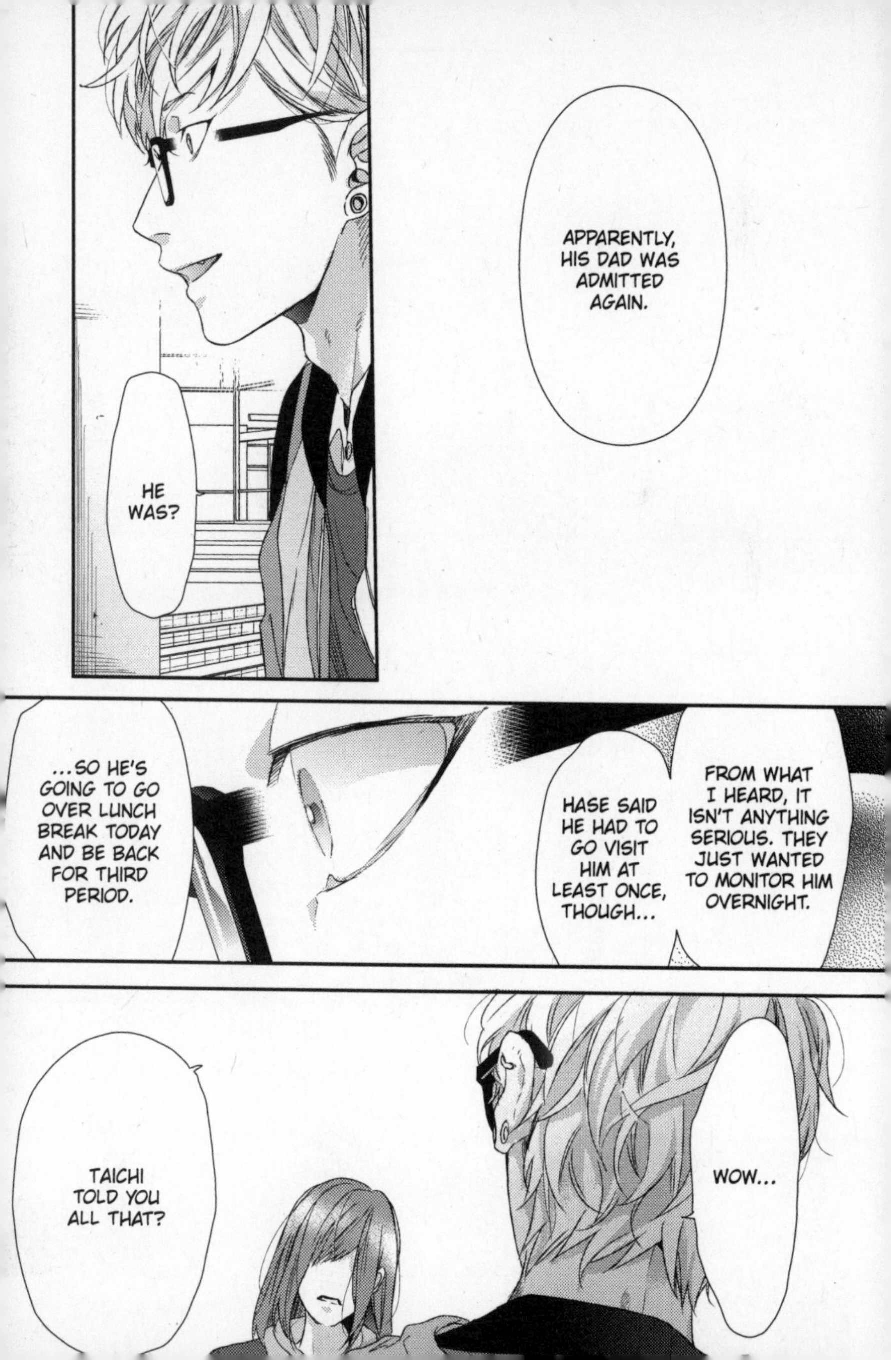
APPARENTLY, HIS DAD WAS ADMITTED AGAIN.
HE WAS?
FROM WHAT I HEARD, IT ISN'T ANYTHING SERIOUS. THEY JUST WANTED TO MONITOR HIM OVERNIGHT.
HASE SAID HE HAD TO GO VISIT HIM AT LEAST ONCE, THOUGH...
...SO HE'S GOING TO GO OVER LUNCH BREAK TODAY AND BE BACK FOR THIRD PERIOD.
WOW...
TAICHI TOLD YOU ALL THAT?

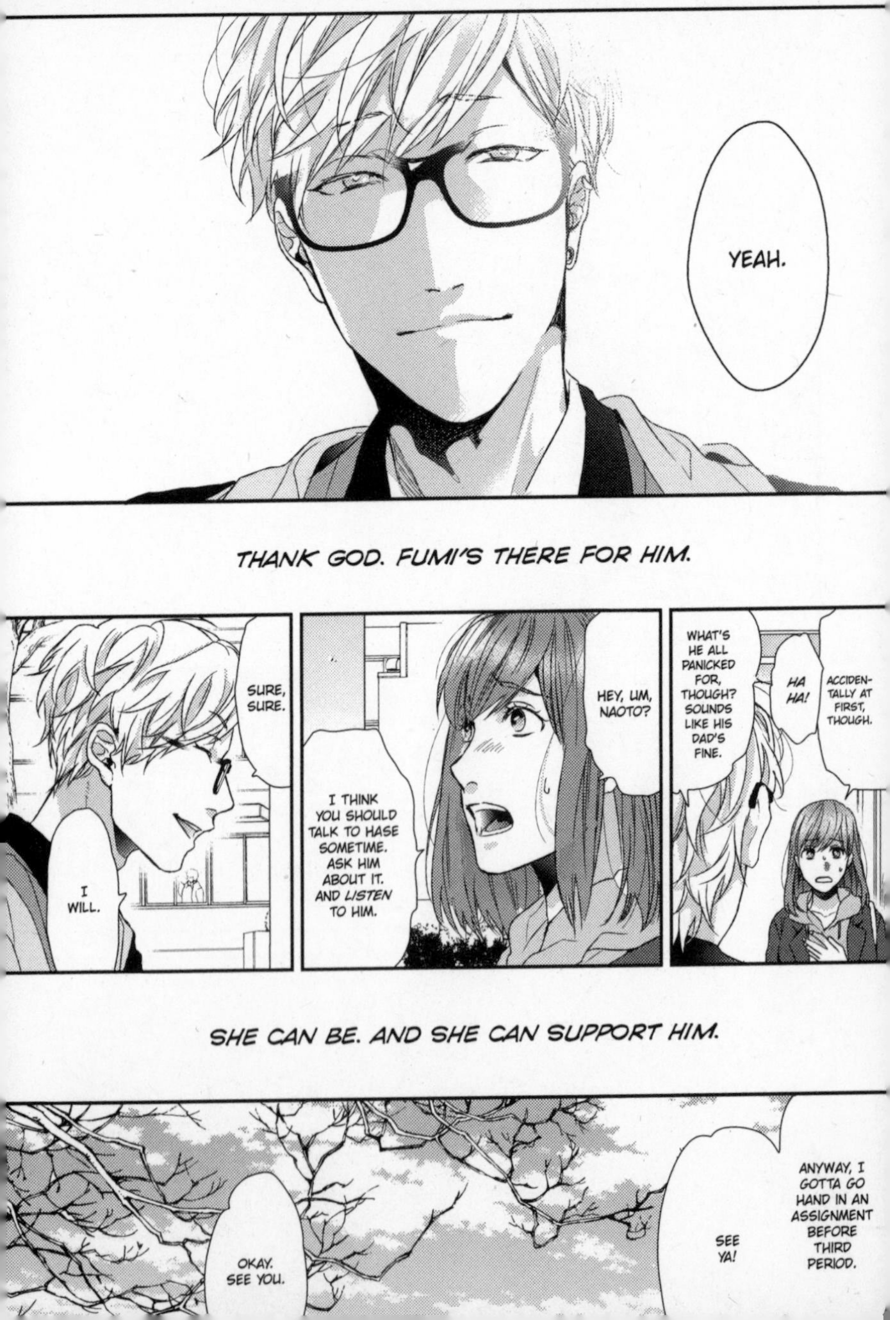
YEAH.
THANK GOD. FUMI'S THERE FOR HIM.
ACCIDENTALLY AT FIRST, THOUGH.
HA HA!
WHAT'S HE ALL PANICKED FOR, THOUGH? SOUNDS LIKE HIS DAD'S FINE.
HEY, UM, NAOTO?
I THINK YOU SHOULD TALK TO HASE SOMETIME. ASK HIM ABOUT IT. AND *LISTEN* TO HIM.
SURE, SURE.
I WILL.
SHE CAN BE. AND SHE CAN SUPPORT HIM.
ANYWAY, I GOTTA GO HAND IN AN ASSIGNMENT BEFORE THIRD PERIOD.
SEE YA!
OKAY. SEE YOU.

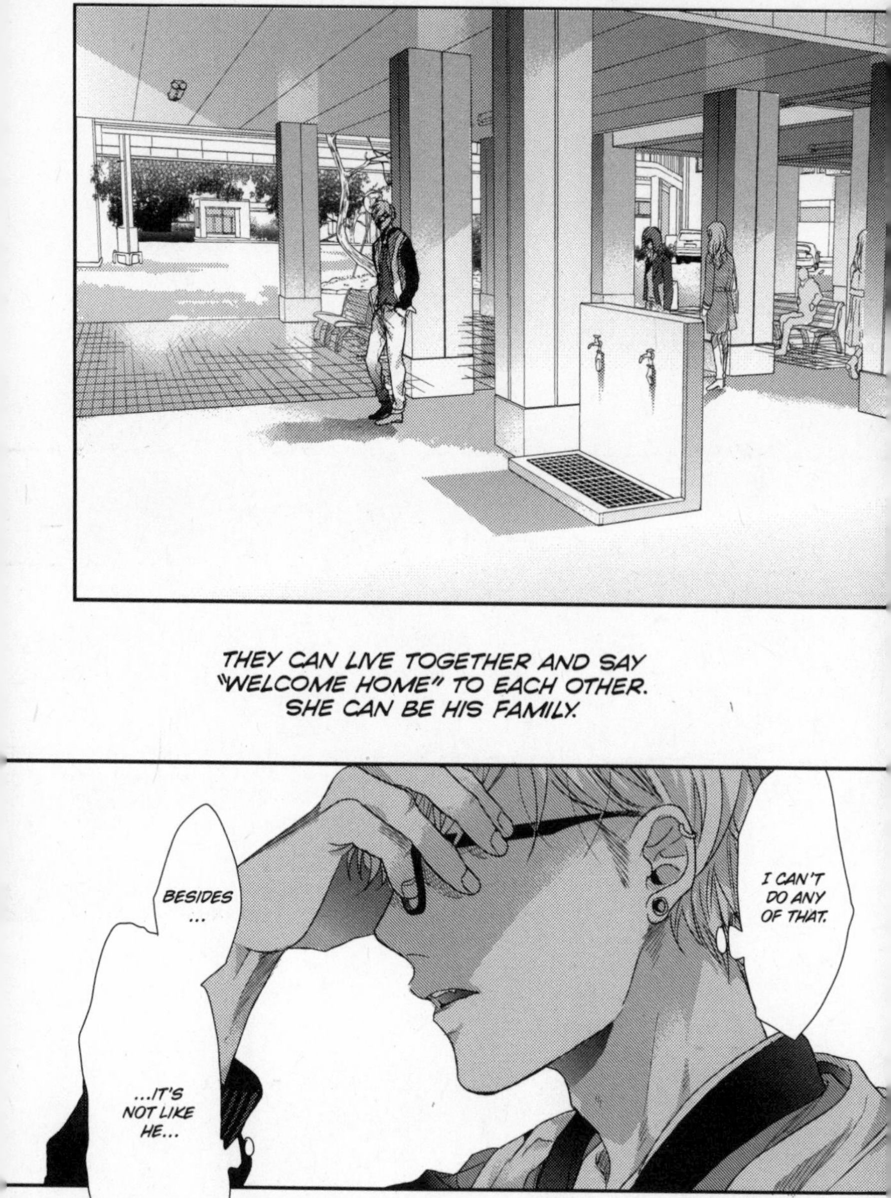
THEY CAN LIVE TOGETHER AND SAY "WELCOME HOME" TO EACH OTHER. SHE CAN BE HIS FAMILY.
I CAN'T DO ANY OF THAT.
BESIDES...
...IT'S NOT LIKE HE...

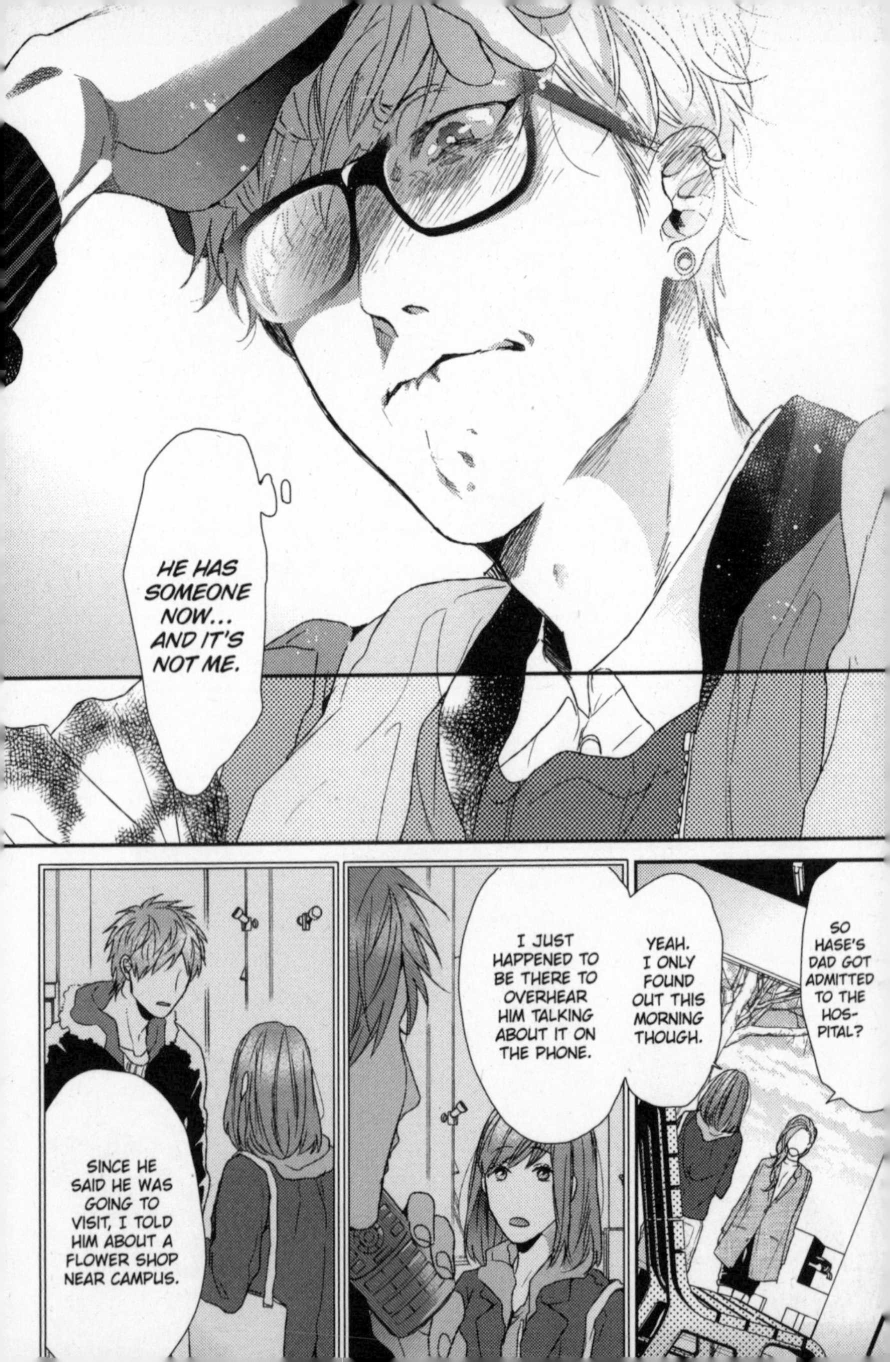
HE HAS SOMEONE NOW... AND IT'S NOT ME.
SO HASE'S DAD GOT ADMITTED TO THE HOS-PITAL?
YEAH. I ONLY FOUND OUT THIS MORNING THOUGH.
I JUST HAPPENED TO BE THERE TO OVERHEAR HIM TALKING ABOUT IT ON THE PHONE.
SINCE HE SAID HE WAS GOING TO VISIT, I TOLD HIM ABOUT A FLOWER SHOP NEAR CAMPUS.

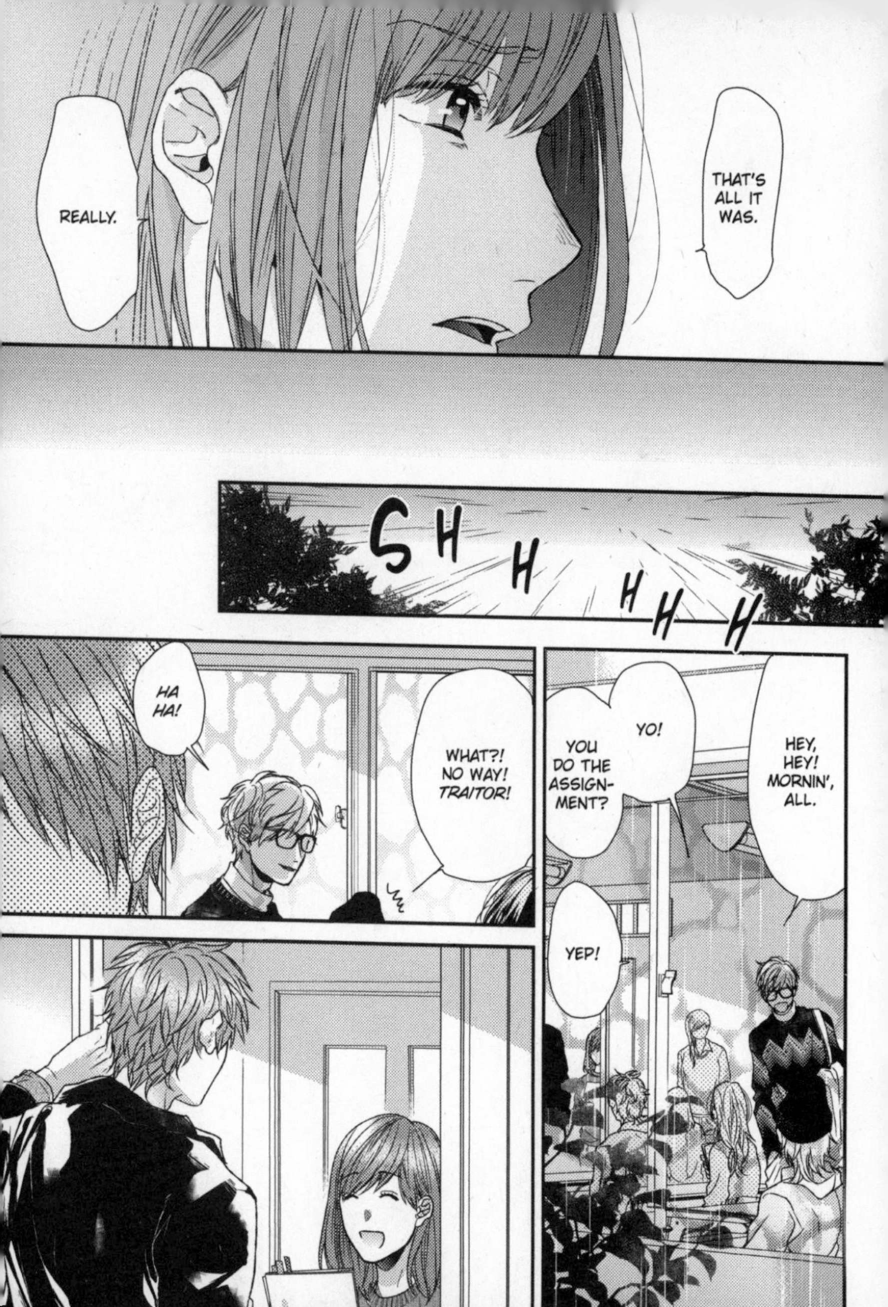

THAT'S ALL IT WAS.
REALLY.
SHHHHHH
HEY, HEY! MORNIN', ALL.
YO!
YOU DO THE ASSIGN-MENT?
YEP!
WHAT?! NO WAY! *TRAITOR!*
HA HA!

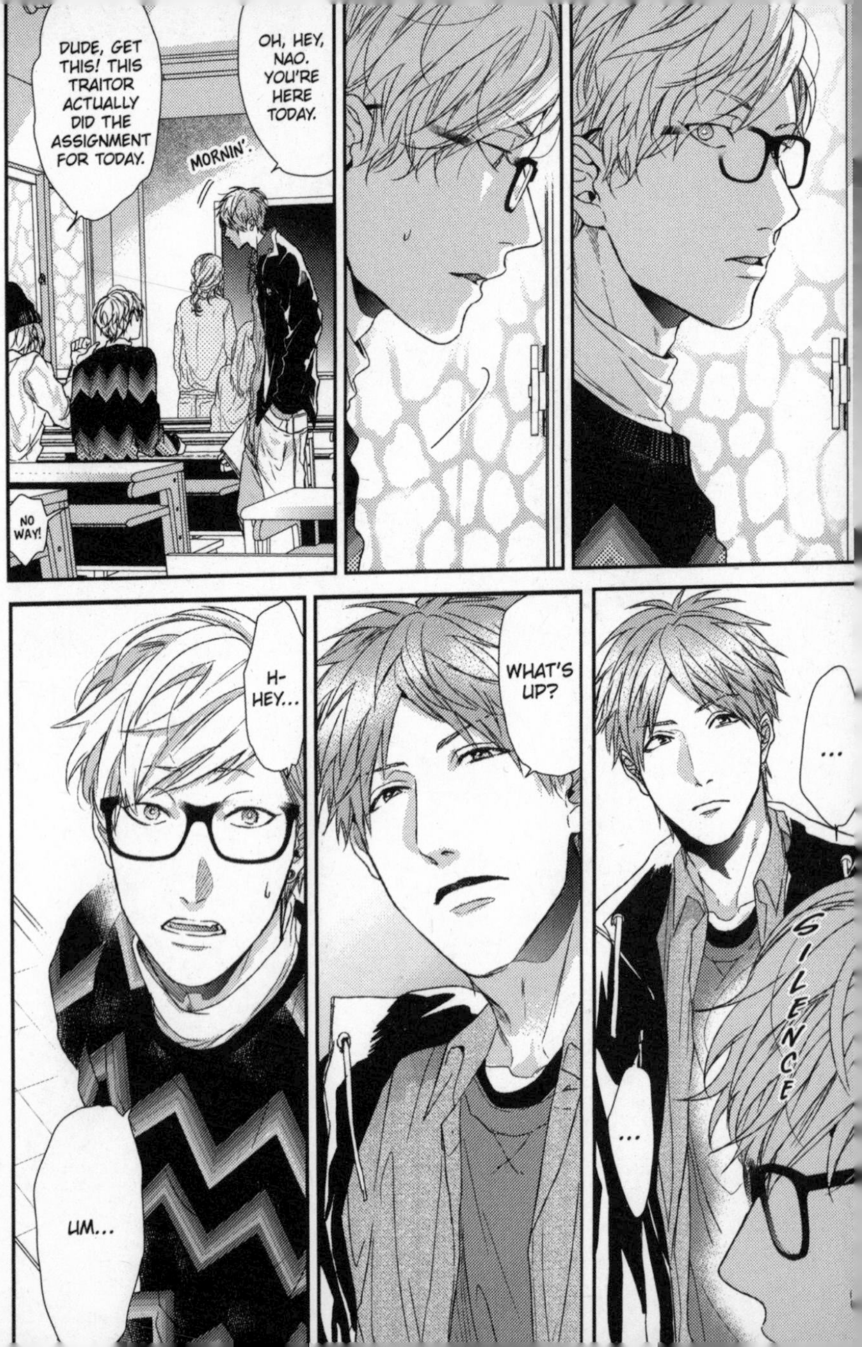
OH, HEY, NAO. YOU'RE HERE TODAY.
DUDE, GET THIS! THIS TRAITOR ACTUALLY DID THE ASSIGNMENT FOR TODAY.
MORNIN'.
NO WAY!
...
SILENCE
...
WHAT'S UP?
H-HEY...
UM...

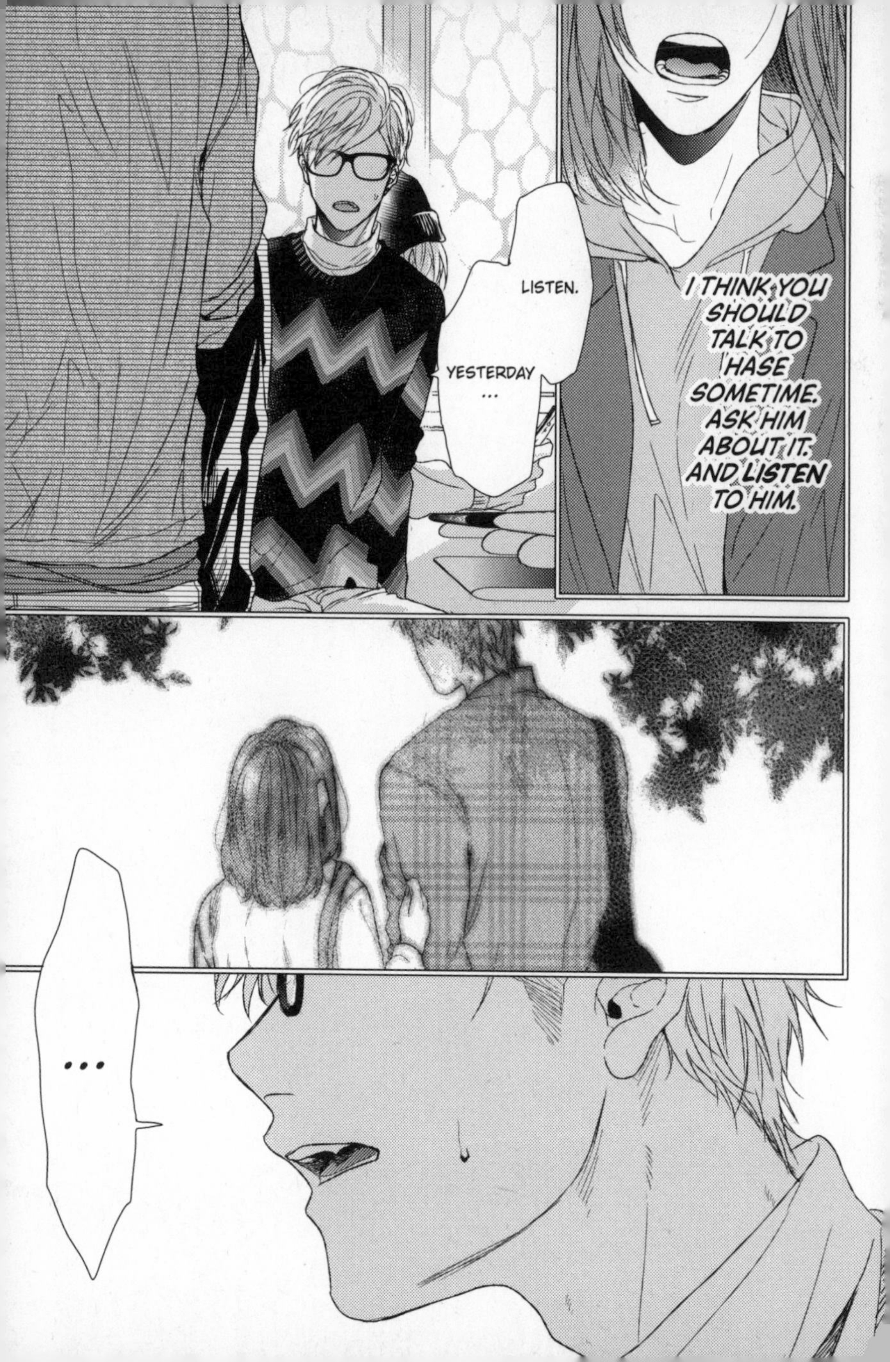
LISTEN.
YESTERDAY ...
I THINK YOU SHOULD TALK TO HASE SOMETIME. ASK HIM ABOUT IT. AND LISTEN TO HIM.
...

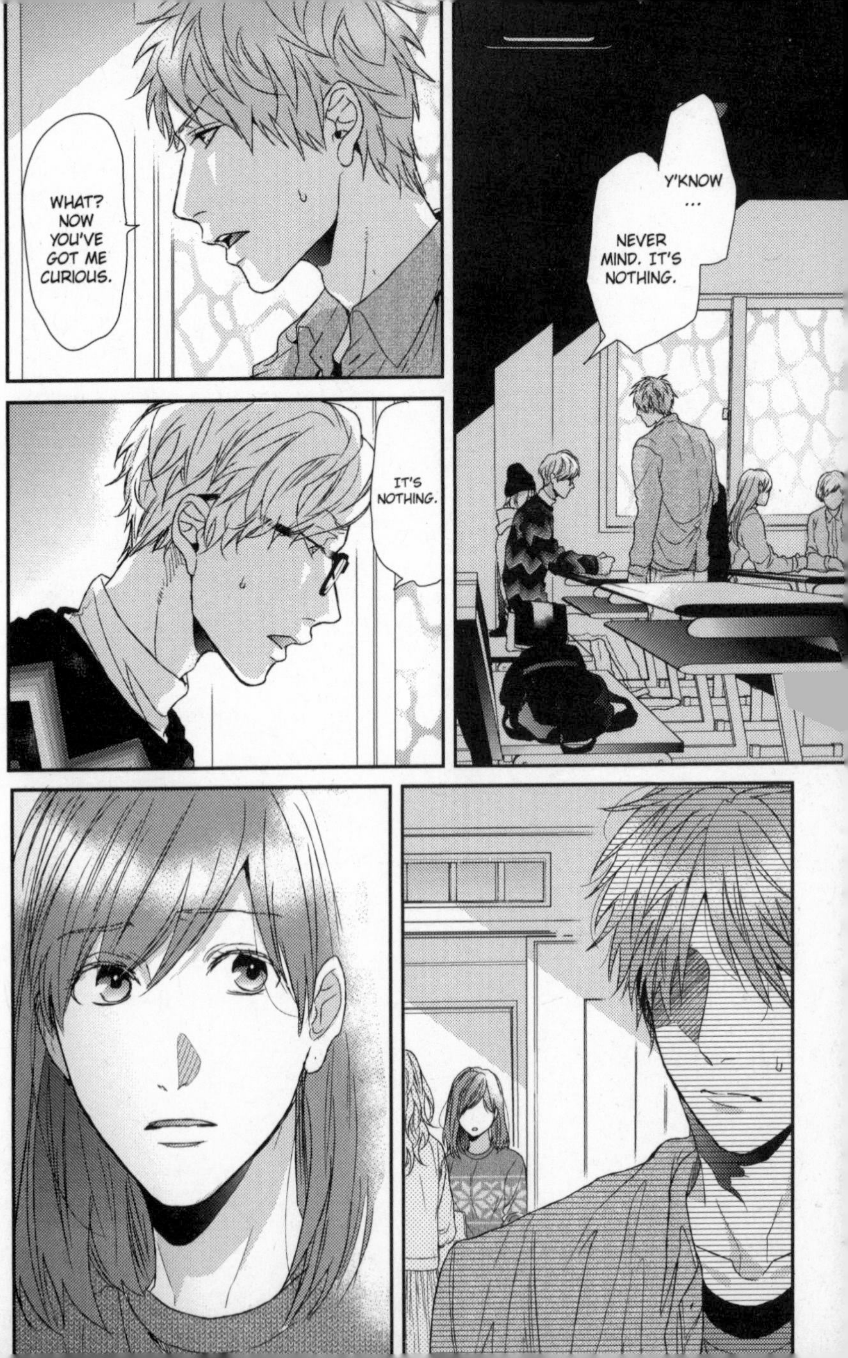
Y'KNOW ...
NEVER MIND. IT'S NOTHING.
WHAT? NOW YOU'VE GOT ME CURIOUS.
IT'S NOTHING.

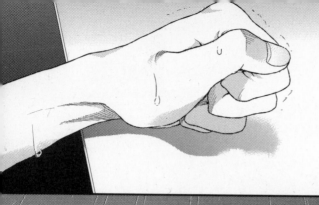

I CAN'T DO IT.

I JUST NEED TO ASK HIM... TO TALK TO HIM AND SPEAK THE WORDS LIKE I ALWAYS USED TO DO.

IT WAS COMPLETELY NORMAL FOR ME TO TALK TO HIM ABOUT HIS DAD AND HIS FAMILY.

BUT... I CAN'T.

IT JUST DOESN'T FEEL LIKE HIS PERSONAL LIFE IS MY BUSINESS ANYMORE.

IT'S NEARLY A MIRACLE WE WERE ABLE TO GO BACK TO BEING FRIENDS...

...BUT I'M THE ONLY ONE WHO CAN'T ACT LIKE EVERYTHING IS NORMAL.

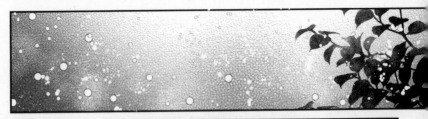

MURMUR
MURMUR
MURMUR
TAICHI AND I HAVEN'T REALLY SPOKEN SINCE THEN.
HEY, GUYS!
CHECK OUT THE NEWS!

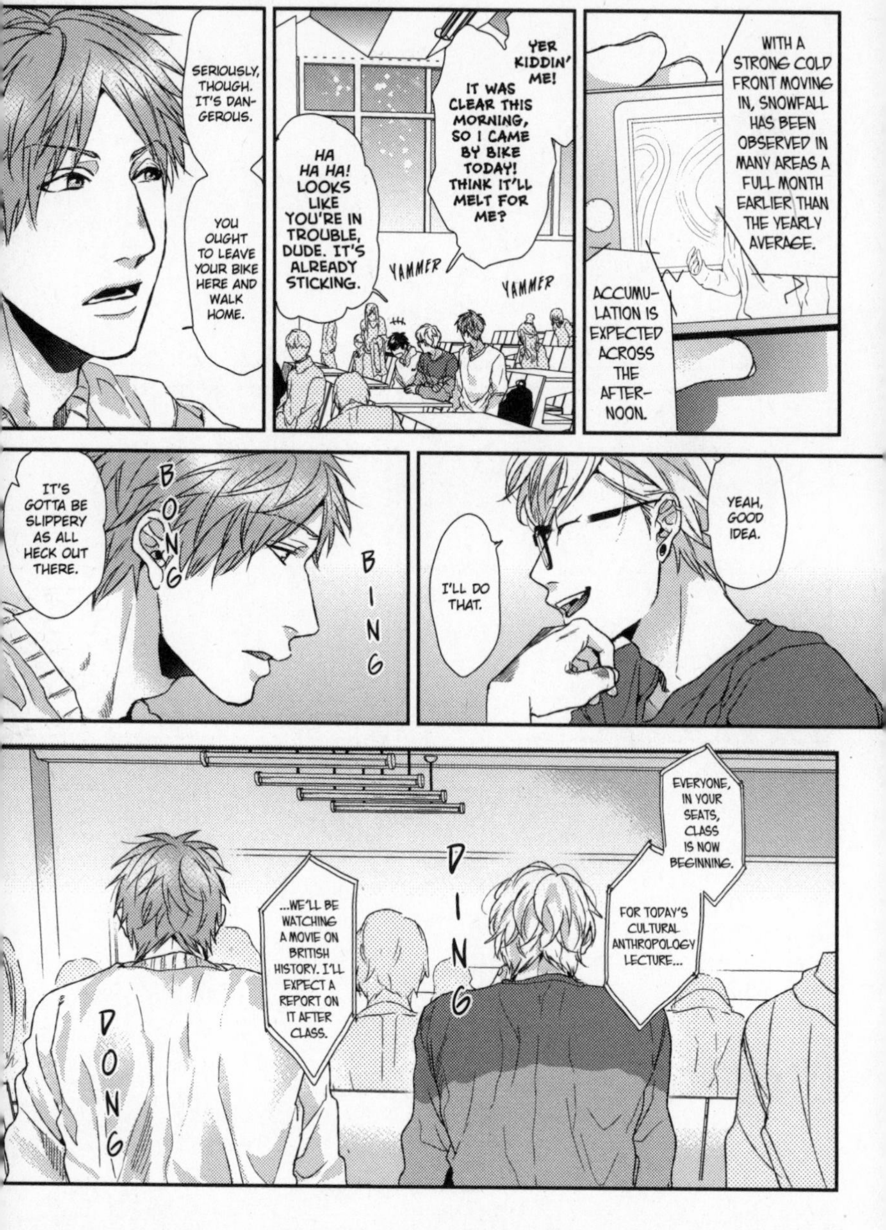
WITH A STRONG COLD FRONT MOVING IN, SNOWFALL HAS BEEN OBSERVED IN MANY AREAS A FULL MONTH EARLIER THAN THE YEARLY AVERAGE.
ACCUMULATION IS EXPECTED ACROSS THE AFTERNOON.
YER KIDDIN' ME!
IT WAS CLEAR THIS MORNING, SO I CAME BY BIKE TODAY! THINK IT'LL MELT FOR ME?
HA HA HA! LOOKS LIKE YOU'RE IN TROUBLE, DUDE. IT'S ALREADY STICKING.
YAMMER
YAMMER
SERIOUSLY, THOUGH. IT'S DANGEROUS.
YOU OUGHT TO LEAVE YOUR BIKE HERE AND WALK HOME.
YEAH, GOOD IDEA.
I'LL DO THAT.
BING
BONG
IT'S GOTTA BE SLIPPERY AS ALL HECK OUT THERE.
EVERYONE, IN YOUR SEATS, CLASS IS NOW BEGINNING.
FOR TODAY'S CULTURAL ANTHROPOLOGY LECTURE...
DING
...WE'LL BE WATCHING A MOVIE ON BRITISH HISTORY. I'LL EXPECT A REPORT ON IT AFTER CLASS.
DONG

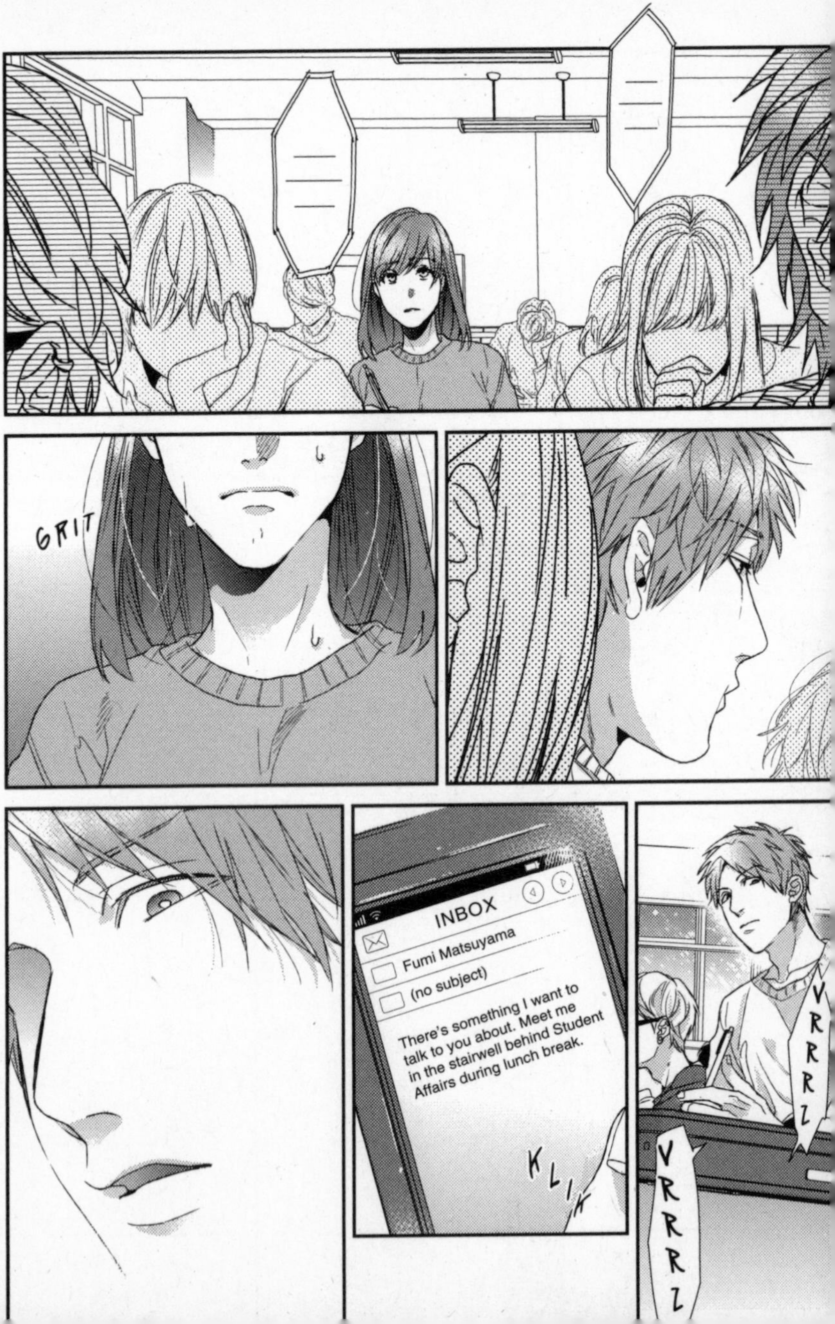
GRIT
VRRRZ
VRRRZ
INBOX
Fumi Matsuyama
(no subject)
There's something I want to talk to you about. Meet me in the stairwell behind Student Affairs during lunch break.
KLIK

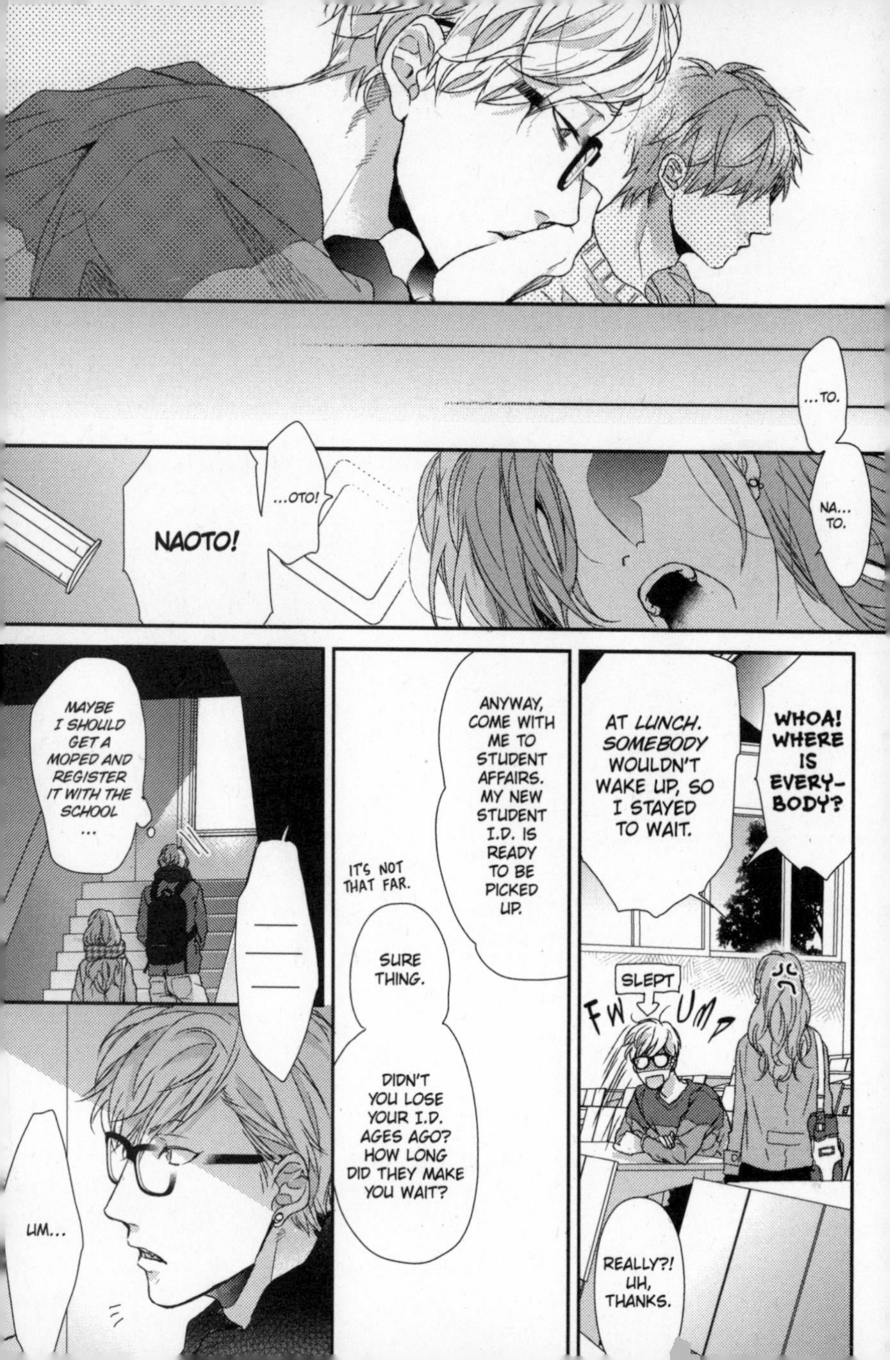
...TO.
NA... TO.
...OTO!
NAOTO!
WHOA! WHERE IS EVERY-BODY?
AT LUNCH. SOMEBODY WOULDN'T WAKE UP, SO I STAYED TO WAIT.
SLEPT
FWUMP
REALLY?! UH, THANKS.
ANYWAY, COME WITH ME TO STUDENT AFFAIRS. MY NEW STUDENT I.D. IS READY TO BE PICKED UP.
IT'S NOT THAT FAR.
SURE THING.
DIDN'T YOU LOSE YOUR I.D. AGES AGO? HOW LONG DID THEY MAKE YOU WAIT?
MAYBE I SHOULD GET A MOPED AND REGISTER IT WITH THE SCHOOL...
UM...

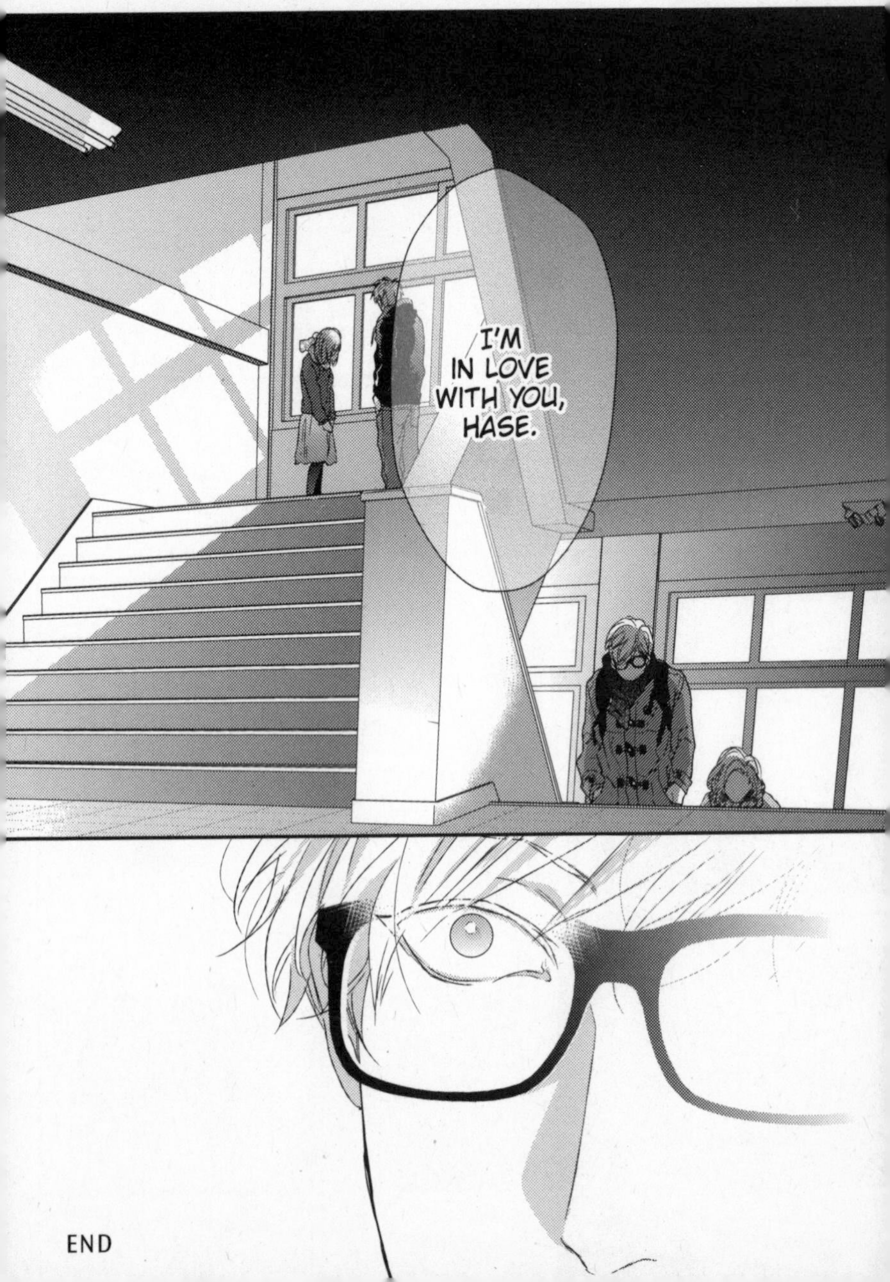
I'M IN LOVE WITH YOU, HASE.

END

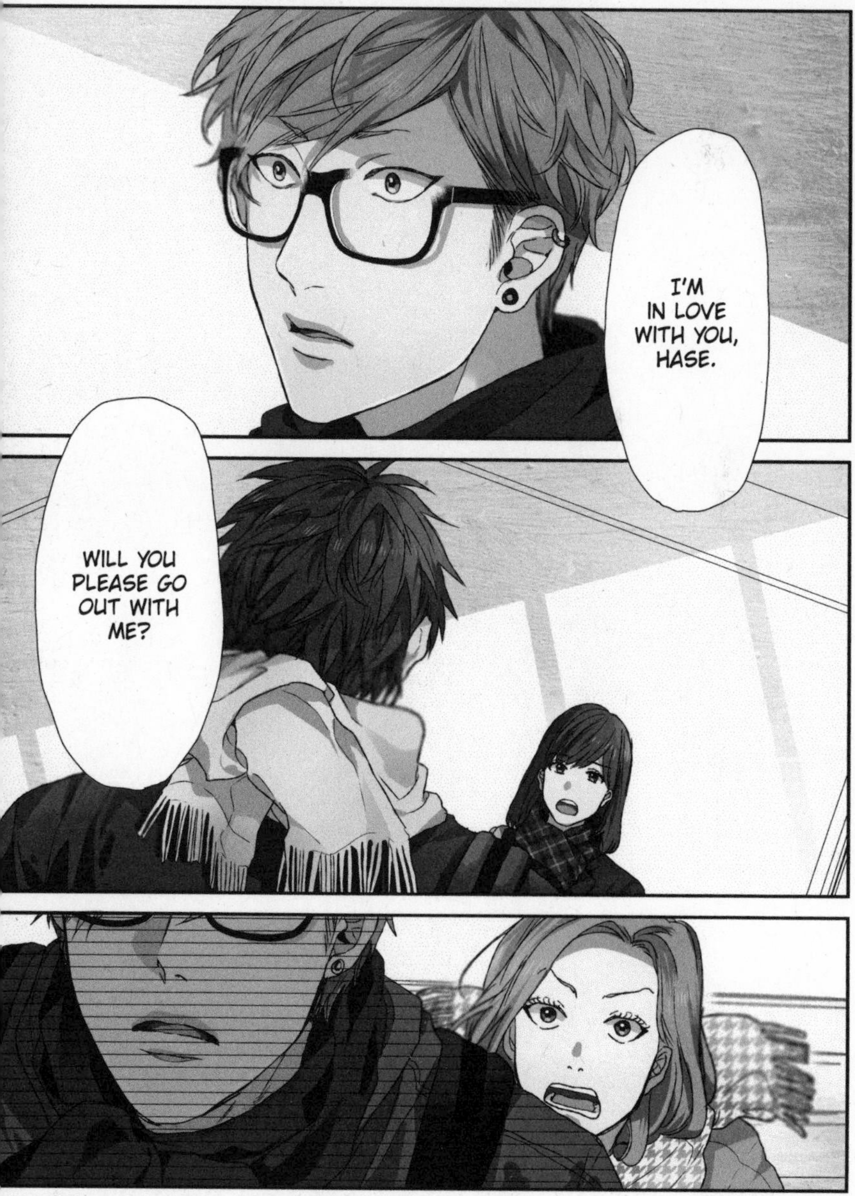
I'M IN LOVE WITH YOU, HASE.
WILL YOU PLEASE GO OUT WITH ME?

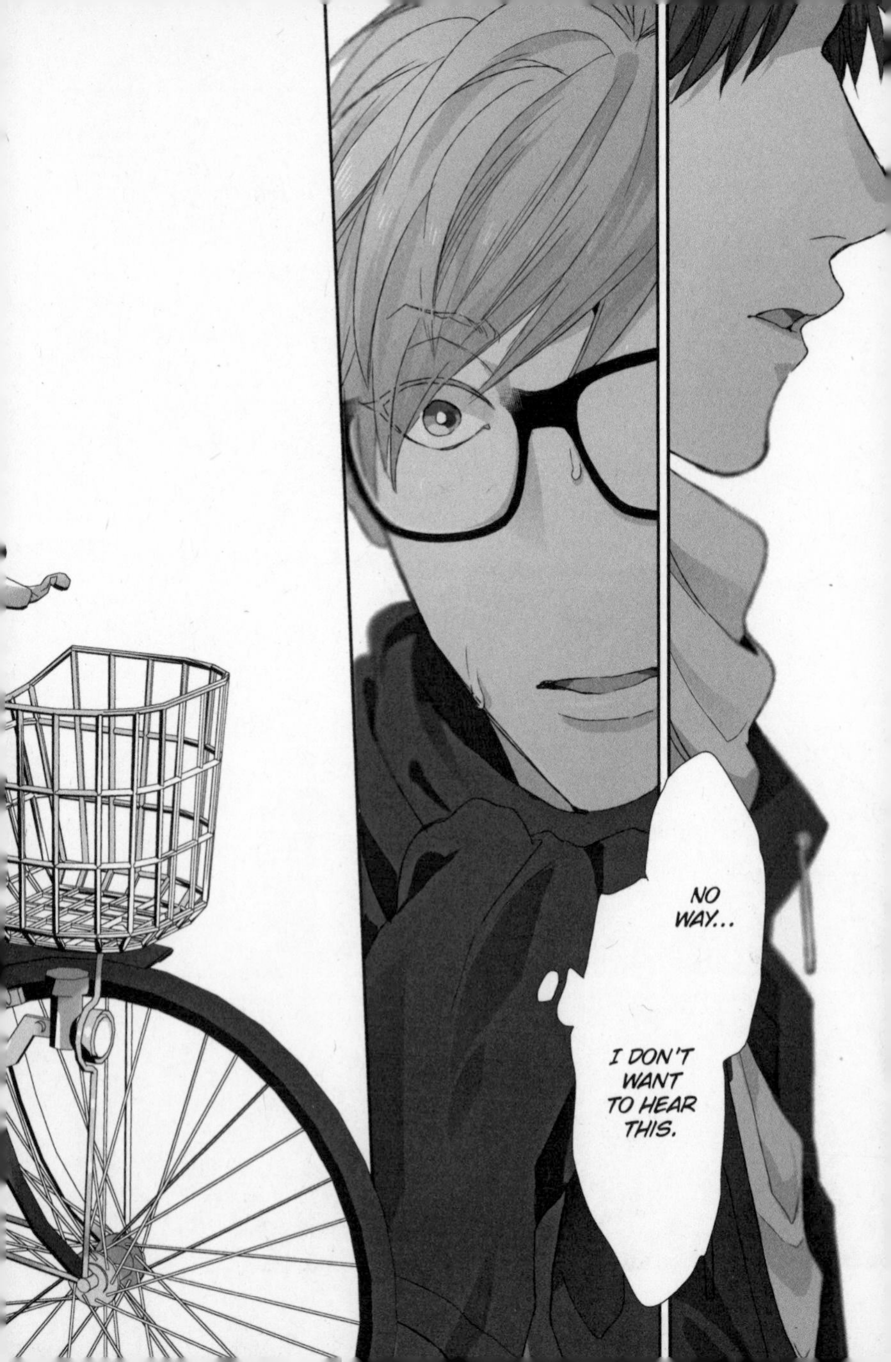
NO WAY...
I DON'T WANT TO HEAR THIS.

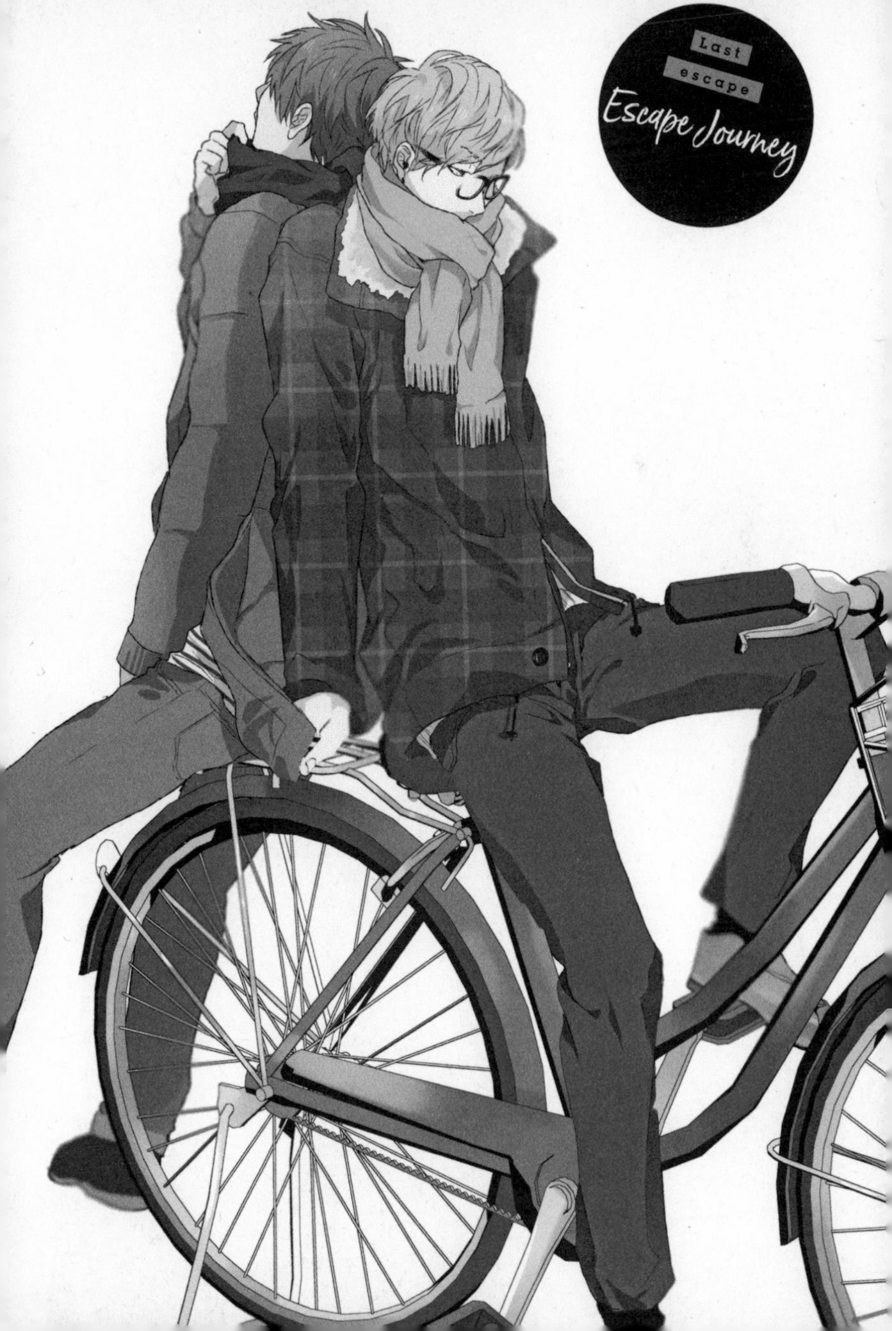
Last
escape
Escape Journey

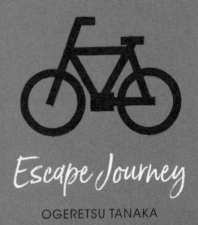

Escape Journey

OGERETSU TANAKA

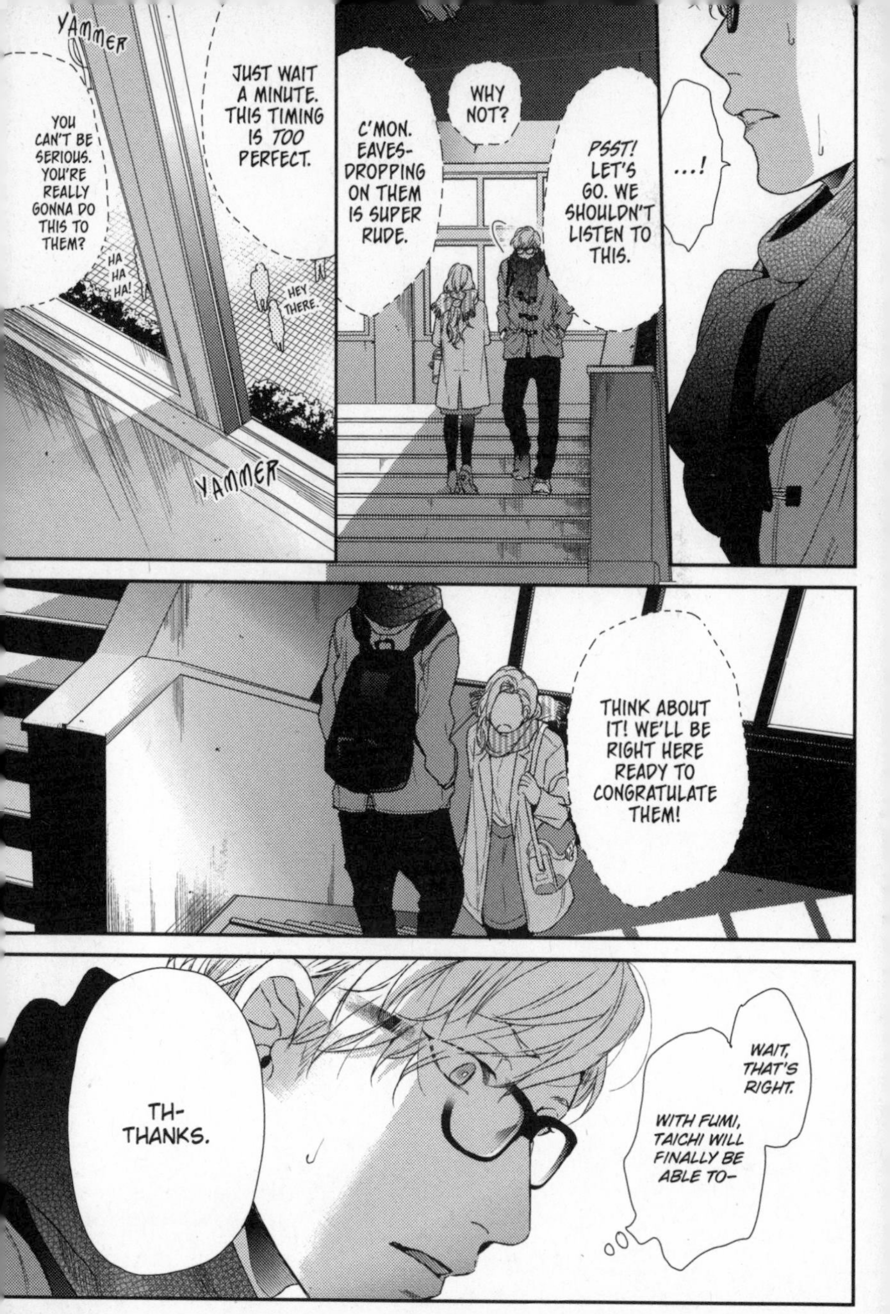
…!
PSST! LET'S GO. WE SHOULDN'T LISTEN TO THIS.
WHY NOT?
C'MON. EAVES-DROPPING ON THEM IS SUPER RUDE.
YAMMER
JUST WAIT A MINUTE. THIS TIMING IS *TOO* PERFECT.
YOU CAN'T BE SERIOUS. YOU'RE REALLY GONNA DO THIS TO THEM?
HA HA HA!
HEY THERE.
YAMMER
THINK ABOUT IT! WE'LL BE RIGHT HERE READY TO CONGRATULATE THEM!
WAIT, THAT'S RIGHT.
WITH FUMI, TAICHI WILL FINALLY BE ABLE TO–
TH- THANKS.

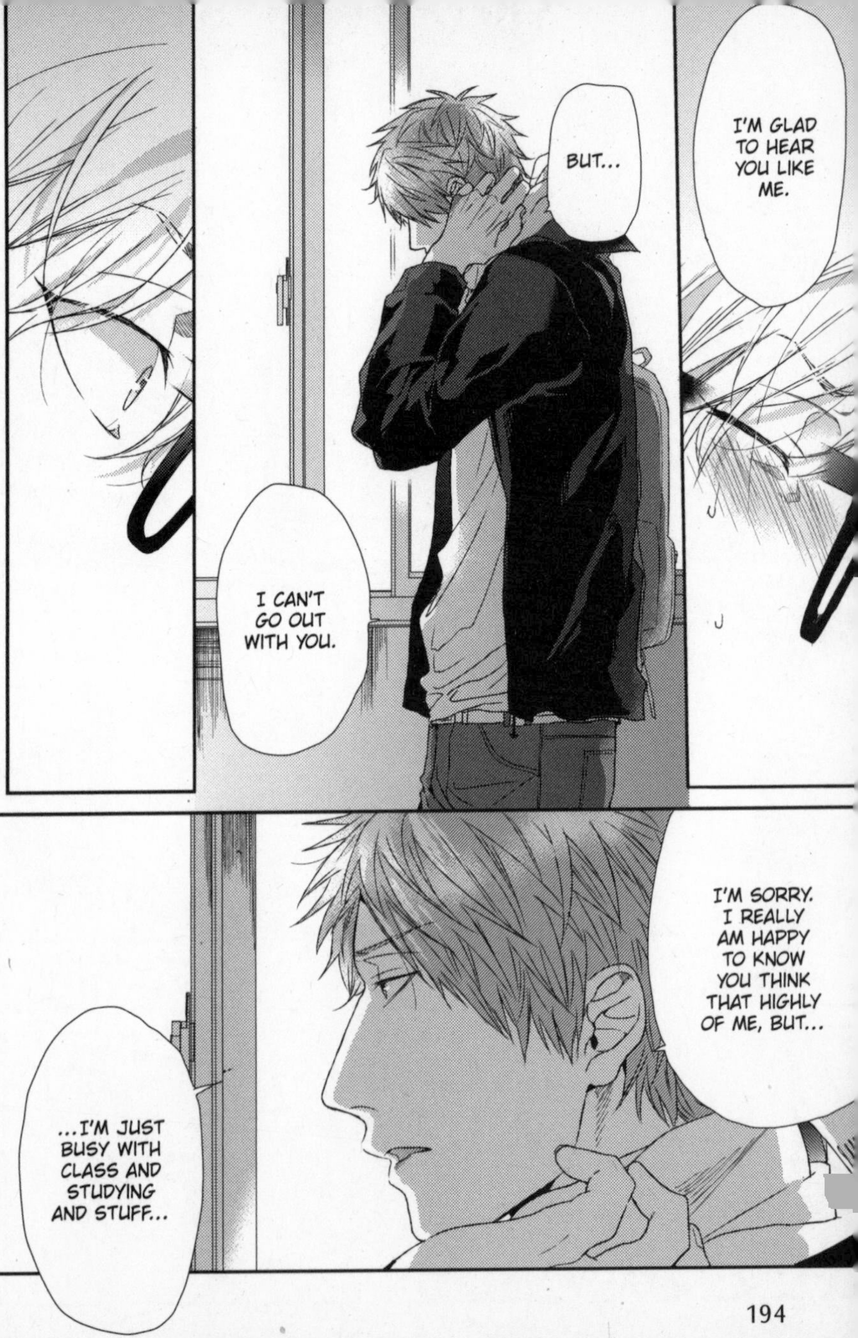
I'M GLAD TO HEAR YOU LIKE ME.
BUT...
I CAN'T GO OUT WITH YOU.
I'M SORRY. I REALLY AM HAPPY TO KNOW YOU THINK THAT HIGHLY OF ME, BUT...
...I'M JUST BUSY WITH CLASS AND STUDYING AND STUFF...

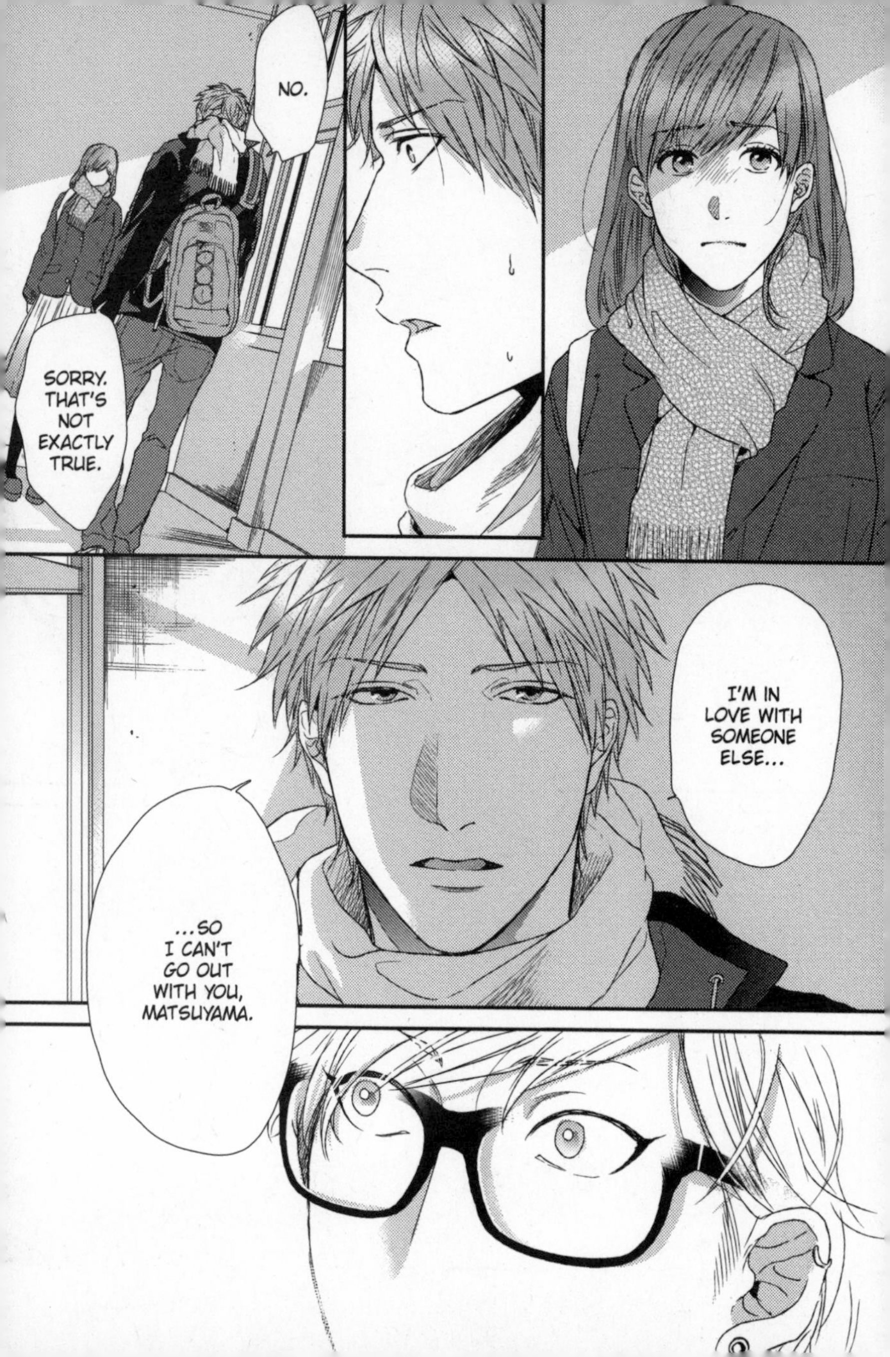
NO.
SORRY. THAT'S NOT EXACTLY TRUE.
I'M IN LOVE WITH SOMEONE ELSE...
...SO I CAN'T GO OUT WITH YOU, MATSUYAMA.

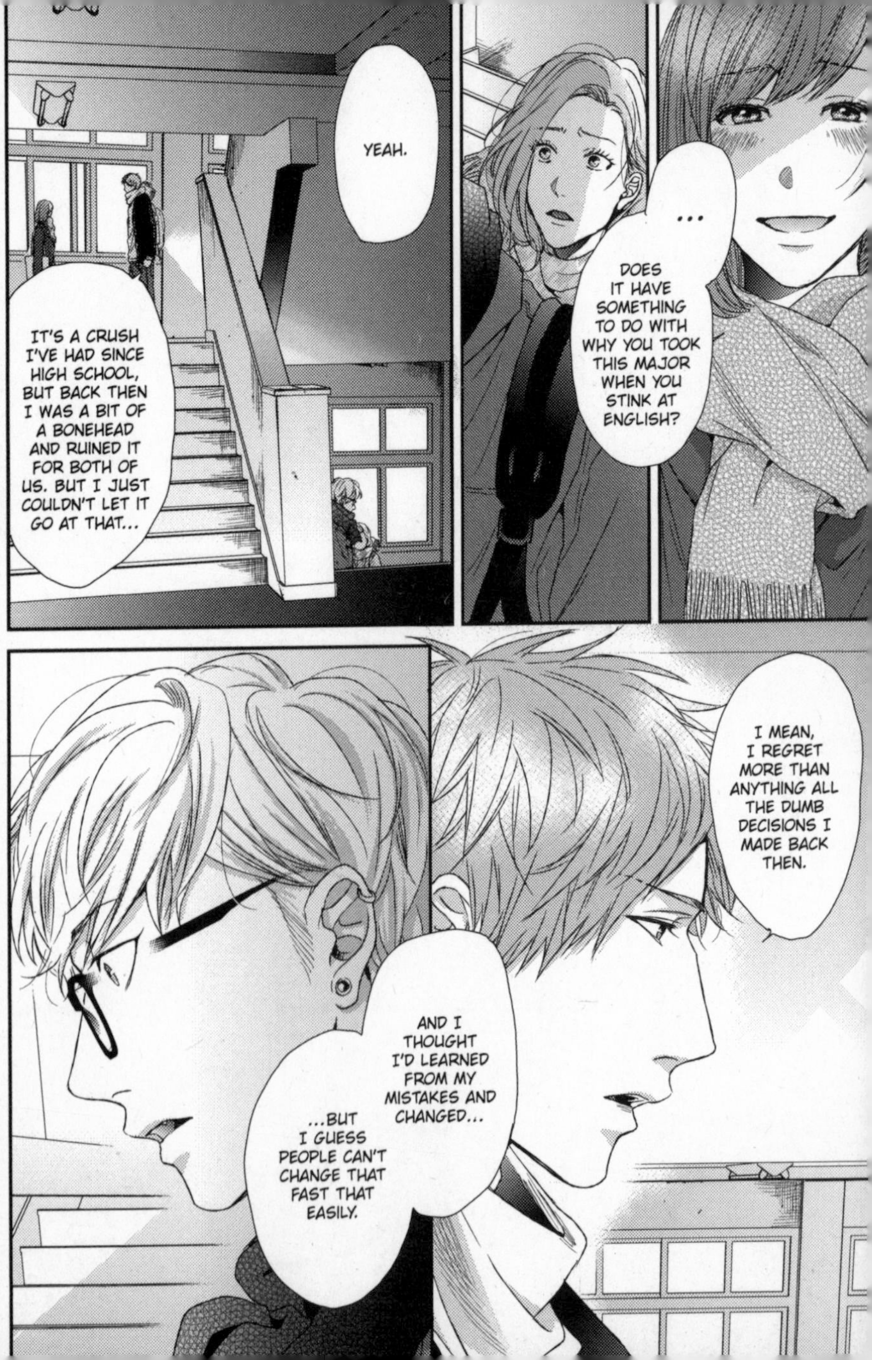
...
DOES IT HAVE SOMETHING TO DO WITH WHY YOU TOOK THIS MAJOR WHEN YOU STINK AT ENGLISH?
YEAH.
IT'S A CRUSH I'VE HAD SINCE HIGH SCHOOL, BUT BACK THEN I WAS A BIT OF A BONEHEAD AND RUINED IT FOR BOTH OF US. BUT I JUST COULDN'T LET IT GO AT THAT...
I MEAN, I REGRET MORE THAN ANYTHING ALL THE DUMB DECISIONS I MADE BACK THEN.
AND I THOUGHT I'D LEARNED FROM MY MISTAKES AND CHANGED...
...BUT I GUESS PEOPLE CAN'T CHANGE THAT FAST THAT EASILY.

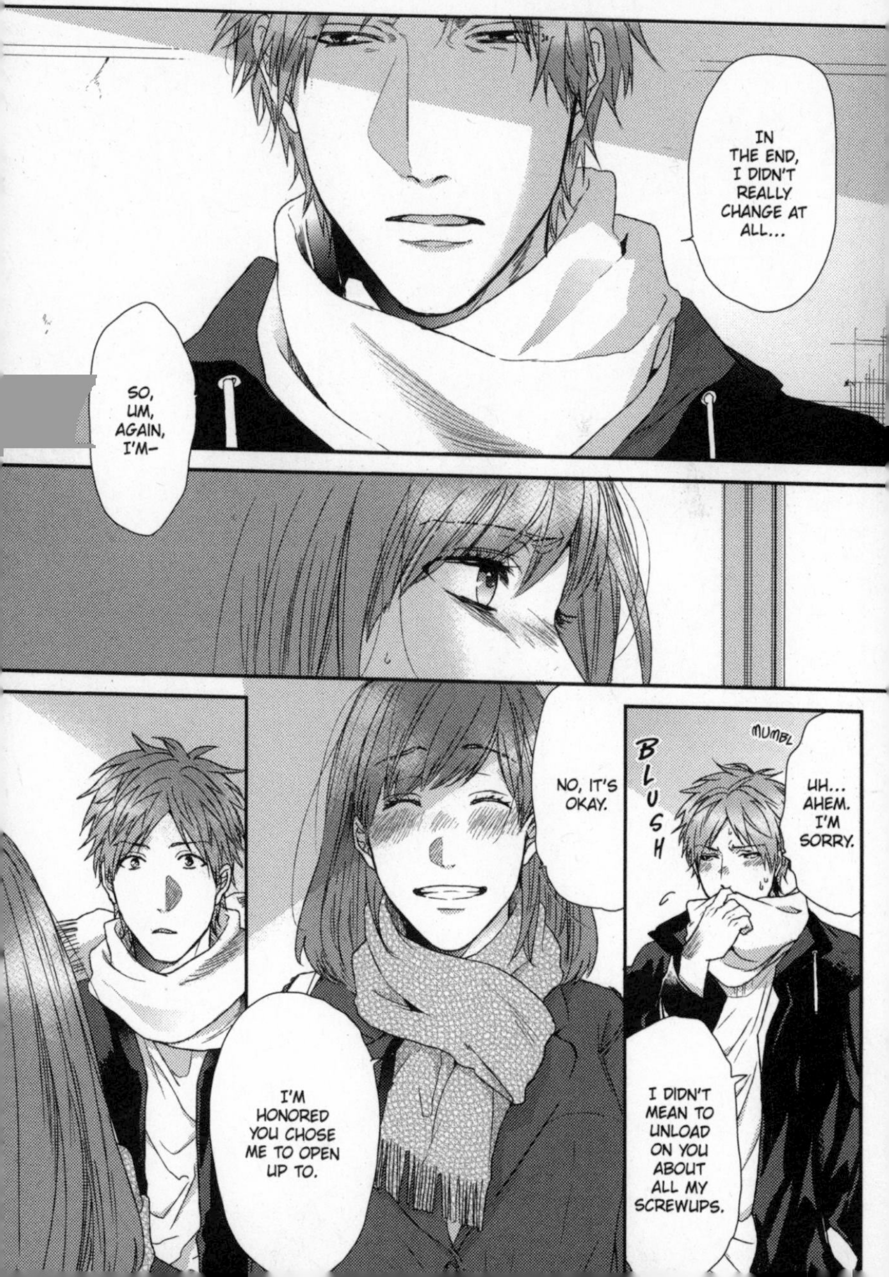
IN THE END, I DIDN'T REALLY CHANGE AT ALL...
SO, UM, AGAIN, I'M-
MUMBL
BLUSH
UH... AHEM. I'M SORRY.
I DIDN'T MEAN TO UNLOAD ON YOU ABOUT ALL MY SCREWUPS.
NO, IT'S OKAY.
I'M HONORED YOU CHOSE ME TO OPEN UP TO.

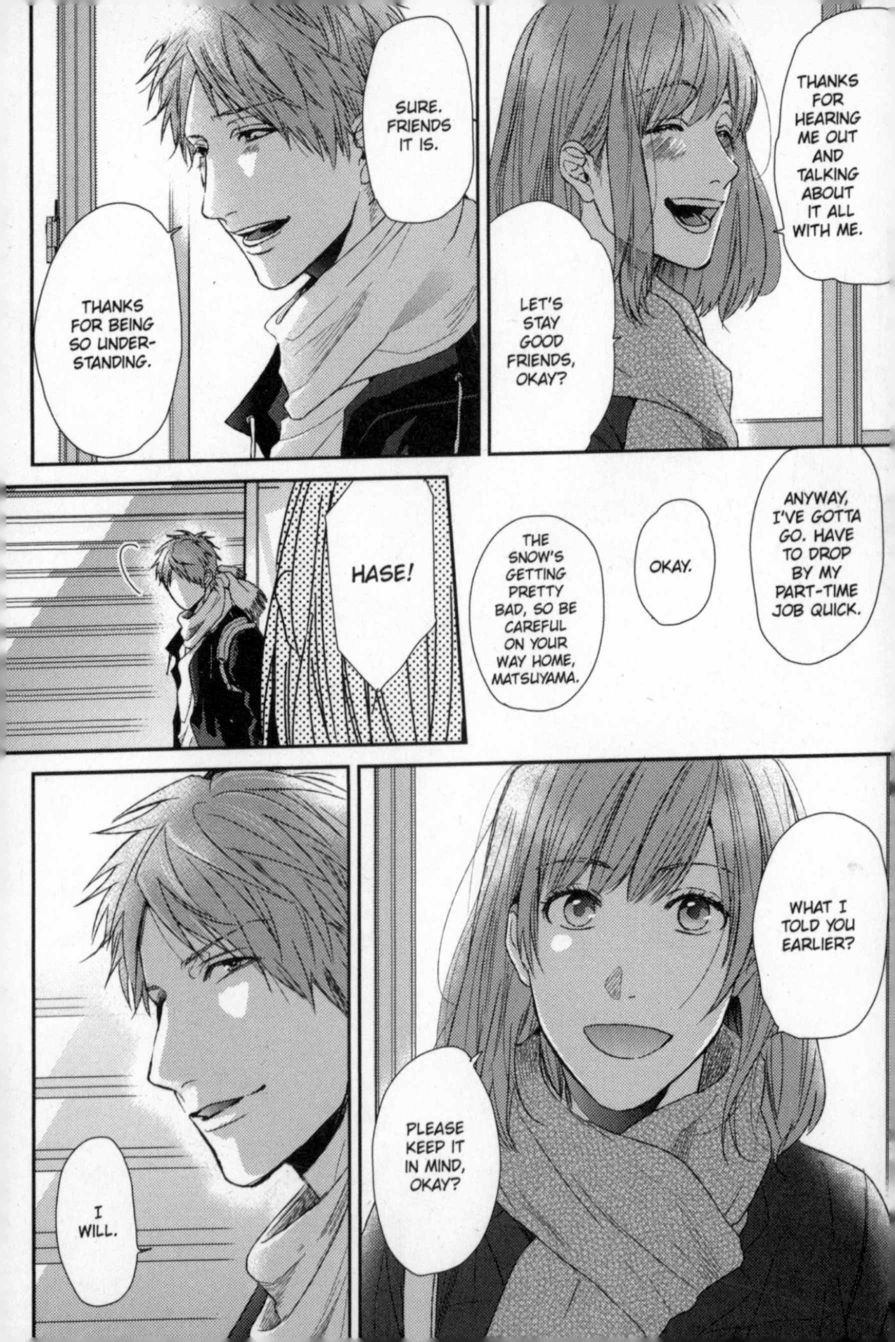
THANKS FOR HEARING ME OUT AND TALKING ABOUT IT ALL WITH ME.
LET'S STAY GOOD FRIENDS, OKAY?
SURE. FRIENDS IT IS.
THANKS FOR BEING SO UNDER-STANDING.
ANYWAY, I'VE GOTTA GO. HAVE TO DROP BY MY PART-TIME JOB QUICK.
OKAY.
THE SNOW'S GETTING PRETTY BAD, SO BE CAREFUL ON YOUR WAY HOME, MATSUYAMA.
HASE!
WHAT I TOLD YOU EARLIER?
PLEASE KEEP IT IN MIND, OKAY?
I WILL.

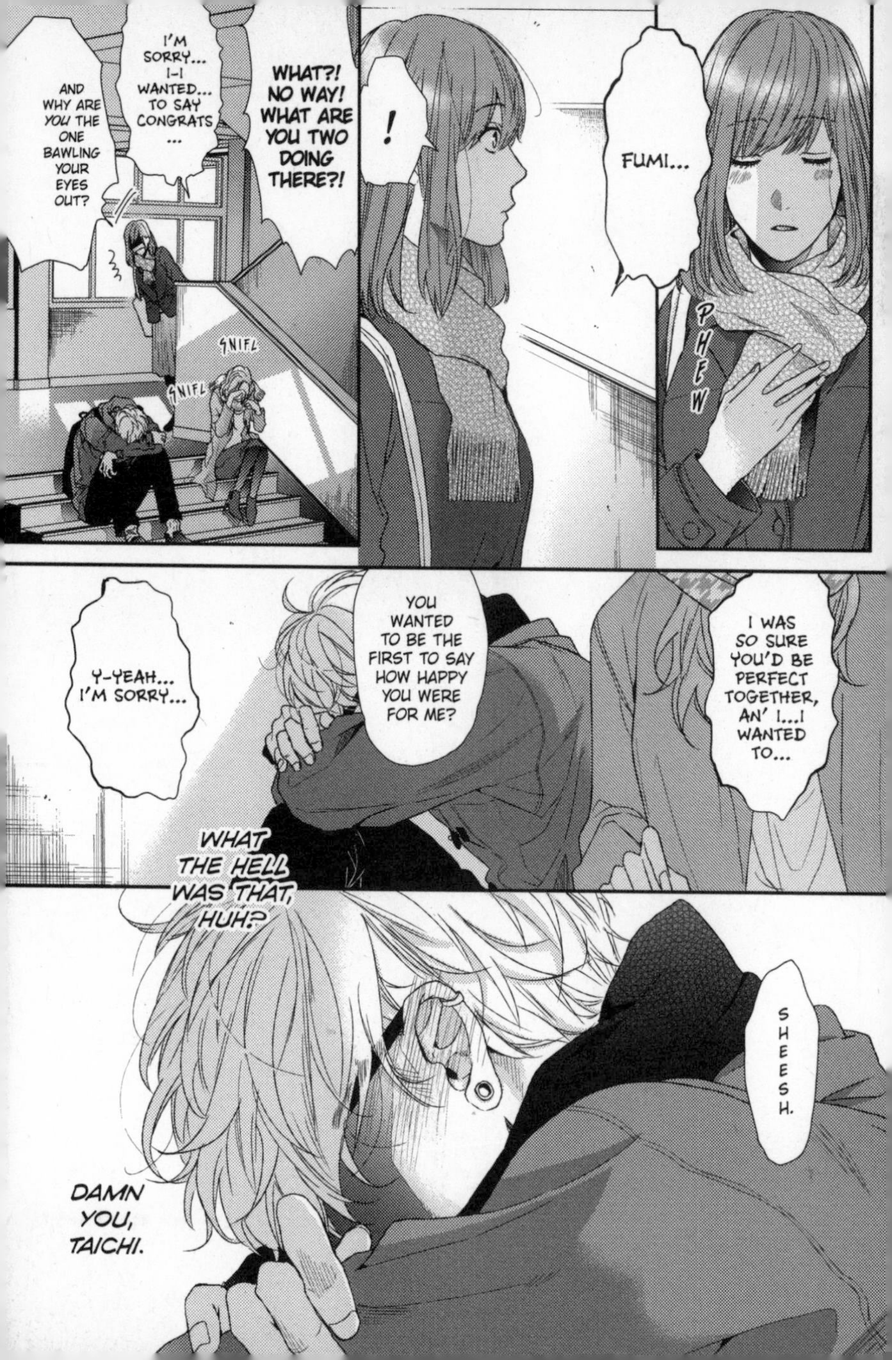
FUMI...
PHEW
!
WHAT?! NO WAY! WHAT ARE YOU TWO DOING THERE?!
I'M SORRY... I-I WANTED... TO SAY CONGRATS...
AND WHY ARE *YOU* THE ONE BAWLING YOUR EYES OUT?
SNIFL
SNIFL
I WAS *SO* SURE YOU'D BE PERFECT TOGETHER, AN' I...I WANTED TO...
YOU WANTED TO BE THE FIRST TO SAY HOW HAPPY YOU WERE FOR ME?
Y-YEAH... I'M SORRY...
WHAT THE HELL WAS THAT, HUH?
SHEESH.
DAMN YOU, TAICHI.

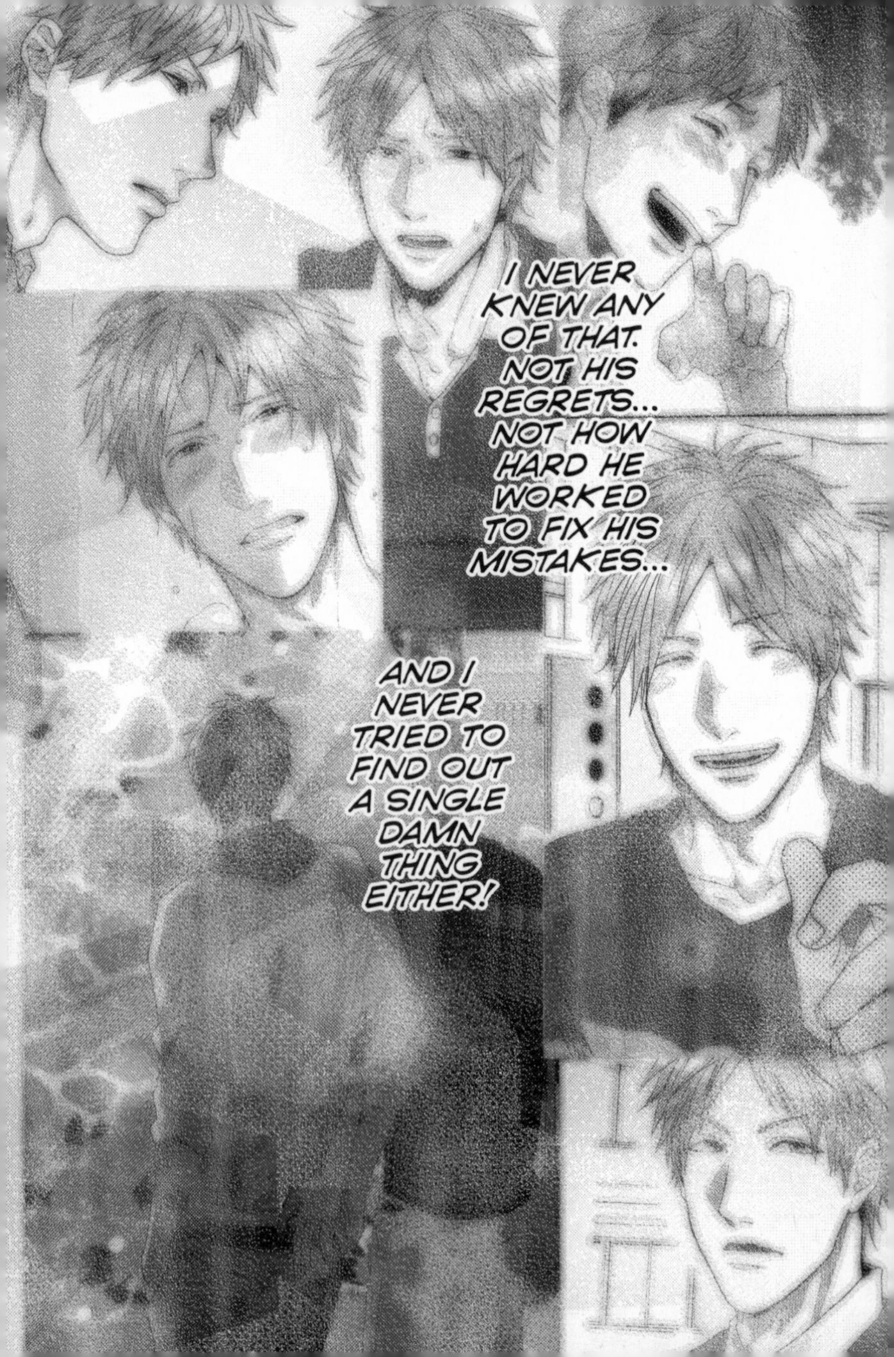
I NEVER KNEW ANY OF THAT. NOT HIS REGRETS... NOT HOW HARD HE WORKED TO FIX HIS MISTAKES...
AND I NEVER TRIED TO FIND OUT A SINGLE DAMN THING EITHER!

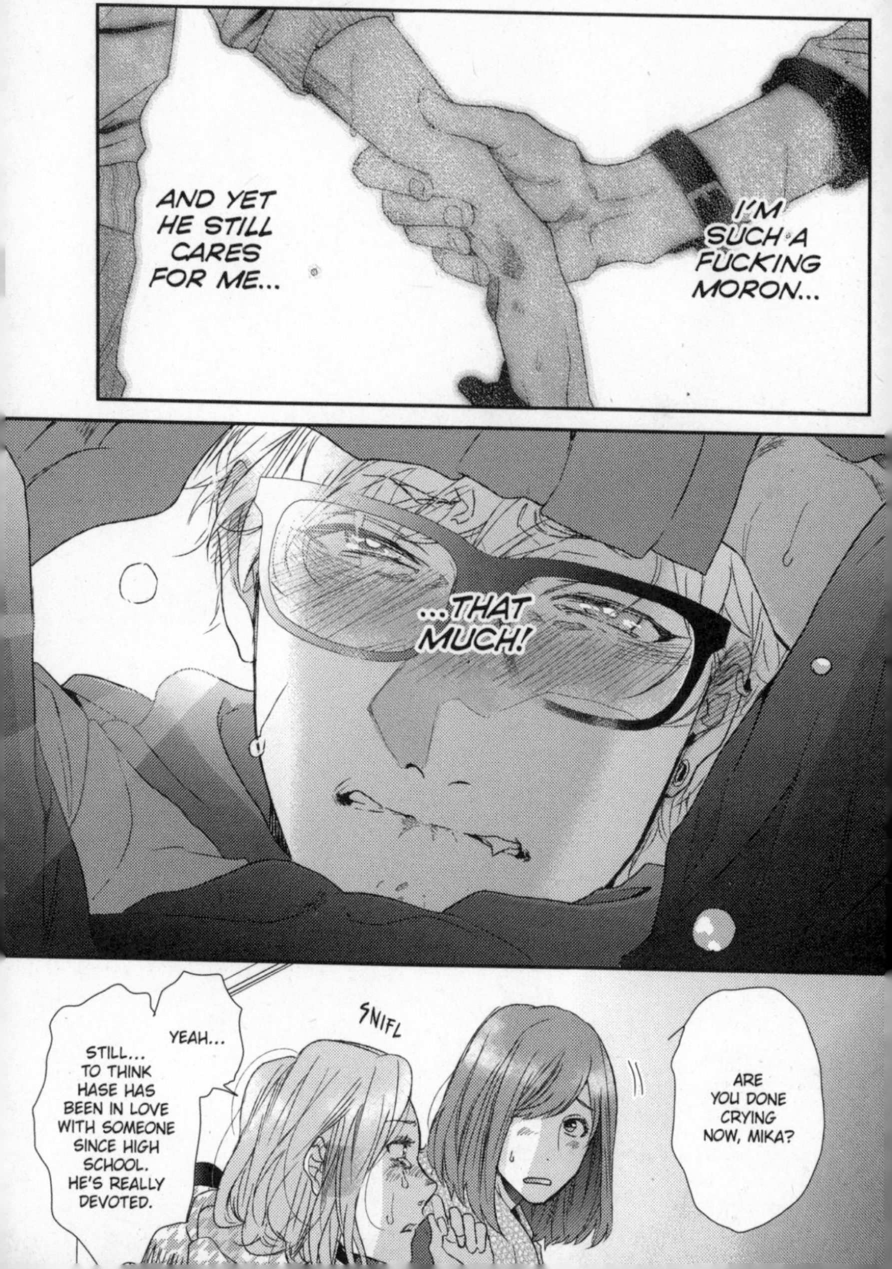
I'M SUCH A FUCKING MORON...
AND YET HE STILL CARES FOR ME...
...THAT MUCH!
ARE YOU DONE CRYING NOW, MIKA?
SNIFL
YEAH...
STILL... TO THINK HASE HAS BEEN IN LOVE WITH SOMEONE SINCE HIGH SCHOOL. HE'S REALLY DEVOTED.

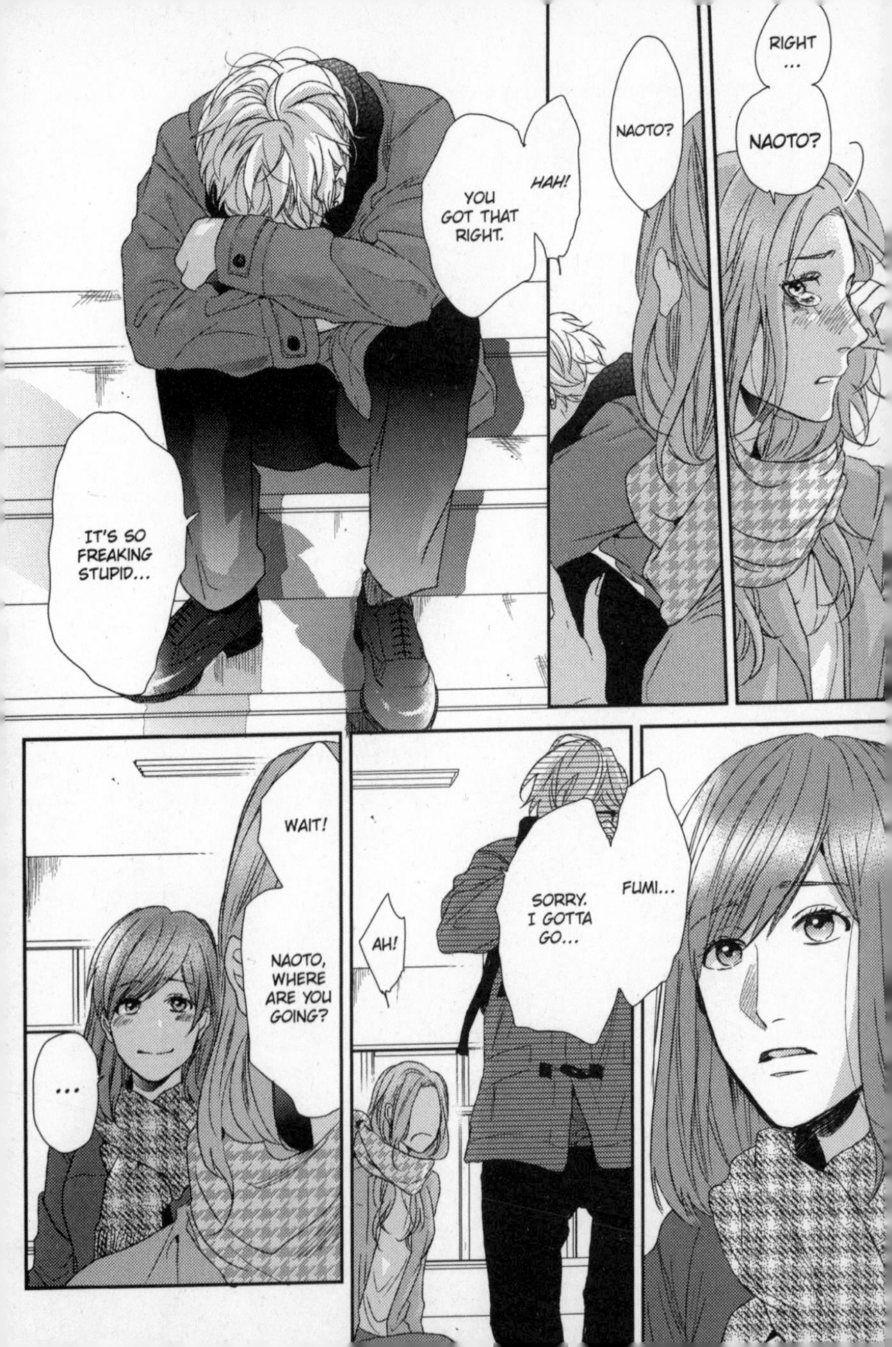
RIGHT ...
NAOTO?
NAOTO?
HAH! YOU GOT THAT RIGHT.
IT'S SO FREAKING STUPID...
FUMI...
SORRY. I GOTTA GO...
AH!
WAIT! NAOTO, WHERE ARE YOU GOING?
...

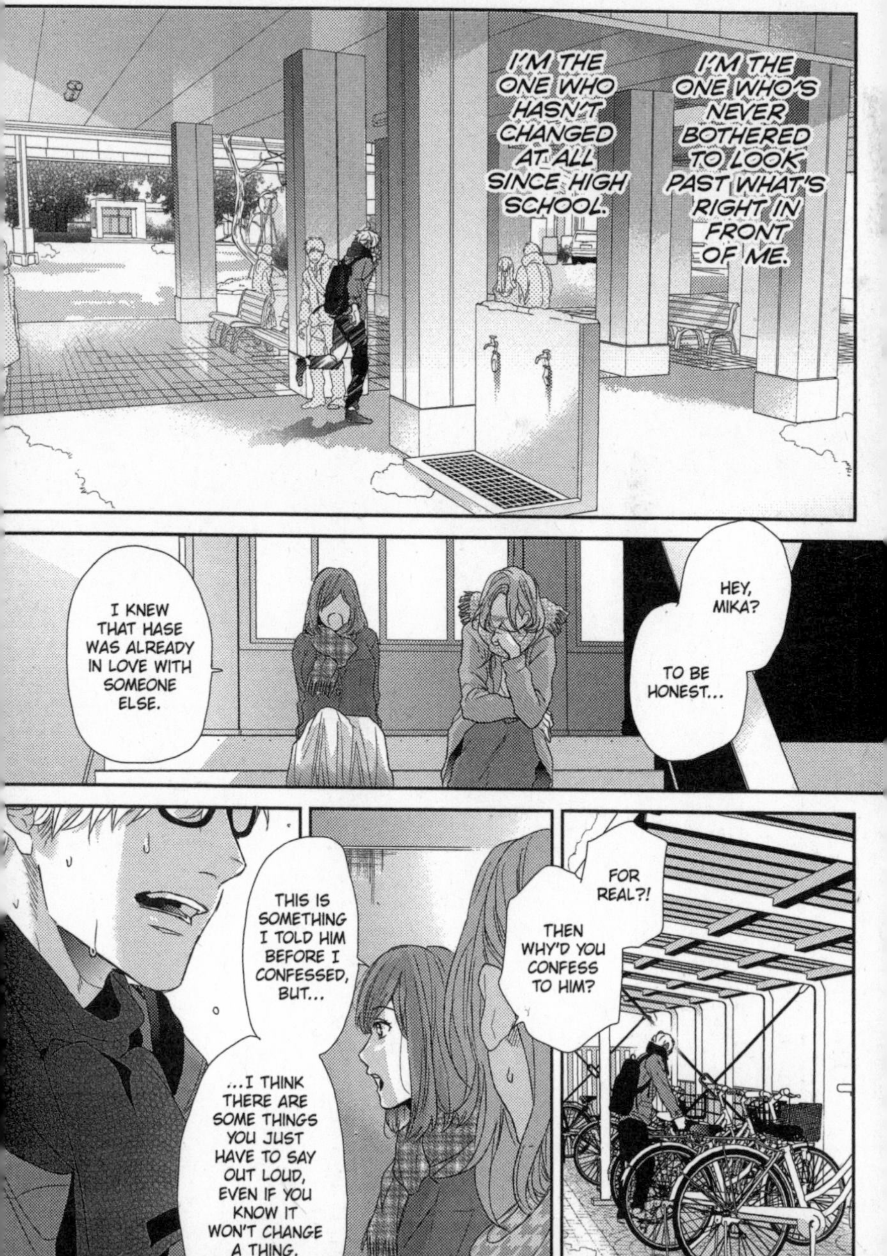
I'M THE ONE WHO'S NEVER BOTHERED TO LOOK PAST WHAT'S RIGHT IN FRONT OF ME.
I'M THE ONE WHO HASN'T CHANGED AT ALL SINCE HIGH SCHOOL.
HEY, MIKA?
TO BE HONEST...
I KNEW THAT HASE WAS ALREADY IN LOVE WITH SOMEONE ELSE.
FOR REAL?!
THEN WHY'D YOU CONFESS TO HIM?
THIS IS SOMETHING I TOLD HIM BEFORE I CONFESSED, BUT...
...I THINK THERE ARE SOME THINGS YOU JUST HAVE TO SAY OUT LOUD, EVEN IF YOU KNOW IT WON'T CHANGE A THING.

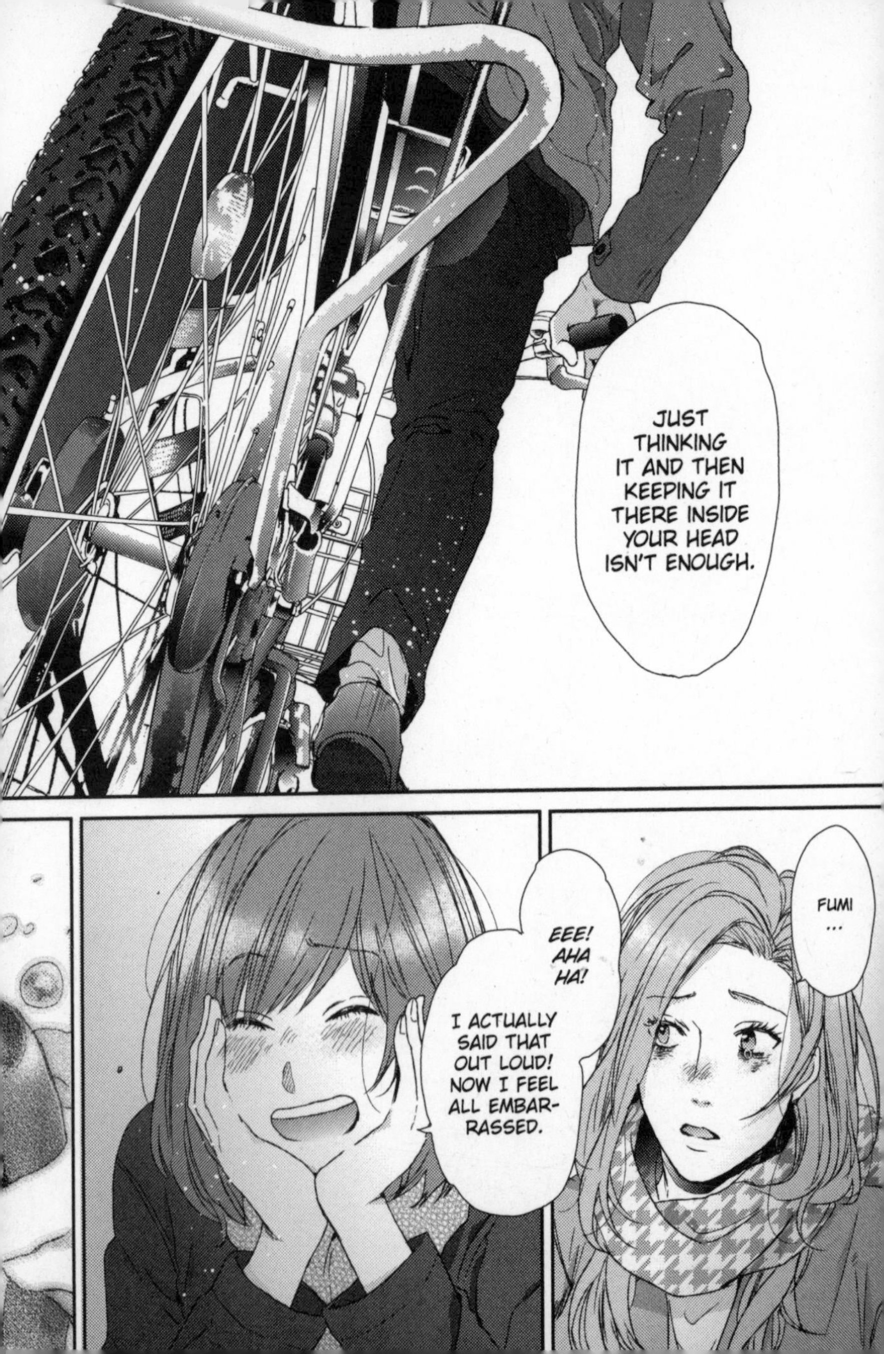
JUST THINKING IT AND THEN KEEPING IT THERE INSIDE YOUR HEAD ISN'T ENOUGH.
FUMI ...
EEE! AHA HA!
I ACTUALLY SAID THAT OUT LOUD! NOW I FEEL ALL EMBAR-RASSED.

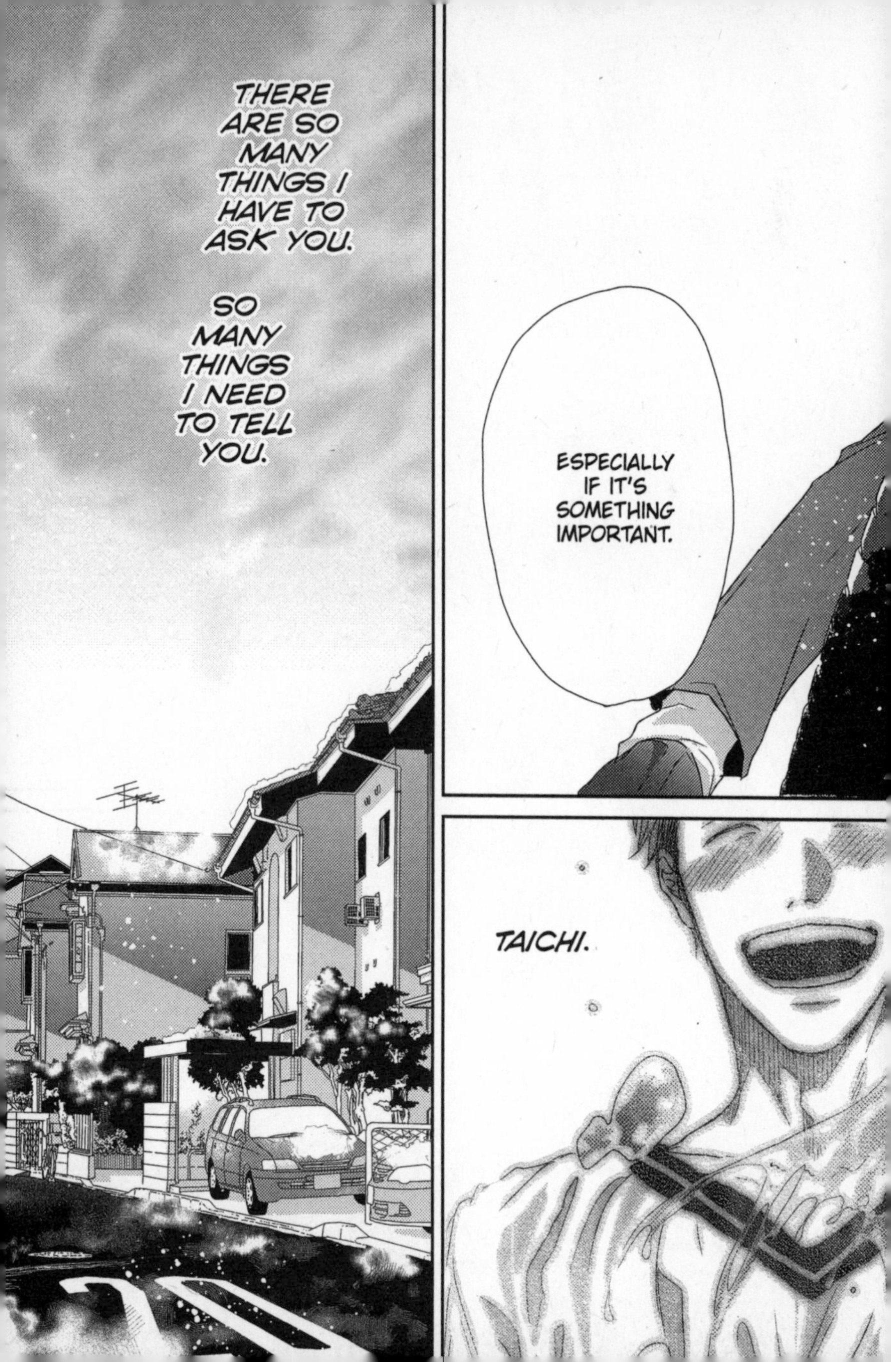
ESPECIALLY IF IT'S SOMETHING IMPORTANT.
TAICHI.
THERE ARE SO MANY THINGS I HAVE TO ASK YOU.
SO MANY THINGS I NEED TO TELL YOU.

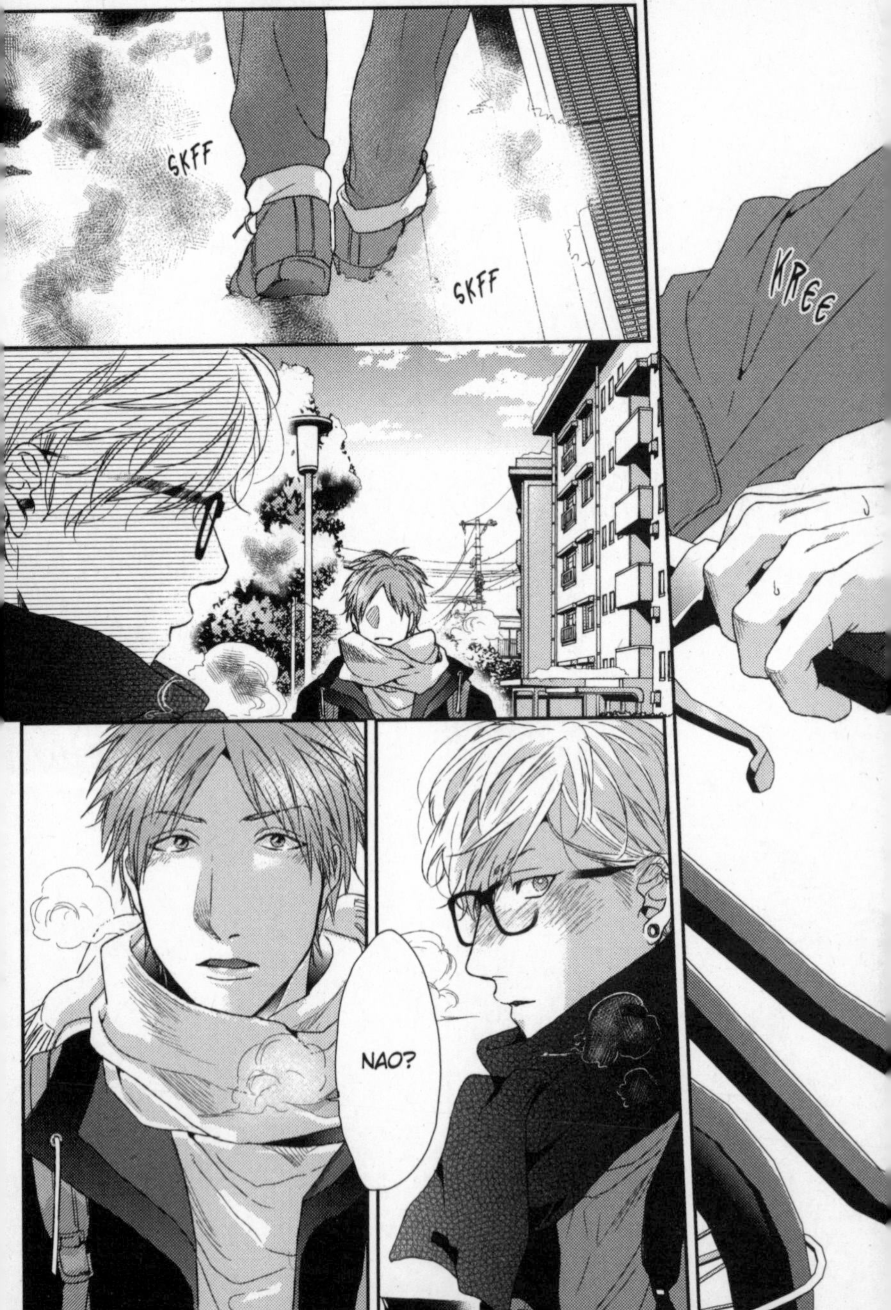
KREE
SKFF
SKFF
NAO?

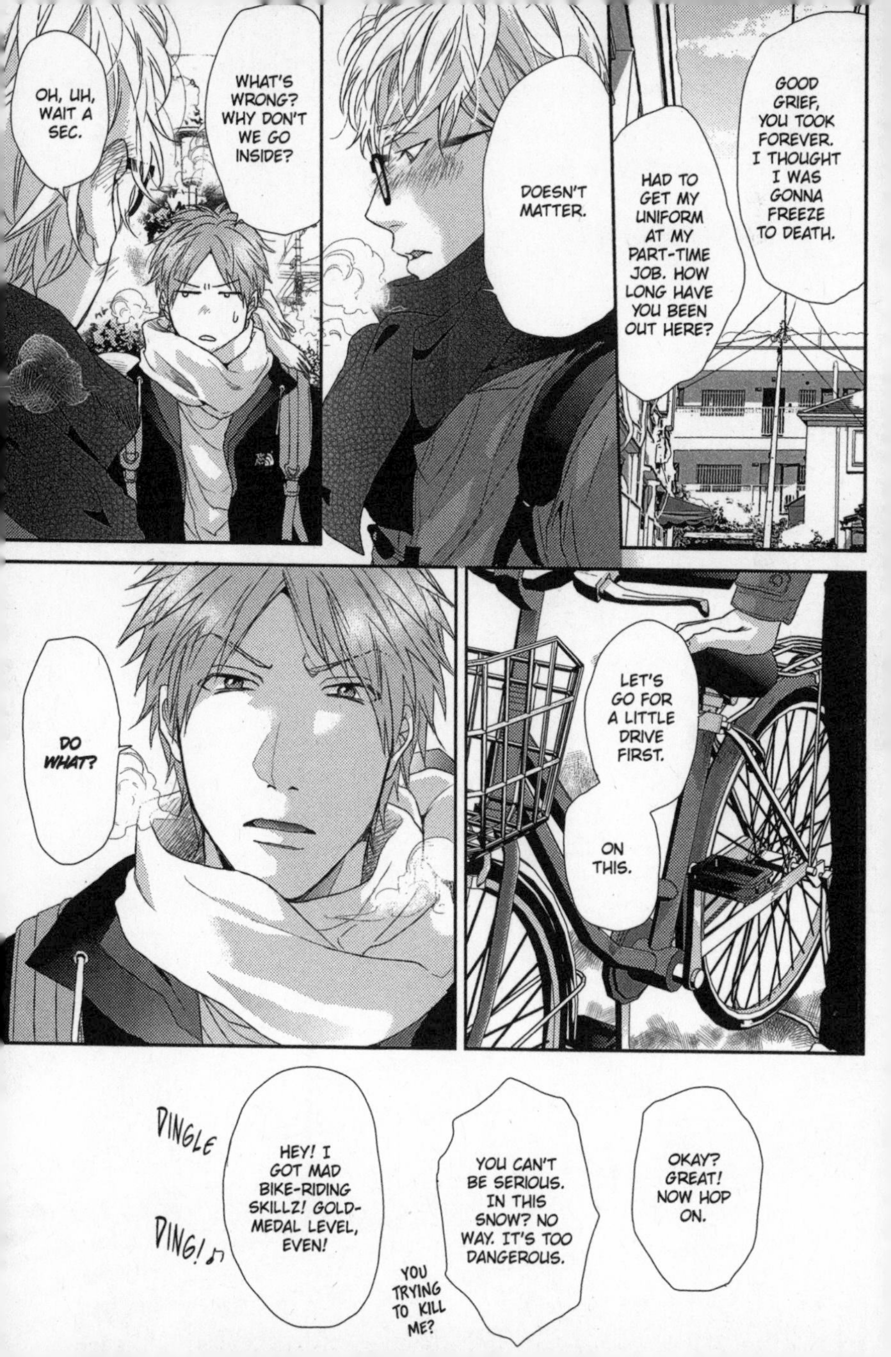
GOOD GRIEF, YOU TOOK FOREVER. I THOUGHT I WAS GONNA FREEZE TO DEATH.
HAD TO GET MY UNIFORM AT MY PART-TIME JOB. HOW LONG HAVE YOU BEEN OUT HERE?
DOESN'T MATTER.
WHAT'S WRONG? WHY DON'T WE GO INSIDE?
OH, UH, WAIT A SEC.
LET'S GO FOR A LITTLE DRIVE FIRST.
ON THIS.
DO *WHAT?*
OKAY? GREAT! NOW HOP ON.
YOU CAN'T BE SERIOUS. IN THIS SNOW? NO WAY. IT'S TOO DANGEROUS.
YOU TRYING TO KILL ME?
HEY! I GOT MAD BIKE-RIDING SKILLZ! GOLD-MEDAL LEVEL, EVEN!
DINGLE
DING!♪

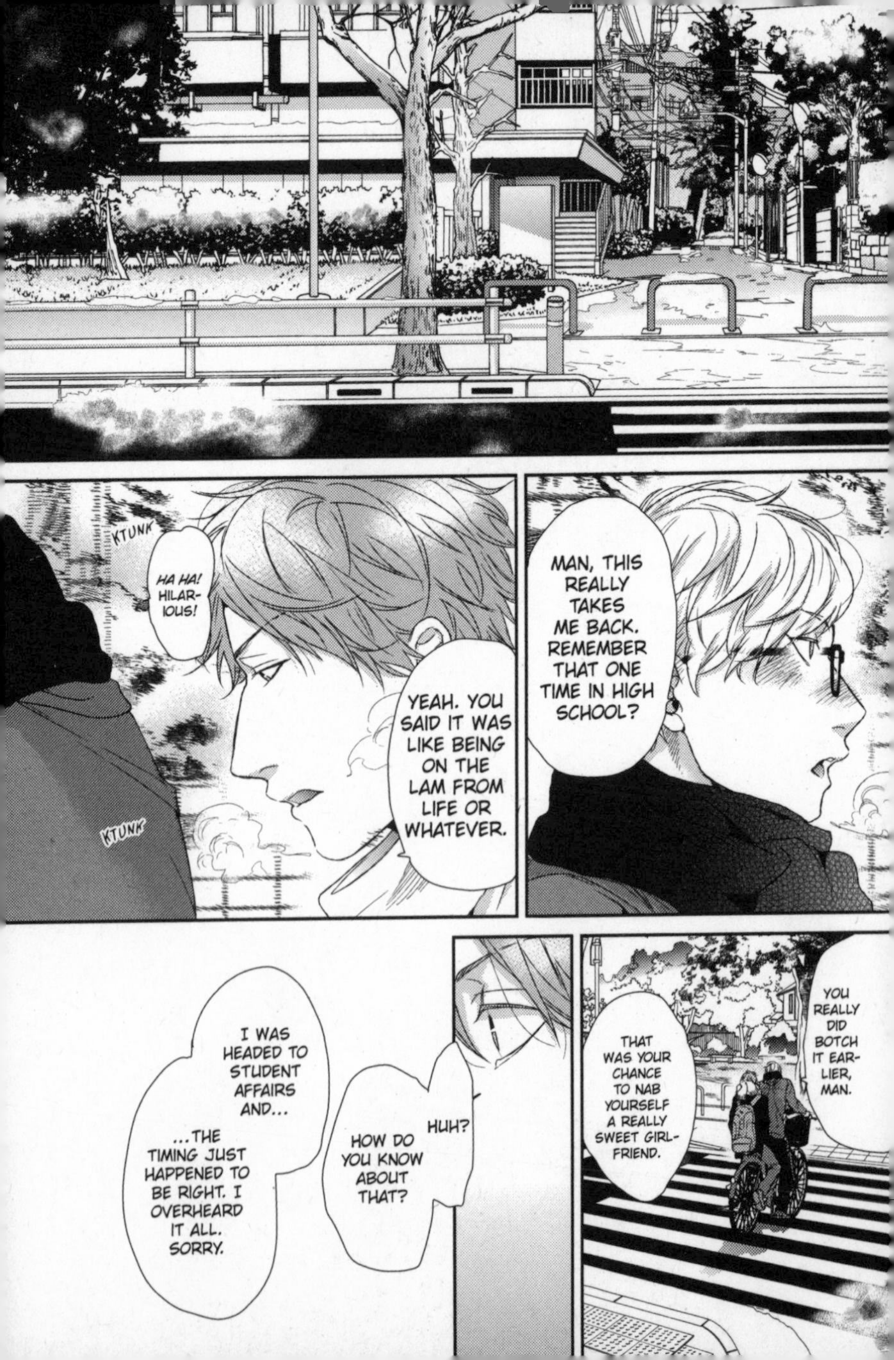
MAN, THIS REALLY TAKES ME BACK. REMEMBER THAT ONE TIME IN HIGH SCHOOL?
YEAH. YOU SAID IT WAS LIKE BEING ON THE LAM FROM LIFE OR WHATEVER.
KTUNK
HA HA! HILARIOUS!
KTUNK
YOU REALLY DID BOTCH IT EARLIER, MAN.
THAT WAS YOUR CHANCE TO NAB YOURSELF A REALLY SWEET GIRLFRIEND.
HUH?
HOW DO YOU KNOW ABOUT THAT?
I WAS HEADED TO STUDENT AFFAIRS AND...
...THE TIMING JUST HAPPENED TO BE RIGHT. I OVERHEARD IT ALL. SORRY.

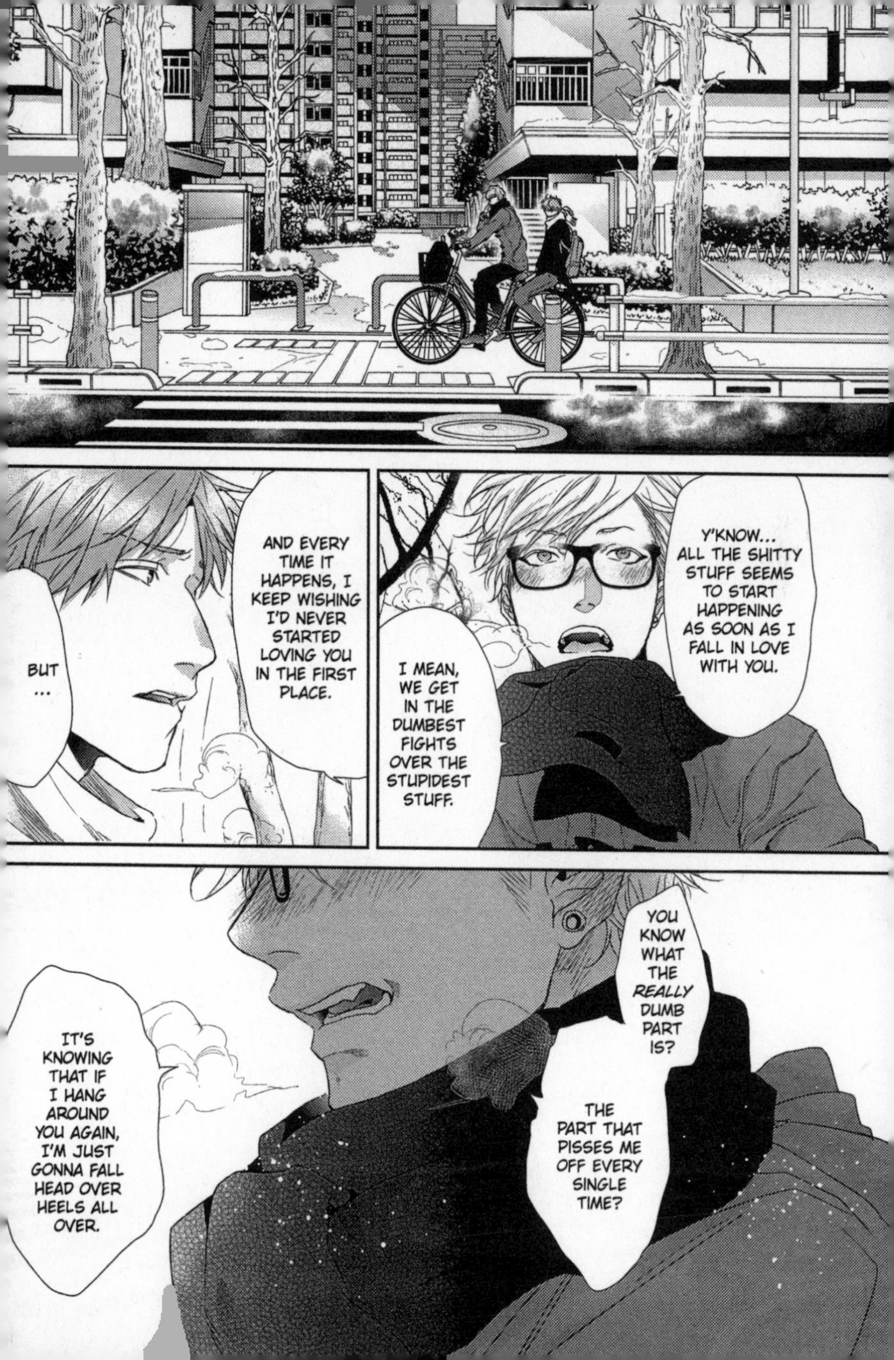
Y'KNOW... ALL THE SHITTY STUFF SEEMS TO START HAPPENING AS SOON AS I FALL IN LOVE WITH YOU.
I MEAN, WE GET IN THE DUMBEST FIGHTS OVER THE STUPIDEST STUFF.
AND EVERY TIME IT HAPPENS, I KEEP WISHING I'D NEVER STARTED LOVING YOU IN THE FIRST PLACE.
BUT ...
YOU KNOW WHAT THE *REALLY* DUMB PART IS?
THE PART THAT PISSES ME OFF EVERY SINGLE TIME?
IT'S KNOWING THAT IF I HANG AROUND YOU AGAIN, I'M JUST GONNA FALL HEAD OVER HEELS ALL OVER.

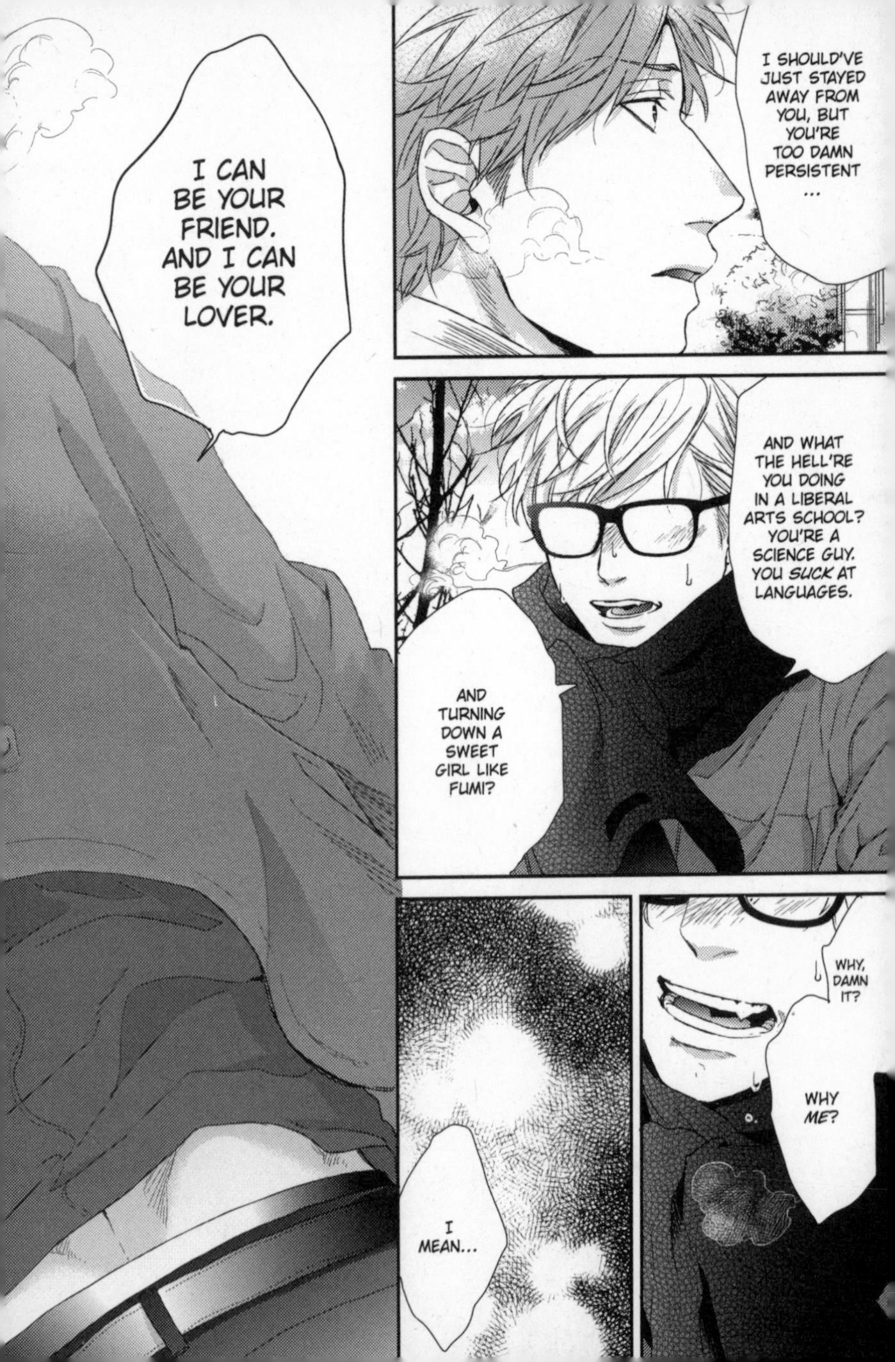
I SHOULD'VE JUST STAYED AWAY FROM YOU, BUT YOU'RE TOO DAMN PERSISTENT...
AND WHAT THE HELL'RE YOU DOING IN A LIBERAL ARTS SCHOOL? YOU'RE A SCIENCE GUY. YOU *SUCK* AT LANGUAGES.
AND TURNING DOWN A SWEET GIRL LIKE FUMI?
WHY, DAMN IT?
WHY *ME*?
I MEAN...
I CAN BE YOUR FRIEND. AND I CAN BE YOUR LOVER.

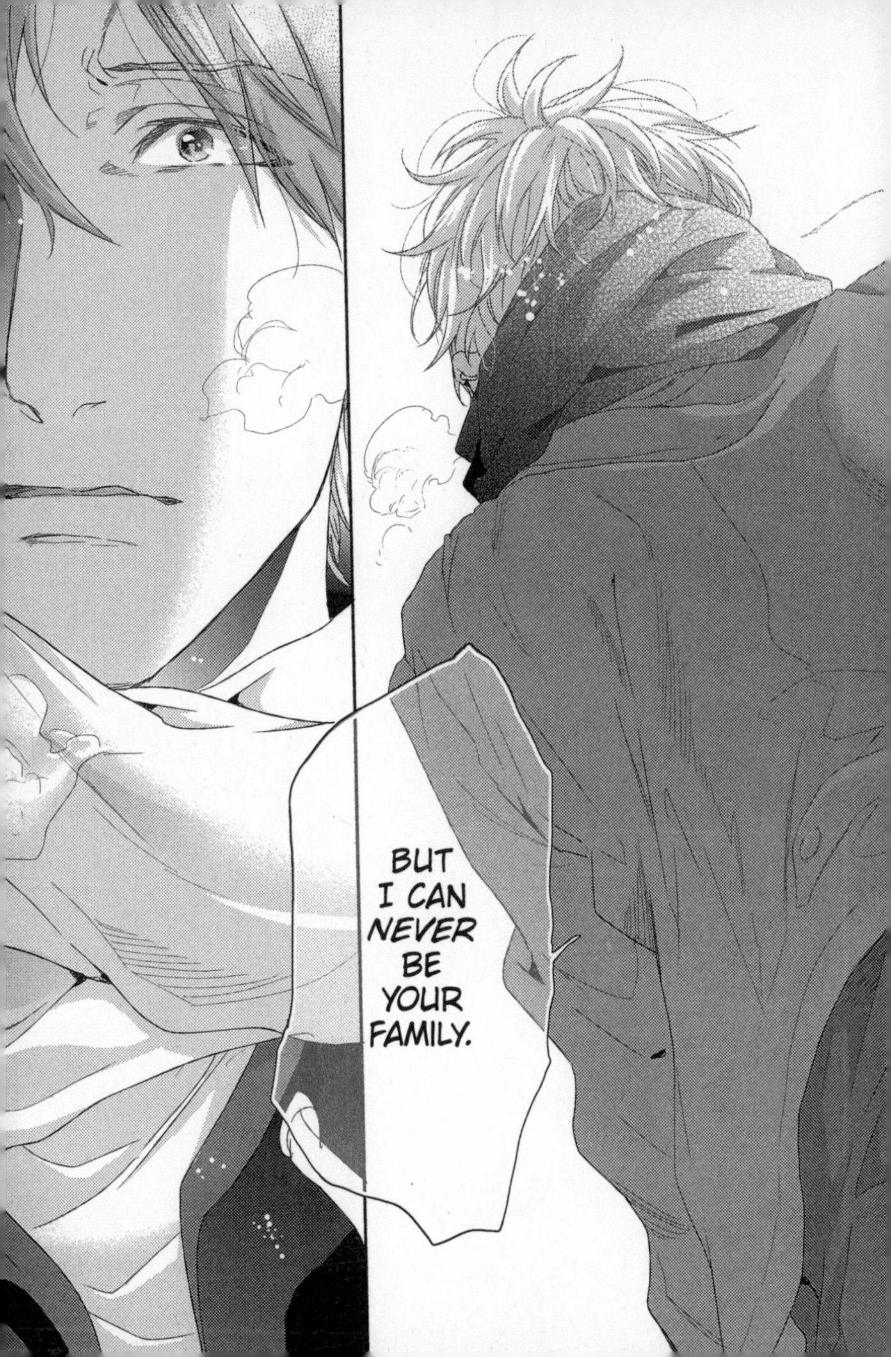
BUT I CAN NEVER BE YOUR FAMILY.

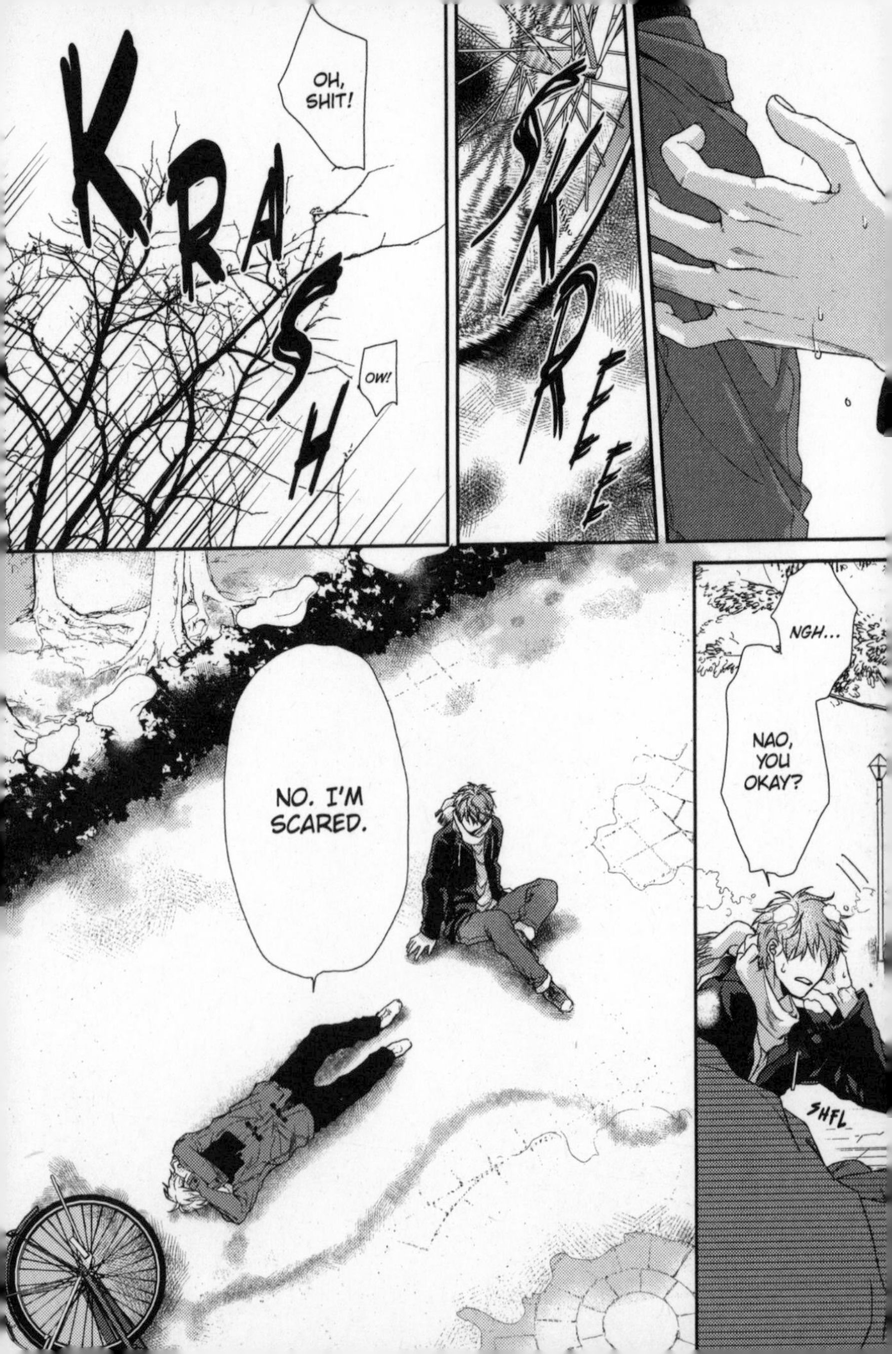
SKREEE
OH, SHIT!
KRASH
OW!
NGH...
NAO, YOU OKAY?
SHFL
NO. I'M SCARED.

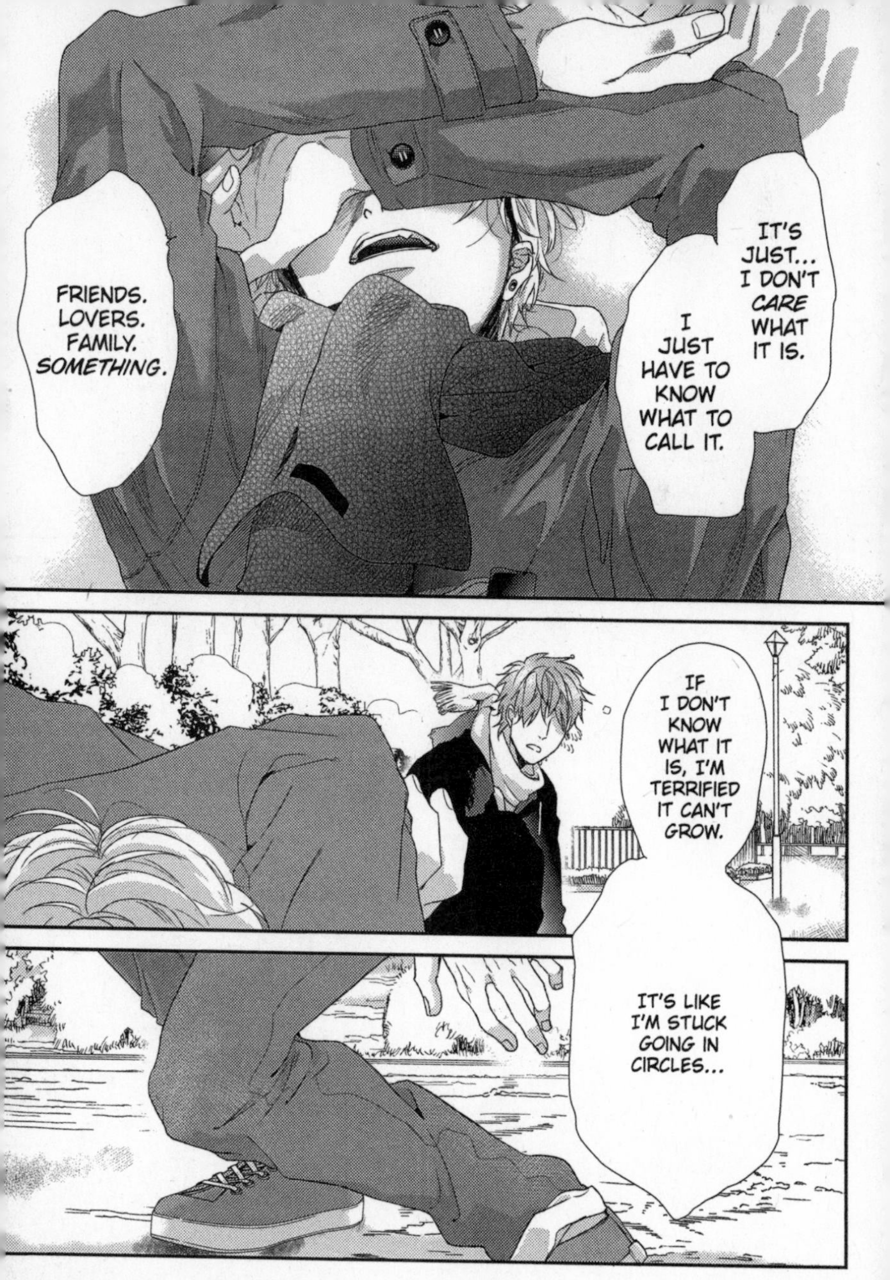
IT'S JUST... I DON'T *CARE* WHAT IT IS.
I JUST HAVE TO KNOW WHAT TO CALL IT.
FRIENDS. LOVERS. FAMILY. *SOMETHING.*
IF I DON'T KNOW WHAT IT IS, I'M TERRIFIED IT CAN'T GROW.
IT'S LIKE I'M STUCK GOING IN CIRCLES...

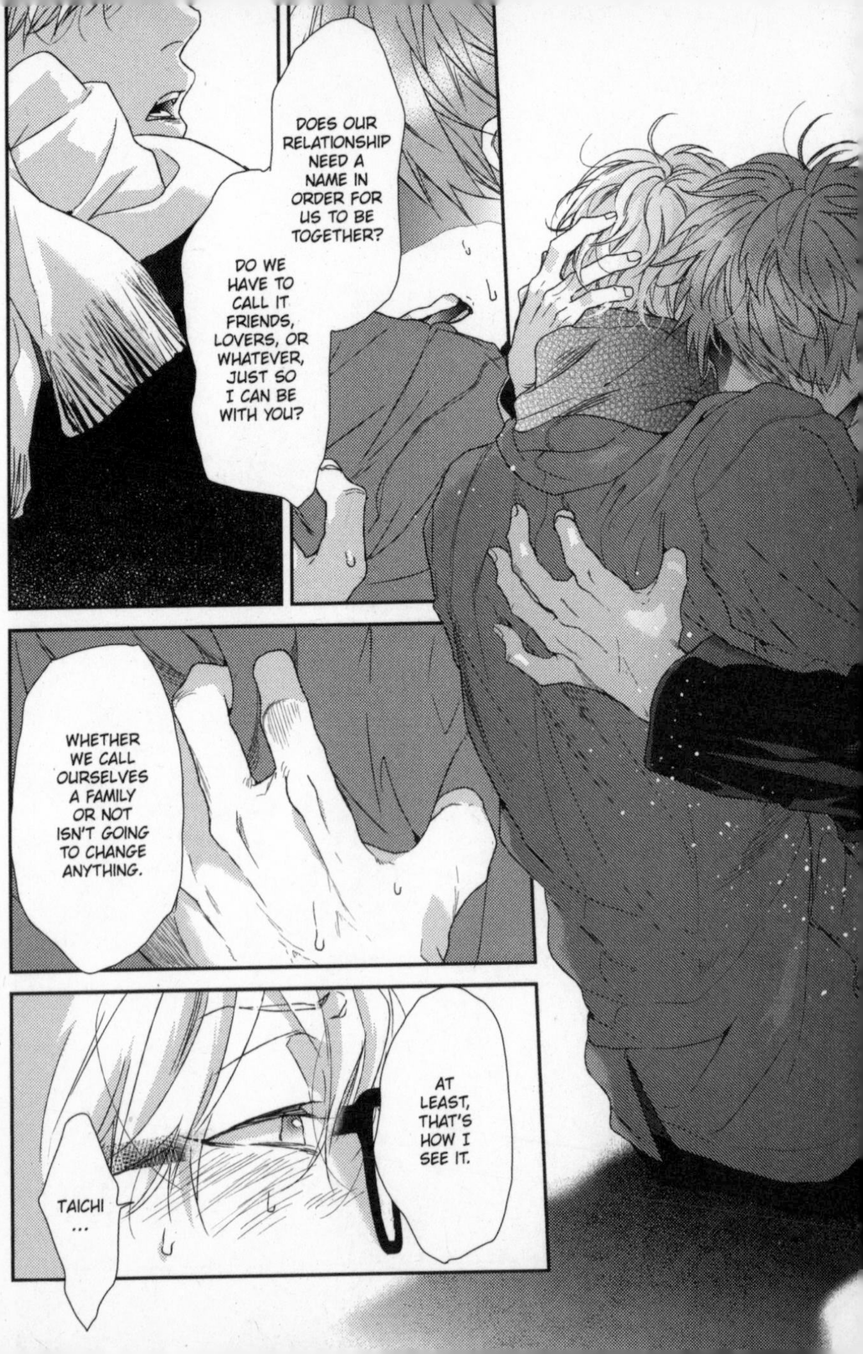
DOES OUR RELATIONSHIP NEED A NAME IN ORDER FOR US TO BE TOGETHER?
DO WE HAVE TO CALL IT FRIENDS, LOVERS, OR WHATEVER, JUST SO I CAN BE WITH YOU?
WHETHER WE CALL OURSELVES A FAMILY OR NOT ISN'T GOING TO CHANGE ANYTHING.
AT LEAST, THAT'S HOW I SEE IT.
TAICHI...

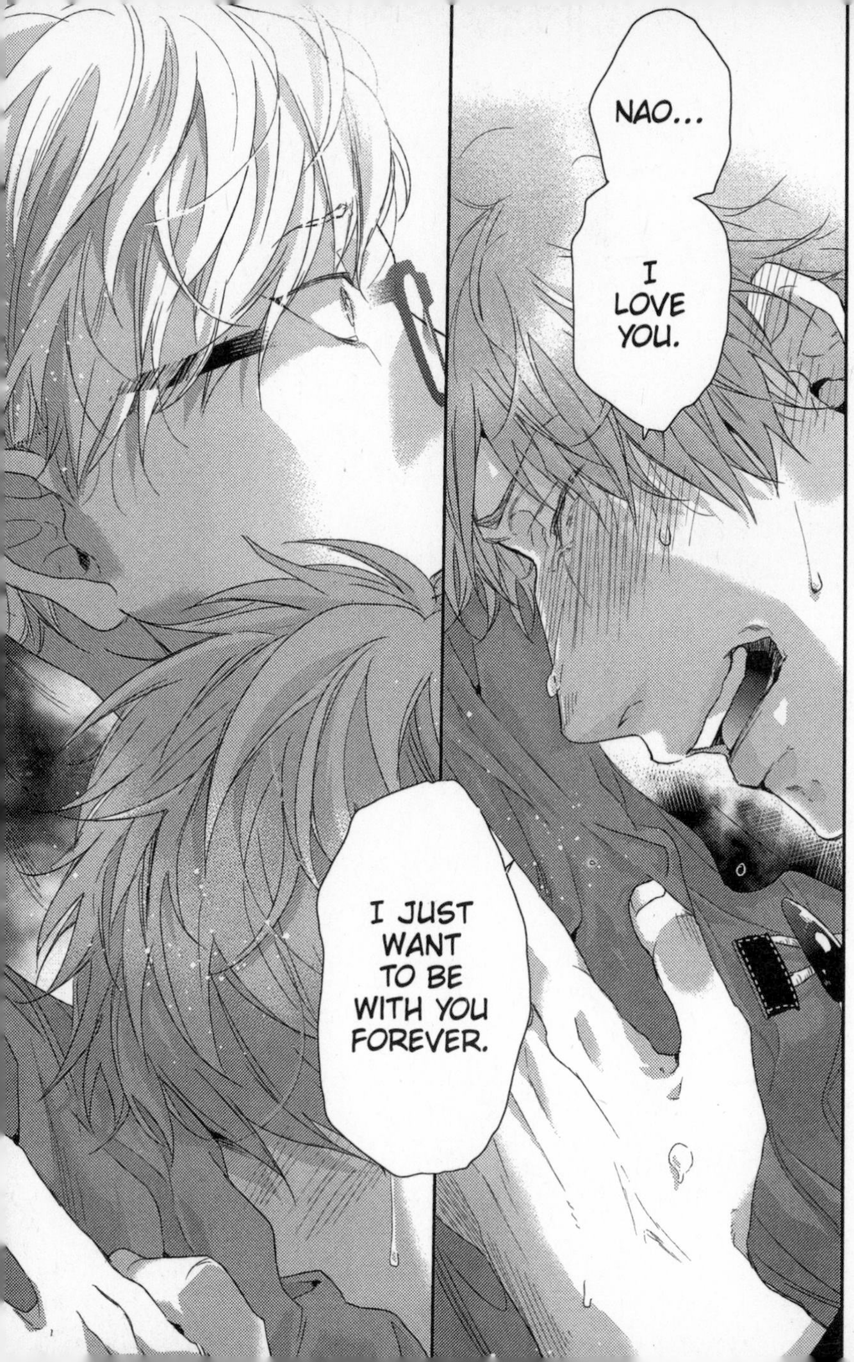
NAO...
I LOVE YOU.
I JUST WANT TO BE WITH YOU FOREVER.

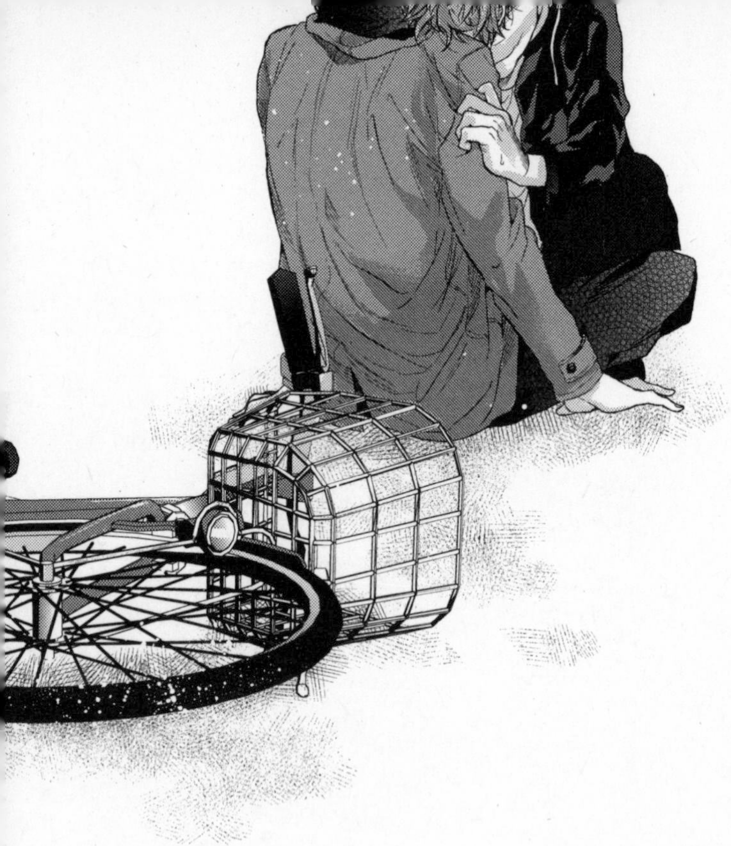

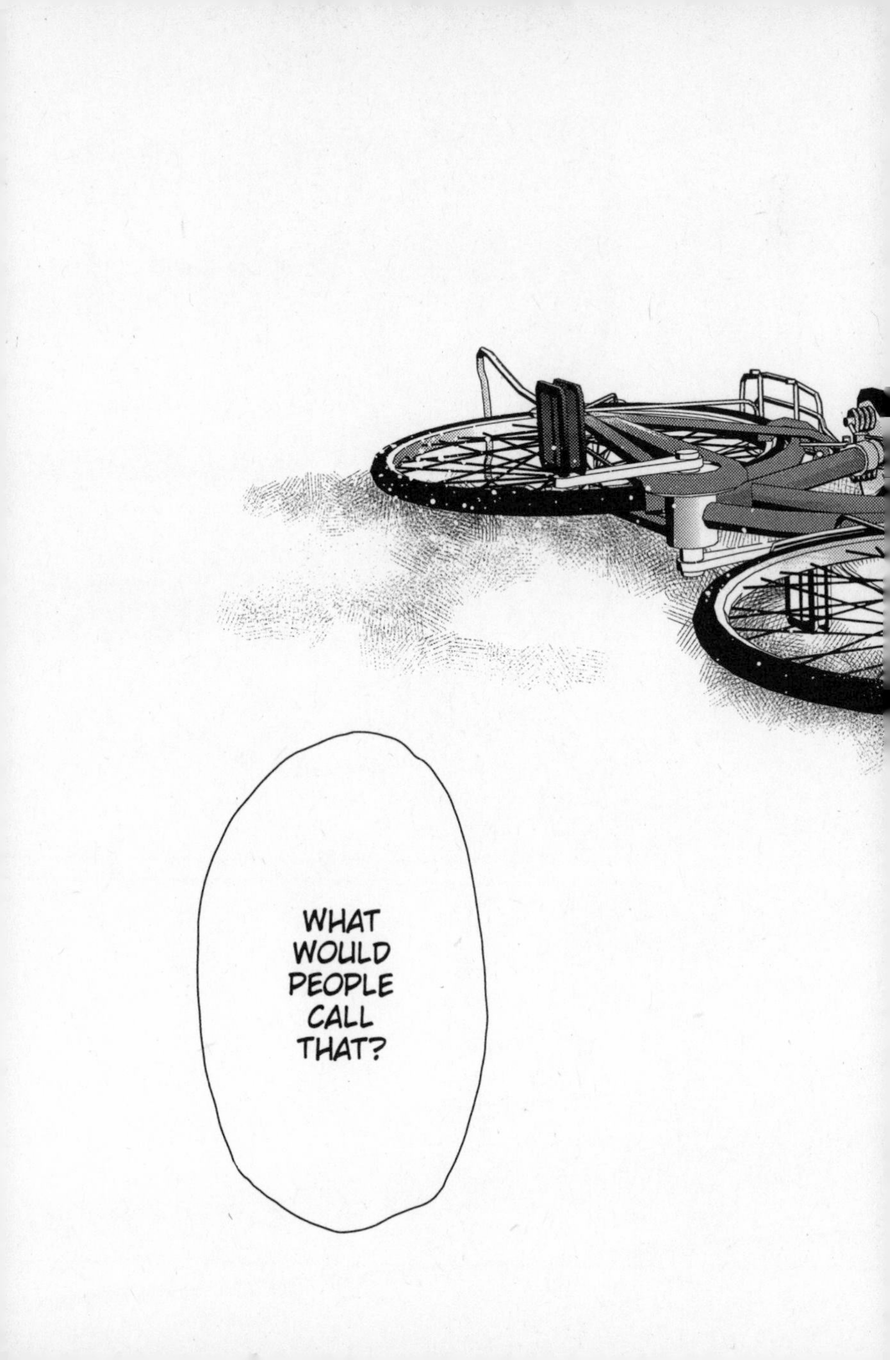
WHAT WOULD PEOPLE CALL THAT?

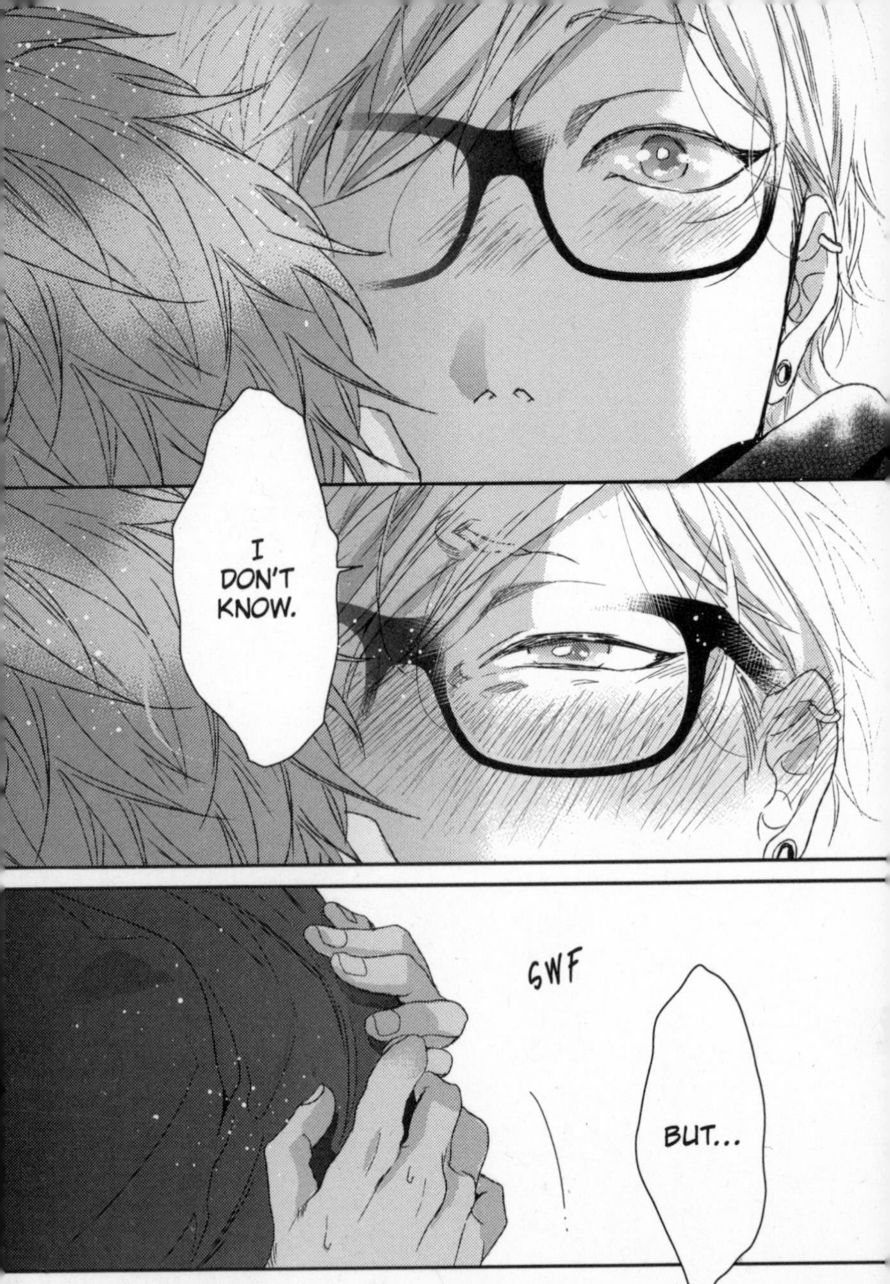
I DON'T KNOW.
SWF
BUT...

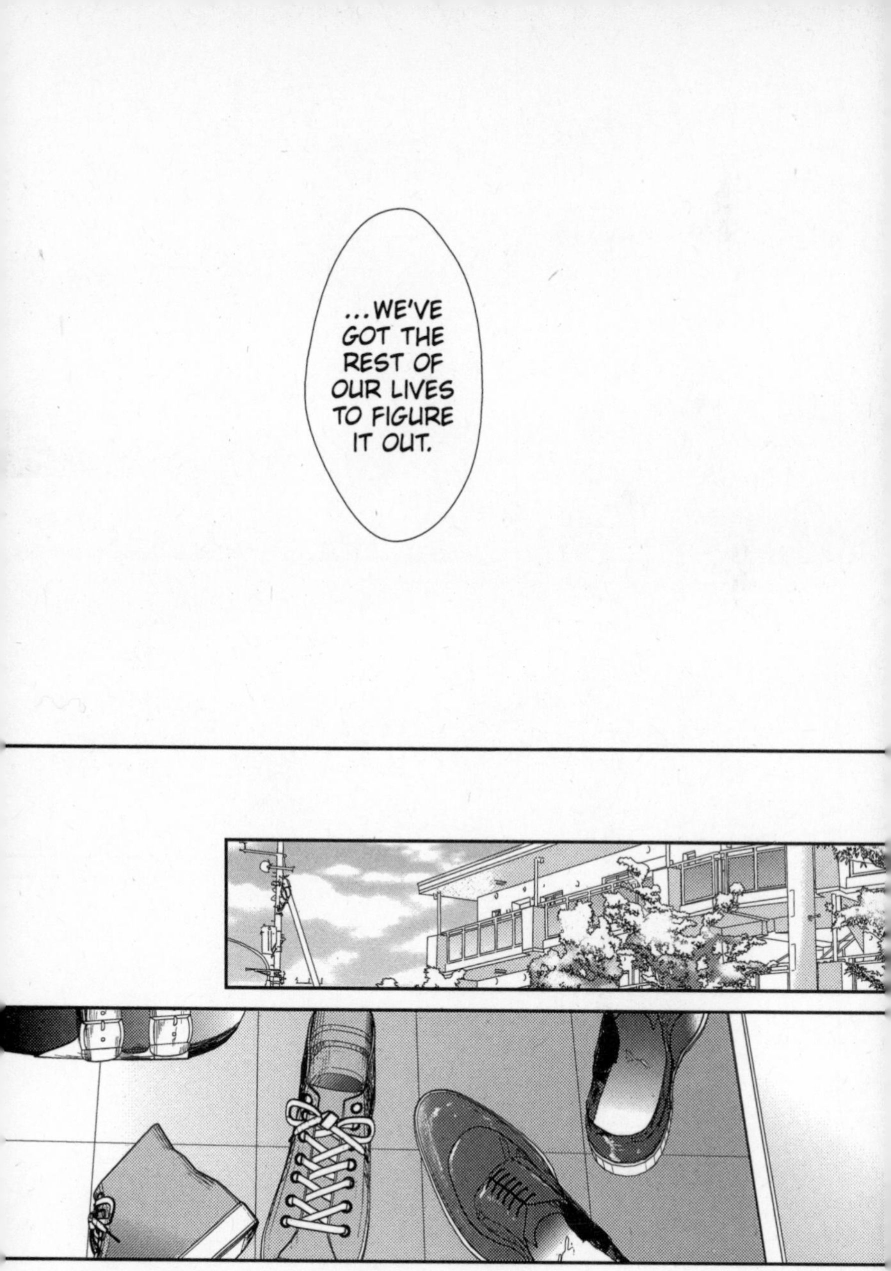
...WE'VE GOT THE REST OF OUR LIVES TO FIGURE IT OUT.

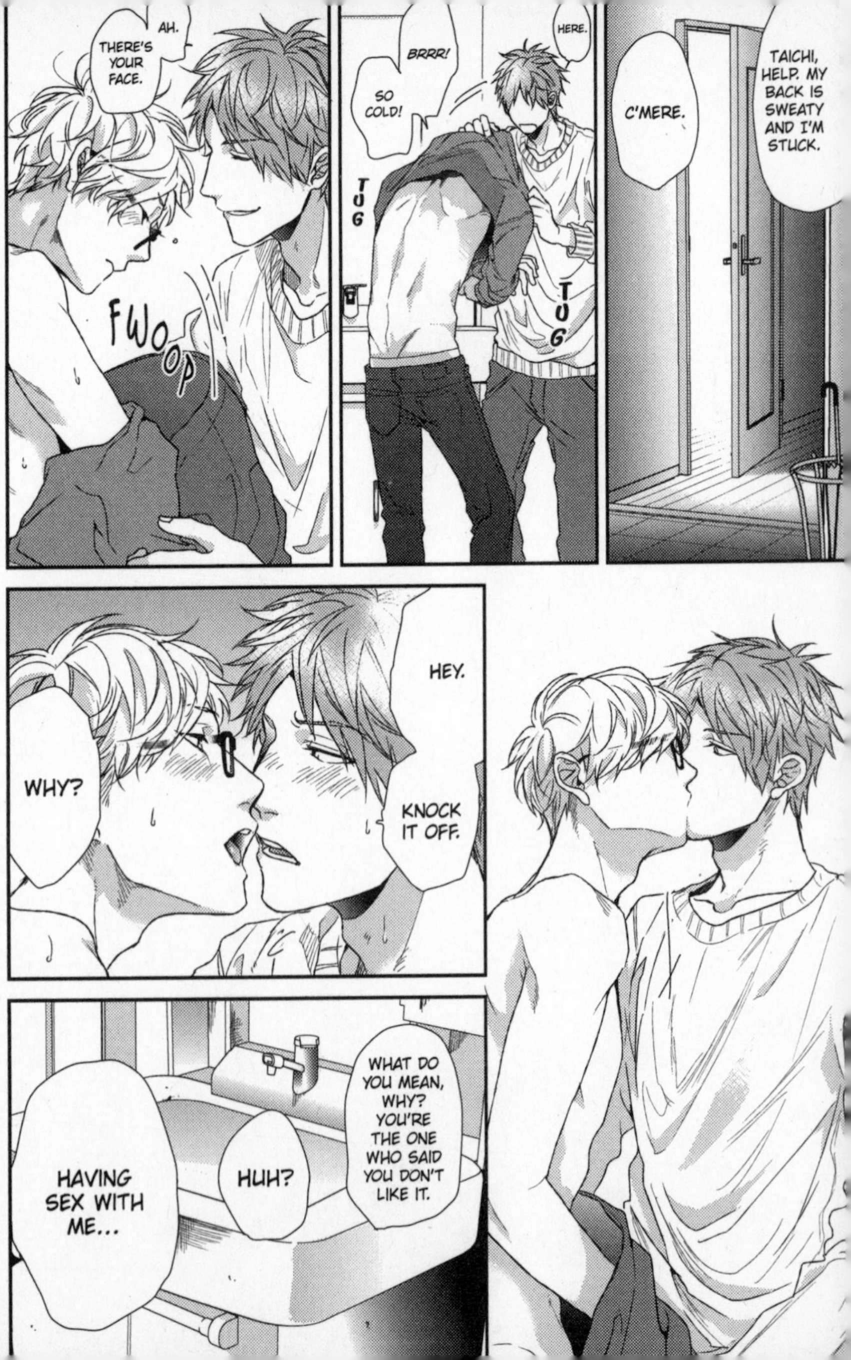
TAICHI, HELP. MY BACK IS SWEATY AND I'M STUCK.
C'MERE.
HERE.
BRRR!
SO COLD!
TUG
TUG
AH.
THERE'S YOUR FACE.
FWOOP
HEY.
KNOCK IT OFF.
WHY?
WHAT DO YOU MEAN, WHY? YOU'RE THE ONE WHO SAID YOU DON'T LIKE IT.
HUH?
HAVING SEX WITH ME...

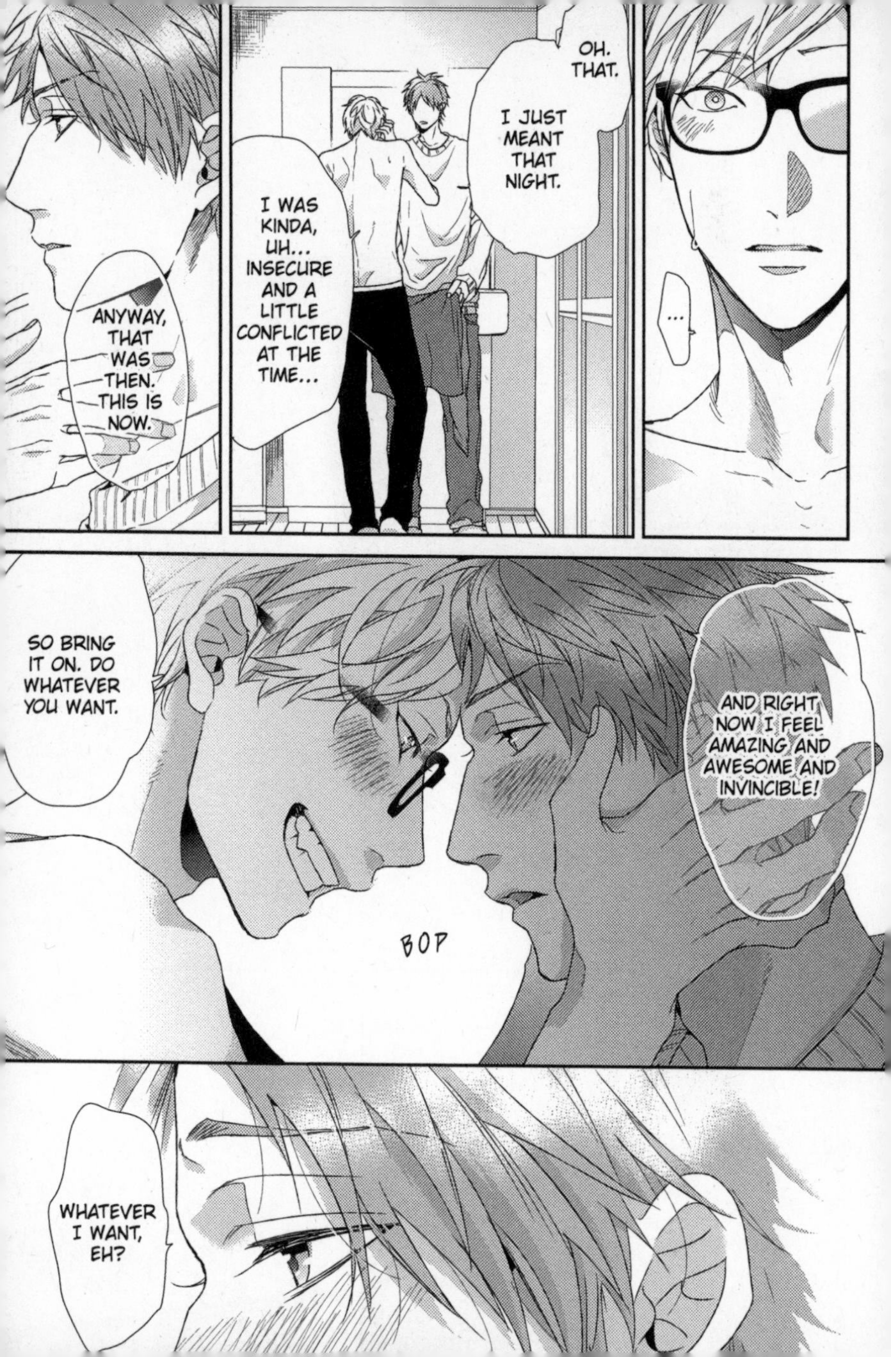
...
OH. THAT.
I JUST MEANT THAT NIGHT.
I WAS KINDA, UH... INSECURE AND A LITTLE CONFLICTED AT THE TIME...
ANYWAY, THAT WAS THEN. THIS IS NOW.
AND RIGHT NOW I FEEL AMAZING AND AWESOME AND INVINCIBLE!
SO BRING IT ON. DO WHATEVER YOU WANT.
BOP
WHATEVER I WANT, EH?

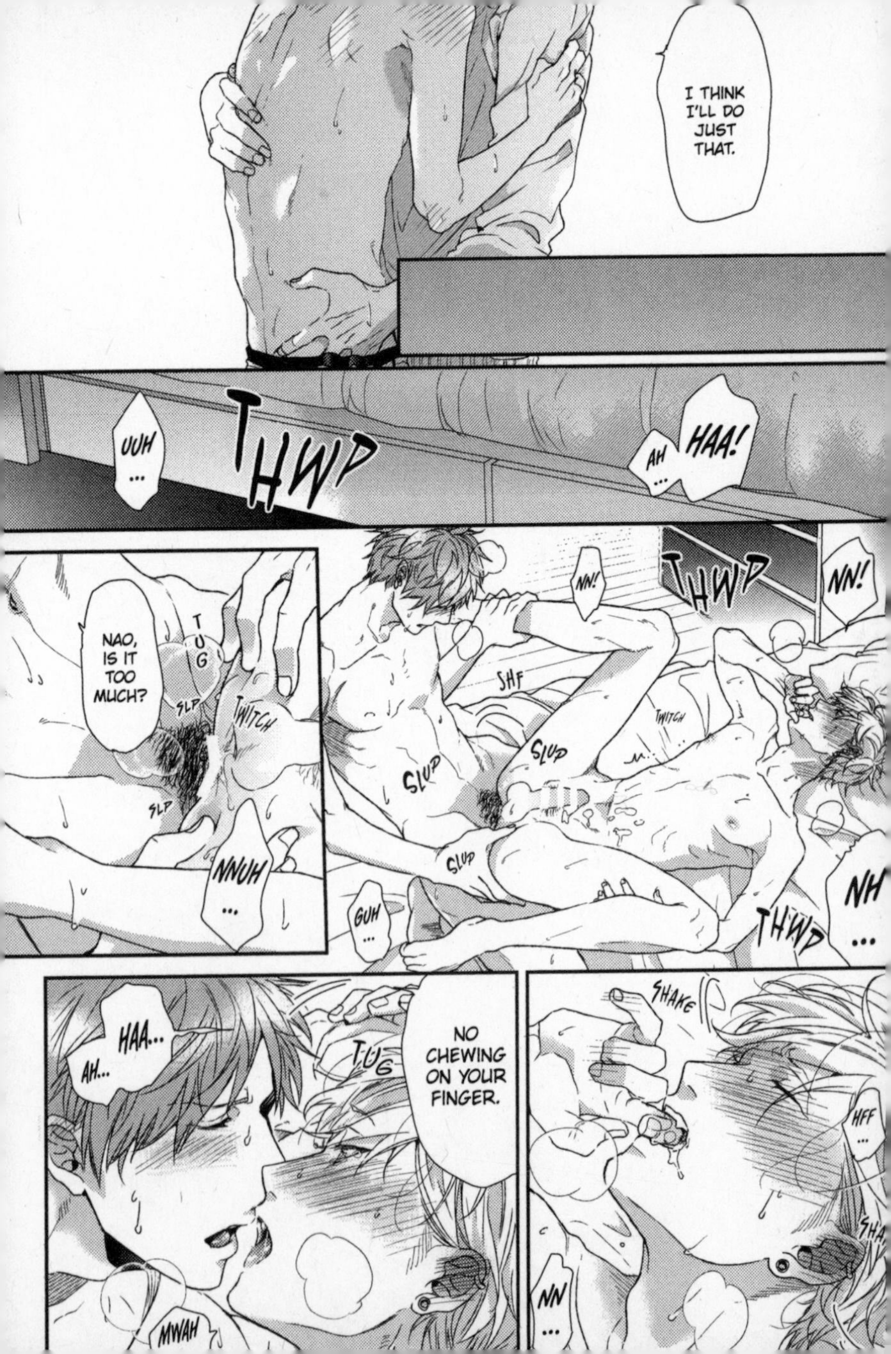

I THINK I'LL DO JUST THAT.
AH... HAA!
THWP
UUH...
NN!
THWP
NN!
SHF
TWITCH
SLUP
SLUP
SLUP
NH...
THWP
GUH...
NAO, IS IT TOO MUCH?
TUG
SLP
TWITCH
SLP
NNUH...
SHAKE
HFF...
NN...
NO CHEWING ON YOUR FINGER.
TUG
AH... HAA...
MWAH

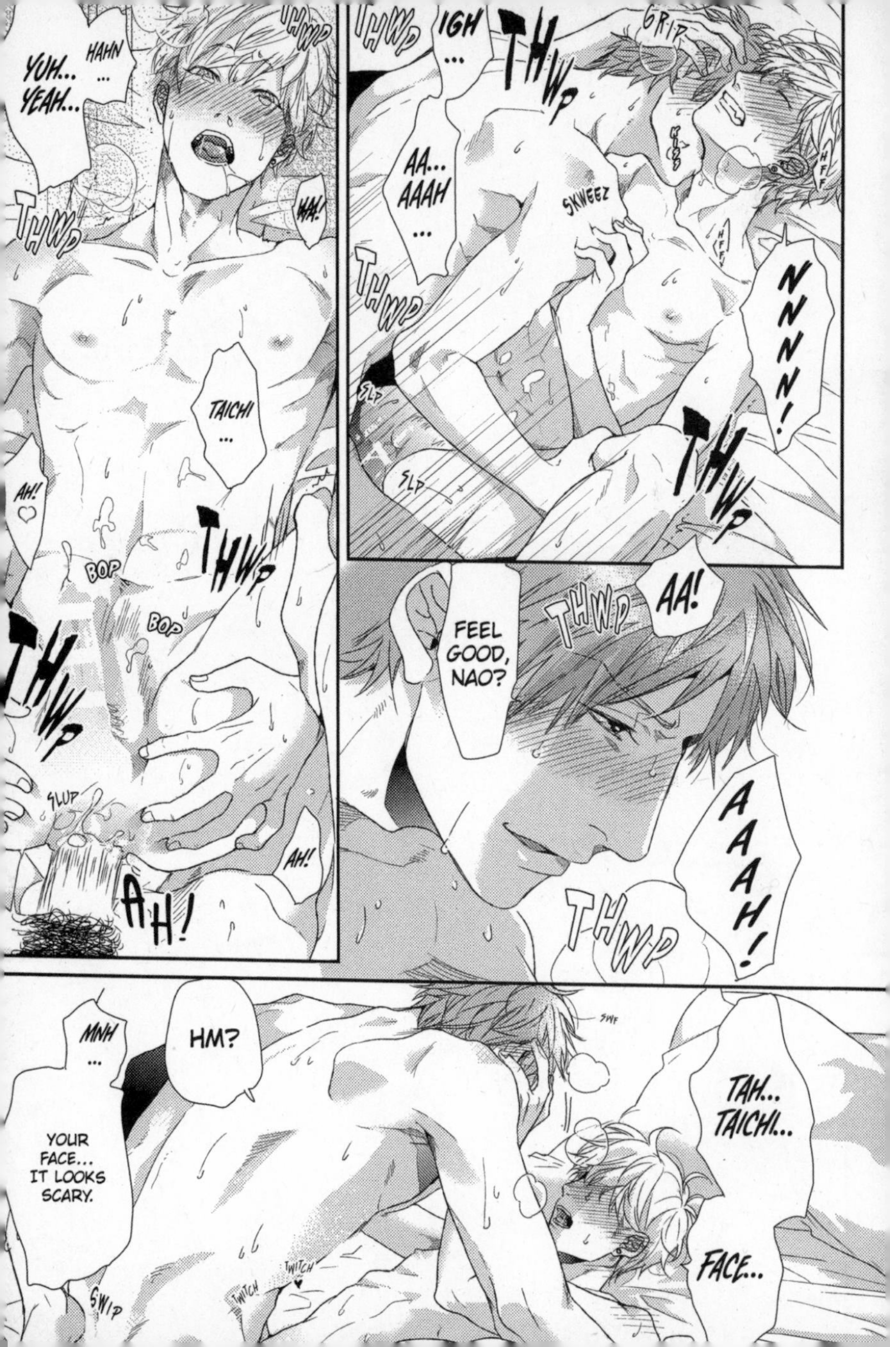
GRIP
THWP
IGH ...
THWP
AA... AAAH ...
SKWEEZ
HFF
HFF
NNNNN!
THWP
THWP
SLP
SLP
AA!
THWP
FEEL GOOD, NAO?
AAAAH!
THWP
THWP
HAHN ...
YUH... YEAH...
HA!
THWP
TAICHI ...
AH! ♡
THWP
BOP
BOP
THWP
SLUP
AH!
AH!
SWIF
TAH... TAICHI...
HM?
MNH ...
FACE...
YOUR FACE... IT LOOKS SCARY.
TWITCH
TWITCH
SWIP

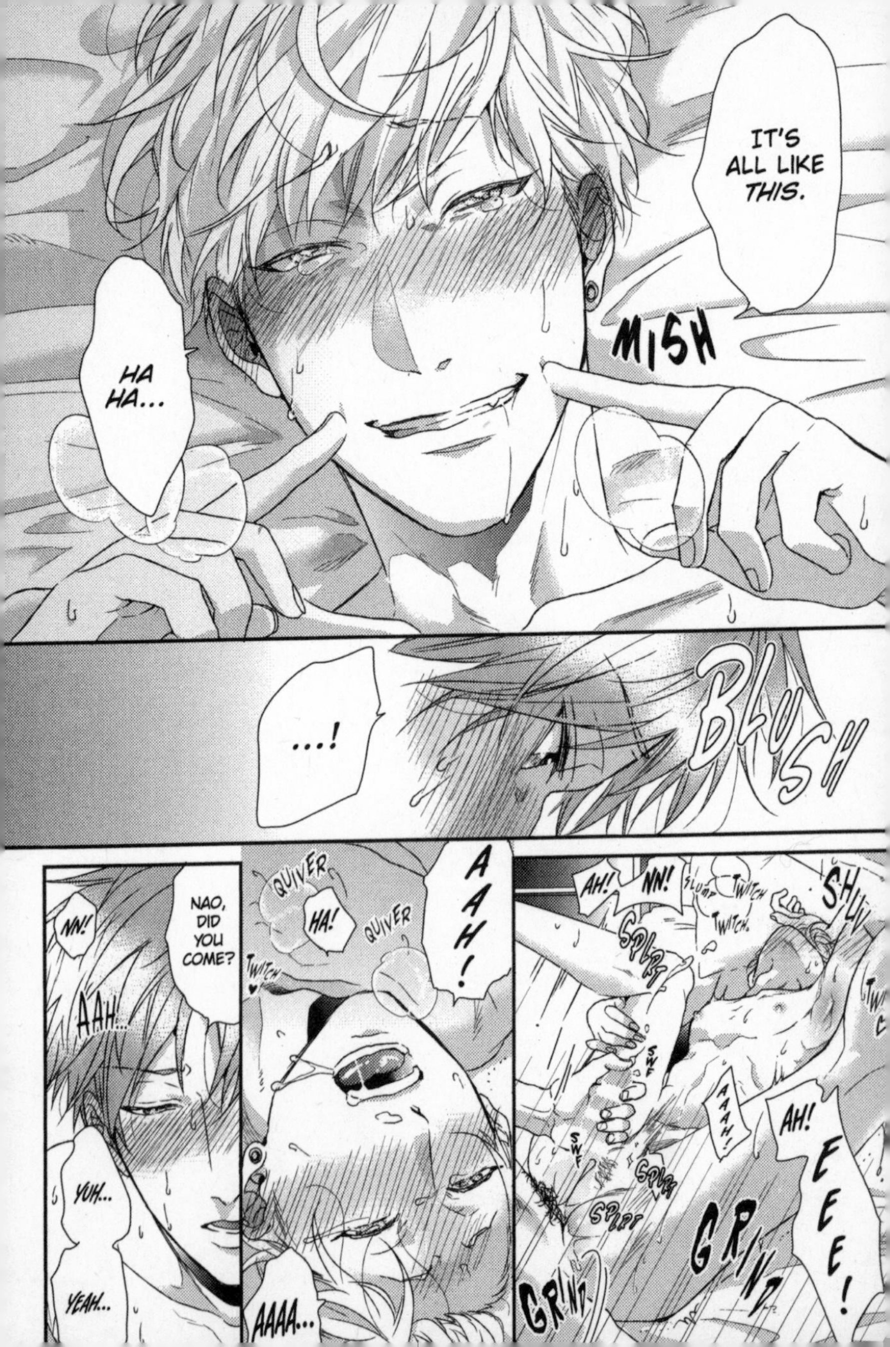
IT'S ALL LIKE THIS.
MISH
HA HA...
BLUSH
...!
SHUV
TWITCH
TWITCH
SLUMP
NN!
AH!
SPLRT
SWF
AAAAH!
AH!
EEEE!
SPLRT
SPLRT
SWF
GRIND
GRIND
AAAH!
QUIVER
HA!
QUIVER
TWITCH
AAAA...
NAO, DID YOU COME?
NN!
AAH...
YUH...
YEAH...

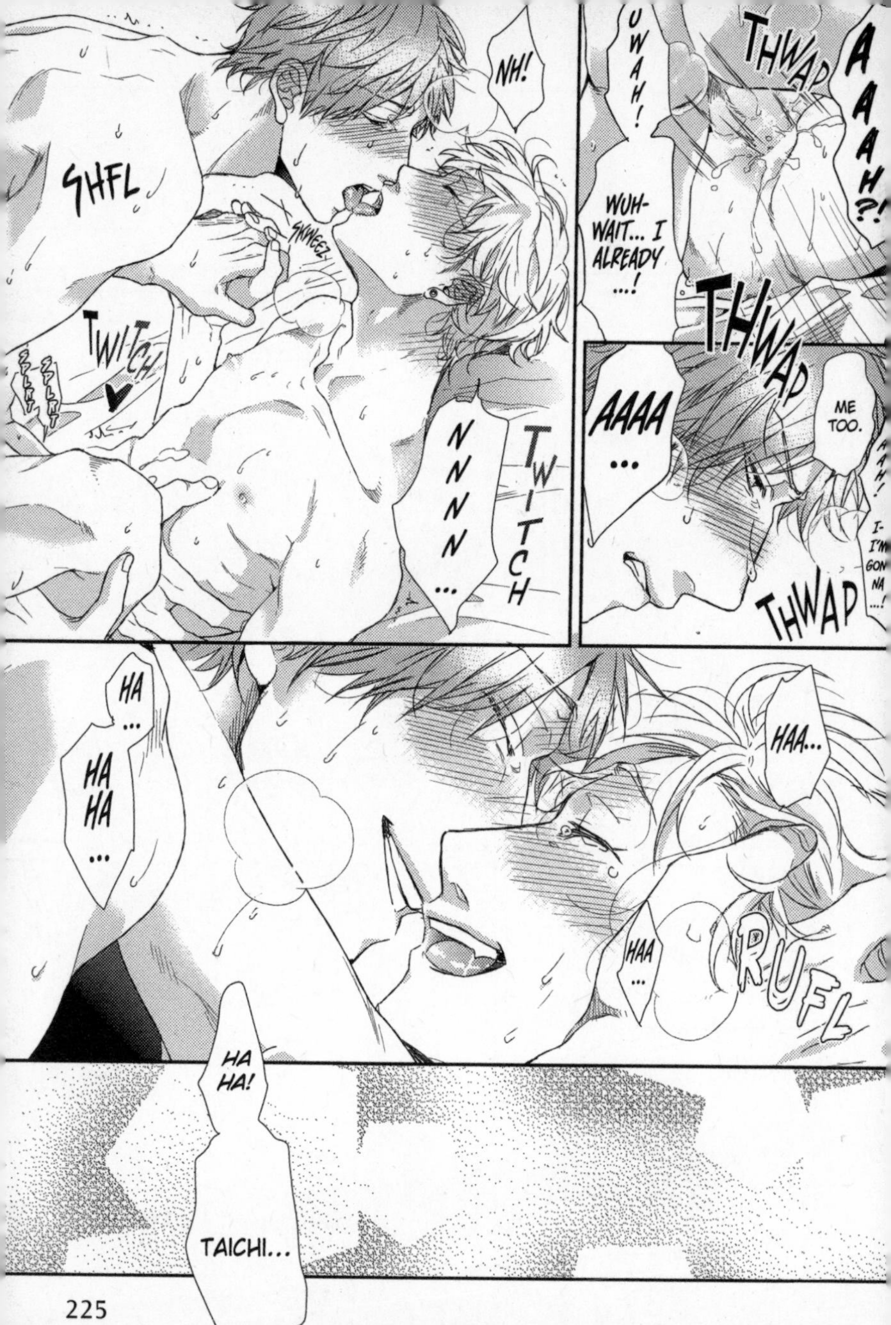
AAAAH?!
THWAP
UWAH!
WUH-WAIT... I ALREADY ...!
THWAP
ME TOO.
AAAH! I-I'M GONNA ...!
AAAA ...
THWAP
NH!
SHFL
SKWEEZ
TWITCH
SPLRT SPLRT
NNNN ...
TWITCH
HAA...
HAA ...
RUFL
HA ... HA HA ...
HA HA!
TAICHI...

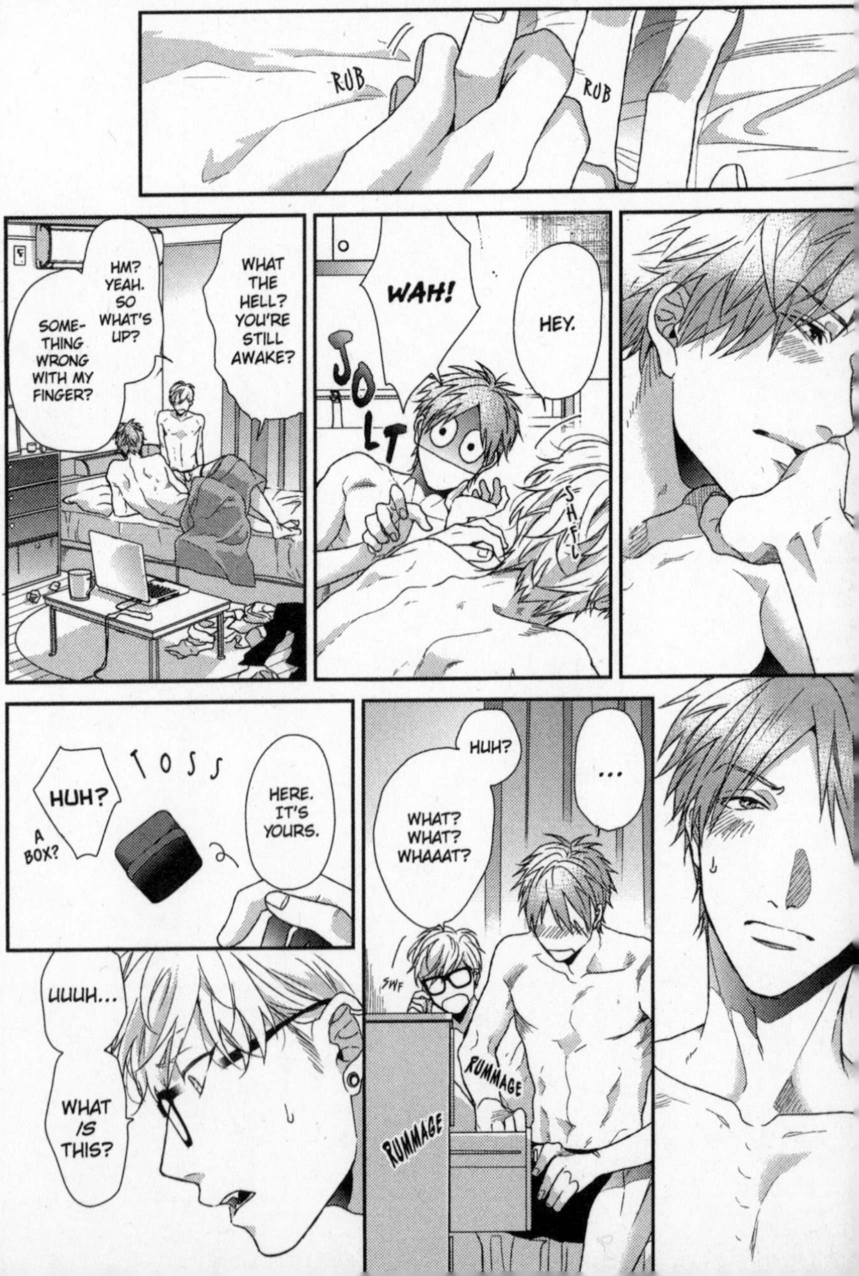
RUB
RUB
HEY.
WAH!
JOLT
SHFL
WHAT THE HELL? YOU'RE STILL AWAKE?
HM? YEAH. SO WHAT'S UP?
SOME-THING WRONG WITH MY FINGER?
...
HUH?
WHAT? WHAT? WHAAAT?
SWF
RUMMAGE
RUMMAGE
HERE. IT'S YOURS.
TOSS
HUH?
A BOX?
UUUH...
WHAT IS THIS?

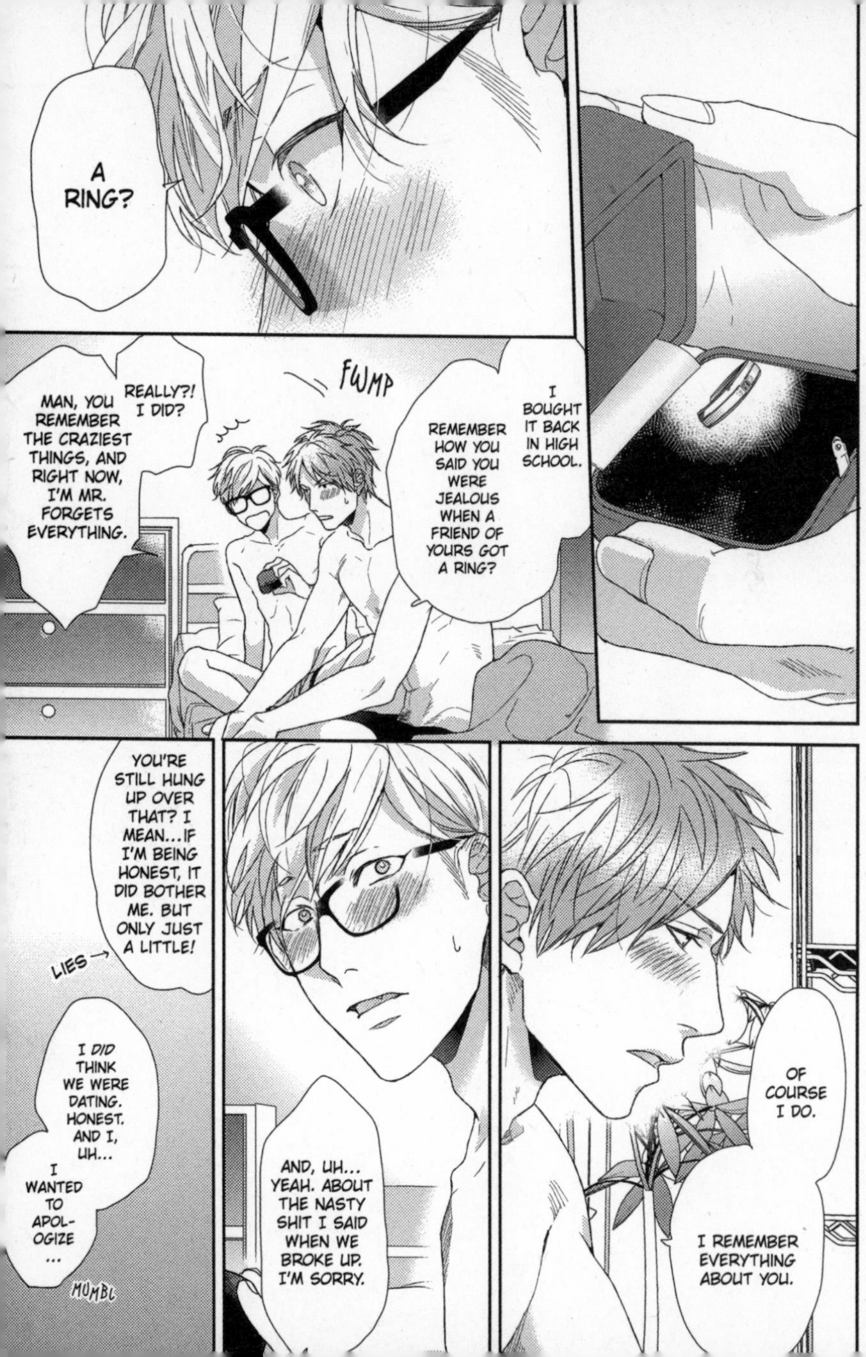
A RING?
I BOUGHT IT BACK IN HIGH SCHOOL.
REMEMBER HOW YOU SAID YOU WERE JEALOUS WHEN A FRIEND OF YOURS GOT A RING?
FWUMP
REALLY?! I DID?
MAN, YOU REMEMBER THE CRAZIEST THINGS, AND RIGHT NOW, I'M MR. FORGETS EVERYTHING.
OF COURSE I DO.
I REMEMBER EVERYTHING ABOUT YOU.
AND, UH... YEAH. ABOUT THE NASTY SHIT I SAID WHEN WE BROKE UP. I'M SORRY.
YOU'RE STILL HUNG UP OVER THAT? I MEAN...IF I'M BEING HONEST, IT DID BOTHER ME. BUT ONLY JUST A LITTLE!
LIES →
I *DID* THINK WE WERE DATING. HONEST. AND I, UH...
I WANTED TO APOLOGIZE ...
MUMBL

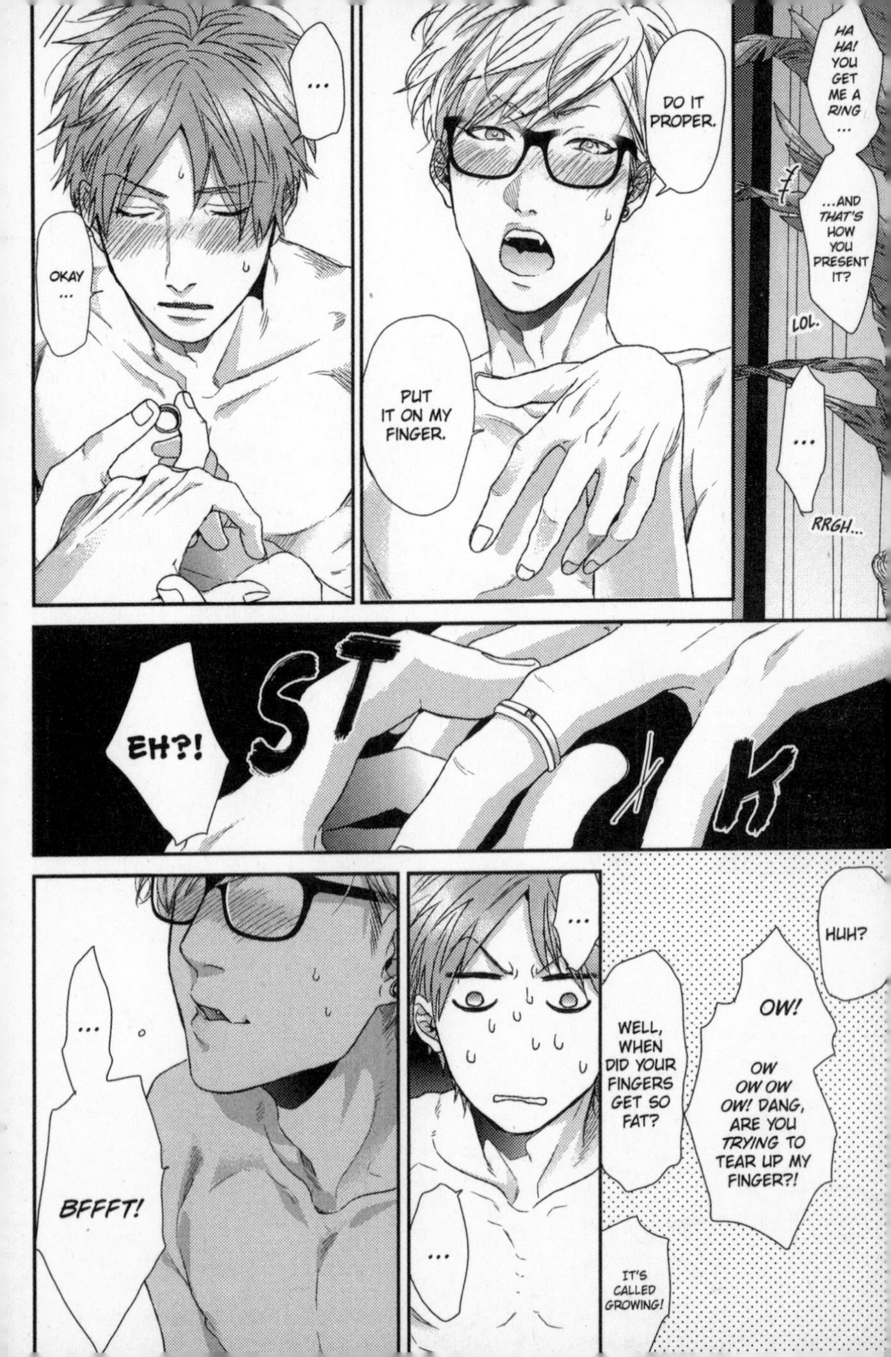

HA HA! YOU GET ME A RING ...
...AND THAT'S HOW YOU PRESENT IT?
LOL.
...
RRGH...
DO IT PROPER.
PUT IT ON MY FINGER.
...
OKAY ...
EH?!
STK
HUH?
OW!
OW OW OW OW! DANG, ARE YOU TRYING TO TEAR UP MY FINGER?!
...
WELL, WHEN DID YOUR FINGERS GET SO FAT?
IT'S CALLED GROWING!
...
...
BFFFT!

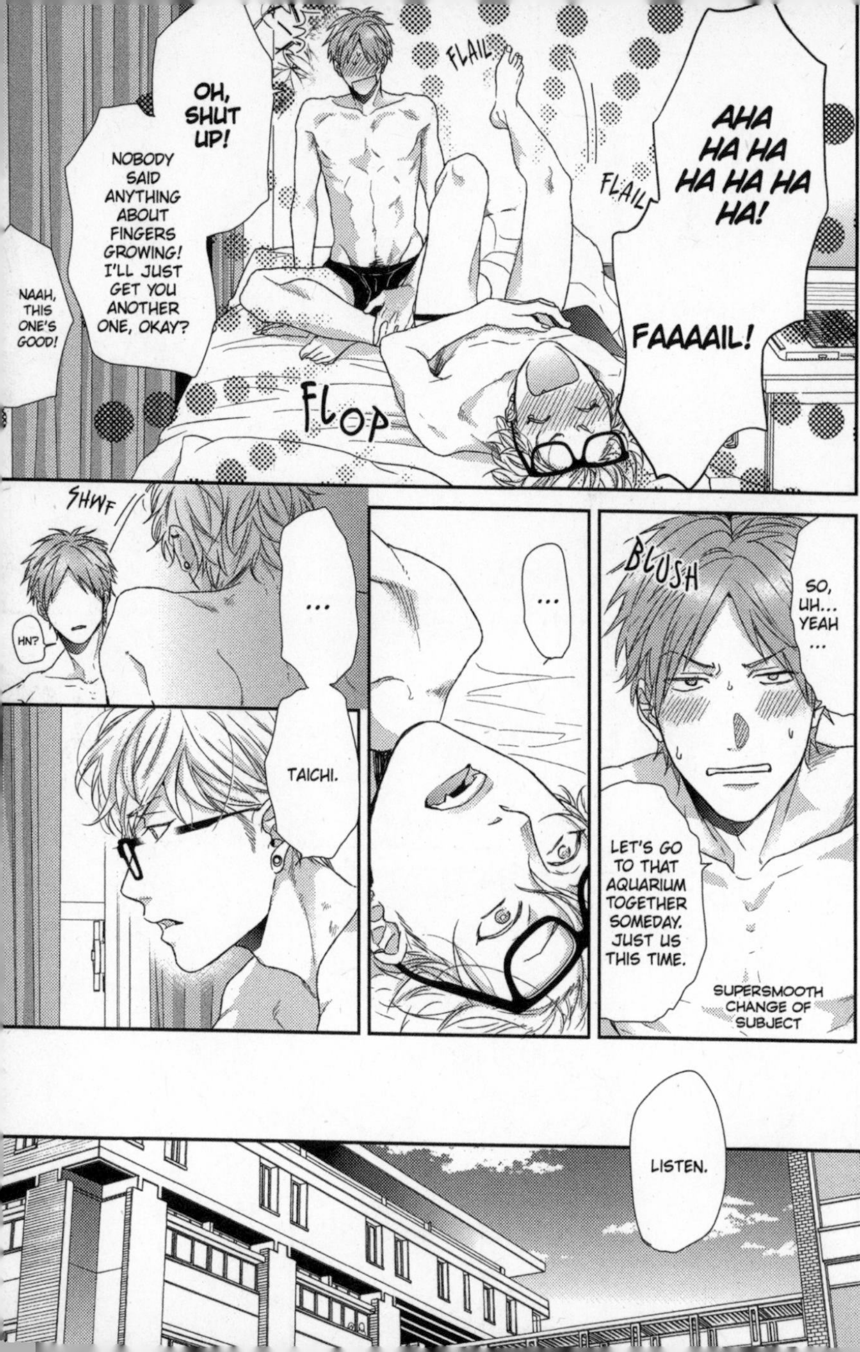
AHA HA HA HA HA HA HA!
FLAIL
FLAIL
FAAAAIL!
OH, SHUT UP!
NOBODY SAID ANYTHING ABOUT FINGERS GROWING! I'LL JUST GET YOU ANOTHER ONE, OKAY?
FLOP
NAAH, THIS ONE'S GOOD!
BLUSH
SO, UH... YEAH ...
LET'S GO TO THAT AQUARIUM TOGETHER SOMEDAY. JUST US THIS TIME.
SUPERSMOOTH CHANGE OF SUBJECT
...
SHWF
...
HN?
TAICHI.
LISTEN.

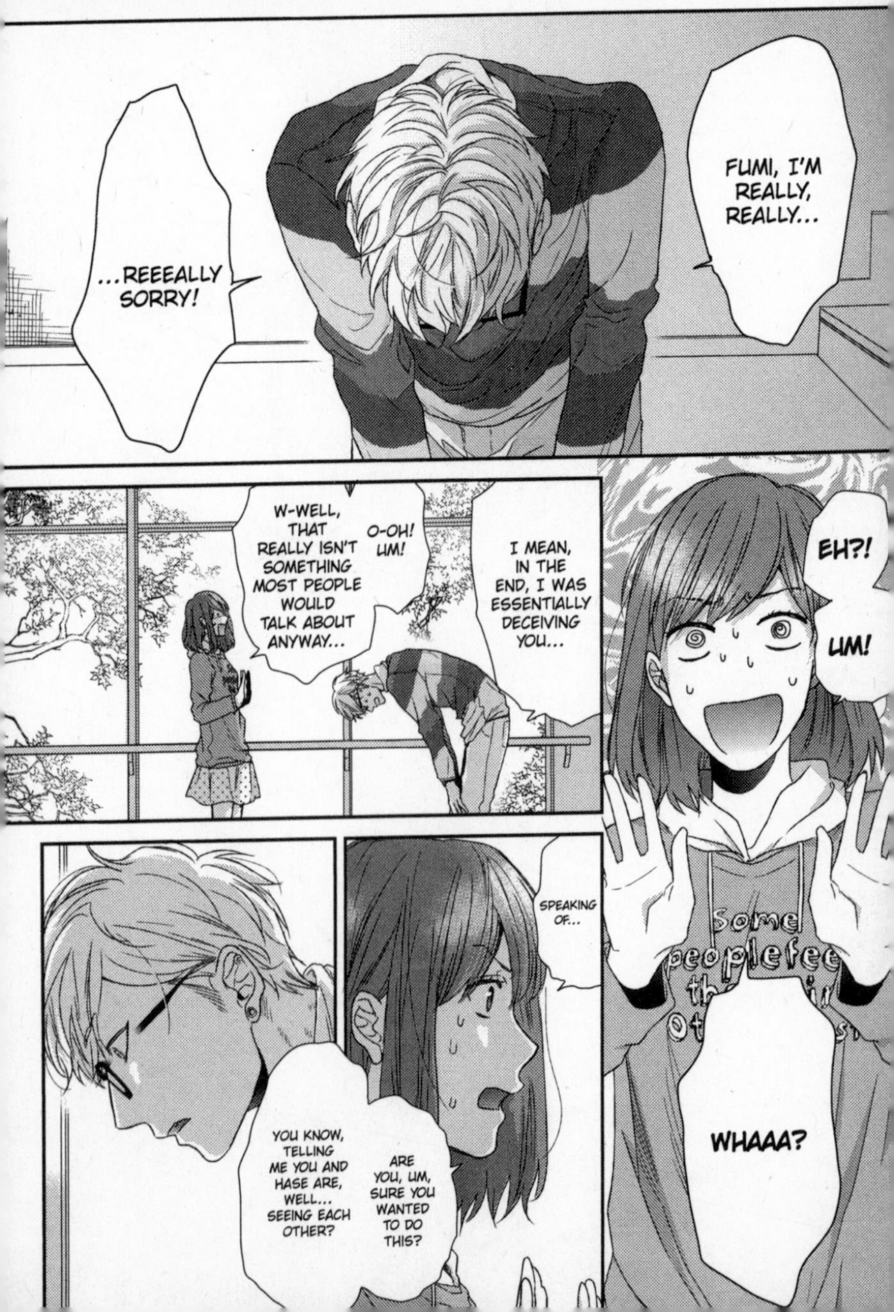
FUMI, I'M REALLY, REALLY...
...REEEALLY SORRY!
EH?!
UM!
WHAAA?
I MEAN, IN THE END, I WAS ESSENTIALLY DECEIVING YOU...
O-OH! UM!
W-WELL, THAT REALLY ISN'T SOMETHING MOST PEOPLE WOULD TALK ABOUT ANYWAY...
SPEAKING OF...
ARE YOU, UM, SURE YOU WANTED TO DO THIS?
YOU KNOW, TELLING ME YOU AND HASE ARE, WELL... SEEING EACH OTHER?

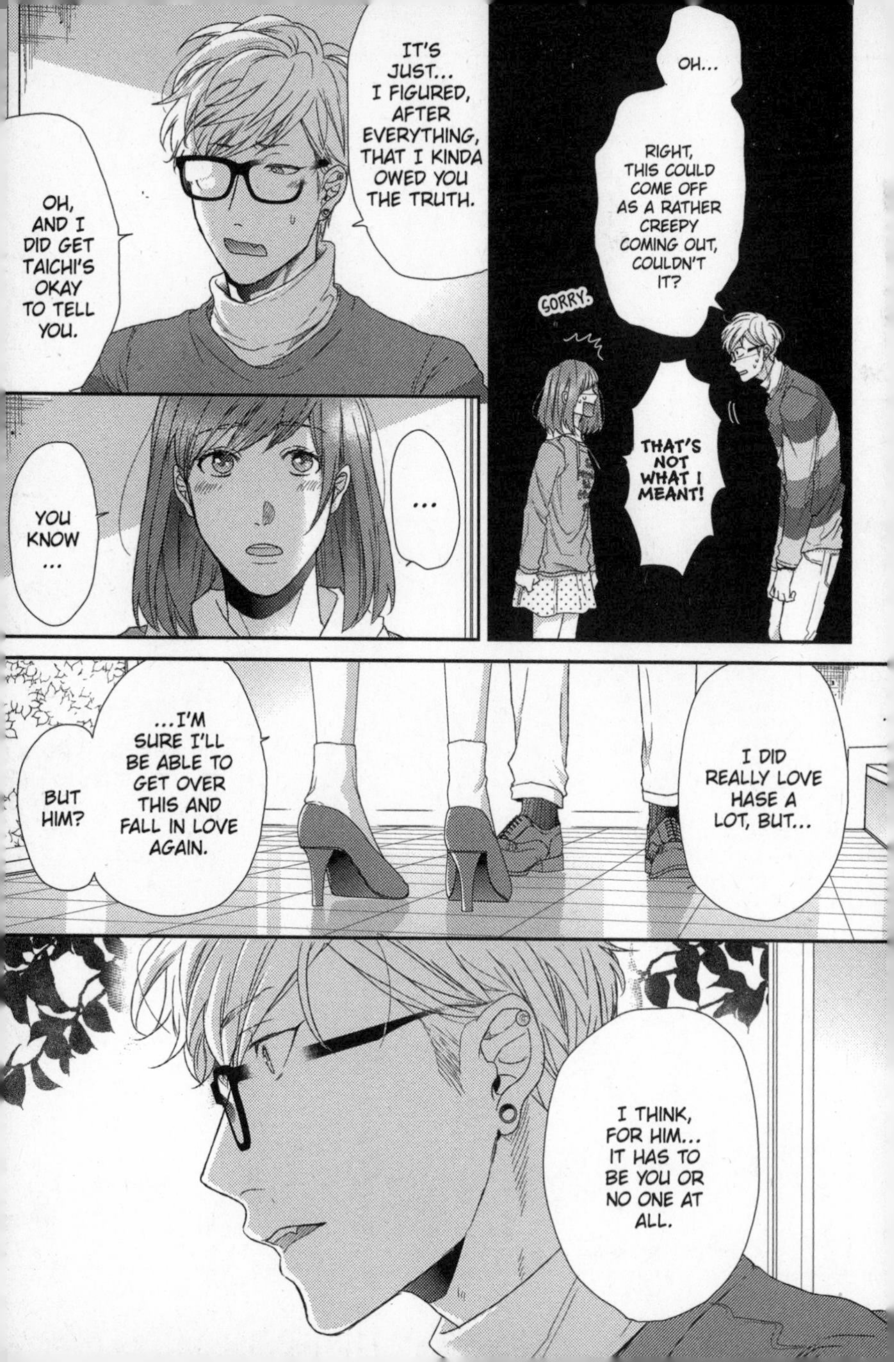
OH...
RIGHT, THIS COULD COME OFF AS A RATHER CREEPY COMING OUT, COULDN'T IT?
SORRY.
THAT'S NOT WHAT I MEANT!
IT'S JUST... I FIGURED, AFTER EVERYTHING, THAT I KINDA OWED YOU THE TRUTH.
OH, AND I DID GET TAICHI'S OKAY TO TELL YOU.
...
YOU KNOW ...
I DID REALLY LOVE HASE A LOT, BUT...
...I'M SURE I'LL BE ABLE TO GET OVER THIS AND FALL IN LOVE AGAIN.
BUT HIM?
I THINK, FOR HIM... IT HAS TO BE YOU OR NO ONE AT ALL.

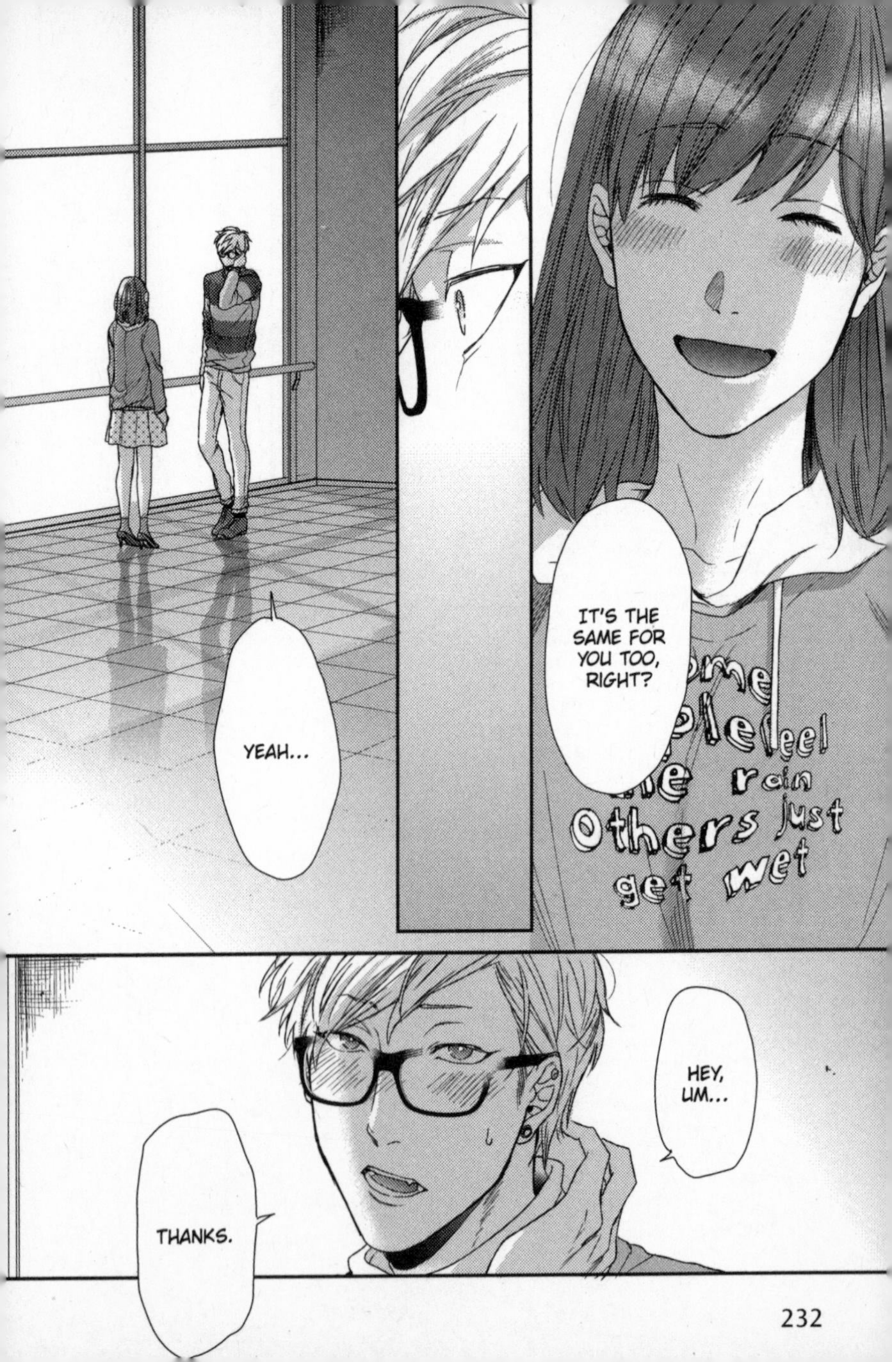
IT'S THE SAME FOR YOU TOO, RIGHT?
Others just
get wet
YEAH...
HEY, UM...
THANKS.

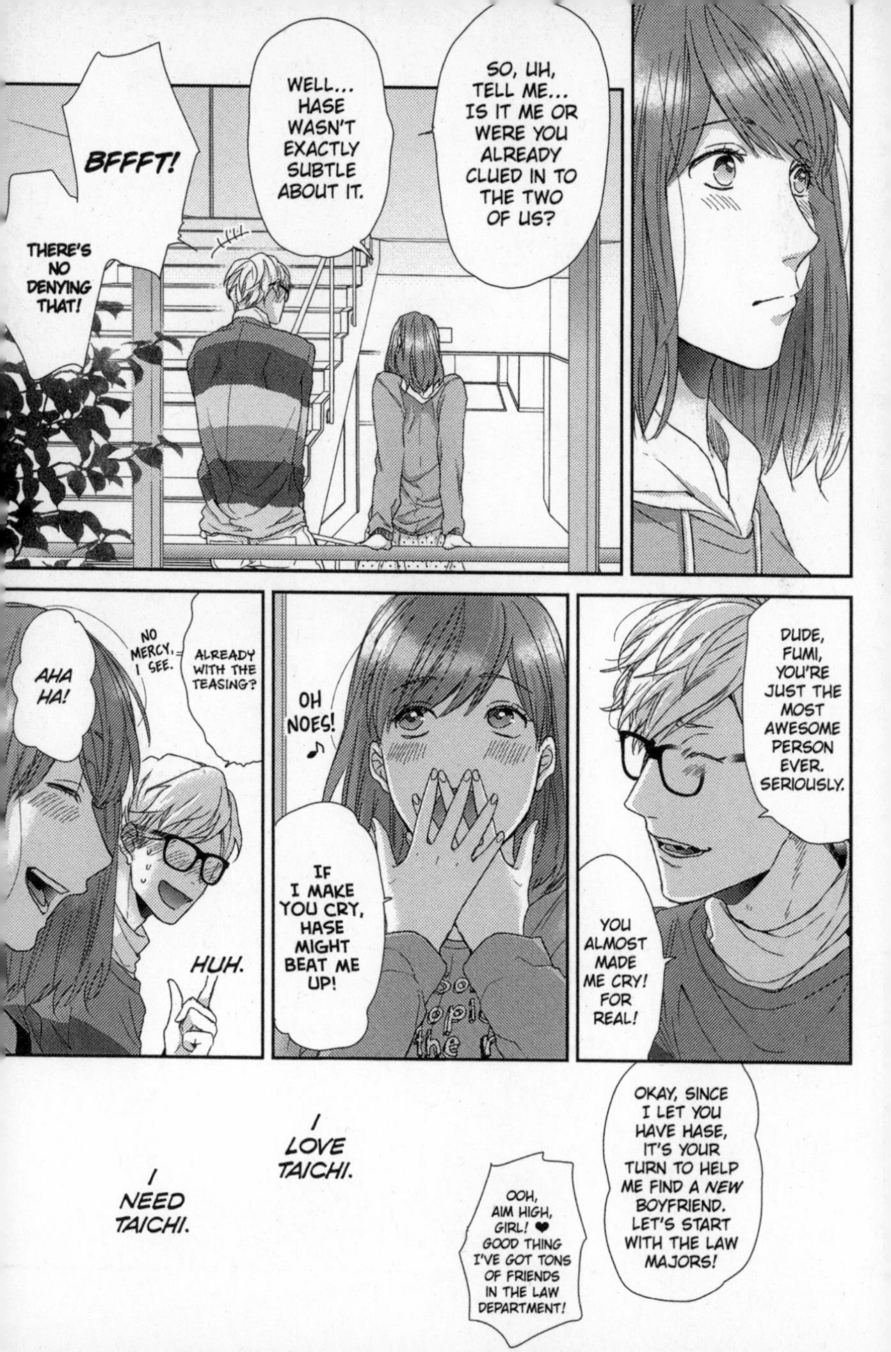
SO, UH, TELL ME... IS IT ME OR WERE YOU ALREADY CLUED IN TO THE TWO OF US?
WELL... HASE WASN'T EXACTLY SUBTLE ABOUT IT.
BFFFT!
THERE'S NO DENYING THAT!
DUDE, FUMI, YOU'RE JUST THE MOST AWESOME PERSON EVER. SERIOUSLY.
YOU ALMOST MADE ME CRY! FOR REAL!
OH NOES! ♪
IF I MAKE YOU CRY, HASE MIGHT BEAT ME UP!
ALREADY WITH THE TEASING?
NO MERCY, I SEE.
AHA HA!
HUH.
OKAY, SINCE I LET YOU HAVE HASE, IT'S YOUR TURN TO HELP ME FIND A *NEW* BOYFRIEND. LET'S START WITH THE LAW MAJORS!
OOH, AIM HIGH, GIRL! ❤ GOOD THING I'VE GOT TONS OF FRIENDS IN THE LAW DEPARTMENT!
I LOVE TAICHI.
I NEED TAICHI.

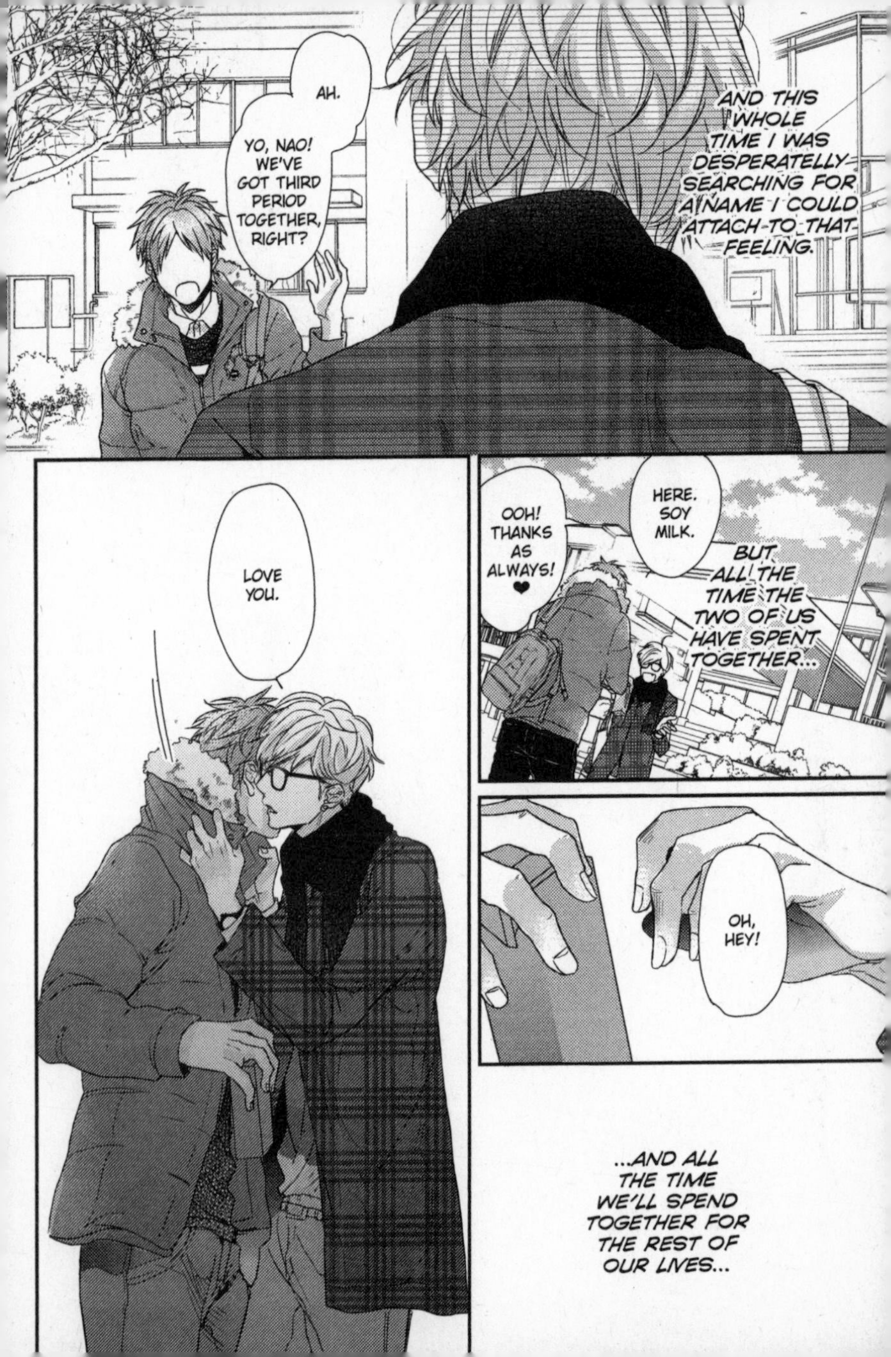
AND THIS WHOLE TIME I WAS DESPERATELLY SEARCHING FOR A NAME I COULD ATTACH TO THAT FEELING.
AH.
YO, NAO! WE'VE GOT THIRD PERIOD TOGETHER, RIGHT?
HERE. SOY MILK.
OOH! THANKS AS ALWAYS! ❤
BUT ALL THE TIME THE TWO OF US HAVE SPENT TOGETHER...
OH, HEY!
...AND ALL THE TIME WE'LL SPEND TOGETHER FOR THE REST OF OUR LIVES...
LOVE YOU.

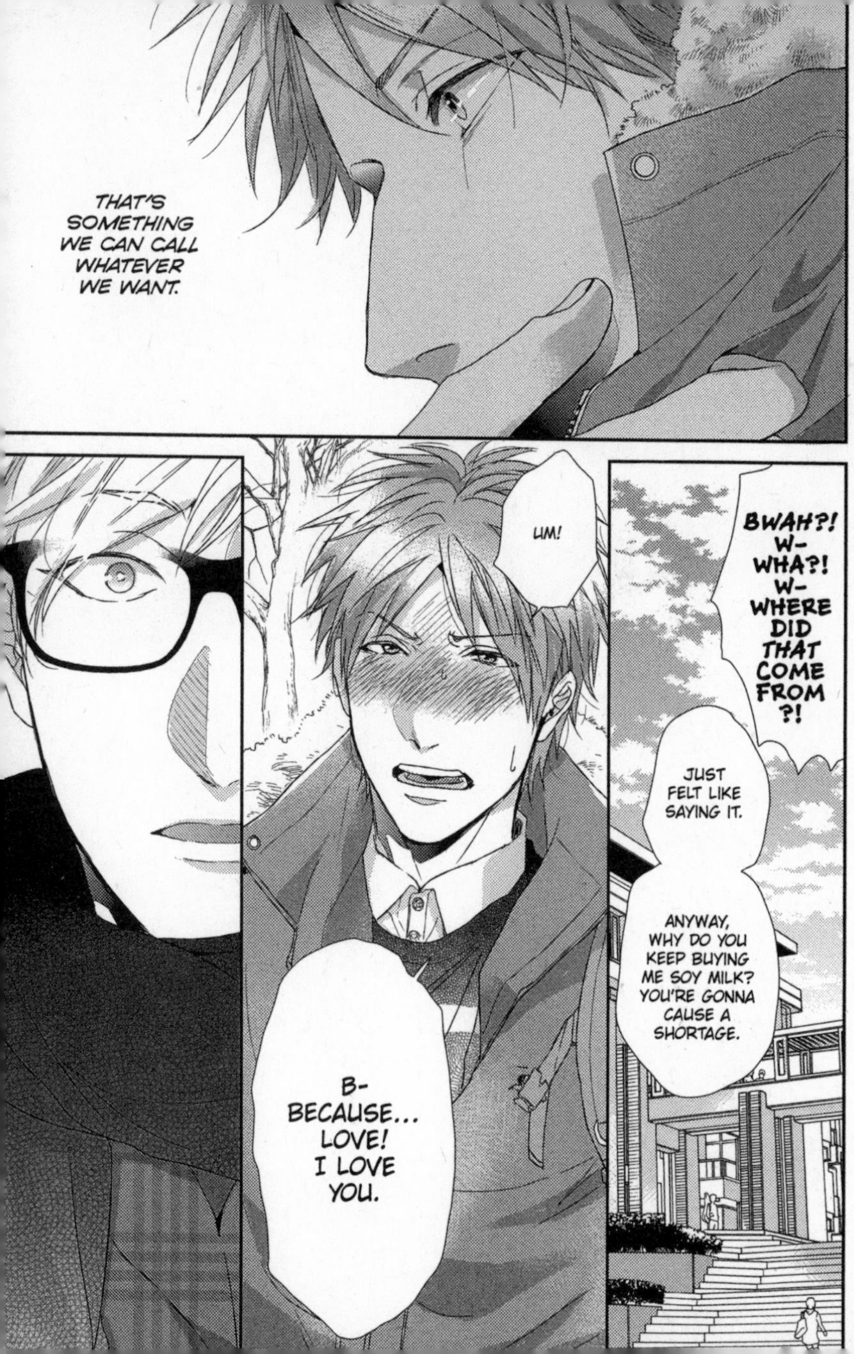
THAT'S SOMETHING WE CAN CALL WHATEVER WE WANT.
BWAH?! W-WHA?! W-WHERE DID THAT COME FROM?!
JUST FELT LIKE SAYING IT.
ANYWAY, WHY DO YOU KEEP BUYING ME SOY MILK? YOU'RE GONNA CAUSE A SHORTAGE.
UM!
B-BECAUSE... LOVE! I LOVE YOU.

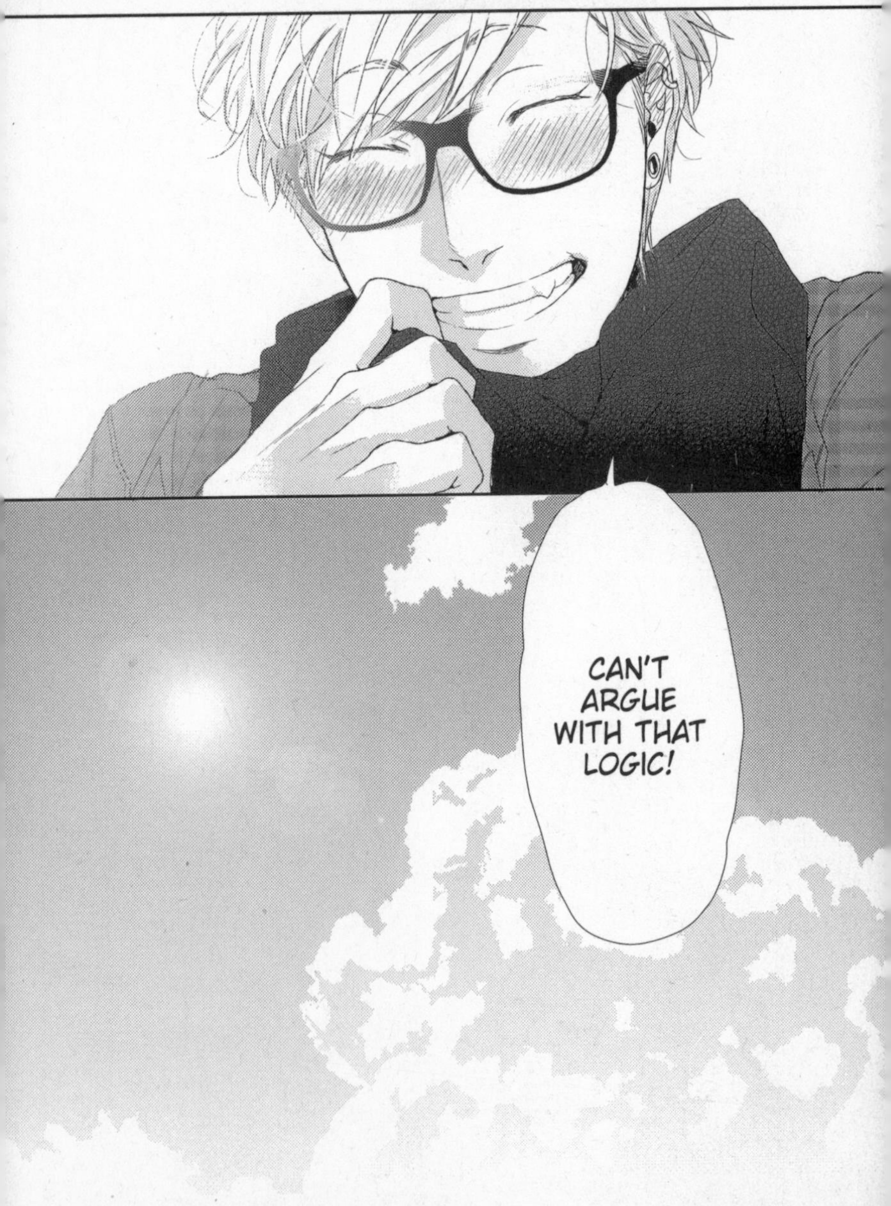
CAN'T ARGUE WITH THAT LOGIC!

Escape Journey / END

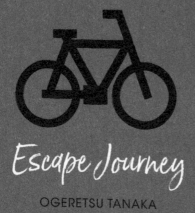

Escape Journey

OGERETSU TANAKA

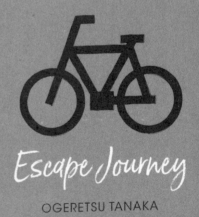

Escape Journey

OGERETSU TANAKA

Escape Journey
Bonus Story

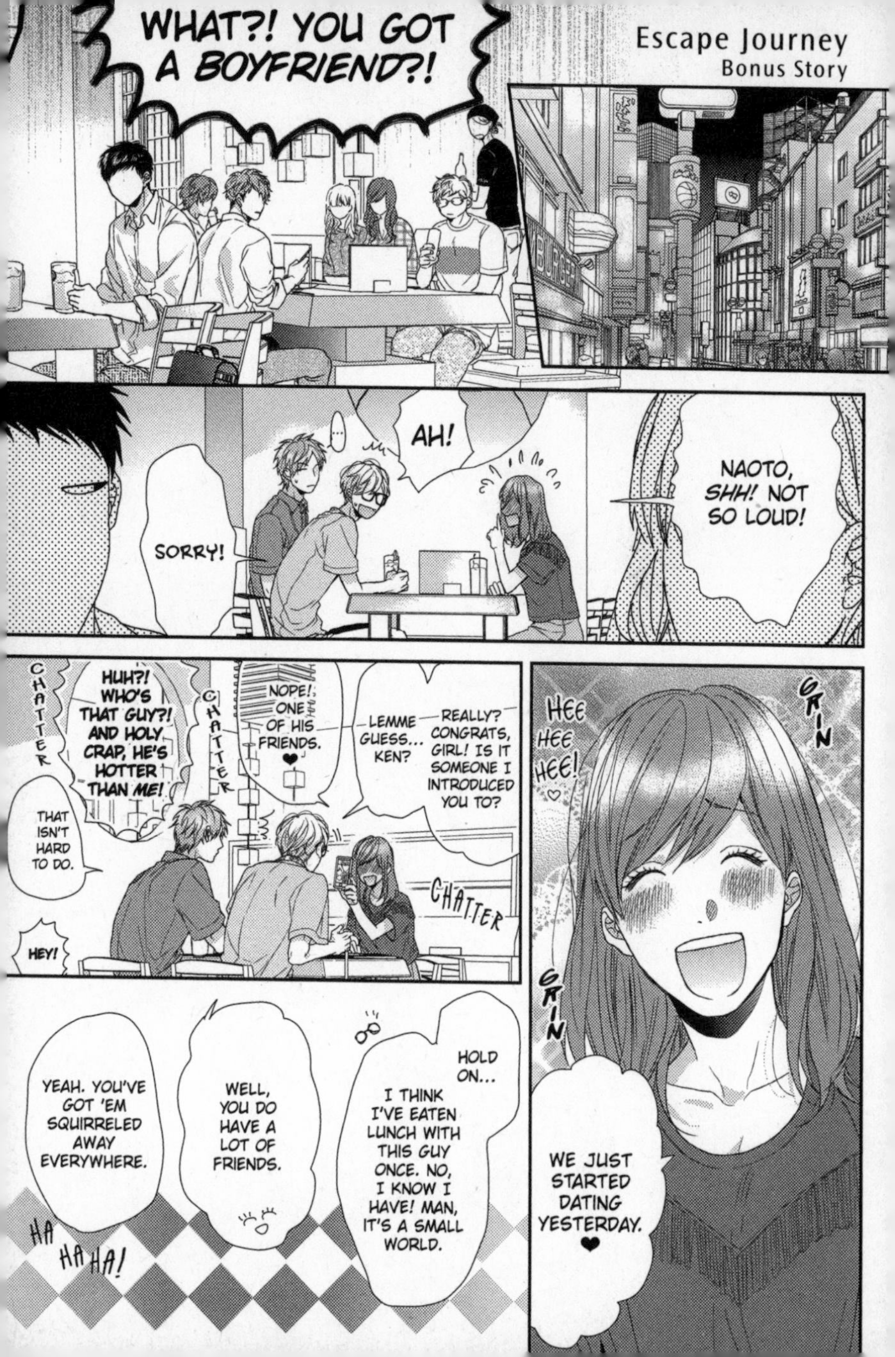
WHAT?! YOU GOT A BOYFRIEND?!
NAOTO, SHH! NOT SO LOUD!
AH!
...
SORRY!
GRIN
HEE HEE HEE! ♡
GRIN
WE JUST STARTED DATING YESTERDAY. ❤
REALLY? CONGRATS, GIRL! IS IT SOMEONE I INTRODUCED YOU TO?
LEMME GUESS... KEN?
NOPE! ONE OF HIS FRIENDS. ❤
CHATTER
HUH?! WHO'S THAT GUY?! AND HOLY CRAP, HE'S HOTTER THAN ME!
CHATTER
THAT ISN'T HARD TO DO.
CHATTER
HEY!
HOLD ON... I THINK I'VE EATEN LUNCH WITH THIS GUY ONCE. NO, I KNOW I HAVE! MAN, IT'S A SMALL WORLD.
WELL, YOU DO HAVE A LOT OF FRIENDS.
YEAH. YOU'VE GOT 'EM SQUIRRELED AWAY EVERYWHERE.
HA HA HA!

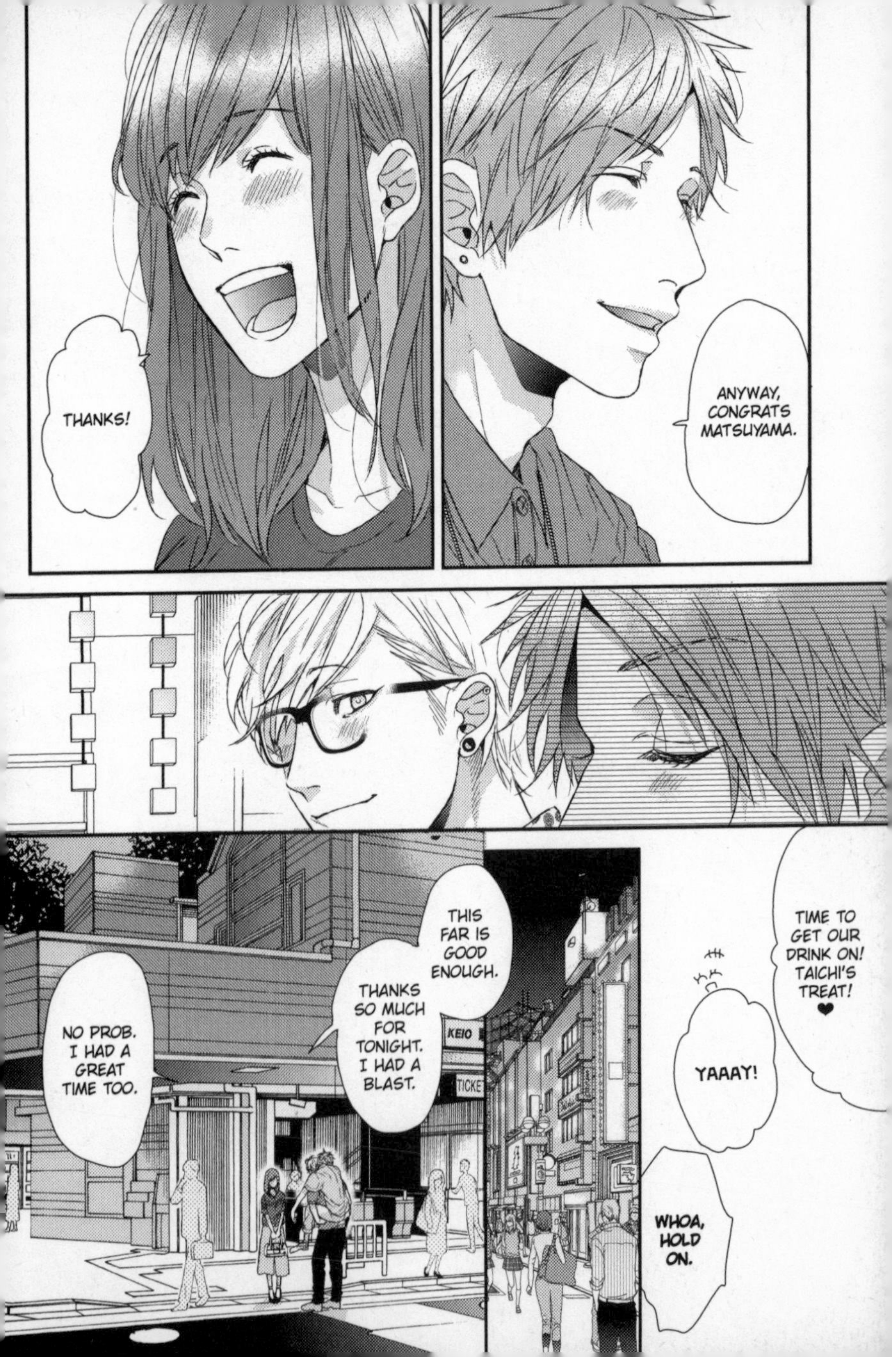
ANYWAY, CONGRATS MATSUYAMA.
THANKS!
TIME TO GET OUR DRINK ON! TAICHI'S TREAT! ❤
YAAAY!
WHOA, HOLD ON.
THIS FAR IS GOOD ENOUGH.
THANKS SO MUCH FOR TONIGHT. I HAD A BLAST.
NO PROB. I HAD A GREAT TIME TOO.
KEIO

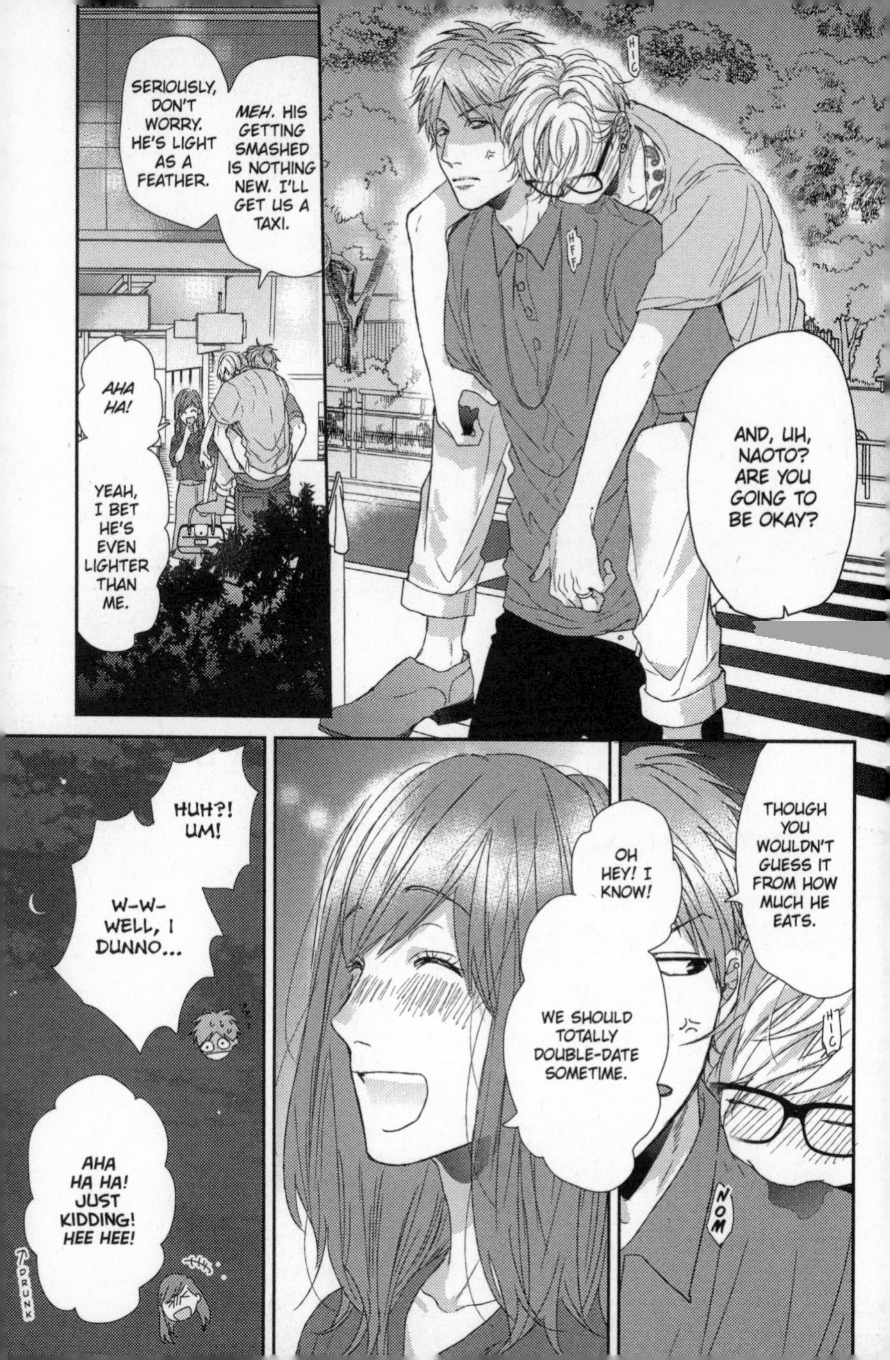
HIC
HFF
AND, UH, NAOTO? ARE YOU GOING TO BE OKAY?
MEH. HIS GETTING SMASHED IS NOTHING NEW. I'LL GET US A TAXI.
SERIOUSLY, DON'T WORRY. HE'S LIGHT AS A FEATHER.
AHA HA!
YEAH, I BET HE'S EVEN LIGHTER THAN ME.
THOUGH YOU WOULDN'T GUESS IT FROM HOW MUCH HE EATS.
HIC
NOM
OH HEY! I KNOW!
WE SHOULD TOTALLY DOUBLE-DATE SOMETIME.
HUH?! UM!
W-W-WELL, I DUNNO...
AHA HA HA! JUST KIDDING! HEE HEE!
DRUNK

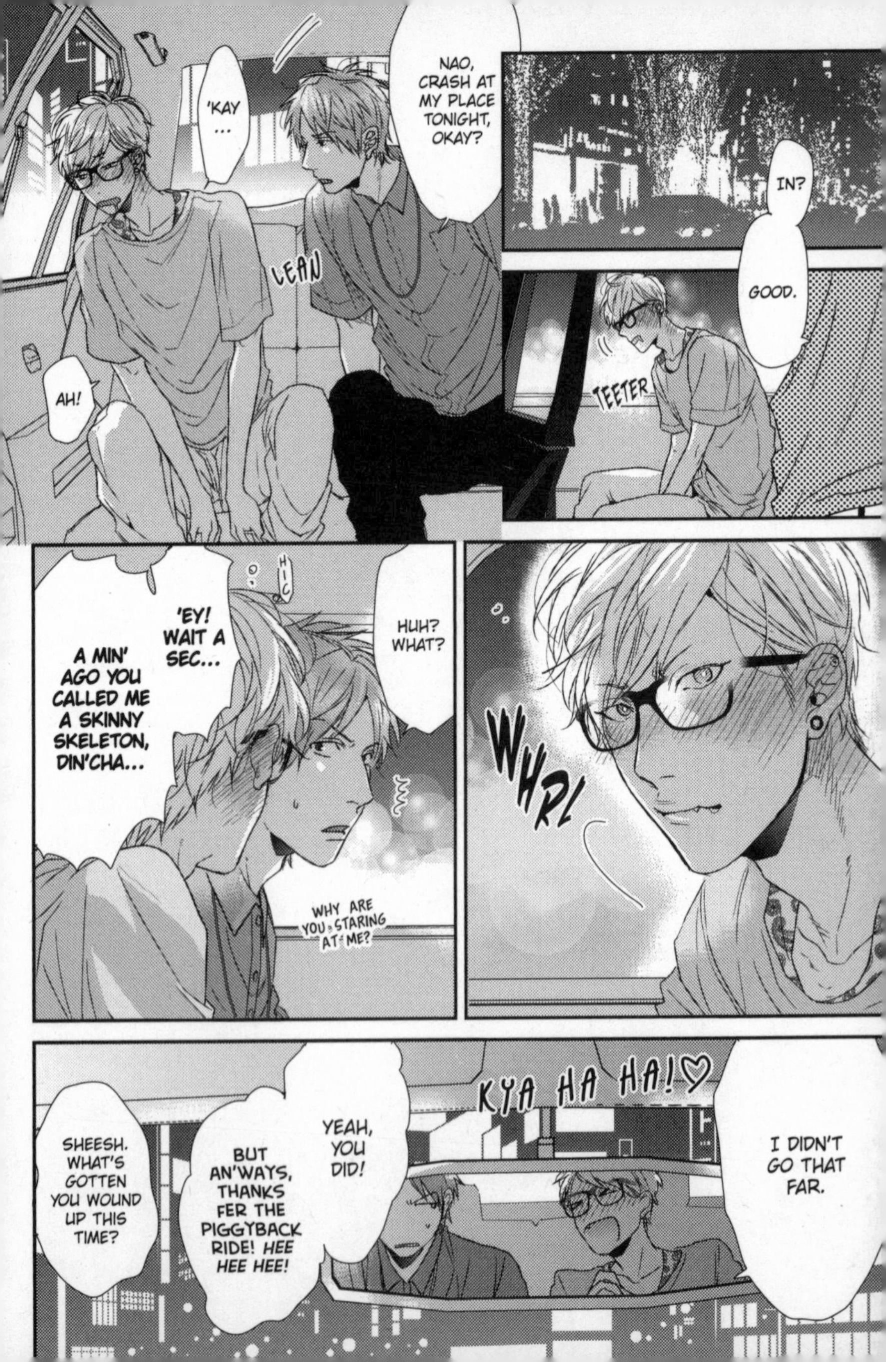
IN?
GOOD.
TEETER
NAO, CRASH AT MY PLACE TONIGHT, OKAY?
'KAY ...
LEAN
AH!
WHRL
HUH? WHAT?
'EY! WAIT A SEC...
HIC
A MIN' AGO YOU CALLED ME A SKINNY SKELETON, DIN'CHA...
WHY ARE YOU STARING AT ME?
I DIDN'T GO THAT FAR.
KYA HA HA!♡
YEAH, YOU DID!
BUT AN'WAYS, THANKS FER THE PIGGYBACK RIDE! *HEE HEE HEE!*
SHEESH. WHAT'S GOTTEN YOU WOUND UP THIS TIME?

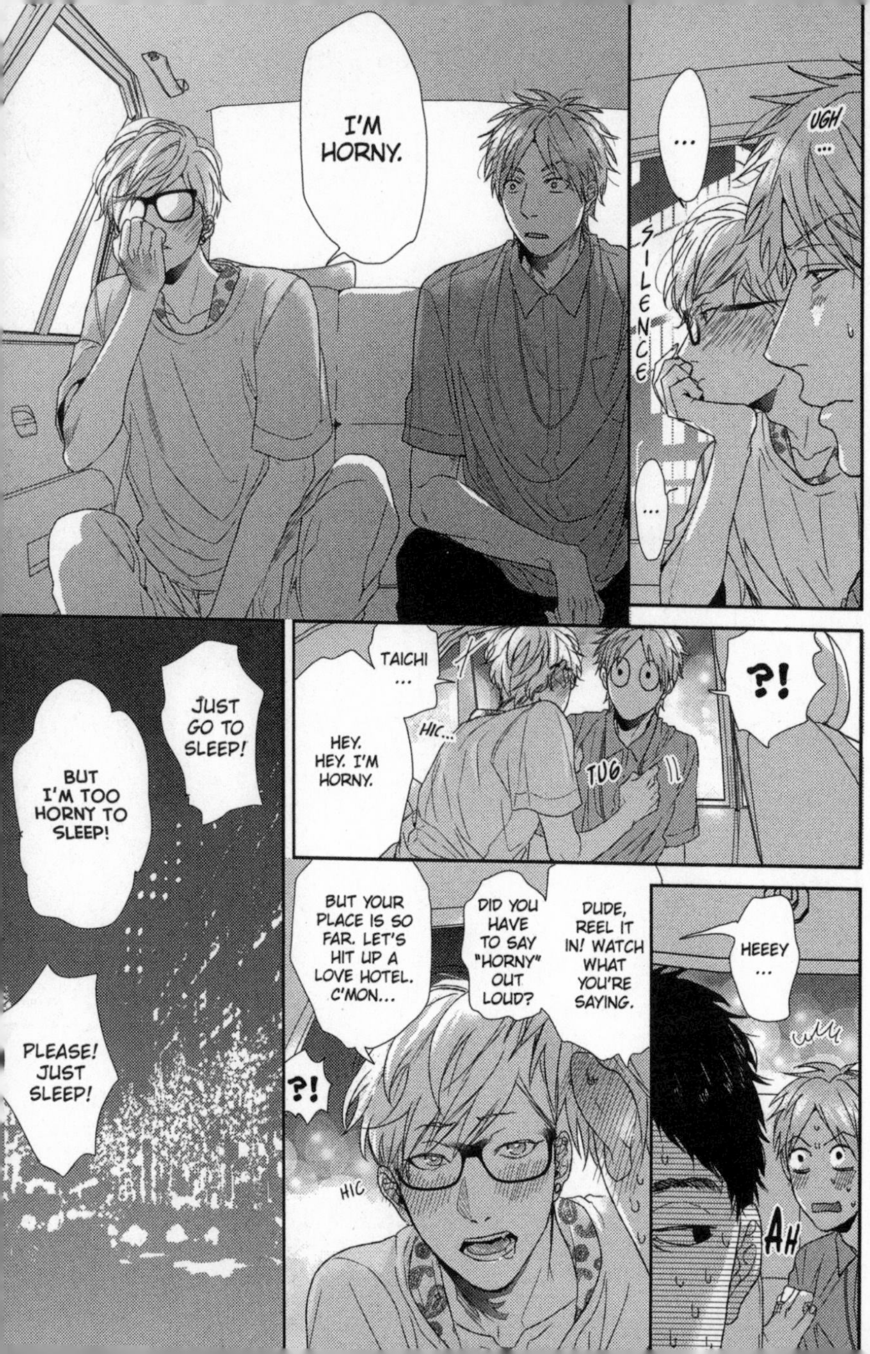
...
UGH ...
SILENCE
...
I'M HORNY.
?!
TAICHI ...
HIC...
HEY. HEY. I'M HORNY.
TUG
HEEEY ...
AH
DUDE, REEL IT IN! WATCH WHAT YOU'RE SAYING.
DID YOU HAVE TO SAY "HORNY" OUT LOUD?
BUT YOUR PLACE IS SO FAR. LET'S HIT UP A LOVE HOTEL. C'MON...
?!
HIC
JUST GO TO SLEEP!
BUT I'M TOO HORNY TO SLEEP!
PLEASE! JUST SLEEP!

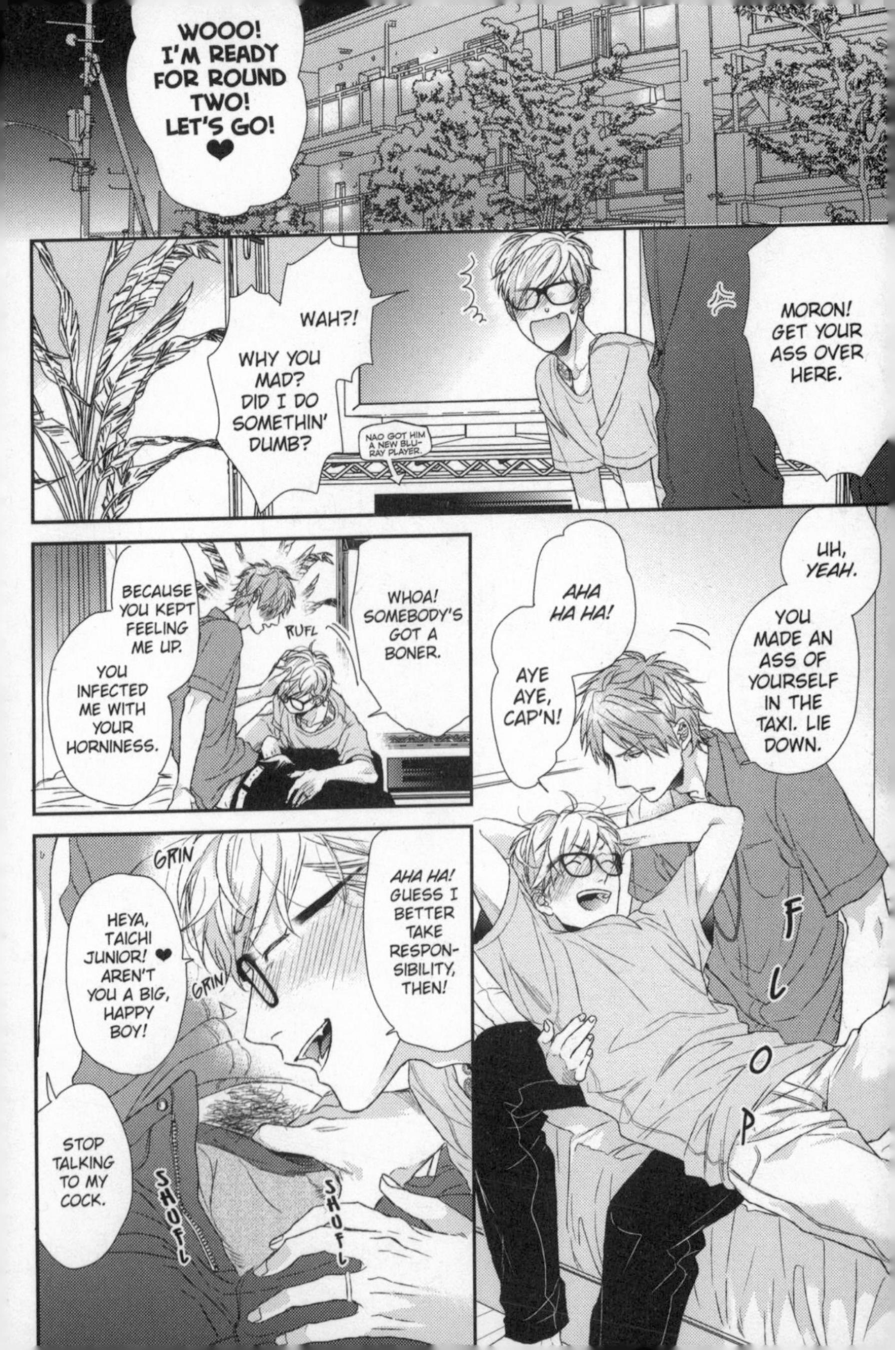
WOOO! I'M READY FOR ROUND TWO! LET'S GO! ❤
MORON! GET YOUR ASS OVER HERE.
WAH?!
WHY YOU MAD? DID I DO SOMETHIN' DUMB?
NAO GOT HIM A NEW BLU-RAY PLAYER.
UH, YEAH.
YOU MADE AN ASS OF YOURSELF IN THE TAXI. LIE DOWN.
AHA HA HA!
AYE AYE, CAP'N!
FLOP
WHOA! SOMEBODY'S GOT A BONER.
RUFL
BECAUSE YOU KEPT FEELING ME UP.
YOU INFECTED ME WITH YOUR HORNINESS.
AHA HA! GUESS I BETTER TAKE RESPONSIBILITY, THEN!
GRIN
GRIN
HEYA, TAICHI JUNIOR! ❤ AREN'T YOU A BIG, HAPPY BOY!
SHUFL
SHUFL
STOP TALKING TO MY COCK.

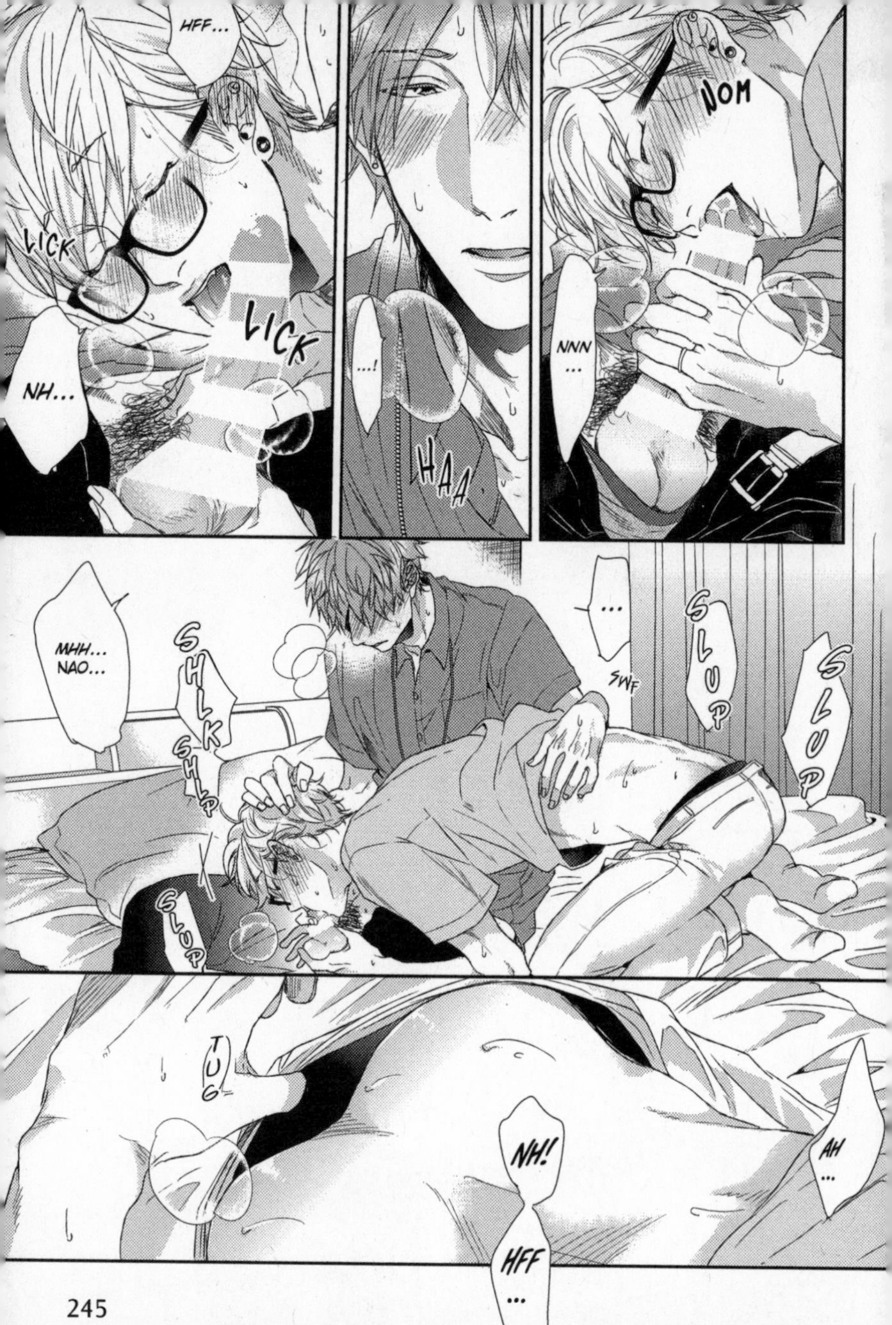
NOM
NNN...
...!
HAA
HFF...
LICK
LICK
NH...
SLUP
SLUP
...
SWF
SHLK
SHLP
MHH... NAO...
SLUP
AH...
NH!
HFF...
TUG

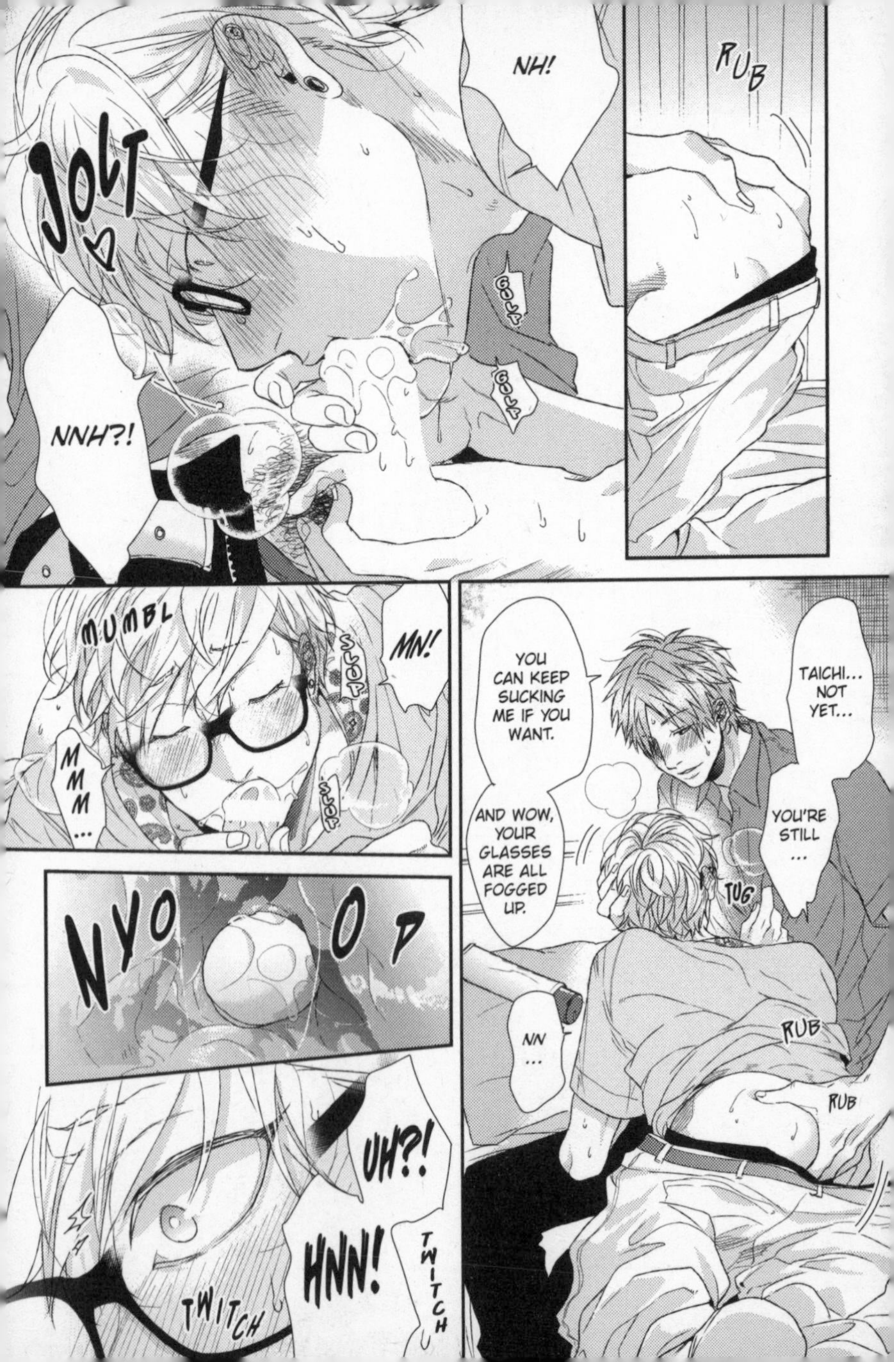
RUB
NH!
GULP
GULP
JOLT
NNH?!
TAICHI... NOT YET...
YOU CAN KEEP SUCKING ME IF YOU WANT.
YOU'RE STILL ...
AND WOW, YOUR GLASSES ARE ALL FOGGED UP.
TUG
RUB
NN ...
RUB
MN!
SLOP
MUMBL
SLOP
MMM ...
NYOOP
UH?!
TWITCH
HNN!
TWITCH

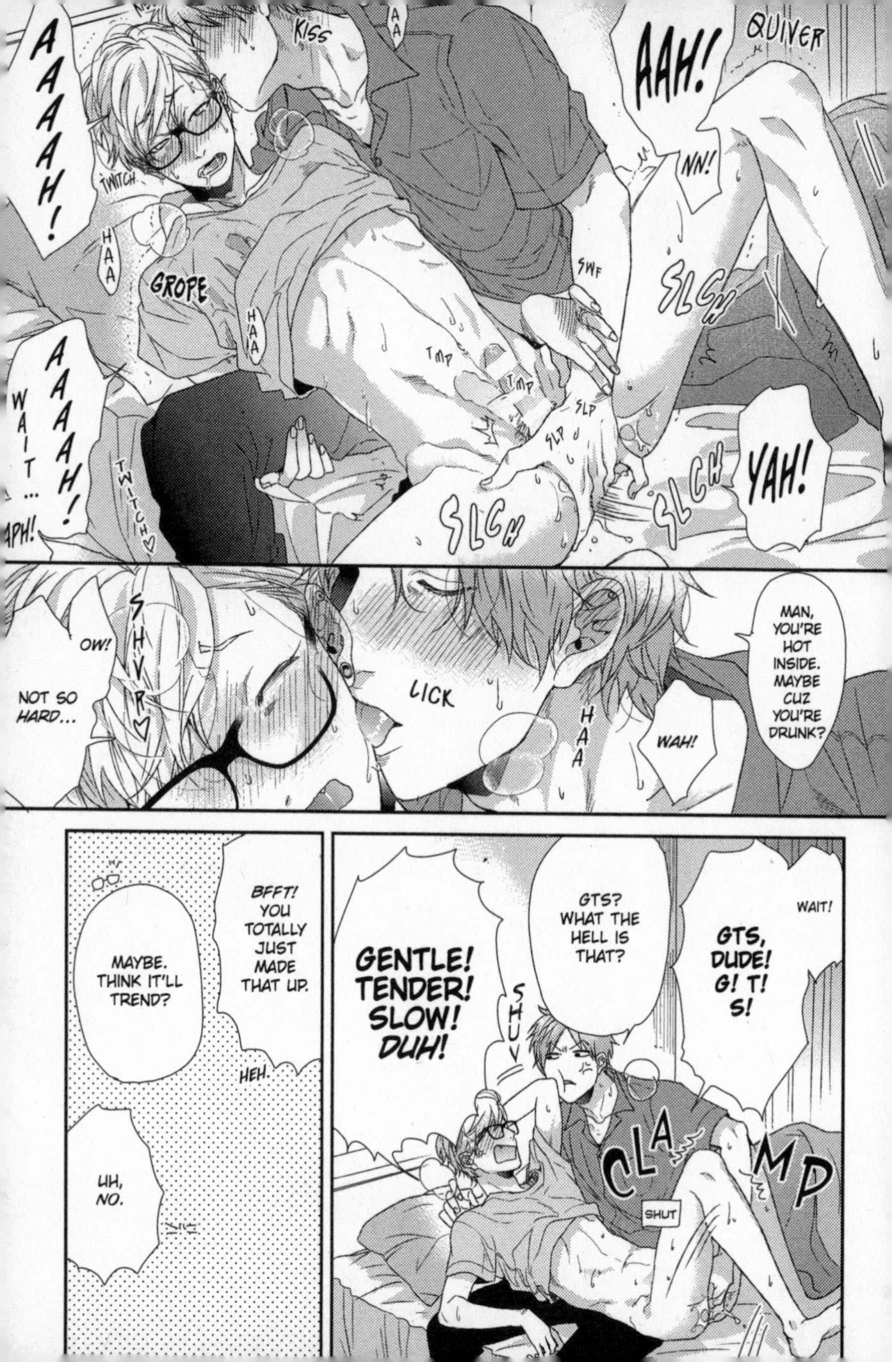
QUIVER
AAH!
NN!
SLCH
SWF
YAH!
SLCH
SLCH
SLP
SLP
TMP
TMP
AA
KISS
AAAAAH!
TWITCH
HAA
GROPE
HAA
AAAAAH!
TWITCH♡
WAIT...
MAN, YOU'RE HOT INSIDE. MAYBE CUZ YOU'RE DRUNK?
WAH!
HAA
LICK
SHVR♡
OW!
NOT SO HARD...
WAIT!
GTS, DUDE! G! T! S!
GTS? WHAT THE HELL IS THAT?
GENTLE! TENDER! SLOW! DUH!
SHUV
CLAMP
SHUT
BFFT! YOU TOTALLY JUST MADE THAT UP.
MAYBE. THINK IT'LL TREND?
HEH.
UH, NO.

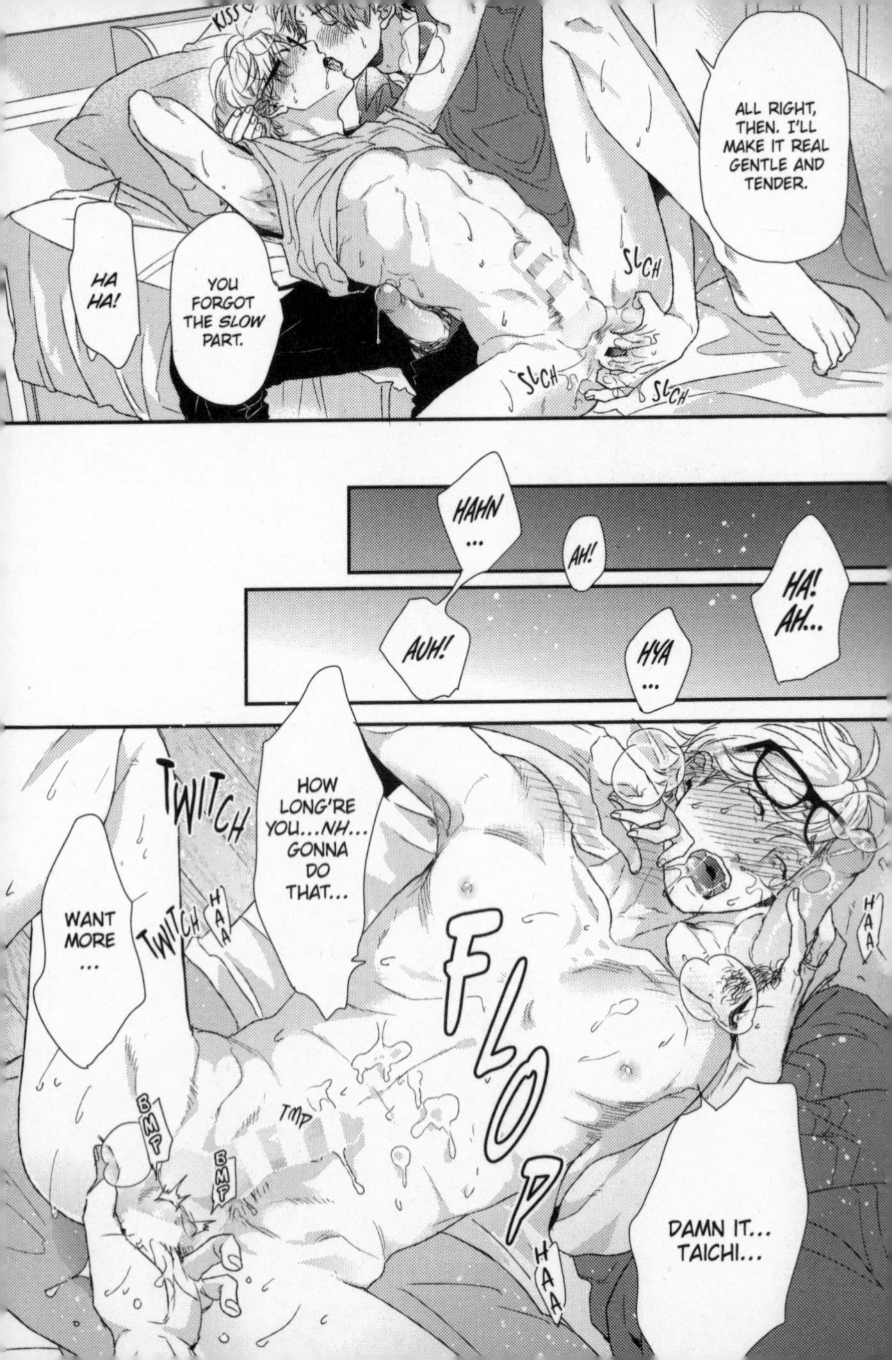
ALL RIGHT, THEN. I'LL MAKE IT REAL GENTLE AND TENDER.
KISS
SLCH
SLCH
SLCH
YOU FORGOT THE SLOW PART.
HA HA!
HA! AH...
HYA ...
AH!
HAHN ...
AUH!
HAA
DAMN IT... TAICHI...
FLOP
HAA
HOW LONG'RE YOU...NH... GONNA DO THAT...
TWITCH
TWITCH
HAA
WANT MORE ...
BMP
BMP
TMP

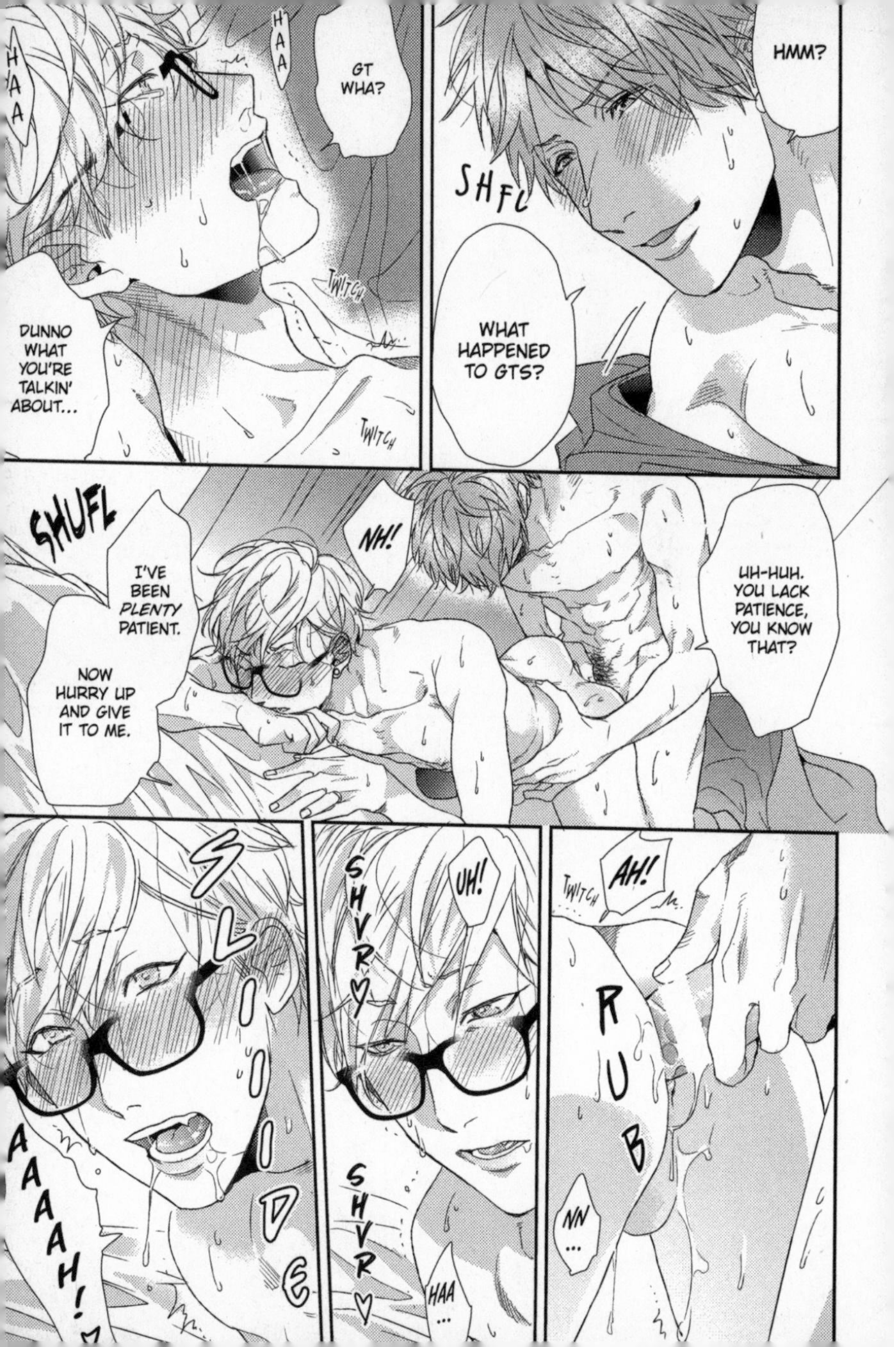
HMM?
SHFL
WHAT HAPPENED TO GTS?
GT WHA?
HAA
HAA
TWITCH
DUNNO WHAT YOU'RE TALKIN' ABOUT...
TWITCH
UH-HUH. YOU LACK PATIENCE, YOU KNOW THAT?
NH!
SHUFL
I'VE BEEN *PLENTY* PATIENT.
NOW HURRY UP AND GIVE IT TO ME.
AH!
TWITCH
RUB
NN ...
UH!
SHVR♥
SHVR♥
HAA ...
SLIIIDE
AAAAAH!♥

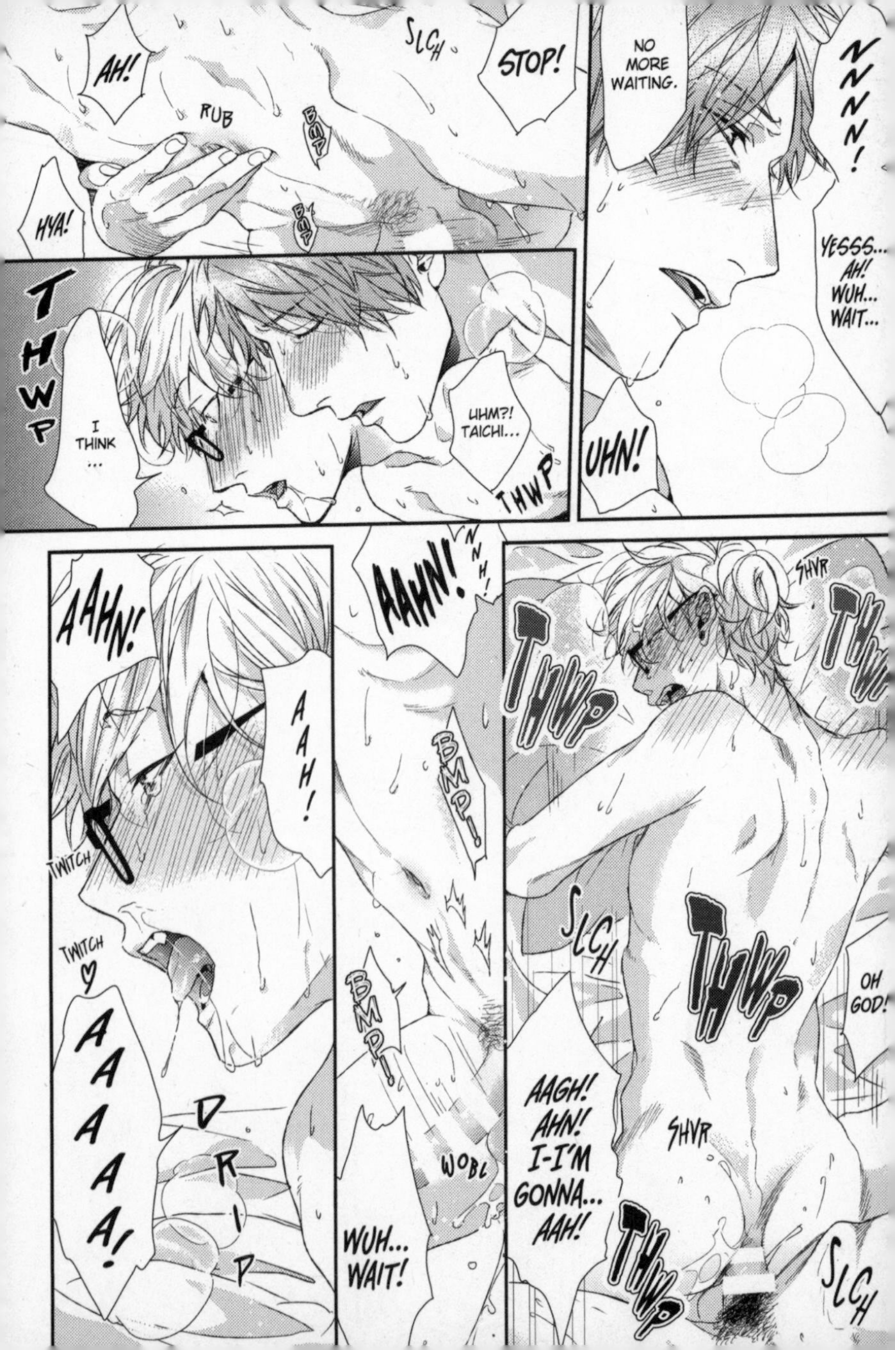
NNNNN!
NO MORE WAITING.
YESSS... AH! WUH... WAIT...
UHN!
STOP!
SLCH
AH!
RUB
BMP
BMP
HYA!
UHM?! TAICHI...
THWP
THWP
I THINK ...
SHVR
THW
THWP
OH GOD!
THWP
SLCH
AAGH! AHN! I-I'M GONNA... AAH!
SHVR
SLCH
THWP
NNH!
RAHN!
AAH!
BMP!
BMP!
WOBL
WUH... WAIT!
AAHN!
TWITCH
TWITCH
AAAAAA!
DRIP

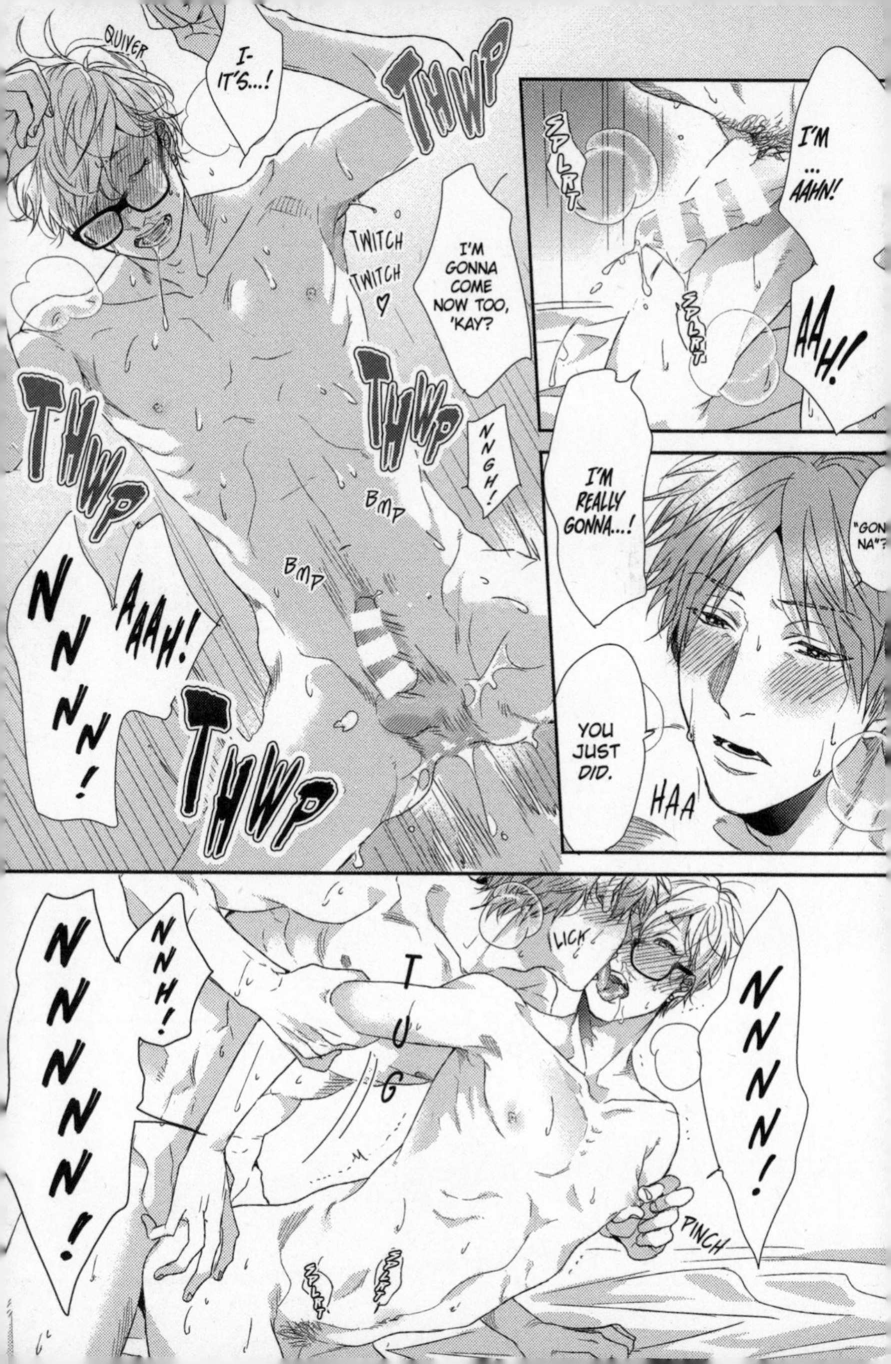
I'M ... AAHN!
SPLRT
SPLRT
AAH!
I'M REALLY GONNA...!
"GONNA"?
YOU JUST DID.
HAA
QUIVER
I- IT'S...!
THWP
TWITCH TWITCH ♥
I'M GONNA COME NOW TOO, 'KAY?
THWP
NNGH!
BMP
BMP
THWP
AAAH!
NNNN!
THWP
NNNNN!
LICK
TUG
PINCH
NNH!
NNNNNN!
SPLRT
SPLRT

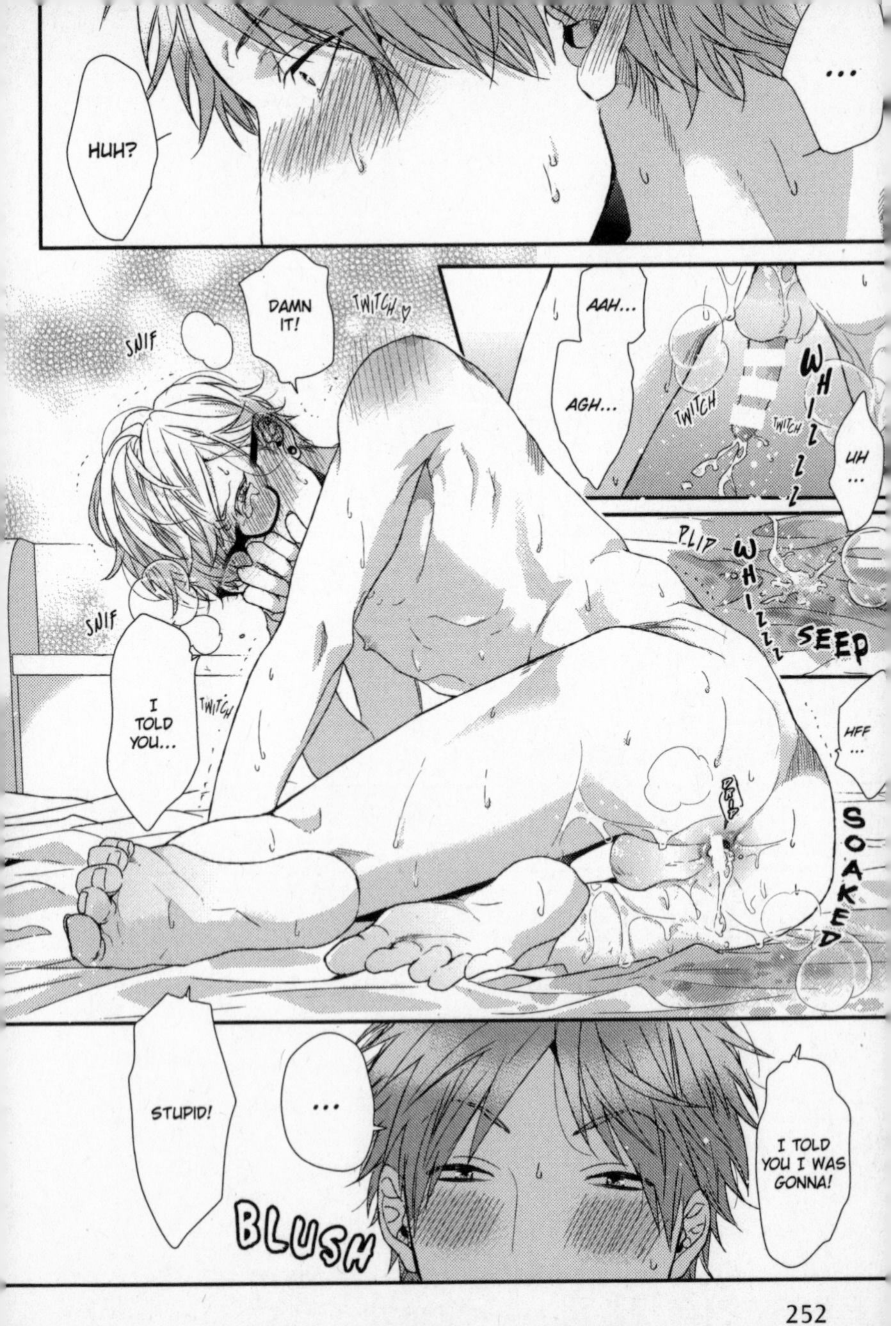

...
HUH?
AAH...
AGH...
WHIZZZ
TWITCH
TWITCH
UH...
PLIP
WHIZZZ
SEEP
HFF...
SOAKED
DAMN IT!
TWITCH
SNIF
SNIF
I TOLD YOU...
TWITCH
I TOLD YOU I WAS GONNA!
...
STUPID!
BLUSH

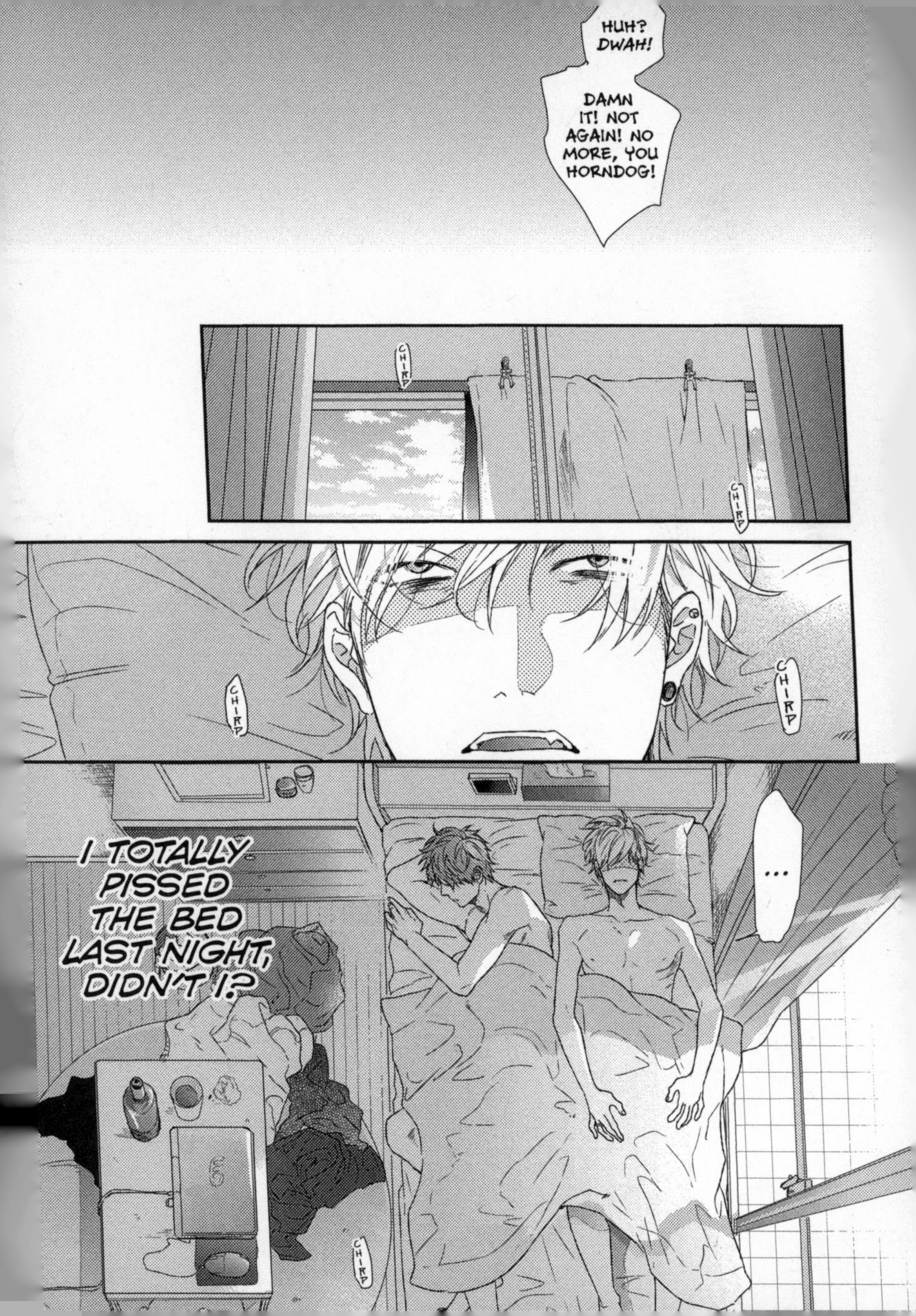
HUH? DWAH!
DAMN IT! NOT AGAIN! NO MORE, YOU HORNDOG!
CHIRP
CHIRP
CHIRP
CHIRP
...
I TOTALLY PISSED THE BED LAST NIGHT, DIDN'T I?
CHIRP

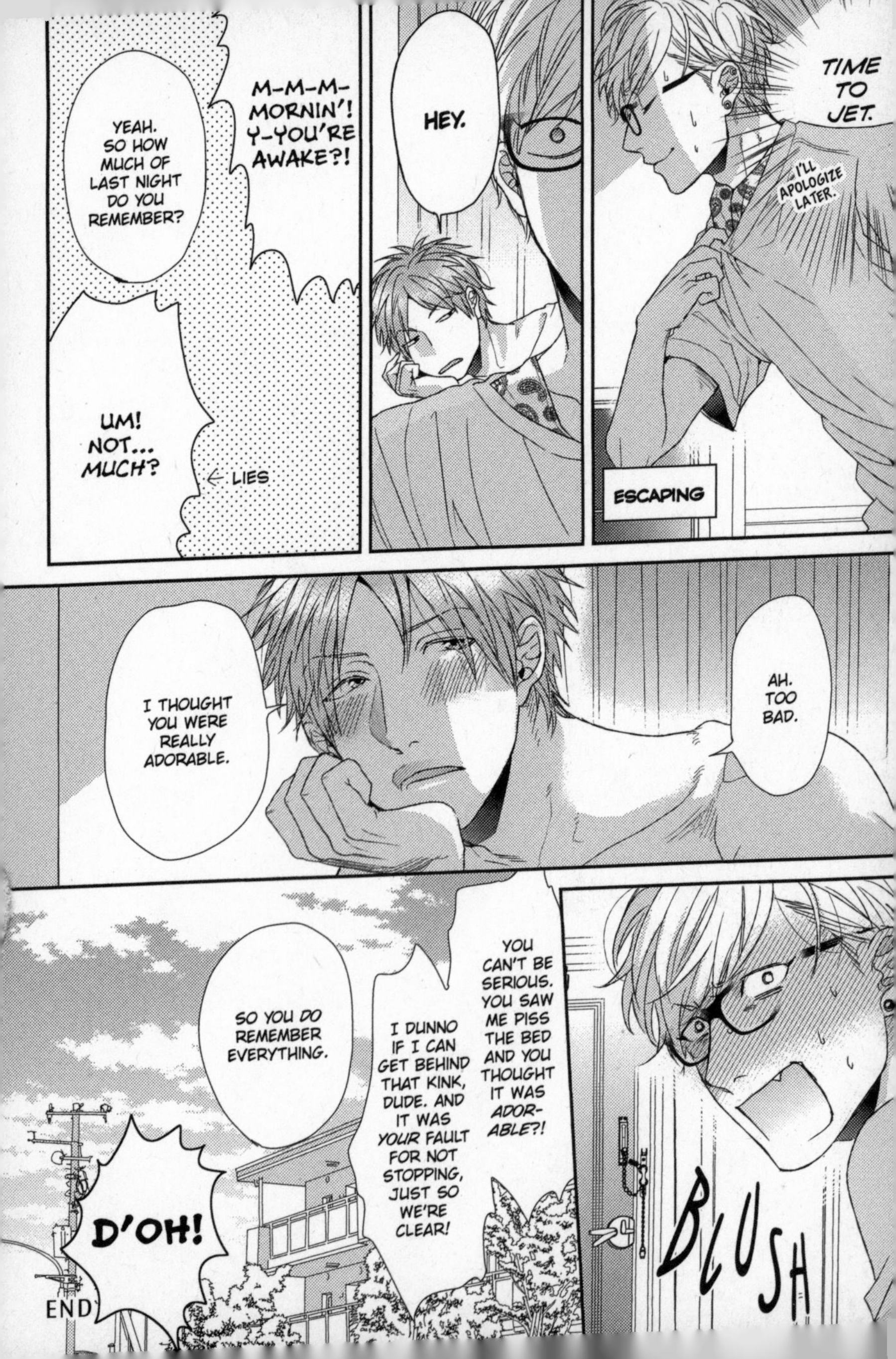
TIME TO JET.
I'LL APOLOGIZE LATER.
ESCAPING
HEY.
M-M-M-MORNIN'! Y-YOU'RE AWAKE?!
YEAH. SO HOW MUCH OF LAST NIGHT DO YOU REMEMBER?
UM! NOT... MUCH?
← LIES
AH. TOO BAD.
I THOUGHT YOU WERE REALLY ADORABLE.
BLUSH
YOU CAN'T BE SERIOUS. YOU SAW ME PISS THE BED AND YOU THOUGHT IT WAS ADORABLE?!
I DUNNO IF I CAN GET BEHIND THAT KINK, DUDE. AND IT WAS YOUR FAULT FOR NOT STOPPING, JUST SO WE'RE CLEAR!
SO YOU DO REMEMBER EVERYTHING.
D'OH!
END

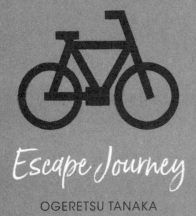

Escape Journey

OGERETSU TANAKA

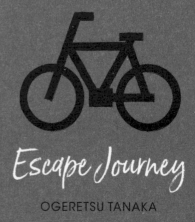

Escape Journey

OGERETSU TANAKA

AFTERWORD

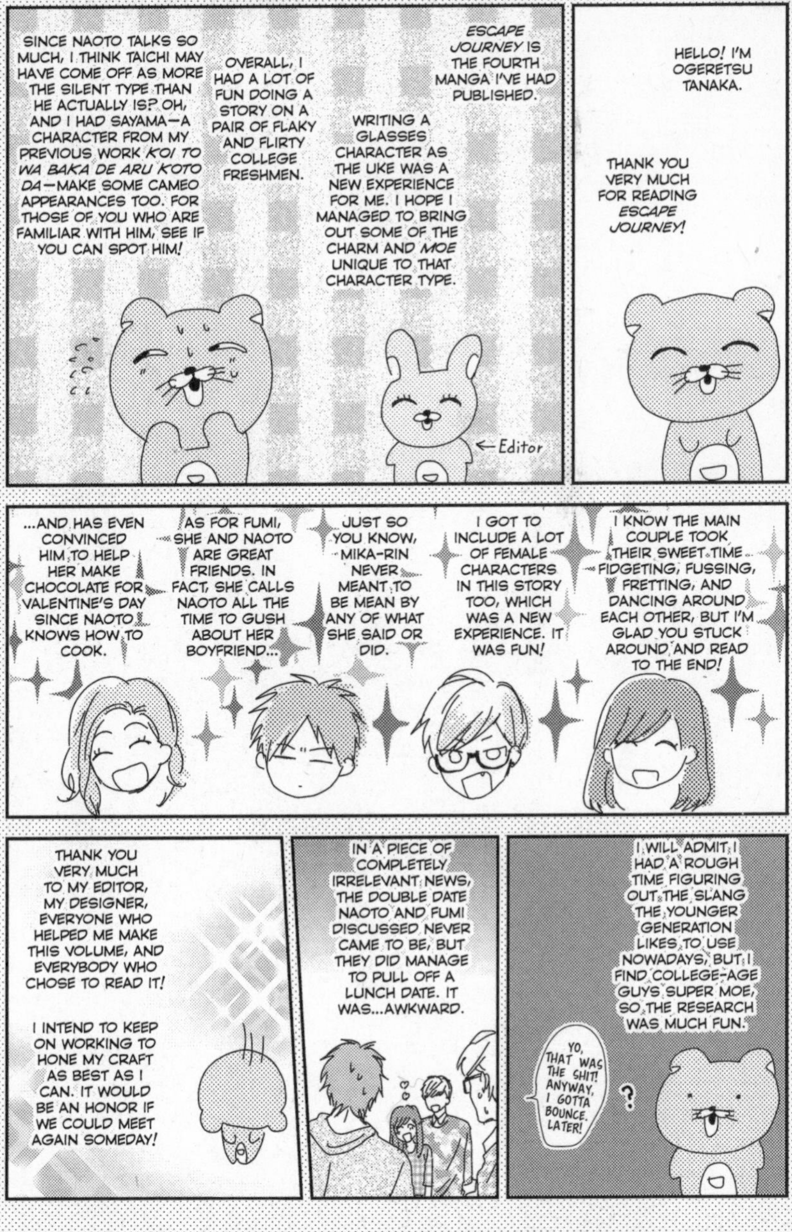
HELLO! I'M OGERETSU TANAKA.
THANK YOU VERY MUCH FOR READING *ESCAPE JOURNEY*!
ESCAPE JOURNEY IS THE FOURTH MANGA I'VE HAD PUBLISHED.
WRITING A GLASSES CHARACTER AS THE UKE WAS A NEW EXPERIENCE FOR ME. I HOPE I MANAGED TO BRING OUT SOME OF THE CHARM AND *MOE* UNIQUE TO THAT CHARACTER TYPE.
OVERALL, I HAD A LOT OF FUN DOING A STORY ON A PAIR OF FLAKY AND FLIRTY COLLEGE FRESHMEN.
SINCE NAOTO TALKS SO MUCH, I THINK TAICHI MAY HAVE COME OFF AS MORE THE SILENT TYPE THAN HE ACTUALLY IS? OH, AND I HAD SAYAMA—A CHARACTER FROM MY PREVIOUS WORK *KOI TO WA BAKA DE ARU KOTO DA*—MAKE SOME CAMEO APPEARANCES TOO. FOR THOSE OF YOU WHO ARE FAMILIAR WITH HIM, SEE IF YOU CAN SPOT HIM!
← Editor
I KNOW THE MAIN COUPLE TOOK THEIR SWEET TIME FIDGETING, FUSSING, FRETTING, AND DANCING AROUND EACH OTHER, BUT I'M GLAD YOU STUCK AROUND AND READ TO THE END!
I GOT TO INCLUDE A LOT OF FEMALE CHARACTERS IN THIS STORY TOO, WHICH WAS A NEW EXPERIENCE. IT WAS FUN!
JUST SO YOU KNOW, MIKA-RIN NEVER MEANT TO BE MEAN BY ANY OF WHAT SHE SAID OR DID.
AS FOR FUMI, SHE AND NAOTO ARE GREAT FRIENDS. IN FACT, SHE CALLS NAOTO ALL THE TIME TO GUSH ABOUT HER BOYFRIEND...
...AND HAS EVEN CONVINCED HIM TO HELP HER MAKE CHOCOLATE FOR VALENTINE'S DAY SINCE NAOTO KNOWS HOW TO COOK.
I WILL ADMIT I HAD A ROUGH TIME FIGURING OUT THE SLANG THE YOUNGER GENERATION LIKES TO USE NOWADAYS, BUT I FIND COLLEGE-AGE GUYS SUPER MOE, SO THE RESEARCH WAS MUCH FUN.
YO, THAT WAS THE SHIT! ANYWAY, I GOTTA BOUNCE. LATER!
?
IN A PIECE OF COMPLETELY IRRELEVANT NEWS, THE DOUBLE DATE NAOTO AND FUMI DISCUSSED NEVER CAME TO BE, BUT THEY DID MANAGE TO PULL OFF A LUNCH DATE. IT WAS...AWKWARD.
THANK YOU VERY MUCH TO MY EDITOR, MY DESIGNER, EVERYONE WHO HELPED ME MAKE THIS VOLUME, AND EVERYBODY WHO CHOSE TO READ IT!
I INTEND TO KEEP ON WORKING TO HONE MY CRAFT AS BEST AS I CAN. IT WOULD BE AN HONOR IF WE COULD MEET AGAIN SOMEDAY!

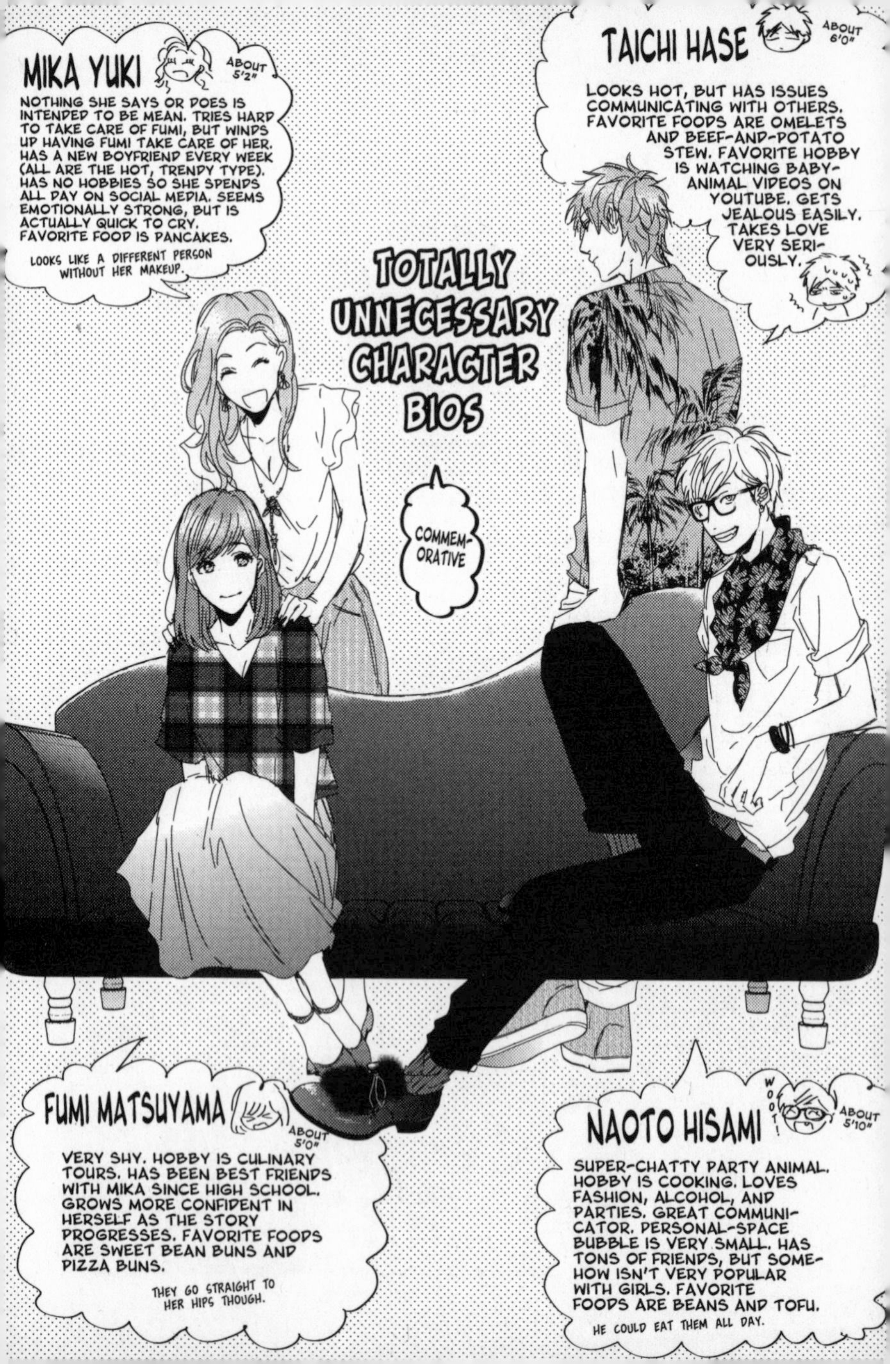
TAICHI HASE
ABOUT 6'0"
LOOKS HOT, BUT HAS ISSUES COMMUNICATING WITH OTHERS. FAVORITE FOODS ARE OMELETS AND BEEF-AND-POTATO STEW. FAVORITE HOBBY IS WATCHING BABY-ANIMAL VIDEOS ON YOUTUBE. GETS JEALOUS EASILY. TAKES LOVE VERY SERI-OUSLY.
MIKA YUKI
ABOUT 5'2"
NOTHING SHE SAYS OR DOES IS INTENDED TO BE MEAN. TRIES HARD TO TAKE CARE OF FUMI, BUT WINDS UP HAVING FUMI TAKE CARE OF HER. HAS A NEW BOYFRIEND EVERY WEEK (ALL ARE THE HOT, TRENDY TYPE). HAS NO HOBBIES SO SHE SPENDS ALL DAY ON SOCIAL MEDIA. SEEMS EMOTIONALLY STRONG, BUT IS ACTUALLY QUICK TO CRY. FAVORITE FOOD IS PANCAKES.
LOOKS LIKE A DIFFERENT PERSON WITHOUT HER MAKEUP.
TOTALLY UNNECESSARY CHARACTER BIOS
COMMEM-ORATIVE
NAOTO HISAMI
WOOT!
ABOUT 5'10"
SUPER-CHATTY PARTY ANIMAL. HOBBY IS COOKING. LOVES FASHION, ALCOHOL, AND PARTIES. GREAT COMMUNI-CATOR. PERSONAL-SPACE BUBBLE IS VERY SMALL. HAS TONS OF FRIENDS, BUT SOME-HOW ISN'T VERY POPULAR WITH GIRLS. FAVORITE FOODS ARE BEANS AND TOFU.
HE COULD EAT THEM ALL DAY.
FUMI MATSUYAMA
ABOUT 5'0"
VERY SHY. HOBBY IS CULINARY TOURS. HAS BEEN BEST FRIENDS WITH MIKA SINCE HIGH SCHOOL. GROWS MORE CONFIDENT IN HERSELF AS THE STORY PROGRESSES. FAVORITE FOODS ARE SWEET BEAN BUNS AND PIZZA BUNS.
THEY GO STRAIGHT TO HER HIPS THOUGH.

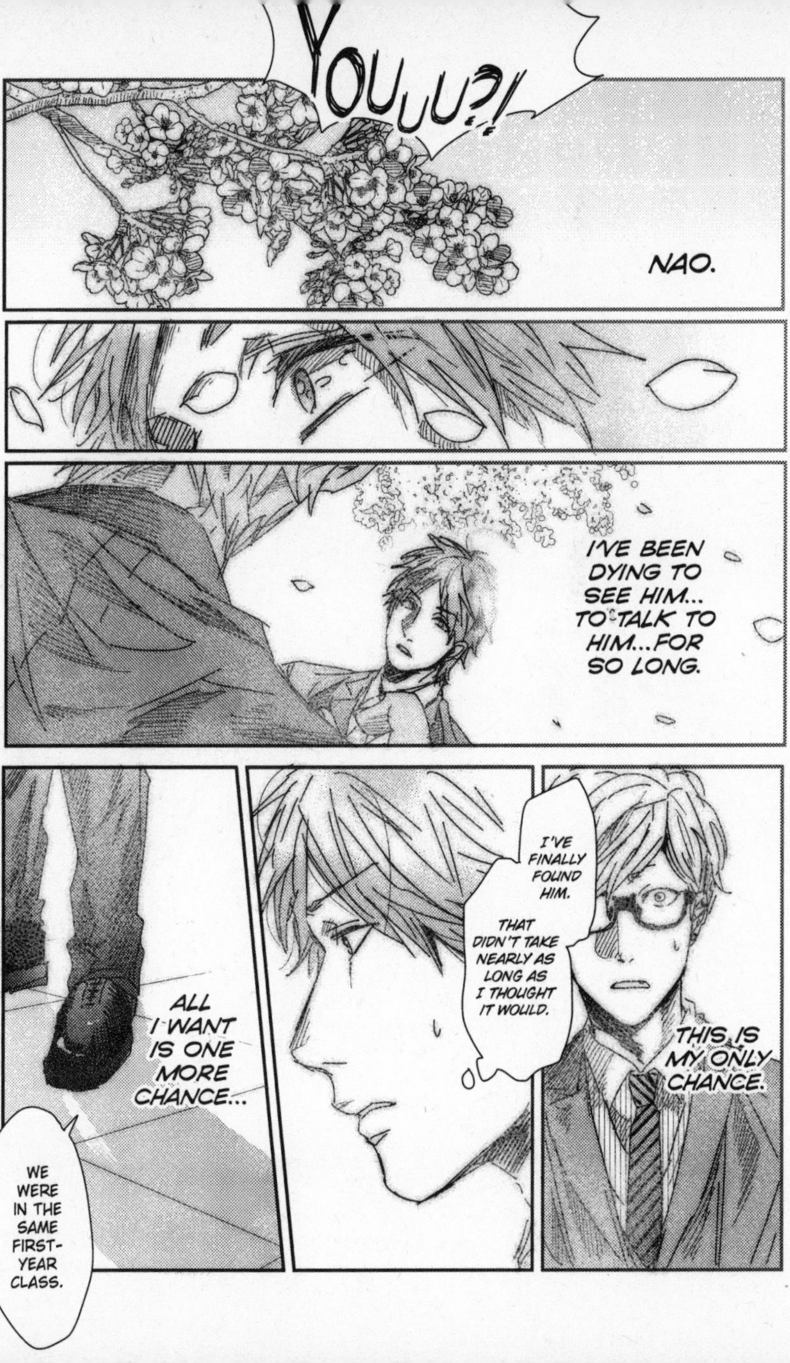
YOUUU?!
NAO.
I'VE BEEN DYING TO SEE HIM... TO TALK TO HIM...FOR SO LONG.
I'VE FINALLY FOUND HIM.
THAT DIDN'T TAKE NEARLY AS LONG AS I THOUGHT IT WOULD.
THIS IS MY ONLY CHANCE.
ALL I WANT IS ONE MORE CHANCE...
WE WERE IN THE SAME FIRST-YEAR CLASS.

About the Author

In addition to creating boys' love, **Ogeretsu Tanaka** also creates non-BL stories under the pen name Tanaka Marumero. She was born on July 3 under the sign of Cancer and has an A blood type. You can find out more about Ogeretsu Tanaka on her Twitter page, **@tanaca_**.

Escape Journey
Volume 1
SuBLime Manga Edition

Story and Art by **Ogeretsu Tanaka**

Translation—**Adrienne Beck**
Touch-Up Art and Lettering—**Mara Coman**
Cover and Graphic Design—**Shawn Carrico**
Editor—**Jennifer LeBlanc**

Escape Journey ① © 2015 Ogeretsu Tanaka
Orginally published in Japan in 2015 by Libre Publishing Co., Ltd.
English translation rights arranged with Libre Inc.

libre

Printed in the U.S.A.

Published by SuBLime Manga
P.O. Box 77010
San Francisco, CA 94107

10 9 8 7 6 5 4 3 2 1
First printing, September 2018

www.SuBLimeManga.com

For more information

on all our products, along with the most up-to-date news on releases, series announcements, and contests, please visit us at:

SuBLimeManga.com

 twitter.com/**SuBLimeManga**

 facebook.com/**SuBLimeManga**

 instagram.com/**SuBLimeManga**

 SuBLimeManga.tumblr.com

SUBLIME

MANGA

One hot guy + One funny-looking guy = One hilarious couple!

His Favorite

Story & Art by Suzuki TANAKA

Awkward Yoshida is hated by all the girls in school for his perceived closeness with hot guy Sato, who uses hanging out with Yoshida as an excuse to turn them all down. If Yoshida is merely an excuse, why does Sato taunt him in private about "his favorite"? Is it possible Sato's feelings run deeper than friendship? And what could he possibly see in the funny-looking Yoshida? Watch Yoshida's life turn upside down with hilarious results!